FRIENDS & ENEMIES

FRIENDS & ENEMIES

A Life in *Vogue*, Prison, & Park Avenue

BARBARA AMIEL

PEGASUS BOOKS
NEW YORK LONDON

FRIENDS & ENEMIES

Pegasus Books, Ltd.
148 W. 37th Street, 13th Floor
New York, NY 10018

First Pegasus Books edition October 2020

Library of Congress Cataloging-in-Publication Data is available.

ISBN: 978-1-64313-560-1

10 9 8 7 6 5 4 3 2 1

Printed in the United States of America
Distributed by Simon & Schuster
www.pegasusbooks.com

"*Let's talk about Me.* The great unexpected dividend of the feminist movement has been to elevate an ordinary status—woman, housewife—to the level of drama. One's very existence as a woman . . . as *Me* . . . becomes something all the world analyzes, agonizes over, draws cosmic conclusions from, or in any event takes seriously. Every woman becomes Emma Bovary, Cousin Bette or Nora . . . or Erica Jong or Consuelo Saah Baehr."

Tom Wolfe, "The 'Me' Decade"

"Unless you wear pearls with Chanel, a hat and unseemly bust."

The Intelligent Feminist's Guide to Survival

CONTENTS

The Last Flight

There never was going to be a right way to write this book. *Memoirs*—God what a chilling thud the word has with its suggestion of a sequence of banal insights. Years ago, sitting in Claridge's tea room in London, a publisher intent on dragging a book out of me said I should write mine as fiction. "You'll find it easier," he said. At the time, neither of us had the faintest idea of what troubles lay ahead for me, which would read like fiction no matter what the genre.

The dozens of memoirs I'd like to read, of fascinating, inaccessible lives full of contradiction and great achievement, rarely make the page, probably because the putative memoirists are too busy achieving: Marie Curie, Clara Schumann, Joan of Arc, Catherine de Medici, or even Coco Chanel—whose demi-memoir was carefully constructed like her work, all scissored skills hiding the body beneath. The Dowager Empress Maria Theresa of Austria, mother of sixteen surviving children including Marie Antoinette, was tied up running the Holy Roman Empire for forty years while she jotted down her thoughts, unfortunately scattered in letters and archival sources, not always translated and full of anachronistic words. George Orwell said he wouldn't dream of writing his because "in an autobiography you had to tell absolutely the whole truth."

Memoirs of survival under god-awful circumstances attracted me for different reasons as I aged. When you are reasonably young and reading Aleksandr Solzhenitsyn or Primo Levi, the notion of facing death is hellishly exciting, largely because you neither understand death nor feel its existence. Death, insofar as you grasp it, is that chalky-white-faced man with a scythe and sort of black headgear popping up in an Ingmar Bergman film. Death exists to be romantically invoked—rather like an interesting piece of fabric worn to emphasize very alive, pretty eyes. When you are old, about the last thing you want to see coming around the corner is a damn scythe. One clings to false teeth and thinning bones with unbecoming tenacity.

Nothing in my own life has been sufficiently original to please me. Pamela Winefred Paget, later Lady Glenconner, is the sort of woman I should like to have been if, as was evident early on, I couldn't be an Anna Pavlova, Golda Meir, Edith Wharton, or latterly in this post-gender world, a Tom Stoppard, Dmitri Hvorostovsky or Woody Allen sans the Mia thing.

Pamela, daughter of an amateur scientist, took part in her aristocratic father's experiments by throwing herself off an omnibus backwards as it went along London's Park Lane at thirty miles an hour, to demonstrate his theory that the force of air behind her would see that she landed safely on her feet, which she did. She also had treacle poured in her ears, which led to his invention of a very successful sign language. Later, with her mother Lady Muriel, she helped newly born Czechoslovakia get on its feet, and then turned to rescuing distressed British subjects from Soviet Russia with special attention to dental care for the elderly, an area too few of us think about in our charitable giving. This is a life worth living if you have no special talent in some field of human endeavour. Admittedly, such a life requires a bit of luck in the parentage you get. As yet beyond one's control.

My own parentage neither added to nor subtracted from my chances of an original life. Both parents deviated from the ordinary only in ways that were largely unhelpful to me apart from their dollop of physical attractiveness. My birth coincided with World War Two's outbreak, but the sole discomfort I suffered came from the British government's commendable determination to see wartime children grow up straight-limbed and strong. This meant the nightmare of the brown bottle and tablespoon of cod liver oil every morning, together with something vile pretending to be orange juice. So while the Luftwaffe bombed the bejesus out of Great Britain, I was happily playing in London's greenbelt, hanging out with the blood red poppies in my grandparents' garden planted around our small Anderson corrugated-iron bomb shelter.

Those poppies stayed all summer and I rather dwelled on them at bedtime. They were sleeping like me, perfectly safe, with petals closed up so the planes overhead couldn't hurt them. There was other life outside that I worried about, most especially the butterflies with their kaleidoscope wings folded tightly under night skies lit with the red glow of explosions over London. We had fields full of silver-studded blues and purple emperors at the end of our lane. Wading into waist-high grass and seeing clouds of rainbow colours flutter up before me was a walk through the looking glass to a world of heart-stopping beauty. "No danger," said my grandfather in his role as our local air-raid warden when I voiced little fears about these enchanted insects flying high into propellers, "They can dive-bomb better themselves."

Seventy years later, those butterflies, or at least their butterfly relatives, became a living metaphor to explain my life. At first I felt uneasy putting that down on the page, as if this figure of speech were too neat—a contrivance or simply a writer's device. In the end, the image turned out to be pretty much on the mark.

The war ended. By five, I could read and write quite well, blessed with a Russian-born grandmother who had been a schoolteacher. Less than ten years later, our family emigrated, in this case mother, sister, a stepfather I adored and a less divine, red-faced baby half-brother. My butterflies stayed behind. In Canada they lived somewhere else, certainly not on the bright new homes of the government-assisted housing estate we moved to in steel-town Hamilton, with gardens that were still only piles of bulldozed earth. I'd run about looking for them, but all I saw were painted ladies and red admirals, alone or sometimes in pairs, never clouds of them, and anyway they were wearing rather ordinary city uniforms. Their magic had been taken from them, just as my childhood had been left behind in England. All I brought with me—apart from my treasured school mackintosh, beret and a few books from the hundreds of cheap Penguin and Pelican editions that had lined our London shelves—was a vague feeling that I would be a writer.

I wrote to be clever and impress my father. I wrote because I was lonely and the enjoyment of writing and pasting together a make-believe local newspaper was a good game for a small child in 1940s and '50s postwar England. I wrote to explain why music made me cry and burying dead birds in the garden did not. I wrote to win book tokens in children's magazines, to keep busy and not irritate my mother, who, when the war was over and her London job with the Red Cross finished, found me a bit in the way.

Having long come to terms with the failure to meet my own writing ambitions, why I write seems far less important now than the worry of why anyone would read these memoirs. I am white. I am Jewish. I am female but not one of the "sisterhood." And I am seen to be reasonably well off. Chronicles of the Damned, really. And that's just for starters.

I have become a misshapen piece of work that is the object either of derision or of indifference. By now there has been sufficient material published in newspapers, magazines, books, and film and television scripts concerning my husband and myself that I am genu-inely and though God knows I hate to use the word, "authentically" unsure of what I am. I doubt anyone can credit confusion about one-self, but believe me, you do finally arrive there. I can't say whether it is after the fifteenth or the fiftieth negative article or the third or the fourth chapter of one of the half-dozen books that dissect you with a hacksaw, but at some point you leave outrage behind and a worm constricts your chest. You see the person they are describing and look at yourself. While you know their "facts" and "anecdotes" are more often than not total fiction and the function of some need to make a quick buck or name for themselves after a magpie run through the clippings, you also know with an awful dread that there are genuine facts about yourself they don't know that probably are monstrous and every bit as nasty. Things get muddled then—you want to scrape their mud off yourself but find in the process you are throwing some of your own back on. Ultimately, there's no justification for writing these memoirs other than to set the record straight, to rationalize the whole endeavour by clinging to the notion that even imperfect, highly flawed people can be interesting and perhaps their experiences might help someone, although frankly I can't see myself as a Florence Nightingale for the confused-female set.

The allegories I draw from nature are my second nature. Wherever life blew me, I could usually find my way to a copse, although the most difficult place of all was Florida's flat empty land surrounding its prisons. It was in Florida, at a stop on the way to the weekly prison visit with my husband, that I saw my first Monarch butterfly. You couldn't miss it in that bright early-morning sunscape of trash cans and crumpled paper cups, so intense the colours and so large its wings as it did a parabola over a little triangular patch of wildflowers growing off to the side of the service area at Turkey Point on Interstate 95. I suppose by then I was emotionally strung out with those 4:30 a.m. drives to Federal Correctional Institution Coleman and the knowledge of the visit ahead. The butterfly was a moment of loveliness in a horrible place. But now I looked at it with an adult's knowledge of the dark, not the bright and beautiful world of a child.

My husband finds it odd that I get help in difficult times by immersing myself in the universe of people who lived in sheer hell, like the 1946 memoir of Władysław Szpilman's two years hiding in Warsaw, memorialized in Ronnie Harwood's Oscar-winning script for Polanski's movie *The Pianist*, or the diaries of the Jewish professor Victor Klemperer, who lived through the war in Dresden. He thinks it slightly mad, certainly idiosyncratic, to cheer oneself up by soaking in human atrocities, war and persecution.

From that first sighting in Florida, the Monarch's story became an active part of my library of desperate lives. From its birth to its death is almost always a blink, a near-hopeless gamble against tractors tearing up their milkweed, wasps and tachinid flies parasitizing their bodies, and humans with chemicals of destruction. For the one out of a hundred eggs that survives to adulthood, a full life may be eight weeks of sun and nectar. Then there is the final progeny—the single miraculous generation of monarch butterflies born at summer's end.

This fluttering eighth of an ounce of invisible stamina will fly some 3,200 kilometres from Canada to an oyamel fir tree in a mountain sanctuary in Mexico, without aid of a Baedeker, GPS or any previous visit, and at the mercy of food shortages, winds and temperature drops. The entire journey is a Death Valley ultramarathon. And though almost every human being under the sun has their own difficult journey, often tragic, few can ever capture in writing the uniqueness of the experience. Our literacy can't quite equal the mute Monarch's display, no matter how we cloak ourselves in colourful wings of language.

Perhaps my interest was sparked by some emotional transference— certainly the Monarchs I raise each summer from collected egg to butterfly are about the closest I'll ever come to giving birth. That moment, seconds only, when the newborn Monarch comes out of its cage clasping your finger, then with one glance, a quick check of fluttering wings, and the life you have reared flies to freedom. Perhaps it is a function of old age, paying tribute to the determination needed to physically battle on. After the long journey to Mexico, after three months hanging on through storms and drought, the very same butterflies—wings often torn—come down the mountain to get water. Their colour is faded but the gossamer structures still beat against air. Destiny is irresistible. They must find the ground to mate and the milkweed to lay eggs, so having refreshed themselves, they rise up once more on battered wings towards cloud and sun to make one last flight— to create new life at the point of death. It will need three or four generations to make the same journey back that the miracle autumn generation travelled in one go.

My husband and I went through a good seventeen years of difficulty. Hades for us; nothing so apparently dramatic for the onlooker. "You must write about what happened," my acquaintances blithely say to me. "I can't wait to read it," says the publisher discreetly, not referring to the heavily lapsed contract. Tell us, who are your tachinid flies, who are the human predators? Tell us how it felt to have your own metamorphosis from fame to infamy, "Cut to the chase and give us the real story," they all say, and I know they want good upscale gossip, names, horrors that have remained unspoken, perhaps a betrayal or two of my husband.

A writer, though, writes for herself and by herself. No matter how much we want to satisfy readers, the mind veers off to its own interests. And I write now from a brain not helped, I suspect, by the years of medicines I chose to take, stimulants of one sort or another to keep it working—helpful aids unavailable to butterflies. This book is simply an account of a woman's life that, like a migrating Monarch, ran into a late autumn storm that continued with droughts and predators to this, the very last flight.

PART ONE

CHAPTER ONE

Vera's Secrets

There must be a way to get past the childhood years, so tedious for the reader unless you are reared by a troop of gorillas or have the writing skills of Émile Zola. Mine started in Chorley Wood, Hertfordshire—evacuated to my grandparents' home at the beginning of the Second World War—a safe place for a Jewish child in 1940's Europe.

"Doesn't she read yet?" asked the man they called Harold, who turned out to be my father, on leave after escaping from a prisoner-of-war camp in Italy.

"Darling, she's only three and a half."

"Can she play anything, 'Chopsticks' at least?" he asked, sitting at the piano. I remember the sounds and watching his hands fly over the keys but not much more.

We moved back to our battle-scarred house in Hendon, in North West London—my baby sister, my mother Vera and Doris, a part-time scullery maid. The ceilings were cracked and a few windows gone, but the apple tree at the end of the small garden and the bird bath were still there. Harold never came home when the war was over. The postwar divorce was loud. Neither parent particularly wanted "the children," but someone had to bring us up, so we were made wards of the court in the custody of my mother.

Vera wore bright jumpers and lipstick and laughed with the lodgers we sometimes took in. She was busy dating, and my sister, Ruth, was often away in a convalescent home—she was quite unwell as a child—so it was helpful all around to send me somewhere just for a night or two so the house could be *kinderfrei*. I never knew the people in whose homes I found myself but they were all kind to me, possibly friends of my mother or friends of a friend. This presented the usual childhood problems. Whenever I went to sleep in unfamiliar surroundings, my great fear was that I might need to go to the lavatory and wouldn't know where it was. If I left my room at night to search the strange house, I was afraid the people I was staying with would hear me and send me home with a note to my mother that I was a nuisance and "selfish"—a label my mother used whenever I did anything out of order.

The other problem was the presence of ticking clocks. The ticking would get louder and louder, insistent as it went on. Put in a bedroom I had not slept in before in a house I did not know, and the clocks would burst upon me, hidden in places I could not find at first, like concealed little bombs. I would lie with eyes open anticipating the next dreaded tick with its elongated tail of reverberation, hoping for it to end, but I couldn't muffle the ones outside my bedroom and the ticking never entirely stopped.

Even so, I almost preferred being in an unfamiliar house to my home on the nights my mother went out and left me alone. The metered gas fire in my bedroom having burned out a shilling's worth and no longer giving off the warm yellow-red light, the house empty and dark, I was too frightened to move. Fear came washing down through the suffocating black of nighttime. I was in a coffin and the lid was closing slowly down upon me.

"Don't be so silly," my mother would say when I told her how frightened I was alone at night. I have no idea where I had seen a coffin—a film, perhaps, or in my mind's eye, listening to an Edgar Allan Poe story on the BBC. But at night that wooden dark lid materialized. If I had not been so paralyzed with fear, I knew I could have touched it—poised above as it was, coming to crush out breath and life at an agonizingly slow pace.

Apart from these wrinkles, childhood was perfectly pleasant. I dreamed that one day I would be a radiant beauty, if not quite a violet-eyed Elizabeth Taylor then certainly with the delicate wide-eyed allure of a Vivien Leigh, who had made a deep impression on me when I first saw her at the Gaumont Cinema in Hendon Central in *Caesar and Cleopatra*.

I took it for granted that I would grow glorious breasts like London's nude Windmill Girls, who my grandmother took me to see in matinee performances in the late 1940s. "Heroines," said Grandma. "They were nude every night of the Blitz, darling. Hitler himself couldn't make them put their clothes on. Have another boiled sweet, dear," she would say, offering a rare treat in those postwar days of rationing and binary burlesque.

I wanted to be "so attractive," which was how I heard people speak of my mother, although her large grey eyes deep-set above high cheekbones, her tiny waist, full bosom and perfect legs were, in my father's family, taken as unmistakable signs of shallowness. The word *clever* was worshipped by them both as the highest praise and the most decisive put-down. "So clever," my aunt would say sarcastically if I made a remark she considered pert. My blood would drain. At night in bed I worried about how to become cleverer. This focus on clever would unfortunately become something of a problem for me in adult life, when I realized that my intellectual ambitions were greater than my intellectual muscle.

My mother wanted to raise me properly, which included ballet and piano lessons, extremely commendable on her part, but the grim little truth was that eventually the ballet teacher would ask for my two and sixpence in front of the other little girls and I didn't have it. I would carry home notes about unpaid fees. I was instructed to please my father, on our infrequent custody visits, with my school marks, my appearance and my piano playing so that he would send us more money. I needed no instruction. Dancing for approval was a natural instinct.

We just needed a bit more of it, and if the walls of the Hendon house weren't quite as wretched as those in D.H. Lawrence's "Rocking Horse Winner" home where they constantly moaned "there must be more money," our walls were not beyond reminding me that I was failing in my assigned task. Without "Harold's help" my rapidly growing feet would not get larger-size ballet shoes or the needed school plimsolls. Vera's dreadful headaches would continue as I thoughtlessly grew out of everything and for reasons I could not understand this state of affairs would lead to my failure to become a debutante in "a beautiful white dress"—a particular fixation of Vera's, impenetrable to me but seemingly of great importance.

At the time, all the women I knew worked: they were chemists, barristers, doctors or employed in factories with funny names like ICI. Even my maternal great-grandmother, still alive at the end of the war, widowed after a Russian *pogrom*, escaping to England with her four children and speaking no English, graduated in 1899 as a professional midwife in London and went into business for herself in 1901 with a smart brass plate outside her front door. My paternal grandmother, never seen by me in anything but trousers with a cigarette hanging from her lower lip, widowed early in the war, ran a small confectionery shop on Commercial Road in the heart of London's heavily bombed East End. Great-aunts made cold cream in backrooms to sell during wartime's cosmetic shortages. This matter-of-fact approach to work might explain why later on I found the incessant whining of North American women about glass ceilings so tedious. On the whole, middle-class North American women, unlike their counterparts the world over, have always seemed a bit spoiled to me, but perhaps that's unfair.

Each parent's family mildly vilified the other. There were lengthy recitations about the money my father owed for "you and your sister's expenses." On visits to my father's side, my clever aunt had her own Pandora's box of horrors. "Your mother," she would say, "only got your father by never letting him touch her before the marriage. Neurotic, of course, but not as bad as her sister Kate. Has Kate tried suicide this week?"

My dear Aunt Kate, a medical doctor by profession, was a severe depressive, and as her illness intensified, she also had attacks, I was told, during which she thought she was a dog, although the breed was never specified. I would have got it later in life, as I liked her enomously.

Electric shock treatment didn't help her although it had an unexpected effect on me: when I saw Jack Nicholson strapped down in *One Flew Over the Cuckoo's Nest*, I tore out of the cinema in a terrible state, thinking of dear Aunt Kate's grey hair shoved into a cap, her glasses removed and her head constrained. My date thought I had no stomach. Aunt Kate and her husband resorted to the very popular suicide method at that time of turning on the coal-gas oven in their kitchen and stuffing the gap under the door with rags. Later on it was a botched hanging and then success with sleeping tablets. Most families, I think, have had some brush with this sort of bewildered human being.

A few years after the divorce, my younger sister and I waved goodbye to our mother as she went off on her honeymoon with our favourite "uncle," as we referred to our new stepfather. "Be good, children," said our mother. We were not. Ruth and I were sent to Devon, to a holiday residence for the daughters of army officers. On the first Sunday there, a large-bottomed lady with a matter-of-fact manner addressed us at breakfast:

"All girls will line up for church in the front hall at eleven, please. Gloves and hats."

Hand up. "My sister and I can't go."

"Why not?"

"We're Jewish."

That night, to confirm my difference, I knelt by the bed— unaware that kneeling was not part of my tradition—and spoke some mumbo-jumbo that sounded to me like the Hebrew I had heard. I had gone to lessons in an Edgware synagogue as a small child but had been withdrawn early. Next day we were sent home from Devon as "unsuitable."

My mother appeared a day or two later. "Why did you have to tell them you were Jewish?" she said. "There was no need for them to know."

Helpfully, when I was six, I won a place at North London Collegiate School (about twenty years before twelve-year-old Anna Wintour arrived) and all unhappiness vanished for me. I loved this school, loved my monitor's badge, the cedar trees, the avenue of limes and the grey-white stone walls of Canons, built on the site of the former home of the Dukes of Chandos, situated amid winding stairs and follies covered in wisteria and ivy.

However, the new marriage resulted in the necessity of my taking a letter to school written by my mother explaining to the headmistress that after three years at NLCS as a Jewess, I was that no longer and would now attend Christian prayers. The movie-star good looks of her new and younger husband were tempered by the slightly awkward fact that he came from a working-class family unfamiliar with Jews and apparently not very fond of them.

"Darling, you see you can't be Jewish anymore," my mother told me. "You'll like it very much. You can attend proper prayers instead of going off to that little rotunda with a few Jewish girls to recite Hebrew with that awful Miss Senator."

"Mummy," I asked, "does that mean you and Grandpa and Grandma and Daddy aren't Jewish anymore?"

"Barbara, dear, this is our little secret."

The notion was puzzling after a childhood that had included a lot of references to my very wrinkled Great Grandma Isserlis, a direct descendant of the great sixteenth-century rabbi Moses Isserles, the Rema, and frequent lectures on the importance of my heritage, whatever it was, but in my own mind I was still Jewish anyway. The only conversion that took place was in my mother's mind. The lure of seeing what actually went on behind the closed doors of morning prayers at my school was strong: I would attend as a Christian—rather like a costume party. Perhaps, gradually, I would get the straight blonde hair too.

At times, I did wonder what being Jewish meant. Both my parents had Jewish parents. I wore a tiny gold mezuzah around my neck, given to me at birth, with a little hinged door that opened to reveal Hebrew lettering in black ink on a piece of rolled paper. I had noticed that my aunts had mainly red hair and I thought this might be a sign of being Jewish. My father and uncles had very dark curly hair, and my own was much the same, with skin that tanned easily without burning in the moderate English summers.

"If you go in the sun much more," my mother would threaten,

"they will think you a darkie." Her maternal instincts usually surfaced to guard my appearance. When I fell off a horse and had stitches in my knee, she insisted I tell my father I must have plastic surgery to eliminate the scar. "No one will marry you and you won't be able to model." Neither of these dire warnings held much worry, as I had no interest in either fate.

There was no stew in my mind over "identity," though it was a bit of a hash. Heaven was in the sky, I thought, but not for us. We had no afterlife. Being Jewish was a secret society whose rules insisted on excellence at school, prodigious reading and a love of classical music—preferably with the ability to play the violin or piano. The rule that as a Jew one should try to be more British than the British was also etched into my consciousness without any factual under-pinning. It simply was.

"Girls," said my mother one day in late summer. "We have a secret. We're going to Canada in November. You mustn't tell anyone, not even Daddy and Grandpa and Grandma." Now our house was up for sale and strangers walked through my bedroom and the garden, dismissing both as "very small," not really seeing my special apple tree with rhu-barb underneath it, and always talking about the shortcomings of our house with the real estate agent. Gradually, books and toys were boxed up and "donated." The warmth of familiar objects was slipping away.

If I adored my new stepfather, which I did, I worshipped my own father. So tall, broad-shouldered, handsome and very funny, revel-ling in my good school reports. The excitement of our rare custody visits was so intense that I almost never slept the night before, trying to think of how to entrance him and keep his attention in the only house the court permitted us to visit him in—that of his sister's, in Hampstead, which was filled with my ambitious cousins, oozing self-confidence. The strain of trying to match the achievements of these precocious well-off cousins, polished up with their private piano lessons and paraded about in front of my father by their demoniacally competitive mother, light years away from the lackadaisical atten-tions of my mummy, made the visits something of a Spartan ordeal.

I'm not sure why I enjoyed it so much. Either early masochism or ruthless competitiveness of my own, I suppose.

On our last custody visit, after tea, my father pulled me up on his shoulders in the Hampstead garden and I buried my face in his thick dark wavy hair, which had a faint smell like a mixture of lavender and shearling, familiar and comforting. He dropped Ruth and me off by the Finchley Road tube, where we were getting the 113 bus back to Hendon. We were leaving England in two weeks and now he knew it.

"Babar"—his nickname for me from the Jean de Brunhoff story— "do your lessons and send me photos and letters." He kissed me. There was no way I could know that it was in fact the very last time. I watched from the upper deck of the bus as his waving figure turned into a shadow and then nothing. He would kill himself just four years later, when I was fifteen and he was thirty-nine. In death he was praised as a man who charmed everyone, played the piano well, and loved tennis, detective novels, classical music, and women with blonde hair. He was said by his doting sister to write marvellously; and a few minor pieces had been published. Sylvester Amiel, the firm in which he and his younger brother were partners, was a respectable if somewhat left-wing group of solicitors in a set of rooms on a ground floor in Gloucester Place, W1. He was one of those people who could still be referred to, once he had left life early, as a man of great possibilities.

This charming solicitor also left his second wife and their two children quite destitute after using up all his life insurance and the education funds for my sister and me, mortgaging his own home to the hilt, creditors everywhere and no savings, in an attempt to cover up his embezzlement of clients' funds. He took his life listening to Wagner in his mother's flat in St. John's Wood while she was abroad— a rather cruel thing to do really when a hotel room would have been easily available. When he was discovered, the radiogram arm was jumping back and forth at the edge of the record, *Die Meistersinger*, and a half-eaten green apple was beside him. That at least was his sister's romanticized version after we ratted out that her account of his dying from his World War Two injuries was bogus; his brother—who made good every penny my father embezzled—had a shorter version: "He shot himself in Mother's flat."

My relatives left me unaware of Anthony, my half-brother whose brain had been injured one day after his birth. The hospital nurse, carrying two new-borns in her arms for maternal visits, carelessly let a swing door bash into Anthony's head. The severe brain bleed was not diagnosed for another two days. For seven years his doting mother cared for him at home until my father's suicide necessitated her working day and night to pay household bills as well as a private facility for him. He was supposed to die in a few years but inconveniently lived to thirty-three, just a few miles away from me in London. My father's increasingly wealthy and intellectually striving family wiped him from their memory. A nurse who remembered a little said that he spent most of his life lying silently in bed. "He never spoke," she said, "but when we played music on the wireless, he opened his eyes and smiled." A child might still be cooed over. A grown retarded male needs shaving and washing, has all the drawbacks including incontinence and none of the pluses of a baby. By the time I knew of his existence he was dead.

London's days drained away so fast that last autumn of 1952 before we were to emigrate. Just before the boat train, I accidentally smashed a crystal ashtray while packing, and shards of glass lodged in my right palm. I thought the pain quite wonderful, well worth it, since I couldn't possibly go to Canada with such a wound. The local cottage hospital sewed it up, but it quickly became infected and I was subjected to antibiotic shots of some sort in my stomach every day on the *Empress of France*. They hurt like blazes.

"The ship doctor says," my mother told my stepfather dramatically, "that if the gangrene can't be stopped, the boat will have to put in at Newfoundland so they can amputate below the elbow." With hindsight it seems unlikely that the ship's doctor used the word *gangrene* except in some notional scenario, but this was the word my mother used. The crisis, real or imagined, seemed to excite her—I rather think she would have liked me better if I had one less hand or eye—and she began telling passengers at dinner in the economy-deck dining room. Then everyone got seasick in the November waters of the Atlantic and my mother lost interest.

Canada for me was super-clean, neither bomb sites nor hedge-rows nor affectionate grandparents to counter my mother's irritation with me. Still, I had a string to play out. I would be going home soon. I auditioned for my father in letters to him. I was happy, observant, trying to be a clever child drawing pictures in words of a fascinating new world that he would want to hear all about.

My letters, sent to the only address I knew—his office—never reached him. They were intercepted by his family. Each day I looked for the letter that would call me back to England. I daydreamed in a perfect technicolour fantasy starring myself as a sapphire and emerald-green wonder of imponderable beauty. My father was demanding this magical child be returned. I would go to London and be Jewish again. In the meantime, I babysat, picked fruit, collected pop bottles and brought discarded coat hangers to dry cleaners in a wagon to get refunds, all towards my fare back to England. Just before he killed himself, I received the only letter my father ever sent to me. "The old world staggers," he wrote, "in the face of the new. We need iron in our souls and our backs. And there is none."

The day I learned of his death was a chilly April day in Hamilton, 1956, with small hints of sun. I was summoned to the telephone in the house where I was renting a room. My mother was calling from St. Catharines, where she now lived with my sister, stepfather and half-brothers. "Your father's dead," she said. "He killed himself." I was silent. "He went mad," she continued. "I expect you'll go mad too." And then she hung up. I suppose she was terribly upset. When you're fifteen you don't analyze very much. I thought, I won't go to school. I have a perfect reason not to go to school. But what, I won-dered, does a person do when they hear the father they loved so much has killed himself? It seemed to me that the correct gesture was to walk by the sea.

My way of dealing with difficult moments was automatically to observe rather than feel. John Masefield's poem bubbled up: "I must go down to the seas again, to the lonely sea and the sky" and so on.

Unfortunately, there was no sea near Hamilton, Ontario. I walked down to Lake Ontario's Van Wagner's Beach, which was quite deserted, a bit of wind over the sand and the beach's pop shop boarded up with Coca-Cola signs. Near it was a shallow stream with a small bridge. I sat on the edge swinging my legs. I wondered what would happen if I jumped into the water. I heard a car behind me and it was a police car. "What are you doing?" the policeman asked. "Nothing," I replied. "My father died," I said, "and I wanted to think about it." Perhaps it was my English accent and proper school raincoat that reassured him. He drove away. Next day I wrote myself a note for the teacher. "Dear Mr. Lewis: Barbara was away from school on Tuesday because her father died." Signed Barbara Amiel. It was accepted.

Mother's remarriage was a terrific success, produced two children and lasted for over fifty years. But the union made my sister and especially me something of a handicap for my poor neurotic mother, who felt my love of classical music and literature was a constant rebuke to her new husband; and in the near-identical features of my face she saw always my father.

Vera was becoming a little more hysterical all the time, and since she had rather a yen to attempt suicide with phenacetin painkillers whenever I lived at home, I quite understood the feelings of my stepfather that it would be best if I lived somewhere else. My sister and I had got into a reasonably synchronized routine after a bout of her sobbing, and when the bathroom door was locked for too long we could push it open with one sharp shove and get her to the local hospital for a quick stomach pump. I parted from my family at first involuntarily when I was fourteen, leaving the younger and more withdrawn Ruth behind, and then off and on depending on Vera's state, quite happily renting different rooms till my last year in high school.

An unpredictable element was my mother's see-saw rediscovery of her maternal role, which resulted in my arrival at high school now and then to discover she had telephoned the parents of classmates to ask for money to help send me to university. Her moods swung erratically into some world where only my stepfather could function. This world was exciting, full of fantasy events that daily placed her in the centre of life-threatening dramas that left her little time to worry about more mundane matters. When my maternal grandfather made a visit to us in St. Catharines, I was quickly retrieved from the room I was living in outside town to complete our happy family. After a week he took me aside. "Don't believe everything your mother says," he suggested gently. "She does imagine things a little."

Children are malleable and take life as it comes. No one told me how lives were supposed to be, and so I didn't feel shortchanged. Between editing my high school magazine, writing the Collegiate Corner column for the *St. Catharines Standard* and working after school at any job I could get, I found a place for myself. I had no parents to give me rules and regulations. I'd say I did pretty well, though some of my deficiencies were a bit awkward later. Kitchens didn't come with the various rooms I lived in, and when I first married I hadn't the vaguest idea how to make a cup of tea or coffee. I lived largely on malted milkshakes from the nearest drugstore, with an egg in them for nourishment.

I saw the considerable benefits in my situation. My home was entirely portable: I carried around a photo of my father in a black leather frame; promoted to colonel, he was in uniform with the Sam Browne cross strap on. He smiled rakishly with the smile I had loved, the same teeth and eyes I had. I kept two or three books from our home in Hendon: Penguin paperbacks in orange and red with the little penguin looking alert and friendly on the front cover and spine—*The Black Girl in Search of God* and *The Moon and Sixpence*, with my father's signature in one and my mother's maiden name scribbled in the other.

The memory of real homes with real furnishings passed quickly. Dating and getting to college were my two high school fixations. My all-girls school in England had not prepared me for boys, but this was a subject that, unlike Latin, I grasped naturally and with rather too much enthusiasm. I seemed to go from extraordinary peaks of infatuation to the gloom of abandonment. My reach exceeded my grasp. It was one thing to get membership in the desired sorority in exchange for writing rather larger-than-life accounts of our volunteer work for the head chapter, and quite another to hang on to the sort of boys that sorority girls normally had as their steadies. The type of boy I was drawn to never really varied. He was always tall and beefy. I looked for confidence and languor.

Confidence came in buckets with the tall blond boy who was the son of the St. Catharines mayor and with whom I fell desperately in something with. But he was seeing me only as a sticky plaster for the temporary break-up he had with the lovely dark-eyed sorority sister who lived in a splendid house on the better side of town. Thrillingly, he invited me to the most longed-for party on New Year's Eve at a home in the posh Glenridge neighbourhood.

My knowledge of party dresses was rather limited. "Can I wear Bermuda shorts?" I asked, thinking of a very nice blue, white and green plaid pair on sale at the shop where I was working. They were summer cotton and at a knock-down price since it was winter.

"No," he said, "not for a New Year's party." Unwisely, I bought them anyway and was so excited with my purchase that I put them on with long white knee socks. Perfect, I thought. The mayor's son, so tall, so broad-shouldered and so conventional, did not. "I told you," he said as I got into his car, "not Bermudas."

His former girlfriend was in dark red cigarette trousers and perfect little ballerina pumps. He ditched me in front of everyone. I cried, which of course made the whole thing that much more humiliating. I didn't yet have the common sense to see how to handle such occasions, and my sense of drama was from the beginning highly developed and not, I fear, unlike my mother's.

I bought a hat and swing jacket to wear to church without the slightest religious hesitation when I found out that St. Thomas' Anglican was the Sunday destination of boys from Ridley College, the local private school. The swing jacket was on sale and a rather nasty shade of grey but utterly up to date. My calculation was rewarded by an exciting encounter on the church steps with a very tall ginger-haired boy from Bermuda, of all places, wearing the coveted blazer, who promptly asked me to the Ridley dance. I asked him in return to our collegiate dance.

"Who's that little Negro boy dancing so well?" he asked as we tried, awkwardly, to jive in my high school's decorated gymnasium.

"Not a Negro, actually. He's Stanley Feldman and he's Jewish. So am I."

"Never mind," he said with much kindness. "Don't say anything if you come to Bermuda and no one will know." I had not taken this aspect into account when I went trawling at St. Thomas'.

My true high school sweetheart was tall, dark, broad-shouldered and confident enough in himself to be indifferent to my eccentric manners, my championing of peculiar causes in 1959, such as legalization of marijuana, and the unease of his parents at my itinerant addresses. In his arms and presence, the zoetrope flashes of yesteryear were shut out and I felt safe. Still, he was not Jewish and his parents seemed ambivalent about me. By the end of high school my single social ambition was to meet a Jewish boy at college and become part of a community. My high school steady became a prominent and accomplished scientist and married a Montreal Jewish girl. When I tried to reconnect with him a few years ago, as sometimes people do towards the end of their lives, he would not take my telephone call.

About forty years after graduating, a classmate died. Among her belongings were the little notes each of us had written partying at her house in our last year of high school. We were to predict our state five years hence. The small brown envelope was still sealed, and I opened it up, curious to know what my eighteen-year-old self had written. The pencil writing was faint but perfectly legible and commas non-existent: "In five years from now I'll still be carrying a torch still trying so hard to be that independent person I want to emulate and probably be damn miserable in the bargain. I'll be chasing the pot of gold at the end of the rainbow and will probably find it's empty."

Perhaps I wasn't as happy as I thought.

CHAPTER TWO

Crime and Poets

I arrived at the University of Toronto by bus in 1959 with a matched three-piece set of Skyway luggage, thinking I looked hellishly smart just like the ads I'd seen of stewardesses poised with overnight bags on the portable steps to a plane. I had no idea what one actually put in the tiny train case with a mirror in its lid, but the set was on sale and the three powder blue vinyl pieces came to $22.50.

I'd scrambled together the first payment of my college tuition and three months of residence fees with my usual confidence that I'd find a job to pay for the rest. The St. Catharines chapter of the Imperial Order Daughters of the Empire had bravely awarded me a bursary without ever meeting me. I have no idea how the patriotic blue-rinsed ladies ever found me, but their forty-dollar cheque arrived each month of my first year—a lifesaver for school books, records and Gus Caruso hair sets.

My high school graduating marks were foul in anything that required homework, given my after-school jobs, but a teacher told University College of my family "circumstances" and amazingly up turned a Leonard Foundation bursary for four years. Mining magnate Reuben Wells Leonard must have heaved in his coffin. He especially specified that recipients must be needy young white Protestants— never more than 25 per cent of them female—who would become leading Christian citizens in the Empire. Those not meeting Leonard's criteria were "excluded." Thank God I didn't know this at the time because I might—probably not—have had an attack of conscience and lived up to my view that death wishes should be respected.

Being thrown into collegiate middle-class life after my sort of existence was like getting tossed into the dry cycle of a washing machine: you tumble from one faux pas to the next. There, finally, they were—Jewish males asking me out: these glorious stacks of Davids, Murrays, Jeffreys, all excitingly in dentistry, med school, architecture and, inevitably, law school, and apparently from families wealthy enough to give them brand-new cars and a seemingly endless budget for dining and playing. Their families owned "cottages" for summer fun; they asked me to "openings" and invited me to classy restaurants that were a maze of pitfalls: finger bowls, the deadly bread basket with objects to be torn into pieces by hand and put somewhere on the table, menus written in French, and other unfamiliar rites. The fact is, I had never gone to a sit-down restaurant in my whole life, nor to any movie that wasn't at a drive-in, an essential location for necking rather than film-watching. Now I went to cinemas and theatres—which meant working out a method of concealing my spectacles till the lights had gone down and whipping them off at film's end. I had never purchased a handbag, just had a wallet, so specs had to be put in a pocket. The wardrobe problems were absolutely goliath. Clearly Bermuda shorts would not be the answer.

Weekends I worked days, plus two nights a week, but that money was to help bridge the gap to cover funds for tuition and residence plus personal needs. The Dean of Women solved that. Her policy was to put like with like in residence, and her selection for me was inspired, though perhaps not in quite the way she would have wished. My roommate, Judith, was a Jewish girl born in wartime Europe, hidden by Catholic nuns and then smuggled out to South America. She had starlet looks, rather Jean Simmons or more appropriately Haya Harareet of *Ben-Hur*. She was extremely intelligent, quiet, and skilled at shoplifting, though coming from an economically comfortable family she had no need to do this—more the thrill, I suppose. I had never thought of this route to the needed garments for myself, but the possibilities were stratospheric if only I could get the nerve. I got it in spades, exceeding my roommate's wildest expeditions.

"Dear Mother," I wrote in my note accompanying a navy blue with red-and-white trim knitted dress and matching jacket, "I thought this would look marvellous on you. Love, Barbara." No response. Perhaps it was the "Made in Israel" label, which I hadn't noticed when hoisting it from the shop. Embellished cashmere sweaters, a memorable Nina Ricci dress—I was in clothes heaven. (Look, the progression is not exactly news: shoplifter early on, shopaholic late in life.) Naturally we were caught—during an urgent trip to get new winter coats. I had my eye on a wonderful belted loden-green number, just the thing I thought to wear to the dreaded Toronto Maple Leafs hockey games. (Words cannot describe the horror of college dating in Canada. Hockey night, a favourite rite of Saturday evenings, was the Bataan Death March for me.)

"Just a moment," said the voice as a hand descended on my newly loden-clothed shoulder. The department store detective spent a lot of time trying to figure out which one of us was "the brains behind this." I was the obvious choice, since Judith was in funds and I was not. Neither of us outed the other. The shivering fear of a hand on my shoulder is imprinted in my larcenous heart, never to leave. The spree required more money to pay back the store for all the confessed thefts. I took on night work, sitting in my room with telephone books and long lists of names, credit ratings and addresses to be matched up and put next to underlined telephone numbers as possible mugs for boiler-room stock salesmen. After that, when necessary I decked myself out from Toronto's recycling shops, which had not yet been called "vintage."

An after-school job I had while in high school at Levitt's Fine China came to my rescue as I took my first tottering baby steps to full membership in Toronto's Jewish community—a community for which I was fundamentally unsuitable given my take on life and politics but didn't realize at the time. Levitt's gave me a virtual Oxford degree in china and crystal tableware (though sadly not on how to use its pieces), and I could soon distinguish Minton china from Coalport and Spode's Imari pattern from Royal Crown Derby's Imari at twenty paces.

This knowledge lay dormant until an encounter in the Toronto Forest Hill home of a young man I was dating. Waiting in the hall for his mother to appear, I could see the living room furniture of a beige brocade zipped up in heavy see-through plastic covers. On the other side of the hall, the dining room, in semi-darkness, was laid out for "company," with plates and stemware. The house seemed like the film set for a horrible murder. Maternal scrutiny materialized. My surname did not bring a warm smile: it didn't match any name she had encountered either at bridge games or bar mitzvahs.

"What lovely Irish Belleek," I said, having sized up the tableware. This had a slightly mollifying effect. Frankly, I thought Belleek was out of place on a semi-formal dining room table, not liking parian and bisque china at this point in my nascent snobbery, but I kept such judgments to myself.

As it was, until university, trying to hang on to my Jewish identity in Canada had been a little tricky. I always wore my tiny gold mezuzah conspicuously over sweaters, had never removed it even in my "Christian" days, but there hadn't been many takers. Mind you, it was only three-quarters of an inch long and the Hebrew scroll was concealed behind the little hinged door at the front. Excitingly, Danny Strub of the Strubs kosher pickle family did walk me partway home quite often in grade eight, but I think it was because he had a series of really bad styes on both eyes that puffed up with pus for most of that year and he was not yet ready to take on the appropriate girls. I would read and reread the *Hamilton Spectator*'s social pages and obituaries to see the Jewish names—Sobel, Koski, Cohen—and learn of their weddings, fundraisers and deaths. This gave me a strange comfort and sense of kinship. I remembered hearing of bar mitzvahs in our London circles where no one questioned the identity of a descendant of Cracow's great Rabbi Isserles and Tel Aviv's Rabbi Moshe Amiel, but it all seemed so far away and irretrievable. The newspaper photos of Jewish events to which I would never be invited were a tangible lifeline. Whenever I saw the appellation *Jewish*, whatever the reference, I felt reassured that we did exist.

In Canada in those far-off days, it was perfectly all right for your homeroom teacher to try to save your (Christian) soul. Every Monday morning in my grade eight class the routine was the same: "Stand up, those who did not attend church on Sunday," Miss Addleton would ask. I stood up alone. The class looked at me with interest. I could not bring myself to explain. The phrase "because I am a Jew" seemed rude, and so I remained stubbornly mute, unable to give her the explanation she might well have accepted.

Eventually I gave in and was baptized and confirmed in a small Anglican church after taking confirmation lessons. I hoped so much that at my First Communion I would be lost in some glorious transcendental rapture, but apart from liking the hymns, nothing very rapturous took place. The whole episode bothered me, and so on the day after I gave the valedictory address at W.H. Ballard Public School, I went to the minister and asked how I could become a Jew again, thinking perhaps there was an Anglican decontamination rite.

"My child," he replied—and this illustration of the church's easy pragmatism has never left me—"when you stop believing, you are a Jew."

The following summer, when I was fifteen, I boarded with a Polish Catholic family who only charged me a dollar a day for a bed in the basement and one big meal. No Jews on that circuit. When I rejoined my mother in St. Catharines I screwed up my courage, polished my mezuzah and ventured into the B'nai Israel synagogue one afternoon, thinking the time had come to assert myself. "Hello," I smiled.

The response was not open arms. The ladies there that day told me in no uncertain terms to leave and come back during Christian Brotherhood week. Similarly, the interviewer at Toronto's Jewish Community Centre at Bloor and Spadina, where I went to seek possible financial aid for university, was very polite as she explained that they only helped Jewish students. I explained that I was such a person. She smiled. Perhaps only a Jew could imagine that a student would fake Jewish identity in order to get money.

Looking back, I quite see the problem Canadian Jews had with me sixty or so years ago. Insofar as I had any visible family, my mum was an ersatz Christian and my stepfather just an English bloke. My Sephardic surname, not Ashkenazi with the comforting ring of Levy, Cohen or something with "berg" or "stein" at the end, was no bloody help. Being penniless, working at strange jobs and living alone in various rooms at different points did not denote the lifestyle of a nice Jewish girl.

Well, I thought, to blazes with them all. Now I was crossing the campus to the Sigmund Samuel Library to read in the stacks, crunching the snow underfoot and staring in wonder at a startling blue sky, all so exhilarating that it brought on a mental mazurka. I took out more books than I read, grabbing titles and piling them up on my desk together with books I bought from the University of Toronto or Christian Science bookstores. Santayana's reflections, essays by Isaiah Berlin, Berenson on Italian Renaissance Art, Spinoza—great chunks of the lexicon of Western thought with an absolutely sticky affection for anything written by George Orwell, and Albert Camus's non-fiction. I skipped lectures to go to jobs, read or sleep in, and dated with manic ferocity. Nothing merited attention for too long apart from music.

In my second year, someone gave me an old and very ugly standing record player that had a grumpy look as if it had seen too many years in a basement. Every requiem mass—Gounod, Verdi, Bach, Mozart, Brahms—every oratorio and sacred cantata were now roommates along with the great cantors. And on the occasions when, like almost every student under the sun, finding some aspect of life too sublime (or enervated) and contemplating some passionate embrace of Thanatos or wondering if the ladder to the clouds could better be climbed by flying off the windowsill, my rapture would be accompanied by the glorious sounds of Bach's cantata *Liebster Gott, wenn werd ich sterben?* That particular cantata's nerve-bleeding beauty, pleading for death, was almost unbearable, illustrating, I suppose, the concern of both Plato and Aristotle that music could play to "disordered" or "perverted" emotions rather than the good.

My small class for Honours Philosophy & English was not exactly standing room only, and each year it was virtually halved by failures, nervous breakdowns and dropouts, confirming my view that I was in the right place. In Whitney Hall, my residence, I was enjoying the pleasure of regular dinners every night after arriving at a less than appealing five foot seven and a half, and weighing in under a hundred pounds—and not from anorexia. Everyone else seemed to be trying to lose weight, so I got as many servings of potatoes as I wanted. This was a home—until the dreaded Christmas and summer holidays arrived and residences closed, everyone went back to their families, and I was stuck, shuffling around, trying to find rooms to let.

"Who's that?" I asked one of the girls in the Junior Common Room in November of my first year. "Forget it," was the reply. "Jewish, but he doesn't date Jewish girls. Only models and older women." That did it. He was tall, dark, extremely handsome and, unlike many of the young men in the Junior Common Room, very silent, with a curious pigeon-toed way of walking. He wore the collar of his black-and-white tweed overcoat up, framing a face that in profile had a fine curved nose and high cheekbones. "I'm going to marry him," I said. Unfortunately for both of us, I did.

I was bog terrified of marriage as a child, which had absolutely nothing to do with the wet-handkerchief unhappiness of my mother over her divorce. Rather, it was the puzzle of it all. I had neither an emotional nor practical vocabulary to understand family life. As every birthday came, nine, ten, the fear became stronger. On my eleventh birthday, my very first thought was that in only five years I would be old enough to marry quite legally. The thought obsessed me as if, come sixteen, I would be sold into servitude.

Gary Smith was in his second year at Osgoode Hall Law School. A premature greyness ran in his family, and his dark hair was already touched with silver in his twenties. I thought he had an almost predatory cast to his slightly saturnine features. He seemed mysterious, and I interpreted his quiet as a sign that still waters run deep. I was wrong. He was simply a quiet man with not too much to say. He was also in a state that I understood much better forty years later: shell shock. His father and uncle were facing several criminal charges for stock fraud. They had been acquitted once, but the Crown had come back with new charges. Meanwhile the Smith twins were out on bail.

I suppose some might say there was a neat symmetry in the scandals touching my first and last marriages, and on the surface there is a certain irony. Gary's father, Harry, had been president of the Havana Riviera, the Cuban casino that was the crown jewel in the empire of a business associate, Meyer Lansky. In Toronto, Lena Horne sang at the Pyramid Room in the Smith-owned Prince George Hotel. It was for both Toronto and the times a larger-than-life lifestyle.

Perhaps it was the premature world-weariness that changing circumstance had forced on Gary that attracted me, rather than his premature silvered hair. The Riviera had come under Fidel Castro's control in January of 1959, ten months before Gary and I met, ending the Smiths' period of Cuban glamour and connections. The second round of criminal charges against the brothers had just begun. This was my first encounter with lives that had been put into limbo while justice was presumed to be done.

A heaviness hung over their penthouse apartment. Everything was on hold—holidays, travel, work. The trials dragged on and on: acquittals, new charges, convictions, appeals. At the time I was absolutely convinced of the men's innocence and convinced they would be convicted. The two notions lived compatibly in my mind because that was life. And years later, in another piece of symmetry, Gary's father was pardoned.

My potential in-laws had all the conventional views of the early 1960s and I shared none of them. I expected to work after marriage and had no intention of changing my name. "Really," I told Mrs. Smith earnestly, assuming she would appreciate my candour and wisdom, "I think it would be better if Gary and I lived together for a year or two before we actually married, don't you?" She responded with the same heart-attack look as when I brought up the jam jar of insects from the mattress in the room I was renting for identification. None of these ideas had any political connotation to me; they simply made sense.

My engagement was accidental. Gary gave me an opal ring for my birthday. "What's that?" said a properly gimlet-eyed Jewish girl in residence upon my return. Between night and the next day, the gift turned into an official engagement, since a ring could mean nothing else. I managed to accidentally break the opal ring twice. I finally threw it into Georgian Bay.

There was a brief flutter while Mrs. Smith enlisted her sister to go to London and check out my family—just to make certain I was Jewish. My Hampstead relatives, a bit put out by the enquiry, sent the Canadian investigative team to Israel to meet my cousin Saadia Amiel, a brilliant nuclear physicist with the reassuring title of director of long-term planning working for Deputy Defense Minister Shimon Peres. Actually, Saadia was busy perfecting the means to make heavy water for Israel's A-bomb. He promptly put the Canadians in white protective suits and took them around the Soreq nuclear facility at Yavne with instructions from my Hampstead uncle to please radiate them.

They returned to Toronto and gave me clearance. Finally, I was in. Jewish. Accepted. My father's family in Britain, reported the investigative team, were even well off, with children at Oxford. This puzzled the Smiths, who assumed, wrongly, having had no experience of caviar communists, that once my aunts and uncles were informed how poor I was and how many jobs I was holding down, a spigot of funds would appear. Now that I was a confirmed member of the tribe, the Smiths had no objections to their son's marriage. Except my own fear of marriage was only dormant. I managed to hold off wedding plans for the four years of my undergraduate degree, but the tanks were closing in. My response was to become catatonic.

"You'll honeymoon at the Sands Hotel in Las Vegas," said Mr. Smith.

"You'll love Vegas," said Celia Smith, encouragingly. "Jack will show both of you a good time." She was a woman of unbounded generosity and kindness to me. She had several utterly beautiful and expensive evening dresses of hers made over for me. She took me on my first plane trip and my first visit to Manhattan, and gamely went along with my determination to take the open tourist boat in the rain to see the Statue of Liberty instead of shopping.

By "Jack" she meant Jack Entratter, not actually the sort of person you encountered in either Hendon or Hamilton. First a bouncer at New York's Stork Club, then manager of the Copacabana nightclub, where he personally selected the Copa Girls, he was an associate of Sinatra's Rat Pack and moved easily in the mix of grime and glamour that made up a picaresque world of mobsters, entertainers and gamblers. Now, good friend of the Smiths, he ran the Sands in Las Vegas.

"You've never been to Vegas," said Harry Smith, as if that settled it. He combed his silver hair back straight and, like his son, spoke very little and in a voice husky from all his smoking. He would stroke my hair and smile when he heard Gary mention that I had got a very high mark on an essay, and I wanted to hug him. I used to watch him placing his bet on the telephone for Sunday's football games. Phrases like "What's the point spread?" which meant utterly zilch to me, had a sort of knowing exciting ring.

I knew absolutely nothing about casinos in Vegas, nothing about the names the Smith's invoked, like a fellow with pull in New Jersey called Jerry Catena who "knows the governor." "Lansky" had a slightly familiar sound to it. "He's a very nice quiet man," said quiet Gary Smith when I asked. "And extremely polite." Gary acted as an informal chauffeur for Meyer Lansky when they were all in Florida. But I asked around and pretty soon I realized that Meyer Lansky may have had excellent manners but he had other things too, including a leading role in the founding of Murder Incorporated, the enforcement arm of the Italian-American Mafia and organized crime. Visiting the Las Vegas of Entratter and Lansky was too much for my nascent left-wing self-righteousness. Shoplifting was behind me, and I had all the outrage of the reformed: "Going to the Sands," I responded at the dinner table, "would be a honeymoon financed ultimately by men hung on meat hooks." Silence. God knows how they tolerated this over the brisket. After all, I had no way of knowing how involved the Smiths were with the darker side of Vegas life—if at all—and the offer was extremely generous given the times they were facing. A polite refusal would have been sufficient.

One last, over-the-top, excruciating scene had to be played. A pre-wedding cocktail party for Gary and me at the Smiths' home included an invitation to my mother. Thankfully, no response. But alas, Vera arrived unexpectedly at the penthouse, alone and in full Jewish mode. Suddenly she was trying to speak Yiddish, something she had never done in her entire life since Russian, German and English were the languages of our family, Yiddish being frowned on as a corruption. Anecdotes I had never heard and strongly doubted about our family's Jewish practices found wings and flew out of her.

She carried on a one-sided conversation, oblivious to any question asked of her, hearing absolutely nothing and in a world of her own construction. She continued a sort of soliloquy as her still-slim figure moved trance-like from room to room, greeting one and all with a sprinkling of oy veys. The Smiths couldn't quite take it in. Having seen my mother in many roles, this one did not especially surprise me, and I was relieved that she had chosen not to wear a sheitel. She did ask several times for gefilte fish. Unfortunately, the Smiths were serving smoked salmon and caviar. There was nothing for me to do but retreat into my happy world of detachment and melt away.

As did the planned synagogue wedding for the spring of 1964. My fear of marriage was no longer hibernating. Inducements were ineffective. Despite their legal circumstances, a number of things were on offer: a future of fur coats, my own bone china, flatware and crystal, summers at "the cottage," a starter apartment and a probable ascent to a house in Forest Hill. The prospect was beyond ghastly, the price tag too high. My feelings for Gary were evaporating as I fought the losing battle against becoming a suburban Marjorie Morningstar without his support. No matter the acceptance and the trouble to get here, the notion of giving up working and losing the independence I had enjoyed since my early teens was nightmarish. I couldn't do it.

But how to get out of it? This was 1964. As wedding plans proceeded, I stewed in a toxic horror. All right, I finally told myself. If I go through with it, I can leave and never have to do it again. But less than a week before the wedding, that seemed too much. Enter Robert Hershorn.

Hershorn had materialized in my life some time earlier during university, and brought with him a buffet of forbidden fruits. Scion of a large clothing manufacturer in Montreal, where he lived, he seemed worldly and slightly dangerous. A friend of mine was dating his cousin, and so the connection was made. Robert would pick me up in his bright red Mustang convertible and we would end up in his suite in Toronto's King Edward Hotel. This was cheating, of course, but in the best of all worlds, Gary would catch on, break off our wedding plans and the problem would resolve itself outside me. Hershorn's flashy convertible was catnip: there I was, incredibly Nouvelle Vague, driving recklessly around the streets that bisected the campus, rather Jeanne Moreau or Anouk Aimée—apart from Anouk's hair-blowing-in-the-wind thing, which my own locks did not handle. When Robert and I decamped to the Colonnade apartment of my girlfriend, I usually found her entwined on the sofa with his cousin. I could see her but only vaguely, due to dimmed lights and a haze of smoke from many candles and marijuana.

Hershorn was the purveyor of many things, including heroin, to which he was addicted, though that was not entirely clear to me at first. I was just attracted to a man who fit my physical prototype with an attitude I found irresistible, both aloof and with a risky detachment. Actually he was strung out half the time, but a functioning heroin addict does aloof very well. Jewish, tall, large and fleshy, this was clearly a man who could take charge of matters and in addition was rich. His world was all about flying to Mykonos or New York as if he were going to Guelph. He can fix this mess I'm in, I thought as I lay paralyzed, unable to stop the marriage and in dread of it. He was eight or nine years older than me and evil and I more than sensed it, I knew it. Robert enjoyed inducting beautiful young women into his world of hard drugs. He enjoyed cooking the heroin for them, holding the spoon over a flame with reverence as if it were some sort of purification ritual, and then, with the tenderness of a mother giving her baby its bottle, showing them how to inject themselves.

I felt so grown-up: not daring but a little perilous. Montreal evenings, either in his cousin's spartan room with its white-painted walls mimicking a simple Greek island dwelling or in Hershorn's large flat on Pine Avenue, I was like a curious Martian. The shadowy candlelit rooms filled with lolling beings opening their veins and mouths to every intoxicant available, the exquisite black model with her shaved head and wild eyes turning perfectly calm as the drug flowed through her veins, the French-Canadian film directors and the Jewish-Canadian sculptor, the smell of drugs and the pageant unfolding in front of me was a little frightening, but then I was on the other shore. I tried a very occasional puff of marijuana, but alcohol made me sick and heroin or cocaine reliance wouldn't help me get up in the morning for the jobs that paid my fees and rent, so I was safe. Hershorn's Montreal was simply my version of the Paris of William Burroughs. Or my own *La Dolce Vita*, my *Last Year at Marienbad*, the films that I adored and that were having such an intoxicating effect on the artsy set.

There was something soft about Hershorn, rather like the beginning of decay in an overripe fungus or fruit. We may have embraced a few times, even made some love, but very soon it became clear that his first love was heroin rather than women. He told me that his parents were hoping he would marry a decent Jewish girl and perhaps, he theorized, I might be the one. Robert died about eight years later, in 1972, in Hong Kong. The official cause was a drug overdose in his hotel room. Those closer to him said he was murdered in some awful back alley. Either way, his end was always unlikely to be happy.

His cousin, poet and future troubadour Leonard Cohen, close though he was to Hershorn—and the two were virtually inseparable in those early sixties—had no active part in the more seamy aspect of Hershorn's behaviour, though Cohen's experimentation with various mind-altering substances may have been encouraged early on by Hershorn. In fact Cohen was the good side of the two cousins, or, more accurately, as Ruth Wisse wrote in a 1995 essay, Hershorn was "the dark side of Leonard's celebrity."

But hell, any moral strictures I had were conveniently deep-sixed as I watched these ugly scenes taking place. That might have jeopardized the fun I was having walking up Montreal's Mountain Street with Robert, Leonard and Leonard's girlfriend, Marianne, on nights when fine rain gave each street lamp a halo and the railings and paving stones a shimmer—while I gritted my teeth in despair because Marianne's blonde Scandinavian hair remained gorgeous and straight while my Jewish hair went utterly frizzed. Besides, it was fun going to Claude Jutra's first feature film, *À tout prendre*, with my first experience of flashbulbs when I emerged from Hershorn's car at the premiere.

I telephoned Robert from Toronto. "I'm supposed to get married this Sunday with lots of guests and I don't want to."

"I'll come and get you," he said, as if there was absolutely nothing strange about a woman he had been dating a few months earlier calling him on the eve of her wedding. As the plane with the three of us took off from Toronto for New York, I felt weightless, ecstatic with relief at leaving Rosenthal china and thank-you notes behind.

The evening that was supposed to be my wedding night was spent in Times Square with Leonard Cohen holding one arm of mine and Robert the other, marching me around in the night air. Earlier on, in the Taft Hotel, a small group had gathered. I remember sitting on the floor next to the splayed legs of a fellow hanging over the arm of an old overstuffed chair as a cigarette was passed around. Someone must have laced it with hash or LSD. The result was catastrophic. My system went into overdrive. I began hallucinating.

God only knows why people actually want to go on psychedelic trips that turn one into an agitated, vomiting mess without the slightest resemblance to a rational human being. The brightly lit New York streets seemed to be both day and night at the same time. Worse, the experience was terrifying because there was no sequence to help me. The mind tried to clutch some moment to put all the sensory input flashing by in order, but when sequence is removed there can be no organization. The two men alternated pouring coffee in me and taking me on firm walks in fresh air until the nightmare passed. After a day or so, I went back to Toronto alone.

Leonard watched his decadent cousin dating a Jewish girl, who neither drank nor took drugs and was working her way through Graduate School, with detached amusement and summed it up in a poem he wrote for Robert about me—or at least a poem I was told was about me. Robert gave me a copy of Leonard's handwritten lines. For all I know, this might have been boilerplate in Hershorn's seduction technique.

For Robert:

> Who saw them fall
> Their zeppelin thighs
> Illumined by flames
> From their garters
> Who saw blood
> Leaking from their eyes
> Who saw them fall
> Into a ruin of powder
> Into a nest of ashes
> Who saw them burning
> Who watching them
> Saw at last at last
> One rise from the ashes
> Bright and cool
> As a twelve year old
> From the ocean

> *Leonard, Spring 1964*

I thanked Leonard and he just smiled.

A month or two later, on a very bright July day, I married Gary Smith, having spent the night before in a hotel room with Hershorn, who had arrived in Toronto with no syringe and called begging me to hop over to a drugstore and get him one. When I returned home, all smudged and weary from bed with Hershorn, I knew the idea of marriage was absurd, but my sister, with whom I was sharing a couple of small rooms for the summer, was adamant.

She cleaned me up, ignored the tears streaming down my face, dismissed my protests that I couldn't get married, didn't want to get married, mustn't marry, and marched me into the car waiting for me. In the front seat, spineless and still weeping like a soap opera anti-heroine, I was squashed between her and Gary. "You're going to get married," she announced. She never had an easy time as my younger sister.

We had lived together during my year at graduate school when I was no longer eligible for residence. I was modelling for Eaton's catalogue (god-awful rayon house dresses were my beat), studying at night and taking vast quantities of codeine, which Ruth watched with horror.

My codeine habit had begun in Hamilton when I was fourteen or fifteen and working after school at a drugstore. I flipped hamburger patties and made rather good banana splits and milkshakes behind a small counter that seated about eight people. The drugstore closed latish, and the walk home was about two miles. There was no bus to the Roxborough Park housing estate where I lived with a mechanic and his family on the far side of the disused runway of the old Hamilton airport. For someone in their mid-teens, the pay was quite good and I had lots to eat, although the smell of grease became anathema. But my legs ached so. The druggist gave me a couple of over-the-counter tablets that contained codeine. The effect was remarkable.

After taking the tablets my spirits got a hit of euphoria. Energy rose too as the discomfort stopped. I didn't realize it was the codeine and didn't know that codeine was a morphine derivative. From that point on, codeine was a staple in my diet. All I needed then were an occasional couple of pills. All I need now are a couple or at max three or four a day. The pills were easily available and there was a cheap formulation called C2 that I could get in the twenty-four-hour drugstore minutes away from where Ruth and I lived.

But occasionally, some sort of clichéd mental anguish would hit. I have no idea why or what—to analyze it would be about as useful as a psychoanalyst asking me about the spots on my childhood rocking horse. I simply wanted to blank feelings out or view life through some jazzed-up euphoria. So, with stonking predictability, I'd gobble more and more of the tablets in search of nirvana and the added pleasure of induced exaltation. Given the oxygen-eating phenacetin content of those small C2 pink pills, taking too many could be dodgy and very occasionally lead to the banality of a hospital oxygen tent rather than any state of bliss. My sister saw what was happening and turned me in to the Alcoholism and Drug Addiction Research Foundation (ARF), whose clutches I quickly escaped after they put me in a ward with heroin addicts—at the time they had rather limited facilities for housing patients. Ruth was taking a B.Sc. in psychology and spent a fair amount of time at the infamous 999 Queen Street mental hospital. She already had enough on her plate—coming home bruised from patients throwing chairs at her—without having to put up with a barely conscious strung-out sister. I've never asked her, but I'm pretty certain her insistence on my marrying was because she saw it as the only means to save me from myself.

"We're there," she said as the car stopped in front of the rabbi's house. "You're going in."

How is it that the very same caress from the very same hands that once sent shivering excitement through me was now unwanted? For at least three years I had barely been able to eat as I waited for Gary's telephone call to set up our weekend date. Now I simply liked my husband-to-be. He wasn't a bully to me. Only he wouldn't release me, no matter what wretched things I did. The marriage lasted seven months. During it, I finally learned how to make percolated coffee. After that, I moved out, my borrowed grocery cart filled with my books and clothes. We parted amiably and with no need of a financial settlement—I was working at the Canadian Broadcasting Corporation and could afford my rooming house, which, with one marriage behind me, was where I was again.

"Barbara," said the impossibly slim, soigné and silver-haired Len Starmer, head of light entertainment at the CBC. "You will be our Miss CJBC." He pronounced the letters in French and did a little tap dance, clicking his fingers to the words. That seemed perfectly normal in the Variety department.

"Sorry?"

"We need an entrant for the Toronto Press Club's Miss By-Line Ball."

"Why me?"

"Your name is French, isn't it? A-miel?" This, in Len's eyes, qualified me as an eligible entrant to represent the French-language radio station of the corporation. "And if you do it, I'll transfer you out of Variety to TV Public Affairs as you requested."

The day was a nightmare. Eating wet, slimy slugs called oysters while being photographed smiling for newspapers did not appeal to me. That evening featured a catwalk contest in dresses, not swimsuits. I managed a whiff of marijuana before the competition to "calm you down," said the acquaintance in the boarding house across the road from mine. I arrived at the Royal York hotel with a melon head and feeling like I was walking on slippery mushrooms. This is not going to be good, I thought—though I could barely think. Uniformed members of the Toronto Argonauts football team, with shoulders that appeared to be seven feet wide, were assigned to walk each contestant down the runway.

"The guys said you were the really hot-looking one," said my mutant seven-foot-square companion.

Before the runway walk came the judges' interview, one of whom was the media magnate and Argos owner John F. Bassett Sr., a tall, good-looking force in Toronto with bushy Wasp eyebrows and a quick wit. Utter fear plus marijuana had made me oblivious to very much, including the interview questions, which seemed disembodied and in freeze-frame. Walking down the runway, I saw my estranged husband, Gary, leaning against the open door to the grand hall watching me. I wondered if I was hallucinating, but no.

"Look," I asked him later with my usual delicacy, "can I use your apartment for an hour or so after this? Privately?" He nodded yes, and I took my mutant football player there for a quick round that was entirely unsatisfactory. Nothing I did seemed to alienate Gary. Turns out the boys on the team had been half-correct: I was the easy one if not the hot one. Isabel, the brunette winner of the contest, quite the most sophisticated and beautiful entrant, must have been a wow in her interview. Six years later she married John Bassett.

In spite of this brief moment of glory on the runway as a doped and fake French-Canadian beauty, my after-hours social life was all but dead. On leaving the CBC offices, I'd slouch back to my rooming house thoroughly dejected, the high point being the consumption of my malted milkshake "with an egg in it please" purchased on the way home. Absolutely no man I was interested in asked me out.

My heart fluttered over the exquisite Tartar features of the CBC's newest boy wonder, Moses Znaimer, a Jew from Tajikistan by way of McGill and Harvard universities. Znaimer cultivated mystery, had a velvet voice, erudite vocabulary and wore the smartest black leather blazers, but made it perfectly clear that his affections were permanently taken by an equally cultivated sloe-eyed actress from Montreal. He bedded me on black satin sheets, stretched smooth and slivery over a round bed, but I had not reached his level of sexual sophistication and was unable to enjoy foreplay while wearing headphones and listening to erotica. Though I grieved at my inability to attract him, there was a certain relief. I could never have dressed as well or copulated as imaginatively.

In my gloom, I managed to uncover a Hungarian second-storey man. He put a couple of guns including a long one under my bed at night when he came in from "doing a job." I thought perhaps he wasn't just a second-storey man since I couldn't see how he would nip across a roof carrying a weapon that size, but he would never be pinned down. He had a certain glib charm and intensity that created some sexual allure. He wasn't really my type, so thin he was almost emaciated, with a rat-like face and the clear blue wandering eyes of a psychopath.

When he had some friends in my room and they seemed to be discussing—when not speaking in Hungarian—a full-scale armed robbery at a Toronto bank with the possibility of a shootout, I decided it was time to exit. Obviously, I would have to go to the police if this was for real. I quickly cleaned out my room when he was "at work" and moved a few streets away. He did not pursue me, although a couple of years later he contacted me through a third party in New York City. He had been arrested in Toronto's Union Station for drug dealing, he said, but somehow had escaped and wanted me to meet him at the Public Library on Fifth Avenue. I didn't.

In 1966, after beginning my appearances on camera at the CBC, a man in an elevator put a business card in my hand and asked if I would be the cover of the first edition of the new *Toronto Life* magazine. He or one of his partners had, I was later told, some feelings for me—apparently this was common knowledge—which may account for a second cover they ran less than a year later: a photo of me in a bikini from the initial shoot, used without advance notice.

After the launch of the magazine, the executive and his wife held a party for the magazine at his Toronto home, to which I had not been invited. Never mind, I thought, I'm going. I longed to wear a new dress of wool lace with its spun dream of bell-bottomed sleeves, scooped neck and the lime green colour that highlighted my eyes and long dark hair.

There is a line in a Tennessee Williams novel about the "anarchistic privileges" of beauty in the young that give the owner a "sort of godly license." I think I had at times rather a large overdose of that. The feelings of the wife were non-existent in my mind; I had a dress, I supposed I looked lovely in it and I wanted what I wanted—to flaunt and taunt—oblivious and uncaring about any damage I might do. Wearing the dress and flaunting cleavage, I recall walking through the rooms of the man's house. I remember hearing voices at a remove and seeing figures oddly blurred. Having displayed myself and talked to no one, I left. The tableau was over. Getting home was not easy. I had no idea where the blazes I was after arriving through the kindness of bus drivers and the directions of passengers.

Shortly after, in retrospect hardly surprising, the magazine executive, a tall, good-looking man, turned up at my new studio apartment behind the CBC building. He'd made no advances previously, not after the one lunch we had together nor after the sunny afternoon I spent having been deposited by him on an unfamiliar steep bank of grass abutting a road and some park, daydreaming at clouds overhead while he followed a more pedestrian itinerary playing golf with friends before picking me up for tea. My behaviour was unmoored, not anchored to reason or feeling. I was happy enough to be driven around, feeling that I was adored and mysterious—albeit loitering palely alongside Metropolitan Toronto roads and cemetery lawns is not quite the stuff of La Belle Dame sans Merci. Self-knowledge was definitely in short supply, and a woman of twenty-five is no sprite, but I seemed to think this was all perfectly natural and would come with no price tag. A married man at your apartment door, however, is no whimsical mystery, and the intent was clear even to a mentally impaired would-be sprite.

I had been told that a group of men known as the Toronto Swordsman's Club had a bet on who would bed me first, but as none of them seemed the least bit interesting to me, none of them achieved this minor goal. I did briefly wonder if this visit was part of the bet. The executive made his advances and I declined. When the message seemed not to be accepted, I did what I later did once more when finding myself with an experienced married man in a similar situation.

"All right," I said in a flat monotone. "Go ahead, perform." Disrobing and lying down, matter-of-fact, stark naked and as still as a dead fish, devoid of the slightest sign of amorous response, deflated advances faster and more finally than physical resistance.

Times, rules and mores have changed, and this technique relied on the male being a gentleman, which the executive most certainly was. I quite see that one would be hard put to offer a deflecting cup of tea to an unfamiliar Facebook date or a hopped-up mini-celeb after displaying oneself bare on a bed, no matter how bored one's attitude. But there was a psychology I had discovered intuitively. A sexual challenge of that sort, in my experience, killed desire faster than mythical saltpetre. No doubt it would not repel a drunken lecher, but my life did not involve drunken people, which is the huge advantage of not drinking myself. As for the lime green dress, well, I saw it in a photo when, fifty years later, *Toronto Life* published their anniversary edition. There it was at some gathering, the dress, me, the cigarette I couldn't inhale. The magazine labelled the photo incorrectly: "The Femme Fatale." Dress Fatale was the story.

My "separated" marital status was the perfect defence against any further marriage, but a couple of years later Gary's family felt we should get a divorce. At that time adultery was the only grounds for divorce in Ontario, and the blame was clearly mine, so I arranged for Len Birman, an actor friend of the film director I was dating, to play the role of witness to my infidelity. Huge mistake: never ask an actor. When the judge asked Birman what his profession was, he took his curtain call: "Your Honour," he replied in the mellifluous voice that had been heard as a voice-over in many a commercial, "I am an actor. My credits include seasons at Niagara-on-the-Lake and Strat-ford, where I played . . ." And so on and so on. "Currently I can be seen in . . ." Next divorce, I thought, I'll get an accountant to testify.

When he was asked to describe how he came upon my adultery, Birman moved into high gear. "I had occasion to bring over a news-paper and ring the doorbell at eight thirty in the morning," he began. The listless inhabitants of the courtroom waiting for their turn to do a standard divorce number perked up to hear the juicy details of a marvellously embroidered description of the debauched scene Birman had encountered.

Now single, past the hump of the necessary first marriage, my life ought to have become lighter, but certain aspects were hampered by the lack of knowledge most home-raised daughters would have had. "You've never wondered why you only have one or two periods a year?" said the doctor incredulously, not knowing Vera, who could not talk about anything to do with my reproductive system without getting faint. I was in some acute discomfort, but the condition was treatable and had an excitingly Jewish name, Stein-Leventhal syn-drome. Had I realized that, I would have gone to a doctor earlier. The contraceptive pill was still illegal in Canada, although allowed for certain medical conditions, and mine was probably one, but my elderly doctor felt its controversial estrogen content too dangerous. Instead I was given prednisone, and suddenly in my twenties I was developing at a fierce rate, which I assumed would deflate when the prednisone stopped. The moon face went but not the moon chest, which later became the source of endless speculation. This led, minus contraception and my belief that I couldn't become pregnant sans periods, to that very condition: four months gone, actually, second trimester, without the slightest idea.

I thought only hillbillies were supposed to go months unaware that they were about to have a child, but had I not got tired of weeks of feeling sick and gradually bleeding a little every day, I would never have gone to a doctor.

"You know what's wrong with you, don't you?" he said.

"Sorry, no."

The news was staggering and depressing as hell. There were two possible candidates for fatherhood: one had more or less raped me. I say "more or less" because I not only knew him, I thought him attractive—he was seeing my married girlfriend on the sly. We had been sunbathing on her apartment building's small terrace, and after she had a quick visit with him a few floors up, she had returned and fallen into a scary semi-conscious state.

I went up to his apartment, telling myself it was to find out what she had been taking. But I'm not sure that was the whole truth. Her boyfriend was something of a rounder, half a dozen years older than we were and very good-looking. It's unlikely that a twenty-three- or twenty-four-year-old girl who visits the apartment of a known rounder in a bikini has a totally innocent mind—even a shirt could have made me more businesslike. His apartment door was unlocked and he was lying on his bed talking on the telephone.

"She looks half-dead," I said. "And she's in a stupor that I can't break. What did you give her? No," I said repeatedly as he pulled me down. "Stop. This isn't why I'm here." His body weight was sufficient to pin me down. I really didn't want to have intercourse, but I can't say I was frightened. In the continued struggle throughout intercourse, which was over in a few minutes—no kisses or caresses there—I was slightly torn, just enough to start bleeding a little. I left the apartment without any hindrance although I didn't get any info on my girlfriend's comatose state, which turned out to be fairly short-lived. I've always thought that while I did repeat "no," my bikinied arrival could well have been taken for consent, and my struggle—in his rather sordid world—just part of the game.

I'm well aware, even if the sisterhood isn't, that women do sometimes say no when they really mean "oh go ahead, persuade me." That's how sexual relations between men and women used to be played. I suppose it was a bad, if time-honoured, thing to do, in those far-off dark days of college life in the sixties. The ambiguity certainly allowed women who wanted to be seduced to believe they were not "easy," and allowed men to rationalize noes that really were noes into consent. For men, it's always best to err on the side of caution, but some things are legitimately perceived as ambiguous: not all matters are black and white; some are grey, whether chromatic or achromatic.

The other candidate had been a man I'd known at university and had bedded only once. Two acts of intercourse four and a half months earlier, and now I was pregnant. My days and nights were nothing but fear and worry about how to terminate the pregnancy. Who could give advice on the consequences of this louche lifestyle? Naturally, I called Hershorn.

"There's a man," he said. "I'll call you back." Which is how I got the name of Toronto doctor Leslie Frank Smoling, who about twenty-three years later was tried with his associate, Dr. Henry Morgentaler, in the case that effectively decriminalized abortion in Canada. The fee was a few hundred dollars and, ever practical, I made money on it by telling each of the two candidates that they were the father. This was greeted by skepticism since both conveniently claimed to be infertile but they paid up anyway.

My abortion was almost comical in its stereotypical features. The storefront had boarded windows covered with paper notices and a backroom featuring a dentist's chair. No anaesthetic but lots of oral Valium. "Are you less than three months pregnant?" asked Dr. Smoling. "Yes," I lied. He was a conscientious doctor, must have quickly seen what we were dealing with, and loaded me up with antibiotics. Mount Sinai Hospital dealt with that night's outcome of the intervention, and the little life inside me was extinguished. My doctor then put me on the contraceptive pill, whose high estrogen and testosterone content completed my delayed development.

Retrospective sentimentality is odious when one is entirely responsible for those fingers closing, the heart stopping and the tiny body being stabbed and shredded. Still, the aftermath: had money been available to support me and my child through birth, might that life have been saved? I suspect not. When a young ambitious woman like me is in pursuit of her career and faces a derailment no matter how temporary, selfish concerns easily override everything. Nor do I think any school sex curriculum or parental guidance will stop unwanted pregnancies, which puts me reluctantly on the side of legal abortion in the first couple of trimesters. Still, having it made clear exactly what is alive inside you and facing what you are doing seem basic ethics. A nearly five-month fetus is not a mole to be removed. At the very least one should know its shape, understand it has developed toes and fingernails, can stretch and yawn, see its fierce little fight for life. "Death comes to the apple, death comes to the cheese," as my former husband wrote in one of his poems. Death came to my fetus. I did not know this would be my single chance at having a child.

After eighteen months at the CBC, I had worked my way up from filing clerk to an on-camera interviewer and story editor. I wasn't much good on television, wooden as a politically incorrect cigar-store Indian, until a film director named George Bloomfield gave me private performance lessons. We met when I was auditioning to ride on a pogo stick for Yardley's Oh! de London commercial. My back was photographed bare while my front was covered with masking tape. I held up a bottle of Oh! de London and looked over my left shoulder.

"Enticingly, please," said Bloomfield, who was sufficiently enticed that after the CBC and I parted ways around 1968, I moved to New York with him. He had finally scored his first feature film, *Jenny*, starring Marlo Thomas and Alan Alda. He was a kind man, with a marvellous sense of humour, ten years my senior, beloved by actors and with his own stylish appearance. Over six foot, on the heavy side and bald with a goatee, he was an arresting sight in the safari jackets he preferred. He was made for the film world of his time.

We lived between locations: London, the Bahamas, New York and Los Angeles—between manna and famine. When he had a feature film, generous to a fault, he gave me charge accounts at Bloomingdale's and Bendel's, which I used with unstoppable enthusiasm. When he was broke, we moved from Sutton Place to Needle Park and made do. Only one thing marred the perfection of it all: I couldn't feel a thing emotionally. Perhaps I had become so terrific at avoiding unpleasant thoughts or memories that I had deadened happiness as well. I really don't know. Something inside me was strangely wrong and came out in small and large cruelties, often to myself, which could be neither excused nor explained by early circumstances.

Bloomfield had a dog, a Hungarian puli named Gogo, as in *Waiting for Godot*. When a puli walks, its long black dreadlocks sway like a curtain, and when you are on the street they herd you. That's what they are, small herding dogs keeping their flock together. Gogo weighed about twenty-seven pounds, and I spent hours parting the cords in her coat and keeping her clean and exercised. We were alone together in New York quite often, and I took Gogo out with me whenever I could. "Gogo," I would call, and she would come to me, her small pink tongue poking out from under her long fringe, panting and tail-wagging with anticipation and those soft dog eyes shining. Pulik have long eyelashes that keep the dreadlocks that cover their faces just far enough away so they can see. Once I found out she didn't mind, I'd pull the hair in front of her eyes into a little topknot so I could look into her eyes.

I had never had a dog and had never really loved anything apart from those high school crushes and my father. I suppose I loved myself, but that flagged sometimes. I loved this dog. I'd stay on the bed in our East Fifty-Seventh Street one-bedroom apartment on sunny days thinking worried thoughts but unsure why I was worried, and she would stay next to me. I could hold her, cry into her dread-locks. I held her and I loved her and I kicked her, hard, really hard in the stomach and groin. I kicked her on those days when I came home from somewhere I couldn't take her, like the nearby D'Agostino's grocery store on First Avenue. I'd open the apartment door and she'd be there waiting for me, jumping up with pleasure at seeing me, and I kicked her viciously. She would never bark, never run from me, only whimper this low mewing sound of pain, and I'd do it again and again. When I stopped she would sigh with relief and lick my shoe and lick my face when I went on the floor to comfort her.

I hated myself for doing this but I couldn't stop. And of course she got ill, bleeding internally and in her stools, and so I rushed her to the animal hospital crying. I wrapped her up, the person that had caused all her sad small whimpers in the face of my continuous torment. She got well, but no thanks to me. I have no idea what caused this sociopathic behaviour. When I eventually split up from George, he brought Gogo to me because, according to him, she missed me and the vet said the reason she had stopped eating was our separation. I couldn't let it happen again and I sent Gogo back. She lived a long, full life in spite of my wretched treatment. I hope my dogs now never sense this.

CHAPTER THREE

Looking for Love

Hollywood was cruel. I saw it from the best possible position, as one who had no ambition to be in movies. James Coburn had offered me a swimsuit-type role in one of his films when I had been there a couple of years earlier for the CBC, but it simply didn't appeal. I suppose too much of Hampstead intelligentsia was left in me. George Bloomfield was up as director for a number of films at the time, which is the fast lane to the loony bin. You "take" a meeting with the money people. "How did it go?" "Terrific." The meeting is always "terrific." The lox and bagels at the Polo Lounge are fresh and you get the distinct impression that everyone has committed to the project with you. Green light. If you are new to this, like Bloomfield, it takes about three months to realize that no one remembers you after the lunch is over except you.

No breakfasts in the Polo Lounge could be good enough to make up for this madness, I thought, but I enjoyed little bits while it lasted. We sat on the floor at Ann-Margret's home on large cushions, hung out at crowded parties with starlets and on-the-move actresses like Susan Anspach and Carrie Snodgress, double-dated with Michael Douglas and his girlfriend Brenda Vaccaro, the consequence of which was to see the only necklace I owned and prized—a silver wire serpent—copied in eighteen-karat gold by Brenda.

The partying of the Hollywood crowd in the swinging seventies revolved around people who were rich, disturbed and took dope with

their therapists. Whatever layer of the entertainment world you inhabited, Quaaludes were in supply like candy to enhance sexual activity
or simply get you "there," wherever that was, which is why I had some
sympathy decades later when Bill Cosby was accused of secretly
doping his groupies with ludes so he could rape them. In those days
everyone had ludes—they were like Smarties and you didn't have to
entice people to quaff them. Even psychologists were publishing
papers on the benefits of Quaaludes in enhancing sexual pleasure.

After making two nondescript feature films, Bloomfield finally
got the one he was waiting for from producer Joe Levine of Embassy
Pictures—a cheery story about two young heroin addicts. This was
clearly a story with Cannes written all over it. Husband-and-wife
team John Gregory Dunne and Joan Didion were writing the screen-
play. Didion's most recent book, *Play It as It Lays*, had cast a pretty
sardonic eye on Hollywood and sent out the message that they didn't
really belong in Los Angeles at all, too cerebral by half. But that was
only my take.

We had story meetings at brother Dominick Dunne's house,
which had a Wordsworthian garden with a stone terrace and a tangle
of perennials and wildflowers—menacing, a bit like the garden in
Suddenly, Last Summer. Didion, finely boned and thin, looked as if she
didn't belong in this world. She created the impression of an intensity
that might ignite any moment to warm you but was more likely to
burn you. I kept my distance. She was the first serious female fiction
writer I had met in the flesh and she had none. In her presence I felt
elephantine and too earthy to ever be a writer.

Casting was held in New York, and Bloomfield took space in
Manhattan's Upper East Side Hyde Park Hotel. I hung around its
slightly shabby, dark-wine-brocade rooms watching actors parade in
and out. But when Al Pacino walked in, the room exploded. He was
the young addict, every movement to the hopped-up look in his
eyes. George ended up casting Pacino in his first starring film role, as
Bobby in *The Panic in Needle Park.*

I couldn't follow what happened next—the film world is snakes
and ladders—but Joe Levine sold Embassy Pictures before production

of the film had started, and while Dunne, Didion and Pacino stayed for the new company, Bloomfield was out. I had been freelancing in L.A. for CBC Radio, shopping interviews quite successfully. Now, back in Manhattan, I thought I had better get more full-time work and help with paying bills instead of freeloading off George. There was a slight hitch when immigration officers turned up at our Fifty-Seventh Street apartment to deport me. Seems an American immigration officer had noted my details at the Toronto airport when George and I first went to New York, and suddenly Bloomfield was facing the Mann Act, accused of transporting me across state lines for immoral purposes, since I had no visa to get American employment. After a series of breast-beating and rather dramatic speeches by him about "the woman I love," the investigating officer responded that "only someone innocent would make such stupid responses," and on noting my education and work experience, helped me get a green card in double-quick time.

George had directed a second film, *To Kill A Clown*, with Alan Alda and Blythe Danner, which by shooting in the Bahamas, editing in England and using a Canadian director happily qualified for several film subsidies if not critical acclaim on release. Getting a third U.S. feature for him was proving elusive. His William Morris agent was forever "at lunch." His business manager Martin Bregman, a man of mesmerizing attractiveness in spite of or perhaps enhanced by his pronounced limp from childhood polio, had the yet-to-bloom Al Pacino under one wing and the ravishing actress Cornelia Sharpe of the Faye Dunaway school of sharp cheekbones under the other. Bloomfield was not going to usurp attention from either. Green card and kinescopes in hand, I went job-hunting and ABC offered me a contract for a pilot documentary project that had something to do with railway bridges. The charm was missing but the salary was enticing. Contemporaneously, Canada's culture lobby was jump-starting a program for feature films, and I simply couldn't nakedly dump Bloomfield after his generosity—so I did it half-clothed. We returned to Canada. To replace his YSL capes and Indian embroidered shirts, I bought him a dark navy "tycoon suit" of proper cut with my earnings from a grimy little job I got at TVOntario writing three-line descriptions of programs. Bloomfield, his suit and his work dazzled a swathe of bureaucrats, and as soon as he actually began pre-production on *Child Under a Leaf*, with Dyan Cannon, I felt it was all right to leave him.

By now it was 1972, I was thirty-one and I didn't have much more to move than the last time. One carload. One change: I had fallen completely, madly and truly in love with a man I had dated with complete indifference five years earlier. Then, I'd had no feelings for him other than enjoyment of his white Triumph sports car in which once or twice I performed fellatio to the fascination of passing truck drivers, all for fun in my indifferent *épater la bourgeoisie* world. My stunted feelings matched a sort of blunted moral sense. The broken heart over my last school boyfriend, who took my virginity in his parked car, was the closest I had come to emotional reciprocation, which is probably why that memory lives like the tuberculosis bacillus, encapsulated in my mind, inactive but forever in my being.

One morning—I have no idea exactly when, but it was early in my second marriage—I woke up with a conscience. It was the damnedest thing. Overnight, my skin seemed to have been pierced with a thousand needles, all of which had become fine antennae, swaying about, searching for ways to avoid hurting people. My hair had been cut. The difficulty was that, caught up by my habitual rhetoric of "let's shock for the fun of it," I continued a muddled psychological posturing, tossing off mals mots about men or human relationships that perhaps I had felt and that certainly were part of the persona I had thought amusing.

"What would you advise women beginning a new relationship?" I was asked by an interviewer around this time.

"Any man should propose to you by the third date," I replied. "If he doesn't, you've failed." I may even have believed it. And sometimes men did propose to me by the third date, and sometimes they left after the first one. But I created the impression of a woman far thicker-skinned and predatory than I was. I knew this and knew it would not help me in my personal life or my work but I couldn't stop myself. The perception of me was that of a cool seductress, rippling and swirling through life. And perhaps when you so describe yourself in spite of yourself, some of the cheaper characteristics do rub off on you.

> Aimlessly, like an iceberg
> you float on
> With most of what you are immersed
> In jealous depths of yourself
> A tip above the surface showing
> to photograph, to dress and to destroy.

George Jonas, "The Absolute Smile," 1967

In 1974 I married George Jonas, a refugee to Canada after the 1956 Hungarian Revolution. Several inches over six foot, he wore German Neophan glasses with pink-tinted lenses that were the rage in 1950s Budapest. In a few short years after arriving in Canada, he had become a radio producer at the CBC and a published poet in English, his third language (after Hungarian, of course, and German). When we first dated, rather indifferently, the only inkling I had of his feelings for me were a handful of poems in his first published book, *The Absolute Smile*. Some named me, some did not. After I returned to Toronto in 1972, and after some extraordinary Sturm und Drang befitting two volatile semi-insane adults now very much in love, we lived together for a couple of years before getting married.

He had the natural ease and manners of a well-bred European, and a sardonic intellect that could splinter the atom. He could view any issue under the sun and tilt the lens to not only give a different approach to the subject but to dissect the issue with wit and honest-to-God brilliance. His writing was in the best tradition of Orwell—economy as a mark of quality. In 750 words he could say what anyone else would take pages to do and even so never touch his originality and depth. We shared a passion for music, especially opera.

Me and role model Great Granny Bertha Isserlis in Chorley Wood, 1941. Bertha, widowed working mum of four children, came from Russia to London in 1891, got a job immediately, studied and graduated in advanced midwifery, 1903. (Courtesy of the author)

My North London Collegiate School uniform, age nine. Absolutely my favorite outfit, unlike Anna Wintour who precociously loathed it, battling with teachers over her stylish modifications. (Courtesy of the author)

Father Harold in wartime
uniform, insert me. Our
resemblance strained my
mother. (Both photographs
courtesy of the author)

My poor half-brother, Anthony, institutionalized for thirty-two of the thirty-four years of his short life.

Grim-faced arrival in Canada, November 1952, on *Empress of France* with sister Ruth. Bandaged hand just visible. (Both courtesy of the author)

My first press appearance, age 14, as winner of the *Hamilton Spectator* contest, "Why I Want to be a Theatre Manager." Answer: fifty free movie tickets to win school friends. (Image courtesy of Hamilton Public Library, Local History & Archives—*Hamilton Spectator* Collection)

First husband Gary Smith, his parents Celia and Harry Smith, and brother Michael. In a preposterous 1963 hairdo, I enjoyed the new-found, short-lived bliss of attending Jewish functions *en famille*. (Courtesy of Gary Smith)

CBC promo pic for god knows what, circa 1965! I was instructed to put on a bikini and pose with famous Toronto Maple Leaf hockey goalie, Johnny Bower, and assorted cast. (© Library and Archives Canada/Robert Ragsdale fonds/neg.#65-13432. Reproduced with the permission of Library and Archives Canada)

Story Editor and rotating host on CBC News' show circa 1967. (CBC Still Photo Collection)

Interviewing controversial "rivers of blood" U.K. politician, Enoch Powell, London 1977, for CTV Reports. (Courtesy of the author)

Interviewing hero Natan and heroine wife Avital Sharansky for *The Times*, London, 1990. (Photograph by Stephen Markeson/*The Times*/News Licensing)

An Editor's work is never done.
Toronto Sun parking lot, 1984.
(Courtesy of the *Toronto Sun*)

Announcement of appointment as Canada's first female Editor of a daily metropolitan newspaper, 1983. Acute shortage of feminist cheers. (Courtesy of the *Toronto Sun*)

Working at home, Toronto, 1984, with a Telegram (an early word processor) and a nightmare of freezes. (Courtesy of Fred Thornhill, *Toronto Sun*)

George Jonas and me, just married at Toronto's Holy Blossom Temple, July 1974. (Courtesy of the author)

Cheeky on-looker snapshot of my "toy boy" companion, Sam Blyth, and myself at a tennis tournament, 1979, prior to our Mozambique nightmare. Blyth became a highly successful entrepreneur. (Courtesy of the author)

Gaunt in Johannesburg, 1980, following prison in Mozambique. (Jan Kopec)

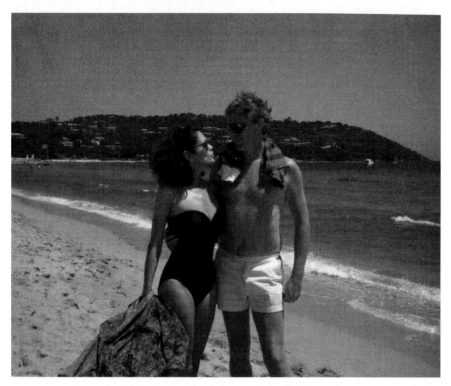

Madly in love with third husband David Graham, St. Tropez, 1985. (Courtesy of the author)

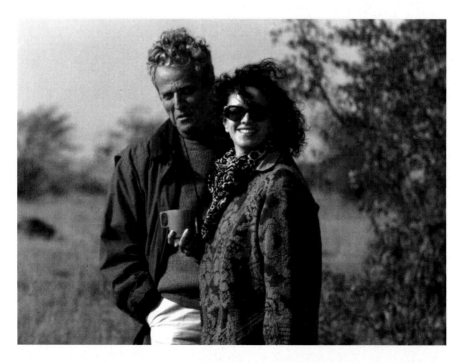

On safari in Kenya with then-companion, famed double-Oscar-winning screenwriter and author William Goldman, 1990. (Courtesy of the author)

There was no foot-dragging this time, no panic and no sleepless nights worrying about the implications of marriage. All I wanted was to be his wife. I was once more in front of a rabbi in his study, with only three other people present. Holy Blossom Temple's Rabbi Gunther Plaut married us with some trepidation. He had no worries about my Jewish credentials. This time it was my fiancé who was up for inspection.

"Do you know any Hebrew?" he asked George.

"No."

"What synagogues have you attended?"

"None," Jonas replied, perfectly politely.

"How can I know you are a Jew?" the rabbi continued, worried that in front of him stood that very rare and exotic creature, a Hungarian Christian wanting to be known as a Jew.

"If I was Jewish enough for Hitler," replied Jonas with continued politeness but a slight edge, "I should be Jewish enough for a Reform rabbi." Given Judaism as practised in the Reform movement, and especially at Holy Blossom, where Rabbi Abraham Feinberg had turned the synagogue into a left-wing rally for nuclear disarmament, the point was not unfair. In fact, Jonas did not have to use the Nuremberg Laws as his passport to Holy Blossom Temple. He was 100 per cent Jewish, though his parents had tried to evade the coming nightmare in Europe by converting to the Lutheran church. It did not help. "The Holocaust," Jonas would say, "was not a TV movie for me."

Our seven years together were intense, and in the last years difficult. He was controlling and I was rebellious. Convinced of the inability of any human being to desist from some form of betrayal, Jonas would often secretly follow me about, although I soon caught on to that. I was not to be trusted anywhere alone—not at the various offices where I worked, not at the TV studios when I did interviews or on-camera set pieces, not at McGill Street, the glitzy new women's club I had joined. "You can have perfect thighs or write," said Jonas in justifying his veto, which was irritatingly true.

Being grounded emotionally gave me the time to focus on writing. Since no magazine would actually commission a piece from the bikinied cover girl of *Toronto Life* magazine—fair enough—I had to do it on spec.

Writing a long magazine piece without any certainty of publication is hell on wheels. I wanted to make a splash and the topic I chose—an exposé of some daft notions at the ARF—was a real investigative bit of work. The addiction centre (which to this day is cutting-edge balmy, dispensing every trend a-blowin' in the wind) was in the seventies plugging the notion of "wise personal choice" in recreational drugs as well as testing behavioural theories on its own unsuspecting staff, a procedure which struck me and some unhappy staff members as questionable. Getting up every morning and self-starting the undercover work leading up to the moment when I got the founding director of the ARF on tape confirming my claims was brutal labour. I researched and wrote for over three months and at Jonas's suggestion took the completed piece to Robert Fulford of *Saturday Night*, quite the best editor in Canadian journalism. The writing and re-writing he made me do was invaluable.

The article was published and I woke up one weekend to a telephone call telling me the *Toronto Star* had a lead editorial about it. This was the first and last time the *Star* had anything positive to say about my ideas. The piece also sparked some sort of provincial investigation, so all in all it was a promising start.

"Well," said Jonas, who had watched my torment over the piece with detached interest. "You've learned how to research. Now you had better learn how to write."

For several years, simply being alone together carried us through. Apart from ideas and sexual chemistry, we shared the same humour and the identical responses to music, which was our second language. There was a downside: his temper, which I knew how to arouse with one look or sentence. Our arguments could extend for hours over such vital (to us) questions as whether or not film could properly be called an art form—this occasioned by my insistence, after seeing Dirk Bogarde in *Death in Venice*, that it could—and in that instance the disagreement ended at about four in the morning with a couple of kicks that fractured two of my ribs. Honestly, every frame of Visconti's film was utterly exquisite, but the question was not of such over-arching importance that it merited so explosive a conclusion. I was not only physically hurt but mentally stunned. Our courtship had included placing me in menacing and contrived situations but never any physical violence. After we married, the violence, though very infrequent, was material and culminated in my receiving a dislocated jaw that required the "I bumped into a door" explanation for the disbelieving emergency doctor.

Intellectually I know that the imbalance between a 125-pound woman and a 185-pound man clearly indicates an unequal power distribution, yet there are psychological aspects here that alter the disparity. I knew every emotional button in Jonas and how to deto-nate an explosion, and I used that knowledge deliberately the way another woman might use vicious sarcasm or a kitchen knife. I knew this too: the human psyche can take only so much damage, and Jonas's had been torn during the first twenty-one years of his life in ways unimaginable to those of us in the free world.

A child of nine who grows up walking on Budapest streets littered with corpses, having to memorize a new identity to avoid having his trousers pulled down for a death sentence by the roving thugs of the Nazi Arrow Cross Party—based on the infrequency of circumcision among non-Jewish Hungarians—is not left unmarked psychologically. Seeing denunciations result in people's disappearances under both Nazis and communists is quantitatively different to our sanctimo-nious whistle-blowing of today (though not qualitatively: encouraging anonymous whistle-blowers is a step towards deforming decency in human beings). Simply put, George had grown up surrounded by betrayal, murder and lies. He had learned to trust no one. And I think he even feared or mistrusted his passionate love for me.

When your husband constantly sees you as someone to be watched lest you stray, the fear almost inevitably becomes self-fulfilling. My ability to exploit his fear and set off an explosion of physical violence became a weapon in my hands: several years into the marriage, when guiltily searching for an excuse to explain my affair with another man, I could press this button, causing the violence that Jonas would hate himself for and that I could use to justify my infidelity. I think ultimately I had the upper hand. When he remarried, he told his very much younger wife of these physical outbursts and promised they would never again take place. In their several decades together, they never did.

One could argue that many people had lived through the same wartime and postwar horrors without hitting a woman. True. And some physical assaults—those used to end an argument on a film or idea—made no sense, fitted no pattern. Something else was at play, and it took me completely by surprise early in our marriage. But ultimately, I think I took advantage of him, not vice versa. Women can fight in many ways that are not physical, and inflict their own terrible damage.

We were dead broke for most of our marriage. His money went to support his former wife and child, now in New York City, and her mother. We lived largely on my earnings—depleted by my shopping stints for both of us. The newspapers described us rather exaggeratedly as a couple of White Russians in exile: Jonas, with his cigarette holder and exquisite accent, impeccable manners, coat over shoulders, and wearing a tie and jacket in an era when no self-respecting writer or producer wore such garments, only dark turtlenecks and sunglasses. In the seven years we lived together, I gave one dinner party, for six people, and it was a fiasco. The lamb I cooked developed an odour that reminded one guest of the smell in the ovens at Auschwitz, where he had been forced to work as a *Sonderkommando*, and he had to exit in a rather upset state. Truly, not the sort of error a hostess enjoys making. Martha Stewart never dealt with these imbroglios.

In 1978, our first book together, *By Persons Unknown: The Strange Death of Christine Demeter*, won the Edgar, a serious prize given by the Mystery Writers of America for best non-fiction of the year, and its earnings allowed us to rent a lower penthouse in midtown Toronto. At the time, *Us* magazine (a project of the New York Times Company to compete with *People* magazine) ran three pages of photos and text on us. The lines describing me played a signature tune I would come to know: "A statuesque, green-eyed brunette, Amiel is a legendary beauty in Toronto, though one observer sniped that her charm lies in 'knowing how to throw her body around.'"

We divorced in 1979, when I decided to leave no cliché unturned, oh God, and, fulfilling Jonas's worst fears, became infatuated with the Younger Man—thus becoming a hot property for every women's magazine similarly infatuated with the topic of the older woman and the toy boy. There were no arguments over division of property because our ideas were really our only valuable property. I left the penthouse and split its rent and maintenance costs for the remaining couple of years of the lease. We shared a lawyer for the divorce. It was a testament to the feelings and need we had for one another that we shared ideas and help in our professional and personal matters for the rest of our lives.

Now, free of Jonas's controlling nature, I could be myself—a thirty-nine-year-old middle-aged infant, going to discos with my young man of twenty-four in totally inappropriate clothing and gyrating to Donna Summer's "Bad Girls" with the predictable awkwardness of my years. By then, I had found my footing as a journalist and was working at *Maclean's*, where I had a column on policy issues, as well as for the *Toronto Sun* and CTV; and, of course, I cared desperately about the Cold War and the growing threats to free speech by the *soi-disant* human rights movements, but my hair was back down to my waist along with my décolletage as I skipped the Cold War barricades one night a week.

Certain aspects of this new fun life were a bit trying. I moved into the slum house previously occupied by three or four equally young or younger friends of my just-out-of-university boyfriend. His former co-residents left behind thousands of fleas from their cats but sadly not the cats themselves, which might have helped put down the rodent infestation. There was also a slightly different focus when it came to my new boyfriend. I now found myself living with a mindset where "the war" denoted Vietnam rather than world war, and communism was an invention of the CIA. Cuba was just a great cheap place to holiday.

That laidback attitude to the history of everything beyond the block on which he was born was the reason behind our ending up in a Mozambican political prison. (Since communism was an invention of the CIA, let's sightsee in civil-war Frelimo-ruled Mozambique without bothering with visas.) I argued feebly against crossing into this communist-ruled country without any entry papers, let alone a handy semi-automatic weapon, but was terrified of appearing to be the middle-aged woman spoiling everyone's carefree fun. Ten days in a political prison doesn't sound like much against the god-awful nightmarish fate some of today's journalists face with years of hostage life and brutal executions, but all the same, being one of only two women in an all-male African prison and catching malaria plus typhoid played hard on me. As a female, I was double-locked in my cell twenty-four hours a day for the private amusement of the cell block chief. On New Year's Day, 1981, for a special celebration, the guards shot some prisoners. I could hear it through the small barred window high up in my cell, and I knew the geography of the prison yard that I had crossed once for an interrogation.

Only the British consul looked for us and eventually secured our release—my beau having, thank God, visited him before our arrest to straighten out how to exit a totalitarian country when we had no entry visas. The Canadian government of Pierre Trudeau positively revelled in disowning me in Parliament when asked why they hadn't helped release me. After I recuperated in a South African hospital, we returned to Toronto, me looking like something the cat had dragged in—how on earth can you get sunken eyes in just eleven days?—to be roundly criticized by newspapers for our negligence in travelling to Mozambique without proper papers, a perfectly justified criticism. Actually, the general press view bordered on notions that I had staged the whole thing to get attention.

Less happily, CBC's queen bee, Barbara Frum, put the Mozambican ambassador on her immensely popular *As It Happens* radio program without the normal courtesy of asking me to take part and counter his bizarre assertions that I was imprisoned after proffering stolen American Express cheques. One would have hoped for more from the icon of the day, after whom the rotunda of CBC's headquarters is named. Perhaps it was just the influence of her producer Mark

Starowicz, later an immensely talented documentary maker but a man whose political affections in the 1970s had led him to accept paid work for a KGB officer operating from Ottawa under the cover of being a *Pravda* reporter.

My boyfriend, Sam Blyth, was a natural athlete—tennis, cycling, sailing, swimming, rugby—with a shock of dark hair and skin as perfect as a peach if a peach could tan. His Wasp credentials were flawless, mother being the granddaughter of Sir George Williams, founder of the YMCA. During nearly two years together he expected me to enjoy these activities, even though, as I pointed out to him, *sail* is spelled s-a-l-e by my tribe. He was full of life, free of angst and determined to make his way in his own travel business, which he did very successfully after some bumpy early years.

How can a man be so exquisitely formed, I thought, with a shoulder-to-waist ratio that was perfection and a muscled stomach flat as an ironing board? I would gaze at him as he slept on hot summer nights with no bedclothes. I got used to living with a man whose eyelashes were longer than mine. In fact, he was altogether so physically perfect a specimen that you really wanted to put him nude on the mantelpiece. My biological clock was now whirring all wheels and I couldn't see why we shouldn't get married. Thank God he could.

For my fortieth birthday, one very chilly winter's day, I came home to my young man's birthday present, which in his absence had been delivered and left on the sagging porch: a rocking chair with, inexplicably, an electric can opener on its seat. The writing was on the wall.

I moved out after two years together, having been unceremoniously dumped for several rather lovely women one after another, all considerably younger than myself. The immediate cause at least left me some dignity: off went my young man, on some incredible bicycle ride from Vienna to Budapest or Novosibirsk with international party girl Anne-Marie Sten. No point trying to compete, but preferable, I suppose, to being chucked for some grim-faced old leftie. Just how he met her is fuzzy in my memory, but it could be that I introduced them, having interviewed her several years earlier for a magazine article.

All I could say when asked what it was like living with a man so much younger was that you spend an enormous amount of energy always having to hold your tummy in.

CHAPTER FOUR

Sexually Incorrect

These days no autobiography is complete without a coming out: "I discovered my sexuality" is a plonking phrase that fills me with utter gloom. The current uptick, "I discovered my gender," usually segues into tales of lavatory discrimination. I have never wanted an emotional and sexual relationship with any gender but male, but like a good number of women—I'm inclined to say most but I have no solid basis for that—I've always had some fantasy interest in women on a physical level.

My irrepressible curiosity made it inevitable that I would try to turn fantasy into reality, sexually speaking. But in the late sixties and early seventies, this was not easy. I found myself tiptoeing around the one or two women rumoured in CBC gossip to be involved with other women, hoping they would make some overture. They did not. Possibly they sensed my basic predilection was not for strap-ons and a life together of domestic bliss, nor even a flirty on-and-off thing, but merely a one-time strong physical urge to "rape, pillage and run," as one of my male friends jokingly put it years later when we engaged in an evening with a third—and very much consensual—woman.

Eventually, in London and Paris, I played out such scenes, but the curious woman who responds to a lesbian overture without making it clear that the involvement is a passing experiment may bring misery to her victim—although in the South of France and the *clubs privés* of Paris, the woman-on-woman thing was often a highlight of everyone's evening, even if I watched rather than participated. Not out of moral repugnance—only that public sex even at private venues with voyeurs hanging around all seemed a bit grubby. This was the flash-and-trash set of the eighties.

Later on in London, a female friend of my then husband came to keep me company while he was away. We went to a film and then back to her small Belgravia mews house and surprisingly (and excitingly) I discovered she had a live-in lesbian girlfriend, hidden socially, whose name I never knew. Their relationship seemed skewed to me, but clear thinking was not helped by the amyl nitrate capsules being popped under my nose. At the time I was descending into the black world of a clinical depression, though like many things in life, you don't know it until it has happened.

I went home alone and next morning there was a tremendous commotion outside my front door: the unnamed girlfriend was begging to come in and making passionate pronouncements to me. I looked out through the chink of the chained door, and her crumpled heap on the ground was slightly unnerving. Shortly, my friend appeared, and the two of them played out a verbal sadomasochist episode whose roles seemed familiar to each. Frankly, I thought both of them potty, particularly in the unforgiving morning light, but the sobs of the first one seemed to be real.

Half-heartedly, apprehensively, I contemplated venturing into the gay club scene in London. My husband was away most of the time and I was not yet established as a British columnist, so life was a bit on the lonely side. Men were off-limits since I was married, but he raised no objections to this initiative.

"Don't do this to me," said a woman I met in the one London gay bar I actually went to—a plain downstairs place off the Fulham Road near World's End, rather like a church basement with a kitchen-counter bar and a few desperately unattractive female couples dancing. I stood like a lumpen piece of clay at the end of the counter until a woman approached me. Chatting to her, a plain, rather oblong lesbian, evidently intelligent if not cultured, was enjoyable, but talking was all I felt up to. When she telephoned next day I explained I really had no interest in that lifestyle. "You ought not to have been there," she said. "It's not for tourists."

I never spoke about similar encounters. I felt no guilt or shame. Society's sexual manners and mores are a foreign language for me. When I muttered views like this to my Canadian 1950s high school classmates after they made offensive remarks about "queers" and "fairies," I was regarded with slack-jawed incomprehension. But my libertarian views on sexuality were inborn. From the moment I was aware of the impulse, without benefit of sex education, parental guidance or swapped views with schoolmates, I assumed everyone had something they were sexually interested in and whether it was your own sex, the opposite sex, the dolls under your bed or the apple tree at the end of the garden, whatever aroused a person was their own business.

Naturally at eight or nine years of age my views on the varieties of sexuality had not fully blossomed or even budded, and if questioned I could not have explained myself. But as each year passed and my attention became more focused, I literally couldn't understand what the fuss was about if someone liked to pull down their trousers and be whipped or needed to flash fleshy bits—disconcerting and probably public mischief when encountered on the bus to school but not traumatizing. Since the *News of the World* and the *Daily Mirror* were among the newspapers I grew up with from the time I could read, I was pretty inured to those staples of the tabloid press—juvenile prostitutes, homosexual priests, murder for "purposes" of performing acts on the victim.

The sexual drive itself is innocent, implanted at birth, as homosexuals know and never tire of telling us. Since aversion therapy is both cruel and useless and you can't excise from the human psyche what is inborn, it seems very mean indeed to outlaw the object of other people's sexual interests just because it's different from yours— unless it is genuinely doing harm to others (like children). When a bunch of consenting adult males were arrested in someone's basement for driving nails into each other's hands or tricky bits, I couldn't see why they shouldn't do this, horrid though I found the notion. The courts thought otherwise on the grounds that even an adult can't give consent to harming themselves, which sounded like a legal technicality to me. We give consent all the time to others inflicting some "harm" to us, when we get tattooed or walk into a dentist's office or see a cosmetic surgeon. I had—and have—a sympathy for people who are genuinely afflicted with a sexual drive that can only be truly fulfilled by prohibited activity, whether or not I personally find the desires repellent. They can't even watch realistic avatars on computer screens in the privacy of their own homes without being arrested or losing their jobs if detected.

Once my somewhat out-of-whack excess testosterone (a side effect of Stein-Leventhal syndrome) hit me as an adult, my own sexual life was bog-standard normal—at least viewed through the lens of today's "sexually active woman." The interpretation of "bog-standard normal" gets modified a bit according to the standards of the day, as do "permissible" and "impermissible" sexual practices, and I've watched it all with some amusement. Heterosexual, homosexual, bisexual, intersexual, transsexual, necrophilia, exhibitionism, voyeurism, frotteurism, gerontophilia, gynandromorphophilia, dendrophilia, zoophilia, pygophilia, agalmatophilia, symphorophilia (the subject of Cronenberg's brilliant film *Crash*)—there are over five hundred different paraphilias, so name your sexual preference and there's a Greek or Latin term that will hide it until society decides to recognize it.

My own rashness got me into a bit of an unwanted stew one Sunday afternoon in Manhattan. Walking along First Avenue, I encountered a man with unquestionably the most beautiful Doberman I have ever seen. The dog was Plato's form of dog, the essence of dogdom. The skin and coat were gleaming, the dog polished without an ounce of fat, prancing along taking in every smell and sound. I was entranced and complimented the owner, who was a tall Afro-American matching the dog in groomed perfection. We ended up in his East Fifties apartment, and during the predictable course of events on his floor he unpredictably sprayed my nude self with a can of whipped cream, probably horrid artificial stuff, but it seemed the dog loved it and very carefully started licking it off me while his owner retreated to the sofa to watch. I was slightly alarmed at the direction events were taking. This was clearly routine for the animal, and I began to worry that I was now a circus act for which the dog may have been abused in training. Keeping my legs firmly closed, I began edging towards my clothes, smiling at both the owner and the dog. The dog was perfectly polite, and his almond eyes simply looked wistful as the whipped cream disappeared beneath my clothes.

"Come on uptown," said the Afro-American gentleman as I wiped and dressed, trying not to show any apprehension. "I've got some friends who'd love to see this." I declined the invitation. The owner clearly thought he was on to a good thing, an Upper East Side English-accented girl with long blonde hair (this was during my attempted Catherine Deneuve of *Belle de Jour* phase), and he followed me back to my apartment entrance, but was blocked by the doorman from going inside. The fallout from this came when George Jonas expropriated my account of the incident and, taking creative licence, turned it into "coupling with a dog" in his poem "The Girls of Whitney Hall," which in turn was picked up by an embittered ex-girlfriend and surfaced in unfortunate ways.

A slight inconvenience of my sexual attitudes was a feeling of some responsibility for the couple of chaps who, after pursuing and dating me, would proceed to consummation—and couldn't perform. The loss of confidence, so shattering to them, was such that I felt it unfair to cut off matters until this hurdle had been overcome: if a man is potent with others, it is simply a matter of time, and while getting there it is not the most thrilling of encounters—lots of forehead perspiration on his part and soothing conversation on mine—you do it. The man's relief when the hurdle is surmounted is worth the trouble—if you genuinely like him—and God, the relief as you can flick them off.

My views on sexuality surfaced in my columns, but at first they were a secondary topic. Back in the seventies and eighties, I was at the Cold War barricades. Gender issues rarely loomed in the world of Maoism and Soviet totalitarianism, where everyone was—virtually at pain of execution—always heterosexual and the regimes had a strangle-hold on politically correct speech. Once Soviet communism was defeated, into that happy vacuum popped, oh Christ, the culture wars.

"Culture wars" is one of two academia-type names for the down and dirty fight between people who want their views on just about everything to be the only permitted ones, and those of us who prefer a society where a variety of opinions are allowed. Another grown-up name is "identity politics," which refers to the same fight in which the loudest, most intolerant group gets to force its values and ideas on everyone else at pain of losing your job and possibly imprisonment if you don't go along. By now this rot has affected every institution we have, from the CBC to our schools and advertising and office chat. There were times when this sort of terrible intolerance came from the right—as in the McCarthy era—but now it comes pretty much from the left, most often in the name of feminism, which began as a perfectly decent movement and has metastasized into a plague of boils on the body politic.

The culture wars revolve mostly around issues of gender, sexuality, religion and terrorism. Even the weather. They all bleed into one another, unencumbered by messy notions of tolerance and free speech. And frankly, in Canada by now, culture wars are more accurately described as culture surrender. *Diversity* was once a normal word referring to a variety of things. Now it means making sure every institution and workplace has the right numbers of whatever is the favoured pigmentation, sexual orientation and race of the moment (some pigmentations and orientations are more equal than others). "Diversity" of views and ideas, a considerably more important application of the word, is dispensable and often plain outlawed.

Speaking as a journalist, today it is as brave to speak or write against homosexuality as it was to speak in its defence when it was illegal. Homosexuals had lives of sheer hell until late in the twentieth century, long after the U.K.'s 1957 Wolfenden Report saw the need to end their repression. But groups born of persecution seem inevitably to become political movements who want not only the basic right to practise their own sexuality or culture without punishments—as they should—but the power to punish anyone who regards their practice as in any way lacking. Acceptance and legalization are only the first step; next you have to admire, love and honour, at risk of job crucifixion or legal consequences. There's a job opening at Gay Pride for a homosexual Voltaire. As well as aboriginal, Muslim, ecological, feminist and Afro-American ones.

Back in 1979, when there was still some semblance of freedom, I wrote a column on a banal issue with a smart, brand-new name. "Sexual harassment" was the term, and "this issue has legs," I wrote. The jumping-off point for my column was a book by two women that claimed working females were unable "to distinguish between consensual and coercive sex" in the office. I couldn't believe that feminism would take up this notion, which essentially reduces working women to brain-challenged idiots. I was wrong. This thesis became a motif of the movement. If all sex wasn't coercive or rape—as Andrea Dworkin later assured us in her jolly little book *Intercourse*—then most of it was.

Sexual harassment is by now so broadly defined that brave is the office male who looks at any part of a female colleague's body but her eyes—respectively—or who asks her out without encouragement. Or with encouragement. She might change her mind about that goodnight kiss and hug the next day. And speaking of redundant terms, we now have "date rape" and "acquaintance rape," although of course we don't actually have "rape" in Canada because the feminists got it removed from the Criminal Code in order to emphasize that it was power based and could include behaviour other than forced penetration—hence the bottomless basket called "sexual assault."

We don't talk confusingly about "dinner-party theft" or "cruise-liner fraud." Obviously, I'm out to lunch in the land of professional feminists, though not, I suspect, most women, but I don't understand how we got here. In modern times, pretty much since the Age of Enlightenment, men and women have always known that non-consensual sexual activity procured through violence, menaces, lack of consent or blackmail, whether in the office, streets or open fields, is and always has been a major criminal offence. Capital punishment for rape was abolished in the U.K. only in 1841. In Canada, murder, treason and rape were capital offences after Confederation. In the

U.S. the last time a man was sentenced to death for rape was a white man in 1974.

And I don't think it is Neanderthal thinking to say that those accused of sexual assault ought to have the same protection in law that everyone else accused of a crime has. Feminism has upended some of the great presumptions of English common law. What the hell happened to the great jurist William Blackstone's "better that ten guilty persons escape, than that one innocent suffer"? Much earlier, the foremost rabbinical ethicist Maimonides, who took a very dim view of presumptive evidence, wrote, "It is better and more satisfactory to acquit a thousand guilty persons than to put one innocent man to death." Hang on to your kippah, Rabbi, if you try that one out on the congregation of your local Reform synagogue.

God forbid a member of your family gets accused unjustly of some sexual or gender offence: whether in Canada, the U.K. or the U.S., pretrial the accuser remains anonymous, with the accused's name in headlines. Rules of evidence are chipped away as well, so the defence faces restrictions on evidence and cross-examination even as sentences become more severe. I'm no ethicist or scholar, but a trial is where we decide whether the complainant or the accused is the victim. Not beforehand in the press. What really galls me is the elimination of the caution judges were once required to give juries in rape cases on convicting on uncorroborated evidence. A caution isn't a prohibition to convict, just a poke in the mind to be bloody careful. That caution is as vital to a fair trial as the caution that you must be convinced beyond a reasonable doubt. We all understand there's rarely a witness to rape, but corroboration doesn't require an eyewitness, only forensic evidence such as a stain, a few skin cells, a hair, even a telephone call to a relative or friend in the post-rape time frame.

The result of the removal of these safeguards has been the persecution and even false imprisonment of innocent people, usually after some wave of hysteria. (Previous hysterias that turned out to be false include false memory syndrome and the "satanic rituals" that put innocent teachers, men and women alike, in prison after tall tales circulated of children being forced to drink blood from sacrificed animals.)

There was a time when victims of rape were afraid to come forward because of police and societal attitudes, but very rarely now. And possibly there are legit reasons for a woman to conceal a real rape. More common in Europe, rarer in North America, raped or adulterous females from some subcontinent or Asian group can genuinely fear for their lives—not from the rapist's assault but from their own families' sense of honour. Some women may be in a real fix after a serious rape, having to explain to spouse or family what she was doing in that part of town that night or perhaps seeing someone she shouldn't because of his relationship to a close friend or a family member. Or the horror of incest. You'd hope that these reasons could be surmounted in the face of rape, but the reluctance to report such rapes has zero to do with society's prune face or macho police attitudes.

A woman may even have difficulty turning in a man with whom she had consensual sex in the past but who went criminally ballistic when she declined to perform. Frankly, it *ought* to be difficult to go to the police: it's a moral dilemma to ruin the life of someone you have known intimately for a time and liked. The Criminal Code does not allow prior intimacy or marriage to even be raised as a defence, and the National Sex Offender Registry commits an offender to a minimum of ten years of restrictions and reporting. So, yes, it has to be pretty damn nasty for a woman to take that step.

To raise these matters is to be a "denier" of rape, which I most fervently am not. Take a public stand against the received wisdom of the eco-aboriginal-feminist axis (the list increases every day as some new lot vies for victim chic) and you are labelled a denier, with all the baggage this word carries from its association with Holocaust denial. You are a denier of child abuse, a denier of the rights of First Nations people. Accept the climate is changing but question humans' role in this and you are a climate change denier and on the wrong side of history as the world faces this crisis. Everything the left tackles is a crisis.

Meanwhile, hello, Ms. Canada. You know a movement has been totally successful when people don't know they are part of it. Canada has become a matriarchy and no one seems to notice: the justice system, education and media have, with very few exceptions, taken on board

ludicrous feminist tropes and ambitions as established truths. A matriarchy will investigate missing aboriginal women long before anyone
wonders about the triple number of missing aboriginal boys and men (or
non-aboriginal boys, for that matter). In a moment of identity-politics
light humour (rare and inaccessible to its practitioners), the commissioners put on the spot about this exclusion of aboriginal males from
their inquiry explained po-faced that "when the concerns of the
LGBTQ community were added to the conversation, separating males
from females is difficult to implement." Which sums up the problem,
doesn't it? That word *conversation* instead of *investigation* is a dead giveaway
of a person with a brain-dead vocabulary.

Myself, I can't believe that if Canadians really sat down and managed to scrub off the received wisdom that coats their brains, they'd
go along with all this. Or perhaps not: righting the perceived wrongs
to women or any member of their axis has become a mainstream
career choice, the road to a place on the courthouse bench, a company
directorship or a job with a corner office. Why give up a good thing
when it pays so well?

No problem for me. I don't care who uses the changing rooms or
lavatories with me. I think it perfectly right that we should all mind
our own business about a person's sexual identity or gender changes—
Nosy Parkers are the bane of existence. We have a popular culture
celebrating sadomasochism in books that have sold over sixty million
copies—fine, if that's your beach reading. But to compensate for this
open-mindedness, we've hung our opprobrium on a few minor vices.
Hence our grim-faced horror if an adult privately views child pornography or pinches a bottom. This is Victorian hypocrisy: legally
murder your unborn child but put dust covers on your computer
screen should a child's photo arouse you. Beats me.

In 2015 I wrote a column for *Maclean's* on Bill Cosby, who was
facing multiple allegations of rape from several decades earlier. If he
was guilty of deliberately doping unknowing girls with Quaaludes and
then raping them, I wrote, he should go to jail for the rest of his life.
But I offered the view that we may never know, since he was unlikely
to get a fair trial after the lurid media coverage. This was two years

before his first mistrial and three before his conviction. At the time, TV screens were repeating interviews with tearful women who had kept silent for at least twenty-five years and some as long as forty but were now suffering post-traumatic stress over a rape they actually couldn't remember or corroborate but could name the celebrity that caused it. They had a name for that in Salem.

My column went through several agreed cuts and changes to soften it.

"Michael," I asked my associate editor, "when is this column going to be given the OK?" Days had gone by filled with requested changes, about 98 per cent of which I had made, and we were up against deadline.

"Editor's out of the office for the day," I was told. "Back tomorrow." He was at the gym, at meetings, at lunch, but not available to OK the column in time for the print issue.

In my thirty-seven years of writing for *Maclean's* this had never happened. Finally I got the message. "If you prefer this to be my last column," I wrote, "would you mind running a note at the end in tiny script that it is my final column. You can do it like the tiny script that ran at the end of my first column in 1978: 'This is the first in a series of monthly columns by Barbara Amiel.' Which became twice-weekly pretty fast.

The column was not published, although it ran online for a short time but without my postscript. The editor of *Maclean's* took me to lunch at the Four Seasons, along with an associate editor and deputy, and suggested that I be "repurposed." In this repurposing my column would vanish; I would do interviews and occasional articles like "the one you did on purebred dogs that was so popular." When I left the Four Seasons, alone and waiting for my car to be retrieved, the doorman said, "I love your columns, Ms. Amiel. I never miss one." Perhaps he was laying it on for a tip. As they say in pop songs, I smiled while my heart was breaking. I was replaced by a nice safe former CBC commentator who I had supported in a column when the CBC fired him for commercial practices they deemed a conflict of interest. All the same, the very fact that I had managed to keep that column for nearly forty years was more of a wonder to me than the ending of it.

CHAPTER FIVE

Woman in Combat

My media career that ended that summer's day in 2015 had begun in Toronto fifty years earlier, in 1965, with the lowest-status job the CBC had, that of a Clerk Grade 3. I had gone to the CBC's Employment Office, as it was heartlessly called before the more caring Human Resources, and quickly discovered that they had no opening for a person schooled in symbolic logic, ethics, Kant and Hegel. I agreed. I was useless. I promised to take speed-writing courses and was sent to the CBC Variety department. After the fiasco of the Miss CJBC contest, I got the promised transfer, and in eighteen months was an on-camera story editor in CBC Public Affairs under the terrifying stewardship of producer Ross McLean, who was a perfect exhibit of rule by fear.

After two seasons he replaced me with Barbara Frum, a wise decision. Mrs. Frum was just beginning her television career and would become a Canadian icon. She was a natural on camera, a genuine talent without artifice or pretensions, and always a reassuring presence. Viewers adored her. Her predictable soft-left views were perfectly in tune with the times. (The interview in which Margaret Thatcher devours her is a classic.) Barbara came with a splendidly supportive and wealthy husband, one son, one daughter and an adopted aboriginal son. Central casting couldn't have done better.

My CBC-TV career having flunked out, I focused increasingly on writing. My column began in 1978, when the somewhat demonic editor of *Maclean's*, Peter C. Newman, decided to launch me after I had some success as the magazine's lead book reviewer. Whatever else he was or became, this did not prevent Newman from seeing some value in me, which frankly I have never understood but for which I have always been grateful. His payment for this in later years was more than a blood-drenched raw pound or two of my flesh, but by then he was short of food.

Newman was of Jewish-Czech origin himself but only when he wanted to be. His shrewd mind saw a career path as a Canadian nationalist, and his clever editing of *Maclean's* took it down that road. A strange, introverted person with mad glinting eyes and a pinched way of speaking, he was another one of the gifted people in television and print who ruled through creating a relentless and mysteriously motivated atmosphere of fear.

"You will alternate columns with Mordecai Richler every other week. The column will be on cultural affairs," Newman told me.

This really was the voice from the burning bush. Richler was a heavyweight writer. His writing was utterly indifferent to the winds of fashion. Blessed with a highly developed sense of irony that got better and better in person the more he drank—Scotch whisky before meals, wine during, and Cognac, Calvados or Armagnac afterwards—he could get away with murder in Canada. His immense talent helped, but his shambled appearance and macho capacity for heavy drinking matched a *La Bohème* view of the writer's life and made his views more palatable. And as a St. Urbain Street, East Montreal Jew, ready to use his own caste and class as satirical fodder, he confirmed his authenticity in a way that none of us could ever match.

His character Virgil in *The Apprenticeship of Duddy Kravitz*, published in 1959, was a superb—and to my mind insufficiently acknowledged—prescient parody of the victim syndrome that would not come to full bloom until some twenty or thirty years later. I loved Virgil, the epileptic who wants to unite all epileptics—sorry, Mordecai: "health handicappers"—to fight discrimination against them. Around 1978, I complained to Mordecai that the field of human rights was getting so crowded with special interest groups that I had decided to write a column on the rights of necrophiliacs. "Too late," he replied instantly. "A Montreal classified ad has already requested that funeral homes stop being selfish and 'share.'" He saw it all.

I interpreted Newman's brief of "cultural affairs" in the broadest sense. The column was an instant success in terms of readership, though it was widely disliked by Anyone who was Anything in elite circles. My writing had the advantage of my early reading of British mags, particularly the "literary" competitions at the back of the *New Statesman* and *The Spectator*, whose winners wrote with droll wit and a perfectly rude sense of humour. I couldn't match them— the best of English journalists left and right have a sense of the absurd that beats all other countries—but it freed my writing from the 1970s deadly Canadian constraint of hypocritical politeness.

My rude columns gave me increasing visibility. At that point, I ricocheted between thinking I was highly attractive and that on close inspection the jig would be up: my front was okay but I had a flat behind. My eyebrows had disappeared after a rather enthusiastic attempt to pluck them in my college years and had never grown back, leaving me with an unfinished look rather like the pairs of eyes from the dolls I had disassembled as a child.

But my appearance landed me on three *Toronto Life* covers and produced a fair number of magazine features with full-page photos and ghastly if demi-prescient headlines like "Barbara Amiel: Aching to Be a Star." Toronto agent Jerry Lodge got me television commercials. Toronto's premier model agent, Bette Milne, looked at me and sighed, "You will never be a model. Perhaps your hands," but I still managed a bit of runway work. So in spite of my wish to play the "I was an ugly child and had a moustache," the fact is that I was pretty decent-looking. It is a separate matter that when your own standard of beauty is the flawless porcelain skin and blonde hair of the mythical Swedish au pair, nothing in the world can ever fully convince a Jewess with combination skin and ever-shiny nose that she really is very attractive.

Once my columns had revealed my shocking classic liberal notions, CBC News and Current Affairs never again used me as a commentator, guest or fill-in. Their commendable rigour in keeping out ideas contrary to their soft-left approach, unlike BBC News and Current Affairs, who welcomed me even as I criticized them in print—as well as CNN and the *New York Times*—kept me off all political programming broadcast by Canada's federal Crown corporation and national broadcaster for my entire life. No doubt the Canadian nation is the better for it.

Never mind, I was great material for CBC's clown world of entertainment and variety. There I sat beaming as a fairly regular guest panellist on *Front Page Challenge*. And for a year or two I was a specialist in the four-minute shocker: TVOntario gave me a weekly opinion segment of that length, carefully counterbalanced by a rebuttal recorded separately by left-winger Laurier LaPierre. CTV's legendary journalist and producer Michael Maclear got me a three-minute commentary bit on their Sunday night *W5* and *CTV Reports* shows in the late seventies, and for a season sent me to make mini documentaries pretty much on subjects of my own choice.

By the eighties I was flying as a journalist. Peeved detractors claimed that my political stance was purely opportunistic, a way of getting attention. I think this might have reflected their own pragmatism but certainly not mine. You really have to work devilishly hard, probably three times as hard as the columnists writing about the same topics from the approved point of view, to keep your job. Underneath the dramatics, I fear I was genuinely something of a "here I stand, I can do no other" sort of a bore.

True, I had become the village idiot for all producers looking for a token someone to balance out the 90 per cent of their program that was dressed-up received wisdom. I was asked to defend capital punishment, which I have always been strongly against, but being pragmatic and needing the airtime, I could at least truthfully say that I thought society had a right, alas, to do it.

I was asked to take positions on all predictable topics because Canadian television couldn't find another female journalist with long hair and a bust to talk in favour of God, against affirmative action and strongly against a state policy of multiculturalism and enforced human rights tribunals. In Britain, I would have been a dime a dozen. Affirmative action has always struck me as basically wrong, although spending extra monies on compensatory education for children from poor schools or difficult backgrounds, and adults trapped in poverty, is a no-brainer. I'm fine with women in combat if they are daft enough to want it or any other largely male job, so long as they can meet the same qualifications as men: I never wanted to be in a burning flat and have an affirmative action female fire-fighter on the ladder, looking equal, helpful and brave but sadly lacking the necessary upper-body strength to rescue me.

I was the media world's "fascist bitch," as theatre director Leon Major kindly referred to me. Actually, the full phrase he uttered when I entered a room at some event was "the fascist bitch in a Givenchy frock." I very much regretted I didn't have a Givenchy frock at the time. I would get them by trunkfuls later.

I played the game to the hilt. I had read about George Bernard Shaw's 1936 visit to Miami, which, incredibly, you can now actually see on YouTube. The great man walks towards the photographers and does a little jig for them. In other clips he mugs. This is Shaw, one of the greatest playwrights in the English language. So when I sweated over a column on legal affairs or détente or the Middle East, I would always couch the beginning in a verbal jig, some grab-your-attention outrageous line or anecdote, and I thought of my clothes and appearance in the same way. I told myself that if Shaw needed to dance a jig for the photographers in Miami to get attention for his genius, I sure as bloody hell needed to dance a marathon to get my views listened to in the Canadian media.

This, frankly, was only partly true. A theatrical personality quite enjoys a level of public conspicuousness. This is hardly a thrilling new insight. Nevertheless, as brazen as we might be, our behaviour says nothing at all one way or another about the value of the contribution after the jig is danced. The ideas stand on their own, for better or worse. For some, myself included, this personality coexists most uncomfortably with social insecurity and even shyness. But it all amounts to the same thing: an inability or disinclination to walk into a room in any way but that of Lucia di Lammermoor at curtain call wearing her bloodstained dress.

There's even more in the stew: a small group both attracts attention and has a singular quality to offend quite unintentionally just by being, as it were. Wherever life plunks us down, our very existence seems to challenge the status quo. This goes beyond the clothes worn or the jig danced. It simply is, and analyzing it gets us nowhere. All I know is that it hinders our life as much as it helps. We grab attention, all right, but don't elicit approval or admiration. When the chips are really down, the full price has to be paid—with interest. I sensed this but couldn't know how very expensive it would be.

When I entered my forties I was pretty damn pleased with my life. Two marriages down plus a two-year stint with my young man and now I was living alone in a smart apartment building in midtown Toronto. I never entertained. My rented one-bedroom, filled with natural light as well as the standing Italian Flos lamps whose halogen bulbs cooked any fly that touched them, had barely any furniture apart from the very large L-shaped desk, crammed floor-to-ceiling bookshelves with my father's photograph at eye level, the best music components I could afford and gigantic B&W speakers, plus the inevitable television set turned on and muted for company. I was forty-two years old and this was paradise. A leased car, nothing fixed, nothing owned. Every time I opened the front door straight into the living room, I felt a hiccup of pleasure that my own work had brought me this.

I very much wanted female chums, but on the whole my school friends had turned left ideologically—or left in the sense of leaving Toronto for Los Angeles or New York. By your forties it's tricky to find single women who haven't established a virtually "closed" set, and no set was attracted to me, for very obvious and good reasons: as far as I was concerned, any dinner plan or movie date could be legitimately broken last minute if a column needed work or an assignment completion. I was unreliable—careless with friends out of an unpleasant mix of selfishness, driving ambition and ignorance. Heaven knows why any female friend hung on, but one or two tried hard.

The consequence of my pole position as Canada's Bitch of Buchenwald was a telephone call. "This is Peter Worthington," said the voice. Which led to a contract to become, first, associate editor at the *Toronto Sun* newspaper and, if that worked out, his designated successor as editor. Worthington was a Canadian original, a rare creature whose talent and extraordinary career included his co-founding of the tabloid *Sun*. His journalism was astonishing in its scope: he interviewed, among others, Alexander Kerensky, who had been minister-chairman of the Russian provisional government in 1917 after the revolution; he somehow managed to be an eyewitness to the assassination of Lee Harvey Oswald. He sufficiently upset Prime Minister Trudeau that the *Sun*'s files were briefly seized and locked by the RCMP under the Official Secrets Act. After a couple of years working with him, Worthington left the newspaper to follow his political instincts and stand in a by-election for the Progressive Conservative Party. I became the paper's editor. Perhaps he had this career change in mind when two years earlier he had hired me.

The *Toronto Sun* and I were not compatible in any way whatsoever, apart from a certain determination to shock and a sturdy belief in a Lockean individualism, a phrase that would have had as much resonance with its core blue-collar readership as a Chinese ideogram. There was a not so subterranean belief that I had obtained the editor's chair, and its office with a dismal potted tree and coat cupboard, via Peter Worthington's bed. Perhaps this helped Canadian feminists swallow the fact that an anti-Marxist female of British birth had become the first woman to edit a daily metropolitan newspaper in Canada (and according to my diligent U.K. assistant, the first female in North America—the second being at a Miami newspaper—to edit such a paper, apart from those who inherited the job through family ownership), but the wistful rumour was not the slightest bit true. Still, the myth comforted the rather jock newsroom, where many had jostled for the position that had fallen into my apparently well-used lap.

I was a shrewd if wrong choice. The managing editor, Les Payette, would have been far more competent in the position. Worthington was irreplaceable, a natural genius at tabloid journalism. I was something completely different. I wasn't bad at making speeches around the country, and my gender lent itself to catchy posters in bus shelters. "The Sun has a New Editor," read one: "Congratulations, it's a girl."

Marketing meetings were my low point. I did everything possible to avoid them. Matters came to a head in 1984, when Pope John Paul II came to Canada. How was the *Sun* going to play the historic visit? Being a Cold War warrior of some intensity and ill-equipped for a tabloid newspaper, I suggested to our marketing meeting that we might want to highlight the anti-Nazi activities of the Pope and most especially his stance against communism in his native Poland. I banged on enthusiastically. My remarks were greeted with dead silence, broken only by the irresistible notion of our marketing director.

"I've got it, and you're going to love this," he said gleefully to the tableful of executives. "We'll sponsor a contest." General murmurs of approval. The *Sun* was mad about contests. I couldn't quite see how to link the Pope with a *Toronto Sun* contest, but I feared the worst. For our marketing director the link was absolutely self-evident.

"Here it is," he said as the cardboard mock-up slid out from under his chair. The words were in purple on a gold background, underneath the *Toronto Sun* logo, the Pope's face and, all around it, balloons with television sets, hockey sticks and skis inside them: "$100,000 in prizes. . . . Can You Guess the Pope's Weight?"

On a hot August day, with the prospect of the deadly three o'clock marketing meeting ahead of me, I tripped along the streets of downtown Toronto. The eighty-five-degree weather, with not a hint of wind, only heavy, humid air, was wrecking my hair. My feet were stuck in high heels and the rest of me in a dress increasingly sticky with perspiration. Lunches in my view were a bloody nightmare. Since I rarely got to the office before eleven, having to leave again at noon was senseless. My usual excuse for not attending marketing meetings or going to lunches was the need to keep up to the minute on the day's news for the editorial I had to write each day, but this subterfuge was not unfamiliar to the publisher.

"When Conrad Black asks you to lunch," he had ordered, looking through the telephone messages spiked on my secretary's desk,
"you go."

About the last thing I wanted to do was go to lunch with
Conrad Black, who I had recently described in the social column
Panache that I ghosted as a man with "acres of untoned white
flesh," which was my way of describing an out-of-shape gentile.
We had first met at the only Establishment dinner I attended. The
evening was at the home of John F. Bassett, the judge of the Miss
By-Line Ball, who happily seemed to have forgotten that early
encounter now that he was happily married to Isabel (Macdonald)
Bassett, the beautiful winner of it. I was seated next to Black and
all I could think to say was that I had read his book on the late
Quebec premier Maurice Duplessis. I had bought the book hoping
it would give me some insight into French-Canadian politics but
had faltered early on. This proved not to be a problem. Conrad
merrily banged on about Duplessis, and with much relief I happily
let him. The dinner was excruciating.

Conrad's path rarely crossed mine: the last time we had met I was
trying out a new form of dressing, namely, concealing my cleavage
in favour of a more demure approach. Unfortunately I hadn't much
fashion sense, and the plain cream wool dress by Gianfranco Ferré
was a large geometric tent with a short cape around the front and
shoulders. I was exceptionally proud of the whole thing. "Barbara,"
said Conrad familiarly and with a devastatingly accurate description
that had not occurred to me, "I see you're dressing like the Pope."

Black was known to me as some sort of a businessman that everyone seemed to revere, a chartered member of the ruling social class
in Toronto. A married businessman and a Christian, he failed on just
about every wicket. On top of that, in our brief encounters at book
launches, his talk was incomprehensible to me. He had an enthusiastic
pattern of speech containing so many historical and political allusions
couched in rotund phrases and unfamiliar words he clearly believed
I understood, that by now I was dreading the moment he would discover I was a total fraud.

I was late for the lunch and fearful, trying hard to think of interests in common. I assumed that we both had a pretty strong dislike of our current prime minister, Pierre Elliott Trudeau, and admiration for America's Ronald Reagan, but I couldn't see where to go from there. Bring them up and there lay a direct path to some disastrous exploration of the roots of Canadian conservatism or perhaps an anecdotal analysis of Madisonian democracy, at which I would fail. I could probably steer talk towards the situation in Eastern Europe, and Reagan's "Evil Empire" speech on the Soviet Union was tattooed on my heart, but what if that led to a discussion of Afghanistan? I could never get the names of the region and its leaders straight, let alone the very word *mujahedeen*—it always came out as "mudajeen" or something worse. I sweated more.

Conrad was sitting in the prime booth at Winston's, the restaurant of Toronto's rich, powerful and very often tipsy. He was perfectly at ease, obviously cool and wonderfully dry. He seemed happy to see me and was wearing the three-piece pinstriped uniform of his class. In his hand was a glass of wine, and my heart sunk. No doubt he would drink several glasses, getting progressively more jovial in speech, while I would be left sitting like the dour abstainer I was.

"Ah," Conrad began as I tried to gracefully slide into the banquette without my skirt sticking to it. "What will you have to drink?" If only wine could turn to water, I thought, which led to a moment of divine inspiration: "I see the Pope has gone to Lourdes," I offered.

"*Ineffabilis Deus*," replied Conrad happily, "December the eighth, 1854." Lunch had begun.

I wish I could say that even then my heart began to flutter or that my opinion of Conrad changed during the lunch. It did not. My unease never left me. Had I known that he was noting my bare legs and damp viscose dress with approval, I might have relaxed.

Conrad Black hadn't the faintest idea that for me he was emblematic of stuffed-shirt Toronto. This was grotesquely unfair to the man, but then I really didn't study him closely. His marital status and the pinstriped look of a financier put him outside my radar. I preferred the private company of outlaws, sometimes even petty criminals, so long as they were European and preferably from east of the Oder–Neisse line. My public escorts varied, but almost invariably I would get bored by the time the waiter brought the entree. Frankly, it seemed like a far better deal to stay home in a comforting haze of chocolates, music, a typewriter and the occasional call to a male friend for a limited-duration late-night visit. I lamented in my column that men could not be switched on and off like a standing lamp, which has always seemed to me a design error.

CHAPTER SIX

Marital Sack Race

Dammit, I couldn't escape this blithering ache for a husband. Any sane onlooker could see that the combination I favoured, and presented, of slightly messy sexual activities, greedy work ethic and snobbish cultural attitudes would not be found in one man—just as any man close to embodying this happy mix was unlikely to find in me the ideal partner for life. If only I had the wisdom of Edna O'Brien, who, after a first youthful marriage of ten years failed, had a desperate love affair and then seems to have stopped the steeplechase. "I didn't live with anyone," she said in a much later interview, "they never moved in. I suppose that gave me more time to write."

In this one area, though, I was a perpetual optimist: around the corner would be my Prince Charming. Ever alert to the possibility of being swept off my feet, the next sweep came unexpectedly when I attended a dull party in Toronto—for which I was very late, possibly because I knew from the tony address that it was bound to be dull. Most of the guests were leaving when I arrived with a current companion from Montreal, a suave and clever Jewish lawyer who felt about me much the way I felt about him: if not Ken and Barbie dolls, we were the matchmakers' mature Jewish version, so we ought to try this on and see if it works but it's very unlikely. Besides, he had a much younger French-Canadian girlfriend in his own back garden.

My future third husband, who had just arrived from London, was still at the party. Apart from the slight inconvenience of his being a

Roman Catholic, David Graham reeked of eligibility: cosmopolitan manner, late forties, well over six feet tall, thick silver-ginger hair, very funny, a successful businessman, never married and a walking photo-op in his casual Burberry. Too good to be true. And it was.

The path of true love never runs smooth, but does it have to be a death march, I thought to myself, as I abseiled through my third marriage. The plus was that in 1984 I returned to London with my Canadian, who resided in the U.K. where he enjoyed its numerous theatres, divorcees, splendid restaurants and intoxicating nightlife all enclosed in a fuzzy tax regime for foreign residents. We ploughed through nine months of somewhat tumultuous dating from Calcutta to Paris before we married secretly in Nantucket after a game of tennis I tactfully lost. He then left for his London home while I returned to my job at the *Toronto Sun*.

The secrecy was necessitated, he explained, by the need to protect his tax status. As a full-time resident of the U.K., it would not be helpful to have a wife with a Toronto residence. My own view, which I pushed furiously to the back of my mind, was that secrecy was a useful tool for a man who had spent forty-seven years as a bachelor to get accustomed to the notion that he wasn't.

Before we each returned to a pseudo existence as singles, though, we flew to New York for a one-night honeymoon in the Carlyle hotel. A starry night was upon us as he pushed open the door to a suite filled with flowers and champagne. I was in heaven. When I came out of the bathroom in my best Janet Reger nightgown, my husband was still dressed and sitting on the bed with his briefcase.

"I've called for a bellboy," he said.

"Why?"

"I just need him to witness your signature."

He pulled an envelope out of his briefcase, opened it up flat on the side of the tan leather, and I knew. This was the marriage contract I had declined to sign, given its rather austere terms. Essentially, I was to give up my staff job at the *Toronto Sun* with all its benefits, including pension and insurance. I was to terminate the lease on my cherished apartment—paid for by me and in a building that rarely had vacancies—in order to sever any Canadian tie that might impede his tax status. In return I would receive—nothing. If we divorced after a number of years, I would get a lump sum of $200,000, rising over a period of years to a maximum of $400,000 Canadian. If there were a child, he would provide for it.

Though in principle I did think separation of assets was a good thing, and although I had no idea of his worth—all I had seen was his two-bedroom garden flat in Belgravia and his small set of offices in Toronto—I assumed that if he needed tax protection he must have something to protect. I felt it would have been sporty to offer some pension substitute to kick in after, say, half a dozen years of marriage, even if I didn't take it up. I thoroughly disapproved of the fifty-fifty no-fault marital property regime in Ontario and had no idea whether our marriage would come under U.S., Canadian or U.K. law, and anyway if the marriage was short-lived, I'd simply go back to the status quo ante. His money was his own.

"David," I said. "I really don't want to sign it and especially not like this on our wedding night."

"Sign it or I leave for London right away."

That travel plan struck me as difficult since it was already close to midnight, but I took his meaning. He'd leave the suite, marriage unconsummated. I had come out of the bathroom worrying about my post-tennis hair and concerned that my improvised bare-faced night makeup of loose powder, lip colour and eau de toilette would not meet his criteria for glamour, only to find that the criteria I had to meet was an altogether different sort of bare face. One minute you're standing in your silk and lace all warm, apprehensive and bridey, and yes of course we had been intimate but it's really a special act when you have just been married, and now I was in a triangle with a Hispanic bellboy, a briefcase and myself. I looked at my putative husband and melted. I signed.

My hunch about the difficult transition he faced in changing his point of view to that of a married man surfaced rather suddenly.

"Will you be seeing Margaret?" I asked before he left in the morning for London, referring to the very attractive divorcee who lived down the street from him and had been his constant date for some time. She had not greeted my entrance on the London scene with whole-hearted enthusiasm.

"She's in Italy for the week," he said.

"Please promise me you won't go there?" I replied, which was probably the wrong thing to ask but the bridal-night scene had something of an operatic *Lohengrin* ring to it already and this was Elsa's forbidden question.

"No, of course not. I'll wait in London till she returns, and you'll be over in about ten days."

I was in my *Sun* office some days later when the telephone rang and his brother informed me that David had been in a terrible car accident.

"Where did it take place?" I asked, thinking I could quickly get the overnight plane to London.

"On the autoroute to Paris. He'd been in Italy. His injuries are very serious. A drunk driver came the wrong way down an exit ramp into traffic."

My reactions were, I think, those of an average new bride, which is to say a mixture of terrible panic and blank rage. Margaret was in Italy. In Paris, my husband had been interested in a very young—just above the age of consent—pretty blonde girl. Actually, in France there is no age of consent, although an adult man is supposed not to have sex with a female before she is fifteen. I couldn't be sure he was going to see her but that's the way his rented car was pointing, although sadly not the car he collided with, and given his proscribed stay at Margaret's it seemed a worthwhile guess. His brother knew nothing of our marriage, only that I had been constantly with David for the past year and our intentions might be long-term—in David's terms. In calling me, he was being a thoughtful brother.

This was not a resounding start to our marriage, but I swallowed and took it in stride. A handsome man that can make you laugh endlessly and make love to you endlessly is rare enough. After he was flown to London, I shared hospital visits with a number of other girl-friends, none of whom knew he was married. This made visiting times

slightly treacherous for me, if not farcical. I watched the play of intimate little signals between David and his harem, smiling like a jolly
good sport which I most definitely was not. I considered putting
strychnine in the wine they were all sharing. David umpired the "girlfriends" around his bed with his usual charm and dexterity, in spite of
one of his wounded legs hoisted by some sort of contraption in the air.
His face was undamaged and his upper torso was peeking merrily out
of the powder blue striped pajamas I had given him. This was definitely teeth-gritting.

His mother, brother and I stayed at David's London flat. One
night, very late, the hospital called. He had a thrombosis and was in
the ICU. The situation we were told was "grave" and we needed to
hurry. The thrombosis had moved upstream from his leg to his lung,
largely I feared because the physiotherapist for his damaged leg was a
gorgeous woman susceptible to David's inexhaustible charm, which
he used to deflect the full regimen of taxing leg exercises into a more
congenial glass of wine together. (This was a private London hospital
with a wine menu.) His brother did a wallet search for insurance
details and came upon our marriage licence. His response was warm
congratulations and then he sent for a lawyer to change David's will,
probably at David's request.

"He's in ICU and close to death," I said. "Is the additional stress
of a lawyer really a positive here?"

I sat alone outside the unit, a non-family member barred from
entering, since I had promised David not to reveal our marital status.
In the wretched neon lighting I reflected on the psychiatric report
that he had given me before we married. At the time I thought it was
hilarious, very North American and ever so trendy—giving your
bride-to-be a psychiatrist's assessment of your sexuality and attitude
to women.

"You might want to read this," he had said in a semi-jocular
manner. "It'll give you some warning." His voice and the rhythm of
his speech always excited me; unlike most Canadian accents, it had a
deep, precise sound, with perfectly placed pauses and no unnecessary
words such as *like* or *you know*. I found this alluring. For a man to have

such legato in his speech, together with that thrilling timbre, was a secondary sexual characteristic for me.

"Should I take some advice on it?" I asked in the same jocular manner.

"From anyone," he said. He handed me the seven-page report, by a psychologist at Toronto Western Hospital, with chunks of redactions.

When I returned from the ICU to his flat, I reread it, this time with a more serious look. Since it had been dated ten years before our marriage, I felt it was probably irrelevant. Some sentences, however, particularly those under the Summary and Recommendations section, had a new relevance. He was described as a "worldly achiever, who, at times, strives for emotional growth and self-actualization." (Whatever the blazes that is, I thought.)

> However he is stunted by his own psychopathology of:
> (a) Difficulty trusting and making a full emotional commitment with people, especially women
> (b) Feelings of insecurity about his own resources, inability to be mature, love and be loved. . . .
> (c) latent sexual and aggressive impulses toward women, which are inappropriately discharged
> (d) possibly ambivalent feelings and conflicts over dependence-interdependence, love-hate.

As far as I could see, that would apply to most men in some way, and most women. The conclusion left me a little more worried.

> It would seem that his relationships have usually been built upon a commercial pyramid of endless transactions with illusionary spiral peaks and very little if any cornerstone foundations. . . . He should continue to be seen by a male therapist, until such time that he has at least internalized some of his problems with women, and has demonstrated some mature behaviour in his relationships with them. Therapeutic progress will to a great extent also depend upon extinguishing the reinforcements David presently obtains

for game-playing, distrust, and immature sexual and passive-aggressive acting out.

This didn't sound quite like a match made in heaven.

The Toronto newspapers made a bit of noise over our marriage when it was disclosed six months later. On cue, a feature article appeared in the Canadian women's magazine *Chatelaine*. There I was, looking radiantly happy in my new London home, holding my latest accessory, a watering can bought quickly at Tesco's so I could hover over the potted plants in my Belgravia garden flat—*garden flat* being something of a synonym for damp. "In London & In Love," said the magazine, describing my "housewifely existence," which was a bit of a stretch. I resigned my *Toronto Sun* editor's job, though remained as a columnist, and left with the dregs of a pension plan. My beloved Benvenuto Place flat went to my gifted cousin, Dr. Robert Buckman, actor, writer, cancer researcher, and father of two, who had decided to emigrate to Toronto from London. I was madly in love.

Pretty soon I realized I was going to have to work. We had agreed that I would make a last effort at the pregnancy I had been sporadically pursuing for the past ten years. David seemed enthusiastic when it was first discussed. Sadly, my attempts at one of the ruinously expensive and con-job fertility clinics that dotted London for last-hope women were going nowhere. My ovaries, blown up by fertility drugs, were ready to explode like overinflated tires. My husband was usually three thousand miles away when my thermometer insisted ovulation was about to take place, and I was bored being a forty-five-year-old layabout with only a weekly *Sun* column and one every other week for *Maclean's*. The old question grew up like an overnight weed: How to reinvent myself.

"Well of course you must write for the London *Times*," said John O'Sullivan cheerily. O'Sullivan was an Irish-English friend who was working for Rupert Murdoch as editorial page editor of the *New York Post*. Murdoch now owned the London *Times*. I was not fool enough to think my Canadian journalism credentials of any value. I had read the British newspapers all my life and I knew I was in deep waters.

I was short on wit, deficient in sardonic humour. In fact, looking at the matter matter-of-factly, whereas in Canada I was a scandalous ideological provocateur, in Britain I could only see myself as a bore.

In due time I got called in to *The Times* by editor Charles Wilson, who fortunately hadn't opened a page of my 1980 book *Confessions* that O'Sullivan had sent him. I carted along a sheaf of my columns. He palmed me off on the features editor, a civilized man who, unsure what to do with an unknown Canadian female journalist, urged me warmly to "try."

In August 1985, Prime Minister Brian Mulroney came to London for a Commonwealth conference, and as possibly the only Canadian journalist in town that week, I was asked by *The Times* if I could "try" a piece about him. Never have I felt the disadvantage of the sobriety of Canadian politics more. British and European politics followed a trajectory from calamity to farce, leaving rich lodes of material to mine. Writing about America was easy in a different way: the United States was both a hellish jungle and a waiting room full of people in analysis ever banging on about their "feelings" while trying to bring peace and love to the world and making fulsome apologies to some obscure tribe for their latest failed attempt. The only distinct thing about Canada was the invocation of its name in the U.K. as a synonym for bland. Still, my Mulroney piece made it onto *The Times* editorial page.

Three months later, Mozambique's president, Samora Machel, had the common decency to die. Thanks to him and his Frelimo communist dictatorship, I had some familiarity with the secret gardens of his land after my stay in his Machava prison over Christmas and New Year's 1980. So while everyone from Margaret Thatcher to the Queen was expressing their fervent anguish at his death—he must have been an utter charmer in person, if not policies—I was dry-eyed and mentioned this to my *Times* contact.

"Well, write something," he said, "and we'll see." My "No Tears for Machel" was featured on the October 4, 1985 editorial page and gave me my first contact with playwright Harold Pinter, who was seated next to me at my first smart literary dinner party that night. This was exciting. A really significant writer. Me next to him. The

Great Man looked at my place card and said warmly, "Are you the horrible person who wrote that disgusting piece on Mozambique's late president in *The Times* today?" With that established, he turned his back on me for the rest of the meal—all four courses. A week later *The Times* asked me to do a piece on TV personality Esther Rantzen, the London version of Barbara Frum.

The breed is not uncommon, and I am certainly an offshoot: clever Jewish girls in the media. There should be a sorority for us. We are ambitious and very often achieve beyond our mental abilities. Esther Rantzen and I both attended North London Collegiate, a spawning ground for the genus, and we both spent the war years in Hertfordshire, a home county of dubious social standing. Our viewpoints may be at opposite ends of the political spectrum but we are of the same stock. Perhaps our great-great-grandparents pushed wheelbarrows in the same shtetl and our more accomplished rabbinical ancestors—we all have rabbinical ancestors—thumbed the same Talmud Torah lesson books. Similarly, given appearance, ideological stance, middle-class upbringing and point of view, though on opposite sides of the Atlantic, the CBC's Frum and the BBC's Rantzen must have been separated at birth.

Esther was setting up a BBC child help phone line, which anyone could call anonymously to report suspicions of child abuse or to seek help. She had skipped beatification for immediate sainthood. Helping abused kiddies is a splendid cause, but Ms. Rantzen, an extremely well-intentioned woman, had allowed her emotions to treacle. In preshow interviews Esther explained that the definition of abuse was elastic: not tucking Daisy into bed at night could qualify as emotional abuse. *The Times* gave me 750 words on Esther's new show. I felt strongly about the matter, knowing full well the sort of nightmare that a malicious or spiteful referral to the U.K.'s children's social services could cause long before serious investigation of an allegation was completed. I went into lockdown on the column.

Nearly ninety hours of rewrites later, I had a column. Not exactly the stuff of Greats, but it was forthright. Two weeks later I had a weekly column in *The Times*. Within a year, I got the runner-up press commendation for columnist of the year, which was a stunner: to this day, after about two or three thousand columns, I have never got any award for them in Canada. Now, in less than a year, I was clutching a scroll, runner-up to an idol of mine—writer Bernard Levin. Meanwhile, I suppose the judges who had to come up with these awards year after year in a limited pool were grateful for a new name.

A treadmill routine set in. Working till one in the morning on my 750 words—and then getting up at five thirty to throw the entire thing out in order to start again—took up five days per column, during which I sat at my Tandy computer looking despondently at the never-ending drizzle, stair rods, mists and just plain rain cascading down on my now limp potted plants, never again to see the blooming purple glory that had graced my arrival.

The telephone never rang, apart from research calls returned. My husband was away 90 per cent of the time, and I grew increasingly despondent in a city where, endlessly exciting as London was, I knew virtually no one. Leaving England at twelve years of age meant I had missed that crucial education after passing my eleven-plus school exam. Those years from Upper Third through to university are the ones that not only lead to friends for life but imbue a natural and spontaneous vocabulary, network and thought patterns peculiar to the culture. Whether it was towns I had never seen or the details of British and European politics, I was at sea without a bloody oar. Appearing on BBC current affairs shows, I hadn't a clue what the British Shipbuilders Corporation was, dreaded any mention of the Irish Question and was still stuck in county names like Cumberland, which the government's 1974 reorganization renamed Cumbria. I barely knew which side of the Thames I was on, and when calls came from the BBC asking "Can you come to Wigan?" I thought of Orwell's *Road to Wigan Pier* and had no notion that in fact I should head not to Liverpool but to Manchester. I lived in the Reuters clippings library on Fleet Street trying to catch up on meat-and-potatoes politics in Britain, and rode a bicycle around Hyde Park Corner to get my head into driving on the left-hand side. I stuck bits of local jargon into my conversation and it sounded like what it was: studied. I cursed my omission of history at college, couldn't name the British kings and queens chronologically apart from spotty attempts that began after 1066. Offa and Egbert were cheeses to me. Worse, I was a fake on two continents now. The British thought I sounded Canadian and, whenever I returned to Toronto, the Canadians thought I was putting on a British accent.

Making friends in a new country has a predictable cycle. You begin with anyone who will take you up, regardless whether you have the slightest thing in common. Suddenly, the woman you meet over mushrooms at the hideously expensive grocery shop on Motcomb Street when you both reach for the last box and have a "sorry," "sorry" moment looms as a possible friend. It took me about two months to realize that the fulsome "Longing to see you again, we must meet" from people encountered at the very occasional dinner or run-in actually was their polite way of saying goodbye. I grabbed on to my husband's English female acquaintances and tried to learn how to dress, behave and talk like them. I knew I looked too "new," too shiny, my clothes screaming "American" or foreigner.

I had been alone quite a lot of my life but never lonely. The excitement of my husband's return visits to London was overwhelming. I'd run to Belgrave Square and buy huge white calla lilies for the hall and plump the flat and myself up and wait for the Burberry trench coat and tousled hair. Then, for no discernible reason, after a few days he would have to leave.

My column began to pay dividends. Two or three like-minded people introduced me around a bit. I joined the Reform Club on Pall Mall, known as the first club you join in London and the first you leave. (I haven't yet.) After two or three years I was at a promising start.

Then my marriage ended in tears (mine), scenes (mine) and despair (mine as well). I was heartbroken, although I had contributed my share to the dissolution.

The immediate cause was my relationship with book publisher George Weidenfeld. There is simply no way on earth to capture what happened in this unnerving scenario and, of course, it is only one side of the story—mine. The entire episode was a bad novel. Weidenfeld, member of the House of Lords, successful publisher, twenty-one years older than me, was a Viennese Jew who fled the Nazis in 1938. He had an extraordinary sense of humour embellished by a wonderful ability to mimic anyone (including Adolf Hitler for one BBC wartime broadcast when they couldn't get the actual tape of one of Hitler's particularly horrid speeches). Exceptionally clever, well read, and adoring opera, he was the consummate European.

Unfortunately he was also very short, plump, and with eyes that could protrude rather alarmingly, especially when upset. Photos show him as having a rather magnetic appearance as a younger man; he had a singular record of attracting beautiful women, including marriage to critic Cyril Connolly's former wife, Barbara Skelton, a femme fatale extraordinaire and previously lover of King Farouk. Skelton had written the second volume of her memoirs, which included slightly unpleasant recollections of her time with Weidenfeld, called *Weep No More*. I did not read it then. I should have. I picked it up when writing this book. Whatever else, her descriptions of Weidenfeld's emotional manipulations were spot on.

Weidenfeld was the best-known party-giver in London for circles that included top politicians, intellectuals, authors, society figures, aristocracy—well, everyone. He lived in a building on the Chelsea Embankment that had an apartment to sell just below his, and David, who had almost no English friends apart from his girlfriends, wanted to buy it. We would share the broad staircase that went by our flat to Weidenfeld's above.

"When he has those big parties," said David, "we'll just put up a sign with 'Coats' and an arrow pointing to our place." Litigation got in the way of this when David rowed with his chosen decorator, the famed John Stefanidis. The apartment was off.

Among my new friends was Miriam Gross, former arts editor of *The Observer*, who invited me to dinner at her home. "Just a couple of people," she said. "George Weidenfeld and one or two others. Why don't you and your husband come?" David accepted. The night of the dinner, I came out of the bathroom to find David lying on the bed, still in his (rather attractive) yellow cashmere crew neck and corduroy trousers—a Canadian uniform of his class.

"I'm not going," he said as the taxi pulled up to our door. "You'll do a much better job alone attracting Weidenfeld's attention and then we can go to his parties. Just tell them I'm unwell."

It was horribly rude. I went alone. As predicted, Weidenfeld was attracted and invited me to the opera for the following weekend. David approved and left town—although I'm not sure he would have signed on to my going to Annabel's nightclub afterwards. My friendship with George Weidenfeld was launched.

George was both a magnificent intellectual and a magnificent poseur. The scope of his scholarship was certainly more formidable than his thorough knowledge of the *Almanach de Gotha*, but "social anthropology," as he put it, fascinated him. I called it gossip. Although he was ridiculed for flitting from one political leader to another according to whose memoirs he wanted to publish, in fact he had undiluted political courage when it came to the most difficult topic in England: that of Israel and being a Jew.

He was not religiously observant, although he became the *chef de cabinet* to Chaim Weizmann, the first president of Israel, and his life-long preoccupation was with Israel's existence and the furthering of good postwar relations between Jews and Germans. His network ran from Pope to chancellor, all across Europe. No man, short of a military one, could have done more for Israel. In certain British publications he was ridiculed and maliciously described in virtually *Der Stürmer* terms.

In conversation he was funny, informed and fascinating. That, together with the circles in which he moved, made him irresistible: being with him, I thought rather calculatingly, gave me access and some status. And, incredibly, many of his acquaintances were reading me and discussing my columns. To have Isaiah Berlin or Michael Holroyd compliment me on the argument in a column was intoxicating. Meanwhile, George acted as if my husband didn't exist, a typically European approach to another's love life and providential, since David all but didn't.

"Miriam," I said, "we've got to get David involved in my friendship with George."

"All right," said George when we suggested this. "You and Miriam put together a dinner party that would make him feel comfortable. You know, some businessmen or friends of yours. I'll ask a few," and he waved his cigar abstractly in the air; the subject was of not much interest. A guest list of about ten people materialized that we thought would be congenial, but when the time came, David remained utterly silent at the dinner table for the entire evening, as if George was a giant spider and he some sort of fly trapped in our sticky social web. It was baffling. "Yes, yes," said George later, butting his cigar in a porcelain ashtray as he leaned back in his armchair wearing the red knitted cardigan he favoured with a yellow shirt and contrasting tie. "He seems perfectly nice. But what do you talk about?"

Gradually, or not so gradually, I could see George was getting attracted to me. He began inviting me to the country homes of his friends when David was away, another world I had never known. Now the serpent's head rose.

In her memoir, Barbara Skelton tells of the triangle that developed between herself, Cyril Connolly and Weidenfeld. She says she became "sexually obsessed with Weidenfeld," although she didn't care for him in any other way and wanted to go on being married to Connolly. My reaction was quite the reverse. Though I loved every minute with George, I not only had no sexual interest in him—I had a positive revulsion. This was not George's fault, but I was still in love with my tall, considerably younger and more physically vital if somewhat less intellectually gymnastic husband.

As the situation escalated, David's own dalliances were scarcely concealed. His single life had never quite ended. At one point, I arrived in New York, where he/we had an apartment, to find our bed still containing spent condoms. On telephoning my car in Toronto, the woman who answered said she was driving and asked me to hold a moment. I later identified her as a gorgeous Jamaican girl. Jealousy overwhelmed me, and I made dreadful scenes. But there is one constant about men that all females know: no matter the evidence, unless you catch them in flagrante delicto, they will not admit to any infidelity, while, unlike women, they cannot absorb any hint of it in their partners.

And I was up to my eyebrows in my own double life: George was now regularly proposing marriage and begging me to get a divorce. I was trying to hang on to the social advantages he gave me without incurring the payment required sexually. This obviously had a short lease. The minute I heard George's suggestion, "Let's spend a cozy evening," I went into semi-paralysis with dread. I knew the code. The only way I could deal with it was to avoid actual body-to-body contact and give him some oral pleasure. Men rarely care whether you like or dislike doing it, since they go into some world where they can live out every fantasy in their heads while you provide, as it were, the background music and sensations.

I wanted nothing in return, which seemed a relief to him. He was embarrassed by my sometimes bouncing breasts (a first, in my experience), which tended to swell at menstrual times, and on one embarrassing occasion when I wore a very loose, completely opaque jersey dress to cover me from neck to wrist to knee—but belted—he asked why they were visibly wobbling under it.

"Perhaps you should speak to Ira," said George, referring to the statuesque Princess Ira von Fürstenberg. "She was telling me she thought it was time to have a breast reduction, and you might want to consider that."

To the onlooker, I was behaving shamefully with George and causing him great unhappiness. Unable to deal either with the bouts of crying Barbara Skelton had described or forget David, I was deadlocked. A cleverer, more decent or more experienced woman could have managed this sort of game far better.

George, on the other hand, was a brilliant manoeuvrer. He would pour out his anguish to his friends, especially those women who formed a sort of praetorian guard about him: they began to look at me as a heartless jezebel leading on this lovestruck swain as if he were a callow youth of twenty-five. "Speak to Gina," he would urge me, mentioning a very clever close friend of his. "Tell her your problems frankly and she will understand." In my desperation and naive belief that women were allies, I actually did this. "I think the world of George," I told her in between my little tearful moments, "but holding him is like clutching death." This brutal simile immediately went straight to George and all over London. A sixty-eight-year-old man of his experience is not a swain; he knew exactly what the problem was and he also knew that if he cried, I would be rendered immobile. I could see him watching me behind his tears and I could hear my voice going from firm to faltering.

"I can't go, George," I would say after he proffered another invitation to the Stresa music festival or a trip to the Weimar republic with friends. "This can't continue." Now that I'd got up the strength to actually say I was through, George would fall back against the sofa, his head lolling on it, sobbing. "How can you humiliate me?" he would ask. "You've promised to come. Everyone is expecting you." This accusation of humiliation always stopped me cold. Guilt seeped through me. The crying would become intense and I would see the tears roll down soft, loose cheeks. I felt encircled by a cobra feigning helplessness, and to say no would be more lethal than going. I would lose the friendship not only of George but, as important, of the several women I really liked, especially Miriam, who were his old friends.

This sounds preposterous—after all, I was not exactly a child bride myself—but the situation, easily resolved on paper, doesn't take into account a feckless quality in me that finds it impossible to let down even the saleswoman who orders a piece of clothing for me and gets sent the wrong design. One quivering utterance of "I did special-order it for you and I don't think it can be returned . . ." renders me helpless: I buy lest I get her in trouble, never mind the expense of buying what I don't particularly like and definitely cannot afford. Of the many holes in my brain, this is one that I simply cannot fathom and that age has not mended.

George had an astigmatic vision in which I was his clever Jewish columnist wife who would run his salon with Clare Boothe Luce brilliance. This ignored my clear and announced horror of ever throwing dinner parties and, importantly, the time I required to write. As for his intense sexual needs, that would all work out. In the meantime, "We'll have a *mariage blanc,*" he would reassure me, which I knew was bunk. "You will live in a little apartment of your own." I had no illusions: he would be there at bedtime, very much part of an anticipated *mariage noir.* He even purchased a small basement flat next door to him connected through a small tunnel arrayed with heating and plumbing pipes, commissioning a mutual friend, Sally Metcalfe, to decorate it. This couldn't have been easy for him— George was not a rich man. Sally must have thought I was brain-damaged as I listened numbly to plans for it, speechless with horror.

The deadlock was broken in 1988 after the *New York Post* page six gossip column mentioned that ladies across two continents were weeping because George Weidenfeld was going to marry British columnist me. A former *Toronto Sun* columnist, Joan Sutton Straus, wrote an indignant letter to the paper that the allegation was false since I was happily married to David Graham. One of David's former girlfriends drew his attention to the exchange, and I was toast. Divorce proceedings by him began immediately.

The break-up was a stew of hysteria and hideously lumpy moments involving me flying back and forth across the Atlantic in pursuit of my soon-to-be former husband. The details would fill a shelf of weepy books. My own view is that my mental capacities never recovered from the fairly lengthy coma induced by an unoriginal cocktail of barbiturates and alcohol that I took during and after one of my beseeching transatlantic telephone calls when David suggested I kill myself, a not unreasonable suggestion given my tiresome repetitions of an inability to live without him. From Toronto, he managed to call the police station around the corner from our Belgravia flat, and I ended up in hospital for about forty-eight hours. Particularly humiliating was his next morning's request to my cleaning lady to FedEx his dinner jacket so he could attend dinner in California with Lee Radziwill.

CHAPTER SEVEN

Blackjack on Steroids

Clinical depressions are fairly common and everyone thinks their own depression is a uniquely vivid nightmare. Mine began slowly, during the last six months or so of my marriage to David Graham, and lasted about two and a half years. When the full grip of what I was dealing with became apparent, panic set in. I think we can all do without another screech about black pits and anguish, so I'll let it go, except to recount two rather unfortunate aspects of my purdah. I had boils everywhere—on my face, under my arms, on my back and neck. Each morning I woke to find another patch of skin that had lurched into something quite horrid.

Then there was the memory problem. This was an acute problem for a journalist. I was now doing a fair bit of political writing for *The Times* and had reasonable access to government ministers. I can't remember—and I'm not depressed now, only old—which minister I was talking to about the 1988 Education Reform Bill, but I had my questions and ploughed through them, making notes. The minister, or perhaps it was Baroness Cox, but I feel certain it was a male, started making little ahem noises.

"Actually, you've already asked me that question, Barbara," said the probably male minister politely.

"Sorry. Let me ask you another one." Question forthcoming.

"Actually, you asked me that too in your previous phone call about five minutes ago."

Unfortunately, I had no recollection whatsoever of making a call five minutes earlier. As I was not on any medication, this could not be put down to the usual excuse of accidental overdose of Valium. I was bonkers. This phase lasted for about six months, and I must say that both Rupert Murdoch and my publishers in Toronto were jolly good sports and kept my paycheques coming.

As my columns got loopier—I recall one about burying Algernon, a toy soldier, in a shoebox in Belgrave Square that really rang bells of alarm—my editors began to discreetly let them go into the black field where unused columns and aging female TV presenters get buried. After my memory returned, I was still a very sad sack, obsessing over my former husband but able to work properly. Perhaps friends in London might have helped me through this, but the ones I had were put off by my behaviour to George.

After about a year, there was a reconciliation with David, on condition that I pay him back for the diamond Bulgari watch he had bought me during our marriage and return anything left of the $400,000 divorce settlement my British lawyer had obtained. I sent his bank $200,000 or so, providentially keeping back $20,000 in reserve. I packed up the semi-furnished flat I had been renting and moved into his new home, a charming little house in Grosvenor Studios, a private gated mews. Up went my bookcases. In came clothes racks. After about a year, that too ran aground when he returned from one of his trips to suggest we get married again. This was a positive note, but there was a catch.

"I'm going on a trip down the Amazon for ten days first," he said.

"Oh, can I come?"

"Well, no. I'm going with . . ." and he mentioned a former, present and future girlfriend—an all-in-one, really.

"Do you have separate cabins?"

"No," said the by now many-ten-times-over millionaire, "but it's purely platonic. I'll buy you the biggest engagement ring on Bond Street when I return." I rung up his about-to-be travelling companion, a woman I knew quite well, and her replies were unhelpful. That was it. No ring could be big enough for any more of that pain.

Being female and all but penniless in London, and approaching fifty, is awkward. London is awash in middle-aged single women, most of them living on not very much money as far as I could see. The one advantage they had was a roof over their heads, either from divorce or family. They had carpets and sets of dishes, lamps with shades of silk or very good card, and upholstered armchairs. I had not managed ten let alone twenty years of continual marriage and had no children needing support payments. Until now I hadn't given the matter a thought. Fiscally speaking, though, I had pretty much the same relationship to the outside world as when I was in my twenties or thirties. "Your husband was rich," said Jenny, one of the several ladies I was consulting about cheap new digs.

"Non sequitur," I ducked.

"You simply must have a table and some odds and sods in storage," said Grace, a divorcee herself, as I contemplated how I could possibly rent a flat in London and furnish it. I had nothing in storage except boxes of paper, mainly research folders with labels like "Family Court" and "Austria—Waldheim," which were unlikely to solve the problem. The only man who seemed interested in helping me find a flat was married and, on my declining his offer of money, he suggested that I must start collecting something so he could contribute to the collection. "What about perfume bottles?" he said.

Grosvenor Studios was now being sold about a year after I'd got settled in it, and I would sit unsmilingly at my desk while the agent showing the house whispered in not so hushed tones that I had just come through a difficult marriage break-up. Difficult! I wanted to say. How about thinking of it in terms of doing Everest during middle age without oxygen or Sherpas? The house was small but quite enchanting—once when I did a CNN stand-up outside it, the interviewer called it the "magic cottage." David offered to buy a mews house and give me occupancy. That sounded wonderful until I saw the lease I would have to sign: of its several personal clauses, one prohibited men staying overnight for any period over six months. That sounded reasonable but I had some experience of how David would both interpret and monitor such a clause.

The prospect of being in a cardboard box on the street loomed. I had a bit of money but not remotely enough for a down payment to buy a real flat. My bank manager was well disposed, but in spite of my new plonking title, senior political columnist at the *Sunday Times* (after editor Andrew Neil had wooed me from *The Times*), he grasped my situation in one question: "Are you on staff?" I was not. No stocks or bonds, property or jewellery, nothing as security apart from my rather perky VW Golf. I was a drifter, dependent on the whims of taste.

Otherwise, my life was moving along quite well. I had managed down the depressive bits, made some friends, turned up quite often on BBC Radio 4's *Start the Week* and *Question Time* on BBC TV. I had reached that bat-mitzvah point in a female journalist's life where a Sunday supplement or glossy magazine celebrates your existence with a one-page profile and a photo of you standing in front of some shelves of books in your home, and there was nothing substantive behind it at all.

Salvation came in the most unlikely shape.

I was working on a column dealing with some proposed legislation to end the cutting-edge horror of date rape. Bored and irritated, I was doing my usual displacement routine and idly flicking through a travel magazine. Turns out Half Moon Cay had a bird sanctuary but hadn't got much in the way of nesting material for birds. Apparently, more female nestless birds than male ones died and they died earlier in their lives. I began to suspect that the magazine had been planted by my ex.

At this sensitive point, the phone rang: "Come to dinner at the Clermont," said the caller in a euphonious voice of rich russet. I was happy enough to abandon the red-footed booby and Canadian Bill C-49 for dinner at a posh London casino. "I'll pick you up at nine," he continued, which gave me time to agonize nicely over what to wear to one of the most expensive restaurants in London.

Joe Dwek was at some point backgammon champion of Europe. We had met at a reception at the home of John Aspinall, the zoo and casino owner, who had taken me around his drawing room in

Belgravia one early-evening cocktail party proudly introducing me as an "honorary man" and "the only Jew here." At that point I hadn't a clue about Aspinall's (known as Aspers) somewhat unorthodox life and views. He proudly proclaimed himself an anti-Semite as he palled around with good friends Jacob Rothschild and Jimmy Goldsmith, two of London's most high-profile Jews. He had opened the first London casino and founded the Clermont Set, a tight group that included aristocrats and high politicians—gamblers all, and some quite notorious, including Lord Lucan, a legendary figure in Britain. Lucan botched the murder of his wife by mistakenly killing the nanny instead and then completely disappeared—helped, it was believed, by Aspinall. He was also a deeply committed animal lover and owned a couple of private zoos where he fostered close relationships between animals and the keepers he employed. His methods led to the deaths of several of them, who were eaten while bonding with his treasured Siberian tigers.

Just why Aspinall had invited me to his reception was a complete mystery to me. A guest told me that my honorary gender was a compliment based on the perceived muscularity of my *Times* column regularly taking on the professional feminist and neo-Marxist crowd. Perhaps one of the very rich men whose company was of such importance to Aspers had mentioned it in passing, although Jacob Rothschild, I was also told, had already dismissed me as "too serious" to be interesting. This I understood. Earnest people are the death knell of any amusing social event or personal relationship, and I was nothing if not earnest. I sweated it.

In fact, I had not been the only Hebrew at that party. Joe Dwek, a charming olive-skinned Egyptian-born Sephardi with a fine-boned face and velvet-smooth voice, had been a guest as well. He had been deciding whether or not to be heartbroken over a model who was living in Paris. The way men view us is always interesting, and listening to what they go through rather helps put one's own fretting in perspective. He arrived promptly for our Tuesday dinner date.

Casinos have their hierarchy, and the Clermont Club in Mayfair was near the very top. Dinner was forcibly intimate in a room where noise was buried in thick fabrics and the lighting dimmed. Out of the blue-black darkness emerged discreet waiters of silky deference, confirming that the customer was a person of such means and taste that this Baccarat crystal, these gold-embossed plates, these heavy silver knives and forks and this melting black caviar were routine for us. I could see how a man of means would feel richer and richer, a member in good standing of a world where nothing could harm one—until every penny was lost gambling after dessert. "What exactly do you do?" I asked Dwek, breaking the British rule of never enquiring directly about such things. "I'm a business consultant," he replied, unhelpfully.

Every now and then I slipped into that torture and self-indulgence to which a certain type of woman—me—is prone. What if it were not Joe Dwek but my former husband with me, huddled this way over the menu trying to read it in this dim lighting, giggling as we once did and ordering teeny glasses of Muscat de Beaumes de Venise. What if he could see me like this, in candlelight with a man younger than myself and rather good-looking, wouldn't he see me differently? Feel differently? The answer was that it would not be better, only more of the same that had led to the break-up, but rationality is in short supply during such musings.

Out of the murky light, a large presence loomed. He had something of a boxer's face, with a very slightly flattened nose, thick, fleshy lips and a complexion that had seen better times. Other than that he was a massive man in a superbly cut suit. About six-two and radiating confidence, this goliath took up all the oxygen around our table. I had no bloody idea who he was or why Dwek was being so deferential. (He was, it turned out, Australian media mogul Kerry Packer, born wealthy and becoming a several-times billionaire through his own business achievements.)

The conversation between the two men was short and muted. "No hurry," said Packer pleasantly as he departed. We finished our dinner at a leisurely pace. As we passed through the corridors lined with Sèvres porcelain and dynasty jade objects that separated the casino world from outside, Joe said: "Kerry wants you to come upstairs. You'll find it interesting."

My column deadline was nagging at me. "Sorry, really can't."

"Just for a few moments," said Dwek and took my arm. I supposed it was not to be missed; a columnist is ever on the lookout for new experiences. Our destination was a very small private room on a high floor. At one end was a counter with a dealer behind it and comfily upholstered bar-stool chairs for about four people. Against one wall was a sofa that could fit three or four, and at the not so far end of the room, a small table with a telephone on it where a man in a dark suit stood silently.

Dwek took the farthest high chair, and Kerry two over, so they were about a thirty-degree angle from each other. The dealer behind the playing table riffled the cards. The man at the telephone nodded. Kerry indicated that I was to sit beside him. Someone asked very softly what I would like and I requested mint tea. Packer produced a cheque book and put it on the table in front of me. The cheque paused for just a second in front of my eyes. It was for £500,000. The card game began. Kerry Packer versus the house.

What I remember most about the evening that was to have some consequence upon the rest of my life was how very quiet everything was. There were five people, a telephone in use, cups being placed on saucers, playing cards slipping out of the shoe, and not a shiver of noise apart from an almost imperceptible sssst of the cards being dealt. It was as if we were all sitting inside some enormous pair of Bose noise-cancelling headphones. As the cards were revealed, Packer would look at Dwek, who would nod or hold up his fingers, indicating, I suppose, the odds as he calculated them. Packer would make a decision; sometimes the decision was unsuccessful, and Packer would write another cheque for £500,000. More often the decisions were successful, and Packer would write more cheques anyway. I lost count of the millions of pounds that were passing in front of me with the casualness of a Visa slip for a cardigan. The only action that interrupted this was that, when Packer was winning, the man in the dark suit would pick up the telephone and make an inaudible call.

Packer won double-figure millions of pounds that night. "Thank you for joining us," he said politely as we walked down a flight of stairs to what appeared to be a reception desk on a landing of gold and white. "The cashier," said Dwek helpfully as we waited. After a moment he asked me, "Cash or a cheque?" I was handed a Clermont cheque for £100,000 made out in my name. "You understand," said Dwek, "that Kerry's winnings are not to be made public."

"I can't possibly take it," I replied, actually meaning it.

"Don't be silly," replied Dwek with a slight tone of irritation, as if he had been through this before. "That's how it works. Kerry will be offended."

I had some fear of being bought, though God knows why since neither Dwek nor Kerry had evinced the slightest interest in me. Simultaneously, in a small patch of my mind lurked the thrilling possibility of keeping it. But out came all the pro forma denials again. Dwek again replied in a tired way as if he knew there wasn't a chance of my not accepting. "Don't be an idiot," he said. "Kerry does this. Just take it and you can cash it right here." This was 1989: I cashed it and found I was holding half a mortgage.

In the cloakroom I handed the attendant a fifty-pound note, thinking I was being very generous. She was an elderly lady, rather frizzled, and took it with thanks but no excitement. "I think the attendant was quite pleased with my win," I said grandly and a bit self-righteously when I joined the two men, as if I wanted to justify taking the one hundred thousand. "You gave her all of it?" Packer said curiously. I felt like a trespasser in a new world.

Early next morning, a Wednesday, and in very good spirits, I sat down again to work on my *Times* column, due the next day. That evening the phone rang. Backgammon and Packer were at a restaurant and I was to join them. Tempting, I said, but quite out of the question. Astonishment. "You can't say no," Dwek said. "You must be there." While £100,000 more than doubled my *Times* salary, my column came first, and missing my deadline would kill it. I went back to work. Twenty minutes later a chauffeur was outside my door. "I'm to bring you to Mr. Packer," he said.

Packer was about three years older than me. I knew something about his reputation for women, his mistress in Australia, the ladies reputedly hired for entertainment during his long airplane flights, and his legendary lines, like the one to the chap he bumped into at a Las Vegas casino. "Don't you bother me," said the man self-importantly, "I'm worth three hundred million." "Toss you for it," replied Packer.

There was something almost thuggish about Kerry, as if at any moment he would abandon all civilized convention, tear his food with his hands and physically maim anyone in his way. That almost primitive ugliness can be very sexually attractive, particularly when presented in an immaculate suit. Men can't see the attraction; they see only the rough edges and find such a statement absurd, putting it all down to money. Money is obviously the soil, the nourishment that creates the man—and enhances him. But by now I've met rather a lot of billionaires and I can vouch that most of them are either sexual neuters or seriously unappealing. Packer's attractiveness was his sheer physicality and the absolute sense of power and safety such a man exudes. I felt no personal interest, but I could see his appeal, although his louche world was far too sordid for me.

When the chauffeur dropped me off at the restaurant, a Chinese or Indian establishment—it seemed to combine both—Packer and Joe Dwek were sitting at a circular table with what appeared to be most of South America. Packer was taking his polo team on a boys' night out. The evening turned into something resembling a family outing. Polo players, Packer and I climbed enthusiastically into cars to go off to a Chelsea cinema that was playing *Pretty Woman*. Packer seated me, the sole female present, next to him. At the moment when the hotel manager in the film looks at the jewellery Richard Gere has borrowed from Beverly Hills jeweller Fred's, and the camera goes in for a close-up of the—very real—ruby and diamond necklace, Packer nudged me contemptuously: "Chicken feed," he said.

Like a video loop, the previous evening repeated itself after the film, only this time with a handful of polo players crowded together on the small sofa in the private room. I sat on the same stool next to Packer, drank the same mint tea, and he won more millions. Each polo player, as well as myself, went home with £100,000. My fear of being down and out in London was over.

In a heartfelt note of thanks to Packer, I mentioned, without giving him details, that he had provided me with the means to continue living in London. He responded with an invitation to lunch. When he came to pick me up, he looked at my shelves of books. "Do you read all these?" he asked, as if it was just barely possible that anyone, let alone a woman, might. I didn't know he was dyslexic. As lunch ended, Packer offered to take me shopping. "What do you like?" he asked. "Chanel?" I declined, and that ended the matter.

In the last months of residence in my former husband's home—he was abroad or, when in London, stayed in hotels—I had met the Oscar-winning screenwriter and novelist William Goldman on Melvyn Bragg's morning Radio 4 program, proving to me that doing god-awful early-morning radio shows had its value. We began dating. Nine years older than me, he was extremely handsome in a Paul Newman way and highly intelligent. He was of course completely in tune with the nightmare of writing and had a wry wit about the hell it provides. "The easiest thing on earth to do is not write," he had said in one of his oft-quoted remarks. "But this is life on earth, you can't have everything."

He lived in Manhattan but had a large, plainly decorated flat in Knightsbridge overlooking Lennox Gardens' square. After a while he wanted me to spend weekends with him in Manhattan, which was a bit of a problem with my column schedule. "I'll take one of the crap script-rewrite jobs," he said, "and use it for Concorde tickets for you." I would leave London on a Friday night and be in New York in time for dinner, and return to London unrumpled on Sunday evening. God, I'm practically Joan Collins, I thought as I sashayed into the Concorde Lounge, becoming a regular. Best not get too used to this.

Given my newfound Packer-based wealth, I was searching for a flat in Bayswater, my absolute dream destination. Goldman was unenthusiastic after he came with me on one excursion. Bayswater was on the other side of Hyde Park from his flat and might as well have been across the Kalahari Desert. "Live on my side," he said. His side, in super-posh Knightsbridge, was completely out of my financial reach. Still, he found a flat three doors down from his. "I'll split the rent with you," he offered. We were thinking of my moving to Manhattan to live with him, and so it seemed an okay thing to do. Stupidly, I didn't think of what this would mean if our relationship went sour.

George Weidenfeld, now a good friend since he was deeply smitten with the wonderful woman who would become his wife, Annabelle Whitestone, was very enthusiastic about this new development in my life. George claimed to have invented Arianna Huffington long before she invented the Huffington Post. He had noticed some physical resemblance in her Greek features to Greek soprano Maria Callas, and commissioned Arianna to write her biography. This was a success story George was keen to repeat with me. "You could become a wonderful Manhattan political hostess," he mused. "Arianna did this. Meet the great and politically connected and have them to dinner in your Manhattan flat." The very notion was proof that George had never quite seen all my limitations. I would rather have drunk arsenic tea than entertained great political figures in Manhattan.

The relationship with Goldman had elements apart from true love. Infatuation was present to a significant degree, and I was immensely impressed with the leonine head filled with the sort of quick insights that made his book *Adventures in the Screen Trade* a classic and garnered him Oscars for *Butch Cassidy and the Sundance Kid* and *All the President's Men*. He turned his book *The Princess Bride* into a marvellous film. The man was a writer through and through: novels, screenplays, non-fiction books. He had the discipline I so admired and the advantage that he loathed social life. He would not be doing the charity galas in Manhattan.

My motive wasn't mercenary but certainly had a pragmatic element. I wanted to get out of London, where my former husband still haunted my nightmares, and I wanted to end the constant fear of losing the means to pay my rent. The Packer money was holding things at bay, but Knightsbridge rents, even at a discount of 50 per cent, could not be sustained indefinitely. I could earn money in New York, but not enough to live in a comfy Manhattan apartment.

I was sufficiently attracted to Goldman that I was jealous as hell
women he was seeing in New York while I was in London— ~~~
death-defying passion was not there.

That Knightsbridge flat three doors down from Goldman's was
by a long shot my happiest residential memory. My flat was the upper
two floors of a converted Lennox Gardens house. A small terrace
overlooked the picture-perfect rooftop panorama and was just large
enough for the metal bistro table and two chairs that came with it.
Waking up in my bed under the sloping ceiling with a skylight overhead wiped away all remnants of my depression. The grocer's around
the corner on Walton Street had fresh roasted chickens, which I alternated with two packs of my favourite Lean Cuisine, chicken à l'orange.
In a colossally happy moment that every female on the planet will
recognize, I was one day discovered by my ex-husband.

He followed me from the Walton Street grocer's where I had
bought my roast chicken. He was buying the old school house a few
steps away that was to become his colossal home, infuriating neighbourhood residents as his renovations turned everything upside
down for years on end. "Where are you going?" he asked. I was
ready. A small shiny lift, immaculately polished, took us upstairs to
my flat. He knew my financial circumstances when we parted but
knew nothing of my luck with Packer or my arrangement with
Goldman, and his surprise on seeing that I was not living in squalor
was palpable.

The flat couldn't compare with his ever more grand residences
but it had the feeling of some luxury and a lot of well-being. All the
recognizable signs of my occupancy were there: the walls of books,
the music components and the photo of my father in its leather frame.
The rooms smelt of my Santa Maria Novella cologne purchased just
around the corner on Walton Street. The flat was feminine and the
femininity was mine. See, see, see, I wanted to shout, I can live without you. There was no need to do it: his baffled face told the tale.
When he left that day, the pain of his existence left me.

CHAPTER EIGHT

Conrad in Love?

It's a shame, really, that reality shows hadn't taken hold when Conrad Black erupted onto the London scene in 1985. A Julian Fellowes type could have scripted aristocrats with long faces mourning newspaper proprietor Lord Hartwell's need to sell a chunk of his family's Telegraph plc to this large Canadian who kept banging on about the Anglo-American relationship when obviously the Anglo-Tuscany one made so much more sense.

The collateral effect was a trill of telephone calls to my usually silent London flat from journos who heard I knew Conrad—an exaggeration at best—seeking nuggets about his personality, politics and favourite tailor. I felt rather sheepish at my threadbare anecdotes. But after all, I had only one lunch and one dinner party to go on, plus a lot of quick chats at desiccated events in Toronto celebrating the opening or closing of something. Still, I did my best.

"Well," I told *Tatler*, or perhaps it was *Harper's & Queen*, "his wife, Joanna, keeps him down to earth." This insight was based on my relief that Joanna was easy to chat with whenever Conrad loomed and was free of any affectation (or long words).

The purchase of an interest in the Telegraph Group was a huge uptick in Conrad's life. London newspaper owners, known in day-to-day speech as "proprietors," were huge celebrities in a way quite unknown in North America. They were thought to hold tremendous influence, and the interest in them assumed supernatural proportions far exceeding anything that the *Washington Post*'s Kay Graham or the *New York Times*' Sulzberger family could enjoy. Conrad was buying instant position in the U.K., onstage and under a merciless spotlight.

On the whole, there wasn't much love for foreign purchasers of the major newspapers in Britain. To say they were viewed as diseased carpetbaggers might be a bit of overkill but not by much. Canadian carpetbagging began with Max Aitken of Newcastle, New Brunswick, who became Lord Beaverbrook, held several cabinet positions and was viewed as a man who could make or break anyone—and did. But then, truthfully, wouldn't you if you could? He was accused of having a blacklist of people, though why this is regarded as anything so evil, I don't know. My hairdresser has one. I suppose it was because as a newspaper proprietor he could enforce his blacklist in a particularly harmful way while the rest of us could only dream. Anyway, Beaverbrook was the start of the legend of press barons, and it is a legend with no happy endings.

Next Canadian up was Roy Thomson, who accumulated hundreds of British newspapers, including the prestigious *Times* of London. "Why do you want to buy more newspapers?" asked one BBC interviewer. "To make more money," replied Thomson. "Why do you want more money?" "To buy more newspapers." His extremely nice son was not made of the same stuff, and under the guidance of a particularly ineffectual advisor, John Tory Sr. (father of Toronto's ineffectual mayor), he threw in the towel and sold *The Times* to Australian Rupert Murdoch. Which was the inglorious end of the Canadian presence on Fleet Street until Conrad Black arrived.

At the time of Conrad's arrival, there were a couple of other suspect foreign proprietors, neither of whom I knew but about whom everyone knew a bit. Roland Fuhrhop, a.k.a. Tiny Rowland, was born in a World War One internment camp in India, which automatically gave him British citizenship. Through one deal and another with murderous African dictator Robert Mugabe, Rowland's company, Lonrho, picked up the marvellously written paper *The Observer*.

Probably the most indigestible newspaper baron on the scene was Ján Ludvík Hyman Binyamin Hoch, whose ringing name sounded like some magnificent seventeenth-century painter's, except he was a Czech Jew who escaped Nazi occupation and fought in the British Army. He renamed himself Robert Maxwell, built up a company publishing, among other things, his own bootlicking propaganda interviews, famously asking Romanian president Ceaușescu why his people loved him so much, shortly before those same people gave him a one-hour show trial and shot him and his wife five minutes after the verdict.

All the same, he was a brilliant publisher, taking the *Daily Mirror* from near extinction to rivalling Murdoch's *Sun*. But his eyes were too big for his tummy, copious though that bit of his anatomy was. Maxwell's purchase of Macmillan Publishers for £6 million required some creative accounting when he allegedly "borrowed" from his company's pension plan without actually mentioning it to his directors or shareholders. This unorthodox and possibly criminal business move—his death ended any chance of a trial—came to light only after he drowned or committed suicide or was murdered (depending which of the rival newspapers you read) while on his yacht. Whatever happened, he ended up floating in the Atlantic Ocean.

The allure of owning a London newspaper seems imperishable. It's the grown-up version of an incredibly expensive debutante's coming out. The most recent foreign proprietor brought unusual qualities even by London's flexible standards. In 2009, Alexander Lebedev, a KGB agent turned Russian oligarch who co-owns *Novaya Gazeta* (the Russian newspaper confirmed in opposition status to the government by the murder of at least six of its journalists, something I don't recommend but notionally wish I could do to a number of Anglo-American and Canadian ones), purchased 75 per cent of the *Evening Standard* from the one remaining British newspaper-owning family, the Harmsworths, headed by Lord Rothermere. Unlike his Moscow-based father, son Evgeny had lived in London since he was eight years old and now runs the U.K. papers.

Evgeny revived the Evening Standard Theatre Awards, always a good thing, with the side benefit of a serious party with long frocks where he could be seen standing next to co-host Anna Wintour (of course) wearing the most elaborately embroidered velvet slippers and jacket—him, not her. As with all London newspaper proprietors before him, Lebedev is unsurprisingly fawned on, which is not his fault, and the articles on him are peons to his good taste, generosity, shyness, brilliance and so forth. Having only met him once or twice in a couple of party rooms in his large Marylebone flat, I saw a rather good-looking, bearded and quiet man of exquisite grooming and probably exotic tastes. Should he lose his money, God help him. Birds of prey sit in wait.

Into this fetid pool dived Conrad Black. Not all of the matters dealt with above had taken place when he first arrived in 1985, but the outlines were clear. This was never going to be smooth sailing.

The notion that someone I knew from Toronto might be coming to town as a newspaper owner was as much a carrot for me as for Fleet Street. My *Toronto Sun* columns were feverish: "The many lives of Conrad Black continue to astonish! Canada does have originals," I wrote in my June 15, 1985, column. I held out the view—in my capacity as a well-known financial expert currently a footstep away from debtors' prison—that this was the perfect time to invest in *The Daily Telegraph*, which was in great difficulties due to unions and poor management.

Breathlessly I wrote that Conrad hadn't yet fallen down. And if he did with *The Telegraph* it would be a wonderful way to go—"with one's boots on fighting the good fight that may allow our society a last chance to survive with civility and intelligence." This was an exquisite example not just of irony, considering what was to come, but more of blasé and blissful ignorance: what did I know about the significance of falling down with or without boots on, apart from a sort of misty Rudyard Kipling view of life's struggles? As for the rot about civility and intelligence, *The Telegraph*, which would in one way or another joyfully stomp on us both, was going to give me a rude awakening.

The collateral significance to me of Conrad's arrival, particularly when in the late 1980s he took over complete control of *The Telegraph*, was something he could not possibly have imagined. To understand, it helps if you are mush after a broken marriage, complete with post-divorce water torture in the form of an unending drip of lectures from your beloved ex-husband about your miserable character.

When you are utterly certain that everything about yourself is loathsome and your nights are spent weeping over the man that left you but periodically telephones just to make sure you aren't over him yet, you'll grasp at anything to break the cycle of despair, even if temporarily. When the mourned husband regularly appears at your door to quickly bed you (raising hopes, among other things) before reiterating how horrid you are and plunging you back into Hades, you search for some sort of lifebelt. When you are challenging your sister's sanity with long-distance calls because, though living in Toronto, she is the nearest person to bore to death with endless repeats of unanswerable and irrelevant questions of the "What did he mean by coming over this afternoon?" genre—in that set of circumstances, an event like Conrad's appearance in London becomes a slash of something to hang on to.

This is how it works: The worst thing about really deep depression is not the black-cloud stuff, it is the vise in which your mind is held, endlessly trapped in past minutiae and with every voice around you outside the funnel you are in. You know that this isn't quite right, those voices are perfectly normal people speaking to you now, in the present; but no matter how hard you try, and God you do, both their replies and your own words are still distanced from you. You struggle so hard to sound normal, but sentences aren't quite under your control and even your facial expressions feel out of sync with what you hear that voice of yours saying. Existence gets increasingly rotten. You can't just "get well." The state doesn't yield to stern self-admonitions and the loud playing of "Land of Hope and Glory."

Every now and then came a minute or at least fifteen seconds where my mind didn't lurch out of my head and disappear under the door. Just then it felt like I had surfaced and now, in this moment, could see things clearly. What an idiot I was, and how marvellous to feel normal again! I'd clutch the moment with relief—all would be all right. Which made the rapid descent all the more wretched. How can it be, I kept asking myself, if I can distinguish normality from this abnormal state, that I can't stay afloat when I surface?

I think perhaps people who have had a clinical depression or an extended reactive one—or whatever it was that happened to me—will understand how anything new from outside that you have special knowledge of, like Conrad's arrival in London, is manna. It's a God-given piece of flotsam, yours alone, to grab and help you swim to shore or at least get through that day or week. You can use it as a conversational patch. Perhaps, if you have something people want to know, you can say it right and no one will notice your state. You hope.

Beginning in 1987 and taking hold during 1988 and most of 1989 was a solid twenty-four-hour-a-day depression during which I was a menace to home and hearth. A rather attractive light fixture in a conservatory got ripped out of the ceiling after a bungled attempt to hang myself from it. I really don't know how people manage to hang themselves apparently easily from bathroom doors or bedroom light fixtures. There must be a trick to the noose that I hadn't got. I certainly did the kick-the-stool-over thing. I became a whiz at collecting sleeping tablets from doctors all over London: Chelsea turned out to be a super-good location for doctors who didn't ask "Mrs. Selby" too many questions.

Clearly, if you really want to do yourself in, you don't have to fly into the Alps; you can just jump in front of a fast train or off a roof somewhere—it doesn't even have to be that high. Life is easy to end. A good razor slash in the bath would do it if you live alone. There was a faint-hearted attempt by me in front of the Baker Street line at the Finchley Road tube station. But I suspect that these failed attempts were all faux, rather like the "insufficient number of pills" Colette ascribes to one of her hysterical French courtesans with a habit of overdosing. What was not faux in those endless two and a half years was the absolute shame I felt as my mind decided to leave me and go missing. I knew this was not the condition that had afflicted my mother—whatever was wrong with her, she could get out of it on cue if she wanted and, anyway, her delusionary structure made her happy.

Occasionally, as I ploughed through this, I'd see Conrad at a London social function or at the British party political conferences I was sent to cover in the large hotels at the slightly rundown seaside locations of my childhood. He was usually surrounded by the upturned faces of journalists, glowing like the petals of some freshly bloomed flower, eager to nod at his views, which he seemed eager to give. Conrad was always friendly and appeared to seek me out. But in my slightly paranoid state and fear for my own equilibrium, his attention was worrying—although it did give me a vague status among some journalists.

The first crack in my aloof attitude towards Conrad came early in 1990, at a dinner party—dinner parties being the battlefield of choice for so much of London life. George Weidenfeld was holding the evening for some famous person in his rather splendid flat on the Embankment, which was adorned with a Francis Bacon "screaming pope" and two marvellously chiaroscuro Giordano paintings. I stood fidgeting in the reception room, my back to the mantelpiece, which, as is custom in Britain, was adorned three deep in stiffies—cardboard invitations, engraved and often with royal or aristocratic crests at the top. I found this was a good place to stand at a cocktail party—passing traffic would gravitate to the mantel, look sideways at the invites, and there was no need to approach people awkwardly.

"Ah, here comes Conrad and his wife," said Aline Berlin to her husband, Isaiah, who was standing directly beside me. Conrad and Joanna always seemed to be backlit when entering, cutting a path through fawning authors, historians, journalists and politicians all looking for some advantage from the pages of *The Telegraph*. These were the glory days of the newspaper. A smorgasbord of intellectuals and historians were spread out that evening, all of whom Conrad feasted on: Noel Annan, Martin Gilbert, Paul Johnson, the up-and-coming Niall Ferguson and Andrew Roberts. I looked at Conrad chatting to Isaiah. How did I not see this, I wondered. Yes, he had lost some weight, but that was not sufficient. My God, he was a very attractive man. Just for a nanosecond I saw it, and then blew the mist of testosterone out of my vision and reverted to my neutral stance.

"Barbara," said Joanna Black as the dinner was breaking up. "We're going to John Aspinall's now. Are you going?" I had not been there since the encounter with Joe Dwek and had not been invited. "Of course you are," said Conrad expansively. "Come with us." The party at Aspers's house on Eaton Square, no mean address, was in full swing when we got there. Filthy rich worlds and lots of pretty girls with pixie haircuts that showed off perfect youthful cheekbones or long blonde hair swinging like a Clairol commercial. They wore beautiful strange clothes that I later realized were either couture or very expensive ready-to-wear and had names with prefixes and suffixes and sometimes both. If the Weidenfeld dinner was the *crème de la crème* intellectually, this was pure *crème*.

The evening was not made in heaven for me. Parties pull up rag tails of depression. I looked over at a group of men: Conrad, Jacob Rothschild, Jimmy Goldsmith and a very large man with his back to me were in a tall stork huddle. Later, when he turned briefly, I realized the fourth man was Kerry Packer. Margaret Thatcher, who had just left office, was watching them. "If only I had had cabinet members like that," she was saying to someone. I had been reading Dian Fossey's *Gorillas in the Mist* and had become familiar with the terminology for a certain sort of male. These are all silverbacks, I thought, and walked dejectedly towards the door, declining Conrad's call: "Barbara, let my driver take you home."

On a warm summer night, I went to the London home of Conrad and Joanna Black. Thank God, my life had picked up. I was emerging quite nicely from depression, and my voice was now my own. I was dating an extremely handsome Greek about town and former escort of Ira von Fürstenberg named Manoli Olympitis. Manoli was younger than me, very socially adept, a graduate of the King's School, Canterbury, and expert in the erotic arts. He had telephoned after seeing me at some Royal Academy event with George Weidenfeld, but I'd had no idea what he looked like, though his name was familiar. On our first—essentially blind—date, when he presented himself, so handsome and clearly younger, all I could do was laugh: I mean, what would a relatively elderly blackbird do when a peacock dropped by?

The few months we went out, including weekends in his Cotswold cottage and a stay at his home in Kalymnos, brought me back to life, even given my acute discomfort at boating with the young ladies his friends brought along, who went happily topless, showing perfectly balanced bosoms. "Don't worry," said Manoli thoughtfully when I later lamented my own sizeable but droopy ones. "Probably time to fix yours up. Just avoid Dr. X. But anyway, when it gets around London that you're dating me, given my choosy reputation in sexual partners, you'll be sought after." I appreciated his frankness, though I wasn't sure that was exactly what I wanted to get around London.

The Blacks' dinner invitation was definitely a step up, a prized possession for any journalist. Conrad now controlled the entire Telegraph group of newspapers and he had also bought my favourite magazine, *The Spectator*, which I had read for thirty years. For this, my usual RSVP regrets for dinner parties were suspended. The invitation didn't include an escort, and I had rescheduled the more exciting evening date with Manoli for later. I was also late, having no idea how to drive myself to Highgate in North London. An A-Z map was on the passenger seat next to me, but I had forgotten my reading glasses and the bloody thing was inaccessible. I rarely had much reason to go north to Highgate apart from visiting its famed cemetery, to sit on a park bench donated in my father's name and brood. Having made a wrong turn somewhere around the Kentish Town viaduct and wondering why on earth a newspaper proprietor would live in this North London traffic hell, my hopes of making dinner were shrinking. Then, voila, I was on Highgate Hill, albeit going rather futilely up and down, until at last I found the small turning to Conrad's home off the road opposite the Research Centre for Transcultural Studies in Health, handy if you wanted pamphlets in Amharic.

Conrad seated me thoughtfully between two elderly gentlemen: TV host Robin Day and Lord Carrington, cabinet minister under three prime ministers, a former secretary general of NATO and possessor of the most droll wit I have encountered. All I remember of the evening is Conrad hovering, asking, "Is everything all right?" and the acerbic remark of one of the men at the table who, on seeing the dinner was plated rather than served à l'anglaise, remarked, "That tells the story, doesn't it. She's no longer interested in him."

Conrad sightings now became a matter of local reporting. Increasingly, noises off spoke with rising volume of marital difficulties. "They are going to separate," I was told declaratively in the summer of 1991 by Manhattan social swan Mrs. Jayne Wrightsman, who was in London at her St. James's flat to do the season. "Absolutely not," I confidently told dinner tables. "No chance of Conrad's marriage falling apart." I believed my words. Everything about Conrad seemed solid, like chunks of granite.

Come autumn, I went into the political triathlon called "party conference." The Conservative Party Conference in Blackpool featured the riveting Prime Minister John Major, unfairly but memorably caricatured by *Telegraph* editor Max Hastings as a man who tucked his shirt into his underpants. Everywhere were dough-faced Tories. Tories tend to be pastier than the redder-faced Labourites and there must be an algorithm for this. I use the word very cautiously. I haven't really a clue what it means.

I was bashing about, trying to perform the miracle of producing some exciting prose on the Tory platform as appropriate to my role as senior political columnist for the *Sunday Times*. As if that wasn't difficult enough, now I was on the floor crawling under furniture like a beetle and meeting several genuine ones as I tried to find a damn phone jack for my Tandy computer. For any would-be journalists who are reading, this is always a part of the profession's exciting and glam life and, Bluetooth or cellular options notwithstanding, you will at many a point find yourself up against the eternal question: "How can I send in my column?" Defeated, I headed for the hotel desk to fax it.

As I stood waiting for the uncomprehending face of the receptionist, I suddenly felt a hand cup and then tap my bottom. I turned around in indignation—to see Conrad. Outrage melted, which was another confirmation of how reactions to the same act can be so vastly different.

"I want to talk to you," Conrad said, which seemed something of a letdown after his greeting. He led me to a large sofa in the middle of the foyer. Columnist Simon Heffer approached, all tippy-toe eagerness to talk to him. "Not now, Simon," Conrad said firmly. I felt suddenly quite important. Conrad had some utterly bogus reason for talking to me, and at the end of the discussion, which on the surface appeared to be about my leaving the *Sunday Times* to work at *The Telegraph*—something I suspected would not be welcomed by its editor Max Hastings—he offered me a ride to London. "I'm going back tonight with Max," he said. "You could come with us and be in London tonight." The idea of being in a car for four or five hours with Max's amused disapproval and Conrad's evaluation of my party conference observations made polite refusal easy.

Once party conferences were over, autumn events kicked into high gear. At a cocktail party at the American ambassador's residence, Winfield House, in Regent's Park, I sat on a club fender taking in the boiserie. Opposite, next to a piano, was Conrad. He beckoned me. "Is Joanna here?" I asked.

"We're separated," he said. "She will not be coming back to live in London. Our marriage is over."

God, I thought. An almost single man in his mid-forties with his position will be torn to bits in a frenzy of frantic hostesses. "The girls," I said, "will be falling out of the trees for you."

"Don't restrain yourself, Barbara," he replied.

I had no idea of the reasons for the break-up but I suspected—correctly, as it turned out—it would not have been Conrad's idea. "I'm usually in New York for weekends," I told him, "but in the unlikely event you find yourself lonely with the children gone, I'd be happy to accompany you to a movie."

A month or two later, I sat in a bistro opposite a cinema on the Kings Road with William Goldman and treasured friend Miriam Gross. Miriam was then the literary editor of *The Telegraph*, which doesn't begin to covey the scope of her brilliance and formidable accomplishment. (Books include *The World of George Orwell* and her own vividly written memoirs, *An Almost English Life*, although for me, her most important addition to my life was the reintroduction of toast, margarine and marmalade, whose bliss I had forgotten.) We were talking about Conrad's changes at *The Telegraph*. I had in fact gone to a concert with Conrad a week or two before, when Goldman was in New York.

Goldman was very cross. "He's got intentions," he said angrily. "I don't like it."

"No," I replied. "He really doesn't. I think he's dating Annunziata Asquith."

I purred over that name, which I thought combined two remarkable qualities irresistible to Conrad: a Highly Catholic Christian Name and a Highly Historic Surname. She was also very lovely—and it turned out she was in fact the companion of the Queen's cousin and photographer Patrick Lichfield. Goldman got quite heated. "Really," said Miriam in a conciliatory but worried tone. "I can vouch for it. They are only friends." As a close friend, Miriam knew my neutral feelings about Conrad. Goldman was not reassured. I suppose a man can recognize certain male behaviour in a more uncomplicated way sometimes than a woman.

Conrad continued to turn up intermittently in my life. One Sunday when, for some reason, I was not in New York with Goldman, he took me to lunch at Arnold and Netta Weinstock's country house in the Shires. Weinstock was still in charge of General Electric, the enormous company he had built, but our talk was of a shared passion—opera, and his favourite conductor, Riccardo Muti. Driving back to London—being driven back by Conrad's chauffeur Sid—Conrad worked on various memos and lists. His briefcase was open on his lap and it was, I noticed, incredibly neat, with a fountain pen set in the little round leather holders of the cover. I had never seen anyone actually use those holders. He turned to me: "Are you all right?" he asked conversationally.

Are you all right? This is scarcely a passion-packed line, and the enquiry is a routine enough question. The words were voiced, however, in a way that made it sound as if he actually wanted to know if I was tired or thirsty or needed anything on this drive back to London from the heart of the Shires. I knew that for the duration of the drive, inside the world that was the back of a Bentley on a Sunday afternoon, I would be taken care of—aspirins, coffee, doughnuts. It was an intoxicating feeling. "I'm doing the seating for the Hollinger International dinner," he said, referring to the annual top-drawer shindig he threw for directors and important politicians, favoured journalists, aristocrats and think-tank types. "Is there anyone in particular you'd like to be seated next to?"

"Yes, actually. Could you put me next to Robert Maxwell?"

"I could. But why?"

"Well," I explained, "I'm planning to live with William Goldman in New York. When I last saw Maxwell he mentioned that I could work at the *New York Daily News*, which he had just purchased, if I ever came there."

"Mmm." Pause, pen taken out of holder and something scratched. "Done," said Conrad. Later he told me this was the moment he decided he had better corner me before I got married again. As it worked out, I didn't sit next to Maxwell. There was an empty seat on one side of me. Maxwell was only a week or two away from his death at sea, and with his agenda I doubt he had much enthusiasm for dining in celebration of Conrad Black.

Conrad's appearances multiplied. I managed to snooker a pair of opera tickets for a performance with Plácido Domingo, and I asked him if he would like to go in return for his bistro and lunch dates. He turned up to my flat early, which I thought was incredibly rude. After I quickly got ready, he led me to my sofa.

Then came the most god-awful torturous speech in haute Conradian style. I was completely flummoxed. He seemed to be asking me to have some sort of relationship, but he might have been describing his relationship with the great literary figures with which his speech was peppered—Tristan and Isolde, Romeo and Juliet,

Héloïse and Abelard. Given the sticky end these couples had come to, I was both confused and not enthused, praying that this encomium would quickly end. Perched on the edge of a cushion, I tried to get a handle on what the hell was going on. I began to grasp that he wanted to start taking me out romantically, which was simply not on my radar.

"Look, Conrad," I said, "I'm really not in the market for an affair." After all, he knew I was involved with William Goldman.

"I'm not asking you for that," he said. "Don't you understand? I'm asking you to marry me."

We had not exchanged so much as a kiss in all the time I had known him. And in my experience, a man who wants to marry you has some physical need for you that will surface before the proposal, unless he is really mucked up. "This is displacement," I told him. "You're on the rebound from your broken marriage and I feel comfortable to you. You should be going out with younger women. Ask Taki to introduce you to some. Or see a psychiatrist." Taki, son of a Greek shipping magnate, with homes in London, New York, Gstaad and Palm Beach, wrote the High Life column for *The Spectator* and was inevitably seen with gorgeous young candyfloss or squiring equally gorgeous toffs' daughters. He had cartloads of them to spare. I believed what I was saying. All the same, when he left, in true schoolgirl fashion I called up Miriam.

"You won't believe what has just happened," I said. I told her.

"Yes, I quite believe that," she said. Apparently, his love life and my place in it had been quite a topic at *The Telegraph*.

Conrad called me a day or so later. "I have been to see the head of the Tavistock Clinic [the country's premier mental health facility] and he is a reader of your columns and has seen you on television. He asked me to tell you that there is absolutely nothing mad about my wanting to marry you."

It seemed to me I was overdue for a mid-life crisis and perhaps this was it—spinning in a miasma of lunatic men in an effort to relive days when I was young and attractive. Not that it is unpleasant to be told such things by men, even if they are temporarily off their rockers.

I called George Jonas, always my redoubt in troubling times. "Well, babe," he said. "These things do happen to you."

The snag obviously was that while having two eligible and highly accomplished men interested in me, I did not love either of them, which even to me felt a bit thick. After all, a woman who finds the words "Are you all right?" earth-shattering ought to be happy for offers of love from the same very solvent, attractive, intelligent male whom she genuinely likes. If it's a relationship you're after, what is missing here? Just imagine never having to listen to another man's life story or explain Vera.

I had gone to Kenya with Goldman the past summer for his six-tieth birthday. Considering him lying in the camp bed next to me, so attractive with his thick silvered hair and aquiline nose, the amusing stories and telling insights he had, together with a trace of our shared Jewish sensibility—surely passion would grip if I could fire myself up. I wondered whether he had the same misgivings over his feelings for me, but unfortunately this is not the sort of thing one can discuss— unless you routinely use phrases like "reaching out." As for Conrad, since I had never allowed myself to think about him in romantic terms, I couldn't possibly respond to his proposal. Conrad was philo-sophical and undeterred. He was sure that, with some perseverance on his part, I would be seized in precisely the same way.

Goldman and I had planned to spend Christmas in his condo-minium in Puerto Rico. I had already begun hideous nightly swimsuit exercises that consisted of twenty-five sit-ups while watching old movies, and languid but generally failed attempts afterwards to touch my toes. Conrad was ringing up more and more, and gradually I had begun to view him through a different lens. The more I looked, the more I enjoyed myself. God, he had me in stitches, and he had that great smell—a man's natural scent either turns you on or is in deadly need of lashings of Acqua di Parma. Action was, reluctantly, required, which was about the last thing I wanted to do: actions equal damn conse-quences, not least being on the hook for the entire Knightsbridge rent.

The cancellation of my trip to Puerto Rico and the revelation of my new status with Conrad were received with explosive fury by

Goldman, who assumed I had been conducting a clandestine affair on his time—and money. I couldn't blame him.

Conrad was going to Australia for Christmas and then to see his children in Palm Beach, where I assumed the reality of his three children's little scrubbed faces would bring sanity and marital reconciliation. Apart from that, the obvious occurred to me—in fact it had been occurring to me more than subliminally after Conrad's proposal. The simple solution was to "quickstart," as my treadmill button puts it, our relationship. Once Conrad had fully appraised my fifty-going-on-fifty-one-year-old body sans the camouflage of clothing, the glamour would vanish rather quickly.

This appraisal was a step I felt I should take with all due haste. If it didn't work in bed, what was the point? Taking a pair of jeans and shirt in my car in case I stayed overnight, I drove, apprehensively and extremely badly, to Highgate the day before he was leaving for Australia. The clothes swung unsteadily on the hanger in the back of the car. I drove up Highgate Hill, forehead to windshield, looking for the unmarked lane to his house, only to pass Conrad standing roadside. U-turn and there I was. *Alea iacta est.*

My conversion to witless and in love was sudden, swift and horrible. Now that the impossible had happened, the notion of being in reciprocated love with a man who was younger than myself by four crucial years and was funny, kind, tall, rich and armed with massive brainpower was worrying. "Do you think," I asked George Jonas, "that he boils little boys' heads?" Jonas shared my fears. We had something of a bleak view of anything good ever happening. "Be careful," he cautioned.

I had one real fear about this marriage, should it take place. Conrad was so large a personality that I was afraid I would get lazy, simply rely on his prominence and stop working hard to get my place at the table. Writing was not an "enjoyable" process for me, although I sometimes had a very good feeling on finishing a day's work—only to think it drivel the next day. Writing was simply all I could do, and my life felt empty without it. Writing was my entry to the world, the currency I used to barter my way, whether at school or beyond. I sensed that I would accomplish much less if I didn't have to fight to secure the ground under my feet. This fear was not strong enough to torpedo my marriage, though I was correct in seeing it.

After Christmas, Conrad returned from Palm Beach reinforced in his determination to make me his wife—full steam ahead. I suggested we have "provisionals"—God knows where I got that term—during which we could both see if marriage was a credible option. Conrad thought I was batty but agreed. By now the press in both Canada and London had its antennae vibrating. I had my first preview of the generous reception our relationship would have from the *Toronto Star*.

The *Star*'s Sunday editor commissioned a story on my blossoming relationship from Susan Kastner, a rather beautiful woman I had known peripherally in university and had seen once or twice when I was married to George Jonas. Kastner had made a mark in the early sixties when she spoofed her way onto Johnny Carson's *The Tonight Show* as a hippie for hire: with her black leotard, blonde hair and striking Zsa Zsa Gabor features, she was a knockout—bright too.

She had approached me when I was editor of the *Toronto Sun*, wanting to do what she described as a semi-satirical column—about the hardest sort of column to write. I wanted it to succeed: apart from Gary Dunford, our pages were top-heavy with straight political opinion, and I hoped she might replace an aging British columnist I had inherited whose politics were, to put it generously, dubious, unless you liked pieces supporting eugenics and apartheid. We published six columns by Kastner but they didn't really work.

Hell hath no fury like a columnist scorned never felt so real. Finally, the satire she had promised: sarcastic, venemous, and a passion that produced some of her best writing. Indeed this would be the first of several such articles, increasing in viciousness. I'm not difficult to satirize, of course. In fact, shooting me is pretty much a fish-in-a-barrel thing, given the volume of material I have written and my undeniable slightly over-the-top use of personal experiences.

Still, in her two thousand or so words, you'd think there might be one teeny plus in my being without a sarcastic follow-up. Nope.

First line: "Attila the Honey and Mr. Money? Barbed Doll and Black Beauty? Lord Con and Lady Barbarella?" Irredeemably nasty, right down to the last line: "Little Lady Barbara. Taken seriously, at last." The *Star* did publish an extremely positive piece by veteran humorist and editor Gary Lautens, greatly appreciated, but regrettably he died one month later. While Kastner remains.

Conrad's courtship was not quite your standard date, dinner and a movie—and not in a good sense. "We're just going to stop off at Claridge's," he said on our first evening after his return to London. "Right," I said, happily balancing on my four-inch Manolos as we climbed the stairs from the lobby to the first floor, hoping he had something slightly rakish in mind. In a huge suite, I encountered two men sitting on a sofa. Both, I knew, had extensive romantic experience, but at this point in their lives they were just fantastically well-dressed and manicured.

Up stood "L'Avvocato," Fiat chairman Gianni Agnelli, Europe's most dashing man, whose style—his Miserocchi driving shoes worn with bespoke Caraceni suits, his watch worn over shirt cuff—was copied throughout Europe and had him named one of Europe's five most stylish men as well as the Rake of the Riviera. George Weidenfeld was ever urging me to go to Caraceni in Milan and have them make me a suit. At Claridge's that elegance was on full display, together with his slightly closed-mouth smile that is in fact extremely beguiling. Henry Kissinger remained sitting. I wondered if Conrad was pulling out the heavy ammunition to impress me or if he was trying to gauge my ability to deal with his friends. We chatted. At least, they did. I felt like a prize heifer at a farm exhibit.

The society side of Conrad's existence was a non-stop tour of Rizzoli-type lifestyles and people. We'd go to dinners at exquisite London homes of families who decorated their houses with items of a quality I normally saw in museums, which is, I suppose, pretty wonderful if you have time to pore over the purchase of early eighteenth-century ewers for your table water. One of the husbands (the wife was American, so she didn't really know) told me the trick of his butler in getting so high a gloss on the silver. It had something to do with boiling the pieces in water with aluminum foil. What it taught me was never to compliment anyone on anything that could lead to a Sotheby's-type lecture.

Frankly, the whole thing was a waft of wealth, fascinating to inhale but in large portions rather queasy-making. Candlelight dinners at George Livanos's house in St. James's were practically Visconti in their elegance. Hanging out with the de Bottons in Belgravia—where, going upstairs, you passed directly next to huge canvases by David Hockney and Picasso, only to sit with a live Bryan Ferry darkly glowering in person—was pretty extraordinary, but frankly not so much as my utter disbelief that the first Mrs. de Botton had put revolving racks for her clothes in their several heated mews garages across the way. Each outfit was numbered and could be viewed on a closed-circuit video system together with the appropriate accessories.

What I couldn't have anticipated, being stuck in my own prejudices, was the level of knowledge such circles obtained simply by virtue of their power and wealth: they routinely had private conversations with prime ministers, industrialists and senior government officials, including intelligence services. On certain subjects they were better informed than any seasoned journalist. This was all very well for Conrad: he got to talk to the men; the Greeks, Venezuelans and Argentinians knew what plots and ploys were being hatched in their respective homelands day by day. I was stuck largely with the women, who, astonishingly, were extremely generous in trying to help me adapt to this new level of society, but apart from a few—Lita Livanos, Patty Cisneros and Beatrice Santo Domingo—hadn't much interest in politics. Lita especially wanted to help newcomer me. "Don't bother insuring any piece of jewellery under fifty thousand pounds," she told me, rather like a useful tip in getting out stains. "It really isn't worth it on your insurance rates."

We got married at the Chelsea Register Office, a familiar destination for couples moored offshore from their own kind. The initial run-up to the ceremony was not promising. "You do know," said the woman across the counter, "that any religious references are not allowed. If you wish to use your own vows they will need to be approved in advance by the superintendent registrar." Should we wish to exchange rings, which we didn't, the registrar recommended "I give you this ring as a symbol of our marriage and a token of our love," which sounded to me quite warm for a superintendent registrar.

We couldn't get married in a church because Conrad had abandoned his Presbyterian upbringing in order to go Roman with a vengeance, not belonging to the school of doing anything by half, and he hadn't yet acquired an annulment, which in my early, benighted days I thought might be tricky given that he had three healthy children from a fourteen-year marriage. No rabbi I knew would marry us, as I didn't know any British ones similar in flexibility to the one I later encountered in Florida, where, after telling the congregation to hold each other close—in itself a rather unusual approach to a synagogue service—he explained that in order to further his spiritual journey he was going to Malibu with a lesbian Buddhist.

Having attended the wedding of Annabelle Whitestone to George Weidenfeld at the Chelsea registry, I knew the routine. Handkerchief at the ready, I had begun to dab, only to find the ceremony was over. The registry official, having duly announced that the building was one in which marriages were authorized to take place, had asked the bride and groom to solemnly declare that they knew of no lawful impediment to their being joined in holy matrimony. After this, the couple called upon all present to witness that they had taken each other to be man and wife, and that was that.

I mentioned this aspect of a registry office wedding to my beloved, who did not seem to quite grasp the situation. Accustomed to heady North American notions of free speech and imbued with the notion that the home of the mother of parliaments could not possibly prevent him from declaiming his religious beliefs, Conrad sat confidently with me in Superintendent Registrar Stephens's office for the routine pre-nuptial chat two days before the wedding. I sensed we were in sticky waters when my fiancé asked the registrar if we couldn't produce a "more resonant rationale for our desire to marry than 'the absence of any lawful impediment to do so.'"

Mr. Stephens, a rather dear man, looked puzzled. "I was thinking of God," continued Conrad. Mr. Stephens looked very glum at this and repeated that any cribbing from ecclesiastical ceremonies such as "love, honour and obey" was out, never mind God. This was catnip. He had no doubt, Conrad responded, of Parliament's right to determine what a civil servant would say in carrying out one of its acts, but Parliament had no right to restrict what we would say at our marriage provided we fulfilled the required formulas first. Conrad concluded with what he thought was a home run. "We have not yet forfeited the right of free expression."

At this point I thought a cooling-off period might help. The point, after all, was our marriage, not constitutional reform. I modestly proffered Mr. Stephens a few sentences I had written in perfect samizdat language. They were horribly pompous, all about human beings are more than blood and flesh and city and state and ending with a vow to my future husband of true love in the name of my fathers and their fathers and their faith and beliefs that have sustained us through time. I wasn't quite sure what my rabbi would think about this, but I was absolutely sure that the Borough of Kensington and Chelsea and the 1949 Marriage Act would take a very dim view of any grinding of glass under the groom's foot into the K & C carpet.

Mr. Stephens read my prose with a look of great relief and pronounced it perfectly suitable. This, unfortunately, raised the competitive instinct of my husband-to-be. "I too should like to add to the ceremony," he said. "I wish to say that were it appropriate, I would pledge what is normal in a Christian ecclesiastical marriage oath, but as that is not appropriate, I would like it recorded that the sentiments in that oath are the ones I hold." Mr. Stephens looked very sad. That, he felt, resembled "a double negative and could not be allowed." Conrad evinced surprise at the sensitivity of the secular authorities and suggested that surely Parliament had more self-confidence than that. "Are you telling me," he asked Mr. Stephens, "that if I mention Christianity, my marriage will be invalid?"

Should I call Place Vendôme, the shop in Conduit Street that was even now hemming the emerald-green short dress overlaid with white lace, which was about the closest thing I thought permissible for a thrice-married bride to wear? By now Mr. Stephens was explaining how the Chelsea registry office was particularly keen to make the ambience of its weddings more friendly and indeed allowed piped music. Unfortunately, last year a couple had requested that the "Wedding March" be played, but after Chelsea took legal advice, that request had to be turned down on the grounds that it was religious. "Religious," I heard Conrad say incredulously through the series of waves that were crashing in my inner ear, making this whole exchange rather distant. "Mendelssohn?" It's all over, I thought, and prepared myself for a single lifetime living on Lean Cuisine's chicken à l'orange.

Happily the ceremony took place with a few minor adjustments. We had very few friends present, since we told no one until the day before. Our home-written wedding vows sound terribly twee to me now; there must have been a few knowing looks exchanged behind our backs as we "performed" our marriage, but our friends kept a stiff upper lip. Miriam Gross was there, as well as the Weidenfelds. Conrad's boyhood chum Brian Stewart flew in from Toronto with his clever broadcaster wife, Tina Srebotnjak. The Telegraph's editor, Max Hastings, attended, having produced a hilarious facsimile of a front page Telegraph with the headline "Black Weds Murdoch Star in Chelsea Ceremony: Media Mogul in Midday Merger with Newspaper Columnist."

Max had us both down cold. "Mr. Black," the copy said, "who purchased The Daily Telegraph from the Berry family in 1985 for five loaves and two small fishes, issued a brief statement from his Highgate home: 'Barbara consented to this outcome on the understanding that I agreed to move out of the North London suburbs and buy a watch. I have undertaken to do both. It will be a wrench to leave Highgate where I have met so many people of sympathetic political and social persuasion'"—a dig at Highgate's foaming socialist MP Glenda Jackson—"'but I am sure that in time I shall learn to appreciate the more salubrious attractions of metropolitan life.'"

The reality of little scrubbed faces—Conrad's children—hit me the second day of our marriage, after we had flown to Toronto and picked the children up to accompany us on our Maine honeymoon, providing a slight disconnect from my romantic dreams. He had arranged to take the children before we made our wedding plans, although I might have put the brake on and delayed saying "I do" if I had known I would take on stepmum duties immediately. Conrad had rented a cottage on David Rockefeller's estate in Seal Harbor. "My parents thought Bar Harbor too flashy and ostentatious," wrote Rockefeller in his memoirs, and in keeping with this stern observation, his own home in Seal Harbor, though spacious and comfortable and hung with priceless paintings, including a Modigliani purchased from the estate of Gertrude Stein, was very subdued.

Our Rockefeller rental some miles away was absolutely spartan. This would have been rather jolly had we been alone, but was less so when accompanied by three stepchildren, six, eleven and thirteen, and their au pair. The children, whose eyes glinted like those in *Village of the Damned* whenever they looked at me, had clearly not received favourable reviews of their new stepmother. On the first morning, that glorious morn when the bride wakes up to her new life in the arms of her beloved and the crisp Maine air and fresh smell of pines wafts overhead, it was not the cry of the plovers, the sweet sound of the sandpipers, but something more resembling the sharp-shinned hawk that greeted me. "Is Barbara Amiel in there?" a voice outside the bedroom door shouted, accompanied by the musical sound of horrid little fists hitting the door. The youngest boy had come to inspect the marriage bed.

Telephone calls from their mother were taken in the corner of the glassed-in verandah with much whispering. Try as I might, I could establish no demilitarized zone. I began to take long walks and return to the house in the late afternoon to be greeted by relentlessly hostile faces. Their mother was in fact holidaying with a former Roman Catholic minister she would subsequently marry, but this point could not be made to children. My husband saw none of this. He saw little enough of his children now that they lived in Canada with their mother, and this was a great treat: the three scrubbed faces were innocent in his presence, and there was nothing to be done but plunge on.

CHAPTER NINE

Savage Rites: The Dinner Party

I was Mrs. Conrad Black. All auguries pointed to a life of unbridled happiness. "Isn't it odd," I said to George Jonas, "that I will actually spend my old age in love and financially secure. Who would have believed after every disaster it would work out? And he's so wonderful. You'll love him." Christ, talk about tempting the gods.

I emerged from the secular embrace of Chelsea Old Town Hall with the slug aspects of my former existence gone. No longer a mollusc, I had a permanent home rather than a series of borrowed and temporary hiding places. My husband was neither neurotic nor elderly, not a sadistic sociopath nor a compulsive womanizer with a Big Love approach to marriage—which is only a mere soupçon of the happy relationships I had optimistically and masochistically embraced—but rather the answer to a maiden's prayer. At forty-seven he was my junior, intellectually far my superior, with all his own teeth, thick hair and a healthy interest in marital relations. He was also rich and Extremely Important, with a company jet. And I adored him. What more could any girl want. Rejoice! Rejoice! as Conrad would say. I did, although I had the sensation that not all the people that knew me were quite so exhilarated.

Previously, I had glimpsed the world of society by proxy through my friendship with George Weidenfeld, who was unflagging in his efforts to upgrade me, a thankless task in his eyes. A new viewpoint was at hand. I had a preview about an hour and a half after getting married.

Ambassador Walter Annenberg and his wife, Leonore "Lee" Annenberg, old friends of my husband, were giving their annual summer lunch. This was not quiche and a glass of wine on the patio but four courses and stiff table linens at Claridge's in honour of the Queen Mother. I had prepared for this more or less as the after-piece to the Chelsea wedding ceremony, by ditching the bare-legged thing, rolling on pantyhose on a hot summer's day, and getting out the modest-heeled shoe.

Here in the main dining room of Claridge's banqueting section was Walter's collection of aristocrats that he had got to know during his time as the U.S. ambassador to London.

"You know the Duke of Wellington and his wife, Valerian and Diana," said Conrad helpfully. I did not. I knew the Duke of Wellington's son, Charles Douro, then a marquess-in-waiting, who in spite of a smashing-looking wife eyed every skirt in London. He asked me to lunch once in their London home—"Apsley," he said breezily, assuming I knew where it was, which I did not. The house, once known as Number 1, London, sits bang in the middle of Hyde Park Corner with traffic whizzing around it, which made escape slightly more complicated than usual.

The men at Claridge's seemed, frankly, a little dried up, although often with rather imposing facial bone structure and piercing eyes; the women with the demeanour and confidence of the handbag-holding ladies-in-waiting of aristocratic background that the royal family chooses for their coterie. Never anything but courteous, unless crossed, at which point they become acidic, they provoke attacks of aphasia in me. (A perfect example of their sting came with this alleged quote from Mary Soames about Conrad. The daughter of Winston Churchill, Mary, to whom the Queen gave the ultimate honour of Lady Companion of the Most Noble Order of the Garter, appeared in the posthumous diaries of Woodrow Wyatt commenting to friends that Conrad Black was "London's biggest bore unhung." She told Conrad this was pure fiction, but it was pitch-perfect for the way her circle would poleaxe.) I was relieved at my decision to wear an un-form-fitting dress for my wedding. Anything smacking of sensuality would have been a hydrogen bomb in that room.

Conrad went happily to his seat next to the Queen Mother as I slithered to mine at a lesser table. "We get on like smoke," he told me of the Queen Mum. "A fascinating woman." I gathered this was because she was a fountain of first-hand history, having met anyone who was anyone during her reign as King George VI's wife, and could regale Conrad with accounts of her visit to Franklin Delano Roosevelt in 1939. I was seated next to perfectly polite and conversationally inaccessible guests. Since one absolutely cannot ever ask "What do you do?" and these people definitely expected you to know what they did, the identity of one's fellow guests had to be gleaned from the place card, which was removed after the first course. Anyway, a card reading "The Duke of Rutland" or "Hon. Margaret Rhodes" didn't lead me anywhere, especially at that early point in my grasp of the hereditary peerage and its jovial use of several names per family, a system that could almost have been created solely to throw honking provincials into the darkness: hence the Earl of Shelburne was in fact son of the Marquess of Lansdowne whose family name was, naturally, Petty-FitzMaurice. I floundered and did a lot of smiling into empty space.

As the lunch drew to an end, thank God, Walter Annenberg got to his feet for the required toast to the Queen Mother. None of us could leave our seats until the royals made their exit, which I expected would not be a problem with the ninety-one-year-old Queen Mother, unlike lingering events with Princess Margaret, who would demand everyone stay with her for hours on end until practically death do us part. Then Walter made a second toast, announcing his pleasure that Conrad and I had just got married and asking guests to join him in wishing us every happiness. There was a polite murmur of agreement, sidelong glances exchanged, and the Queen Mother said to Conrad, "Congratulations. I'm sure you will be very happy." This was the beginning.

That night was the wedding dinner party we were throwing in the private room at Annabel's. I had my "best friends" Annabelle Weidenfeld, Tessa Keswick and Miriam Gross, who was now Lady Owen, there with spouses, all of whom I could enjoy through my buzz of happiness, which for once was not codeine-induced. Conrad's guests, apart from boyhood chum Brian and his wife, Tina, were a little more of a mixed platter: Lady Thatcher and her husband, together with an eyebrow-raised Max Hastings as he looked at Prince Andrew's wife, HRH The Duchess of York (Sarah), of whom he greatly disapproved. Jacob Rothschild was there without Serena, his wife, who I liked enormously, and David Frost, thankfully without wife Carina, who was usually fairly beastly to me.

The decor, such as it was, flowers and the like, had been arranged by Caroline Druion, who had been at the wedding, had flawless taste and was the provider of my wedding dress through Place Vendôme, the shop she and her husband, Seymour, owned. I had done none of it. So at this point the whole evening looked like a pretty easy thing to replicate in one's own home.

Hideously, my worst side also made an appearance that evening: I had banned Caroline Druion from bringing her husband to the after-wedding dinner, telling her that he was, after all, a "shopkeeper" and had nothing in common with Conrad and his friends. In retrospect I cannot believe I did anything so utterly vile: the remark was cruel, pseudo-snobby and ludicrous about a cultivated man like Seymour. Conrad would never have entertained such a thought. My excessive anxiety over this new life with Conrad brought out a poisonous stew of self-importance and insecurity.

During our "provisionals," the subject of entertaining and dinner parties—that is, me throwing them—had never come up. We had travelled together and felt that sharing a barely present bathroom amid the horrors of Davos was a clincher in testing our compatibility: if we could survive that, we could survive anything. As a precaution, I made our marriage conditional on my never having to attend the World Economic Forum again to enjoy its humourless Swiss hospitality run by a Prussian with at least a hundred babbling voices onstage saying utterly nothing of interest because no one dares say anything original in front of thousands of attendees. In between seeing loads of one another, we had lived apart, and I had no dining room in my Lennox Gardens flat. We tried living together there, but Conrad got stuck in the pretend acrylic-encased shower that the attic ceiling made super small. Of course, pre-marriage I had been to one of Conrad's at-home dinners and to his Hollinger dinner bashes, as well as doing the rounds of posh London dinners with him. Incredibly, I had not taken on board the fact that my own home would now be a regular dinner and luncheon destination. The price tag for true love was about to catch up with me: Conrad's world revolved around the stomach-churning need for "us," i.e. me, to give dinner parties. Perhaps this is the point where I can finally apologize to all who had to endure my "entertaining."

At fifty-one years of age I had managed to avoid this particular disease and manoeuvred through life giving only two dinner parties. My monastic approach to entertaining, however, could not survive being married to the chairman of The Telegraph plc, where ex officio I now occupied a social position. At this haute level—or I suppose at our rather haute age—the dinner party is an occasion that almost no one likes, that guests regret accepting, that exhausts the hostess and pleases no one but the grocers, liquor stores and wine merchants. After several thousand years of refinement, the essential elements remain unchanged: you show off the cave, bring back the slaughter, and tear it and selected members of your tribe to bits. Somewhere lurks a Pasteur or Salk of the social life of human beings who will come up with another way to spend time with friends or expand social circles without the necessity of this beastly ritual.

I know the general view is that I just couldn't wait to climb the society ladder and was deliriously excited about becoming part of this fabulous world of party-giving and dinners. To say I would have preferred working in a salt mine may be a little over the top, but not much. There was no transition, not a whisker, between the days of heating up Lean Cuisine dinners for myself to those of entertaining a prime minister, HRHs, industrialists, celebrities and aristocrats of all sorts, society ladies and attached husbands, Great Thinkers and film stars. Wobbles and crashes ensued as I discovered tricky bits—on first encountering the mildly anti-Semitic Wasp world of Palm Beach was one. At such moments panic would set in and I would accuse Conrad of living among bigots, take to my car (which became my escape

module) and drive to some secluded spot to work out how to navigate
my new life. Conrad became adept at talking me down from the tree.
Usually, he would call up George Jonas for advice.

Some London friends needed to recalibrate. Pals in journalism
who as a matter of sanity routinely comforted each other with embroidered accounts of the cloven-hoofed activities of their editors and
proprietors, a safety valve I had often used myself, now viewed me as
on the other side. I thought I was still a journalist, unchanged in this
aspect of my being, but from the perspective of working confrères,
my bed and breakfast was now with the corporate world that in their
view thought only of making money out of compromising their talents. Any disliked viewpoint in my *Sunday Times* columns was now
treated as the pretentious musings of a rich socialite.

It stood to reason that at every dinner in our home, Conrad was
the main attraction. Dinners usually had about thirty guests, many
with an extremely sensitive view of their own importance, so it
became a question of how to seat all of them next to him. We had
moved to a rented house while waiting for our new home in
Kensington to be renovated. The ground-floor dining room was
narrow and bisected by load-bearing pillars. Dinners required two
circular tables, one in each section of the room, which exaggerated
the problem. He clearly could not be present at both tables simultaneously, short of some special effect or cloning. I tried the standby of
moving him around. He was not on for this, since the move invariably came in the middle of one of his best potted recitations of the
history of the world or else required him to leave a lovely female
dinner partner for a less lovely one.

I can't believe this now, what a crashing disaster and childish
effort, but I actually had a life-size photo of Conrad laminated to
cardboard that folded in two places, to sit upright on a chair at the
table that was without him. Conrad's table was always genuinely
the best place to be. His table rocked with laughter, while Outer
Hebrides looked on enviously. In vain did I look for amusing guests
to scatter, but he had invariably snookered them up, and anyway
my conversation wasn't going to inspire them the way his did. I am

not pathologically shy, nor without wit and humour, despite what this book may convey, but I just couldn't turn up the volume necessary to create the bonhomie that works wonders in general table conversation.

Life was a fairly constant social meltdown. Dinner at Karl Lagerfeld's home in Paris was misery given Conrad's delight in speaking his Haute de Gaullian French, and the impeccable chic of the other women present at the table for twelve. Decades of failed attempts at learning French were a bloody curse to me now, as I missed almost everything that was said. Occasionally I was tactless too, which is relatively unusual for me. I had assumed that Richard Gere wearing cropped trousers, a boater and tap shoes while breaking into song and dance in his film *Chicago* was one of those mad mistakes an actor can make when daringly pushing their envelope and that we could joke about it together. This was me at Anna Wintour's home trying hard to do unforced natural party chat:

"What a nightmare for you," I said to Gere. "But really bravely handled."

"Dancing is something I can do," he said coldly and moved on.

Obviously the wrong approach to a Hollywood star. My social nerves were reversed and most of my energy went into worrying about how to present myself. God, the opportunities I missed, if only I could have assumed my journalist persona and listened, questioned and noted details as if preparing for an article.

Everything was flammable, and I sloshed oil over it with what I told myself was becoming modesty but really was my burst-or-boast syndrome. "I don't mean to name-drop," I would tell my Canadian acquaintances, "but the reason I couldn't come to your evening in Toronto was we had to go to a birthday party at Highgrove for the King of Greece that Prince Charles was giving." (Actually this one was a whopper, a 100 per cent total lie; I had been invited to this occasion, at which most of the crowned heads of Europe were present, including the Queen, Prince Philip and the Queen Mum, but I was so stuck in my cringing Hendon persona that I was afraid to go. Conrad went alone, and I wrote a grovelling letter of explanation for my absence to Prince Charles that I pray his private secretary binned.)

On the other hand, some of the social compensations of being Mrs. Conrad Black were terrific. The old saw of never having to worry about getting a last-minute good table at a restaurant came to be taken for granted. And I began to enjoy making entrances and seeing heads turn. I was somebody: it was fun. You get used to it very quickly, and I positively swished. Even better were the seats I could get for concerts and operas and plays. I can't really see why this privilege should have been given to us. Some celebs or billionaires give a place cachet or buzz, but I'm pretty sure that neither the Munich opera house nor the Seattle one needed us for buzz; all the same, one telephone call got us excellent last-minute seats for their sold-out *Ring* cycles. Meeting and socializing with great musicians, screenwriters and artists now happened frequently, although it generally confirmed my belief that artists are best known through their work. It's the Hollywood California syndrome writ large: dimmer than late twilight on politics and social issues, with jaws that practically unhinged if you expressed any deviation from received wisdom—but possessed of a talent you'd die for. This attitude was not shared by Conrad as long as the dim artist was an attractive female, preferably wearing a short skirt.

As I settled into my new position, I began to get oxygen deprivation at the thought of the steep domestic mountain in front of me. So long as I was out of society, I had no need to trump it. But now, thrown into a maelstrom of entertaining and being entertained, the old competitive instinct kicked in. I was consumed by fear of not doing it right. I was no bloody savage, but now I was gathering up homes of monumental size in London, Palm Beach and Toronto, all requiring "decoration." They were not grand by the standards I was about to see—Blenheim, of course; Lily Safra's Villa Leopolda on the French Riviera, bought from Gianni Agnelli, with a special tower just to store her auction catalogues; and Gloria von Thurn und Taxis hanging out in her Schloss St. Emmeram unable to count how many hundreds of rooms were in her Regensburg digs—but for me, my new homes were stupefying. Having not decorated let alone renovated one room in my entire life, this would all have been hilarious and a women's mag "growth experience" had I not taken it so seriously.

Like a homing pigeon, at the suggestion of my new New York friends, I found my way to Léron linens in New York City, a firm that alleges it was founded a century ago in Paris, although I have slight doubts about that aspect of it. But no doubts about its products. Léron makes Pratesi bedsheets look like camping gear. The trouble was, I never asked the prices—I mean, how much can sheets be? I just saw their exquisite designs, handmade sheets to fit your antique four-poster. They saw me coming. "Shall we look at the colour schemes and furnishing in your bedrooms and fix a motif for each one?" asked the clever saleslady/design consultant, who quickly summed me up as a brand-new Upper East Side wife with wallet and no experience, alone, stumbling and without guide dog. "Would you like to match your garden, your bedroom carpets or the birds on the terraces? I think we should embroider the master bedroom linens in four colours."

Then came the invoices for tens of thousands of dollars per set. With a minimum of two sets per bedroom, sometimes three sets, every bed a different size thanks to our decorators, and about twelve bedrooms, the cost was colossal. And the invoices didn't arrive until the work was done. No pre-payment, just sign the order, like one of those nineteenth-century fiction characters signing a friend's note for his gambling debts. And Conrad was oblivious to what I was doing. "Great beds," said every guest, consisting almost exclusively people who had never known much more than drip-dry sheets to begin with.

I lent our London home to the desk clerk and his friend from the Carlyle hotel who were on their first trip to Europe; I lent Palm Beach to my Toronto hairdresser and his colouring assistant as well as assorted dog-friends I later made through my Kuvasz club. My choice of guests had the Palm Beach butler in a slightly morbid state. "Lady Black, your friends in the Nile Guest Room South with the . . . large dogs . . . have arrived with their belongings in a [whispered] brown paper bag."

"Yes, Domenico. Is there a problem?"

"Should I unpack the brown paper bag?"

I practised the talk. Everyone in the antiques and decorating world talks a pigeon English while they angle for your retainer. They were a guild of narrowed-eyed interior decorators, consultants, antique dealers and jewellers flogging antique silver salts from royal tables. At first they trod carefully, an initial parry in which a killer word lurked.

"Yes," they might muse thoughtfully as we talked about a new room. "How do you see that corner?"

I did not "see" corners.

"Perhaps a directoire *tôle peinte* in ormolu and enamel with snuffer on a gueridon? That could be pretty," they might venture. They watched your face, and if you couldn't respond either knowledgeably or semi-humorously—"I'd prefer Jean-Michel Frank and a couple of model giraffes"—they knew they had you, hence another 60 per cent on your bills. God forbid I muddled up a *lit de repos* with a *duchesse brisée*. This was basic decorator-interrogatory, a quick wheat-and-chaff procedure that helpfully categorized one. Bedrooms were always "dressed." Soft furnishings were assessed in terms of the "palette." I spoke none of it.

The set pieces of our entertaining were the summer and Christmas drinks parties—with summer's being the most important. Out went the invites on gold-bevelled cardboard stiff enough to be used as a diving board. "Mrs. Conrad Black At Home" the card announced with more confidence than Mrs. Black felt, who prayed she would be out. These harrowing occasions involved several hundred people trooping through our house to meet, greet and pass judgment on our taste or lack thereof. The lists were drawn up by Conrad, with me insisting on some friendly faces, or so I thought. Since my choices were invariably journalists, I did not take into account a basic truth.

"For every journalist you invite," said Miriam Gross after my first invites had gone out, "you create another ten who hate you for leaving them off." The logic of this was undeniable and would, as they say, be later revealed. But I had never looked at it that way. "Having journalists into your home," said Conrad, "is an invitation to disaster." I was thinking with my journalist head, and it seemed to me that if a working hack could meet the prime minister or the chairman of British Airways over a summer drink, it could be a useful contact. So I insisted we include journalists on the guest list. I should have just opened up my veins.

The parties got out of hand. Conrad bumped into so many people as his days wore on and the list just grow'd.

"How the hell am I going to recognize three-quarters of these people?" I would lament. "Conrad will handle it," replied my newly acquired, matter-of-fact and hellishly efficient assistant, Penny Phillips. Which he did—until the fateful summer party when, after addressing London's Centre for Policy Studies on the virtues of free trade with the U.K. and North America (long a favourite theme of Conrad's and today newly relevant), he went to lunch at Harry's Bar with Tessa and Henry Keswick. "I feel a little faint," said Conrad before passing out. Buckets of ice came tableside to be applied to his forehead and the fire department arrived, hoping, given their unusual speed, for something rather more sinister than a urinary tract infection. Conrad was shot full of antibiotics and ordered to stay in bed for thirty-six hours. "He must not get up under any circumstances for your summer drinks party tonight," said our doctor, clearly miffed that he hadn't been invited. I was left to host the damn thing on my own.

The only certainty was that the former King (Constantine) of Greece and his rather lovely wife would be among the very first guests and I would no longer be able to use my usual escape route of leaving it to Conrad as I fussed with the butlers. Nice as Constantine and his wife were, my efforts at small talk with them in the centre of a large and briefly empty room were wooden.

The staff brought me double vodkas neat, which I sloshed down with two glasses of water, aspirin and codeine, knowing that I would be tremendously sick in about four hours but caring less as I became utterly drunk. "Hello, hello," I was gamely saying on the half-landing outside the drawing room as the house filled up and wave after wave of faces crested on the stairs, interested really only in sizing up who was there and getting past ones that didn't count. Some of the guests didn't seem to recognize me anyway, given that my identity was often fixed by my presence at the side of Conrad. I escaped as soon as I could, sliding past the chairs that blocked the upper floors of the house where I knew trusty friends like Annabelle Weidenfeld would find me.

Like a creeping mould, my houses, particularly the London home, began to need "staff." This is one area where you either have natural talent or not, and it has little to do with upbringing. (My sister is brilliant at this.) Conrad preferred to do business lunches in the small dining room that seated six to eight people comfortably— although once again in his enthusiasm, when we were having a lunch that included Gianni Agnelli, he couldn't resist inviting extras, and my chair was wedged up the chimney. Now that I was in the enter-tainment business, I needed to employ butlers as well as the laundress and cleaning ladies. The cartel of domestic employment agencies kicked in, and the résumés and interviews began.

Staff who had Buckingham Palace on their résumé really im-pressed me, until I discovered that this was a false lead. The Queen having so large a staff, each member does one thing, and they are lost if multi-tasking. They all seemed to know one another or have slept with each other and no one had a good thing to say about another ex-staffer. The romantic politics were as tricky as the household ones.

Then there were the graduates of the butling schools, most notably the academy of Ivor Spencer. In the mid-nineties when I was hunting for butlers, this was still a relatively small field. London was not yet the top choice for the thick wallets of foreign grandees looking for a friendly tax shelter, especially the newly made Russian billionaires. The best butlers moved round and round among familiar homes—the Lloyd Webbers' to the Schwarzenbachs' to the Gert-Rudolf Flicks'—where knowledgeable chatelaines whipped them into shape. The very best of course stayed with their English employ-ers in their London and country homes and had no desire to work for "new people," let alone Canadians. The newcomers—one hoped to find some unmined diamond—arrived with résumé in hand and desperate eagerness. "What is your strength?" I asked one Ivor Spencer graduate. He was ecstatic at the question. "I can," he explained, "fold a napkin a different way for every day of the year."

Senior staff appeared to have an imperative need to one-up you, and in the beginning—well, actually to the end of this phase of my life—they could more or less succeed. "Yes, I have the same set in my South of France place," said one member of our domestic staff to me, almost pityingly and very off-handed, as he looked at the pride of place my Blue John garniture occupied. Another looked knowingly, with slightly pursed lips, after an antique three-foot carved ivory pagoda that I loved arrived from auction. "Mmm," he said, "I remember that from Mrs. Wrightsman's house. It was sent to her as a gift and she didn't know what to do with it." And then came the slightly horrid smile at the notion that her bottom-drawer gifts were my prize pieces. Then there were the coy notes: "In an effort to be completely honest," wrote one recently hired head butler in London, "I have been approached and received a 'muted' offer to put forward my candidacy for a position within a prestigious foreign household. My feeling is that this is nothing more than a well-planned hoax!" A.k.a., salary hike or out I go.

Conrad received none of this. He had grown up with staff and behaved in a manner that commanded respect and affection. One of our butlers, a tall, broad man, showed this affection in an unusual manner. On a Sunday night after returning from a trip abroad, we heard an envelope being pushed under our Kensington front door. The envelope was addressed to Conrad Black. On opening, we discovered a five-pound note inside and a letter enthusiastically thanking Conrad for the wonderful evening spent together the previous Saturday (while we had been in Manhattan). The money, explained the letter, was for payment of the club fees "which I know you never thought I'd pay back." The evening must have been an amazing success with the faux Conrad. "How did you feel on Sunday morning?" asked the letter-writer. "I was teaching at 10 a.m., so I had to get up at 8, when I was feeling 'tender.'"

Tender? Conrad called the man who'd signed the letter (and thoughtfully included his telephone number) to discover that he was genuinely under the impression that our butler, with whom he had spent the glorious evening in a gay bar and then back at our house, was in fact Conrad Black. His disappointment was manifest, but he did ask Conrad out anyway.

Sometimes staff communications simply baffled me. A Paris hotel delivered a fax to me from London full of vile remarks about my "demands." I had no idea what was going on and thought it best to just ignore the matter till I got back. On arrival in London I found another fax in my machine.

> Madam:
> Where to begin?
>
> I must say that I regret sending you that defensive and despicable fax in Paris. Above all I would never wish to upset you as I hope you know I am very fond of you and have the greatest respect for you. I totally misunderstood the request from Rosemary [Conrad's assistant].
>
> I am an ungrateful, servile moron who does not deserve anyone to be good to him.
>
> For what it is worth I have been quite tired for the past two weeks.

I suppose the May 1997 dinner Conrad decided to hold for Katharine Graham, doyenne of the *Washington Post*, to mark the serialization of her memoirs in *The Telegraph* ought to be counted a success, in spite of the potential pneumonia thing I created. Faced with Mrs. Graham, I decided that Conrad couldn't possibly object to journalists at the dinner. Turns out, our definition of journalists didn't quite match. About the closest names allowed were the extremely beguiling and clever television presenter Selina Scott and Charles Moore, who had by then succeeded Hastings as editor of *The Telegraph* (later the highly acclaimed authorized biographer of Margaret Thatcher).

"We have to have some of her fellow publishers," Conrad said, "like Robert Gavron"—of the Guardian Media Group—"Vere, of course"—Lord Rothermere of Associated Newspapers—"and Marjorie Scardino"—CEO of Pearson, which included the *Financial Times*. "And I'd like Diana there."

"Diana?" We had at least five Dianas on our guest lists, but I had a sinking feeling.

"Princess Diana."

Chances were she wouldn't come, I thought. But if she did, it presented the eternal problem of who to seat next to her. We'd met a few times, informally. From what I could see, Diana was a woman of contradictions, quite beautiful, and a mixture of shy coquetry, sharp street wits and great warmth all whipped up together in an intense aura of vulnerability. She was young, we were oldies, and none of our social friends would fit. I cold-called Milan for Marco Tronchetti Provera, head of Pirelli tires, whom I had seen across the room at a Bilderberg function, and invited him. He was a handsome and apparently charming man between wives: no longer with Pirelli heiress Cecilia Pirelli and not yet with the stunning Tunisian model he would marry a few years later. Invite accepted. An old friend of Conrad's, Thierry Despont, a Frenchman, a wonderful dinner partner, funny, unpredictable and clever, a tremendously talented architect and artist, happily divorced and then living in New York—I wasn't sure if he was straight (he is) since he was simply too good to be true—also accepted.

Upon her arrival, Diana took a look at the placement chart before descending to the dining room: "Which one is my hot date, Barbara?" I gave her the details and assumed she'd go for the Italian, but no, the following week, Thierry was dining with her at Kensington Palace. You can never guess these things. Her thank-you note in that big loopy Sloane handwriting, delivered first thing next day, followed the rules perfectly—a charming anecdote about the dinner to personalize it and a compliment for your hostess. "Congratulations—as a first!— seating me between two divorced gentlemen! One would build me a house, the other would provide me with wheels. . . . What more could a girl ask for?!"

The pneumonia peril happened this way: To provide extra seating that night, I had a marquee set up in the garden, attached to the house. Although it was May, the temperature was a bracing seven degrees, no rain, but invigorating gusts of wind. Unfortunately, of the six heaters ordered, only three arrived, of which only one was functional. None of my butlers caught this, since they were throwing plates at one another in a fuss over who would serve which side of the table given the presence of Diana. I was in the main dining room with Princess Di, and Conrad was seated in the marquee next to Kay Graham. On his other side, Anna Wintour was talking to my idol Tom Stoppard, which is why I kept trying to look into that part of the dinner. I saw Anna Wintour's face dead-white in the chill but gamely smiling.

"Madam," said our head butler behind me. I'd been scraping him off the ceiling all week because finally our tuppenny-ha'penny house had managed to come up with guests of the calibre he was used to. "Madam, it is very cold for your guests outdoors. Perhaps shawls?" I knew that he knew every item in my wardrobe, the very drawer my shawls were in, and had probably worn some of same when I was out of town. Should I just send him up for them? No, he'd have to feign ignorance. I slipped out and fetched bundles of then legal shah-tooshes and pashminas, and the old British stiff upper lip came out with a vengeance.

The *Sunday Mirror* ran a double spread on our Kay Graham dinner, with its list of "Britain's top movers and shakers" in attendance, together with photos of some guests arriving at our front door. With its customary deep attachment to accuracy, the newspaper captioned a photo of Wafic and Rosemary Saïd as George and Susan Soros. Anyone who has the slightest inkling of my politics knows that I would have to be gagged, drugged and tortured before inviting George Soros to my home. Quite mutual, I expect.

Everything clicked pretty well that night. By sheer luck I had managed to lurch out of one of the syndromes that haunted my dinners. When entertaining someone I thought terribly important, like

Jordan's Crown Prince Hassan and Princess Sarvath, or friends who themselves entertained in sumptuous style like the Saïds and Lloyd Webbers, a panic would grip me that my table would never come up to scratch. In this state of cold fear, I would keep inviting more and more "names" to buttress the dinner, to get that perfect mix, fascinate all guests, and the result was a table so crowded that it was impossible to lift a piece of cutlery without elbows poking deep into your dinner partner. Truly. Getting in and out of a chair was akin to slipping into a World War Two tank. My guests were unable to move their shoulders left or right during table talk and had to swivel their necks like Balinese dancers. I invited too many people fearing my guests would not be interesting enough. And Conrad invited too many people because every time he met someone, he found them interesting.

One event loomed annually like Erebus over the sunny summer festivities and was viewed with trepidation. This was known as "Bass Week," and it sent shivers through Annabelle Weidenfeld and myself. Mercedes and Sid Bass would arrive like clockwork in London at the height of the season and expect—no, demand—a round of dinners from the British guests they had entertained in New York. The Basses were part of Upper East Side society and important members of the small number we saw regularly on our visits and who I unoriginally termed "the Group." New York society at the time was helmed by Brooke Astor, whose health (and expected demise) was watched over by a small huddle of Manhattan *tricoteuses*, all in waiting for her chair while busily collecting antique dinner services at Sotheby's auctions. Mercedes was not quite seen as pre-eminent successor, although she probably thought she was, but she had two invaluable assets: her second husband, Sid, whose attention she initially obtained when each was married to someone else, by the unusual first move of throwing a bun at him during a dinner at Blenheim or Southampton—choose your source. Billionaire Sid, coming from Texas, had not only oil but also a luxurious private plane and was the largest single shareholder of Disney Inc., where, with Roy Disney Jr., he had appointed Michael Eisner CEO. In addition, he was an extraordinarily amiable man, kind and observant, who appeared to be run by Mercedes. (When they surprisingly divorced in 2011, among other things, he left her with all their grand homes plus the Grand Tier at the Metropolitan Opera House—renamed the Mercedes T. Bass Tier when "they" donated $25 million to the Met in 2007.)

If I pull out every last possible plus, which is like pulling out my own teeth, Mercedes was an exceptionally generous person to her chosen guests. She did entertain us all royally in a New York apartment glittering with Boulle and more Boulle, and no doubt it was my own lack that I remained unconvinced by and unconnected to her humour or conversation. Persian by birth, in profile she looked a bit like Nefertiti and kept her hair short, all the better to create a long neck for her flawless matched twenty-centimetre pearls, when the closest anyone else could come was about a graduated sixteen to nineteen centimetres. She entertained top musicians—she loved Beverly Sills and Valery Gergiev, and Valery in particular loved Fifth Avenue, given how much money he had to raise for his beloved Mariinsky Theatre—although I was deeply and possibly unfairly suspect of her genuine feeling for music. By the second act of the operas I attended in her box at the Met, she was fairly boozy and often leaned over me to talk to Barbara Walters while the house lights were already dimmed and the overture was playing. For anyone who truly cared about music, how was it possible to do this? But we took full advantage of her connections, her invitations to opening night of the best plays on Broadway and her boxes at the opera and Carnegie Hall. She was indefatigable in her pursuit of the newest and best restaurants. "And she's so much fun," said author William Shawcross, who, I deduced, had known her in more spontaneous circumstances than the rest of us.

Otherwise, she was tediously opinionated and spiteful to boot. She did strapless with such refinement that one could imagine her restraining any hint of bosom with masking tape before dressing. I couldn't really believe that she had an internal organ in her or that she actually digested food and excreted it like the rest of us, being so constipated in her manners and determined never to return to her former heavier self. I was chastised by her for wearing white high-heeled shoes. "You don't ever wear white," Mercedes told me. "It's for salesgirls, and not the ones at Bergdorf's." I told this to Annette de la Renta and Nancy Kissinger, and the next time Mercedes invited us to dinner at her apartment, we all wore white high heels. Mercedes survived. In my view, she was a bit like a reformed showgirl gone Park Avenue, and took the rules very seriously. Still, if you wanted to pal around with the Kissingers—which Conrad did—and Jayne Wrightsman—which he enjoyed—you had to take the whole package, which included Mercedes.

"It's arrived," my assistant Penny would tell me. "The Basses will be in London and they've listed their free nights." You couldn't palm them off at a restaurant alone together; Mercedes would want a full-on dinner. "Oh G-d" reverberated throughout our house. Bass Week usually fell in the middle of the season and was shared by dinners in their honour at the Weidenfelds', the Livanoses', the Duffields', Jacob and Serena Rothschild's and ours. There were probably more, and I expect various dukes—Beaufort and Devonshire, at least—were in there punching. But a certain dread was in the air.

The major problem was rounding up guests that would meet Mercedes's criteria. Most of them weren't really up for more than one Bass evening, so competition among hosts was fierce. Coronary arrhythmia was my response, and a prayer for Ebola, and it got worse, not better, each year. For the June 2000 Bass dinner I decided to share the strain with (now Dame) Vivien Duffield, daughter of the late businessman and philanthropist Sir Charles Clore, and throw a joint affair for about sixty at Kenwood House, the former stately home in Hampstead, familiar to viewers of the 1999 film *Notting Hill* where it appears as itself in the location for a film within the film.

"Oh, it's simple," said Vivien when I broached the guest list problem. "Just make sure we get enough dukes and seat Mercedes with them. Everything else is easy."

This North American aristo-fever is familiar enough, but it could vary in its detail: Judith Taubman, wife of billionaire Al Taubman, inventor of the American enclosed shopping mall, had a terminal case. She would interrupt absolutely any activity to take a telephone call from any European titleholder, from thrones long gone to grand houses quite worn out. Mrs. Bass went for the English aristocracy alive and well. Or near alive; age didn't matter. Apart from aristocrats who wanted donations from the Basses for various philanthropic causes (often close to home, such as restoration costs when home was a castle), most of our English friends really hadn't a clue who the Basses were, a notion that would have been incomprehensible to Mercedes. Surely anyone worth knowing would know of her.

For an earlier Bass dinner, I had inveigled Tom Stoppard to come by, mentioning Sid's influence in Disney and friendship with Michael Eisner—this before Tom's jackpot Oscar in 1999 for *Shakespeare in Love*. Mercedes took a look at the dinner placement when she arrived and was overheard by our staff to complain to her husband: "They've put me next to that awful playwright." She apparently muddled up Stoppard with David Hare, whose *Skylight* she had not enjoyed on Broadway, and all dinner long told off Tom for plays he had not written. His note afterwards said he felt that, in the event she found out her error, which he had found impossible to correct, neither he nor Hare would be hired by Disney. The next Bass dinner, I put her next to Constantine of Greece. I cannot imagine what she said, but it must have been a showstopper: Constantine, a man of usually saintly public manners, turned his back on her early on and would not return.

A smallish dinner for Al and Judy Taubman at Cottesmore Gardens in 1997 caused a hiccup that went totally viral later on and grew into a grand mal seizure. Conrad was a director at Sotheby's, Al Taubman was chairman, and the guests were largely his London directors. When a female guest cancelled last minute, Conrad, who felt a need to do the man-next-to-woman seating thing for Judy, called up Eleanor Mills, a writer with *The Telegraph* shortly to leave for the *Sunday Times*. Good sport Mills arrived on about two hours' notice only to meet the icy eye of Judith. Unbeknownst to me, Judith announced, "No reporter from the *Sunday Times* allowed." *Anathema sit*. She had a rule about journalists, and I suppose it was only my marriage to Conrad that permitted me to remain in the room, which she will no doubt regret should she read these lines. Eleanor was sent home.

"Why didn't you just let Judy leave?" I asked later when I found out. "I should have," Conrad replied outside the closed barn door. Seven years later the story surfaced in the press and was recycled everywhere. Here was hard evidence of our high-handed and extremely bad manners—particularly mine—though I had been in blissful ignorance of the entire imbroglio. As the tale gathered moss, it had me throwing Eleanor out via the kitchen basement and possibly in a sack, though that was not specified. The matter was finally sorted out, with Ms. Mills graciously accepting our apology years after the damage was well and truly done.

Conrad's physical presence was the nearest thing to a riot shield. I could peek and he could talk. Unfortunately, Conrad could talk very well indeed, and that often meant we were in a circle of silent upturned faces all looking positively rapt. I sensed, possibly incorrectly, that he was making no friends by sharing his extraordinary grasp of British and American political history. "You see," I would harridan him when we were doing the usual post-mortem, "a lot of these people have to listen to you whether they want to or not and they will resent you for that. No matter how entertaining or informative, nothing helps. You control *The Telegraph*. They may need you or work for you. And they can't wander off."

"No, no. Everyone enjoyed it immensely," he would tell me. "I had calls all day." I was not so sure.

I had twenty-twenty vision when it came to my own shortcomings, and this is one area where it really helps to be both astigmatic and myopic or else you add a warped narcissism to the stew and see nothing but your own deficiencies. But here, right in my line of vision, were the writers, conductors, statesman, talented celebrities, all those people I had read about and wanted to know—kissing my cheeks and thanking me, asking where the loo was, some getting absolutely sloshed and oozing stories and experiences that I never got because I was too busy oozing water, ammonia, salts and sugar. Perspiration. Or endlessly swivelling my neck about—one of the worst things, by the way, a hostess can do—to see if the evening was "going well." A visibly nervous hostess is an icy east wind.

Conrad would sit me down and tell me what an idiot I was. "People don't think you're a fraud. Your dinners are wonderful. Everyone says so." Half of that may have been right, but not having taken a poll I can't tell you which half. Looking at it practically, even though I was just a dolled-up mixture of Hendon and Hamilton in search of an English identity or an Oxbridge level of intellect—or something I would never reach—there clearly are people who surmount being born in a dustbin. Neither Hamilton nor Hendon is a life sentence. Mind you, my manners are. I never raised my voice like a Billingsgate fishwife because that was unnatural for me, but it was also natural for me to be moody and show it and complain to friends about my health (very infra dig), and neglect common courtesies like the writing of thank-you notes or replying to telephone calls, and to say things that were flamboyant or poorly timed. And feel awkward as all blazes when entertaining. It's a popular truism to say the more you know, the more you realize how little you know. I don't feel that way. The more I know, the more I realize how much I have thrown away.

On a more practical level, there was an ancillary reason for my dread of entertaining that only increased as I bounced along being Lady Black. I had great shoes, super clothes, a fabulous chef—and one hellhole of a dining room. Literally. The Cottesmore Gardens house was really splendid but for the location of the dining room, which might as well have been in a Yorkshire coal pit. The house itself was made up of two houses put together by the late Australian businessman Alan Bond. He had, among other things, bankrolled the 1983 Australian win of the America's Cup, and then went bankrupt after an unwise media deal with Kerry Packer (most business deals with Packer being unwise if you are not the Packer side of it) and later served time in prison for white-collar fraud. Conrad got the house for a fraction of its value from Bond's estate. (If you start counting the coincidences and concentric circles here, it gets eerie.) Bond had put the two houses together only with one very primitive connecting door on the second floor.

Through several years of renovations, we had smoothed out the connections, and all floors flowed nicely. But moving the main staircase to get the dining room close to the reception rooms would have cost a fortune. We didn't have the money. Or couldn't justify the expense. And most important, never realized what the result would be. And so the dining room lingered alone on the lowest floor, next to the kitchen (good), looking out onto the small garden (nice), but with no adjoining rooms. The only entry to it was a dark flight of stairs dead up against one wall from the entrance hall (disastrous). In addition, Conrad and the architect had made a decision, later regretted, to have the dining room double-height. The small dining room on the main floor had sliding doors that, when opened, over-looked the downstairs dining room when larger dinners needed both. This was fine in theory, but in practice it turned the main dining room into an open mine with the intimacy given by a ceiling the height of St. Peter's.

Dinner over, the accomplished hostess wants guests to drift easily and happily into sitting areas for brandy and coffee and continue the party. Not in our house. My tummy lurched each time guests had to march up that damn steep flight of dark stairs to where the front door faced them. From there, out they went, like penguins. Rarely did anyone ascend yet another lengthy one and a half flights of stairs to the reception rooms where staff waited with drinks and demitasses.

"Your dining room doesn't work. It's nasty," said Vivien Duffield, as if I needed her confirmation. Easy to say in Vivien's cushy situation. If her small London dining room wasn't up to perfection, she could just add another £10-million Canaletto to the ones on her walls. Vivien had a streak of cruelty that masqueraded as honesty. A shame, because she could be charming, and she almost single-handedly raised the money to renovate London's Royal Opera House. Anyway, no point moaning about our bad decisions. I just tried to make the pit user-friendly.

Colourful frescoes were painted on the upper half walls of bal-conies with glorious birds and cascading fruits and flowers. Lovely but no help. The downstairs walls had a *trompe l'oeil* of draped curtains with more birds, and over that I hung large light-filled Odiot drawings, including the working sketch for Marie Antoinette's dressing table. Attractive, even interesting, but the essential problem remained. We bought six free-standing tripod torchères from Kedleston Hall at auction and placed them around the room with their fifty or so candles lit. "Don't ever sell those torchères," admired Robin Hurlstone, an antique dealer and long-time partner of Joan Collins. But they changed nothing. Dining rooms need to feel intimate. Ours felt exactly like what it was: a large, deep cave that had been decorated a lot.

And every time we gave a dinner, that flight of stairs faced me as I led guests down. I suspected that, had I been a guest myself and looked at the seating chart just next to the descending stairs and been disappointed, I would have felt as though I were going down the Tower of London steps to my execution. Or the pit and pendulum. No way out. But then, as in so much of life, there never was.

CHAPTER TEN

Palm Beach

For about forever, I had heard Palm Beach referred to as a glitter-ing mecca, the *ne plus ultra* of luxury. Just filled with beautiful people who never had bad hair days, who wore gem-encrusted kirby grips, did poolside stuff in gorgeous caftans and went to their own tennis courts behind their own pool houses swinging racquets in zip-pered covers with shoulder straps—unlike mine, which must have had a cover once. At game's end they would jump casually over the net—and have you ever tried that? In my view it's castration time.

Finally, in 1990, David Graham drove me there, after a deadly time at his mother's home on Sanibel, a small, quiet island in the southwest of Florida that's known for its beaches dotted with shells. For me, it was a flat expanse of sand along which tourists with rolled-up trousers and hunched backs searched for relatively ordinary shells to clutter up their luggage. Overhead were clouds of turkey vultures scouring the ground for carrion. "My son is very difficult," David's quite nice but quite stern mother told me as we walked along the beach. "I do hope you will be happy." I should have taken more note of her word of caution and the buzzards overhead.

David said Palm Beach was *the* place to be. Curiously, the sole purpose of our trip then was to look for Conrad's house—David always had an odd fixation on Conrad because of his prominence and reputed wealth. Anyway, we drove up and down looking for a house for which we had no address but which David thought he would recognize as Conrad's by some sort of homing instinct. He didn't. I didn't see the town's magic, only lots of extremely tall hedges. We left the same day.

My first real trip to Palm Beach as a potential resident was before Conrad and I got married. He took me to a big dinner in a very big house on South Ocean Drive that had a ballroom and then he disappeared, leaving me alone to mingle with the host, hostess and guests, a large number of whom were drunk. The place was alight with huge diamonds and shimmering gowns, and the people wearing them were over-tanned, over-made-up and gesticulating with that sort of sway that drunks often have. Suddenly I felt like I was in the Palm Beach version of a Bruegel the Elder painting, but I wasn't sure whether it was *The Triumph of Death* or *The Flight Between Carnival and Lent*. After about forty-five minutes of "No, thank you, I don't drink" and "She doesn't *drink*?? Who brought her? What's she doing here?" I fled to a back marquee, where I discovered Conrad at a table with his wine glass and a long-haired blonde (of course—although, to be bitchy, not an entirely natural blonde), pretty and of indeterminate age. She was weighed down with a mixture of inexpensive beads and the freakily huge real stuff. Just the two of them, head to head. I didn't take kindly to it.

When it came time to leave and the blonde came up to say goodbye, Conrad introduced me to Kate Ford, the late Henry Ford II's widow. I was unenthused. I clammed up when we all said our goodbyes, with that tight mean little mouth I can get, and Kate said: "Honey, you won't get him that way." In fact, she was as decent as they come and turned out to be one of the nicest people in Palm Beach.

About four months later we got married and, that winter, headed once more for PB. "Don't freeze," said Conrad as we were being driven along U.S. Route 1 and the signs began to appear. "You're going to really like Palm Beach." This was one of the few mistakes about me he made.

Our first engagement as a married couple was a party at a long-standing friend's house. "You'll see," Conrad said. "This will be different. The hostess of that other party was a well-known alcoholic with problems and they were rude to you. Sara and Norman are dying to meet you."

He was correct. It was different.

The evening began with "drinks in the loggia," a destination that had been absent from my decorating experience but one I was to come to know well. "Come on in," said Sara pleasantly. I liked her right away. The place was crowded. "I'll be just fine here," I told Conrad. "Go mingle." I felt perfectly at home in spite of the slightly unfamiliar way the men dressed. To be honest, I sometimes thought that genuine Palm Beachers were a mutant tribe of humans that must have come out of the union of a golfer and a Belisha beacon. Azure blue Kiton jackets with black-striped Fedeli shirts and cotton piqué trousers. Engineer-striped polo shirts with bright yellow trousers purchased from the aptly named Trillion shop on Worth Avenue.

Everyone had a glass in their hand and seemed a little excited. "You understand," said the tall red-trousered man with harmonizing bright reddish face who was the very first guest I encountered, "we simply can't let the Jews into Palm Beach."

I swear. This was the opening gambit. Honestly, you cannot make this stuff up. Shoo, shoo, I could hear Palm Beach say to me.

The unlikely topic originated with word now seething around the party that someone of Hebraic origin was not just developing something big in West Palm Beach but, far worse, was making a bid for an authentic Palm Beach home. And not just any home but one by the town's toniest architect, Addison Mizner, in the estate section of Palm Beach proper instead of the condos past Sloans Curve, an area considered appropriate for such people and adorably known as the Gaza Strip. A sort of group activism had gripped the party. The Jews were coming!

"Why can't you let them in?" I asked, genuinely curious and automatically excluding my origins from the question lest the man become embarrassed—though I needn't have worried, as the genus *Palm Beacher* is not handicapped by embarrassment over matters of that sort. Anyway, I thought, his fears are needless. What members of my tribe would want to wear yellow or red trousers in loggias? I turned out to be very wrong on this point.

"They'd turn the place into Miami," he replied. "Big buildings, noisy tourists, everything." I gave him my nodding sympathetic look. "You don't have anything to drink," he said.

"No, I'm in recovery." Which I was. I've led a sheltered life, I thought.

About three nights later I was at a Palm Beach home for a dinner and dance. I was well into my practised version of the fixed-grin-and-tilted-head approach while I foxtrotted, although my animation never approached the frothiness of another newcomer, New Jersey–born Lynn Forester, later Stein, now Lady de Rothschild courtesy of Sir Evelyn de Rothschild. When talking, Lynn uses an extended giggle, irrespective of subject matter, in place of any comma or punctuation mark. My dancing partner, Norman Murphy, and his wife had taken us to lunch the day before at the Palm Beach Bath and Tennis Club, which, it was emphasized to me as we arrived, was very exclusive. As we danced, I realized Norman was well into the Scotch-and-soda or gin-and-tonic part of the evening, and although it had not handicapped his skills on the dance floor, his thought processes appeared loosened.

"I got a letter about you," he said.

"A letter?"

"Yes. They reminded me that my membership would be endangered by bringing unsuitable people into the club. The B and T, you know." He did a lovely full turn, dipping slightly, only to find my shoe was on his foot. Not deliberately but with surprise.

"Unsuitable?"

"They don't have Jewish memberships," he said.

"But I don't want to join."

"They prefer not to have you inside the club."

As we drove home, Conrad could see trouble looming. I could barely speak. "Did you know?"

"I don't believe it anyway. He was just trying to show off."

"Don't believe what?"

"That they actually sent him a letter. Perhaps they telephoned. But Palm Beach is much more than that."

"How much more? Are you a member of the B and T?"

"No, I am not. I belong to the Everglades Club." I knew the Everglades Club. It was housed in a formidable building designed by Palm Beach god Addison Mizner at the end of Worth Avenue, with a huge parking lot, tennis courts and an immense expanse of lawn and golf carts.

"Well, that's a relief at least. I assume I can go to lunch there?"

"I'll check into it. If you can't, we will fight that."

My newly cultivated patina of the well-mannered lady buying playful little place-card holders at Mary Mahoney's on Worth Avenue vanished with a blink. "Check into it? Have you been taking your children and former wife into a club that might, and probably does, in the splendid Palm Beach manner, bar Jews and never tolerate blacks?" Knowing Conrad's total lack of prejudice when it came to colour, creed or diet, I thought I was on a winning wicket. I did not yet know his aunt and uncle were B and T members. Later that season they would visit us after a game of tennis, their racquets neatly zipped up.

"Why did you leave?" asked Conrad, puzzled at my disappearance as his elderly relatives sipped cool drinks.

"I didn't want to contaminate them."

His reply was perfectly reasonable from his point of view: "They are old people who would be horrified to know how you felt. Most people don't have a preoccupation with Jews like you." This was in fact a rational answer, but then most people aren't Jews. Conrad didn't seem to think anything was amiss. If his club was prejudiced, he would change it. "There's a very nice Jewish golf and tennis club," he said. "I go there often. And there's the Beach Club. Anyone can join it. Furthermore, there's a synagogue on North County Road. A very large building."

"But every one of your friends that I have been introduced to so far is a member of the Everglades and the B and T. Why on earth would I want to mix with them?"

Here I was, married to this wonderful man who had only one problem: the town in which he lived for a few months each year had clubs to which he belonged that would not admit his wife. Well, you do feel a bit peculiar, rather like the cow in a field of zebras. I wondered vaguely how the Bath and Tennis Club's membership committee knew of my religion. It's true I bash on about it here, but not there. And it wasn't as if I hadn't tried to at least behave like a Christian. I was dressed in the most gentile clothing I had, having quickly realized this was the way to go. My mother's words to me when I was about six years old came back: "One day," she said, "if you marry a non-Jew he will call you names." This was odd, given that my mother became a non-Jew herself a few years later and married a gentile, but it's the thought that counts.

I turned over the problem of the Everglades Club in my mind. Secretly I wouldn't mind being a member: the parking lot was very handy to Worth Avenue, and the snob factor of membership, with their little insignia on the car windshield, quite pleasurable. I wouldn't have to talk to anyone there. I could even be an exquisitely dressed thorn in their side. Perhaps the co-founder of the Everglades, Paris Singer, son of the sewing machine inventor, had got fed up with assumptions that he was Jewish—the sewing machine, after all, being closely connected with the schmutter business, along with an ambiguous name like Singer—and ended speculation by creating an exclusive club that would confirm his God-fearing antecedence as an anti-Semite. Paris Singer's father had his own question mark, with suggestions, always denied, that he was of Hungarian-Jewish origin—or somewhere "like that." Frankly, in my view, you don't name a male child Paris unless you are Jews from Bucharest. Still, I couldn't quite put aside the larger picture. "I do not wish to join your Everglades Club," I told the beloved. "You can have your clubs."

Matters escalated when it was confirmed that not only could I not become a member, but at the Everglades, a popular destination for dinners and parties, Conrad could not take me in even as his guest. Nor could I go there for a party. "You can take a prostitute off the street as a guest," I said, "if she is dressed appropriately—no T-shirts in the restaurant and no trackpants on the premises—but you can't take your wife there because she is Jewish. This is a blood libel."

This was the idiocy of a few and not of a government, although I must say the bigwigs of the town's council didn't seem too concerned by it and, having met a few of its members later on, I rather thought they embraced it. Nothing about it injured me except that my husband was part of it. I've always thought private clubs or associations should be absolutely free to establish their own criteria for membership, however stupid, but to bar a member from taking their wife or friend as a guest seemed uncivilized, showing a distinct lack of confidence in their members' judgment.

Conrad went on a rampage. He rounded up heavy-hitting seconders to nominate me for the club, among them former U.S. Supreme Allied Commander Europe General Haig, Paul Desmarais, Earl E.T. Smith, former Mayor of Palm Beach, Kate Ford, and a raft of other notables.

"Please," I suggested, "let's not do this. I don't want to be a member."

"This is important," said Conrad.

"To you, but not me," I replied.

But, oh hell. If your husband is gung-ho on it—and Conrad was now in his determined mode—there was nothing to do but graze the Lilly Pulitzer florals. On the appointed day for my interview I arrived with Conrad at the Everglades and was shown up into a small room where several people sat facing me. My hair was blown dry neatly by my fashionable low-profile PB hairdresser, George Elliott, but I couldn't do the daytime Palm Beach thing of pulling it off the face with a headband or tying it at the back of my neck. My head is the wrong shape and my hair not thick enough. I had not purchased a Lilly outfit for the interview. This was an investment I was not prepared to make, and anyway I would have looked faintly ludicrous in her prints.

The interview was a complete letdown. Everyone was extremely polite and listened courteously as I explained I really didn't want to join the club or impose myself on it, only I would like to occasionally have lunch or dinner with my member husband. "Really, I quite understand your right to choose your members and have no wish to interfere with that."

There had been some previous negotiating, of which I was dimly aware, that involved everyone accepting that I was Jewish but quietly letting me pass.

"What would that make me?" I had asked Conrad. "Something ethnically stateless? Or just not what I am?"

"They will accept you as my openly Jewish wife or I will resign from the club," said Conrad. "Don't shirk this. We had to do it at the Toronto Club for Irving Gerstein."

"Do what?"

Turns out Conrad had spearheaded a movement to admit the first Jewish member to that exclusive club. "Myself, Fred Eaton and Galen Weston," he said. "We told the committee we would resign if Irving was not admitted, as there could be no other reason than race and religion." (I remembered this when Gerstein eagerly joined in the movement to chuck Conrad out of the club Conrad had got him into.)

"I really don't wish to pretend to be something I am not," I now told the three or four gentlemen who were looking at me with benign expressions. This, strictly speaking, was not entirely true because I had spent a good deal of my life pretending to be one thing or another. And probably there was nothing to be read in their faces. They had decided beforehand and the whole thing was pro forma.

"Nor," I added, "do I want to be a crusader. If you feel that I am not an appropriate member, I will make no public fuss. This will be a matter for my husband and myself." God, I sounded like I was reading off a prompter with the "Signaling Virtue" speech on it.

Honestly, you can never please your own tribe. When I was admitted as a full-blown, acknowledged, even devout Jew, you'd think I'd switched sides and betrayed my ancestors. The Palm Beach Jewish community rose as one. "You should have demanded an additional dozen Jewish members with you," said Marjorie Fisher, and she wasn't even Jewish but was married to Max Fisher, a super Jew and philanthropist. "Otherwise," continued Marjorie, "they did it because you live in London, are married to a gentile and won't be around much." This became the popular view, and I got a lecture from Al Taubman, who had been turned down when he applied. With customary skill, I'd managed to piss everyone off.

I know that every society has its social order and hierarchy, whether spoken or unspoken. Old school tie, culture, manners, money or merit—choose your criteria for your top lot. Palm Beach does a brilliant job of making those who don't quite fit feel like they are knocking on the front door but entering by way of the back. The whole place feels like a colouring book: the land of the Munchkins or a theme park. The sunsets too glorious. No frayed edges, no potholes, no rundown houses. Do you know that there is not a single poor person after sundown—seriously, search behind the well-bred garbage cans—and nothing but rich people and their servants twenty-four hours a day.

Palm Beach has its own police force and mayor. The narrow island wants to make sure you know that the incorporated Town of Palm Beach is distinct from all the gated communities and towns beyond its borders that wistfully ape its name—Palm Beach Gardens, Royal Palm Beach, West Palm Beach—and the nearby addresses that don't—Manalapan, Hypoluxo. (I am respectfully tugging my forelock to the true home of old money in southern Florida, which is Hobe Sound, no Jews at all and whose ultra-wealthy residents consider Palm Beach altogether too flashy.)

Life in the inner courtyards and loggias of the Town of Palm Beach's private homes was a film trailer of impeccable staff gliding over acres of marble and stone to bring a cool drink. Nothing unpolished or out of place, and curtains in appropriately tropical fabrics, fantastically pleated or delicately transparent, waving in the light breezes. Gardens were trimmed and cultivated with ten-foot hedges that grew in a season or two but never sported an errant hair, lush and thick and topiarized by hordes of Mexican workers. Mansions had fountains that never seemed to go wrong, as ours did, suddenly drying up and leaving the bottom all grungy. "You don't have a fountain man," my butler reproved me. No, I didn't.

There was no sense of workplaces. The Palm Beach veterinarian, the dentist and the optician all worked in charming little houses with pots of exotic flowers lining the porch stairs. There were no office buildings—safe from those Miami-type developers. The air was heavy with the powerful and enchanting smell of night-blooming jasmine, gardenias, moonflower vines and the more overpowering smell of smug self-satisfaction.

In the morning, troops of Hispanic and black workers would drive over one of the three bridges that connect Palm Beach to the mainland to service the homes. In the evening they would all go back—except for the workers in the restaurants and the clubs. Sometimes when I was out walking late, I'd see the black and Hispanic workers taking a quick break at the service door of the Everglades Club—a rushed cigarette, perspiration dripping off their faces, dark skin gleaming and food-grubby aprons. I told myself that they were earning for their families, that I had done similar jobs when young myself, but it stuck in my craw that they were serving a club that would never let anyone of their pigmentation in the front door. And that no one seemed to feel discomforted by this.

Through pelting tropical rains and baking humid days, my husband loved Palm Beach. Watching him strategize all night and worry over his constant battle with Murdoch for top spot in London—*The Telegraph* versus *The Times*—I knew I couldn't take away this one retreat by standing on my dignity, and I wasn't certain I wanted to so long as I could drop in and out. Conrad had been there for twenty years before we married, and even when he had on his fist-face of concentration, sitting in a wicker chair writing endless pages of figures with a fountain pen as he calculated debt ratios or circulation figures, Palm Beach gave him the sensation of being at least partially removed from the nastiness of a rather dirty business war.

Like two sensible (and yes, of course I'm stretching the use of that word ludicrously) adults we came to "the Palm Beach Compromise," which in reviewing now makes utterly no sense. Instead of Conrad's current house in the middle of other houses with a view of hedges and their Hispanic gardeners, we would find a house that overlooked the sea. Not the inland waterway, which was jolly nice and had a lot

of traffic to watch as big yachts came by but was essentially a commercial vista, but the sea. Now that I write this down, just how
getting a house in the same Palm Beach but on the ocean would solve
anything is unclear to me. I kept arguing that we were living in a
bigoted town that had no real beaches and no scenery, only gigantic
insects that looked to me like killer mutations, ghastly humidity and
a tropical climate that was completely opposite to what my doctors
advised for a dermatomyositis/lupus cross, so why were we there?
The "compromise" of a house on the ocean would cure exactly one
of those elements and not the most important. But that's what happened. And I don't think I want to delve into either my or Conrad's
motivation and psychology here.

Okay, I said. Please not a big house that requires "staff." Just one
with a view.

Getting a not-big house with a water view was, as I discovered,
a Palm Beach contradiction in terms. That real estate was just too
expensive for a normal build. Houses on the water would normally
be in the high double million figures, but Conrad found one for the
"bargain" price of just under $10 million, which, after selling his four-
bedroom home on Canterbury Lane, was affordable. The German
owner of the ocean property was facing a triple whammy: a messy
divorce, a prosecution in Germany and a heart attack. He had fled to
Switzerland, where, near death, he was confronted on our behalf,
virtually bedside, by that model of tact, reserve and compassion, by
the female Palm Beach real estate agent.

Perhaps if I had realized that the man for whom the house was
built, Hans Ferdinand Fischer from Vienna, had committed suicide
in 1979, at the age of sixty, presumably in this very home at 1930 South
Ocean Boulevard, I might have hesitated to occupy it. Though probably not. I'm not one for karma, but given the history of our new
London home, Alan Bond and all, I may have worried about the
pattern. The house gave us both a three-hundred-foot stretch of land
fronting on the Atlantic Ocean and three hundred feet backing
directly onto the inland waterway lapping at the foot of the garden,

while boasting one of the very few underground tunnels—permission to build them was no longer granted by the time we bought in 1998—which led directly from the downstairs loggia underneath the road and opened up on the beach.

Though under PB restrictions it was illegal to construct a higher floor overlooking the water, we managed to convert an existing tower-like rooftop space into my workroom: there was just enough room for my desk, some bookshelves and a very tiny daybed. Up there away from everything I was in heaven, and on windy wet days when the rains beat heavily on the windows, I could look out and pretend it was the English Channel.

Our social life was predictable. Conrad had a very soft spot for a smartly packaged woman with "views," TV personality and right-wing author Ann Coulter, who lived in a perfectly normal-sized house on the closest thing to a regular street in Palm Beach. After one evening in her garden, it seemed to me that splendid though she is, she also shared some similarities with the Mad Hatter. I love the titles of her books, such as *How to Talk to a Liberal (If You Must)*—my feelings exactly—and Conrad was dazzled by her quick and witty retorts, the product of a summa cum laude Cornell education and a post-graduate law degree, but of course, as I have repeatedly mentioned, it didn't hurt that she was also over six feet tall with the requisite long, shapely legs matched by blonde ultra-straight hair that provided a Lady Godiva service to her near-absent skirts.

Once installed in our renovated oceanside house, with my usual kamikaze instincts I decided to make a stab at reciprocating one or two of the invitations we had accepted. I had already held a cocktail party for about seventy-five people, to celebrate the closing of a Hollinger underwriting. I'd felt very Manhattan social X-ray because I was at my lowest weight ever and this meant I could fit into the long Chinese cheongsam I had picked up at a vintage outlet to use as a wall hanging—now I was a perfect wall to hang it on. The dress was sapphire blue, with tiny flowers embroidered on it—very Jennifer Jones in *Love is a Many-Splendored Thing*—and it had to be a size minus zero. I was losing weight again at a rapid rate, due not to enemas, pills or starvation, the usual amusements of society ladies, but sheer black-dog pessimism, which I must have been picking up subconsciously or subcutaneously from Conrad, since as far as I could see we were doing very well.

My view that only gay men and metrosexuals like women who resemble skeletons was confirmed next day when Conrad told me that Hollinger's VP of investor relations, Paul Healy, a gay man thrilled that the deal had been done, said to him at the party, "Your wife is so attractive she brings out the lesbian in me."

We had been to several dinners and lunches at Brian and Mila Mulroney's Palm Beach home, which was a perfectly charming house—not on the water. Mila had the knack—perhaps it helps to have been the prime minister's wife—of giving charming lunches and dinners on her outdoor patio. Actually, I think she could have given charming dinners in a pup tent in the Kalahari Desert. Some people can. I decided to skip anything dodgy and simply have a relaxed no-fuss lunch for the Mulroneys on our upper terrace, the only outdoor space that was a normal distance from the kitchen. The view was lovely, and I pictured the breezes gently wafting about us. If only.

I'd purchased a pretty glass table and chairs but not yet tried them out. The terrace, I now discovered simultaneously with sitting down for lunch, was in fact too narrow to allow guests on both sides of the table to easily pull out their chairs. Given we were only four people, I thought we could comfortably serve across the table once we had shoehorned ourselves in. I seated Brian with his back to the featured view because it was the side with a bit more chair room. The sun hove cheerfully into view, bouncing off the blue-and-white awnings, before travelling west with full afternoon rays hitting Brian's neck and back, in defiance of awnings that fell short. I was sitting opposite and could see the sweat first in rivulets and then gushes down his face as he gamely continued the conversation. The temperature was in the nineties, not a hint of wind; this was about the closest I'll ever get to sitting in a jjimjilbang kiln. Most big Palm Beach houses, I now realized, had been built anticipating this problem: their terraces were sufficiently deep that tables could be put far back under awnings and the sun kept out.

The Mulroneys, versed in the polite and political art of tolerating discomfort while dissembling happiness, said not a word. They smiled and chatted, God they deserved a decoration for surviving this, and Brian melted in front of my eyes. I whispered instructions to the butler to suggest we have refreshments inside, to which Conrad ebulliently announced, "We can go inside anytime. Let's enjoy it out here."

"I think Brian may have heatstroke," I said. Brian gallantly dismissed my concerns. Mila looked worriedly at him as his linen shirt filled up with damp patches.

Our lot was wonderfully spacious, a prime location, but frankly the house itself should have been a tear-down or total gut. The truly formidable impediment was trying to amend a house designed by Palm Beach architect John Volk. Widow Volk was on the Preservation Foundation of Palm Beach and the Historical Society of Palm Beach County, was chair of the town's Landmarks Preservation Commission and the first chairwoman of the Bath and Tennis Club Buildings and Grounds Committee. Our architectural design team—Anne Fairfax and Richard Sammons—in the early years of their work and newish to Palm Beach, named the house "the crab" because of its rather unfortunate shape, if not our pace in paying construction bills.

They did a masterly job. When writing this, I went onto their website only to find brilliantly coloured photos of some of the crab's rooms under the curious title of "The Renovation of a Regency House." I clicked, and a heavy wave hit my chest and gut. There it was. Our lost Palm Beach home as if in a time capsule, waiting for us to reopen. The huge reception room filled with light—and those thingamajigs I had forgotten that were the stamp of our Palm Beach lives: Conrad's chess set on the games table; his office with the odd-shaped box behind his Linley custom-made desk, books piled everywhere, and the checkered deep pink material I had loved for his reading chair. All chosen so carefully, photoed when it was newly done and none of us knew we would only have it for a few years.

In order to survive in life, absolutely every human being has to blot out splintered moments or happenings, memories, those bits and pieces tasted but never quite digested. When a piece such as a home you painstakingly created is forcibly and unjustly taken from you and its memory pushed down inside so as not to torment, but then unexpectedly that loss rears up in pixel-perfect pictures—out of reach but in front of you—chosen objects with their own history of acquisition on the computer in blazing colour, the hurt re-emerges, starting in your chest and going into your heart.

Apart from the drawback of its location in Florida, I loved this house best. Clearly I was never going to rival the great society hostesses, but I knew us: this was a refuge of wicker and trellis-lined garden rooms, of deep, comfy reading chairs, of wide marble halls that the dogs sprawled in away from the heat, of French doors that opened from almost every room onto parterres filled with white flowers and beyond them the iguanas lazily climbing along the edge of the water.

Almost best of all, this magical home required virtually no staff to maintain it apart from the daily cleaning lady and our butler/houseman, who lived in Fort Worth across the bridge. Once we drove behind the white gates flanked with two stone eagles, Conrad and I were alone in our world, away from everything. On the evenings when the blood-red sun set and the birds came flying back against a deepening sky, black long-necked silhouettes returning to the mango groves, Conrad and I would sit together talking into the dark about a hundred and one things. That was before the charges against him turned every conversation for the next fourteen years or more into a worrying, desperate exchange about lawyers and legal tactics. Till then, on the terrace, side by side, with the sounds of the lapping inland waterway and the gentle rush of water from the small fountain just beyond the kitchen garden, I thought the sweetness of existence had been given to me.

What else do I remember of Palm Beach, before the memories were inextricably linked with the trips to Florida's federal prisons? For one, ineradicably, Ghislaine Maxwell. Ghislaine was the daughter of the death-by-drowning media mogul Robert Maxwell, who'd named his yacht *Lady Ghislaine*. She was not beautiful but arresting, with a face that had sharp angles, sometimes elfin and sometimes dark. After her father's death, I began to see her, accidentally it seemed, in both Manhattan and Palm Beach.

She had a relationship with financial advisor Jeffrey Epstein, although the nature of it was a bit foggy. At that time Jeffrey was close to a lot of billionaires, including Leslie Wexner, for a time a director of Hollinger. Leslie had a golden touch for understanding women's dreams as founder of The Limited chain of women's stores—Victoria's Secret, Bath and Body Works, and such. He was a warm, gentle man, even shy, perhaps. After his marriage, he left the colossal fifty-thousand-square-foot house he occupied alone on East Seventy-First to Epstein, and went to live in his super-colossal sixty-two-thousand-square-foot home near Columbus, Ohio, with his bride and, latterly, their four children. Both houses confounded me on my single visit to each. There was something withdrawn and impersonal about their luxury. Enigmatic houses, really, like both Leslie and Jeffrey.

Epstein was an unknown quantity to me; we had been invited to his Palm Beach house and I had declined, though Conrad went over one afternoon and they strolled outside talking about economic policies. Jeffrey was a handsome man, but he made me a little uneasy and I couldn't say why. I just knew I would bore him. After all, I was more than twenty years older than Ghislaine, who was in her thirties and a good dozen years older than Jeffrey, and I sensed that the difference was important in their world that had a pretty explicit sensual component to it. It was a rather exclusive if not strange world, not part of visible Palm Beach social life and filled with billionaire toys like Epstein's huge real estate properties—an island here, a mansion there, his private planes that included a Boeing 727, as well as a helicopter and a Gulfstream IV jet.

Ghislaine was renovating a house on Sixty-Fifth Street in Manhattan—we were on Sixty-Sixth, so it was easy to bump into her. "I'm really lost in Manhattan," she said to me one day. "It would be so helpful if you could introduce me to someone that might advise me." My sympathy kicked in and I thought about it.

I thought about it. "You know," I said. "Georgette Mosbacher is a very savvy businesswoman. She just bought Borghese cosmetics. Really generous too, and she knows just about everyone."

"I was thinking of Henry Kravis and Leonard Lauder," said Ghislaine rather decisively. "I'd like to meet them."

Well, I thought, both were extraordinarily successful businessmen, billionaires and very happily married. I'd dined at their homes, including the Lauder residence in Palm Beach, where I met his mother, Estée Lauder, then in her nineties. Easy enough to telephone either Henry or Leonard, but I wasn't quite sure what I was supposed to say. Kravis would certainly ask me questions, so I thought I'd try Leonard. A shame, really, because I would have paid big bucks to see Marie-Josée Kravis take on Ghislaine. I duly called up Leonard.

"You may know of Ghislaine Maxwell and the terrible death of her father," I told him. "She's asked for some advice, I think it's about doing business in Manhattan and she especially wanted to meet you. She may be a little lost after all the terrible publicity. Can you help?" God, I thought, even as I was saying it, the man does have rather a large cosmetics company to run, and what in heaven's name am I asking? "Yes, of course, Barbara. Come around to tea." Ghislaine and I trotted off to the famed Lauder triplex on Fifth Avenue, and there, with tea, china and biscuits all deliciously laid out, were Evelyn and Leonard Lauder greeting us with smiles. I wasn't sure why Evelyn was there, but of course it was the wise thing to do. Almost instantaneously I felt damn uncomfortable and realized, as Ghislaine turned up the charm in contrast to her usual combative, brusque manner, that whatever it was, Ghislaine's agenda wasn't straightforward business advice. Her conversation had no point to it. She answered questions about herself evasively. What a chump I was, wriggling in my chair, overcome with embarrassment. What the blazes were we doing there?

Years later, around 2005, Jeffrey came a cropper in a sex scandal. His Palm Beach home was said to be the headquarters for a sex-trafficking ring using young girls from West Palm Beach, and it was implied that Ghislaine was procuring for him. Besides young girls, big whales were also supposed to be lured into Jeffrey's web, possibly for some sort of compromising set-up—great business whales like Leslie Wexner and hedge fund whales and politicians too, it was claimed. Personally, I have never believed Ghislaine guilty of any crime more than wanting to please Jeffrey or maintain whatever the relationship was—business or personal and likely both. And sometimes, when you are in a vulnerable position, you can be manipulated into unpleasant behaviour.

Jeffrey's 2007 convictions in the Palm Beach trial only proved—as far as that record went, and frankly the record is a pottage of dropped charges, disappearing accusers, questionable testimony matched by questionable settlements all revolving around sticky oily massages and Jeffrey's seedy onanism—that he was guilty of one state charge of procuring a minor for prostitution. Over ten years later the more serious charges were being investigated when his life ended in that New York prison in 2019 before any trial could have made sense out of it all and established guilt or innocence. And as I read about his murder or suicide, questionable like everything else in his life, I wondered if that afternoon tea with the Lauders was a small piece of a puzzle, a tiny glimpse of some aspect of Epstein's life with Ghislaine. Because otherwise the meeting made absolutely no sense.

Anyway, there we were one day—several years before Jeffrey's first round of troubles surfaced—Ghislaine and I, walking along the Palm Beach sand, me glancing enviously at her youthful ability to wear short shorts and look super with no makeup in the full white sun, while we kicked pebbles like normal people do, and out of the blue she said, "I'll bet I'm in charge of more bathrooms and lavatories than you."

Although an unexpected question, I realized this was another Palm Beach abacus to gauge how rich one is.

"You haven't counted?" she asked.

I hadn't, although providing hand towels for powder rooms and accessories like the mandatory orchid and scented candles was another of those fascinating jobs I had added to my list. "Quite a lot," I replied.

"How many?"

"Including half ones without a bath?"

"Yes, and you can count planes as well. Choppers too."

Mine came to an astonishing thirty-nine.

"I win," said Ghislaine. The Palm Beach version of Monopoly, I suppose.

Back when we lived there, you could calculate social acceptance in the 33480 zip code by your social distance from the woman sitting at the apex of its pyramid, wealthy beauty Pauline Boardman Pitt, originally a Philadelphia Drexel Munn on one side and great-granddaughter of the founder of Harvard Business School and Citibank on the other—which, though not part of my lexicon, definitely had the clunking sound of a deeply serious provenance in the New World. In person she is the closest I've seen to Tracy Lord, the character played by Grace Kelly in *High Society* and Katharine Hepburn in *The Philadelphia Story*. Better-looking than Hepburn and more alluring than Kelly, who lacks Pitt's robust sensuality, I thought she was an utter smasher who could dazzle like the sun bouncing off a calm ocean even as she unambiguously communicated to you your status as a minnow. She was close to social perfection in her caste and class, except when she went off the rails. And, without being totally beastly, I must say there is nothing more reassuring than seeing one of these goddesses go off the rails when you can't ever balance on them your-self. It's not quite *schadenfreude*, just a reminder to never despair. Not everything is the perfection you will never reach.

Pauline went off the rails, ballistically, over Sotheby's chairman and real estate developer Al Taubman. Big Al, as he was known, not for anything but his physical size, became gratuitously boring in my view when he decided to enter high society, probably pushed by his wife, Judy. Suddenly his dinner conversation changed from mildly ribald and amusing to serious lectures on the import of bananas. A typical American criminal prosecution got him, not for felonious dinner table conversation, but for some sort of price fixing as owner of Sotheby's, together with his British counterpart at Christie's. This was not viewed as a crime in the U.K., so the Christie's CEO was not charged except in America, which he wisely decided to give a miss in his itinerary.

Taubman was sent to prison. A lot of people in Palm Beach expressed their sorrow and pity over his incarceration. This gave Pauline her opening. She knew crocodile tears well enough to call them. Off went a signed (and published) fax from her to a New York gossip columnist in which she called Alfred "a pig who never does the right thing unless it looks better in high society." I don't think the word *pig* ever publicly crosses the lips of old society unless perhaps speaking of raising heritage pigs for show, definitely well-bred pigs and not the one to which Pauline referred. There was also a side snipe at Judy Taubman, whom Pauline referred to as a woman who denied her origins and called herself Greek. That was low. I have no idea what Judy's origins were, but she was beautiful enough to have been a Miss Israel.

Pauline was unerringly accurate in nailing social hypocrisy, but not quite so accurate in her estimation of Al Taubman. Taubman was philanthropic in places where, unlike Palm Beach or New York City, there was absolutely no social cachet. He never graduated from his alma mater, the University of Michigan, but he donated well over $250 million to the university for a medical research centre and to its School of Architecture, as well as large amounts to help recreate the city of Detroit—not exactly an A-list address. I'm not really up on old society etiquette, but is it really done to send such a note to a newspaper when a chap is off to prison? Probably not the best idea at any time.

Her derailment was attributed to the painful experience of watching her two husbands go through years of torment working up business deals of varying reliability for Alfred Taubman. During that trying time, Pauline—Drexel Nunn notwithstanding—had to take Judy and Al's antics in silence rather than aggravate matters for her spouses. Vexing. When you come from such blue-blood and inherited wealth as Pauline, you may not know much about the fluctuating colours of blood required in the real world of tough business deals that led to Taubman's self-made billionaire status. I did wonder if, after the dam had broken and the note had been sent to the newspaper, Pauline had seen that she was breaching the very code for which she and her world believed they stood.

Of the years that Conrad and I had a home there, I can wistfully remember the blazing sunlight on the spotless streets and the almost erotic thick vegetation, the *boudin blanc* at Chez Jean-Pierre melting in my mouth—actually, anything from Chez Jean-Pierre's menu—and the frustrating lack of anywhere to sit outside with just a short espresso and *pain au chocolat* to munch. Palm Beach then was like those shimmering mirrored balls that revolved overhead at high school dances in the late 1950s: a little world of dozens of beautiful surfaces reflecting absolutely no reality outside—no wars, no diseases, no poverty, hunger or dirt. Such a place is not bad or good; it is a confection of some imported icing sugar, sweet and complete and for the tables of the few.

I remember the beauty of the little vias off Worth Avenue with their vines, sculptures and fountains surrounded by benches to sit and watch the strollers pass by. I remember how safe I felt walking in the cool night air if Conrad had to be away on business for a night or two, on the beach alone on a moonlit midnight savouring that special freedom the ocean gives you.

Later on, I would see Palm Beach through a different lens. It became my own prison.

CHAPTER ELEVEN

Jewels on Park Avenue

"You know," said the real estate agent, a middle-aged woman from Sotheby's New York whose day-timer was filled with boldfaced social names, "this is a J.E.R. Carpenter building." Oh God, Manhattan real estate speak. "Next door, of course," she continued, "at 625, it's a Candela. You really can't do better."

"Mmm," I heard myself humming—my usual enigmatic noise to counter the unknown.

"And best of all, you have a couple of staff rooms at the back."

The thought of hiring New York staff presented itself in all its grimness. "Only one apartment to each floor, and of course this is really the third floor," she was saying in order to compensate for the fact that this was only the second apartment floor and the higher the apartment, the more desirable. I was thinking—well, actually, I was thinking nothing, in case it all suddenly burst and I woke up. This was unreal, too good to be true, buying a Manhattan apartment on Park Avenue at Sixty-Sixth Street. There was a thick cooking smell drifting through the apartment from below. No one mentioned it.

The apartment was a co-op, which meant we had to be interviewed by the board. References were required, and Conrad naturally was something of an overachiever. He obtained glowing letters from Brooke Astor, David Rockefeller, Henry Kissinger, Sid Bass and Mrs. Charles B. Wrightsman. The building, elegant enough, was not quite up to the category of those names, and I wondered whether this would arouse resentment or respect. "Herbert Brownell lived here, you know," said our real estate agent. "He had letters from President Eisenhower and Richard Nixon." Well, he had been attorney general under Eisenhower. He was approved. So were we.

No sooner had we established ourselves as genuine Park Avenue co-op owners when the time came for me (not Conrad, who knew everyone) to learn the names of my new friends. Actually, first came applying for credit cards—Saks, Bergdorf's, Lord & Taylor, Bendel's, Bloomingdale's. I did this largely because it was fun to go into the customer service office and, when asked for my address, say "635 Park Avenue" very casually, and they'd know immediately it was in the most coveted and desirable zip code (10021, which got changed to 10065 when the Upper East Side was split in 2007). Worse, I followed this up by offering a Palm Beach and a London address if they wanted: this was like name-dropping, only better. Next came the name thing.

Any place thrives on gossip, but Manhattan thrives more so because everything is more so there. This was a double whammy for me. I am not averse to hearing good gossip. After all, everyone gossips—geniuses gossip, hairdressers especially, and dentists would if their patients could. I have been known to pick up *People* magazine in the hairdresser's even when there was a copy of *The Economist* right next to it. *Especially* if there was a copy of *The Economist* actually. But if, like me, you can't remember names, you can't actually contribute gossip, which is a social handicap of staggering proportions and right up there with my inability to drink.

Just how I have functioned socially at all becomes more of a mystery to me as I write this down, although I did develop all sorts of bizarre ways of circumventing and hiding these handicaps. There's got to be a reason for my name-blackout, which has haunted me all my life, even when my memory was exceptionally good and I always won those children's games of "How many items can you remember?" after a tray was flashed before us with all sorts of objects on it. But since late childhood, people's names went into a dead end or a tangle of synapses. A further refinement of this is that when I do remember a name, I can't remember which face it goes with. There must be a medical syndrome for this. Perhaps it's a sub-category of disconnection anomic aphasia.

Just recently, a famous historian came to our Toronto home, and after he had long discussions with my husband about the usual—the cabinet betrayals in Salisbury's government or something—he turned to me: "Barbara," said the famous historian, "I can't wait to sit down and have a good long gossip with you." Oh Christ, I thought. I'm no good on Salisbury but even worse on Boris Johnson's girlfriends or the net worth of that newspaper man's son. I'm not claiming some sort of sensitive introvert status, just a state that anyone who knows me will confirm: I prefer small homes by choice—not necessity. Like most people I only remember what I want to remember and that apparently does not include names or juicy anecdotes about people. I prefer my friend Clarissa Pryce-Jones's brown sugar cake to fancy desserts and have no vibrant social explorer in me. But I did try to make it all work in New York.

My ear was always open for the aural distinction between Diane (von Fürstenberg) and Diana, which was usually Diana Taylor, the much-admired companion of Michael Bloomberg, or, secondarily, ABC's star Diane Sawyer worryingly referred to by Barbara Walters who was increasingly afraid of losing an interview to her. We slotted into the small circle of people I refer to as the Group, which was headed by Mrs. Charles Wrightsman (Jayne), heir presumptive to Brooke Astor, and had its nucleus in Mrs. Henry Kissinger (Nancy) and Mrs. Oscar de la Renta (Annette), and included Barbara Walters (between spouses), with Mercedes Bass nearly a 100 per cent member but just completing probation, having come latterly and noisily.

Each of the Group's spouses contributed as orbiting nuclei: Oscar made his ready-to-wear available pre-season with professional altera- tionist and discount. Henry Kissinger provided the gravitas and intellectual sheen otherwise missing. Sid Bass, his plane and Disney connections. In a sea of social sharks, Jayne, Nancy and Annette were entirely loyal to each other. Jayne had no living spouse, but her late husband's exploits in postwar France under the helpful eye of his

friend General Dwight Eisenhower were just mind-blowing. Charlie
Wrightsman acquired and transported to America planeloads of French
furniture, entire floors of parquet de Versailles and walls of boiserie
from some of the finest châteaux in France for dirt cheap prices at war's
end. This enabled Jayne to donate a pile of it to the Metropolitan
Museum of Art, get galleries named in their honour and become the
Group's serious fine furniture and art specialist (and generously give
bits of her collection away—to Jackie Kennedy on loan for the White
House and to the Kissingers for their River House apartment). Out of
war and plunder comes philanthropy. Also new additions to my vocab:
"He hasn't endowed his wing," said Jayne Wrightsman with a slight
put-down giggle, speaking of the Henry R. Kravis Wing at the
Metropolitan Museum. "Endowed?" "Provided the permanent fund
for its upkeep each year."

As a Barbara myself, and very much a new newcomer, my name
understudied America's sage TV interviewer Barbara Walters, whose
obvious contribution to the Group was superstar TV glam. I looked
at some of her early work and God she was a smasher in her heady
days, and even in her later years she could still pull it off. We were
supposed to have a lot "in common" because we were both JJs—
journalists and Jewish. In fact we had very little in common. I could
never say it, but in my view, Barbara was not a journalist. Her TV brief
was to have no views and to worship at the altar of celebrity-dom.
I mean, a journalist can't interview Fidel Castro and let him get away
with saying he has no political prisoners, only counter-revolutionaries
who have committed crimes, and your next question is "When will
you shave off your beard?"

"I'm not there to challenge or judge," Barbara said. "Fidel was a big
bear of a man, charismatic." Yeah, well, in my view you're not there to
give him propaganda time either, and that's essentially what he got, in
his charming, charismatic big-bear way. But Barbara actually worked
hard, which was a novelty in this group. And although at first I choked
at Barbara's lists of the Ten Most Fascinating People of the Year, which
always included some of the ten most boring ones, like Jimmy Carter,
Ozzy Osbourne and Paris Hilton, I quickly saw I should just lighten up.

After all, in pre-Twitter days, someone had to speak up for the millions who believed the Most Fascinating Persons of the Year were Brad Pitt and Angelina Jolie, and I'd be a dead loss or go mute. I'd grow a Pinocchio nose if I put my name to choosing Hillary Rodham Clinton as the Most Fascinating Person of the Year once, let alone three times as Barbara did. All I hoped for was a wink by Barbara to say "Hey, this is how I earn my Park Avenue flat" and I'd understand. But she took her role as a ground-breaking journalist very seriously.

"My" Manhattanites, the few people I had known before my marriage to Conrad, such as Norman and Midge Podhoretz, were never invited to the Group's dinners as the token cultural or intellectual trophy guest—like art historian John Richardson or the Metropolitan Museum's director, Philippe de Montebello—although they were well known to them and the truffled risotto was the lesser for it. The Podhoretzes were the real thing, and Norman's brain could slice any social pretension apart in less than three seconds, had he chosen to waste it that way.

Just why I so keenly wanted to be part of this lot is a mystery, although looking at it pragmatically, not. This was my shortcut to becoming "known" to restaurants and photographers, which seemed important at the time. Conrad had known Jayne for eons from Palm Beach, where he had liked talking to her husband about his exploits as a wildcatter in Texas and postwar Europe. Kissinger was a longtime idol of Conrad's and he was, to be fair, a very funny man and of course incredibly bright, although how one was to enjoy his brains at a regimen of dinner parties, restaurant gatherings, openings, premieres and so on is hard to say.

The one time dinner conversation did get serious was at the Kissingers' house in Connecticut, at a small gathering with Donald Rumsfeld in 2002, when Rumsfeld was defence secretary and the Iraq situation was heating up, with weapons of mass destruction notionally hurtling about. Rumsfeld was justifying the invasion of Iraq. The whole matter baffled me.

"As far as I can see," I remarked quietly to Henry, "all Saddam Hussein wants is to sell his oil to the West at the best price he can, be rich and have his country to himself. He's no threat to us." Henry, who was in favour of U.S. military intervention, poked his elbow into my rake-thin side, encountering a rib, and muttered *sotto voce*—as much as a dark German-accented voice can do *sotto*, "You may win the argument with that, but then we'll have no invasion." Essentially: Please shut up.

Our apartment was next door to the Candela building where Henry Kravis took his new wife, Marie-Josée, to a triplex of magnificent proportions—never publicly photographed, and decorated by Jacques Grange or François-Joseph Graf. (I tended to get these names muddled, particularly when the jeweller Laurence Graff complicated conversations.) Ours was a standard $3-million apartment that was badly in need of work, so we put another couple of million into restructuring and redecorating. We were not in competition, but on the day that Henry Kravis walked into our half-renovated apartment, I knew that however hard I tried, our place was like his staff quarters.

I had seen just a few rooms at his next-door palace when we had gone there for dinner: layer upon layer of exquisite fabric, walls covered with artwork that could have taken pride of place in any royal collection or great museum, carpets of exotic beauty, and surfaces punctuated with such decorative touches as hopelessly desirable collections of antique German Kunstkammer objects in turned ebony and ivory.

Conrad swears he told me that Henry was coming by, but I know that is a total lie because had I known, I would have been feeding pigeons in Central Park. Henry's small, natty figure gingerly stepped over the tins of paint and the crumpled drop cloths. His eye quickly took in the entire dimensions of our new home, which at 4,600 square feet was, in my mind, the ideal roomy size even if it could have comfortably fitted into just one of his reception rooms next door. Satisfied, he exchanged a few pleasantries with Conrad and left. Our London interior decorator, David Mlinaric, was doing the apartment, but I felt as if I had been caught, à la Rosie the Riveter, with paintbrush in hand, no makeup, hair in rollers and, like the apartment itself, definitely wanting.

In those heady Manhattan days, we would go to our apartment every September and October for business meetings, and if I had to be honest, I'd say this, too, played a major role in my enthusiastic joining of the Group: we got to the September openings of my favourite places—the Metropolitan Opera, Carnegie Hall, the Lincoln Center's Alice Tully Hall—with no trouble, with wonderful seats in their private boxes and, as a topper, the pièce de résistance, the place to bring out one of the gorgeous long frocks from the new season's haute couture.

Had Nancy or Annette ever "let me in"—that is, let me speak to them normally over a coffee or spend an afternoon in a park or garden—I would probably have found them interesting company and perhaps they me. Both read substantially, and Henry's travels to China must have given special insights. Annette and I were both mad animal people—but in the decade we ran around together, we never once did anything informal like that which might have brought out shared interests apart from Paris gossip about the frightful debacle at some défilé de mode. Although God knows I tried. "They really like you," Conrad would say, and I would think, Yep, and I have a bridge to sell.

The bite in the air of a sunny autumn day walking along Fifth Avenue next to Central Park never, ever tired me. When you have means, all the sores of New York are invisible. You put paper money in the upturned hats of the sidewalk flute players. When you are idle, every stranger you pass has some charm, some eccentricity, and the bumping of elbows and shoulders that would irritate if hustling to work holding coffee are simply amusing aspects of the great metropolis. You marvel that this is not a movie you are watching but life itself. In those years of New York life, the months and days leading up to the late autumn of 2003, I was through the door that led to a world of as much music, beauty and excess as I chose. The nightmare of entertaining was left behind in London.

In our first year of marriage, before we had our Manhattan apartment, Mercedes Bass had given a birthday party for Sid at an Upper East Side restaurant and choreographed it with her usual energy. We all had red T-shirts with "Sid Is the Brightest" in black lettering on the front. We did not, however, put them on. That night Conrad had a fainting spell and collapsed on the shoulder of Barbara Walters. Sitting opposite him, I heard his rasping breath and then saw the shudder as his head went backwards before he slumped into an eerie, pasty-faced unconsciousness. Oh Lord, I thought, I am about to become a widow.

Sitting in the emergency waiting room between that evening's gunshot victims with Oscar de la Renta, who had insisted on leaving the party to accompany me to the hospital—yes, he was all that the obits said, kind and generous—I was resigned to a brief memory of a happy marriage. The male nursing aide who took us back to the room in which a conscious Conrad was lying pale as a kabuki in soiled trousers looked relieved when I volunteered to clean him up. My husband had lost consciousness from the pain of passing a kidney stone.

Mercedes sent out a large framed photo of all the guests in our fancy togs and jewellery. It's really a photographic intarsia of faces snapped at the restaurant before Conrad passed out, mine pasted between Evangeline Bruce and Mica Ertegun. I have a wide smile. I know my smiles, and that one is genuine, all happy and hopeful. (I haven't managed that smile for over sixteen years now.) On the shoulder of my black dress is a 1940s brooch from Tiffany's in London, pavé and small full-cut diamonds with two lovebirds in tiny rubies, a birthday present from Conrad. The frame included cut-outs from at least one other occasion. In one headshot, Mercedes is wearing one of her huge pearl necklaces, and in another, a torsade of emeralds.

My concentration on jewels as a fulcrum for description is not accidental. For an early birthday after my marriage, two of the Group gave me four soft green suede travelling cases for jewellery from T. Anthony on Madison Avenue. I still can't decide whether this was generosity or bitchiness. They were about eight inches square and three inches deep, fitted with removable pouches and detachable rolls for rings. I'd never seen anything like them. If I had any costume jewellery to transport, it would go in plastic roll-ups from drugstores with see-through compartments.

"Tell Conrad to fill them," joked Annette de la Renta, a little tartly I thought. Jayne Wrightsman's note was gentler: "The way things are going," she wrote, "these will soon be filled. It's the only safe way to go." For some reason I thought an explanation for my lack of jewellery, which evidently had been noted by the Group, was owed. This was an unfortunate habit of mine and always resulted in far too much information being given. I didn't want them to think Conrad lacked generosity. Of course, both Jayne and Annette had their own money—Jayne from her late husband and Annette from her mother, Mrs. Charles Engelhard Jr., in both cases hundreds of millions, independent of the jewels and art they owned.

"Conrad," I pointed out defensively, "has already had to fit me out from top to bottom. I came with no dowry." Yep, I really did say that. I earnestly explained the situation as I saw it: I had come to this marriage late in life, it was my fourth, and I had arrived essentially penniless and sans jewellery. Even my clothes, and I had a lot, were inadequate for a life of gowns and tiaras and lunches at the Four Seasons and dinners at La Grenouille. My wardrobe was filled with good sportswear and a couple of cocktail dresses I adored, but the handbag and accessory thing, let alone jewels, had not entered my line of vision.

What I had were large "purses," as they were called then in Canada, misshapen from being stuffed with research and with bottoms stained with water and salt after being plonked down on wet restaurant or office floors. Evening clutch bags were not even a notion in my head, nor evening coats, jackets and stoles, nor tasteful cover-ups like the marvellous little black satin cropped jacket lent to me one frantic occasion by Marie-Josée. (Though I did come across a photo of me presenting some trophy at Toronto's Woodbine Racetrack and there I am, around 1984, standing in a black dress with spectacularly big bad hair, spotted stockings and, lo and behold, a little cropped white jacket lined with pink. Where or when I got that, I have no idea. The jacket never resurfaced.)

When I entered Manhattan's society life in 1992, my serious jewellery inventory was a Bulgari yellow gold and diamond Parentesi watch from one marriage, a yellow gold men's Bulgari watch on a black leather strap, a small pair of gold half-hoop Cartier earrings with a pavé diamond X on them, and a pair of inexpensive silvered shell earrings from Fred Leighton that David Graham had given me (after our divorce) for my fiftieth birthday. My sole luxury item of clothing was a black mink coat that I had since made into a throw for Conrad's study. I had no rings apart from a lovely plain eighteen-karat gold serpent ring from George Jonas; Conrad's Tiffany engagement ring, with its 3.5-carat diamond; and a couple of plain wedding bands. Frankly, jewellery had never much interested me.

Annette and Jayne looked blankly at me as if I were the abominable snowman while I explained my lack of adornment. Undeterred, I just had to continue. It was logorrhea. "My writing income has always been perfectly adequate for my life up till now," I said solemnly, without the codicil that it simply didn't envision balls, Fendi Alta Moda furs and stays at vacation homes with a little more complicated of an itinerary than Canada's Georgian Bay cottages or my Bournemouth days. Now it was villas in the Dominican Republic, huge ranches in Colorado and bloody palaces in Marbella, with special needs that involved authentic Navajo jewellery and large amber necklaces that were dismissed unless the beads contained perfectly trapped and fossilized flies. Then there was the cost of an extra season each year called "resort" and sometimes more specifically "cruise," demanding special jewels.

"Just bring patio jewellery," Texan philanthropist Lynn Wyatt once suggested perfectly seriously when I flailed helplessly about packing for the South of France, where she and her husband had an exquisite villa above Monte Carlo. Patio jewellery, it turned out, meant huge, perfectly spherical and polished turquoise beads alternating with full-cut diamonds. "Lily"—Safra, who owned the Villa Leopolda, alleged to be the most expensive home in the world—"has the very best turquoises," said Lynn helpfully.

Naturally, there were almost normal people at the events we attended who didn't come with jewels from S.J. Phillips on Bond

Street, owned by the Norton Brothers (the "Bandits of Bond Street," Jayne Wrightsman bantered delightfully, or accurately described by Anna Wintour in an editorial letter, "the highlight of London trip . . . especially captivating are the estate prices, those dazzling romantic reminders . . ."). Normal rich people managed perfectly well to get by without Graff's pendant earrings of twenty-carat D-flawless diamonds, but they were not on our team. They were those *other people*, out there, very nice but not really part of our set. (Though even some artsy or working members were part of this vast jewellery leap-frog.)

"Pretty, isn't it," said Diane von Fürstenberg, seated next to me at a private dinner in the Metropolitan Museum for one of their friends, organized by Anna Wintour and Annette in one of the seemingly monthly Big Dinners honouring each other. She extended her wrist delicately, turning it as her head tilted, appraising it, her face framed by that dark lustrous tightly waved hair high off her forehead. She was referring to her bracelet, which looked about three or four inches wide, of perfectly cut, seemingly flawless diamonds—round ones, ovals, pear-shaped, all exquisitely worked in together and gleaming with furious intensity. "Barry gave it to me," she explained, meaning her husband, Barry Diller. I had admired it, so she was only responding to my compliment, but in my mind (not hers), when she stuck out her wrist and looked sideways at it herself, I was reminded of the scene in *The Sopranos* when Carmela drives her new Porsche, a gift from her husband, to show it off to a glum Ginny Sack, whose cars have been lost to FBI forfeiture. Carmella's cover for showing off the car is to take Ginny away for a spa date. "Is that new?" asks Ginny, looking at the shiny SUV. "Oh, the *car*?" says Carmela offhandedly. "Yes, yes. Porsche Cayenne. Like the pepper." A gift from Tony, a gift from Barry.

Having carefully explained my situation to Annette and Jayne, an explanation that in retrospect did neither Conrad nor myself any favours, indicating that I was both unnecessarily gauche in my talk and bereft of jewellery, I was left out to dry. The only explanation could be either that Conrad was not rich enough to decorate me in haute jewellery or that we were both indifferent to the matter—either explanation being damning.

Fine, I know it's balmy to react to such exchanges that others might easily take in their stride, especially if they work at *The Guardian*, *Independent* or *Toronto Star*, but rise to it I did. If only, instead of endless rows of bottled supplements for strong nails and creams to stop acne, I had something to kill, contain or heal my acquisitiveness, competitiveness and characterlessness. Failing on all three counts, the immediate solution for me came in the form of the Avon Lady of jewellery.

Ana Cristina Alvarado had the plumage of a tropical bird, which was appropriate given that she was from Central America. She worked for Piranesi, a New York City jewellery company, and what she did was traipse between New York, Palm Beach and London visiting clients with her collection of about three hundred sample pieces. Piranesi appeared to be owned by two North African Jews, brothers who specialized in Colombian emeralds for a private clientele and had some truly gorgeous stones, but the company's work as I knew it lay in the many pieces of ready-to-wear jewellery in the middling price range, made for them by various manufacturers. Nice enough, but sometimes a little crudely set, with a machine-made feel, unlike the delicate pavé settings of a Verdura or the spun grace of Buccellati. At that time, a top piece could cost $150,000, while most pieces cost somewhere between $7,000 and $60,000. Piranesi specialized in a lot of bang for less bucks, though the brothers themselves had, in true Oriental tradition, not much respect for bric-a-brac that had little value in the stones.

My purchases fell in the $4,500 to $35,000 range, and since I was embarrassed to tell Conrad, I was forever worrying about payment. Ana Cristina's special quality—beyond her patience and knowledge—was the payment plans she devised for her clients. Her invoices were complicated by the various postdated payments, exchanges and credits she allowed clients to make.

Journalists were still being paid well in those times before the internet killed us. With my *Times* contract, my *Maclean's* columns bringing in $2,400 a piece, plus features and columns here and there in American publications, and with no rent, telephone or food bills, I had some money. I thought the pavé diamond heart earrings I bought for $35,000 were gorgeous, and, for the money, they were; the Giovane emerald drops were more so, but then with my unhappy eye I quickly realized that they were barely the jewellery equivalent of a bridge line of clothing, never mind haute couture (today anglicized to "high jewellery"). Still, I tossed my hair back to show them off and longed for the day when I could afford one of Ana Cristina's $75,000 emerald bracelets.

The rot began one day at lunch in London. We were five at Mosimann's, sitting down for a pleasant interlude. "Your earrings," said John Gutfreund, formerly chairman of Salomon Brothers; known as the "King of Wall Street," he had a year or so earlier been deposed. "Did you buy them?" He was referring to my new Giovane emerald drops. I wasn't quite sure what the best answer would be, having learned that truthfulness is often not a useful currency in such circumstances.

"Conrad bought them for me," I replied, thinking that would show his devotion together with restraint on my part.

"They're the wrong colour," said Gutfreund. His tone of voice left no room for any other interpretation than derisiveness. My inner voice said, What a nasty thing to say. But I squirmed and probably flushed—a jewellery parvenu trying for a Ritz address while staying at a Ramada Inn. "Probably a lot of oil in them and it hasn't done much good," continued John. Honestly, I waited for the loupe to appear and pulverize me. "Tell your husband to ask these two ladies," he said with a nod at his wife, Susan, opposite me, and Princess Firyal of Jordan next to her. "They know their jewellery."

I looked up this business about oil in the encyclopedia when I got home and supposed that, yes, given their price, they must have been heavily treated with oil to give them a better appearance and bring them closer to the colour of the dark green emeralds from the deepest mines of Muzo or whatever. I won't wear them anymore, I thought. I didn't stop to think that getting upset by this was something of a flaw in me slightly deeper than any fissure in my emeralds. I should have laughed, or passed Gutfreund off as an unpleasant idiot, which he clearly was, but it cut. In retrospect, it's easy to groan over what an idiot you were, but that's rather like the clever comeback that occurs to you only that evening in bed.

My jewellery eyes were opened, though. I could see that there was no ceiling, no limit to this. Should you acquire the requisite D-flawless diamond ring of at least twenty-five carats, you would be outshone by the 2.5-carat hopelessly rare red diamond or the necklace of perfectly matched pigeon's-blood unheated rubies.

Many of the more telling and brutal moments took place in Jayne Wrightsman's Fifth Avenue apartment at the little lunches she often had for a few of the Group, at which she seemed to take delight in egging people on. "Mercedes will die," she said to Annette de la Renta and Nancy Kissinger, "when she sees the new diamond Henry gave Marie-Josée. It's bigger than hers." General giggles. Some months later, we were all lunching at Jayne's on the day of a charity dinner being hosted by Evelyn Lauder for people with AIDS. The theme that year was red and black—as in Valentino, not Stendhal—and this time Annette, Nancy and Marie-Josée Kravis were seated around the table. Conrad had just given me a smashing pair of ruby and diamond earrings from Graff, which Jayne had already seen. I was in raptures over them; still am. "Red and black," said Jayne to Marie-Josée. "So you'll see Barbara's wonderful new ruby earrings tonight." My heart sunk. I could hear the thump as it cratered into my stomach. I reached for the bread. "Barbara," Jayne rebuked, "bread is not the staff of life." They all thought I weighed too much. Christ, I thought, my Graff earrings are very lovely with their almond shape and little rubies interspersed among diamonds, but in carat weight they are no match for a Kravis jewel. I knew that Marie-Josée would not hold back, and we were to be seated together that night at the same table as the Lauders.

Bingo! Marie-Josée appeared in earrings with rubies the size of pigeon eggs, never mind their glorious pigeon's-blood colour, and, inevitably, with her dead-eyed smile, she asked to see my "new ones," partly obscured by my hair. Would I have done that, I wondered, if I had Marie-Josée's wardrobe of jewels, thinking probably not. I'd wear some red or black item of clothing to follow the theme, but knowing the economic circumstances of a "friend" relative to mine, I'd leave the competing heavy ammunition at home in favour of one of the many other pairs of stupendously glorious earrings in my safe, something neutral, perhaps, like diamonds or pearls. And if I *were* wearing rubies, I certainly wouldn't flash my bigger ones and ask to see the smaller pair. Marie-Josée gave no quarter even in friendly times.

I wondered, too, about Jayne. "Tell Conrad to buy it for you," she said one day as we looked at pouches full of jewels, this time in London, from the visiting Italian jeweller Angela Pintaldi. I demurred. "Aren't they rather big?" I asked, looking at the strings of huge pearls interspersed with turquoise and amber. "Can't ever be too big," said Jayne in an ellipse of the ladies' credo "can't be too rich or too thin." Pintaldi was considered a "fun" jeweller and therefore was considered to have nothing that couldn't be purchased in multiples: bracelets to pile on, necklaces and rings galore. Strangely, I never saw any of the ladies wear these purchases. Perhaps they were for staff or nieces or just a way to spend an afternoon. Jayne is a kind and extraordinarily elegant woman, I thought, but why does she make me feel so terribly small? The fault is not in our stars but in my eye, yet sometimes I thought it might just lie in a teeny desire to see me wriggle a bit.

As my reputation as a lover of fashion grew, one or two of my British friends used me as a cover. One weekend, staying at a good friend's country home, her husband confronted me with not so mild accusations of having led his wife into "reckless extravagance, Barbara," with her recent purchases of several Pintaldi pieces. I had no idea she was a client of Angela's and I knew nothing of Angela's recent visit. Pintaldi, being of some rather social Italian family, was not unfamiliar to the British set. I sensed there was a myth being built here that was not flattering to me, but I was not quick enough to see the ramifications it would have. I made an apologetic noise and didn't give my friend away.

The curious thing is that since I didn't really "feel" the beauty of jewellery, how had it come to be a necessity? No matter how much you look "into" a stone, there isn't really that much to see. It's just a big sign of wealth. I've got mega bucks, the thing screams, even as you rhapsodize about its eternal flame or some such balderdash. There is no special beauty inside a gem, no matter how brilliantly it is cut. It's dazzling, I suppose; the colours can be vibrant or ice, but what else? I wish there was a metaphysical answer, but nothing has changed since cave days: it's status, adornment, wampum, a means to barter— or transport wealth easily across borders.

One exception: I'd kill for the jewels of the Nizams of Hyderabad. This is passionate jewellery unmatched in the world: turban sarpechs of curved erotic beauty from the Mughal dynasty; peacocks, flowers, tigers and lions worked into jade and gold bracelets; necklaces of diamonds, carved rubies and emeralds. My favourite decoration has always been the riot of Indian jewellery I bought in palmier days from London's Eileen Coyne, who would visit the bazaars and shops at Jaipur, bring back some nineteenth-century piece she'd found and make it up for me. Not terribly expensive, something like a carved jade belt buckle encrusted with semi-precious stones used in a necklace and weighing a ton, if not costing it. This was my jewellery thing, and I did that thing well.

The only time I was really put on the spot in London was with Hannah Cranborne, wife of then Viscount Cranborne—the cadet title before he became the seventh Marquess of Salisbury, the bluest of blue blood in Britain, and she the bluest of about-to-be marchionesses. We were going over for tea at their London *pied-à-terre*, and although I normally dressed simply, for some reason I had on a large (bad) emerald ring set in two trillion-cut diamonds. The minute Hannah greeted me I knew this was too flash, and at the doorway I quickly slipped it into my handbag. Her eye caught it.

"What did you put in your handbag?" she asked.

"Oh, nothing," I said, holding on to my clutch bag for dear life. Normally this would have meant, in any language, "I don't want to speak about it," but it felt like Hannah wanted to show me up for some reason.

"No, I saw you put something shiny in."

"Just a ring that was hurting me," I replied.

"Oh do let me see it. Look, Robert." She reached for my bag. "Barbara has a ring in her handbag."

This was absolutely pure bitch. She must have her reasons, I thought. Perhaps she wants Robert to give her better jewels than the wife of a tradesman like *The Telegraph*'s proprietor. I gather that Emily, Dowager Marchioness of Salisbury—Hannah's great-great-great-mother-in-law, I estimate—somewhere in the eighteenth century got into a huge row over the family jewels and refused to hand them over. When she died it was revealed that she had been selling them off to finance a high life, and what she was actually flaunting was largely paste. Anyway, who knows what motivates marchionesses? And that day, Hannah was in a mood.

The jewel theme ratcheted up stratospherically with the entrance of Joel Arthur Rosenthal into my sphere of consciousness. Known simply as Joel by the ladies of the Group, his jewellery moniker was his acronym, JAR. "He's the Cartier of our times," Henry Kravis told me, echoing the judgment of Christie's jewellery man François Curiel, adding that collecting JAR was like collecting great paintings. In this, as in so many other investment matters, Henry turned out to be dead right. "You must have some JAR," said Jayne. "Marie-Josée gets his little pink leather boxes under her pillow all the time."

My pillow had earplugs under it. Humans are like any other carnivores. When they sense vulnerability in a member of their pack, they either toy or go for the kill. Were they stalking me, I thought? Why are they forever banging on about this? The answer was that I should care far less, but that insight was years off.

Unlike just about every other jeweller in the world, Joel was said to choose his clientele rather than the other way around. I'm not entirely convinced of this, but I'll buy it as far as it goes. His rudeness was legendary, but tolerated because of the exceptional artistry of his work. His clients seemed to revel in the fact that he was nasty to other people and tolerated them.

His shop was on rue de Castiglione, a little lane off Place Vendôme next to the Paris Ritz. No name on the door, no merchandise in the curtained window. A man let me in—clearly not *the* man. He asked my name. "Mrs. de Botton said there was a necklace of pearls that I should look at." The response to this was not quite but close to supercilious. It appeared that JAR had few ready-to-wear jewels. After disappearing, the unknown shop assistant returned with a necklace—two rows of very small natural pearls with delicate pavé diamond links. Perfect understated taste, and a quality of pavé work I had never seen before. The price was US$325,000—completely out of reach.

JAR was now the Minotaur in the labyrinth, and the only ball of thread I had was what I could spin out of my work as a journalist. An exhibition of his work was coming to Somerset House in London, a distinction not unconnected, I suspect, to Jacob Rothschild, good and close friend of several JAR clients and the man largely responsible for the restoration of Somerset House itself. The opportunity for a feature piece in *The Telegraph* loomed and I told Sarah Sands I could get it. But Joel was playing hard to get. I canvassed, pulling out every name to recommend me to him. The interview was granted.

The metaphor of the Minotaur turned out to be rather apt. Joel's arresting face could only be described as having certain resemblances to the drawings of the mythical bull, with hooded half-opened eyes but no visible horns, which were, I suppose, his prices and temper. We talked and he rhapsodized at length about his work, his future and especially about his writing, an aspect of him I did not know. He sent me a portion of a manuscript, which seemed, unlike his jewellery, slightly laboured with self-conscious insights. He had gone to Harvard, and writing was the work at which he longed to excel.

The syndrome is not unfamiliar: the master surgeon wants to be a poet, the film star wants to be a writer/director, the jeweller a philosopher, the need to be other or more than what one does so well grips very hard in some, and usually in those unsuited to the desired realm.

My article was highly complimentary, but not a puff job either. "The exhibition has 400 pieces, of which perhaps close to one fifth are masterpieces. Any serious artist from Coleridge to Picasso needs a body of work to set off his truly exceptional pieces and this is Rosenthal's," I wrote, hoping that the proximity of his name to

Coleridge and Picasso might offset the following comment: "JAR does flowers in bud, flowers opening, flowers blooming—and flowers fading. The fading flowers look exactly like that—wilting and on the point of death—which may be an acquired taste." The friend who had recommended to Joel that he see me thought the article was terrific. "He'll love it," she said.

Like hell. I received a six-page handwritten letter from him that accused me of trivializing him in an article that would better have graced the gossip columns. "Banal trivia better for gutter readers and the Daily Mail. Where is the depth and insight?" he asked. Scalding criticism and disappointment from an author *manqué* really pissed off. There went my JAR in the event I ever had enough money to get a piece.

Once, later, when I attended the European Fine Art Fair in Maastricht, I spotted Joel looking intently at a tiny green diamond in a wall showcase. I followed him around the booths watching which pictures he stopped for, and one of them he lingered at and came back to several times was a small oil of a side street in Italy at sunset, the walls lit with shadows giving it a strange moody perspective like Tintoretto's *The Stealing of the Dead Body of St Mark*. I purchased it. The price was minimal and I liked it very much. The painting would be the closest thing I could ever get to that pink leather box.

CHAPTER TWELVE

The Group

I can't blame the Group for what happened to me. Each of them knew who they were, even as I vacillated between thinking I was an exceptionally sensitive person and a total fraud. But I wanted to be like them, and then I thought, No, God, no, there's more to me and why don't I just settle on becoming a sensitive transvestite or a displaced Karakachani and end this muddle. It would be extremely helpful when writing a memoir of sorts to know who exactly you are, even if you edit out the nasty bits and exaggerate the good. But I had already started another instar: changing and assuming a new shape, both physically and mentally, neither for the better. The fact is, I became a caricature of the Group. Incredibly, now that I think of it, I managed to so arrange myself that I finally flipped into that no man's land where songs like "The Windmills of Your Mind" make sense.

There we are all together: frozen in time in a photo now in one of the many coffee table books about Oscar de la Renta. New Year's Eve, 2000. Oscar draped us over a sofa in his Dominican Republic home in the manner of the famous Cecil Beaton pose: Annette, Nancy, Mercedes, Jayne and the two Barbaras all tarted up in our long gowns and the glittering paste tiaras that had decorated our dinner plates. God, I felt so glamorous and cock-a-hoop spending New Year's there with them all, in spite of the fact that my blue silk Oscar de la Renta gown was creasing like mad and shows up next to the creaseless others.

"We can't go on like this," I said to Conrad that night.

"What do you mean?" What I meant was, we were always guests—guests in the Dominican Republic, guests in the Hamptons or Connecticut, guests in their boxes at the opera or the openings of Carnegie Hall, guests at the charity tables that cost anywhere from $25,000 to $100,000 a table and the galas that came with them. We weren't giving this set any social status they recognized; they were giving it to us as far as this stratum of New York went, and we weren't even paying our way with donations or buying the odd seat. Conrad had no embarrassment. He was a bloody fish swimming in the sea of the people—billionaires or typists, he enjoyed people. "We give value," he said. I suspected that while his excellent dinner table conversation was valued by some hostesses and their guests, the shorter and richer husbands often looked peeved.

That millennium New Year's, I went as usual at a few minutes after midnight to telephone George Jonas, a call we had made each New Year's since we divorced. "Good luck, babe, let's hope for a good year," he said. He didn't tell me he had just been diagnosed with Parkinson's.

Being with the Group meant you got photoed for the *New York Times* social pages or *W* or *WWD* rather a lot, and I quite liked that. No nasty editorial stuff with it, just a photo of you and your frock. It came with baggage, though—more concern about my appearance, as if that were possible given my total immersion in myself. In Paris, my dermatomyositis hit infuriatingly, and I woke up to swollen heliotrope eyelids and the less-fashionable butterfly rash deepening on my face. That's shot it, I thought, particularly since now I knew why I was teetering on my high heels. Those god-awful inflamed muscles were giving way.

"Barbara," said the first Mrs. Bass, who I only knew by sight but who was in the Ritz elevator with me. "Is it sun or allergy?" I explained. "Let me get you something that will help temporarily," and she came back to the lobby with a tube from her dermatologist. "I always have this with me," she said. It was some prescription cream, great stuff that temporarily slowed the reddening scales and cracks until I could get back to London and a good slosh of intravenous immunoglobulin.

On our return to New York, Anne, Mrs. First Bass invited us to the ballet gala she was chairing. "I'd love to see her again and take her to lunch," I told Sid Bass. "She was so kind. I don't suppose [second Mrs. Bass] Mercedes would mind?" This, I thought, was a judicious though unnecessary enquiry. Apparently not.

"I'm afraid she would. You'll have to choose. Anne said some very unpleasant things about Mercedes." In the Mercedes ascendancy, Anne kept her lesser patronage of the ballet while Mercedes swanned at the opera. Park Avenue divorces apparently included charity splits and no-speaks territory that had to be respected by friends of each side. Madness. Still, queering Mercedes would be a major problem in the Group. So Anne Bass got put in a box, lid shut tight. What a ghastly person Mercedes is, I thought. I felt wretched caving in, but rationalized that I had enough uphill climbing in the Group without adding more ankle weights.

"Nancy asked me to tell you, once again," said my staunch husband, "that you shouldn't be so insecure. They really like you." Certainly everyone professed love for everyone in the Group. But this was American pro forma social courtesy. The rudeness was in not professing—at any opportunity, privately or out loud and emotionally, and preferably in a fulsome but joyless toast—love for every damn person with whom you interacted socially. However, I tied up my shoelaces and invited Jayne and Annette to lunch at my apartment— an agonizing prospect for me and obviously too agonizing for them. They accepted and then, on the morning of, cancelled. "So sorry, can't make it."

Still, I gushed—George Weidenfeld would have been proud of me—and played the game with enthusiasm, even when my attempts to reciprocate a season of invitations to the opera or a country house in Connecticut by sending extravagant gifts (in my terms) went unremarked or, worse, remarked:

"I gave the silver bracelets you sent me to my nieces, and they loved them," said Nancy Kissinger of the two Angela Cummings

braided silver cuffs I'd sent her after a Thanksgiving dinner. My fault
for asking if she had received them after a month of agonizing silence
and my fear that someone opened the package and thought they
were napkin rings. Did she mean she showed them to her nieces or
did she regift? Less humiliating was the dead silence I didn't break:
the crocodile wallet I had agonized over at Bergdorf's for one of the
ladies—was it too showy or was it the wrong part of the crocodile?—
and the Lana Marks gold lizard evening bags together with the Hermès
washbag for someone's husband. Both must have been received but
never commented upon, even as they profusely thanked one another
for a book on planting bulbs.

Every Christmas the gifts would arrive for me. So exquisitely
wrapped. You can't imagine the ribbons and paper and satin and silks
that were lavished on a box. None of your Hallmark and Papyrus
ready-to-wear wrap. And the boxes: papier mâché creations and gilded
cardboard. One of them could buy a hundred meals in stricken Africa,
a truism of which I was to be made acutely aware. And while I wrote a
note of thanks for Jayne's knitted sable stole from the haute couture
and the box of Manolo Blahnik shoes in absolutely my taste and size
(Lily Safra's gift), I had a feeling I just wasn't getting it right. This was
atonal dissonance on a John Cage level. Jayne can help me, I thought.
She'll have the answers and know the melodies.

Since Jayne was about twenty years older than the others and an
old friend of Conrad's, I rather looked on her as a sympathetic ally in
my new world. The straws a drowning person clutches. Jayne was the
Group's deity, an infallible source of knowledge about high-society life
as lived in the thinnest of its ozone layers. She had nothing to lose, I
reasoned, and would help a newcomer. After all, in her life before marriage to Charles B. Wrightsman she was a salesgirl, albeit with a good
private school education and at an elegant shop. She must have had to
learn the ropes herself. And I had questions, God, I had questions—
about social etiquette and practical solutions for which my self-education
in Hamilton and St. Catharines, never mind the Reuters library in
London, had not prepared me.

But I simply could never get Jayne alone for that heart-to-heart.

It was on par with arranging a private audience with the Pope. I would arrive at her apartment after we had arranged to have a little lunch or a cup of tea, "so just the two of us can have a real chat," Jayne would say, and be shown happily into one of her sitting rooms to enjoy a warm greeting from Annette. Or Nancy. One of the Group would always be there, as if a witness was needed. I could hear the telephone conversation: "Darling Annette. Barbara Black is coming over for tea today. I'm at my wits' end what to talk to her about, you know how she is. Can you come by?" All I really wanted to ask was where to find good silver antique chargers large enough to take twentieth-century dinnerware. Or where did Annette find the wonderful hurricane lamps in her Manhattan drawing room? (To this I got an answer from Annette: auctions for early eighteenth-century ones or, for flawless copies, John Rosselli on East Seventy-Third Street.)

There was one piece of invaluable advice Jayne could have given me—not the location of the best glove shop but the element that she had by now made a physical part of herself: Don't show your happiness in public. If you must, keep it very low-key. Don't talk about it. Keep it only for your lifelong close friends. She had watched me, knew my weakness, and saw I didn't understand this. Personally, I think she veered between wanting to warn me on Conrad's behalf and wanting to see where this delicious spectacle of a woman without boundaries might lead. Had she given me that advice, the wretched errors I was about to make might have been tempered. As it was, I must have been an entertaining sight, thrashing about looking for harbour, gussied up with a hook in my mouth.

Occasionally, a newer and younger woman in the Park Avenue world would ask me out, and I'd get hopeful that conversation might turn from home decor or self-decor into world decor. And it did. The young wife of a private equity CEO leaned intensely across the table at a small restaurant on the Upper East Side of Third Avenue where the two of us were lunching. She was so pretty in a natural way— quite unlike the stiffer Manhattan women I knew.

Her husband was a hands-on philanthropist and art collector who championed causes with an energy usually reserved for corralling wild horses, even while running a very successful investment fund. Their age difference probably measured about the same as their height disparity—he was six foot six and she must have been close to a foot shorter. She had brought me the loveliest set of mousseline scarves from Charvet in Paris in varying shades of pink and orange. I wondered if she went through the same agony over gifts I did.

"What do you think about Africa?" she said even before we had ordered food, so I thought it might be a new sort of salad.

I played for time. "I'm sorry. Africa?"

"I want to end world poverty," she said, "and I wondered if that would be the place to start. What do you think?"

God, I thought, I'm her intellectual Jayne Wrightsman. "I will have to think about this," I promised helplessly. There was so endearing a dewy freshness in this woman who actually wanted to end world poverty. It's a toss-up, I thought, who will eat her alive first— the New York ladies or the contemporary Idi Amins. Turns out she was far smarter than I. In due course, and as her husband became ever richer, she became chairman of the New York Public Library Board for a lengthy period and published a book not on poverty in Africa but on the spiritual significance of city parks and squares around the world.

The group's dining rooms were often the battlefields and, at first, losing a bit of blood over gold embossed Russian Imperial porcelain seemed fair enough. I did wonder who on earth did the washing-up when each of Nicholas II's dinner plates was worth tens of thousands of dollars and the big pots decorating the table, I was reliably informed by my dinner partner, were "eighteenth-century Younzheng crackleware, quite lovely and she got the pair bidding against Lily Safra for under a million. "Such shimmer went a good way at first to compensate for conversation, which reached its peak in a discussion of a new wing of some museum or the latest Stoppard play on Broadway, the opening night of which everyone had attended but they never discussed what the play actually meant. I suppose it sounds like compensatory intellectual condescension on my part but frankly the saving

grace of any dinner party anywhere—short of exposure to some rari-
fied creature like the Queen of Englnad or Mahatma Gandhi—is not
the tableware but the table talk. Scrambling for topics when I was
seated next to the inventor of the hedge fund, Henry Kravis, at some
wedding dinner, I was thrilled at his unexpected opening sally to
me, which was in reference to his wife: "Marie-Josée," he said, "has
a terrific interest in China." I plunged.

I had just been rereading *Prisoner of Mao*, the 1973 book by Bao
Ruo-Wang, and could never understand why it was not better known.
Enthusiastically, I began. Henry's French-Canadian wife was, after
all, an economist and a member of the Hudson Institute, so her inter-
est made sense. He listened with his customary politeness, and when
I had finished the first spill of enthusiasm, turned to me and squelched.
"I was referring to her interest in antique porcelain."

Never mind one's views of this group of Manhattanites, my banging on about why they didn't take me to their bosoms or hang out at
coffee shops with me requires about fifteen seconds of reflection if
your dial is set to normal. By post-fifty-five years of age, people have
their own groups of friends, shared memories and a way of life. "My
wife was dead right . . . she says life's too short to spend it in breaking
in new people," Gus Trenor announces in *The House of Mirth* when
he walks out of a lavish gathering thrown by newcomers to his circle.
Nancy and Annette probably had good chats during wellies-and-
trowel activities at their respective Connecticut homes on weekends.
Jayne had to rest in bed when she wasn't on her non-stop social calendar, needing days of serious famine to make up for any tedious but
necessary public display of appetite. As for shared interests with me,
they had either long passed or never had much in politics, policy or
even music. And all of them had, just like Wharton's Trenors, seen,
embraced and waved goodbye to many a newcomer, as indeed they
would to us.

I had read enough Edith Wharton and ought to have known what
I was facing. Little had changed, including the backbiting. The opera
had moved to Lincoln Center, the holiday homes were more fashionable in the Hamptons than Newport, and it was just possible to live

downtown if you were a one-off like Anna Wintour or a filthy rich and truly accomplished bohemian like Diane von Fürstenberg. Still, the possession of an opera box in the Grand Tier ruled. The homes, the dressmakers, the carefully curated conversations on appropriate topics with appropriate behaviour at dinner tables remained fenced in by unspoken rules.

Though clearly I was no *House of Mirth* Lily Bart trying to pay my dress bills for Fifth Avenue parties on modest means, nor *Custom of the Country* Undine Spragg trying to break in from a small-town Apex background, I shared aspects of both fictional characters, and just as Lily and Undine would crash in different ways, I met the Park Avenue wall of silence, the *omertà* of a group who had staked out their territory over several decades of proven sustainability and knew that "new" people might turn out to be fireflies of only a season or two. Why give away precious tips and inside knowledge unnecessarily?

Being a trophy wife—which I sidled up to, although I failed on a number of key counts such as age—obviously predicates a trophy husband, and they could vary by shape and size but not wealth, which at that point required a basic few hundreds of millions. Many of them were experienced in polishing up the second or third wife to the top-tier level. Conrad was a dead loss at this game. But I got word that the most valuable ally in maintaining trophy looks was the New York cosmetic dermatologist Dr. Patricia Wexler.

Pat Wexler was at the cutting edge of everything. In the 1990s she sucked out fat from my behind, after pinching me all over and lamenting that I had very little fat to give, while I lamented that my behind was the one place I didn't want to give it up. This fat was spun and then injected into my face, usually to fill in under my eyes, where I never had bags, only sunken pockets, and at the bottom edges of the face where bone deteriorates. The look was amazing, except I had an unfortunate proclivity to bruise. I would spend unsuccessful hours with zippered nylon LeSportsac bags full of little pots of Kevyn Aucoin concealer mixed to mimic my skin colour, which fooled no one—the bruise just looked yellow and could last for two weeks in spite of laser therapy to break it up.

On returning to London feeling very "refreshed" after a successful Wexler pit-stop and being gaily greeted by all, I had the misfortune to encounter Jacob Rothschild at some large gathering. Jacob, who had dismissed me earlier as "too serious," now had a new brief. "You look," he said, peering quizzically at my face full of my behind, "completely different. What have you done?"

True, most middle-aged American women that Jacob encountered (read "rich," because the only middle-aged women Jacob would have bothered noticing were the ones that could give money to the various charities he headed) were transforming themselves alarmingly with extreme plastic surgery. I stood his remark out defiantly—after all, I had not had plastic surgery—and turned the query back on him with a syrupy enquiry about his own health, implying he looked a little "tired." In fact, Wexler is an artist who would not permit her patients to overdo it. "No trout lips," she would say as I begged her for the sultry look of the time. "Your own lips are just fine. And we don't need chipmunk cheeks," she would narrate, syringe in hand, poised above my sunken eye sockets. God, the pain was excruciating.

I liked Wexler on a personal level very much, her American matchstick-thin legs crossed and her blue eyes peering out from under her dark red Louise Brooks bob, but our politics rarely coincided. Her heartfelt repulsion about the election of the "crooked" Donald Trump—well founded, she thought, in light of her personal experience with his former wife Marla Maples, the details of which, infuriatingly, she would not disclose—were sufficiently strong that I could see the possibility of any exchange of political views upsetting her to the point of some momentary wrist tremor translating into giving me a Quasimodo face.

"I hope you're all Republicans," Ronald Reagan famously said as he went into surgery after the assassination attempt. For a few hours, as Pat Wexler's needles twisted into my face, I became a Hillary Democrat. For the services of Pat Wexler, I'd sing the praises of Glorious General Who Descended from Heaven and the Great Sun of Life Kim Jong-il.

Thinness crept up on me. Perhaps it was the mimicking of the Group's attitude to bread, butter and desserts—items that were the outer circle of hell and never to pass lips—while salads, which I personally hated, were rejoiced over and anything gratinéed or sauced (always on the side anyway) declined. Slimness was a product of "sensible eating" (hah!)—also known as taking diet pills—and, of course, one's "fast metabolism," a favourite phrase of the obscenely thin who are either starving themselves or purging between courses in their scented (with Manuel Canovas Palais d'Eté candles) bathrooms. I went native symbiotically by just not eating much, and very soon I too was on target to becoming a Tom Wolfe social X-ray.

"Don't ever lose your cleavage," Oscar had said to me on our first visit to the Dominican Republic, long before that millennial New Year's. I was climbing out of his swimming pool in my Liza Bruce swimsuit, white, partly transparent like Elizabeth Taylor's in *Suddenly, Last Summer*. I had no idea what he was talking about—how could you "lose" your cleavage? The gimlet-eyed ladies, sitting poolside in their caftans or white trousers, said nothing as I grasped the stairs and clambered out. And only a year later the plump cleavage had gone, together with one-third of my body weight, and I was still a whale compared to Annette or Jayne.

Like the poses in a daguerreotype or a series of vivid *tableaux vivants*, the memory of those women standing in one another's homes, just out of my reach, remains locked behind my eyes. All around them the proof of their status: eighteenth-century cabinets of sycamore and satinwood marquetry, the rich colours of carpets from Doris Blau's emporium, chairs and sofas upholstered in silks from worms fed exclusively on mulberry leaves, an inlaid mother-of-pearl games table with its exquisite cabriole legs. And the legs of the women next to these symbols, always thin as my grandmother knew, standing like storks in slender black high-heeled shoes of classic simplicity, all so proper in their gaiety, so confident, so sure. So little-black-dresses and large matched South Sea silver-white pearls together with splendid art deco necklaces from Boivin, Fouquet and Cartier. I knew they were flesh and blood, but I couldn't see those legs ever standing in movie lineups or exiting a taxi. Limousine legs. Though I had spent as much money as many of them on my appearance, their poise could not be bought.

But this constellation, so plotted and chased by me, was well on the way to irrelevance and extinction, without visible achievement. Many of the socialites were second or third wives, and they were childless. The Group would live on for a while, their names purchased, endowed and inscribed in museums, hospitals and opera houses or on the labels of the clothes companies they had built like Carolina Herrera and Oscar de la Renta. But endowments run out, companies are sold. In time they would be replaced by bigger donors, or the buildings would see the fate of Ozymandias.

Some names would continue on through children from previous marriages. Members from South America with part-time residences in the few chosen blocks along Park and Fifth avenues seemed more likely to have offspring equipped and determined to carry on the elegance of their families—the Cisneroses, de Ravenels, Santa Domingos, and the sons and daughters of the U.K. aristocrats who had dropped in and out of the Group's dinners in the ritzy co-ops and charity balls of New York, as well as seemingly imperishable names like the Gettys and Rothschilds. Like their parents, they would create beautiful homes and exquisite, if smaller, gardens. Their expensive dressing would continue but we preferred a pared down simplicity rather than the escalating ornaments of the billionaire nouveau riche. The focus of their philanthropy would move from the arts to a smorgasbord of ecological issues— climate change, clean water, the endangered species of the animal world—often highly commendable and in keeping with disengagement from the "elitist" worlds of arts such as opera, ballet, and music.

But all around the group I knew, celebrity culture was taking over, and whatever else film stars and reality show superstars possessed, little time was spent contemplating the fine arts of living or manners. The sway of the Group was virtually over, although, just like the Romanoffs, they would never realize it until the end. Still, like Plato's prisoners in the cave seeing only shadows of the world outside, they had no desire to escape and no realization that they were chained. And I had manacled myself to them.

CHAPTER THIRTEEN

The Telegraph Gauntlet

We had agreed. After our marriage, I could continue to work for Rupert Murdoch at the *Sunday Times*. I was about as close to happy there as any columnist could be, which is to say I was not quite suicidal once a week when trying to think of a bloody column topic. I may be considered unbalanced or just masochistic, which I absolutely am not—well, maybe slightly—but I really liked working for editor Andrew Neil. He kept sending me on assignments for which I was so clearly unsuited that writing and reporting became a challenge again, and I was a happy nervous wreck. Then, in 1993, the price war between *The Telegraph* and Murdoch's News Corp began. Murdoch was confidently predicting to all who would listen—a very large and densely packed hall—that only three London broadsheets would survive his attack and *The Telegraph* would not be among them.

"I'm sorry, Barbara," Conrad had said in his extremely serious voice that means I will brook no dissent, "but you simply can't keep working at the *Sunday Times*." I had been working there before our marriage and kept on even after the price war began. But one of Murdoch's tactics was to offer *The Telegraph*'s best writers rich contracts to get them to defect. "It will not set a good example for our people."

"I've been doing a column there for over twenty-five years," I whinged. "You know *The Guardian* and *The Independent* would rather

I'd been drowned at birth, and as far as *The Mail*, *The Sun* and the *Evening Standard* go, well, I'm not a tabloid writer." This was not entirely true. Tony O'Reilly, who I liked enormously, had bought a share of *The Independent* and, on a stay with him and his wife Chryss Goulandris in Ireland, had told me that if ever I left the *Sunday Times* he would see that I got a job at *The Independent*. Being shoehorned into a newspaper that way is definitely not ideal, and I had a strong inkling that the editor, Ian Hargreaves, although a cypher to me, would not take kindly to such a matter. "Anyway," I told my husband, "Max won't want me at *The Telegraph*."

"Oh yes he will," said Conrad firmly. I feared the worst.

Max and I met in a hotel tea room. I believe it took place in Claridge's, except I was so uneasy it could have been the Sheraton Skyline at Heathrow. It was clear he had been sent there against his own better judgment by "the Chairman," as he regularly referred to Conrad when not calling him "Proprietor."

Hastings was everything I feared: the nearly seven-foot-tall hunting and shooting Englishman who spoke in a way I had trouble understanding because words stuck somewhere between his throat, back of mouth and sardonic smile. He had both a vocabulary and British references that were utterly unknown to me. I knew he was an excellent editor, military specialist and reporter, and a writer of considerable merit in his own right. He also had a special mocking air for anything that was a bit off. I was a bit off. Ever since Conrad had got *The Telegraph* to run a photo of me in 1987, when I was working for Murdoch and won a Women of Distinction award, Max had been distinctly suspicious of Conrad's personal interest in me, and our marriage of course confirmed that.

We had a cup of tea brought and tried to converse.

"Erm, the Proprietor suggested we talk," said Max unhelpfully.

"Erm, yes," I answered. This was always my default position. When in the presence of adversaries or foreigners, I automatically fell into the rhythm of their language. Max gave me a semi-sardonic smile.

"You are coming to us, I gather?"

My move. I was petrified I was back on the target range and arrows were about to whiz by my head. Max would now discuss some white paper or debate in the House of Lords that I might have missed and delight in mentioning, "by the way" to Conrad, that I still had some work to do catching up on my new home—as if I had stepped out of the Kalahari Desert on my first visit to a big city. I had come a cropper on this a few years earlier when being interviewed by the CEO of *The Telegraph*, Andrew Knight, a very feline man with retractable claws. At Conrad's suggestion, long before we were married and even before I had a column at *The Times*, Knight saw me about a job, and in an absolutely horrible exchange he asked me my view on some education bill or political dispute being debated in the House of Commons. I could not answer and had done a wobble. He seemed very pleased by that, and out came the claws as he followed up with more smiling questions.

I gave up my column in the *Sunday Times* around August 1994, very reluctantly and unhappily, doing only a couple of odd jobs for them afterwards. Shortly after our encounter, Max left the *Daily Telegraph* for a tabloid newspaper in a rather shabby series of events: Conrad had worked hard to keep Max, whose qualities as an editor he never doubted, including negotiating at Max's behest a super-enriched contract with special provisions to help the tax aspects of Max's ongoing divorce—unaware that at the very same time Max had agreed to go to the *Evening Standard*. This was not the best side of Max. He was certain Murdoch was going to win the price war, the strain of the newspaper battle was nerve-racking (one *Telegraph* executive succumbed to a stroke, another to nervous breakdown) and Max's military prowess notwithstanding, he had no taste for sinking ships, especially ones off Canary Wharf in the Docklands: captain off the boat first, passengers be damned.

After doing a couple of book reviews for *The Telegraph*, I got a column under the editorship of Charles Moore (Eton, Trinity College, grandson of Bt. Sir Alan Hilary Moore; significance of these credentials to come). The pluses of working at *The Telegraph* were not evident to me. At Murdoch's papers, after my marriage, while I had put up with some critics of my columns labelling me as nothing more than a rich and spoiled society woman, at least I had been safe from the stocks reserved for nepotistic writers who got their jobs only because they were married to the proprietor. That protection gone, the buns were hurled at me. And it was a horrible position for Charles Moore: he couldn't fire me, he couldn't treat me as a normal columnist (though he did his best) and he was stuck with me knee-deep in cement. Of course I felt like a bitch, but writing came first.

There was a further handicap: at *The Times* and *Sunday Times*, my position on the Middle East and Israel was not a contentious one. At *The Telegraph* the ambience was, to put it mildly, very different, and I was, to a few of the journalists and several of the more senior editorial people on the managing side, a veritable Jud Süss. I really felt sometimes that they were (mentally at least) swinging incense after I telephoned—never mind appeared in person—just to cleanse the air. Conrad's support of an Anglo-American alliance was well known and bad enough, but his support of Israel was positively smelly. God, he even owned the *Jerusalem Post*, which had been taken from a proper left-wing Peace Now (at any cost) newspaper to a supporter of two states but with secure borders for Israel. And horror of horrors, he was a personal friend of Benjamin Netanyahu. Though he had been writing supportively of Israel for years before we met, now it was put down to the ravings of his mad "Zionist" wife. That was a problem in the making that, as years went by, only increased.

With a blind optimism unusual for me, I hoped to make friends with colleagues at the paper: I was particularly fond of Sarah Sands, the deputy editor to Charles Moore. Sarah was witty and a very talented writer of the colourful gossip and popular arts sort. Around the paper, she and the intellectual Moore were known as the Actress and the Clergyman. This notion of a friendship was one of my more delusionary ideas: apart from close friend Miriam Gross, who I had known before my romance with Conrad, the idea of a proprietor's wife being a real friend of any *Telegraph* employee was madness. How could any journalist at the paper pal around with me and speak frankly or joke or be sarcastic about their working life? They couldn't, which excised about 90 per cent of conversation. And if they did spend any time with me outside the paper, they became tainted as someone playing up to the proprietor's wife. I suppose I thought I could be like some student prince and whip off the costume of royalty and go incognito to drink beer with fellow students. The trouble is, crossing over from the editorial floor to the executive one after years of being a journalist goes against the grain: you don't feel as others see you.

Sarah tried, in her way. "I'm going to have a drink with John Malkovich at the Savoy," she said in an after-work telephone call. "He'd like to meet you." Puddings and chocolate biscuits! Malkovich loomed large in my dark matter, and I was excited as hell. Also, might this be an actual overture of friendship from Sarah?

Quick dash to bathroom to tart up my hair. Being an avid glossy-mag reader when not poring over Proust, I'd just read a piece about ways to give a limp hairdo "quick bounce and volume." Thus, I enthusiastically rolled up a chunk of hair, framing my face in a long-handled round brush, and sprayed it heavily to create those becoming waves the magazine promised me. Unfortunately, the magazine had neglected to warn about the life-and-death situation faced if using a brush with natural bristles. My hair wound easily on the brush—but would not unwind. The tangle was sealed for life. A difficult choice awaited. I could leave the entire brush in with the long handle simply a projectile coming out of my forehead and get to the Savoy. Or . . .

It was too late to go to a salon and have it removed professionally, so after about thirty-five minutes of struggle, the lure of Malkovich won. I had to cut the brush free right at the front of my hairline and part, leaving a line of exposed skin on the top of my head that I first tried to camouflage with permanent marker but resorted to a combination of that and shoe polish. The brush with the attached seven inches of hair went into a plastic bag so that I could show them tangible evidence for my lateness.

After arriving at the Savoy and anxiously wittering about the cause for my delay in slightly breathless detail and apologizing, I pulled the hairbrush with its fringe out of my handbag. It must have

been like the moment when the head is pulled out of a basket after
an execution, except fortunately there was no blood dripping from
the brush—only my tresses. Sarah smiled. Malkovich seemed not
to understand.

I turned sixty that December. In late November, we sat in the small
dining room in London going through the usual post-dinner ritual
of "must-do" vanilla files: lists of messages and tasks. Would I appear
on the BBC show *You and Yours*? Sounded ominous. Could I debate
at the Oxford Union? Not on your life. A publisher wanted to talk
to me about doing a book on the relationship between America and
the Middle East. A lifetime's topic, I thought. The butlers were quar-
relling over shifts. Linens had to be chosen for the Palm Beach house,
and Sotheby's was having a furniture auction with two pieces our
decorator thought would be "splendid" for the downstairs loggia.
I threw in the towel after reading a request from the BBC to appear
on a program with the call-in question "Are American lives more
important than Afghans?"—one of the up-to-date BBC formulations of the "When did you stop beating your wife?" sort.

"I need a chocolate biscuit and tea."

"Just one more," said Conrad, and handed me a largish brown
envelope.

"Not the bloody hurricane insurance from Palm Beach again."
I was in a battle over certification for our ocean-facing windows.
"Please, later. They have pages of god-awful questions that I can
never answer fully enough for them."

I opened the envelope with one of my small moans of exaspera-
tion, well honed after three husbands. In it was a small lump of tissue
paper and a black Graff box. Unwrapped, it was a diamond ring with
a GIA certificate confirming that this was a D-flawless twenty-seven-
carat diamond. "An advance birthday present," said my husband.
"Wear it with the ladies." Just like that. More fun, I think, than under
the pillow.

On my actual birthday we were in New York. "We're going out
to dinner at La Grenouille," said Conrad. Very posh, I thought, for a

birthday dinner. I loved the place and had formed a close attachment ever since a Donna Karan crocheted sequined jacket of mine had attached itself to the maître d's jacket in one of the very narrow pathways between tables in the jammed room. We were, for an agonizingly embarrassing few minutes, Siamese twins *en face*, while diners, including comedienne Joan Rivers, watched our pantomime as we tried to separate my loops of silk crochet and sequins that had encircled his buttons and breast pocket pen. Eventually, scissors were required.

As we arrived this time, I saw Nancy and Henry Kissinger hurrying in ahead of us. She was wearing a long frock. "Something must be on," I told Conrad, slightly miffed that we weren't going. The entrance to Grenouille is quite small. Nancy and Henry were being ushered upstairs. So were we. "They're here for your birthday," said Conrad jovially, who appeared not to know after nearly ten years of marriage my aversion to anything resembling a dinner party for me—something I had skilfully avoided in the "we love you" rotating dinners of Manhattan society.

I was not certain the party was really for me, given that the seat of honour on my right was filled by Donald Trump—a man I had never met before but to whom Conrad was trying to sell the Sun-Times Building in Chicago. (He did.) On my other side was Henry Kissinger in dual capacity as my friend and a Hollinger director. He and Trump talked happily over me. I knew at least two-thirds of the people there, but I'm not sure they all would have been my birthday party choices: most of my London friends—the Keswicks, Miriam Gross and the Pryce-Joneses—were missing.

Conrad's happy indifference to the nuances of New York social life and their marital gymnastics was apparent in his seating arrangement, as ex-wives and new wives sat facing one another looking slightly frozen. Nothing compared to the daggers between editors Anna Wintour and Tina Brown, who were embroiled in some battle that neither of them will now remember but at the time made the handy sightlines Conrad had organized between them akin to a high-voltage electric fence.

I had one previous birthday party in my life, my seventh birthday, when I tore my ear on a rose bush in our Hendon garden playing Murder in the Dark. Fifty-three years later I was overwhelmed—if underdressed, since the invitation specified black tie and it had been followed with a vengeance. Sadly, not knowing the nature of the evening, my huge ring was at home. "Underdressed," you understand, translates into the most understated little black dress by Chanel Haute Couture that ought to have cost about one-twentieth of the price I'd paid and probably cost one-fiftieth to make.

The shock of this assembly—and there they were, Annabelle Weidenfeld, Nancy, Annette, Mercedes and Jayne among the guests—both unnerved and moved me. I stood rooted next to a large potted plant, its foliage providing temporary camouflage, and looked down at this bevy in evening gowns apparently assembled in my honour and started to cry. "Oh, for heaven's sake," said Annette crossly, and I stopped. I wondered if she could even count up the number of dinners and parties in her honour.

Conrad gave the most incredibly embarrassing and fulsome encomium about me, and as it continued past five and then ten minutes, I could see the shifting in seats and the eyes that turned from his face and began to focus with uncommon interest on place settings. A soprano and tenor from the Metropolitan Opera sung the duet from *Samson and Delilah* where she seduces Samson in order to learn the secret of his strength and betray him to the Philistines. A favourite aria of mine, though perhaps not the best choice metaphorically speaking. Out of the corner of my eye, I could see Henry and Marie-Josée Kravis, who had arrived late and were sitting on a wall banquette exchanging eyebrow-raising glances.

Women's Wear Daily ran a large photo of me, and the society columnist Suzy (Aileen Mehle) gave the party two columns, publishing most of the guest list. Lists were now part of our lives. Best Dressed lists, Most Influential Political Hostess lists, Best Parties, Most Wanted Guests, Power Couples, Media Power Couples, the *Sunday Times* Rich List. Junk, because while some of the names heading the lists had a passing relationship to reality, others were clearly arbitrary notions drummed up in an editorial meeting according to the needs of the magazine or its editors. Photos of us at various events appeared regularly in newspapers in the U.K. often accompanied with fair-to-snide comments, in New York papers with generally admiring comments, and in Canada with semi-fawning comments so long as Conrad remained a presence in the print biz. The *Toronto Star* played the role of Caesar's slave, reminding us not only of our mortality but also of our flat feet and various evils.

In spite of my knowing that such lists had utterly nothing to do with real accomplishment, only the throw-your-idea-in-the-hat atmosphere of an editorial conference, and meant as much as a list of the best ice creams or the newest restaurants—probably less—it still felt a little heady, not quite those clouds riding overhead that you had looked at as a child but a pleasant breeze just beyond the reach of most earthlings. "Don't be ridiculous," says Meryl Streep playing Anna Wintour in *The Devil Wears Prada*, when her assistant Andy (Anne Hathaway) hesitates at following her celebrity-career path. "Everybody wants to be us." I had a bit of that feeling.

We were now to be painted for London's National Portrait Gallery. Conrad already had a rather handsome photograph of him there. Our portrait was to be done by India Jane Birley and involved a lot of going to the Abbey Road area in St. John's Wood. The result was a rather odd facsimile of Grant Wood's *American Gothic* sans the pitchfork but definitely with the woman's pinched and grumpy look. There was a frightfully embarrassing dinner hosted by the chairman of the gallery at that time, Henry Keswick, at which the painting was unveiled. Its presence did not help appetites, nor did the *sotto voce* comments that burbled along underneath pro forma words of admiration. I wondered, vaguely, whether this was how India Jane saw us or if she was simply bored and spoofing on the assignment.

And the parade went on: our Kensington house, more or less finally furnished, was featured in the decorator's pornography magazine, *Architectural Digest*, though we kept our names and faces out of it. The coverage was important to our interior decorator, David Mlinaric, who I think was making an American push. After the photographers got through with staging, I could have sworn that our drawing rooms looked almost Fifth Avenue, so long as you didn't look for the Boulle, Klimt and bejewelled Fabergé snuff boxes. We did manage a Tabriz carpet and eighteenth-century Chinese leather screens. And of course we had the bloody "Napoleon chairs," as I called them.

"They're far too big and must have cost a fortune," I complained of the Empire furniture suite, noting with some panic that the set came from the stratospherically priced Paris antique dealer Aveline. "Why would we want them?" The two sofas and four chairs featured the most voluptuous gilded caryatides and ought to have been in the gallery or enfilade of some great palace.

"Do you have any idea who sat on these?" my husband said incredulously. With that question I knew I was dead. Turned out the bottoms of Cardinal Consalvi, Talleyrand, Pius VII and Napoleon himself had sat on them.

"How do you know?" I countered, even as I knew this was an approach any removal plans of mine could never survive.

"It's all documented by Aveline. They furnished the room in which Napoleon and the Catholic church signed the Concordat of 1801 and then went from the Château de Marbeuf to Joseph Bonaparte, King of Spain, and thence to Marshal Suchet." What can you say after that? Bottoms, after all, matter.

As the new millennium rolled on, the hostility towards me among the small but vocal-in-corners group at *The Telegraph* could be charted in direct relationship to the increasing hostility towards Israel—on the face of it a wacko notion, but true. Terror acts by Islamic extremists were still being attributed to the Israeli-Palestinian dispute, which was a providential coincidence for those who disliked me and my writings on the issue. My instinct to avoid working at *The Telegraph* had been correct, but once I was there I did my best.

Readers' letters were heavy and largely positive. Though my marital status protected me and Charles Moore was supportive and very decent, I knew there were poisonous pockets of dislike at the paper. I couldn't really put my finger on it—after all, one couldn't expect to be loved or liked—but there were not so subtle references to how my political views on the Middle East were going down with *Telegraph* journalists. It struck me as bizarre that my politics were translated into such personal dislike: after all, I rather admired some of the people whose politics were utterly opposite to mine. Perhaps this was just what we now call fake journalism, designed by competitors to upset matters at the paper, and really I wasn't the evil cuckoo in the *Telegraph* nest. I couldn't exactly do a poll of attitudes, so I decided to go to the paper's emblematic staffer, the legendary Bill Deedes. Could we have a cup of tea, I asked.

William Francis Deedes, Baron Deedes, KBE, MC, PC, combined a number of qualities of the British in one package, and although I barely knew him apart from a nodding acquaintance through his son Jeremy, who also worked at *The Telegraph* as its managing director, I was hopeful of his blessing—though God knows why. Deedes belonged to a particular group of Englishmen whose lineage included at least three of, choose 'em, such attributes as a public school education, family peerage (generally minor), upbringing by nannies (in Deedes's case it was a butler), strong Conservative Party connections (in this, Deedes was an overachiever, having three hundred years of a Deedes sitting in Parliament and he himself having been a minister in the Macmillan government even while editor of *The Telegraph*) and a distinct reserve when outside their own group. One instinctively knew such a type would not like anyone from across the Atlantic unless perhaps they were old-family New Englanders.

But all the same, Bill Deedes was a seminal figure at the paper, highly regarded, said to be at least part of the model for the infelicitous reporter William Boot in Evelyn Waugh's satirical novel *Scoop*, presumably the result of the encounters between Waugh and Deedes when both were covering the 1937 war in Abyssinia. Now in his mid-eighties, his extraordinary fortitude as a journalist covering stories in places as remote as Africa and his friendship with the late sentimental and very un-British Princess Diana led me to hope he might be a rather mellower specimen of his class. And since he was very much in the loop, I thought he might explain what the difficulty was.

The point was, Deedes had in his gift the power to bestow the paper's Good Housekeeping Seal of Approval on me. In truth, I thought Deedes would see that I was a "likeable" enough person, not a pushy North American Jewish woman who had married the proprietor and was now trying to interfere with the editorial thrust of the paper's Middle East reportage. His uncle, after all, had been Brigadier-General Sir Wyndham Henry Deedes, after whom a street in Jerusalem is named in honour of his fair-minded work in the British Mandate for Palestine, and Bill had lived with him for five years.

Mildly confident that sympathetic help was at hand, I set out for the Stafford hotel in St. James's, which was his choice. I had never been there, and the dark polished doors and slight gloom of the lobby gave me pause. This was not the corporate comfort of the Inn on the Park, nor the cozy atmosphere of Deedes's favourite haunt, Paradiso e Inferno, a not inappropriate name for our meeting, as it turned out.

Deedes was a thin, spry man whose face at his advanced age was made up of sharp bones, rather like a refined edition of Malcolm Muggeridge's cranium. We sat on a sofa with the tea in front of us. I saw no point in beating about the bush. "Do you think," I said, "that it is wise for me to be working at *The Telegraph*? I do sense some unhappiness about it." I had given hostage to fortune and was hoisted on my own petard by Deedes's unexpected answer.

"Yes," he said. "I think you should leave."

The punch in the stomach was short and swift. I had gambled on a direct approach and lost. "But where would I go?" I replied. "I have to keep writing, and Murdoch's papers are out and *The Independent* and *Guardian* are left-wing and wouldn't have me."

"Have you actually tried *The Independent*?" the fruit of England's loins replied. "Your columns are well read. Anyway, I see you've been writing for the *Evening Standard*. Why don't you go to Veronica Wadley?" He lifted his glass of water and sipped it, his pale eyes not exactly focused on my face but looking over my shoulder to the middle distance. "You see," he continued while glancing away from me, "it is not in the interests of *The Telegraph* to have the wife of the proprietor on its pages. This presents a problem for your editors and colleagues." No quarter asked, no quarter given. He seemed carved in blue ice, with an aura of frosty English integrity hovering over his skeletal face. He never once looked at me directly during our conversation, fearing, I suppose, that he would turn to salt. Social distancing was part of his genetic make-up. Come the COVID-19 hysteria and he would need no dots on the floor, no instructions about two meters apart. We were, if not quite invisible, subterranean dwellers. Troglodytes.

Well that's put pot to it, I thought. Clearly no success in my likeability offensive, all that bonhomie and my working at being ordinary insofar as my marriage would allow. I had been delusionary. The world may have seemed to be my oyster, but as Mr. Wilde might remark, I had used the wrong fork.

There was a coda to this unpleasant, colder-than-liquid-air meeting, which I would only learn about years later. In 2007, Bill Deedes died, and his authorized biography, *The Remarkable Lives of Bill Deedes*, by Stephen Robinson, was published, although I didn't read it until a decade later. Deedes had made its publication conditional on his death for reasons that became apparent. One of Bill's many lives involved a twilight relationship with a colleague at the newspaper over fifty years younger than himself. In 1994, at the suggestion of Max Hastings's deputy editor, the eighty-year-old Deedes had been paired up with a new writer, Victoria Combe, a graduate of Cambridge and, at twenty-seven, decidedly good-looking.

Victoria had not yet got a permanent job at *The Telegraph*, but with Deedes's ardent mentoring, she soon did. A warm friendship developed that resulted, according to Robinson's book, in some animosity around the newspaper as Victoria garnered more attention and opportunities than more experienced colleagues. Deedes and Combe travelled together extensively, and whatever the nature of their relationship—more likely unchaste in Deedes's imaginings and purely chaste, if somewhat opportune, in Victoria's behaviour— it kept Deedes busy at work for several years, including the last, difficult ones, when his wife was dying of cancer. Deedes's marriage split, and his children resented the time and care he gave Victoria.

The old bugger, I thought. Just how helpful was his little pas de deux with Victoria for "the interests of *The Telegraph*"? Manners are the hypocrisy of a nation, said Balzac, and the English have very good manners indeed.

CHAPTER FOURTEEN

The Bloody Anti-Semitism Chapter

It's hard to be objective about why people who don't know you dislike you. A man who claimed to have edited me at *The Times*, though I didn't recognize his name, told a profile writer that I "simpered" when turning my copy in; another told an interviewer that I once edited my copy while resting my breasts on his shoulder. Some feat, given that every column of mine was edited by telephone, fax or email, so perhaps he had a post-natal weaning thing about mammaries. Before my marriage and then our troubles, editors pretty much told me I was pleasant to work with. Still, the intensity of loathing that Conrad and I evoked played a crucial role in our story. Had the media firestorm not been so destructive, the facts might not have been so obscured. But hey, you live high by the media, you die low by it.

In the U.K., the strongest animosity was roused by my support of Israel, which was a real shocker to me. I came home to London in 1984 full of the gung-ho assumptions I had been taught since a young girl about the British character: a people and society of fair play, built on a scaffolding made up of such general truths as the Magna Carta, Blackstone's ratio, Dicey's parliamentary sovereignty, the playing fields of Eton and the Marquess of Queensberry rules. I was brainwashed with this before I was twelve years old. Later, I added George Orwell's view of England—hypocrisy and class distinctions, yes, but "No party rallies, no Youth Movements, no coloured shirts, no Jew-baiting or 'spontaneous' demonstrations," he wrote. And I believed all this rot and had absolutely no idea that it would not apply to Jews in Britain who supported Israel.

In Canada, my opinions on the Palestinian-Israeli dispute were fairly unremarkable and even popular with a lot of readers, but in Britain they were rat poison. In return, I quickly understood that rat poison was what I would get back. Sadly, a lot of the time the poison was dispensed by people who were accomplished, decent and the sort you'd like to spend an evening with—if only they were not anti-Semites. Murderers, cannibals and terrorists are regarded with more sympathy in large swathes of the U.K. elites and media community than the media supporters of Israel, although come to think of it, if you are identified as a Zionist, you are considered to have committed at least two out of three of those crimes by proxy.

I never thought I was a Zionist. If I'd been asked before the creation of Israel in 1948, I would have said that creating a lifeboat for Jews in the middle of the Arab world was potty, a contradiction in terms. No matter our five-thousand-year link with the area. Never mind our chant "Next year in Jerusalem." Don't go there, I would have said—that's no safe haven no matter how good we are at growing tomatoes in sand. "A land without a people for a people without a land" became an early Zionist view. Well, there was no Palestinian state. But there were people.

Actually, not to give a history lesson here (though I will), but "Palestine," the biblical home of the Jews, was until the twentieth century ruled by the Turks as part of the Ottoman Empire. Arabs and Jews living there were subjects of Sultan Abdul Hamid II. And it's not a total stretch to blame the French, just a little, for today's Israeli-Palestinian conflict. The Hungarian-born playwright who covered the Paris trial of the French officer Alfred Dreyfus for a Viennese newspaper was, like Dreyfus, a highly assimilated Jew, by the name of Theodor Herzl. After watching an innocent Dreyfus convicted, Herzl had a revelation: praying "Next year in Jerusalem" at the end of Passover seders wasn't going to be enough. Political Zionism was born with his 1896 pamphlet, *The Jewish State*.

Herzl tried to get money from the Rothschilds to buy Palestine from the Turks—people did actually think about buying countries back then—and failed, just as Donald Trump couldn't get the Danes to help him buy Greenland. After the Ottoman Empire was defeated and the Turks went home, the great powers played really bad chess over the Middle East. As various bits of desert were split up, the British Balfour Declaration, of 1917, promised "a national home for the Jewish people," and in the very same sentence told the Palestinians that "nothing shall be done which may prejudice the civil and religious rights of existing non-Jewish communities in Palestine." There you have it—selling the same piece of real estate twice. Or in the words of my former husband George Jonas, with whom I never tired of discussing this subject because his views were so much more temperate and informed than mine, Palestine became the Twice-Promised Land.

The Jews were more flexible than the Arabs about accepting any deal for a homeland, probably because we were getting bored with evictions, ghettoes, pogroms, gas chambers, and generally nasty things. The British turned 80 per cent of Palestine into the Hashemite Kingdom of Jordan and told the Arabs and Jews to divide the remaining 20 per cent between themselves. The Jews very reluctantly said okay. The Arabs said no way, and said no again when the UN voted for partition of the land in 1947. After that UN vote, Israel declared itself a state in 1948, and the Arabs attacked it within five hours. And it's been attacked ever since in the outright wars of 1948, 1956, 1967 and 1973 and the unceasing terrorism of Hamas and Hezbollah, among others, because to the Palestinians, a Jewish state, no matter how small, is a catastrophe—the Nakba.

If you lose wars, you generally lose territory, and so the Israeli 10 per cent became about 30 per cent, and included a good bit of the West Bank (captured by Jordan after the 1948 war and taken by the Israelis after the 1967 war). Then the Israelis gave back some conquered territory—Gaza to the Palestinian Authority and the Sinai to the Egyptians—which only infuriated Palestinians and their supporters more. When you compress history this way, the back and forth of territory sounds like casual moves in a game of Monopoly and I suppose it was for the great Powers who began it: now it is no game and the consequences for all involved are quite terrible.

"Why don't you follow Ben-Gurion's example when he said 'never refuse to refuse'?" I asked Palestine Liberation Organization spokeswoman Hanan Ashrawi. "You've been offered partition since the 1933 Peel Commission and land for a country since the 1947 UN resolution. Plus endless road maps giving you land for peace if you will only formally recognize Israel as a Jewish state." Her answer was straightforward: "We are an all-or-nothing people," she said, "not like the Jews." It's tricky when only one side of the two-state solution wants two states. Any state of peace with a Jewish homeland would be a victory for the Israelis and a defeat for the Palestinians.

Once Israel as a Jewish homeland became a fait accompli, the world supported it right through its first twenty-five years, when praise was heaped on those plucky Jews turning the desert green. But then supporting Israel became inconvenient and bloody irritating. Palestinian terrorists hijacked Lufthansa Flight 649 in 1972 and discovered they could get cash, hostage swaps and loads of publicity for acts of terror. After that everything went haywire. Hello to intrusive security checks at airports, profiling of passengers, handbag searches and increasing terror threats, making ordinary travel and even ordinary life increasingly difficult and dangerous.

Of course, no one would say this was a part of the reason for being pissed off at Israel. No, it was for far higher moral reasons: it was the Israelis' dreadful military "occupation" of "Palestine." It was the terrible poverty of the Palestinians caused by Israel's border regulations. It was the murder of civilians and the desecration of Islam's holy sites by the land-greedy Israelis. But you could only swallow this with a large dose of double standards and mendacity.

You had to overlook the state of war the Arab world had declared against Israel from the day it became a state; the moral difference between terrorism and counterterrorism; the refusal to recognize Israel as a Jewish state to this day by various Palestinian governments and terror groups that still vow to wipe it out whether by war or demographically by the right of return; the vandalizing of Jewish holy places in Jerusalem when it was under Arab control; the determined effort to keep the Palestinians in camps and poverty instead of an oil-rich Arab world taking them in.

The fallback position at most dinner tables of the Great and Good in Britain was that they were not anti-Semitic—God no, some of their best friends were Jewish if not they themselves—but they were against the heinous policies of the murderous State of Israel. Now that South Africa had abolished apartheid, there was a vacancy for Most Evil Country, and Israel was tailor-made for the job. "It's not anti-Semitic," Miriam and I were both told separately with hauteur time and again. "Lots of Jews [among elites] agree with us." Personally, I think there's a central casting for house Jews.

Clearly there are policies of the Israeli government with which you can strongly disagree without being anti-Semitic—after all, about half the Knesset does it every day. And here's where it became—and becomes—a problem for me: I don't have a foolproof way of distinguishing between those who legitimately dislike the policies of the Israeli government or who think the creation of Israel was a mistake—which includes Jews—and real anti-Semites. I just don't. All I can say is, one gets a gut feeling. But the gut is splendid for digesting food, and less reliable in digesting ideas.

I interviewed Soviet refusenik Natan Sharansky for The Times. He had spent nine years in prison, much of it in solitary confinement, after protesting the refusal of an exit visa for Israel. Sitting next to him was extraordinary: you try to see what it is that makes a man, in his case one so quiet and rather small, give up health and freedom and wife and family for a principle. Sharansky came up with a test to identify anti-Semites, which is, I grant you, a curious thing to do, but the question is so vexing, and perhaps part of his time in solitary confinement allowed him to think about such matters—or at least helped him survive. Anyway, after his release and emigration to Israel he was in charge of monitoring anti-Semitism as a minister in government. His test is interesting, as you would expect, and I think it's helpful but not definitive.

Old-style anti-Semitism has us baking bread or whatever with the blood of Christian children and plotting to take over the world. New-style anti-Semitism is more subtle, and unless it's coming from the right—which these days is barely a fraction of the anti-Semitic movement and has been replaced largely by the left—it is disguised as criticism of Israel. Sharansky's test is called the 3D test: the first *D* stands for demonization, in which Jews no longer drink blood of Christian children but the Jewish state is compared to the Nazis and Palestinian refugee camps to Auschwitz. Those comparisons, he says, quite rightly, are "not legitimate" and are anti-Semitic. The second *D* is for double standards. Judging Jewish behaviour by a different yardstick than anyone else and, in the case of Israel, when the UN and its adherents single out Israel for human rights abuses while giving tried-and-true abusers like China and half the Arab world a pass (as the Boycott, Divestment and Sanctions movement does), and when the Israeli ambulance service alone among the ambulance services of the world is denied admission to the International Red Cross—these double standards are not simply anti-Israeli but anti-Semitic. The third *D* is delegitimization. Modern anti-Semites, Sharansky says, try to portray Israel as the last vestige of colonialism and "alone among all peoples in the world," with no right to exist as a Jewish homeland.

These may be necessary ideas in the mind of an anti-Semite, but they aren't in my view sufficient to identify one. People holding these ideas may not dislike all Jews, just Israel. Very rare, but just possible. Hold these ideas, as the BDS does or even *The Guardian* with its support of the Palestinian right of return, and it's basically a euphemism for sanctioning the end of the Jewish state. At the very least, it's skating on thin ice, and underneath that ice is anti-Semitism.

Your average suicide bombers make no distinction between Israelis and Jews when they passionately murder them in French delis or synagogues across Europe. Anti-Israeli journalists are so eager to believe terrorist propaganda that they will report massacres of civilians by the Israeli army that never took place, as in the Battle of Jenin—which is not to say that every Israeli soldier carefully checks for civilians when entering a town infiltrated by terrorists, but at least killing civilians is not the loudly stated aim of Israel's army, its government or its people.

"Rarely in more than a decade of war reporting," wrote *The Times'* Middle East correspondent emotionally, "have I seen such deliberate destruction, such disrespect for human life." Actually, she had seen nothing, but rather than say that or check more sources, she took her account of the battle from Hamas, the militant Islamic terror group funded by Iran. The indisputable truth later acknowledged rather grumpily by the British press was that no such behaviour by Israeli troops had taken place. There are lots of examples of this kind of reporting in the U.K. press.

Happily for the British press, they could peddle their diseased views quite safely. The Political Cartoon of the Year award for 2003, presented at *The Economist* HQ, went to Dave Brown's depiction of a grotesque and naked Israeli prime minister Ariel Sharon eating an Arab baby—on the front page of *The Independent*. Not surprisingly, this quite upset the Israeli embassy, not to mention Prime Minister Sharon, and they complained to the Press Complaints Commission. Then Brown credited Francisco de Goya's horrific painting *Saturn Devouring His Son* as his inspiration, and you could hear the sighs of relief—although I don't quite follow how that cleansed the cartoon of anti-Semitic intent. Goya's Black Paintings could just as easily be cited as the inspiration for a number of cartoons in the Nazi rag *Der Stürmer*. In fact, I'd say the *Der Stürmer* cover of issue 25, in 1933, was closer in style to Dave Brown's cartoon than Goya. Unluckily for Julius Streicher, publisher of *Der Stürmer*, he did not come up in front of the U.K.'s Press Complaints Commission and was hanged after the Nuremberg trials.

U.K. journos and media can bravely say what they like about Jews, knowing that even wonky Jewish Defense League types won't come to blow out their brains like Islamic extremists invading *Charlie Hebdo* in Paris. Which explains why *The Independent* could publish Dave Brown's hideous cartoon but were afraid to publish the Danish cartoons of Muhammad. Terror works. People who torch buildings because of a cartoon and murder civilians and blow up planes are clearly medieval fanatics—they've taken the time machine back to the Middle Ages and the Jews haven't. And that's another thing.

No one wants to say that they dislike Israel because they are cowards and afraid of Islamic extremists; they come up with something more presentable and say—probably like the editor of *The Independent*—it is not terror alone that makes them yield to terrorists' demands. They act because it is the right thing—a desire for justice. Which is really deadly. To quote George Jonas, "Terror is victorious when it persuades the terror-stricken that they're motivated by a sense of equity . . . [when they] think they're acting out of an abundance of goodwill rather than an abundance of caution."

I'd hazard that part of the world's problem with Jews is that we are rather like weeds that develop resistance to herbicides or a staph virus that is antibiotic-resistant. The Babylonians, Assyrians, Hittites, Seleucids, Vandals, Goths and Saracens either conveniently dispersed, blended in or simply disappeared as cohesive peoples. But no matter how hard societies through the centuries tried to get rid of us, there we were: rebuilding our Temple, mucking out in ghettoes, always popping up in one country or another and traipsing across Europe to find the friendliest dukedom or village around.

The minute I became a known factor in London—Zionist Alert!—I started showing up on less salubrious lists: *Private Eye*'s Bore of the Week and Horrid Hackette references. The *New Statesman* launched its list Dangerous Idiots, and I had the distinction of being one of their first two nominees, "predictably," said the *Evening Standard*. Most of this had to do with my writing on the Middle East, although I don't doubt that my perceived anti-feminist stance, among other things, was extremely vexing to the saucepan-bashers at *The Guardian* and *The Independent*.

At *The Telegraph*, where my column now appeared weekly, I was a source of multiple embarrassments to the editor, although being a gentleman, Moore never indicated this in any way directly. The columns I wrote on Israel numbered about 20 out of 160, but who's counting? Well, I am, actually. I got *The Telegraph* to send me all my columns so I could do just that, and it was heartening to see how many times I bashed feminism, the BBC and the International Criminal Court, among many other topics. In my defence, I should point out that after the 9/11 attacks, Islam itself was a key issue, quite apart from the Israeli-Palestinian dispute, as was the never-ending war in Iraq—which I remember being forced to write about by *Sunday Times* editor Andrew Neil for my first five columns with the paper in January 1991. The Gulf War and Operation Desert Storm in Iraq and Kuwait were hot topics in which I had zero interest. The assignment was pure torture.

Behind the ordinary anti-Israeli lot at newspapers and television were the highbrow battalions backing up ordinary journos. Intellectually, they scared the bollocks out of me. They had CVs you'd kill for and quite often came from families with some aristocratic link. The most persuasive of the lot and pacesetter of the anti-Israel pack is A.N. Wilson (Rugby, Oxford's New College—founded 1379—and St. Hugh's). He's a seriously good author, historical biographer, novelist and sometime journalist—a man of genuine accomplishment whose intentions may be honourable and whose fine mind can handle many subjects but who has utterly no insight into himself.

He believes he is a friend of the Jews and Israel. He is adamant that he is not an Arabist. He refers routinely to the time he spent on a kibbutz in Israel. He writes of the six million Jews killed in the Holocaust and laments that they did not escape to Britain. "What concert halls we'd have, what universities, what dentists," he wrote in 2002 as suicide bombers were ravaging Tel Aviv. "How infinitely impoverished we would be without the great ethical teachings of the Torah, especially the ten commandments; without the haunting spiritual poetry of the Psalms," he lamented in 1995.

On the other hand, writing in 2002 of the "paranoia" felt by British Jews leaving the U.K. because "they think this country was no longer a place where they could feel easy," Wilson said: "None of my much loved Jewish friends or in-laws live in Israel, thank God, but if they did I'd be sending them one-way tickets to come home. . . . There [Israel] was an experiment, started in 1948 and so far failing disastrously."

I know this kind of philo-Semite, as ANW describes himself. If only Israel would remain a country of symphony orchestras and great writers (and wonderful orthodontists), then perhaps he wouldn't want to deport all those Israeli Jews out of their homeland. It is the grubby-mannered, elbows-out, noisy Jews with their in-your-face national pride, and the rough militaristic Israel (which wants to survive as a Jewish homeland and not a *judenfrei* Islamic one) he hates—the Israel that has spoiled his uplifting vision of Jews sitting at their piano stools or making the desert bloom green with their hands for their Arab brethren rather than red with the blood from Arab suicide bombs.

The giveaway is his Israel "failing disastrously." The only democracy in the Middle East, with a functioning judicial system that actually jails Jewish settlers who attack Arabs rather than naming squares after them and declaring them martyrs, a red-hot economy, high-tech inventiveness, plus a world leader in medical and pharmaceutical innovation. And all this while living in what is politely called a rough neighbourhood, which makes it tough to just be about psalms and straight teeth.

Like all nationalities and tribes, Jews embrace the refined with the vulgar, the musical with the unmusical, the honest with the crooked. Israel's domestic policies towards their Arab minority citizens are far from perfect. There's little doubt they have broken international law by sending soldiers across sovereign borders (usually necessarily, in my mind, but I'm a supporter), and some of their actions have been counterproductive, mildly speaking, to retaining Western goodwill. But absolutely nothing Israel has done can be discussed in the same breath as terrorism: murdering murderers or responding to stones with bullets can be debated (as it has been by Israeli Supreme Court president Esther Hayut, who asked where danger to life entered the picture when an Israeli soldier shot and killed a fleeing stone-thrower), but what is beyond debate is the deliberate murdering of civilians sitting in restaurants or shopping or the use of your own people as human shields. And while I'm clearly not an expert on the Christian conscience, I'm baffled by the notion that 43 per cent of the world's Jews—about 6.5 million—should commit suicide by policy or, in A.N. Wilson's generous offer, take airline tickets to yet another dispersal and exile.

To my mind, rude chat about any group or religion, whether at dinner tables, on social media, even in horrible cartoons or vicious columns—though painful if you are its target—is not a problem for the law. People ought to be able to say or draw what they think, even if it's very stupid. And anyway, it's far safer to have people showing their colours in the open than concealing them. Putting historian David Irving in an Austrian jail for denying the Holocaust is wrong. People should be able to deny the Holocaust without being jailed, even though they are either mad or at the very least bad. Totalling up the number of anti-Semitic rants on Twitter isn't useful either. Inventing new laws such as "hate crimes" is unnecessary. If motivation is to be taken into consideration, then consider it at sentencing. Whether or not the number of anti-Semitic "incidents" is going up depends on how you total these things: yelling of playground names or obscenities is horrid, but surely not a crime to be counted in some lump of statistics? Whatever else, Britain remains a place where Jews live in greater safety than anywhere in Europe.

Still, the social stuff, unimportant as it is, can be testing and sometimes pops up in situations where etiquette demands you grin and bear it. At an incredibly posh post-wedding bash filled with royalty and every billionaire in Europe, I was seated next to HRH the Duke of Gloucester. In his defence, I expect His Grace was in a rather grim mood that evening, having just moved his ninety-three-year-old mother out of Barnwell Manor, her home of fifty-seven years, and been pilloried all over the tabloid press for this cruelty. I rather sympathized with his predicament—having to bear the cost of a large estate to placate one elderly person.

All the same, HRH, first cousin to the Queen and eldest male descendant of three kings of England, asked, after noting my place card, what my husband did. An unusual question in etiquette terms, but ever ready and willing, "Newspaper proprietor," I answered, fairly certain he knew. "The lowest form of humanity," said the duke with as much gusto as his clenched jaw and glottal-stop postalveolar approximant would allow, "rather like the Israelis." A twofer. In deference to HRH, I protested very politely, trying not to aspirate the wrong consonants. The duke's response was to turn aside and not speak to me for the remaining two hours. I would have liked to brain him, but look, it was a wedding celebration.

Among even very good friends, the issue could peek out unexpectedly. Once, my husband and our host were having one of those semi-competitive conversations to which Conrad is prone, this time rhyming off great British companies of the Empire. "Anglo American plc, which became De Beers, is another," said Conrad.

"No," replied our host, a man of substance and great business achievement himself. "That's a Jewish company."

His wife, concerned, tried a slight corrective measure. Her husband was undeterred.

"Well, the Oppenheimers. They're separate, not really British," he explained. Nothing remotely anti-Semitic.

Still, it's the old question of loyalty and the nation-state. How many generations need to be born in France before one is accepted as "French"? How many hundreds of years before a Jew is truly British? If ever.

Closer to home, it surfaced a number of times each year at *The Spectator*. Given my reverence for *Speccie* writers one and all, that was like being pricked by a Bulgarian umbrella. I've never been a close friend of Taki Theodoracopulos, wealthy Greek man about town and boats. It's hard for a non-drinker to enjoy him fully, since he is the original legless man riding a bike. But I found him decent, totally loyal, and though his writing was high-class gossip, really, had he put his mind to it, he could have been a significant writer. His wit and imagery could be absolutely ineradicable. "But back to Gstaad. A few weeks ago while entering the Palace Hotel," he wrote, "I saw the Dowager Empress of Japan, Hirohito's widow, went up to her and bowed deeply, à la Japonaise, from the waist down. But upon closer inspection it turned out to be Valentino, whose jet-black hair and stretched skin makes him a twin of the Empress." Ever since, I can't see a photo of grand couturier Valentino without seeing the empress and Taki's bowing.

Such wonderful aperçus, though, were sometimes replaced in Taki's columns by little adjectives and adverbs about "pushy" Jews or the "hairiness" of this or that named Jewish person, usually in the middle of one of his more serious columns. Given my own hirsutism, for which I endured years of electrolysis, I tended to be sensitive on this point. I defended our friendship and his columns to Jewish friends, usually by changing the subject.

But the column that really did it was when Taki dug up the old trope about the malevolent influence of Jews on U.S. policy and included a scalding denunciation of Israel. "The way to Uncle Sam's heart runs through Tel Aviv and Israeli-occupied territory," he wrote in reference to Marc Rich, a Jewish American philanthropist who squeezed a pardon out of Bill Clinton (supported by big-shot Israeli politicians) even before he had stood trial. Actually, all that pardon demonstrated was the power of moolah with Clinton. As a topper, Taki added that Rich's so-called philanthropy, which included various museums, art and cultural centres in Israel, was misnamed given that it went to "those nice guys who attack rock-throwing youth with armour-piercing missiles."

I hold no brief for Rich, don't have a clue whether he was guilty of the U.S. tax charges against him. But it happens I was once in an open jeep with two Israeli soldiers who were showing me around the Arab quarter somewhere by East Jerusalem for a *Times* column, when just like that, pffff, the air was emptied of all sound. The streets became eyeless as shutters magically closed over open shopfronts. Largish stones were hurled at us with some speed and force. The situation did not bring a moment of epiphany, nor was I seized with the notion of dialoguing. The two army lads looked scared stiff. Personally, I would have felt a lot better with some armour-piercing missiles in my safari jacket pocket rather than a comb and Kleenex.

Finally, all of this stuff about what was and was not anti-Semitic or anti-Israel came to a head in late 2001, at a now legendary party at our London house in honour of *The Spectator*'s editor at the time, Boris Johnson. Ah, Boris.

This was early in Boris's picaresque career, before he had become mayor of London or a cabinet minister. Or a prime minister. He was a thirty-four-year-old, six-foot-plus mass of blondness topped by an endearing thatch of hair that was forever in his eyes and brushed back with one hand and contrived spontaneity. He wrote marvellous, often hilarious columns that were impossible not to read. His tutor at Oxford is reputed to have said he was "the brightest pupil I ever had." Women adored him. Older ones wanted to mother him while younger ones could find themselves facing a range of activities beyond the pleasure of his company, including abortions, miscarriages and the bearing of love children. No one complained. Even his second wife, a lawyer, stayed the course for twenty-five years. I thought him quite wonderful, and yonks ago in those pre-high-political-office days, most male journalists rather liked him. They were undone by his combination of wit, shuffling self-deprecation and self-parody.

Guests were invited to our home to celebrate "the Boris Phenomenon," and the invitation was decorated with illuminating quotes from Boris's life that illustrated his skill at sidestepping awkward promises he broke or questions he did not want to answer. "I will not run for Parliament if I become editor of *The Spectator*" was in the upper left of the invite, a solemn promise he made to Conrad on being offered the editorship. Two weeks after he was appointed editor, we learned he had thrown his hat(s) into not only one but two constituencies. Boris kept both the editorship and his newly won parliamentary seat. When interviewed on why he was going into public life: "Well, they don't build statues to journalists, do they?"

The guest list was largely *The Spectator*'s, and while I knew most of the people, many were social strangers to me. The mix included a Nobel writer, semi-royals, boldface names in journalism as well as authors, historians, celebs and some very gorgeous women, including one of Conrad's crushes, Elle "The Body" Macpherson. You really didn't have to worry about conversational lacunae in a group like this.

Naturally, our handling of the party was being happily dissected, as was Conrad's handling of *The Telegraph*, including possible promotions and appointments. Short of donning earplugs and horse blinders, there was no way to avoid the halted conversations or elbow nudges whenever I ventured across the floor to the side of the room largely peopled by detractors. This called for my ghastly forced rictus, helped by a surreptitious belt of vodka, the alcoholic beverage of necessity, which comes out in desperate moments and is paid for with desperate headaches later on. With the second shot, the teeth and smiles melded into a half-grimacing fresco, and I bolted into the little lavatory behind the drawing room that no guest knew about.

One of the things I was always forgetting was that almost all the people there were at least twenty years younger than me, some thirty years younger. If I was constantly disappointed in not being one of their "pals," apart from the reason that I was married to the proprietor, I didn't take into account this vitally important age gap with its differing expectations. These were people who, married or not, partnered or not, were still very much in the sexual game—their flirting, their looks, their banter were aimed at a variety of ambitions. In your thirties you think more carelessly than later on. Acclaim and achievement had come already to many of the guests, but not yet the frustrations that follow. In those earlier decades, you generally have less tolerance, and your wit and humour are perhaps more sharp but the focus narrower. Certainly more unforgiving.

Still, an exceptionally interesting group, even engaging, and those who I did not know I suspected I would have liked to have known. Except perhaps for one man. The French ambassador, Daniel Bernard. As the evening wound down, I ended up at a table that included Ambassador Bernard. The subject of Islamic terrorism came up just as I was trying to smash up my île flottante without totally dissolving meringue into the caramel sauce. The bombings of 9/11 had taken place a couple of months earlier, and while in Ramallah and similar places the Arabs were jumping with joy on rooftops, the

London version of this was a more subdued told-you-so, eyebrows-raised observation that the U.S. was asking for it with its unconditional support of Israel.

The French ambassador's contribution to the discussion was to memorably remark that the current troubles in the world were all because of "that shitty little country Israel. Why," he asked, "should the world be in danger of World War Three because of those people?"

I was chattering away and didn't hear the fatal remark. Conrad, who had been doing the rounds, had just landed at our table. He did hear it. "I'm sorry," said Conrad, who thought he must have misheard or perhaps it was a language problem. "Could you repeat that?" The ambassador happily did—in French and English. Afterwards, when Conrad told me, the point as I saw it was not that Bernard thought that Israel was a horrible notion but that the climate was such that he thought it was perfectly normal for an ambassador to say so as if it were a truism. America is rich and vulgar; Italy, chaotic and sienna; Britain, an island ally; and Israel is a shitty little country.

Leaving for Christmas in Toronto that week, I was pushed for a column topic. The ambassador's remark struck me as a catchy way into a larger discussion of Islamic terrorism and so I quoted it without actually naming Ambassador Bernard, but when completed, the column didn't have much verve. "I'm sending in a fairly boring column," I apologized on the telephone to Charles Moore from Heathrow. This wasn't fishing. The column was good enough to run, but sometimes you hit a home run. Not this one. Which had the accuracy of my stricture to Leonard Cohen in 1965 not to make records because he couldn't sing.

My veiled description of the French ambassador in my column—"the ambassador of a major EU country"—hit headlines when reporters did a magpie run of EU ambassadors and Daniel Bernard happily outed himself because from his point of view, why not? He had said nothing remarkable. His remark ricocheted around European newspapers, yet I was pilloried for having broken the rules of decency by writing about a conversation that took place in the presumed safety of my home. The ambassador's comment itself seemed to be viewed as unexceptional.

At *The Telegraph* a sign went up over the loos: "Room for shitty little things." *The Guardian*'s take was, "Every Salon Tells a Story—That's Why the Lady Is a Hack." Ever-friendly Deborah Orr, writing in *The Independent*, mentioned that when on holiday she found Israel to be a "shitty little country," which I suppose is a perfectly legitimate opinion of a holiday destination and probably not altogether inaccurate for her, given the significant difference between British etiquette and the rather abrupt, often peremptory Israeli manners. Her piece than segued into one of those riffs on the difference between anti-Zionism and anti-Semitism and for good measure she suggested, disarmingly, that I was rather like an abused adolescent who had taken too much therapy. Now, she wrote, in this addled state I saw anti-Semitism under every table in London just because "a lot of London dinner tables are in fact anti-Israel."

In Canada, the *Toronto Star* printed strong criticisms of me from, surprise, surprise, Ryerson's perennially left-wing and sometimes even hard-left chair of journalism—honestly, someone should fumigate that place. The French press went wild. No column I had written had received so much international attention, including positive comment on it in the *Wall Street Journal*. For a nanosecond I was internationally known as a columnist, albeit a bad-mannered one.

But my manners and the ambassador's remark were not the point of my column, only a grabby lead into a discussion of how Islamists were overplaying their hand, from their rejection of the Oslo Accords to the attacks of 9/11. The headline of the column was "How Islamists Are Overplaying Their Hand." That went unnoticed.

My fault. If I wanted the column to be read for the reason it was written, then I should have resisted the temptation to include any details that could identify Ambassador Bernard. What I did was rather like the publishers of *Playboy* magazine who, after printing short stories by significant writers or conversations with eminent people, just can't understand why readers skip the in-depth interview with John Updike in favour of in-depth photos of naked women.

Getting attention with a catchy anecdote for a piece of writing is always a two-edged sword. Instead of a discussion of Islamism, I had created a discussion of dinner table etiquette. A month later the ambassador was given a posting in Algiers. A year and a half later he died prematurely, at sixty-two. No rejoicing over that, my first kill.

CHAPTER FIFTEEN

The Lady's for Burning—in Haute Couture

A couple of months before the *Spectator* party, Conrad had finally become Lord Black of Crossharbour. *Crossharbour?* I'd had a bit of gag reflex.

"Can the wife choose a different name?" I asked, knowing the answer but thinking the question might promote a rethink. Else you could predict the beastly puns ahead.

"This is quite traditional," said Conrad. "Max Aitken, the first Canadian peer to own a newspaper, became Lord Beaverbrook, named for the small New Brunswick community near where he lived, which also had the advantage of a distinctly Canadian ring."

"We live on Cottesmore Gardens," I heard myself saying a bit plaintively. "And . . ."

My voice was lost under Conrad's recitation of how Canadian Roy Thomson became Baron Thomson of Fleet, of Northbridge in the City of Edinburgh—the addresses of his first newspapers in Scotland and London. "Crossharbour," Conrad continued, "is the district in which both the offices and printing plant of *The Telegraph* are located—as well as the closest light railway station." I tried to visualize Conrad on a train platform, never mind a light one.

Own or control a large U.K. national newspaper and a title will loom. A peerage is all but attached to whomever is Proprietor of the *Daily Telegraph*. Before Conrad, *Telegraph* proprietor Michael Berry became Lord Hartwell, before him William Berry became Lord

Camrose. The Harmsworth family, who control Associated Newspapers Ltd., became the Lords Northcliffe and Rothermere. Matter of practice. Alas, Canada's peerless Prime Minister Jean Chrétien had other ideas. No way bloody Conrad was going to be a Lord while he was around. "*Passe pas, hostie!*"

Conrad was to be the sole Canadian in history who, while holding dual U.K./Canadian citizenship, and residing in London, would not be allowed to accept the U.K. peerage unless he renounced his Canadian citizenship. His motive was low revenge, stemming from a small-beer sponsorship "scandal" the *National Post* (then owned by Conrad) had dug up involving him.

Just in case it worked out in Conrad's favour, I was quietly playing the sound of "Lady Black" to myself. I rather liked it, although I was sufficiently imprinted in childhood to think it completely mad that a Jewish woman from Hendon who had emigrated to steel town Hamilton, Ontario, would have a title. There was an impostor quality about my elevation: "Small titles and orders . . . to help unhappy commoners," from a Gilbert and Sullivan operetta.

Knowing myself though, I was pretty certain that if the title came through, I'd manage to overcome these qualms. I could feel the lure of my assistant making hair and restaurant reservations for "Lady Black."

"You have no idea," said my friend Miriam Gross, who had just become Lady Owen after her husband Geoffrey Owen, a former Wimbledon Centre Court player and Editor of the *Financial Times*, was knighted, "how fast you get used to being called Lady when people speak to you."

I felt sorry for Conrad—in a way. I mean, if you will bang on most of your life about how great Canada is to anyone who will listen and you feel so deeply about being Canadian, which he genuinely did, you probably ought not to put the beloved to the test and see if your affections are returned. Which they were not.

Canadians by and large supported Chretien's highwayman ultimatum, "Your peerage or your citizenship," largely because they didn't have a clue about the issue and the precedents supporting Conrad's case. Conrad chose his peerage, while vowing to reclaim citizenship when Chretien left. I mumbled about the folly of giving up his Canadian passport. "You must get as many as possible, just in case," my mother would say, suggesting one day I would have to flee, possibly an insight into her perambulations regarding ethnicity.

Conrad has always wanted to play an active role in policy and international affairs but knew his electoral chances were about on par with a dead herring's. Now, a member of Parliament's Upper Chamber, he could finally take part. Canadians, with the exception of notables such as Ken Thompson (himself a peer, although not active in the Lords), went wacky trying to outdo one another in spite. His peerage was described as a narcissistic need to ride with hounds and lunch with the Queen. "How many fancy dinner parties and weekends of foxhunting can one tycoon fit into his hectic schedule?" snickered Geoffrey Stevens, then managing editor of *Maclean's*. The splenetic comments revealed a basic illiteracy concerning the role of working peers, which was astonishing. For years as a practicing hack in Canada, I had been aware of the Lords' debates and used the Hansard transcripts as research material.

Conrad's sponsors were former prime minister Margaret Thatcher and Peter Carrington, one of Britain's greatest statesmen since Churchill, both described by then *Globe and Mail* columnist Heather Mallick, as "that clot Conrad Black and his ancient friends." For good measure she added Henry Kissinger to the ancient-clots list.

Now that Heather herself is coming into her sixties, I don't think it comely to be cruel. But just in passing, while conceding Henry Kissinger is elderly, he was still advising governments on foreign policy in his nineties and did open U.S. relationships with China, while Ms. Mallick's opening of relationships is largely confined to a more mundane sphere. He has written over twenty-five books (one of which, *World Order*, he wrote when he was ninety-one and which Mark Zuckerberg put in his book club). As for Lady Thatcher, she cleaned up the decades-long so-called British disease on coming to power in 1979, after three male prime ministers before her had failed. Class and union warfare had peaked with gravediggers on strike and graveyards locked, rotting garbage piled up on the pavements with happy scampering rats, hospitals closed (emergency cases only), bread out of supply one week, milk the next—courtesy of rotating strikes. An era is named after her, and so extraordinary was her role in British history that her funeral was attended by the Queen, who previously had attended only one other PM's funeral, Sir Winston Churchill's.

I think some Canadian journalists looked around the news-room and felt special and brave throwing mud at great names like Kissinger and Thatcher—or indeed Conrad—when in fact they were simply mouthing the zeitgeist of the drain they inhabit: it takes courage to oppose what your friends say, no courage at all to echo. They remind me of those Hollywood actors at the Oscars who get up on stage and act as if they were the unknown student in front of tanks in Tiananmen Square, voicing positions on every-thing from gender issues to President Trump: they may or may not be correct views, but in that closed shop of the mind, they know everyone in the theatre agrees with them to resounding applause. What's so brave about that?

Miriam was right. By the start of 2002, I was fully accustomed to being "Lady" Black. One of the three or four hereditary Jewish peers and the most prominent, Jacob Rothschild, sent me a coaster for my coffee cup with "Her Ladyship" on it. Point made. And the point was this, which we knew but most Canadians didn't get: we knew very well that a working peerage had absolutely nothing to do with aris-tocracy in the substantive sense. We hadn't suddenly been reinvented as a titled family.

In social terms, Conrad's new title meant bugger all. I had met a few of the real hereditary peers, dukes, marquesses, earls and so on, some of whom had been a serious part of British history, some not, some living in dilapidated circumstances, some managing to steer clear of the National Trust and hang on living in their magnificent homes. And those few I had met were a different breed, with their own language and values. You cannot "join" up. No point in even trying to, although I'll admit I found the desperate antics of some of the Americans trying to do just that pretty amusing. While the

hereditary aristocracy sometimes recognize—briefly—your value
and even accomplishment, in their eyes you are transitory. You come
and are gone, your name and house pass, leaving no mark in any
meaningful way—just as prime ministers come and go. A working or
honorary peerage is a one-time chance to participate in the affairs of
the nation and then it goes poof with you into the grave. But for a
man like Conrad, that one-time chance was all he wanted.

The ambiguity of our finances continued as, in 2002, the *Sunday Times*
welcomed Conrad onto its Rich List for the first time as a British citizen,
albeit at number 271 with a modest (in such a list's terms) £121 million
attached to his name. At the same time, the business pages were talking about "Black's coming downfall" and the end of his business life.
"Don't believe any of it, good or bad," said my husband.

Conrad's fist-face appeared more and more of the time. His telephone conversations were incomprehensible. "Return equity swaps,"
he would say, and then, "With a vendor take-back participation we
could use Jack's lions."

Me afterwards: "Lions?"

"No, not lions. Liquid yield option notes. L-Y-O-N."

None of it made sense to me. I knew in 2001 that some activist
investor with an 8 per cent share in Hollinger was writing letters
demanding Conrad take a pay cut, which was received with predictable
enthusiasm. Activist Investor was also demanding the share price be
raised—as if Conrad wanted to see it plummet. Truth is, Activist
Investor hoped the stock would dive so he could buy it cheap and be
such an irritant that he would force Conrad to either buy him out or
do cartwheels. This is called greenmail. Don't ask.

Days were stuffed with business, with Conrad fluctuating
between worry and exaltation as we travelled between London and
New York. At eight o'clock, wherever we were, came a quick shift
into evenings of social splendour, mingling with a vast swathe of
elites, some purely social and some brainy—the two are quite separate and do not coexist in 99.999 per cent of human beings. Conrad
belongs to that infinitesimal proportion combining the two, which

may account for his anatomically large cranium. After theatre, concert, dinner or some celebratory occasion for some well-known person, we'd be home by midnight (late for New York, early for London), change out of our evening clothes and start the midnight-to-three work shift. I felt it was inevitable that burning the candle at both ends would lead to a meltdown. Conrad, on the other hand, thought that with his exceptionally hard work and the influential contacts made through some of those grand glittery evenings, he'd power through any business crisis.

In this frantic atmosphere, it was no surprise that I would slip up. Like Chamberlain at Munich or, more aptly, Napoleon invading Russia, I made a colossal mistake, although in the swirl of matters it seemed a really good thing at the time.

"Please," said *Vogue* editor Anna Wintour, "do our age issue. I really need you." Could any request have sounded more innocent? The *Vogue* "Age Issue" was a fixture back then, the thinnish August edition selecting a well-known woman or aristocratic supermodel to represent each decade of a woman's life from her twenties to her eighties before the massive September magazine came out.

Perhaps a woman in her sixties ought not to have been so flattered to be asked to represent the decade that definitively marks the start of the swift slide into irrelevance and, further, to represent it in a clothes magazine rather than a compendium of Great Thinkers of Our Time. But I didn't even have a qualm to brush away. Six pages of photos and a profile in American *Vogue* for a vain woman is so shallow it allows no thoughtful dredging. This is My Moment, I rhapsodized—internally, you understand, while dredging every crust of sang-froid I could find. Indeed, it was about to be a bloody Immortalized Moment, though perhaps not of the sort I wished.

And, frankly, it was generous of Anna to ask me. For all the money I spent, she knew that my fashion sense was, to put it politely, uneven, even though earlier that year she had put me on the *Vogue* 2002 Best Dressed list: this cunning achievement relied on separating women into various categories, thus encompassing just about everyone who touched her circle. I was put on the "Vixens" page together with Jennifer Lopez, Daphne Guinness and Sally Albemarle, while the "Swans" page had the *crème de la crème* of dressers, including Aerin Lauder, Marie-Josée Kravis, Annette de la Renta, Anne Bass and C.Z. Guest. "Goddesses" were Kate Moss and Madonna, and a glorious Nicole Kidman got the number-one full-page spot. Forty women were chosen all told, and I had a small tingle of pleasure at seeing the absence of Mercedes Bass, a base emotion. Triple bollocks, if only I had insight concerning myself and stayed the hell away from any interview, so many cards might have fallen differently.

"You'd be wonderful," said Anna. "And we'd have Mario Testino do the photos and André the clothes." A Testino–André Leon Talley–*Vogue* collaboration, with Anna overseeing it to make me look good. What could go wrong?

I had not done a media interview since I'd married Conrad, and when I saw the press's venomous reaction to that happy event—especially in Canada—I got a good whiff of the danger. I was interviewed once sometime before my relationship with Conrad had begun, for Rupert Murdoch's short-lived magazine *Mirabella*, but I was, after all, working for Rupert. I skipped print and TV requests for "personality" interviews and kept my working profile up with the more serious TV appearances that were expected of most political columnists.

Sir Robin Day's BBC show *Question Time* was torture but unavoidable, as it was the most prestigious political show on the BBC. Day was an institution in British life. He had been president of the Oxford Union, and it showed. "What do you mean by that?" he would say snappishly on live television after an obscure rebuttal from either audience or one of the four guest panellists. His political memory was rather like Conrad's, absolutely deadly, making it hard to finesse a question or answer. However, his formidable mind was laminated to an attitude about women that was slightly uncomfortable.

After my first appearance, he told me, "I watched it in the screening room and I cannot decide whether you created such a stir because of what you said or what you looked like." He was given to overtly sexual remarks as well as being a tactile man, and by today's febrile standards would have been severely reprimanded, if not charged with sexual harassment or assault. I found dealing with him perfectly easy—at heart he was a gentleman, even if the heart was not the primary organ focusing on you, and any advance was easily declined and had absolutely zero effect on being asked back on his show.

The evening before my first appearance on *Question Time*, I was hyperventilating at a reception at 10 Downing Street and all I could think about was the chilling nightmare to come. Cold sweat—God, why had I accepted. My friend John O'Sullivan, op-ed editor at *The Times*, took me up to Thatcher and told her how frightened I was. The Iron Lady did her thing. "Be yourself, Barbara," said the PM, her eyes fixed on mine in an unwavering stare and her hand on my arm. "Be yourself and you have nothing to worry about. I read your columns and you will be splendid." The thought of Mrs. T. perusing my work was in itself scary. I went home and prepared as best I could (Dalmane, I think) for the next evening's encounter with Robin Day.

My debut went fairly well. Once the question is on a subject that interests me, my terror diminishes and I get quite involved. Apart from the head-over-toilet-bowl discomfort of throwing up a sort of green porridge before each appearance and the ever-present danger of being revealed as a political idiot, there was no worry the questions would be personal attacks.

Anna's invite, on the other hand, was the serpent in the Garden of Eden. I suppose I said yes because I wanted the publicity, wanted to stay in with Anna and loved the huge embossed envelopes that meant another *Vogue* invite to a premiere where Conrad could flirt with such stars as Nicole Kidman and I could dress up with no starchy dinner attached. And underneath, I rather hoped it would make me an important fashion lady and, by osmosis, one of Anna's coterie.

I had introduced Anna, at her request, for one of those inevitable New York power women lunch things, which were by definition helplessly trendy—in this instance the Matrix Awards for "Women Who Changed the World in 2002." All the usual suspects in attendance (read: several hundred power women). Conrad was one of four men there—Shelby Bryan, who was Anna's beau; a mid-luncheon appearance by Bill Clinton, who was another presenter (which struck me as slightly contradictory given his relationships with less powerful women); and Walter Cronkite.

Onstage I just plunged right in with my intro—foot straight into the mud. Everything I had seen of Anna led me to believe exactly what I said when I emphasized her bravado in the face of the envy of her print peers who put down fashion glossies. "Anna and I move in different worlds politically and socially. But I'd like to have the following in common with her," I said. "She is principled. She never whines; she never temporalizes. She doesn't complain when the envious try to debunk her editorial achievement by consigning her to the pigeonhole of fashion. . . . Ladies and gentlemen: a brilliant editor-in-chief—Miss Anna Wintour."

Having introduced her, Anna proceeded to confound me. She dreads public speaking engagements, obviously either didn't hear me or couldn't improvise, and had a prepared text that was a defensive litany of how her peers treated and put down fashion magazines. What she said was certainly true. What I'd said I thought was true. We should have conferred before the lunch.

"How could you introduce Anna?" said the *New York Times* reporter who'd accosted me reprovingly outside the luncheon. "Really, she's not a serious person."

"Not serious? Only successful?"

"Well, she certainly isn't politically aware," he'd said. As if the *New York Times* was.

"OK," I told Anna, "I'll do it. The 'Age Issue.'"

At that moment, there ought to have been a rumble of thunder in the clouds and the grinning face of Beelzebub peeking through.

"We'll have Oscar do a dress for you," said André confidently. About three weeks later my assistant, Penny Phillips, wrote in her notes, "André Leon Talley rings to say 'there is a HUGE drama about your bustier for the Oscar de la Renta dress.'" The dress materialized and it was hideous. Not the dress, but the dress on me. I felt like a lampshade.

"Show me your haute couture," said Talley, wanting to find outfits for the rest of the spread. "Do you have a favourite outfit?" And there he was, terrifyingly large as life, *Vogue* editor-at-large André Leon Talley riffling through my two London walk-in wardrobes—if not a horror show, certainly a nightmare in the making. Finding something suitable for the image of me as a political columnist was a bit dodgy, given that all my writing is done in what *Vogue* would consider clothes from a bin in hell. As for the Paris stuff, Yves Saint Laurent Couture was my wardrobe's backbone, and that was ruled out. Saint Laurent had banned *Vogue* from its fashion shows after Anna had revealed that she thought his clothes were out of touch. *Vogue* responded with a blackout on Yves Saint Laurent.

By the 1990s, Yves was unwell and erratic, and he or his team were really doing the same old thing year after year. I bought his haute couture because I had no idea he was "doing the same old thing," since I hadn't known his thing before. "Those dreadful lesbian suits," said Jayne Wrightsman, looking at my newest Saint Laurent Couture suit. "Why do you buy them?"

I can't remember who came with me or if I was alone the first time, in 1997, when I walked up the short flight of stairs at 5 avenue Marceau to Yves's haute couture salon, but for me it was my ascent to the celestial—in fashion terms. Everything was hushed, so well bred. I remember best of all in those fittings in the high-ceilinged rooms, the little man with jet-black hair and impeccable suits who would step back, clasp his hands and look at the clothes on me without seeing me and rhapsodize, "*C'est sublime.*" Then the *flou* or *tailleur* team could breathe again and leave. Inside that salon with its gold chairs and sofa, all the metaphors about being in a velvet box rang true.

Hélène de Ludinghausen, the *directrice*, sat in a corner, smoking, occasionally making a remark in her raspy voice to the client or staff. Or explaining quite wonderfully how she was going to get her special chickens over the English Channel in spite of customs regulations. She was the perfect link to the ghosts in that salon, some of them still alive. Later on I read her remarks in a *Vanity Fair* article on Palm Beach: "Palm Beach to me is the epitome of everything that's gone wrong in America," she said. "Because it's all based on money, not accomplishment anymore. The men play a little golf, not much, and

fall into the stupidities of the women—the gossip, the intrigues. After
a few weeks here, they're even more obsessed about their seat at
dinner than their wives are." Bingo. I kicked myself on reading her:
here was another person I had missed knowing, even though at the
time I clearly recognized her superior qualities. I assumed she would
not be interested in me because, unlike most of her clientele, I did not
have that sort of "money."

I tell you, there was a magic in that salon. All those circles that
Saint Laurent touched, intersecting and breaking apart in a dance of
fashion, elegance and decadence. In person, they would have as little
interest in me as I would have in them, but as a pageant of icons and
tableaux vivants in my mind they were irresistible: favourite client
Marie-Hélène de Rothschild, fashion jeweller Loulou de la Falaise,
muse Betty Catroux of the straight blonde hair and bangs, model
Veruschka, his breakthrough black model Mounia, and then Catherine
Deneuve on his arm; all the baking-hot coloured days of Marrakesh
and the hashish-filled nights with Loulou and her husband Thadée
Klossowski, a young, sexy and competitive Karl Lagerfeld stealing
and sharing boyfriends with Yves. I thought of them as the enamelled
figures on some preposterous fusee bracket clock, gilded and dancing
around in a circle as the quarter-hours struck.

My buying of couture had a short but manic life from 1998 until
late 2002, a period during which Saint Laurent in person and creativity
was all but absent. Then, in 2002, he announced his retirement and
put on his last couture show with a lot of the old designs reprised:
marvels of embellishment by Lesage, designs from Jean Cocteau.
I spent the last of my already way-over-limit budget on them. It
didn't occur to me that if these items had to be altered when my size
altered, which it did drastically as I shrunk, or a button was lost, I
would be in a pickle.

Sorting through my wardrobe with André's critical eye was a
horrifying epiphany. I realized hundreds of thousands of dollars spent
were ashes stylistically. I pulled out a Jean Paul Gaultier tailored outfit
that seemed a wonderful choice, probably because it was relatively
tame—no bare buttocks, which was a phase Gaultier was going

through. When I'd ordered it, I had played around with the revealing blouse underneath and demanded matching trousers just like one of those rich society women the designers loathed who took their imaginative designs and picked away at their originality till we might as well all have been in an institutional uniform. "Mmm. We can use it," said André, looking a bit worried.

Next time he appeared he had with him a Carolina Herrera ready-to-wear outfit I would never have thought of buying and which was marvellous: a "simple" silk blouson of large violet flowers on a lighter violet background, its long, full sleeves cuffed preposterously with sable, and paired with her red-and-grey-plaid wool trousers.

"Mario's a little upset," said André ominously when Testino arrived at Cottesmore Gardens. "He had a bad time in the last shoot." Upset? He was rigid with fury and resentment at having to do this pedestrian assignment, which had no artistic challenge apart from the lack of artistry in my being. To add to the gaiety, Mario and his hairstylist were barely speaking and on arrival each departed rather dramatically to separate floors. They only came together on the issue of my hair, which, both said, separately, was horrible and "not modern." I rebelled—foolishly, because I didn't understand that in a fashion shoot, you were better off wearing some outlandish hairstyle than your daily look.

Mario sulked his way through the shoot. "Couldn't we have some music to make her more . . ." His sentence petered out in a shrug. A scan of my music confirmed his barely hidden contempt for my irrelevance.

"We had a terrible time at the last shoot in the country with Amanda [Harlech]," said André in an attempt to comfort me when he was not comforting the hairstylist or running between floors to effect a reconciliation with Testino. "She was on horseback and her hairstyle was combed up high on one side, a nightmare, absolute nightmare. I didn't like what they did AT . . . ALL." André often spoke in capital letters. My everything was just so boring to this team that the hairdresser and Mario washed their hands of me and I was left to backcomb my hair into something perfectly suburban. Depressing, since I had fantasized about being pals with Testino and hanging in his studio next to Kate Moss.

"I'm sending you an interviewer for the piece I think you'll really like," said Anna afterwards. And I did. Julia Reed was the most intelligent and personable interviewer I have ever known. I liked her so much that I didn't want her to suffer what I had suffered during the many profiles I had written—when the subject of your profile bars you from really seeing their house, clothes, book, music choices, room furnishings—their life, as it were. This is the Great Profile Curse, and from the start of my journalism career, I stipulated that I would do profiles only of people I could actually spend days with.

The subject of a profile usually acts rather like a house being staged for a sale: you see them in a designated room, possibly two, with a few curated books on a table and utterly nothing that gives any glimpse into their character—acres of square-foot bland. The only exception to this was Britain's Tony Blair. When researching a cover profile for the *Sunday Times* magazine, I stayed in his home in Sedgefield, in the north of England, before he had become leader of the Labour Party. At night I crept downstairs for a glass of milk and a furtive telephone call to the chap I was dating, Conrad Black, and then wandered around.

The Blairs' house was completely open to me during my stay there, and the incredible disorder of it all—the children's toys lying about, dust everywhere (not unexpectedly, given two working parents, young children and an old house), and the piles of magazines and papers on the floor—was extremely endearing and softened my natural hostility to the politics of Labour. Less so Cherie Blair, who hated me, in fact made no pretense of anything else, which I rather admired, and whose morning presence in the kitchen or brief encounter outside the shared bathroom atop very narrow stairs was so frosty I could see her breath. But this freedom to roam around was unusual. Given the more usual experience of being sidelined in an anteroom by whoever I was writing about, I decided I would not inflict the same restriction on a fellow journalist, particularly one I liked.

"Go anywhere in the house," I said to Julia breezily. "Look around, open drawers. There's nothing to hide. My workroom is on the top floor." And I went upstairs to make myself a cup of tea, which might as well have been hemlock, while she nosed around.

And she did. When she came back from her tour we continued talking over tea and biscuits.

"You have a lot of clothes," she said in a bit of an understatement and with a smile. There was nothing malicious in her tone. It was, after all, a matter of fact.

"Yes," I replied. I had a pat explanation. "When I was at the University of Toronto in the late fifties," I told her, "I was going out with the man I would marry, whose world was one of rich Jewish families where the daughters always had super clothes. I hadn't a penny, so I went to the second-hand stores—a little shameful in Forest Hill circles. At a party of one of his best friends I wore a lovely little brown silk outfit with tiny white polka dots and a draped skirt. Very chic. I had bought it the day before for somewhere around twenty-five or thirty dollars at a shop on Yorkville named L'Elegante. The mother in whose home the party was looked at me through her cat's-eye glasses. Then smiled just a little nastily. 'My daughter Corinne,' she said, 'had a dress made for her just like that. Only we got rid of it because it had a cigarette burn right there.' And those manicured nails travelled across to the inside drape in my skirt where in fact there was a very small burn hole I had not noticed."

There was no way to convey to Julia the sick feeling I'd had. I was the original second-hand Rose in Corinne's clothes. Please, God, open up the floor. "Corinne, come and look at—what's your name, dear?—Barbara's dress." I had countered with a stumbling story about this having been my mother's dress, also specially made for her, but it was hopeless. I was nineteen years old.

"That's when," I continued to Julia, "I decided to never be in such a situation again. And since then"—I made a grimace to her and spoke in a deep voice, all capital letters itself, to indicate the slightly self-deprecating humour of the situation—"I have an extravagance that knows no bounds!" The story was absolutely true and my feeling at the time so devastating that the damn scar tissue is still there and on cold days flares up, but I doubt it had much relevance to my consuming love of fashion.

Extravagance that knows no bounds. How many times have I regretted that line? My love knows no bounds. Her jealousy knows no bounds. Shakespeare could give it the setting that made it work when Shylock (in Arnold Wesker's rewrite) presciently says, "Seeing what men have done, I know with great weariness the pattern of what they will do, and I have such contempt, such contempt . . . My contempt, sometimes, knows no bounds." The words sounded melodic to me, and they were going to be the noose around my neck.

When Julia quoted my words in the lead paragraph of her article for *Vogue*, I couldn't blame her. I would have done the same thing myself. She put the remark in context, narrated the second-hand Rose aspect absolutely accurately and let it proceed, naturally, into a description of all she had found in my home. The cause was not helped by the claim in the article—which was splashed over the double-page spread of me in the Jean Paul Gaultier Haute Couture, with Fred Leighton jewellery on loan via André—that I was married to "one of the world's wealthiest men."

"One of the world's wealthiest men!" Conrad said on seeing it. "What rubbish." I thought the tagline that I was "on deadline" while dressed in haute couture was the rubbish, although the photos captured the essence of my desk, which did not, unlike me, have to be made up for the occasion. After Jayne Wrightsman read the article, she looked concerned. "Anna should have protected you more." I had no idea what she was talking about. Protected? From what? It wasn't Anna's responsibility to protect me from myself.

The press had a small flutter over my *Vogue* appearance. *The Guardian* suggested that "Telegraph subs who handle her eccentric columns will be excited to learn that the 61-year-old Lady Black owns a dozen Hermes bags, 30 to 40 jewel-handled Pellegrino handbags"—a reference that baffles me; wish I had just one—"and an Imelda Marcos–style shoe collection including Blahnik and Chanel flats . . . In just one of their four homes."

In a column titled Blackwatch, *Private Eye* thoughtfully pointed out that while "Daily Telegraph staff have endured many months of cost-cutting and belt-tightening, at least one hackette at the paper isn't feeling the pinch. With perfect timing, Telegraph columnist Barbara Amiel (who is also the wife of proprietor Conrad Black) has chosen this moment to invite American Vogue to inspect her wardrobe." In Canada, journalist Judith Timson called it "fashion porn," which I think was pretty accurate. As was her judgment that I was a "study in the reinvention of self."

This was the last year I would be at the couture. André Leon Talley had shaken my confidence so I had asked him if he would help me in the future. "Ready-to-wear," I suggested, "would be the best route for me."

Legendary Vogue editor Diana Vreeland discovered André; Anna Wintour quickly recognized his talent as one of those mortals blessed with the eye of an eagle, the taste of a Hubert de Givenchy and an other-world originality when it comes to fashion. Myself, I quickly realized this was going to be a pricey venture no matter what level we kept it at. André decided I should be introduced to the shops around NYC and benefit from the discount they gave to VIP customers. The first was Prada, where I had never shopped. The sales manager looked at me skeptically after André's introduction.

"For a discount, I will need material for our files," she said. "Could you send me clippings on yourself so I can forward them to the head office." I sent them the *Vogue* article and a few photos from *Women's Wear Daily* and the *New York Times*. This gave me qualified admission to the private client's room upstairs in their Madison Avenue store.

"You must have this," André said, pulling out an unstructured small lime-green crocodile handbag shaped like a soft-sided coffee cup and attached to a metal ring that could handily go around your wrist if dancing, I suppose. Then came a top with navy plastic triangles attached, edged in a nasty green Teflon sort of material, and matching trousers. All of which I was too embarrassed not to take but

I could see that this sort of thing, even with the very generous discount on offer was going to mount up. The *coup de grâce* to our wardrobe relationship came in July.

The *Vogue* article was about to come out and the haute couture houses were having their autumn/winter 2002/2003 shows in Paris. André was on task. The faxes came in fast and furious and were absolute masterpieces of fashion-speak—a little-recognized genre—as well as Andre's now poignant descriptions of the late Karl Lagerfeld.

His first fax, hot off the Paris runway, was Wednesday morning, July 10: ". . . the moment of perfection, yesterday at Chanel. BB, order like there is no tomorrow. The collection is a masterwork, the finest Karl has done in his entire career! Also, Anna has said you can order the same little black, she ordered, and we made a coat from another dress. Tell Beatrice to do exactly the same for you . . . it is the little short black Audrey Hepburn dress, worn under a very strict nun like tunic. We turned the tunic into a beautiful coat, zips up the front to wear over the dress."

Wednesday night: "Steer clear of anything edged in sable at Balmain; the sable is not the finest and therefore it will date badly. . . . You are going to want to be in Chanel, for its sheer perfection. . . . Chanel is younger, refined. It is like nothing, yet it is everything. It is mostly black, white. You are going to flip for the severity, married to the frivolity and explosion of fantasy. Trust me. Annette [de la Renta] and I have seen this stuff longer. Anna ordered three things. . . .

"Chado [Ralph Rucci's ready-to wear line] prices are couture, but the quality is couture. Of course I do not expect you to think of ordering a matte crocodile jacket for $70,000, the ballgown is $80,000 . . . but there are sensible prices like ten thousand for the workmanship. Double face sable trousers. Gold handbags like bamboo baskets. . . . He will be the future to look for things that don't absolutely pull you down when the bon de commande is presented."

I had a sinking feeling as he talked about "sensible prices"—the same feeling that had come upon me the year before when Anna had told me to dash down "immediately Barbara" to the YSL ready-to-wear shop in Manhattan to pick up this must-buy trench coat in python. She had got one and the price was "quite reasonable."

Her price was clearly very different to the one I was offered.

André's fashion diary to me continued: "Karl's dinner organized by Anna last nite (sic), where Oscar and Karl danced the merengue was brilliant. Annette wore Karl Lagerfeld Gallery. The orchestra was marvellous. . . . Listen, someone told me there was an item in the paper about your legs up in the air on the Concorde from some unhinged chair. I was told this at the reception, I thought it was gossip, but someone said they had read it in the London papers? Are you recovered from that incident?"

(I was.)

"Danielle Steele ordered ten looks from Balmain including the bride's entire look. For San Francisco. Go figure."

André is a far more complex man than these faxes reveal: in them he was doing a job for me. My husband shared my fondness for André, whose accomplishment as an extra-large-size, gay Afro-American man in the viper's nest of fashion has been entirely due to enormous talent, perseverance and hard work, all at the cost of any personal life whatsoever. How he obtained his graduate degrees in French Studies is extraordinary given that he was brought up by his grandmother in segregated Durham, North Carolina, where she was a cleaning lady and his grandfather a sharecropper.

He would have been invaluable had I discovered him at the beginning of my foray into haute couture. But I was at the end. The huge outlay embarrassed and worried me. And I didn't know how to tell him. After all, I had solicited his advice and he was dutifully giving it to me. But the bills were being dumped in Conrad's lap.

The final fax came the next evening:

"Hold everything. It's at Gaultier that you will let it rip. Forget everything I said about Chanel." A list of nine possible looks followed.

"This collection was a romantic masterwork, the best haute couture Gaultier has ever done in his career. You don't have to go to Chanel, not even for number 16. I would spend it all at Balmain and

Gaultier, with most of the big investment evening choices at Gaultier. You will be so very, very pleased as—I know you love Gaultier. I loved it, there is such beauty and modernity! Much love, André Leon Talley."

I ordered nothing.

Then the August 2002 *Vogue* appeared on newsstands. I quickly dashed out and bought six copies of it, hoping that the woman who outed the burn on my second-hand dress in Toronto was still alive: if she was, she'd read it, because those rich Forest Hill ladies all read *Vogue*. I didn't see the interview's potential as a lethal reactant because I hadn't yet grasped the new ingredients in the American business culture.

At this point in time, social media and "celebrity wardrobes" had not yet taken hold. When they did, photos of girls, never mind women, with hundreds of pairs of shoes, outfits galore and loads of handbags would be something to be admired and proudly shown off. In terms of shallow display, I was ahead of my time and behind in the number of handbags. After ten or eleven years of avoiding interviews, I had mucked up. My desire to see myself memorialized in *Vogue*, to make the cut as a fashionable woman, had been my undoing. I might as well have constructed the guillotine in my walk-in clothes cupboards and lain down beneath the blade.

CHAPTER SIXTEEN

Summer Storms and Autumn Thunder

There was nothing to indicate that 2003 would be the year in which the curtain would rise on act 1 of our very own opera, set in madness and played out in a shadowy world where we seldom knew what would happen next, only that it would be hellishly bad. Any opera addict knows—especially if, like me, you're an addict of Wagner and just about anything Russian—that almost every opera follows an absurd plot, ending with fabulously musical deaths splattered everywhere and the tenor on his knees crying, "Ignominy! Anguish! Oh, my pitiable fate!" as the curtain falls to huge applause.

We had a packed house watching us but no applause.

There were small signs of the jolly new order to come that I didn't recognize. When I tried to buy two Wolford bodysuits in Bloomingdale's, the saleslady, who had just complimented me on my Hermès handbag, did a rapid reassessment as she announced with a note, of slight triumph I felt, that my Bloomingdale's card was declined. This had happened earlier in the day, when I was trying to buy a pair of shoes at Bendel's.

"That's not possible," I said, politely, now that she was clutching my packaged bodysuits, showing some reluctance to hand them over. I insisted on the impossible—call upstairs—taking wry comfort from evidently having made her day. There are greater tragedies in life than the declined credit card, but it certainly does bring joy to the messenger. Even the bloody ATM machines seem to up their screen brightness when declining my withdrawal. "Try another amount" is not a reassuring message when you've asked for $150. I managed to wheedle out the info that my Bloomingdale's credit limit was now cut to $100, but didn't twig what was going on. I simply thought this was just another one of those irritating and argumentative computers or some unfathomable muck-up because of all my various social insurance numbers getting muddled.

I had three social security cards—from the U.K., Canada and the U.S.—with three different names to go with them—single, married and titled. The thought of traipsing up to customer service to explain that Lady Black of Crossharbour was the same person as the Barbara Amiel who got her Bloomingdale's card in 1972 wasn't inviting. I just left it.

I didn't know that forces inside Hollinger's New York office were sabotaging my credit references.

Otherwise, everything seemed perfectly normal. We hit Washington for the White House Correspondents' Dinner and New York for Anna Wintour's big bash for the Costume Institute at the Metropolitan Museum, whose theme that year was "Goddess," which I thought was redundant given that was pretty much how most of the guests saw themselves on a daily basis. Anna was all in white, with a white ostrich jacket and very black sunglasses. By 2003, my confidence level had finally pretty much stabilized, allowing me to enjoy some gala events, so long as I wasn't in charge of them. My attendance at big events like the Met Gala would of course confirm the description of me in columns and profiles as a "socialite," which was irritating, but then I thought, well, it has a whiff of Audrey Hepburn in *Breakfast at Tiffany's* or even Babe Paley at Truman Capote's legendary 1966 Black and White Ball for *Washington Post* publisher Katherine Graham. So what if it didn't seem to take account of a full-time writing job as well as executive functions.

Conrad had, thank God, finished his 1,296-page single-volume biography of Franklin Roosevelt, and plans were being made for publication in late fall. "Let me do the publication party," said Marie-Josée Kravis, and Annette de la Renta said, "I'll co-host," which

Conrad thought was pretty great. Two social heavyweights to bring in the crowds.

May arrived, bringing spring, and for the first three weeks it *was* spring—emotionally speaking. Conrad and I split the social calendar. The Mariinsky Theatre was having its gala three-hundredth-anniversary celebration in St. Petersburg and I desperately wanted to go, but for some reason an invite didn't materialize. Probably just as well: Dmitri Hvorostovsky was singing, and my adulation of the Siberian Tiger might have fused my wiring. Instead, I went to Montreal on May 1 to do my much lower-kilowatt performance for Israel Bonds at a synagogue that was filled with the most polite and accepting audience I'd ever had. They were so gracious I almost felt guilty about accepting the $20,000 fee. I mean, the right thing to do would be to donate it to the cause. But then I thought, Look, for over six weeks I had worked on my speech to the point of near dementia. I justified taking the hefty fee on grounds that if you do one free, every Jewish organization under the sun invites you to speak. All the same, it was wrong.

Wrong. The theme of the year.

That same day, Conrad went alone to a big dinner at David Rockefeller's in New York—a split very much in my favour, I thought, given Mr. Rockefeller's anal-retentive personality playing Noble Patriarch of America's most iconic Wasp family, hell-bent on avoiding controversy. Then, joining the great spring migration of North Americans hell-bent on "doing the season," we flew to London, right into the belly-up season of pink food. *The Telegraph* always had a garden in the Chelsea Flower Show, which is pretty much the season's start. The Queen arrived, gloved, and with a very glum-looking Prince Charles searching for ecological developments to enhance his magnificent gardens at Highgrove. They stared at the *Daily Telegraph* garden.

"Oh Lord," I had uttered as we arrived at this year's garden, which was named, with unerring prescience, "The Wrong Garden." The water in its fountain ran uphill, or rather it looked like it was going uphill but that was illusionary. Usually, I loved our *Telegraph* garden, especially when Arabella Lennox-Boyd did it. This garden was the feat of engineer James Dyson of vacuum cleaner fame, who explained, "The starting point was unconventionality. We wanted to investigate the idea of wrongness as a design principle," as if that was an explanation. The critics wrote admiringly of how his entry "challenged our ideas of how a garden should look." I dare say. I hated it.

During the bang-up Cartier dinner in the Chelsea Physic Garden that evening, my body decided to put on a little sideshow of its own. "My dear," said Nicky Haslam as we sat down, everyone lingering to turn about and see if their placement was up to scratch, "is something wrong? Your hands are a very odd colour. Shouldn't we do something?"

My fingers were now blue. Secondary Raynaud's is a minor syndrome, collateral to my dermatomyositis, but I hadn't had an attack for years. Usually my fingers would go white halfway down before I noticed it, and getting to all blue was an impressive first. Finding warm water fast does the trick but hurts like blazes and your hands turn a bright scarlet. Looking back, frozen hands, declined credit cards—ironic billets-doux from somewhere. The Cartier dinner was a fitting line to be drawn under the enjoyment of normal times.

Two days later we were in New York City for the 2003 Hollinger International annual shareholders' meeting. No herbaceous borders here, just nettles and thorns. The meeting was held in a hideously gloomy room in the Metropolitan Club on Sixtieth Street, just east of Fifth Avenue. Anticipating a bit of badmouthing by the activist institutional shareholder Tweedy, Browne, Conrad had suggested to Donald Trump that he make a statement at the meeting expressing confidence in Conrad's management of Hollinger, given the recent deal they had made together for the sale of the Chicago Sun-Times Building as co-developers, a deal that turned out to be highly profitable for both parties. Donald bought some Hollinger stock to make himself eligible to attend.

I was horrified. I had nothing against Donald Trump, who, in our brief meetings, had always been pleasant, but no matter his considerable business successes, I couldn't see him as the best source for a credible vote of confidence in Conrad's dealings. "Wrong note for that meeting," I pleaded to Conrad. "Too razzamatazz for any prickly institutional activist. He will have the reverse effect you want." I had always wiggled uneasily in my seat at Hollinger board meetings, fearing they were altogether too jovial and that we were losing serious directors as Conrad narrated stirring tales of his battles with Murdoch. They wanted dull and figures. They always got the figures, but dull was not a word in Conrad's life.

"Melania is so beautiful," said Conrad, speaking to one of his stronger motivations. "She'll be a pleasure to see at the meeting."

She was and is beautiful. The meeting, though, was about as ugly as they get, short of a shoe- or chair-throwing session. The day before, we—all the Hollinger executives and directors—had been sent a not-your-best-friend letter from a New York City law firm on behalf of Tweedy, Browne, third-largest institutional investor in Hollinger. As far as I could understand the terminology, Tweedy, Browne was demanding Conrad and Hollinger executives return all management and non-compete payments made, totalling US$74 million, plus damages and interest. Horrid words like *usurpation* and *misappropriation* were sprinkled throughout the letter.

If Conrad was upset, he hid it from me. One of the singular qualities of my husband is his ability to absorb pain and his determination to never show it or to worry me. This spared me considerable worry of my own, but it had its downside: I remained in the dark as to the extent of our problems for far too long. Conrad repeated a mantra I was going to hear him say to one and all for the rest of my life, day in and day out, on television, at dinner, in courtrooms, in bed and in my nightmares—which though true was not exactly the poetry by which I wanted to live and die: "These payments were approved by the audit committee, discussed by the directors and revealed in full to the SEC"—the U.S. Securities and Exchange Commission—"in multiple filings. Our corporate lawyers in Toronto and Chicago approved and signed off on everything." No, not quite the elegant epitaph I pictured for my gravestone, but still, okay. Fine, that should do it, I thought.

Tweedy, Browne had also filed a form with the SEC demanding a special committee be established to investigate all payments to Hollinger executives. Although "special committee" had the sound of organizers of a school prom, they were in fact the business world's flavour of the month, and while in our blind madness we thought they were simply an additional if cumbersome layer of protection for shareholders, they were a Trojan Horse for taking over or, as in our case, stealing a company from all shareholders, every single one, big and small.

As the meeting wore on, a nondescript investor with a bald head and small fringe of hair like a tonsured monk stood up and accused Conrad of theft. "Stealing," he said. Conrad replied tersely with real anger: if that was what he thought, he should sell his stock, likely at a decent enough profit, and get out. This was not banter. Our board of directors, up for re-election, sat grimly in the front row with hang-dog expressions and almost visible bubbles over their heads: "What am I doing here? What do I need this for?" All the directors were there except Henry Kissinger, who, not uncharacteristically when trouble is in the air, begged off in favour of a meeting of the Eisenhower Foundation. Rather like getting a headache to avoid sex, I thought.

After Donald stood up to commend Conrad on their deal, the largest institutional investor, Southeastern Asset Management, stood up almost heroically in that lynch 'em atmosphere and said that Conrad and his executives had earned every cent of their disputed fees after having created $2 billions' worth of assets, and they would be satisfied with the phasing out of the super-voting shares (which confer extra votes per share). Conrad had already conceded this would be done over a period of time. "Black Caves In," read the headlines.

I knew that just about every media company, including the *Washington Post*, the *New York Times*, Rupert Murdoch's News Corp, and Associated Newspapers (which owns *The Mail*), had the same super-voting shares in family or friendly hands in order to keep control, as does Canada's Torstar, but neither the Sulzbergers, the Rothermeres, the Grahams nor the Honderiches were under a media spotlight.

Next item on the Tweedy, Browne agenda was our chef, or rather his cost. Apparently one-third of our chef's salary was paid by the company, which, though I didn't know that, seemed pretty damn fair. Admittedly, when you hire a chef who, fabulous though he was, demands same-day caviar from the Caspian Sea, the bills do mount up. I had tried to monitor kitchen expenses after asking one day how it was possible for five carrots to cost twenty-five pounds sterling, really, and as for the fresh lobster—had it been flown in that day from Maine on the Concorde? I did a special committee investigation of one into the carrot scandal but got nowhere. The answers, when they came, were usually delivered by puzzled blank faces whose grasp of their native English suddenly failed and whose fallback position was that things were "very expensive" that particular day due to weather, always terrible climate problems, and we did need fresh ingredients.

"We will set budgets for the meals," I said purposefully, and gave said budget to the house manager and went back to monitoring the *National Post*, having earlier taken on the job of executive VP editorial for Hollinger. I tried, wishfully, to think of one dinner or lunch at our homes that had not been for a business reason or with a business component. Conrad told shareholders that all subsidies of this sort would end. I crossed my fingers and prayed this would mean giving fewer dinner parties. Since *The Telegraph*'s offices were located in the Docklands, quite a few people balked at going there, and so it made sense to hold business lunches at our Kensington house. At the end of the meeting, Conrad, as rehearsed, proposed the establishment of a special committee of the Hollinger board to "clear the air and look at and report on all the contested payments." Some members of the audit committee, and the directors, brightened up at the prospect of additional fees.

Conrad was up to date on everything in the world of newspaper publishing—and, of course, about FDR from christening cup to burial—but out of touch with the deadly bog of American corporate governance. He had absolutely no idea of the scope and power of a special committee. I had even less. We both thought, Oh goody, we'll just have a special committee check everything out and this unhappiness will end.

I was not encouraged when Marie-Josée Kravis, one of our directors, came up to me as we were beginning to exit the Metropolitan Club's gloom. She was wearing her impassive face with a very smart day suit: "A special committee," she said to me. "That's the end." The words were tossed out indifferently. She'd had some experience with them on other boards.

"That's what she said?" Conrad asked me later. "I wish she had discussed this with me before I agreed to the committee." All the same, Conrad thought the meeting had gone very well. "We've come through it," he said.

Outside the Metropolitan Club, press lined the covered entrance right up to the curb. Flashbulbs and hostile questions. Okay, here goes, deep breath, I thought. Up yours, I was silently thinking as a frazzle-haired journalist poked a mike in front of me and triumphantly asked what it was like to be married to an accused thief. Don't you wish you had a husband as good-looking and clever as mine, I wanted to reply, but kept my peace. When a *Sunday Times* journalist asked Conrad if he was overpaid, he replied that he thought not but the journalist probably was. My tone-deaf inner voice was humming along at what a lovely day this was—the weather so sunny and clear, without any of the humidity that proper summer brings to New York City. Thank God that meeting is over, sung the voice, here's Gus our driver, yes, look, we have a car and driver of our own, and now we can escape all you nosy reporters and post-mortem over tea and chocolate biscuits. I was not depressed, in fact I was a little self-satisfied about the merits of my position and husband, unaware that this was anything more than a normal business battle.

After all, what was life with Conrad without a business struggle. He battled from continent to continent. For example Australia, when he was fighting to get control of the Fairfax newspaper group, which he did. My highlight memory of those battles with Australia's Rupert Murdoch, Kerry Packer and a couple of prime ministers was the Australian Senate hearings on foreign and cross-ownership in the media, which ought to have been titled "How to Screw a Large, Cross and Foreign Canadian." I sat demure and bored in the front row, attempting to look keenly interested like a responsible foreign partner's spouse.

The newspaper wars in London had been going on since the second year of our marriage, and early on, when I was not yet accustomed to the almost daily jog from euphoria to despair, Conrad found me atop a ladder against the wall of my workroom—I never called it an office; that made it sound as if I were an accountant or obstetrician with a real profession—in our rented Belgravia home. I was trying to open the high windows. "What on earth are you doing?" he asked, reasonably enough. I looked down at him. "Deciding whether to die on the battlefield or in Chester Square," I said matter-of-factly. Fighting Murdoch, who is a combination of every opera villain going and then some, is scary. Stab Scarpia or even Mephistopheles in the back and in florid arias they would accuse you of dirty dealing. Backstab Murdoch and he would shrug it off as normal business practice. But there was a qualitative difference in this new Hollinger battle. This one was within its own shareholders. And the press saw an opening.

Newspapers are utterly fascinated by themselves and their own. Together with the larger-than-life profile of my husband, the mix was toxic. His views were antithetical to the left, and we had provided a God-given opening for *The Guardian* and *The Independent*. But this time it was not simply a question of *pas d'amis à gauche*. Murdoch's London and New York City papers, from his tabloid *Sun* and *New York Post* to the broadsheets of *The Times* of London, were on our jugular as well. *Pas d'amis à droite*. The two of us were about to do our own Charge of the Light Brigade.

"Is the Party Over for the Blacks?" was the tabloid take, and "Ultimatum for Lord Black" was the more restrained broadsheet approach. In Canada, the old knives were resharpened for the "Lord" Black who had deserted his country for foxhounds. To add a note of gaiety, another unnamed source reported on our summer party and added, "Some guests couldn't help noticing that Lady Black's hair seemed to have grown rather spectacularly. Surely she can't have had hair extensions?" Odd, I thought, that the length of my hair was now part of the brew. This was the time, too, that photos of me in dresses began to appear not in *W* and the glossies but in the business pages as examples of our/my excess.

Senior former employees found themselves overwhelmed by newly discovered feelings of moral responsibility. They had to speak up. Max Hastings, in his 2002 memoirs, wrote that Conrad was "seldom unconscious of his responsibilities as a member of the rich man's trade union." Hmm. I thought back to the lengths Conrad had gone to protect rich man Max's not inadequate income at the time of his divorce. And then there was the eighty-year-old Peregrine Worsthorne, former editor of the *Sunday Telegraph* and High Tory, so emollient when he wanted something from Conrad, now gratuitously vituperative, offering *The Independent* a nasal quote, calling Conrad's friends—a list that included Margaret Thatcher, Henry Kissinger, Richard Perle, Lord Carrington, Mangosuthu Buthelezi and Jimmy Goldsmith—"certainly not my definition of the great and the good. Conrad bestrides a very small world like a colossus." Knowing Perry's vanity, I suspected he had practised that quote in front of the mirror in case the BBC came calling.

As the summer wore on, I knew that something was going the way of Chelsea's "Wrong" Garden. Conrad was looking for an investor among the large funds to come in as a partner and privatize Hollinger. "This is the way to go," he said. "Get out of the spotlight and manage the company for long-term benefits, not these short-termers who want to sell everything and run." Correct thinking, but getting out of the spotlight at this point was rather like rethinking strategy when in a tumbrel en route to the Place de la Révolution.

Given the value of real assets, there ought to have been no trouble with either a refinancing or a major investor, apart from the usual Marrakesh bazaar aspect. But we didn't realize how advanced the plotting against Conrad had become. The special committee had retained Richard Breeden as its counsel. We knew nothing about him apart from his position as former head of the SEC. "A good man," director Richard Burt told us. Compared to what? Felix Dzerzhinsky?

The summer was a *folie à deux*. On the one hand, we were attending parties and socializing in what I thought were regular London season gatherings, plus quick coffees with girlfriends in Harvey Nicks. What I didn't quite twig to was that quite a few of our more casual "get-togethers" now had a different agenda. Conrad was in search not only of investment but someone to tell him what the blazes was going on.

In principle—I shouldn't use that word because it wasn't present in a single one of our directors—Conrad's own directors should have and could have told him what was impeding his ability to get the necessary refinancing. They knew, and remained silent. Behind Conrad's back, the special committee's Breeden was warning investors and banks that something fishy, possibly even criminal, was going on at Hollinger, and that warning was enough to deter. Blocking refinancing would turn out to be contrary to both Hollinger's and shareholders' interests—only Breeden and the expanding network of lawyers (including his own firm) and accountants he employed would profit. But Conrad had no ability to respond to secret allegations. The directors cowered, heeding their lawyers' cautions and Breeden's threats that they might be implicated if any wrongdoing was found. Oh, for just one principled and "brave" man.

Conrad thought Blackstone Group chairman Stephen Schwarzman might be the man—he was not only the most successful financial investor in America but unusually straightforward; if he knew anything, he would tell Conrad. So we had both Stephen and his wife to lunch and dinner and also visited them in their New York apartment. His wife, Christine, was very thin, young and lovely and much warmer than the other wealthy Manhattan and Palm Beach wives, but quite high-strung, and I was always a bit worried that if I got too enthusiastic in my views she might break apart like that exploding pumpkin Edward Fox shoots in *Day of the Jackal*.

Stephen has large spaniel eyes and, as the summer went on, there was a look of concern in them that puzzled me. A friend, jeweller Dorrit Moussaieff, had just married the president of Iceland, of course, and was giving an appropriately smashing dinner with him in her Cadogan Gardens flat. She had seated me next to Stephen.

"How is Conrad doing?" he asked.

"Fine. He's just about wrapped up the refinancing," I said. At that point Conrad was negotiating with the Carlyle Group and it was at the last stage, the one before the lawyers give the final OK to the agreement.

"I'm glad," said Stephen. Pause. Spaniel eyes fixed on my face, searching . . . for what? I believed what I was saying, so nothing to find, nothing held back. He divined that. "I really hope it goes well for him." There was a diminished cadence in his voice, not patronizing; it sounded like genuine concern, which I found worrying. Why would he be concerned? I knew Conrad had been talking to Blackstone about refinancing as well. But then he had been talking to lots of people to get the best deal.

A year or so earlier Conrad had talked to Henry Kravis about the global investment firm Kohlberg Kravis Roberts, which Henry had co-founded, taking a stake in Hollinger so it could go private. He respected Henry and thought KKR a good bet, but hadn't mentioned it to me for whatever reason. Now, try to imagine the worst possible way to find out about your husband's financial dealings. Does the name Marie-Josée Kravis come to mind? It should.

I was lunching in Harry's Bar with Joan Collins. Given her star status, we had been placed in the table she favoured against the wall. A voice greeted me, not altogether warmly, and I looked up. It was the inevitable Marie-Josée, the absolute epitome of elegance. She is blessed with exquisite features, dark hair and a manner so cool it could get you through a power cut of several days in a hundred-plus-degree weather.

"I heard the dinner went very well," she said, effectively to both of us, since Joan and I were sitting next to one another against the back wall. She was referring to a Hollinger event to which she and Henry had been invited but had declined to attend. I opened my mouth to thank her, but she had more to say. "The first thing Henry would do if he decides to go into Hollinger would be to cut out its big dinners. They're unnecessary." The remark was delivered with a hauteur that matched her clothes—in fact outdid them. Whether or not Henry's view was correct, and I expect it was, Conrad had come to the same conclusion. Still, the time and place for that little critique, which could only be construed as one of those "my husband's wallet (read: penis) is bigger than yours," was not en passant as I lunched with a friend.

I do distrust people who can say unpleasant things without blinking, and Marie-Josée's eyes remained perfectly expressionless. She disappeared into the back room of Harry's. I repeated it to Conrad, and all he would say was that Henry's company was looking at Hollinger's refinancing plans. He never rose to any bait that criticized Marie-Josée, which could drive me potty. Sometimes you really do need your spouse to get down in the gutter with the rest of the world and gossip with you. But they had been good friends. "Henry has very impressive, first-rate people" was all he would say.

As the summer days of 2003 began to shorten, the London season tightened. Tom Stoppard gave his annual garden party, where I could admire him along with a few hundred other people. Stoppard is tied with the late Dmitri Hvorostovsky for my two super-great extramarital pashes, but Stoppard now has the edge, being alive and with a history stretching back to my twenties, when I first saw *Rosencrantz and Guildenstern*.

So strong grew my adoration of Stoppard as I saw more and more of his work that it overcame my acute discomfort at encountering his close friend Jeremy Irons on the few occasions we were invited to Tom's flat. Just like Bryan Ferry, Irons has served a chilling purpose in my life: I am invisible to them both. Neither Irons nor Ferry seem to believe in the bother of making a new female acquaintance much over the age of consent. And I don't blame them for a moment. This is a perfectly understandable law of nature, which you try to outwit when clothed in the allure of your husband's newspaper empire and your own writing. That doesn't cut it in the land of heartthrobs, where you are simply a middle-aged woman advancing steadily into the twilight zone of incontinence underwear. I suppose I might have been "interesting" to talk to on some level, but by that point in a man's life they have all the interesting females they can handle—just never enough physical sex.

Summer wore on. *Lohengrin* was playing at the Royal Opera House with the legendary Waltraud Meier and Robert Dean Smith, who would go on to sing Wagner at Bayreuth. Came the annual Serpentine Summer Party, and then Elton John and David Furnish had their late-June White Tie and Tiara Ball, the last one we would attend. Which is a somewhat more benign application of the insightful "you never know when it is the last time" that David Graham winningly said to me pre-lovemaking on a Lake Country weekend when he was claiming reconciliation after our divorce but was actually in the throes of a passionate love affair with a six-foot blonde American plastic surgeon. I am happy to report that this particular young blonde Amazon ended up stealing his credit card numbers, and less happy, though not, I confess, distraught, to report that she was eventually murdered in her Chicago garage—drugs, I think. My indifference to her bloody end arose from a bizarre incident in which she sent David over to my London lodgings after our divorce with a condom firmly attached by surgical glue to his relevant part, together with her instructions to make love to me. Given my rather weak emotional condition, the consequent distress this caused on revelation of the situation and explanation of why it was that our embraces could not bear fruit did not seem to me to be so very amusing.

Like everyone who does the London season, it all ends up with an inability to find any waistband that still fits after countless helpings of summer pudding and smoked salmon. Some well-heeled friend had recommended I speak to her latest find before I left London for Toronto, a fitness guru who apparently monitored everything, including your complete food intake. This would help Conrad, I thought. Very cautiously, I had a Mr. Bean come to the London house, where he explained, reasonably enough in his lights, that, yes, his program to get us healthy required first a full study of our lifestyle, starting with me.

I have always loathed the word *lifestyle* and never as much as when it means someone is going to ask absolutely asinine questions insofar as they are applicable to any life I lead. My life has no style; it has always been a precarious mix of gutter and ballroom, of intense work and absolutely unhealthy play. Still, came the predictable questions: How much sleep do you have? Per night? Average in a week? What do you have for breakfast? What is your training regimen? What are your goals?

Goals? Regimen? Had such lunatic vocabulary hit cardigan-and-common-sense Britain? I had thought asking about one's "goals" was a North American preoccupation, but now it was obviously a by-product of increased emigration to London of wealthy Manhattanites.

A long questionnaire was left at the house for me to fill out. For people who love questionnaires about themselves the way some love psychoanalysis, Mr. Bean was probably ideal. How could I explain that, without my mix of Carnation evaporated milk and Ribena to swallow my 20 milligrams of codeine at somewhere between midnight and 3 a.m., I could not write a bloody line, let alone calculate what my "goals" in fitness were, and that after doing this for the past forty years, I was unlikely to recalibrate. Mr. Bean came on a Very Confidential basis because, as I explained to him, I didn't want the newspapers to start shovelling it at me. He understood. "I shan't even mention I've seen you to the people that recommended me."

A couple of days later my assistant, Penny Phillips, put a snippet on my desk from Ephraim Hardcastle's gossip column in the *Daily Mail*. After taking a whack at Conrad for spending company money on the papers of Franklin Roosevelt (turned out to be a great investment), his eye turned to me. "There is more positive news to report. His wife (pictured) Barbara Amiel (Lady Black in private life) has decided that she and the somewhat portly fifty-eight-year-old Lord Black must improve their physical fitness. Friends say Barbara has decided on a programme costing thousands in which experts will study every aspect of their lives, interview members of their staff in both London and Manhattan, and study their diet. Whatever arrows are fired at them by critics in financial circles, the Blacks will henceforth be in fighting trim."

After reading that, I got the feeling you get on seeing parsley stuck in your teeth when the night is over. If only I had known, you think. When gossip columnists are questioning your financial circumstances rather than the usual "Does she or doesn't she?" you get the picture fast: people are talking non-stop and exclusively about your husband's business problems. All the emails I had been getting from friends and the concerned looks asking essentially the same question—"How are you?"—had not been referring to my physical health.

As the days shortened, my worries began to leak out of Pandora's box and surface, often in the form of itchy eczema. We were in real trouble. Hollinger's loan notes were coming due, and in the ordinary course of events would simply be refinanced. The list of companies Conrad had approached to invest in Hollinger's refinancing, and their rejection of the same, was considerable. "I don't understand it," he would say, worried, puzzled. "We've got great assets. They're managed extremely well. We've beaten Murdoch in the price war. This is simply a question of ripening assets to sell them all at the right time. Everyone I approach are all very interested, work hard going over our company, and then make all the right excited noises after finishing satisfactory due diligence, only to abruptly flake off. I never can get a good answer why, and people with whom I've always had excellent relations can offer no good reason."

Blackstone, KKR, Warburg Pincus, Quadrangle, Madison Dearborn. I heard all the names and watched as the same thing happened. Initial meeting, lots of interest, due diligence on the company completed after swarms of accountants and money managers circled and landed on the financials, followed by great enthusiasm—Conrad's spirits reviving, intense negotiations and exchange of emails and draft deals. I'd listen to the telephone conversations, sitting in the library with him, watching his fist-face of concentration, noting his assumed matter-of-fact air to the person at the other end of the line, even though in fact I knew he was desperate, and my hands would be knuckled. The conversation would end, and Conrad would turn to me: "Well, I think that's it," he'd say. "We've got an agreement. It just has to have the final runover by their lawyers." He would retreat to our terrace with his evening glass of wine that was evolving into his evening glasses of wine—not more than two or three, but to a non-drinker like me it was still a worrying amount. After the first couple of collapsed deals, I could no longer feel any relief when I heard "we've got a deal," only increasing worry, because I knew there would be another level of stress on him. And then, always, it was all off. His calls not returned. Dead air.

We would wait apprehensively, wishing that the telephone, which had forever rung, would end its silence and ring again. When you have lived with the sound of non-stop telephone calls for years and in a flash, just from one day to the next, everything goes silent, it is like finding yourself on the moon's crater. When finally someone could be contacted, and usually it was the junior to the desired contact, there was a cul-de-sac of words. "We don't think this is for us. I'm afraid it can't be done," some lawyer or other would report.

Only Stephen Schwarzman gave us a glimpse of what was going on. "We'd like to buy," he told Conrad, "but have to wait until the special committee process is over." Which was useless because Hollinger's notes were due very fast, the cash wasn't there, and the special committee's report would take a number of months, we thought. And anyway, what did the special committee's report have to do with the status of Hollinger Inc.? If Conrad's understanding of what was going on was nil, mine was nil minus a hundred. But when I looked at Conrad, increasingly pallid and exhausted, it was as if I could see past his flesh to the veins and arteries where a huge thrombosis was relentlessly working its way up to his heart.

By the autumn, the newspapers were giving Hollinger daily death notices. There was rarely a day when one or another paper in London, Toronto or New York would not write about the desperate situation of the company. Depending on the format of the newspaper, tabloid or broadsheet, the crisis would be blamed on our lifestyle or on the fiscal structure of Hollinger. We were twisting in the wind. Most of it was inaccurate, even in the *National Post* in Toronto, which Conrad had founded as a conservative oasis in the great Canadian left-wing desert.

In Canada, Paul and Jackie Desmarais were opening a new addition to their fabulous 21,000-acre estate in the wilds of Quebec, two hours north of Quebec City. The thick invitation arrived with promises of a weekend combining planned activities with lazy times in the exquisitely furnished rooms. British friends were flying in for the celebrations at the main house, Cherlieu, modelled on a sixteenth-century Palladian villa. There was to be a Russian evening of dinner and dancing, "white tie, long dress, decorations," followed by a barbecue and western party the next night. I wondered if Conrad was going to look for financing there.

The prospect of such a weekend was too daunting for me and I begged off. Conrad once more set off alone, partly because he had enormous affection and respect for Paul Desmarais, and partly, I think, because as the vicious attacks on him in the U.K. press mounted, he wanted to "show the flag"—a phrase I was growing to hate. (I would see this legendary Quebec residence a decade later, when Paul was seeing his old friends one by one to say goodbye before his death.)

In spite of the biting headlines and sarcastic newspaper cartoons, I had absolutely no notion that I was in the last days of our own *ancien régime*. I hung on to some sense that, ultimately, Conrad would tie up loose ends, not nooses. We returned in September to London and went through the motions of social and business life.

By the end of the month, finally, a deal was made with Bain and Company, a reputable Boston global management consultancy. An acceptable term sheet was negotiated that would privatize both Hollinger's Canadian and U.S. companies and leave Conrad and Bain as equal shareholders and managing partners. The deal was approved by Bain's lawyers. Hallelujah! The relief that Conrad had a deal was tremendous.

As for the special committee's investigations, the Toronto auditors assured Conrad everything was in order, every deal approved, filings with the SEC made, company filings listing every transaction in order. Hollinger in-house counsel in Toronto and Chicago (where the American corporate offices were based) had signed off on every deal and assured Conrad there was nothing under the carpet for the special committee to dig up. "All Tweedy, Browne is doing," said Conrad, "in spite of their noise and fury, is complaining I am paid too well. The accretion in values covers that." For a second or two in corporate time he had some of his natural enthusiasm and bounce back.

On October 13 we said goodbye to the staff and our driver, left our Cottesmore Gardens home and got aboard the company plane for New York.

The gods are not entirely ruthless when they are about to impale you: this would be the final trip Conrad would take on that plane, which, much as he liked it, wouldn't be a death blow. Far more of a kick in the lower anatomy would have been the knowledge that this was also the final time he'd be in his London home, the final day he would sit in his roomy and decidedly eccentric office at the back of the house, converted from the disco it had been for the former owner to make space at the window for his desk with its large ship models; the last time he would eat, sleep and be in his own home in Kensington. I think it would have near killed him had he known.

In late October, Bain and Company, at the very point of closing, pulled out of the deal. "Why?" asked Conrad. "The externalities," replied a member of the Bain team. We hadn't a clue.

INTERMEZZO

A rockslide begins in silence. The steep hills of granite sit, quite sure of their dominance. They stand firm even as water gathers deep below them. Gradually the erosion begins and the coming danger is manifest in a hairline crack or sometimes a little spray of pebbles. Pressure fights stability, and disaster waits patiently for some triggering event, ordinarily a rainstorm or some idle whim of the earth. Small rocks break off, tentatively. Dust hangs about, suspended in the silence. The calm is a *ruse de guerre*. Water defeats stone and the granite crumbles in a cumulative shift, rock upon rock, till the very landslide itself creates a second storm as it forces the air beneath it out. Nothing can stop it.

I've tried to look back and see when our rockslide began. I can see the cracks and pebbles all right. They are all those dates in my diary accompanied by a sick feeling of the ground being undermined by some force I didn't understand. For many years I could not see the beginning. Others could, and I should have—after all, I had climbed the face of those rocks, kicking them with abandon, indifferent to their laws. Later, I knew that there never were gentle slopes, only sequences of misjudgments without malignant intent that had built to this explosive point. But at the beginning, for us, the noisy calamities, one after another hurling down on top of us and dissolving ordinary life, began the afternoon of October 29, 2003.

I sat sipping coffee in an open storefront on Third Avenue and made a call to my husband. "Everything all right?" I asked routinely. "A disaster," he replied in an unexpectedly dull voice. I immediately set out for home. The sun, as is always required on disaster days, was shining brightly. The East Side moms that had so delighted me moments before now turned into chatty roadblocks, silly women with Hummer-style prams and hanging paraphernalia to be dodged. My husband, when I reached him, was very still. On the wall facing him was a picture by a favourite painter, Christopher Nevinson, showing some of his favourite things—ships in New York's harbour. The painting was a wash of olive and silver hanging next to the windows overlooking Park Avenue. A tiny stream of sunlight had managed to slip past the higher buildings opposite our second-floor apartment and threw some illumination on his face. The painting's silver ash frame matched my husband's ashen face. He sat upright and rigid. A pharaoh with no purpose.

"It's finished," he said. "This is the worst day of my life."

What if I had known then what I know now? What if I had known that we were about to become a scandal in London and New York, our lives gruesomely dissected with a butcher's delicacy and a thief's honesty by Vanity Fair, The New Yorker, the Sunday Times, the BBC, CBC, Uncle Tom Cobley and all?

What if I had known that for the next two years, with a short break of a few phony weeks in the summer of 2004, we would wake up to pages of faxed newspaper clippings, sometimes as many as fifty, rarely as few as ten, every day, every weekend, with headlines that claimed my husband was "disgraced," had "looted" hundreds of millions of dollars from the company he had created?

What if I had known the stories would, through a type of angio-genesis, grow their own deviations, malformed, malevolent, till the speculative had become the thing itself creeping over media and dinner tables for the next dozen years, only slowing down after every last bit of poison could be wrung from it and the matter would be used up, just as we were, with a contented sigh that we had been "finished"?

What if I had known that my husband's name would become a synonym for greed and failure, a cautionary tale for little children, and that at sixty-three years of age, after a lifetime of work and apparent success, I would lose every job I held, be accused of taking money for work not done, and be ridiculed in the public eye as a contemporary Marie Antoinette—what then?

We were about to become, just as newspapers and magazines gleefully and correctly predicted in the weeks following, shunned by our smart New York friends, who only weeks earlier had professed to "love" us. With a few extraordinary exceptions, London acquaintances carefully retreated, reminding each other of their early suspicions of my husband and of the demise of Robert Maxwell. In Toronto, we were poison among the circles in which my husband had moved since childhood, but an addiction for journalists.

And if I had known, there was nothing to be done. Had we the gift of prophecy, we might have sold some stocks or exercised some options and arranged for monies to be transferred into foreign bank accounts or even our own domestic accounts, just to pay all the many dozens of lawyers we were about to employ. We had no great stashes of cash, no preparations for the onslaught we were going to face. We'd thought we had nothing to hide and so we had no cover. We sat balanced on our highly visible lifestyle, one where telephone calls to the prime minister would be returned the same day, where invitations to dinners and celebrations, written on implacably stiff cards, appeared at an improbable rate, where holiday greetings would come from world leaders, the royal family and statesmen across Europe, from film stars and industrialists. Though any onlooker could have told me that such a life—suddenly achieved—ached for indignant comment and would offer little help when ex officio armour was breached, incredibly, stupidly, I had no concept of the brutal momentum of downfall.

And anyway, I would have said that the social and material "downfall" of two people is in itself only a small personal tragedy. If presented with a similar scenario involving someone else, I might have mused—with breathtaking arrogance—that in a world where people routinely suffered the loss of life to dreadful diseases or the loss of their liberty to brutal dictatorships, what was so special about losing one's job, being dropped from the clubs one belonged to or being forced to resign from the boards and positions held in the community? We had our health.

In spite of all homilies repeated to me in childhood, the admonitions that a reputation was a human being's most precious possession, I could never have foreseen the psychological consequences a total demolition of our reputations would bring. I lacked the imagination. What does a person do, anyway, if they can foresee what is to come? What if you knew, at this very minute, out of the blue and with no time to prepare your defence, that the personal details of your life were to become public property to be scrutinized and then bowdlerized by complete strangers—your letters, your emails, your thoughts, the drawers in your bathroom, the shelves inside your mental cupboards? And if they were not actually open to the stranger, if the medicine cabinet was ruled out of bounds by some stroke of luck, specialists would profess to know what was there anyway, and each cream and potion would be listed in the pages of some newspaper or in the chyron beneath CNN news. Everything you had built professionally would crumble, accompanied by careful explanations that this was meet and proper given the wrongs you had done. How, if one fully believes oneself to be innocent, how do you deal with this?

The half-life to come for over a dozen years, battling calumnies and deceit that even well-disposed friends came to believe, lay ahead. For the first twenty-four months we would exist as wounded snails, withdrawn inside what shells we could create. Each month the perimeter in which we could move became smaller, the noose drawn a bit tighter. We would retreat a little more, and more would be demanded from us—more money, more money, more money—till every shiver in the trees, every telephone call or ring of the fax whispered then yelled the need for more money. There would be no other consideration in our lives. Banks on whose boards my husband had sat for several decades would not give us mortgages on our homes in case the property was forfeited or word got out that they were helping prop up so tainted a name. Courts would demand millions and then more millions before even a shred of evidence had been produced or any charge laid. There would be no more evenings for me spent writing columns or arguing over editorial budgets; we talked almost exclusively to lawyers and officialdom in a little world that felt increasingly remote from any sort of reality, while all around us rejoiced in our discomfort.

As it was, on that October day in New York, knowing nothing and fearing little, I ground the Jamaican Blue Mountain beans in our kitchen and made us both a cup of coffee.

PART TWO

CHAPTER SEVENTEEN

Exit Inch by Inch

The lead-up to the awful day had us routinely observing the social rites of a Manhattan autumn. I had no notion of how we were being viewed, but a pair of doomed marionettes might cover it.

We'd done the opening of the Metropolitan Opera and Carnegie Hall, courtesy of the customary generosity of the Basses. Everyone was too wonderful for words, which was the problem—no words. Perfect manners, air kisses, and not a word said about the huge headlines trumpeting our coming fall. Agreed-upon social manners dictated no reference be made to looming icebergs. It was unnerving, almost spooky.

Through September, October and even some of November, we were still on the regular invitation lists. We sashayed out to dinner with a slightly reserved Jayne Wrightsman, who admired the little black outfit I was wearing. "Who did that darling suit?" she asked. "Donna Karan," I replied, and her interest noticeably waned. A Madison Avenue shop. Not Paris. Not dear Oscar.

In late September the first arrow: Hollinger's special committee was claiming everything on my computer for their investigation and would be taking away my hard drive and for good measure cutting our high-speed T2 lines and access to the servers. My heart absolutely cratered. What did any of these Hollinger business beefs have to do with me? I held no shares, took no non-compete payments. How could some ad hoc group of unknown sticky-handed investigators take away over fifteen years of work—my writing, columns, research, all my email correspondence.

The game had begun in which the target is slowly stripped naked and then cut inch by inch. We were informed in stiff-as-starch terms that our server was Hollinger property and we could not copy or remove anything on it. In movies, people just type in some code, preferably at night, holding a flashlight, and everything is copied and downloaded in less than a minute or two. But in 2003 I had absolutely no idea what to do.

Earlier in the year I had been roped into a speaking engagement: an old flame and friend, Hungarian-born filmmaker Robert Lantos, was being feted at a huge fundraising dinner in Toronto for Canadian athletes going to the 2005 Maccabiah Games in Israel. "You'll hate me," said Lantos, "but I'd be so grateful if you'd be the keynote speaker." Back in July, thinking it a good cause, I replied in a one-word email (now excitingly available to the special committee's investigators): "OK."

The usual fears before making a speech to over a thousand people who've actually paid a lot of money to hear you (or more likely be seen doing good while wearing great outfits) began as I crossed the Sheraton Centre Hotel lobby towards its Grand Ballroom. Usually, I rather liked the little frisson that came from being the night's keynote speaker and wife of Conrad Black. But now a quite different feeling crept over me. Although the sound of hundreds of largely Jewish participants has a pretty high decibel count, for me there was a sense of parting the Red Sea, and not for any Promised Land. Bubbles of silence excluded me as I walked past guests. I was an oddity, a kind of Elephant Man: I had grown tumours, and onlookers were nudging each other. I was unaware at that point of quite how heavy the exclamation-point headlines and newspaper coverage was of the accusations against Conrad. A day later, October 29, I returned to New York.

A late fall day in New York is the perfect time for walking. It had everything—blue sky, crisp sunlight and, lifting my spirits, the prospect of poppy seed palacsintas on Little Hungary's Seventy-Ninth Street. John Ruskin named the association between mood and weather a "pathetic fallacy" because, he wrote, it was a false feeling. Still, I was flooded once more with a happiness I wanted to share. I telephoned Conrad.

From that moment, those short seconds of drained words, following which I returned to our apartment, from that point as I saw my husband's grey-faced despair and half listened to the background wail of sirens in the Manhattan streets below, idly noting that my so-called walking shoes were pinching, nothing could stop the landslide that had begun. A planet can take millions, perhaps billions, of years to form, but it can shatter in an instant when something veers off course and the collision with a larger force destroys it.

Conrad was fifty-nine years old, and thirty-seven of those years had gone into building his publishing empire and his private company. Both would splinter in days and be a memory in a month. This is not a mystery novel, and all readers will probably know the formal end to our events even as today, my husband, seventy-four, like the metaphorical phoenix of the Greeks and the Talmud, rises again from the ashes. So, what I now say is no spoiler. Everyone knows.

Except then, no one wanted to know the one essential detail: the truth. Who, after all, wants to go backstage and ruin the make-believe? Why should they bother, anyway? And what you can't predict when such calamity overtakes is human character, about which one had written so much: how friends and enemies will behave and who those friends and enemies are. How I hated that effing phrase I was to hear so often: "You'll find out who your real friends are." Nine times out of ten it sure as hell wasn't the person spouting this bit of polluted redundancy.

Wednesday's child is full of woe, my mother had said when happily informing me I had been born on a Wednesday, and this Wednesday I was living up to it. Conrad's VP finance and his in-house Toronto counsel had telephoned with small, shaken voices. "It does not appear," they told him, "that all the non-competes had been approved by the independent directors." Conrad knew the implication immediately. This was the match. The bonfire ignited.

Once there is an accusation that you have sidestepped the rules and wrongly taken money from the company, you're done. It would take years for those allegations to be revealed as false. Meanwhile, the special committee, with its extremely prestigious lead counsel, former head of the SEC Richard Breeden, had proclaimed Conrad a thief and fraudster. Present yourself for execution.

From here on, the figures of "stolen" money escalated every day; each news bulletin, every crawler on CNN, NBC, ABC announced almost daily that the committee had turned up millions of dollars more in unapproved payments taken by Conrad and his henchmen without anyone knowing. Now, with horror, we understood the *on dit* behind our backs and why refinancing had been so impossible.

Actually, we had set ourselves up in part. Conrad had been a vocal foe of the corporate governance movement, which while touting transparency and accountability in company policy—perfectly good aims—often seemed to him nothing more than a cover for hijacking companies from their founders. In would come the grey men of administrative governance who in many cases would do little but enrich themselves at the cost of shareholders.

Pretty much all his life Conrad had felt immune to the consequences of speaking your mind publicly. He had the confidence that comes with a privileged background, and one hell of a brain that had built this extraordinary company of newspapers. So long as he spoke the truth and acted honestly, he felt completely confident in his ability to walk any tightrope or financial situation.

He loved words and pithy phrases. "Corporate governance terrorist" was his name for the sort of person Breeden would turn out to be, and it was not appreciated. Without fully understanding the strength of the spirit that was now terrorizing the business community in the U.S., Conrad had made himself into a high-profile, juicy target. Richard Breeden was virtually known as Mr. Corporate Governance, and he had been invited inside the tent by Hollinger's special committeee as their counsel.

Conrad and his associate David Radler had been selling off the American community newspapers at peak profitability to realize their value. A billion dollars in capital gains had been added to Hollinger's balance sheet from these sales—this was part of the accrued value that Southeastern Asset Management had praised at the raucous share-holders' meeting that established the special committee. The buyers wanted to protect themselves with non-compete agreements with Conrad. Those non-competes went for approval both to Hollinger's audit committee and then the full board for discussion and final approval.

Even as Conrad was trying to refinance Hollinger, Breeden was warning financial funds and banks not to touch the company—there were transactions including these non-competes that were very questionable, possibly criminal, and the special committee was investigating.

A whiff of wrongdoing is enough to derail any re-financing, it doesn't have to be proved, and the directors sat fearfully and silently holding hands with their lawyers lest they be implicated. No one wanted to tangle in this. No one took the initiative to question Conrad or asked to see the signed approvals. Conrad was boxing in the dark. And the speed with which a rabbit punch can be publicly administered to a man who has spent most of his working years build-ing a company is shocking. More incredible in fact than in fiction. But there it was. Conrad was a couple of steps away from being out of the ring and flat on his back.

When it became apparent that all non-compete payments had in fact been revealed and listed publicly numerous times, the special committee's investigators adroitly switched paths. Ah yes, the direc-tors had been informed but "misled" and "misinformed": some of the non-compete payments were never requested by the buyers of the newspapers being sold to them. This too was proved false in the trial findings, but that was still years off.

The whole thing hit like a personal weapon of mass destruction. At this point, what you need, frantically, is pots and pots of money. Cash. A Daddy Warbucks. Lawyers will have to be hired, and U.S. lawyers as well as Canadian ones. The American lawyers will require upfront payments of millions because, unlike us, they knew this could become a battle of many years and needed to make sure they had a paying client. Canadian lawyers had lower fees, but they too want to see the colour of your money.

In the abstract it was interesting—if it hadn't been happening to us. We were about to be ensnared in the American lawyers' version of a pyramid scheme. You put down your retainer and each lawyer you retain then recruits another "specialist" lawyer needed to opine on what has already been opined, only to conclude with the rote phrase "unfortunately this does/does not come under the jurisdiction of . . . but let me refer you to . . ." Throw in the Department of Justice, SEC, FBI and the legal counsel of the U.S. Postal Service, and you can easily match the Great Pyramid of Cheops. The private practice lawyers extract every last dollar you can raise in retainers and fees, while the government seizes and confiscates your property before any civil or criminal trial in order to hamper your defence. At the base of this pyramid, and the only people who put money into the scam, are the accused, namely us.

"We are going to attend," said Conrad when I tentatively asked if perhaps this was a reason to skip the Literary Lions dinner on November 3. He was back in fight mode. And unlike good times, when I could easily absent myself, now to do a no-show would be akin to a Benedict Arnold. All I could think was that we were about to be *thrown* to the lions, never mind how well read they were. The dinner is an annual event put on by the New York Public Library to raise funds and honour one or two authors. Importantly, it imparts a touch of intellectualism to the charity galas and is considered the highlight of the cultural life of New York. As far as I could see, it gives a lot of people who have no idea what the inside of a library actually looks like the chance to see one—albeit that night, exquisitely decorated by socialite-cum-decorator Susan Gutfreund, there was little evidence of anything so deadly as shelves of books.

Conrad had been recruited as a donor by HRH Princess Firyal of Jordan, who was co-chairing the evening with Annette de la Renta. She had got him to pledge $100,000 as a "benefactor." Just what we needed.

Firyal was not your common fundraiser with sensible low-heeled shoes, earnest heart and a mission. She had married the brother of the late King Hussein of Jordan and, after delivering herself of two sons, divorced him. Whatever else she did or did not get, she managed to keep her HRH title. (Titles from royal marriages turn out to be bitterly fought over, rather like the family pet, and their owners need the claws of Bengal tigers to keep them; *vide* the ex-wives of two of the Queen's children, Sarah Ferguson and Princess Diana, both of whom lost their HRH on divorce.)

Firyal's next beau was the legendary Greek shipping multi-billionaire Stavros Niarchos, rival of Aristotle Onassis. The story is that Stavros, in trying to win Firyal's affections, started off sending her insultingly small gifts, like a sable coat, which she returned cut into tiny pieces. As this is a family publication, I won't give the details of the doubtless apocryphal story of what was said to be the gift that won her over, apart from her genuine affection for Stavros. Getting Conrad to pledge $100,000 for the New York Public Library was small stuff for Firyal. Paying it turned out to be more major for us and the subject of vicious gossip—but it was paid.

All I remember of that evening, apart from thinking how dark and crowded it was as I advanced into the bower of flowers and vines that Ms. Gutfreund had created, was the bright white fox stole draped over Marie-Josée Kravis's back. I remember it because the previous season of YSL Haute Couture had featured that white stole together with a black version. "It's so Hollywood in white," I dismissively told my vendeuse, Virginie, at the haute couture salon, thinking she would admire my refined taste as she pointed out its merits. "I'll take the black."

Now I saw the black one I had was boring; the white, spectacular. Dammit. This was always happening to me: spending a fortune to be ordinary. That night I was wearing a sleeveless store-bought gown from Carolina Herrera's Madison Avenue boutique. I remember this not because, like some of the ladies, I kept a diary of what I wore so as not to repeat at any public event, but because I got an email from the psychiatrist monitoring my medications: "Saw your picture in the paper for the library benefit. You definitely need to drink some protein shakes. Hope the Wellbutrin is kicking in?"

Two days after the disastrous telephone call of October 29 came gallows humour. Canada's *Globe and Mail* released its list of Hall of Fame companies, and honourable mention for Best Acquisition went to "Hollinger Inc.: Conrad Black's holding company bought 58% of London's Daily Telegraph for $67 million in 1986. . . . Today, it is said to be worth $1.6 billion." Well done, Conrad, I thought. Lucky shareholders. And now came my own little Hall of Infamy win.

Back in July, Toronto fashion doyenne Jeanne Beker had asked me for a column for her new magazine, *Fashion Quarterly*. She was sure that there was a place for something other than dull navy parkas and hockey nights in Canada. "Could you write about real jewellery?" she asked. "Especially, please, stones, diamonds," and whatever else I really, really, really didn't need to be writing about in twelve-point type for publication in November 2003.

"It looks great," Jeanne emailed me in November. "You're going to love it." Well, it did look great. The first issue's theme was glitz and jewellery, and the blue-and-white cover was a perfect backdrop for its title, "Ice Cool Bling." No fault of Jeanne's, but I did not love it.

I had sent her photos of myself "wearing one of your gorgeous pieces, to illustrate the article," as asked. The photo selected did not actually feature one of my own pieces, though Jeanne would not have known that—it was a necklace on loan from S.J. Phillips in London and it went with the strapless YSL Haute Couture evening gown I was wearing, provenance helpfully provided by me and noted. This was at the opening celebration of the extraordinary fifty-five fountains donated to London's Somerset House by Lily Safra at a cost of something like £8 million.

Jacob Rothschild, who had a close relationship with Lily and her billions, was hosting the evening to thank her, and attending were the Queen and the Duke of Edinburgh. I knew greeting Her Majesty the Queen with possibly the lowest curtsy HM had ever seen would be the summit of Lily's social ambitions, and as she sunk to her knees I thought, Well, she deserves it. Eight million pounds is a lot of fountain.

My necklace was not even really a necklace, as Jacob Rothschild, who greeted Conrad and me in the courtyard, pointed out. He looked at it with a careful spot-on aristocratic eye and said, in that languid voice he has, "You're wearing a tiara around your neck."

"Yes," I replied. "The Norton brothers"—the owners of S.J. Phillips—"converted it into a necklace."

"Rather large," said Jacob. "Is it comfortable?"

"Diamonds, Jacob," I replied, "are always comfortable." Actually, it scratched like blazes and I gave it back the next day.

The column I wrote for Jeanne's magazine, titled by them "A Girl's Best Friend," was not quite as glaring a gaffe as my interview to *Vogue*, but its timing was worse. Breezily, chattily, I talked about my indifference to jewellery until Conrad had taken me to a night at Annabel's in London hosted by jeweller Laurence Graff. Long-legged models wearing diamonds blazing like fire under the hot lights came down the runway. Truth is, the evening was bloody warm and I was bored.

Laurence generously put a 100-plus-carat kite-cut diamond in my hand, "just so you can see it close up." I wrote: "I was hooked." In fact, I wasn't. I'm a clothes horse beyond any rational level, and the notion of wearing a 100-carat kite diamond in my cleavage was grotesque, but the line worked in the piece and the piece worked—if it had been written by anyone but me.

As the negative newspaper stories mounted up, I quickly assumed I was for the dust heap. "Do you still want me to write this week?" I emailed Sarah Sands at *The Telegraph* on November 2. She did. And was enthusiastically supportive. "First-class reporting again," she emailed after I submitted my column on the UN Human Rights Council in action. Sarah had got a very reluctant UN to give me press accreditation. "Thanks for finding the time to do it. Sorry everything must be a bit hellish for you at the moment."

Back at the home front in London, the usual domestic tantrums were in full swing. I was holding the fort, precariously, against a slew of requisitions for uniforms, extra debit cards and new accounts, as well as stalling the dreaded request for meetings to "discuss" household organization and the "reporting chain." Showing the indubitable spirit that made the Commonwealth great, our domestic team found the strength to rise above the negative news stories about their employer in order to confront real issues. Nothing, it seemed, could dampen the enthusiasm of our house manager, a determined Australian. He was convinced this would be a good time for him to travel to Florida and make sure the Palm Beach house was ready for us. "Circumstances may make this inappropriate," I replied. Too ambiguous. Better I should have said, "We'll probably be broke in a few weeks so don't go," because he did go to Miami to speak to agencies about housekeepers for us. Undeterred, he next turned a beady eye on our New York apartment. He had heard that our daily cleaning woman "was struggling with her work load." Turned out she was facing domestic problems and needed both a social worker and psychiatric help, which we had obtained for her, and probably should have shared. An opportunity, he thought, to have a review of applicants for a house manager, and he proposed to send over his deputy. "Is there a green card issue?" he asked.

In the first couple of weeks of November, there was an eerie lacuna of uncertainty. On the sixteenth, Conrad set out from our apartment for Hollinger's offices on Fifth Avenue to discuss "a way forward." Hot coals or ground glass must have been something akin to the emotional pain he felt walking across the marble-floored lobby of the offices he had leased at a knockdown price from Alfred Taubman. On arrival, he went into his office—just days before his desk was expropriated.

The way forward turned out to be a greased chute to a pit full of snakes. Rather than the expected informal meeting, Conrad faced a well-rehearsed special committee attended by their counsel Richard Breeden. This was the very first time Conrad had met him. Conrad sat, nominally, as chairman at the head of the table, as Breeden coached what essentially was the committee of public safety to sentence Conrad to the guillotine. When the meeting was over—after continuing the next day—Conrad had been forced to "temporarily" resign. He should have gone into that meeting as any American business executive in the aftermath of the formation of a special committee would have: with a legal team of his own and possibly two fully armed security men.

"What's Breeden like?" I asked Conrad.

"He looks like one of Beria's men," he said, referring to the chief of Stalin's secret police.

"Dead face? No twitch as they sentenced you?"

"I think we can make a deal," said my ever-optimistic husband.

Over, I thought, we're toast—not because I was a bloody Cassandra doomed to be right and never heard, but when you're standing back watching and not sweating over the heavy lifting, you see patterns.

My husband is not a stupid man. But the ambush was so unexpected that he didn't grasp Breeden's intentions. I shudder to say it—Anne Frank, forgive me—but Conrad still believed that human beings were good at heart, or if not quite that, certainly with a measure of decency. With no proper lawyer, he signed an agreement thinking it would protect both the ordinary shareholders and his rights as chief executive and controlling shareholder of the company he had built. I watched as, within a week, six of the eight points protecting him were violated, ashes in our eyes and mouth.

Conrad's "temporary" resignation was met with crescendos of jubilation. Glorious financial times ahead for Hollinger were predicted. Conrad's surname became a running metaphor: "Black Days at Hollinger," "Blackouts at Hollinger," "Conrad's Black Eye," "A Black in the Red." Since there is effectively no libel law in America, anything could be and was said about us. *Time* magazine, on December 1, 2003, reported that "Hollinger announced last week that an internal inquiry had uncovered $32 million in questionable payments, including $7.2 million directly to Black and $16.55 million to Hollinger's Canadian parent company. None of these payments were authorized by the board or the relevant committees."

On the night Conrad's resignation was made public, I watched a BBC reporter on CNN stand outside Hollinger's offices on Fifth

Avenue quoting an unpleasant and grandstanding poseur, Herbert Denton, who liked to think of himself as a crusading activist: "Lord Black is getting out with hundreds of millions of dollars. Shareholders get nothing."

We had at that point, possibly, $20,000 in cash, and my income as a *Maclean's* and *Daily Telegraph* columnist, plus anything else I could write. There were no overseas accounts, no safety deposit boxes or caches of money anywhere. Our running expenses were paid out of Conrad's income, and Richard Breeden had declared that would be cut by 95 per cent, effective immediately, while, humiliatingly, Annette de la Renta and Princess Firyal were talking about how we hadn't yet paid our Literary Lion pledge. We did not yet realize that when we came to sell items—and we had homes, furniture, art and my jewellery—they would be blocked or seized either by the U.S. and Canadian courts or, in my case, by fears of prospective buyers that they were purchasing items I had no right to sell.

Watching the TV news in our apartment, I saw once more the dreaded chyrons. This time, newspaper magnate Conrad Black had "looted" his company of hundreds of millions for his personal extravagance, this being discovered in investigations by the special committee. In the hysteria following the Enron and WorldCom scandals, it was enough to make an allegation entirely without proof that would ultimately destroy Hollinger, a nearly $2-billion company of hard assets, and rob the shareholders of virtually everything. This was the business version of the sexual "me too" denunciations to come in 2017.

I remember freezing on the sofa, shaking inside but silent because Conrad was next to me watching the denunciations. All I could see in that small room where Conrad worked were price tags: the invoices for the small mustard-and-red fringed sofa on which I was now huddled facing the carved accusatory griffins on his dark mahogany desk. It had not been expensive, I remembered, but was so handsome. Behind me was a white plaster George Washington bust on a pedestal that, when he looked up from his desk, Conrad could see. "I cannot tell a lie."

I started frantically sending off emails to friends in London and

Toronto explaining that these stories were false and all payments were authorized. But who could believe that *Time* magazine would tell an outright lie without even benefit of the *alleged* word? I should have saved my staccato breath and just counted my now arrhythmic heartbeats. And so you bash on. Normal life has to be played out. In Canada, my former husband George Jonas had been admitted to hospital with bad angina, and a second heart attack was feared. I flew to Canada to meet with his wife. I was ashamed to admit that I was grateful this attack had occurred in Canada, where medical bills could be largely covered by insurance, unlike the first attack in Arizona, whose bills we had paid.

Just a few days before Conrad's resignation, a request had been forwarded to me by my London assistant from Maria Ebrahimji, editorial producer at CNN International, asking me to participate in a news show about President George W. Bush's upcoming visit to London. "We are going to be doing a few Q & A programs on Bush's trip and I would love to have her join Gaby Hinsliff"—political correspondent for *The Observer*. "We have been wanting to have her on the program for many many months now (her schedule is always so busy!)."

Keeping my columns going and working was my thread to sanity. I'd been on CNN a few times before I married Conrad and once afterwards when attending Princess Diana's funeral. This was a bit of normality, I thought—I had written a column on George Bush in *The Telegraph* a couple of weeks earlier, and having me comment on his London visit made sense.

My previous CNN appearances had been done on location, but this time, in their Manhattan studio, I was seated alone in an empty box with a blank screen in front of me and sound coming through earplugs, probably standard practice but unfamiliar to me. The room seemed so small, the walls and ceiling so suffocating with no windows. The opening questions were fairly normal, with the other guest contradicting me on-air, but everything was civilized and run-of-the-mill until the interviewer changed the subject. I don't have a transcript, but essentially she suddenly said that I must be feeling the pressure now that my husband had been forced to resign and accused of looting the company.

This was an ambush. "This is unfair journalism," I replied. The events surrounding my husband, I said, "are unfortunate, they are difficult, but they have absolutely nothing to do with my role as a journalist." I realized we had become "news of the day" and, from a journalistic point of view, I knew I was fair game. If you don't ask, you don't get, but nevertheless I felt garrotted. Later I watched myself on the show and it was shocking. True, I had no TV makeup and the lighting was thankless fluorescence, but the face on that TV screen looked like a trapped animal's even before the unexpected questions. My eyes were fixed and almost bulging. This was the face of a hunted woman. I was furious with myself. How could I have thought I was in any state to do such an interview?

Next up was the saga of the publication of Conrad's magnum opus on Franklin Delano Roosevelt, scheduled for publication in November. This ought to have been a fabulous time for Conrad, the culmination of years of work, and under normal circumstances he could have revelled in the laudatory pre-publication reviews he was getting. *Publishers Weekly* called it the "best one-volume life of the 32nd president," all 1,280 pages.

Canada's Heather Reisman had planned a signing session for his book at her Indigo store in Toronto. Conrad handled the huge crowds with courtesy and wit. Coming out of the store, he was greeted by a circle of reporters and made the single mistake among his ad hoc comments throughout the years of ambushes to come. On being taunted by a reporter about how the Hollinger share price had risen overnight on news of his exit, he quipped back, "I made fifty million bucks yesterday. That's a flameout I could get used to." It bore a resemblance to a Trumpism.

On hearing it—and God, I think it was on a video and audio loop, I saw and heard it so often—I flinched. We couldn't sell those shares, and our finances were getting stretched, to put it mildly. But I could see the pain and frustration that impelled Conrad. He was like a great animal chained up to be tormented with pointed sticks and branding irons for the amusement of jeering spectators.

The American launch party was scheduled for November 26. I dreaded the likely judgmental eyes, the behind-the-hand whispers. Perhaps I could line up some support from one or two people I knew were likely to attend. Or at least get some reassurance that in their eyes, at least, I was not the profligate caricature I was reading about. My first thought was the one other journalist who was in the swim with Upper East Side society—Elizabeth "Lally" Weymouth, daughter of Kay Graham, owner of the *Washington Post*.

Lally Weymouth was an almost beautiful woman and certainly not lacking in brains, but her appearance was impaired by a manner that at times could be shrewish. She had all the trappings, but unlike other society ladies she had published at least two non-fiction books, and worked hard at keeping her hand in the *Washington Post* and doing important interviews. Her dinners were distinguished by the unusual mix of guests. She was the granddaughter of Eugene Meyer, descendant of a line of distinguished rabbis, although her own identification with Judaism was problematical. Her mother was half-Jewish through Meyer and had, as far as I could see, a very ambivalent attitude to this. Kay often remarked, in a not altogether friendly way, in fact rather rudely, on my own identification as a Jew, as if it was somehow poor taste on my part to reveal it. Why on earth, she said, referring to the tiny Star of David necklace I wore under my blouse, would I want to draw attention to it?

I could never decide whether Kay's bluntness was the legendary toughness attributed to her—you know, the woman who stood behind her reporters' so-called Watergate exposé—or more likely plain rudeness. I'm told she could be charming, though I never saw it. I did see a lot of leeway and excuses made for her because of her status. Rude powerful people who are brusque are inevitably explained as "shy," and when they happen to behave warmly with normal politeness or unexpectedly ask about the health of your children, they are invariably described as "charming," while such behaviour in others is taken for granted.

I valued Lally's opinion simply because she was among the social set but not quite of it, and so as I beat my wings against the glass jam jar I was now in, I thought I'd sound her out before the Lions' dinner. She responded immediately. "Four Seasons Grill," she said, which was pretty much a larger jam jar full of power-lunchers. She was as usual dressed in black and as usual incredibly slim. The booth she had against the wall was one of the room's prize locations. As I sat down I could see a number of people who had done business with Conrad or knew him, staring as if I were some sort of white rhino that had briefly come to munch. Lally got down to tacks pretty fast. Unsolicited, she told me how she lived without showiness (which was largely true) because "that's best." Which, I could now belatedly see, was very true. "I don't spend on clothes," she said. "I don't do any of that made-to-measure Paris stuff. I was brought up to be simple."

I couldn't help noticing her necklace as she spoke, set against her very simple black dress. It was an opera-length strand of perfectly matched golden or perhaps silvery—time dulls some distinctions—15- or 16-millimetre South Sea pearls, very becoming, very valuable and appropriate to an heiress of the *Washington Post*—even after the newspaper lost 95 per cent of its value and was sold.

Her remarks were clearly a distillation of other people's views besides her own and had just a hint of a rehearsed quality. She must have pondered what to wear when delivering them. Did she hesitate for a moment before taking the pearls out of the velvet-lined box in her safe? The implication was very clear: Conrad's troubles were the combined fault of me, Yves Saint Laurent and jeweller Fred Leighton. Now I knew where the wind was blowing.

I tried to brush off what she was saying but, looking into the darker corners of my mind where cobwebs knitted over the dirt and debris heaped on top of my mental Pandora's box, I wasn't sure that I could. Was it possible that Conrad's fees were exorbitant because of me? He'd assured me they were par for the course in the type of deals he was doing, but I still can't help thinking as I look back that marrying me was a disaster for Conrad. Just because his circle in New York and Palm Beach wore couture, why did I have to wear it? His first wife hadn't. I bought insanely, and I gave away less insanely but happily—bags to staff, Chanel jackets to cleaning ladies, private donations to distressed animal lovers or kennels, gifts that had no tax receipt. I bought and gave with exuberance.

"You did go overboard spending now and then," said Conrad when I questioned him. "But not into perilous waters. I was watching and would have stopped you."

In fact, I am certain I was a disaster. Take our four homes: a wife is supposed to manage household expenses, not ignore them. I tell myself that having had no experience of a normal home upbringing, it was bound be catastrophic when thrust into a world of wealth and society at fifty-one, but if I could learn the details of French porcelain and the uses of a *surtout de table*, I was not so stunted that I couldn't understand the need for budgets. Making up a budget for four homes just never occurred to me. Conrad and I never had a financial discussion except for my haute couture budget, which I blew by double each of the four years I was in that world.

When married to George Jonas, whom I more or less financially supported, he watched with resignation as I bought clothes and took on more and more work to pay for them. "It's an addiction," he said of my love of raiment back in 1975, "but it's better than alcoholism or kleptomania." Turned out it wasn't.

According to the special committee report published later in 2004, I had been paid $1.3 million over five years, or $230,000 a year, of which $142,000 was the annual salary for VP editorial. And my income was actually probably more when you added the various fees for speaking or freelance writing that I did outside Hollinger. I winced as the newspapers thundered on about it. What was the figure made up of? Column fees? Director's fees from different boards? There was something called "bonuses," and I remember having been sent two cheques by David Radler, president and chief operating officer of Hollinger. "What is this for?" I asked him in a note. "Just take it," he said. If that tally was accurate, where did it all go?

There were taxes, of course, that I filed and paid yearly according to tax treaties in the U.K., Canada and the U.S., but I had no idea how much they were, as the accountants simply drew on my bank for payment and I wasn't much interested in seeing my tax returns—never

had been since I started needing an accountant to file them for me
in 1976. I gave George Jonas $60,000 a year because he really needed
it, and he always gave me good editorial advice, better than I gave
him, I thought. (Both of us ran each other's copy by one another and
I gave my pedestrian views on his draft manuscripts. "You're my best
editor," he would comfort me.) I donated about $30,000 a year to
charities, official and unofficial—largely opera and animal welfare or
their distressed owners.

The rest must have been sheer happy squander. The small stuff was
books and CDs. The heavy ammunition must have been the "needed"
jewellery from Anna Cristina Alvarado, the Chanel jackets, the
Hermès bags, the Manolo Blahnik shoes in crocodile and buttery soft
leathers and the splurges on Angela Cummings jewellery that I liked,
although the ladies in the Group saw her work as insubstantial trin-
kets. God, how stupid could I be? I had been supporting the Wertheimer
(Chanel) and Dumas (Hermès) families. I still had no stocks, bonds,
art, real estate or expensive cars. True, the special committee's report
turned out to be so libellous that Conrad ended up getting $5 million
in damages from its authors, but to this day I can't forget the sums they
listed me receiving.

Some women are naturally thrifty—like my own sister—and I was
naturally a spendthrift. There was not a shred of financial prudence in
me. With a recklessness that never left me, I put aside absolutely nothing for a rainy day, convinced that whatever happened in life, I could
always work my way out of it, work at two jobs if necessary, work
longer or harder, and besides, here was a pair of exquisite black suede
gloves, unlined, smooth and supple as silk. I had to have them.

Lally's words found their mark.

It was upon us now—we had the attractive invitation to the Kravis–
de la Renta book launch featuring a picture of the FDR book cover.
How will they handle this, I wondered? Awkwardly, was the answer.
The day after Conrad's resignation as Hollinger CEO, and about a
week before the party, we received unfortunate news from the
co-hostesses.

"There's been a difficulty sending out all the invitations," I was told by Conrad, who had got it from Annette or Jayne. "Marie-Josée's secretary," he was told in a confused account, "misplaced the invites or the secretary lost a large part of the guest list." Or the moon over 625 Park Avenue where Mrs. Kravis lived had turned dark with frogs. Perhaps the invitations had gone to Never Never Land to await Mrs. Clinton's scrubbed emails.

Mrs. Kravis herself had already resigned from the Hollinger board in late September under some pretext or another. This was not the first time a board had seen the smart heels of her Gianvito Rossi shoes when trouble loomed. Conrad, who'd had some small role in advancing her pre-Kravis status when he invited her to various forums while her marriage to conductor Charles Dutoit was breaking down, and had been her friendly acquaintance for about twenty-five years, was no longer useful to her. Indeed, he was a burden in the making.

On hearing of the so-called muck-up with invitations, I knew we were in for Manhattan's chic version of the Unsinkable Molly Brown's party. We had no way of knowing how many invites had actually been sent out, but clearly some hadn't—perhaps there were important business and social contacts the Kravises preferred did not know of their role in this party. The Grill Room at the Four Seasons, which under normal circumstances would have been jam-packed for the launch of an already acclaimed book on FDR by Conrad Black, was about to resemble a wake. Conrad had to drag me there. Mrs. Kravis, Mrs. de la Renta and Mrs. Kissinger plus husbands were, to their credit, in attendance, however reluctantly. And later they accompanied us to the after-launch dinner being held by Jayne Wrightsman. It would be the last time our "group" were all at dinner together.

My husband and I seem to have been at two different parties that evening, in what must be a magnificent example of his glass-is-half-full versus my glass-is-virtually-empty approach. Or, were he not the man I adore and admire, I'd say he was stark raving mad. In the room next to us, a reception was being held for the new book by former Treasury secretary Robert Rubin, aptly entitled *In an Uncertain World: Tough Choices from Wall Street to Washington*. The sound of voices and laughter indicated that clearly was the place to be. Guests were looking in at our group and scurrying past. Our room was an archipelago of empty spaces.

Looking for succour, I spotted Ghislaine Maxwell of the many bathrooms. She had been importuning my friendship before our crash with repeat invites for us to go to Jeffrey's island and relax, but I thought it might be rough sledding, marooned on an island counting kitchens or plunging my cellulite next to her toned thighs in the swimming pool with no way out but a rowboat. Still, we were friends—so putting on my "so good to see you" face, I headed for her. She bolted. Turned that sharp tight little turn when you really want to get away, and that was it. "We had Jim Wolfensohn and Mayor Koch come from their party to ours," said Conrad ebulliently later. I felt as if the room had been the deck of the *Flying Dutchman* with a ghost crew of guests.

In the second *Vanity Fair* article about us (I think there were four altogether, which in a back-handed way is a compliment to our infamy), writer Duff McDonald quoted an unnamed (of course) guest who said, "That room is usually a rat fuck at these kinds of parties. But there was plenty of walking-around room this time." McDonald reported that "the normally flamboyant columnist Barbara Amiel . . . kept a low profile, wearing a coat with a high collar. According to one guest, you couldn't see her face unless you happened to be staring straight at her." I can't remember exactly what I was wearing, but definitely would have worn such an item had I one in my wardrobe. Sadly, nothing was shielding my face except possibly the wish written all over it that I wasn't there.

One of McDonald's informants for the article was happy to be named, and talked about the book launch he was not at: "'I'm on the board of Rockefeller University, as are Nancy Kissinger and Annette de la Renta,' said Christopher Browne, managing director of the New York investment firm Tweedy, Browne and Black's chief adversary among Hollinger shareholders. 'Annette came up to me at a meeting in November and said that I was doing wonderful things over at Hollinger. I said "Yeah, but are you still throwing him his book party?" She said, "What can we do? We didn't know he was so greedy.""" Perhaps she said it, perhaps she didn't. She never gainsaid the remark, and it really hurt Conrad. Probably the most accurate description of the party was Tina Brown's assessment in a piece published in the *Washington Post* on December 4, which began: "It's odd how fast grandeur becomes gloomy when the miasma of misfortune sets in." Good line.

In November and December alone there were hundreds if not thousands of negative press stories on us from all over the world. There was nothing in my life to draw upon and give me some idea of how to handle this with any shred of dignity. I remembered a phone call out of the blue in 2001 from Mercedes Bass. "You'll be reading about this tomorrow," she said to me right off the bat. "But Sid sold his Disney stock at a huge profit. He didn't have to do it but it seemed financially the right thing to do. We're very happy about it." I had no idea what she was talking about. I supposed this was just the excited call of a wife who wants to spread good news. Mercedes had never telephoned me before and her speaking voice was a little tighter than usual and the words came out rat-a-tat-tat.

"Wonderful," I said. "Congratulations." I did see coverage on the news. Sid had apparently invested in a lot of stocks on margin and now brokers were calling for payment. He had to sell a big chunk of his position at Disney to pay up, which cut his share position from 14 per cent to 4 per cent—still the largest single shareholder. Apparently, no one could understand why a man as rich as Sid would be buying on margin. He was left with a billion or two, hardly a death blow, but clearly to Mercedes it was a humiliation to be headed off by these odd calls to her acquaintances.

My own specialty in these last months of 2003, and certainly for at least half of 2004, was in firing off emails to everyone explaining that it was all going to be okay. Unnecessarily long explanations of the role of activist investors and asset stripping were included, and I'm not surprised no one seemed to have read them. After all, I hadn't really listened to what Mercedes was saying. "Take what you read with a pinch of salt," I wrote to Sarah Sands at *The Telegraph*. "This will all straighten out shortly." Conrad told me it would, and so I believed him—for the first two years.

My December birthday came and went. In one of those macabre ideas to which Hollinger was now prone, a birthday greeting was sent to our New York apartment, where we were holed up like resistance soldiers in hiding. The inscription marked "this auspicious occasion and send you every good wish for happiness today and in the future." The card was signed by the New York office, including Hollinger VP shareholder relations Paul Healy (a sychophant of Christopher Browne), who, having pried himself loose from licking Conrad's shoes, was now doing his murderous best to cut him off at the knees.

Our New York society friends struggled on gamely a few more months, like some intrepid expeditioners in the jungles of the Amazon. Of the Group, Barbara Walters lasted longest, and during our final lunch, in late December 2004 at Harry's opposite the Plaza hotel, she proudly showed me her invitation to Donald Trump's upcoming wedding. I remembered on the spot why I was told it was rude to tell other people about events to which you had been invited. This was a failing Barbara never got over—her invitations to the Geffen yacht were particular triumphs that could not only be used for preening but also as an excuse for being too busy to see you, as in "Sorry, but I'll be busy packing for the Geffen yacht." When I mentioned the Trump wedding to Conrad, he had Anna Wintour let Donald know we would be delighted to come.

On New Year's Eve, 2003, Annette and Nancy telephoned me from the de la Rentas' home in Punta Cana, Dominican Republic, full of warm greetings. I was very grateful but found it curious that they did not mention Conrad, ask to speak to him or even extend wishes to him. "Goodbye, Barbara," said Nancy warmly. "So long," I said, which was a sign-off I almost never used.

So long Park Avenue and Fifth.

Cecile Zilkha, former president of the Metropolitan Opera and in the early stages of lymphoma, invited us to the opening performance of *Salome* that March. She assured us there would be no press, and no intermission as the opera is one act only, and even offered to arrange a private elevator to take us to her box. I had not quite grasped how fragile we were thought to be until her kind message was delivered. We gratefully declined the elevator. Anyway, the minefield turned out to be right there in the box next to us, containing, among others, the Basses and Barbara Walters. Mercedes's Persian eyes in her strangely white face—the arsenic kabuki-like makeup favoured by many of Park Avenue's senior ladies—glommed onto me as she leaned over the partition before the overture and loudly berated me for not keeping in touch with her. The exchange lasted a minute only, mercifully concluded as the orchestra began. Her box's occupants rushed out at the opera's conclusion.

Next day, being a chump from Mars, I took Mercedes at her word and sent her an effusive email. What the hell, I thought. "Dearest M: Lovely to glimpse you the other night . . . We bash on. This will end and I remain convinced that my darling will be vindicated. But it is tiresome while it goes on. P.S. you're right I didn't reply to your sweet message of February 9, which I read out loud to Conrad the MINUTE it arrived. I think sometimes I am simply afraid of being a liability . . . I mean after three months of nonstop negative press, you begin to think that perhaps there is some truth to the rumour that one has a very nasty disease and next thing you know, you're looking for rashes all over yourself etc. If it weren't for sane friends, and they have kept me afloat, I'd have committed myself long ago!!!!! xxxx." It was "gush, gush," as George Weidenfeld had counselled. There was no response from Mercedes to that nor to the following three emails I sent.

Bravely, Jayne Wrightsman gave the last supper for us at her home on Fifth Avenue. There were only two other guests, each of whom appeared to be in terminal pain. Buñuel could have made a good film of it with script by Beckett à la *Endgame*, with Conrad and me in dustbins. Robert Pirie, bibliophile, banker and lawyer, one of the very few American patricians who always acted with generosity and loyalty, was clearly in agony—his leg culminating in a foot the size of a melon resting on a pillow—and Barbara Walters was suffering from some sort of virus. The evening was painted in the sombre tones of Renaissance chiaroscuro. I could see a vanitas in a corner of the room, figuratively anyway, looking like a bowl of rotting fruit. I had been in those rooms several dozen times with guests scattered merrily around Jayne's sparkling treasure trove, and those evenings were always jewel tones, never light pastels. But that night the air was full of pain and murk. Jayne would never cease keeping in contact with both of us through letters and telephone calls so long as she was physically able, but she would never again see us in public or invite us to her home.

The final goodbye from Barbara Walters came in December 2005, just after criminal charges were laid. Her email had the ring of sincerity, though emails have made feelings easier to exaggerate while less meaningful by the very ease of moving the texted sentiment around. I was sitting blankly in Toronto, another birthday past and looming ahead another Christmas and New Year's to remind us of better times. The criminal indictments had come down a week or so before, but we had over a year before the case would go to trial.

Barbara's email confronted the delicate problem of how to write to people in our situation. By now I could do a handbook on the etiquette of communicating with the accused, the convicted, the innocent and the incarcerated while being upbeat and conversational, so I can easily see the difficulties people had of striking the right note. Barbara decided to cover the keyboard, and I think she did it fairly well, apart from her irresistible need to talk about new invitations.

"Dear Barbara," she wrote:

> It is a cold messy day in New York, a Friday, and I have a few moments and as you have been so much in my thoughts, I am writing this little note.
>
> I have to tell you first of all, how moved and impressed I am by the dignity you and Conrad have shown during these terribly difficult months. To keep your head when all around you are losing theirs, is a great feat.
>
> I miss seeing you but very little has changed. Jayne still had her charming little dinners for Jacob Rothschild. They are informal and Mercedes comes in a ballgown. What else is new? Oscar and

Annette are off to Punta Cana for the holidays. I will go down
for a few days and then spend the New Year here in New York.

I have been working on a two-hour Special which airs
December 20th from 9 to 11 p.m. It is called "Heaven. Where
is it? How do we get there?" I am very proud. I travelled all
over the world to do it, with interviews from the Dalai Lama
in India to a would-be suicide bomber in a high security prison in
Israel who is certain he is going to Paradise and I am going to hell.
I talked with Cardinals and Rabbis, with Imams and Evangelists.
It was fascinating for me to do.

My phone just rang. Cecile Zilkha, evidently very well, inviting
me to the Metropolitan Opera gala on April 9th. Isn't that absurd?
I said I was already committed. I may run away and come live with
you in Toronto.

You know, I hope, that I am praying (even though I don't
believe in heaven) that all goes well for you and Conrad. Perhaps
it is a good thing that a trial or hearing will finally take place so
that Conrad can at last present his case.

I hope the holidays are not too difficult.

As always, barbara

She made an effort where none of the other Group did.

Perhaps because I was unseasoned, those first couple of years were in
some ways the most painful. Six or seven years in and your nerve
endings, which never become completely cauterized, don't register
pain over small things. Losing status, money, reputation and security
is a shock when it happens all within a few days. The feeling of falling
down that elevator shaft is impossible to capture. And gradually you
realize, falling, falling, that you still haven't reached bottom and you
can't even see it.

Since I couldn't yet fully grasp the case against Conrad, I didn't
have the protection of what would come later, understanding the facts
behind the whirlwind of accusations and knowing, profoundly, that

my husband was innocent and being relentlessly persecuted for crimes that hadn't taken place. The habits of my profession are both a help and a hindrance: even with Conrad I couldn't be sure until I knew and understood every detail. Once grasped, there was absolutely no shame. In fact, his persecution was almost a matter of pride.

Later, too, you become less self-centred. The feeling of friends abandoning you yields to a more sensible outlook: people have their own lives, their own problems, you are not the centre of their universe and those who were social friends are quite reasonably living in another sphere. Their absence is not some terrible character failing on their part but rather the way of the world. What is less forgivable are those friends who, instead of carrying on with their own lives and using you only as an occasional dinner table anecdote, now become enthusiastic participants in tearing you apart. That may also be the way of the world, but it is less seemly.

For myself, once this exclusion began, I was just as happy not to be sought or seeking out. In dog parlance, I had been socialized late in life, and our isolation, though utterly awful for my husband, was not as difficult for me, having only experienced this life of Conrad's for the past eleven years.

Some memories leave paths, scars where they have touched the fleshy cortex; others pass over without a mark. Sometime in 2004, as the cold winds were buffeting, I sat with George and Annabelle Weidenfeld in the tea room of the Carlyle hotel. There's a rosy feeling in that small tea room just outside the formal restaurant, as if you are encased in deep burgundy velvet, another time and place far from worldly grit and grime. Me, my dearest friend Annabelle, and George brimming with his anecdotes. The taste of a good cup of Earl Grey. Then, in quick succession, the moment fractured into shrapnel bits, each piercing flesh.

First came unmissable six-foot-seven Mathias Döpfner, the forty-year-old brilliant star of Germany's Axel Springer publications which include *Die Welt*. Conrad and I were fond of him. He manages his ambitions with principle and without malice. He smiled at me and then motioned to George, who rose from our banquette and followed him into the bar. Mathias was in town to talk to Hollinger about Springer's possible purchase of *The Telegraph*.

Almost on his heels came Lynn de Rothschild with her throaty giggle at her own wit or good fortune. It is not unpleasant but at the best of times a bit unnerving. I needn't have worried. Not half a dozen months earlier she had sent me a caressing email—I had a number of them from various people—which appeared to be requisite before dropping us: "This must be hell for you," wrote Lynn, "but know I am thinking of you. Remember that which does not kill us makes us stronger. Call if I can do anything." I looked up and smiled at the woman who had sent those supportive words, but I must have been wearing the Tarnhelm, *Götterdämmerung*'s magic helmet that renders one invisible.

Lynn beckoned to Annabelle, who rose, and the two of them stood talking directly behind me in full voice about their evening plans and the dinner parties for later that week and the upcoming schedule for London. Lynn departed in a sand-and-beige waft of giggles and goodbyes to half the tea room without even a nod to me. Perhaps there was no awareness on her part, only the selective vision of the socialite: where Fifth Avenue leads, as Mrs. Wharton wrote, Lynn followed. She really didn't see me.

In December 2003, the SEC had sent me a fifteen-page subpoena for every document relating to specific Hollinger matters since 1999, to be submitted to them within ten days—actually five days, since they had sent the request via the Torys law office and it didn't make it to my fax machine for nearly a week. It was not reassuring to see that it defined "documents" as "including but not limited to, any handwritten or typed records, notes, correspondence, memorandum, contracts, agreements, journals, logs, calendars, diaries, cheques, bank statements, account statements, reports, summaries, studies, analyses, minutes, bulletins, notices, schedules, drawings, diagrams, pictures, telephone messages, drafts, final versions, originals, copies or annotated copies or any other paper, writings or prints." And that before they got to their definition of electronic material required. I think they allowed me to keep my dreams and nightmares off the list—unless I had transcribed them.

After I picked myself up off the floor—girls from Hendon aren't used to receiving fifteen-page subpoenas from the SEC—I looked again at the subject matter this was to cover. Nothing here that I can help them with, I thought, since the focus was non-compete payments and the resignation of Hollinger officers. But then one of Conrad's lawyers or possibly accountants explained that everything from the household purchases of cheese and nuts for dinners that may have been subsidized by Hollinger would be included. The SEC would decide.

I made a decision as well. I would not comply. The request was absurd. I had no lawyers of my own, and Conrad's were far too busy to start looking at household bills. I went upstairs and took a comforting dose of codeine with a large glass of Ribena and Carnation milk.

CHAPTER EIGHTEEN

Valley of Past Friends

Our Manhattan apartment had become a bunker. And the doorbell kept ringing, practically non-stop, even as the telephones went silent—apart from creepy lawyers' calls. We told the doormen not to let people come up, but we no longer had credibility with them; we were "under investigation," which is the open sesame to a doorman.

Ring, ring.

Nervously: "Can you get that, Conrad, please?"

"I'm on the phone with the lawyers." Ring, ring. "Barbara, please get that. I can't hear on the phone."

So the subpoena would be thrust into my hand or the urgent letter from Gordon Paris, the new nondescript and, from the shareholders' point of view, ruinous CEO replacing Conrad.

Even the junk mail seemed to get into the Hollinger spirit: Bergdorf Goodman's invites were now addressed to Lady Conrad Lack, and my Leica camera renewals to Black Lady. Various staff members were taken off the Hollinger payroll with two weeks' notice and told that it was up to us to reimburse them if they were to be kept employed. This seemed particularly unfair to people like our New York driver, Gus, an Argentinian immigrant with wife and children.

Gus drove Conrad in the city, but as we were there only about four months a year, the rest of the time he ferried Hollinger people about, did all manner of errands and jobs for them, and acted as property manager for both the corporate apartment downstairs and ours upstairs. Given the rather exotic tastes of some Canadian Hollinger directors who stayed in the corporate flat, this was a necessary function.

Although most of the Canadian directors would be unknown outside Canada, the name of Allan Gotlieb, Canada's former ambassador to the United States, made a mark briefly in 1986 when his wife, Sondra, slapped her social secretary on the occasion of a dinner she was giving for then prime minister Mulroney and then vice-president George H.W. Bush. Myself, I have never wanted to slap anyone, but there have definitely been times when hanging and quartering would occur to me.

When Allan Gotlieb became a director of Hollinger Inc., Sondra became my problem. Allan would book the corporate apartment in his name, but usually only Sondra would show up. She was a particularly difficult woman, especially if she drank, which may have been behind the social-secretary slapping that gripped Washington, D.C. But the more awkward matter was cleaning up after her—our household staff rebelled when she was a guest.

"They won't do it," Gus told me.

"Why?"

Sondra appeared to be a rather messy woman. "There's Vaseline everywhere, as well."

"I'm sure you're mistaken or exaggerating. That simply couldn't happen—it must be a pizza sauce of some sort. Mrs. Gotlieb is an accomplished author of many books and a columnist for several publications." Which she was and is—a really good writer, with messy habits.

"Why is the mixture on the walls and floor?"

Ring, ring.

"Conrad, there's a man standing in our foyer and I don't recognize him."

"Call the doorman and see who it is."

"He said it was an urgent message to be hand-delivered to you only." I put aside hopes of the lottery, since I hadn't entered one, and the notion of a nice billionaire calling to save us seemed rather far-fetched. But an insistent doorbell has to be answered sooner or later. And so they came, the civil suits. Some new "derivative action" was forever being served from some new legal firm representing some new claimant—honestly, at times I thought Canada had at least fifteen provinces and held my breath for claims on behalf of Native peoples. Surely someone had invested in Hollinger on their behalf, making me yet another atrocity in the lives of our indigenous peoples.

For us, the days of the week now fell into a new sort of pattern: Monday, Tuesday, Wednesday, Thursday and, for crissakes, it's Friday. That was the favourite torment day of the Hollinger International people. I think they sat around having snacks and drinking Red Bull devising some new memo or fiat to terrorize us over the weekend.

Toronto was Conrad's great last hope. This was the home of Hollinger Inc., the Canadian holding company that controlled the American company and held the majority of its shares. Its four independent directors could be a bulwark against the madness of the fulminations in New York at Hollinger International. They had the power to stop the American company and the special committee in its tracks, or at the very least delay them while we got a grip.

They were, apart from Allan Gotlieb, fairly nondescript people, but nondescript souls are often the sort who suddenly distinguish themselves in a moment of danger. These ones did not. Their names mean nothing to anyone outside Canada and very little to most Canadians, apart from one of the directors, Fred Eaton, the senior member of the great retail family, whose great-grandfather, Timothy, founded Canada's first department store, which became a chain of beloved T. Eaton stores all across the country—which, 130 years later, under the skilful management of Fred and his brothers, went into bankruptcy.

For a moment in time, the four Canadian-based directors could have helped thousands of shareholders and employees keep their pensions and jobs—and at the very least provided a formidable barrier to the Ontario Securities Commission's destruction of the company. But they had other agendas. It can be intriguing to see how sentient human beings of normal intelligence and some accomplishment react when suddenly given power. In this case it was not edifying—rather like watching a cluster of invertebrates devouring a vertebrate: leeches do that with frogs; the spineless centipede can overpower an exquisite vertebrate coral snake. Our four directors had little backbone and much venom.

I'm not sure why they behaved this way, but as an amateur psychologist I'd speculate that weaker people sometimes resent the benefits that a stronger person confers on them. Instead of seizing the moment to help Conrad, they may have seen it as a moment to get even for the times his accomplishment had made them feel smaller.

The sole female on the board had been my choice, the fifty-something never-married daughter of the high-achieving and rather wonderful Laura Sabia, a Canadian feminist. Maureen Sabia was the girl in my high school class who wore stockings when the rest of us wore bobby socks; she drank tea from china cups when we were hanging out at drive-in root beer stands. Probably every classroom has the girl that makes everyone else feel a bit grotty.

Maureen had a legal background, and when she joined our board she was working out of her apartment as a "corporate governance" consultant and trying to sort out a direction in life. Fussy to the point of neurosis, always a bridesmaid and never a bride in her working life as well as her personal life, she would make a career out of non-executive directorships and various bureaucratic chairperson and directorship positions, not actually running a business herself but preaching to others about how to do it. Her time at Hollinger would be a springboard for her when suddenly every company needed a female non-executive director. She was, I think, my greatest disappointment, since I had fought hard to get her on our board both as a vote of thanks to the kindness of her mother, who when I was alone in St. Catharines had befriended me, and as a chance for her to reconstruct her life.

The fourth director, Doug Bassett, was a rather jolly and amiable chap, nephew of the great Canadian media magnate John F. Bassett who had judged me at the disastrous Miss By-Line Ball. Doug inherited the running of Baton Broadcasting and was without the venom of the others. He simply went along.

We had an emergency conference call with all four directors: the moment seeks the man—and woman—for the turning point and avoidance of much misery to come. But there was no bang here, only a whimper. Instead of asserting their independence from the American hysteria hell-bent on destruction and avarice, our four directors, like a team of synchronized swimmers, demanded a copycat process to New York's. Conrad, they all insisted, had to resign as CEO immediately or they would resign. They had their ethics. And not much else, I thought.

I listened to their serious and "more in sadness than anger" little speeches. I can't stand false sanctimony. Conrad was not going to resign from the Canadian company he had built and in which he was the majority shareholder, so the directors, every one of them, solemnly submitted their resignations. Well, that at least, I thought, solves the vexing Vaseline question: no more Sondra Gotlieb. A silver lining to every cloud.

I was on the call, listening as Conrad asked them to just give him a little more time. He was in the thick of negotiations with the reclusive British Barclay brothers, who had agreed to buy all of Hollinger Inc. in a complex deal that would give them *The Telegraph*, which they had pursued for many years, while allowing certain other assets to be purchased by Conrad or sold by the Barclays. Had the deal been completed—and cynic and pessimist though I am, this was close to the making, since the Barclays couldn't give a damn about the frenzy in the U.S.—Hollinger shareholders would have benefited greatly and the four directors seen very large sums for themselves. Of necessity, the negotiations were extremely confidential, and the directors had not yet been involved.

When the meeting was over, I didn't put down the receiver—it wasn't a deliberate manoeuvre to overhear them; I was just rather stunned. I quickly realized they were continuing an informal meeting without us. Conrad, utterly despondent, had hung up. He had expected some loyalty from them at least. Back in the Toronto boardroom,

Conrad's blood conveniently out of sight, the assassins shucked their high-priest robes and the sepulchral tone affected during the meeting, and went into fits of laughter. I listened as each person tried to outdo the other in spurts of self-congratulation.

Gotlieb opened the fun. "Did you catch me? I really think I should win the Oscar for best performance and tact," he said in reference to his mimicry during the conference call of a "concerned" director. I thought of all the favours Conrad had done him. Gotlieb had had a distinguished career in the diplomatic service and had become an advisor to the bank Julius Baer, but, as he explained to Conrad on returning to Canada in 1989, he needed an income. Conrad made him publisher of *Saturday Night* magazine, chairman of the Hollinger International advisory committee, which required him to send fifteen letters a year, and, more importantly, recommended him to Sotheby's as their new Canadian chairman. Given that Conrad was a director of Sotheby's and its owner, Al Taubman, was a friend and Hollinger director at the time, the letter carried weight. "Once again, let me appreciate your thoughtfulness in recommending my name to Sotheby's. I hope you had no trouble detecting my enthusiasm," Gotlieb wrote to Conrad in December 2000. His current work, he wrote, involved "only modest time commitments." Old favours do not require a man to act against his own judgment, but they might lessen amusement at your benefactor's predicament. Allan, like his wife, could not be mistaken for a person of character.

Maureen: "When Barbara started worrying about Conrad's reputation . . ."

"I nearly burst out laughing at that," said the formerly honourable Fred Eaton. Conrad had been a director of the T. Eaton Company and had tried hard to help steer them through a course that might well have avoided the bankruptcy four years earlier. I had made a plea during the conference call for them to consider what they were doing in the light of destroying a man's reputation. Fred Eaton, it turned out, "nearly burst out laughing" at this. Given Fred's decades of friendship with Conrad, I didn't expect such glee and petty spite in his boardroom desertion.

"We know whose reputation she's worrying about, and it's hers," contributed insightful Maureen. "Well, that's it, and about time. I've had it with Conrad's protestations that he's solving this. No more of his con, con, con. I won't take it. Give him another week! As if he thought we'd wait any longer."

Much self-satisfied laughter. General agreement and noises off.

Now it was scrape-the-barrel time. Good people who once would have jumped at the request to be a director of Hollinger turned Conrad down—politely—with letters that always began with some mention of how "flattered" they were to be asked and ended with a self-effacing note that they were not going to be of much help at this time. In the end, Conrad had to rely on names that others came up with.

And they were truly trash and, latterly, when Conrad had lost all control, all but outright crooks. The first lot, who told reporters they were "new brooms," did set some records: they made themselves the highest-paid directors in the world, giving themselves about $100,000 a month in fees. Like flies to sticky paper, they endeared themselves to an equally obtuse and weak judge whose lust for power and profile matched theirs for money. He would rubberstamp their requests and hand out rich emoluments costing shareholders tens of millions.

Hollinger was a magnet for scum. There's glamour attached to a newspaper company that you don't get sitting on the board of a tire maker or widget producer. Thieves and hustlers came in cartloads. Turf wars broke out. After the dust settled, the bully-in-chief, with a name totally unfamiliar to me but with a scabrous mind that would obsess on ways to harm us, was a lawyer and money manager (his), Wesley Voorheis, assisted for a time by his second-in-command, another bully, Newton Glassman. Their first act was to launch an "oppression suit" against us—definitely a first for me.

"Who have I oppressed?" I asked a truly oppressed and depressed Conrad.

The judge now running Hollinger through these noxious proxies heard the claim of an oppression suit—sadly, not a wonderful bondage outfit by Thierry Mugler—and unhappily denied it. "There's no grounds for oppression here," said a disappointed Ontario Superior

Court Justice Colin Campbell. "However"—he cleared his throat—
"some action needs to be taken."

"Why?" our lawyer Peter Howard asked reasonably enough.

"Mrs. Black will be removed as a director," ruled Judge Campbell.
Conrad having resigned that morning, he had to settle for me. He
couldn't actually come up with a reason, so I assumed there had been
another one of the many legally dubious têtes-à-têtes in chambers
that had not been to my benefit.

Conrad was a dead man barely walking. What could I do? I got in
silly DVDs like the entire *Sex and the City* series and we watched it at
night together. We were like characters in a lifeboat, no shore in sight,
rations running down and clashes of temperament in the winds.

Conrad's public mentions of my behaviour throughout these years
was always positive. God, he practically had me as a saint in the extraordinary "Valentine to Barbara" that he surprised me with in the *National
Post*, written from his prison cell. I sounded so devoted in his narrative,
like a Joan of Arc confronting the enemy and always protecting her
Dauphin. And basically, I was on board for whatever happened.

But just as people on a lifeboat can start driving one another mad
after the initial glow of survival, I began to get pea-green with sea-
sickness. There was a period in New York where I went overboard.
I can't remember whether it was in December 2003 or the following
January, as the enemies' V-2s ramped up their blitz, but I was gripped
by stony anger for about ten days straight. Conrad was coping with a
thousand and one cuts, magnificently, never taking it out on me and
trying to absorb everything. I, like the bandaged mummy in a horror
film, walked stiffly and silently from room to room, never looking at
him, as if seeing his face would be the final indignity.

"Can't you bear to look at me?" Conrad asked. I never answered.
I don't scream or throw a scene, but, far worse, I simply go dead silent.
In fact, I *couldn't* look at him. My inner voice was blaming Conrad
for this nightmare that was only beginning, and naturally I had a
hundred and one reasons, none of which had anything to do with
why this was happening.

When finally I spoke it was to say, "I told you," which is the phrase every human being could do without their entire life unless it prefaces something like "you would be a terrific success." But no. "I told you something terrible would happen if you continued to spend so much time on the Roosevelt biography."

This referred to the single serious fight of our marriage, sometime around early 2003 in London, before the troubles surfaced. I was jealous of Franklin Delano Roosevelt. You can see the madness of it. I think I knew at the time that it was really my jealousy of Conrad's ability to concentrate every spare minute in his life so passionately, for days, months and years on end, writing a serious book. While, as I saw it, my spare minutes when not doing my job as a columnist went to bloody staff and menus.

"No good will come of this," I had said ominously at the door of the ground-floor room where he worked surrounded by paintings of cardinals and the bust of Margaret Thatcher, not to mention the death mask and hands of Joseph Stalin. When not in agony over Hollinger matters, he was researching, reading and writing *FDR*. Everything was Roosevelt this and Roosevelt that. My hostility had reached the point that to cite the thirty-second president of the United States was to start an explosion of invective from me. The New Deal was not working in our marital life. "All your attention is on FDR and nothing else. Something awful will happen." This dramatic line was based on nothing factual. I had absolutely no prescience that I would be correct in foreseeing that Conrad's demi-isolation from the weedy world of U.S. corporate practices was going to absolutely kill us. I was just mad as hell that he was inaccessible to me. Conrad, on the other hand, was writing an absolutely brilliant book that would be universally admired as the greatest one-volume biography of Roosevelt.

At this point it was past two in the morning and I didn't feel like working any more that night. "Don't bother coming to bed and waking me," I said morosely in a challenging tone, using the age-old tool of the neglected wife.

"I'll go to the guest room," he said, which made me even more unhappy, "if this is what our marriage has come to." And slammed the door in my face. Interrupting his bout of late-night writing was, as every writer knows, the wrong thing to do, but I felt totally in the right. To hell with FDR.

Now, in New York, the only alleviating factor to my B-movie performance as a bitch was that I couldn't carry it through our night-times. I certainly tried a couple of nights, scrunching up on my side of the bed, flinching exaggeratedly if a foot or toe touched me, but after a few nights as an immobile lump of stone, I clung to him for infusions of support, and then would wake up and become as horrid as ever. After about ten days I came to my senses without us ever discussing it and, after that, apart from the perennial "I can't go on," I had virtually no slippage again.

In the first few months of 2004, Conrad was still chairman of the Telegraph Group, so he wanted me to "show the [damn] flag" and go back to London. Old habits die hard, and before I left, I called up my "good friend" Abbey, the manager of the Manhattan Manolo Blahnik shop. "Abbey, I think the situation calls for a pair of mood-lifting shoes," I said, trying to emulate an upbeat voice. "You've got quite enough," she replied brusquely and hung up. How poisonous must one be when even the New York vendeuses wish to distance themselves?

Conrad was never going to be living in London again, but I made trips back to keep the train on the rails. Leaving a large house totally in the hands of domestic staff can be unwise. I avoided London friends on the first quick trips back but returned soon to see the stalwart William Shawcross and his wife, Olga. They took me to dinner at Daphne's, an easy restaurant, after a literary party where Joan Collins and I were ringed by paparazzi. Suddenly, out of nowhere it seemed, half my face was paralyzed, apart from a tic in one eye.

"Look, I'm very sorry," I muttered through semi-closed lips and a rigid cheek. "But something seems to have happened to my face." Olga and Willy looked on sympathetically. I mean, what do you say to that? And it seemed to have enfeebled my mind as well. Half my vocabulary disappeared up Chelsea's Draycott Avenue. I loved time with the Shawcrosses and now I was a bloody demi-mute. It's hysteria, I thought, and I expect that's what happened. After all, you can only go on play-acting *It's a Wonderful Life* before the mind and body, exhausted, have a bit of a revolt and go on a brief strike. I could think well enough for writing alone in my room but my words wouldn't quite make the full trip from mind to tongue. (Conrad told me a similar semi-paralysis happened to him on occasion. Years later, I was told that it was probably stress-induced Bell's palsy; the editor of this manuscript had seen the same syndrome in his family. I found that comforting, because giving it a medical name made me feel less like a drama queen.)

A social Alzheimer's was impeding me, which, together with small outbreaks of social Coventry, was a diabolical mix. You aren't quite sure who will cut you until it happens and you find yourself with a smile and an outstretched hand falling back limply to your side. To be honest, that sort of thing never fussed me, except I couldn't aim my own darts in the right direction: my bad memory, encumbered by circumstance, medicines and short-sightedness, handicapped me in the most embarrassing ways. At Santa Montefiore's literary party, I chatted warmly and revealingly to a woman I thought was Minette Marrin, an author and journalist (and good friend of Miriam Gross) whom I very much admired.

"I hear you're selling your house," she had opened, smiling. "What do you plan to do? Will you stay in London?" There was something of a relief in speaking to a friend, and so I began chatting away, like a stopped-up sink that's had Drano poured down it, glad to share real feelings instead of my pretend ones, until, with a sinking feeling, as her questions mounted, I suspected this was not after all Minette.

Unfortunately, she turned out to be Veronica Wadley, past deputy editor of the *Daily Telegraph* and now editor of the *Evening Standard*, an attractive woman and protégé of Max Hastings who bore the considerable handicap of marriage to a spectacularly bad yellow journalist and author named Tom Bower. He had written a very nasty piece about Conrad and now came smarmily up to me holding out his hand. At that point I realized my error and refused to clasp it. He sneered like a cobra. Blast my bloody memory and eyesight, I thought. Honestly, Minette and Veronica don't look at all alike, apart from

having that automatically engaging manner a British female journalist has when interviewing and in search of information.

We were in exile proper for about twelve years, and beleaguered outside the trial and prison process for another four. The one thing that
upset me was the black hole, always expanding, containing the faces
and voices of good friends who died during that time, now permanently out of reach except in some haunting moment when they are
captured in pixels on a television screen or in a newspaper cutting.
Looking back at it, so many people in London had been dear to me
and life was brutal to them. No time, no chances to say goodbye or
enjoy them. David Tang's generosity, Josephine Hart Saatchi's abun-
dant warmth. No possibility to thank David Frost for his kindness in
inviting me time and time again onto his television programs to discuss the news even after I became the greedy wife of the "disgraced"
Lord Black. All doors closed.

The trips to London now were increasingly painful. By the end
of 2004, our home in Kensington felt as if it were cryogenically preserved. All the furniture was there, sitting upright next to perfect
curtains and pelmets, tabletop photos arranged in silver and tortoise-
shell frames, but the house was no longer breathing. Conrad had
always been its heart. When he was not there to descend the stairs at
an appropriate pace and with no sign of haste no matter how late he
was, and he was always late, to joke in the entrance hall with the staff
as he always did, the rooms were lifeless.

At night, without Conrad, I'd work very late and then go downstairs to lock myself in our bedroom. The house was full of bits and
pieces of my husband that were like discarded tissues—crumpled and
useless. To one side was his dressing room, with a wardrobe of much
of his winter clothing waiting for his return. I'd walk in it and smell
the jackets, burying my face in the dark navy and black of merino-
wool tweeds and cashmere blazers that I had insisted he get to replace
his Eaton's Pine Room suits, the velvet smoking jackets in navy, green
and burgundy that Henry Keswick favoured.

Each morning I faced his Andy Warhol portrait, so handsome. Agate eyes staring at me. *The Telegraph* was no longer delivered first thing in the morning, and there was no 2 a.m. chat in bed as we read through its pages: "Conrad, have you seen the leader?" I was alone. I couldn't imagine we would ever sell the house—I'd have been happy to see Palm Beach go, and at that point it was worth more than our London home.

London, when all was said and done, was the city that came closest to home, perhaps because of early memories, perhaps because it was such a challenge culturally and intellectually that it kept me feeling alive no matter how cruel the journalists became, or perhaps because it was where I really had the women friends I wanted. So much effort had gone into putting down roots and groping through all the cultural thickets. And perhaps because of, shut away, the memory of the father I had loved so much and our Hampstead days together.

The reality was that, for whatever reason, I couldn't quite place myself, and when, after selling the London and New York residences, I wrote a column in which I called myself "Lady Black of No Fixed Address," it was not self-pity, only the reflection of a state of mind. One doesn't choose to feel rootless. It is not a gypsy outfit you put on to either add allure or create a persona. For some reason, I simply could not find a home, either psychologically or physically. And now it was too late. All roots had been pulled up and withered. Languages forgotten.

But the imprinting of early years always remained ready to pop up. Why else could the sight of poppies in a picture or a film bring back so acutely the meadows of childhood; why else would cliffs overlooking grey seas churning in the winds and the discomfort of a pebbled beach be so intensely satisfying, while the magnificent Great Lakes of Canada were so profoundly uninteresting? Why did I love the Atlantic in Palm Beach only when stormy and grey? Why would the smells of London, even the unpleasant—to me—smells of Indian food cooking still be preferable to the antiseptic pavements of Manhattan's Upper East Side or the clean pretty sidewalks of Toronto's Yorkville? Rain, smog, Fry's chocolate spread and Ovaltine. Childhood, I suppose.

Canada had been extraordinarily generous to me, and no one had to do a selling job on it. I could see that the people were far easier, far more tolerant, that the air was cleaner both in fact and in a philosophical sense, that the pavements were not covered with blood because in effect the country was so very new. One didn't have to work at being a Canadian; it was a warm bath. Essentially, I thought it a more decent country than either America or the U.K., but not really a good fit for me. Always, from the earliest days until now, even in the best of times, I felt as if I spoke a slightly different language, one that was not better but simply my language.

Please, God, I thought, don't take London from me. I've worked at and puzzled out re-entry to life in the land where I was born since returning permanently in 1984 and nearly got it. But it seems God was on holiday.

CHAPTER NINETEEN

Madame Jenah

The snow was falling outside our Toronto home that evening, so cold, so chill, that even the flakes were getting discouraged. Earlier I had been trying to explain in a little meeting I called for our domestic staff that they should not admit anyone through the gates they did not know and certainly not take delivery of any envelopes. They were doing their best, but occasionally a dry cleaner would come in and hand over a registered letter instead of clothes. Photographers had managed to get on our property and take pictures of the indoor swimming pool. I was never quite sure if it was owls or the *Toronto Star* hooting overhead.

We had no security apart from my adored three Hungarian pulik, Moffat, Monty and George, all named after members of Conrad's family. I hadn't been thinking when I got the dogs—I wanted them so much—and of course I was always away and so by default the pulik came under the loving but somewhat indulgent care of our German house manager, Werner, and sadly I had to watch them, dreadlocks flying, march away into his house at the end of each day.

The evening I went missing, Werner had left the house. Inside now was quiet, apart from the low murmur of Conrad on the telephone to lawyers. Always lawyers. He had lawyers for this and lawyers for that. Conrad's situation had been evolving wildly, like some sort of invasive shrub that you cut back but it returns ever more resilient. "This is war," he would say to me grimly.

And this was still early on. We had another dozen or so years to go, and had I known that, my walk might well have taken on the colour if not the courage of Oates's Antarctic "I am just going outside and may be some time." Difficult moments had piled up. There was the over-the-telephone firing of Conrad as chairman of Hollinger, which I tried to stop with my quaint suggestion that the board might first want to see some evidence of the alleged malfeasance. This suggestion did evoke, from Henry Kissinger, a murmured "Perhaps we should . . . ," followed by Richard Breeden's curt dismissal of Henry's mumble and straightway asking for a vote. Henry voted in favour, with one of his pro forma explanations that this was not to be construed as a personal affront to his long and enduring friendship with Conrad. With friends like that.

I can't remember precisely what sent me into the snow. Possibly the letter from the Internal Revenue Service telling me my U.S. tax returns since 1999 had been reassessed and I owed them millions based on such perks as my travel on the company plane (which Conrad never allowed me on unless he was on it as well). That IRS demand was faxed to me page by page in London one evening, and it felt like a hand reaching out from the machine and grabbing my throat.

Or perhaps it was yet more pages of grim demands in language I simply didn't understand, telling me this new "verified derivative complaint" included a prohibition against the complaint being viewed by any unauthorized individuals. As far as I could tell, the only unauthorized individuals lived in Togo, since the contents of these filings were usually in the press the next day.

All the contents of my filing cabinets—decades of column research, newspaper cuttings, personal credit card accounts, bank statements and readers' letters—were packed and strewn everywhere in my Toronto workroom and along the halls, to be taken away and scrutinized by Conrad's lawyers as well as Hollinger's. I could only hope it would improve their understanding of the Middle East. The telephone numbers—day and night—of one of Conrad's lawyers was taped to every telephone, since we were warned that the RCMP could execute search warrants on the house on behalf of the American authorities at any time. "They prefer to come late or in the early morning, like 4 a.m.," we were told. Everywhere felt uneasy, shaky. I had packed up all sorts of personal mementoes and love letters, insurance files of furniture, art and clothing, and taken them to the basement of George Jonas's house in the middle of the night.

What small thing had been one small thing too many? Cumulative, I expect. I think the RICO charges that included me were a bit more of a shock than some of the other assaults. I had heard of the Racketeer Influenced and Corrupt Organizations Act in gangster films and later in *The Sopranos*, when Tony, in a session with his psychiatrist, complains of everything falling apart because of RICO. "Is he your brother?" she asks.

"How," I asked Conrad's lawyers, "how can I be a defendant in a RICO suit?"

"Because Conrad is the majority shareholder in his private company Ravelston, which controls everything, and you own shares."

"No, I don't," I told them. "I don't have a single share of Ravelston stock. Never did."

But it didn't make any difference. It was like trying to correct an error in Wikipedia, which, until 2019, always gave me an extra husband, as if four weren't enough. Taking all these demands together, plus the earlier fifteen-page SEC subpoena, I felt a little overwhelmed. Any one of them might send you for a walk in the snow. But mainly, I think, it was the fact that as these documents rained down upon me, I had no lawyer. No one to represent or speak for me.

"Look, I have some money of my own," I would say to Conrad's Toronto lawyers. "I'd really like to hire a lawyer of my own."

"It's not in Conrad's interests," they would reply from a defensive huddle. "Someone new can't be brought in at this point." It appeared there were all sorts of court-restricted documents that couldn't be shown to other lawyers. I mentioned my worry in passing to Conrad, but he was preoccupied, understandably, with the terrible blows he was taking, and to his lawyers I was a bit of a collateral nuisance. Perhaps they didn't see it that way—they were working hard for him— but I don't think they quite understood my fear.

"Your interests are not identical with Conrad's," George Jonas would say. "You must get your own representation." And I would nod and say that yes, Conrad understood that. But I was lying. Not that I wasn't understood or was misunderstood—I was just one piece too many.

"You don't realize," said one of Conrad's junior lawyers, "that most of the large law firms in Canada are involved in Hollinger matters anyway on one side or the other." We were a real plus to the Canadian legal world, true, but what the junior meant was that it would be near impossible to find a firm that wasn't "conflicted," to take me on independently. I didn't care about the large firms: if I couldn't have Conrad's big guns, somewhere there must be a Canadian lawyer who would help me, even if he was in a one-room office on the outskirts of town.

Lord, it was the triple crown to the stars. There was a $200-million lawsuit against Conrad, and he replied with a $750-million one, and Hollinger came back with a billion-and-a-quarter-dollar one. I was added to the list of defendants in the billion-plus one. I'm not pleading little girl lost here; I'm not exactly mentally deficient, but this was absolutely beyond my comprehension. When a suit for a billion dollars arrives on top of everything else, you feel like a giga-gigantic tractor is coming to squash you.

The snow wasn't so deep, perhaps three or four inches at the very most, but it was firm. Our property is large, a number of acres in an area of north Toronto called the Bridle Path. Conrad's father had originally negotiated with the zoning authorities to make all lots in the area a minimum of two acres and he had built the first road there. We had a driveway running about three hundred yards off the street to our front door. This year, I had asked if the snow removal could wait as long as possible. When earth and stone and trees are made into one clean sweep of gently undulating lines by the drifts, the eye rests. No one was coming to see us socially or with good intentions, so I reasoned I needn't worry about easy snow-ploughed access to the house.

I put on my boots and coat and left the house. I couldn't face talking to Conrad anymore that night about our problems, but if

I was there, how could we talk of anything else? I knew he was attempting some agreement to sell his voting stock, so I left him a note in the hall to "make yourself a good deal." We knew our phones were tapped, although we weren't sure by whom, but what did it matter—it was all the same side and not ours. We had bought cell phones, the kind where you buy time and have no contract so you can throw them away and get a new phone and number—and I didn't bother taking one with me, nor my wallet. I took the emergency kitchen keys so I could open the small side gate to get out of the property.

The streets were deserted, but they always are at night in our residential north end of Toronto. No nearby coffee shops or cinemas. Though it was bitterly cold, there was little wind, and even though it was still snowing just a little, there was room for a moon to illuminate all the front lawns of white and the vacant lots running to the ravines. At some point I decided to go into a ravine, sit down and think things over. What could I do? It was checkmate. Every way out was blocked unless I wanted to act "against Conrad's interests," as the lawyers said. I was ready to go to prison for contempt, thought it would be an improvement on my current situation. "You don't know my wife," Conrad had told his team. "She'll demand jail rather than go along with this." The lawyers just laughed and said that if I didn't reply to a subpoena or suit, all that would happen were heavy fines.

My nose was running; I wondered if I had frozen mucus on my face. I had taken three or four Valium tablets before leaving, just to try to level out the fear in my stomach that was erupting daily, and perhaps I did feel slightly becalmed. My quilted coat was long and snug, with a hood and drawstring, and I felt secure in it, as if I were in a sleeping bag. After I found a spot in the ravine I lay down in the snow with a scarf over most of my face. My hands were the only part of me that was cold, despite my shearling gloves, and the very tips of my toes a little in their heavy socks and fur-lined Aquatalia boots. Then my fingers went numb and then curiously they got warm and then they didn't feel at all. I scrunched them up inside my coat sleeves.

I wasn't deep in the ravine, but it was steep. If I craned my neck, I could just see the tips of street lights through the trees. I remembered how I would lie down in the park at Hendon and look up at the sky to see my future, then memories and my present situation tumbled around in my head. I'll rest just a moment or two, I thought, and think. I wasn't really used to Valium and it seemed to be creeping up the back of my head with a pleasant warm sensation.

I didn't absolutely freeze, and no coyotes came to gnaw on my body or strange men to mug me. Most strange men and coyotes have more common sense on so cold a night. But something woke me up, and a good thing too. My face was completely numb and my eyes seemed stuck together, but in fact it was my eyelashes iced over a bit. The difficulty now was climbing back up the ravine. I had no feeling in my hands. The one contact lens I wore was stuck to my eye. Grasping the roots as I had coming down was almost impossible, my fingers were temporarily out of action, so I tried crawling, zigzagging to keep my balance on the side of the ravine, which worked sort of well until I slid down again. Eventually I came up with a method of lying on my back and using my elbows to dig into the snow. It wasn't terribly efficient, but then I wasn't exactly at the North Pole, only north Toronto, and I wasn't miles from civilization, only a few hundred yards from a major intersection.

When I reached the top, I felt awful. And stupid. I was very cold. What had I accomplished? I had wanted to wipe my mind and the troubles away, hoped perhaps a solution would come if I could just think outside the house, but nothing was going to sort out that easily. The Valium was wearing off and I didn't have any more with me. I hadn't got a watch on, so I had no idea how long I had been away. Anyway, our house was so large that sometimes I could go for eight or ten hours through the evening before seeing my husband. Possibly Conrad hadn't even noticed I was gone. I had some parking coins in my coat. I walked to a twenty-four-hour convenience shop at a gas station and bought two pocket combs. Then I started walking home.

Our driveway was ablaze with lights. It took me ages fumbling with my keys to manage to open the small side gate—you have no idea how hard it is to manipulate keys when your fingers can't feel until you need to try fast. There were police cruisers, and as I arrived, so did the canine unit. The police had been exceptionally kind and not put out a radio notice to look for me in case the media heard it. George Jonas was there as well, with Conrad. I was not too coherent, and my eyes were very swollen in what apparently was an oddly coloured slightly bluish-white face. Frostnip, they called it, not frostbite.

After noting my absence a few hours into the evening, Conrad had followed my footsteps as far as he could before they had disappeared under the falling snow. My note wishing him a good deal was read ambiguously, especially my explanation that I just wanted to go somewhere quiet, away from this nightmare. I was terribly embarrassed and tried to give an explanation—of which I really had none.

"I wanted to get Conrad a comb," I said. George Jonas looked at me quizzically. "I've got to have my own lawyer," I burst out.

There may be less hysterical ways to get a lawyer, but a few days later, I had an American one for all the SEC and Hollinger suits, and he was one of the best New York civil lawyers going—Gregory Joseph, a man of integrity.

Trying to recount what happened during these really frightful times has unique problems. Whenever I sit down to try to explain the god-awful chain of events, I have to read appalling emails from 2003 onwards, over a hundred volumes of court transcripts and filings, dozens of binders of newspaper clippings and correspondence—never mind the quickie books of journalists, usually relying on some now discredited source—and the whole stew plunges me into a total funk for days.

All the lies and accusations jump off the pages and swirl around like shrieking banshees. Each succeeding month my body let me down a little bit more as if I had chronic flu. The worst part of it all was the irrationality: if you have some dreadful illness, the struggle and wearing down at least make sense. For this, though, there was no reason, no path to follow, no precedents to draw upon. I couldn't count on two plus two adding up to four when it so often added up to five and the court stamp on some filing gave the lie authority. Just pavements giving way under my feet, year after year. I was prey.

I understood the skepticism about our innocence. No smoke without fire, and if we were innocent why did all this happen—I know. But these nightmares do actually happen to innocent people. Perhaps if I had known of something "bad," some crime committed, that would have given me a handrail of sorts.

As it was, I sat listing our errors and our offences as honestly as I could, to make sense of it all. I clearly had an offensive, smug and abrasive personality. We had been too blatant in our enjoyment of what Conrad called "the preferments" of his position. There were just too many photos, too many pictures of us enjoying ourselves all over the place with important people. Hear Conrad on the radio. See Conrad being made a peer—and complaining about the loss of his citizenship. See Barbara prancing around on the social pages of the *New York Times*. Read her fey comments about extravagance and clothes that gave Conrad's enemies an open sesame. People were simply tired of us: tired of our being and our bloody self-importance in the pronouncements we made verbally or in print.

"People generally see what they look for, and hear what they listen for," says Judge John Taylor in *To Kill a Mockingbird*, and it was time to see us pulled down a peg or two—or a hundred. The fight between Christopher Browne of Tweedy, Browne and Conrad was never about Conrad's compensation; that was a side show, window dressing designed to whip up the media—which it did. Black and Browne were simply at loggerheads over the future of Hollinger. Browne wanted to sell and Conrad wanted to keep. Browne's best weapon was to accuse Conrad of malfeasance and leave the corporate governance lot to do the rest. And my husband, like some mouthy Muhammad Ali dancing up and down, fought back, taunting, most inadvisably if accurately, "corporate governance terrorists." Only this contest had no Marquess of Queensberry rules and both contestants got knocked out.

I never met Christopher Browne, but under other circumstances I might have liked him. He was said to be a quiet man. He was certainly a generous one philanthropically, neither flashy nor ostentatious in his style in spite of owning a colossal house in the Hamptons that sold for $147 million after his death—at that time the highest price paid for a house in America—alongside his Park Avenue duplex, which listed for $29.3 million. Perhaps he was genuinely irritated by Conrad's way of life, particularly after reading of his wife, whose "extravagance knows no bounds," while he lived quietly with his male partner, fighting the devils of his own alcoholism. He never saw what happened in the fight he began, although he lived long enough to see corporate governance destroy Hollinger. He died at age sixty-three, only six years after he began the Hollinger fight. Before he died he had come to hate Breeden—but he never budged in his antagonism to Conrad, apart from conceding, "The special committee was a disaster. At least Conrad knew how to run the company. No one else there has a clue."

The air in the first decade of the new millennium was thick with the horrors of corporate frauds: Enron (2001), whose bankruptcy lost shareholders $74 billion, and then WorldCom (2002) went bankrupt, losing investors $180 billion. Hollinger was not bankrupt, had no accounting fraud, had no phony figures and had solid real assets producing a profit every year. But in the post-Enron climate, once an activist shouted about unearned compensation and demanded an "investigation," like all hysterias, whether those of Salem, McCarthyism or the "me too" movement, no proof was needed before sentencing began.

And Richard C. Breeden was—in those days, though no more— Mr. Corporate Governance. His last hurrah was probably the hue and cry that surrounded his four-year delay giving victims of the Madoff fraud the recovered money he was holding on to while billing $38 million plus to the government for his firm's services. In theory, Breeden was working for the Hollinger shareholders, but the actions he took were designed to enhance his own power while staying behind the scenes. As Mrs. Kravis, who knew the corporate governance scene well, living with her enormously successful husband, Henry Kravis of Kohlberg Kravis Roberts, predicted to Conrad: "Breeden will stay forever and destroy the company."

But how on earth were even responsible editors, let alone working journalists, supposed to know that a man of such seeming probity
as Richard Breeden, former chairman of the SEC, could possibly
ever exaggerate, misdirect or be untruthful? You had to know the
Washington swamp to place him. He'd been a fixture with four presidents and worked closely with George H.W. Bush, who appointed
him to the SEC, which turned out to be extremely fortuitous for the
Bush family when George Jr. got into a sticky situation with sales of
Harken Energy stock in 1990, which should have raised concerns
about insider trading but instead got a pass from Breeden's SEC. Odd
for a man like Breeden, who early in his tenure at the SEC said an
accused inside trader "should be left naked, homeless and without
wheels." Breeden had something on everyone—even a president.
Once the financial scandals began, the big-money appointments as
monitor of this and special chair of that got thrown to him like pies
in a Laurel and Hardy movie.

God, the days and nights I sat, teeth clenched so tightly I had jaw
and nerve pain on eating—when I could eat—as Breeden rang rings
around us. We thought we were clever, and we were just so goddamn
naive. Here a judge, there a judge—Breeden picked them and had
them all convinced; everyone wanted to be a hero to the shareholders.
Conrad was blocked from his own company, blocked from using his
shares, blocked from selling them, blocked from negotiating a deal
that would actually have put money in shareholders' pockets—those
waiting pockets that saw barely a fraction of what they lawfully
deserved. And everyone applauded our undoing, at least everyone in
print or on TV or anyone that had a grudge or *schadenfreude*, a bunion
or sore tooth.

"The fall of Conrad Black," said Melanie Phillips in the *Wall
Street Journal*, "is being received in Britain with almost as much glee
as the defeat of Napoleon at Waterloo," with "acres of newspaper
columns . . . gloating." What does a wife do watching this? You make
his coffee with a dash of milk, no sugar, kiss him on the cheek, "You
look wonderful, darling," and send him off to his execution.

Hell's bells, the horror he felt: "On the advice of counsel, I invoke my right under the Fifth Amendment not to answer on the grounds that I may incriminate myself." The words acid in his mouth as he sat in front of the SEC deposition hearing. Perjury is the last refuge of the scoundrel prosecutor with no evidence of wrongdoing—give one answer that is slightly different from another, a legitimate slip of memory, and you are toast. Then the jeers that same evening: "Black took the Fifth, the crook's first refuge," said TV commentators. There was nowhere for us to turn for help, and the real wrongdoing of the special committee and the "new brooms" would only be revealed a dozen years later, when Hollinger was a memory, the shareholders faded into oblivion, and the two of us like worn treads on overused tires.

First, we had to be nuked, radioactive after the publication of Breeden's great opus, the special committee report of August 2004, described by a credulous press as "exhaustive" and, more accurately, a "roadmap for the SEC and criminal prosecution." When I saw it, I thought of squids. Because that's how it worked. The report, informally called "The Hollinger Chronicles," squirted ink all over facts, obscuring everything in great dark clouds of half-truths while its eight arms wrapped their suckers around Conrad and the squid's parrot-like beak tore bits of flesh from him.

The report was the basis for everything to come: the horrible books written about us, the nasty press, the foul atmosphere that led to criminal charges. And it was grotesque in both its distortion and invention. No one was going to read all of it, of course, not 513 pages of charts and figures and bizarre business dealings, but there was a handy summary with catchy phrases that the press loved, like "corporate kleptocracy." We had apparently diverted tens of millions of dollars to ourselves in fraudulent activities, to "line [our] pockets at the expense of Hollinger almost every day, in almost every way [we] could devise," and had stolen 95.2 per cent of Hollinger's income. Actually, the report totalled our theft at about $300 million at this early point. Or was it four hundred? You couldn't tell page to page. Nearly 750,000 pages of documents had been reviewed, stated the report, at a cost to shareholders of US$60 million, money that, like some desert mirage, was there and then on approach disappeared into lawyers' and new brooms' pockets. We were thieves, always had been. But, promised Breeden, it was a new day, a new Hollinger, now managed for the benefit of all shareholders. An uptick in profits and stock valuation was promised.

As the press headlines blared "Personal Piggy Bank for Black and Amiel," Conrad, exhausted with the battles, had dark depressive moments. "They won't be content with a heart attack," he would say to me. "Nothing but my suicide will satisfy them. I'm a period piece. My serious career is over." Then I'd have to do a see-saw act and play Pollyanna. That's how we worked through the whole situation. Each one of us trying hard to balance the other as events changed. But there was no way to counter the special report that was now our obituary.

"Oh yes there is," said Conrad. "I'm going to sue Breeden and the special committee for libel." His lawyers looked at him with that glassy-eyed, slack-jawed look, as if he had finally lost it. Dementia praecox. Patiently, as to a child, they told him it was a waste of money, not possible. Myself, I thought the last thing we needed was another hopeless court case. But Conrad was absolutely unperturbed by their stand. "I am the client," he said. "I will list the errata. We will file. Breeden will never, ever go to court and testify. Cross-examination will kill him. He can't justify his claims." In his Toronto library he sat at an off-line computer I'd had put in—now that we knew our computers were hacked—working on listing the errors in the report and giving the back-up evidence.

I shouldn't say it was small comfort that Conrad was right, but by the time Breeden had exhausted all appeals up to the Supreme Court of Canada to avoid coming to court, Conrad was in prison, largely as a result of the chain of events his special committee report had set off.

"He's offering to settle," said our lawyers incredulously. "You were right."

"He can't offer enough," I said. I wanted to see him in the witness box being torn apart, every last rotten lie exposed. That's the neat part about not being a Christian—you don't have to turn the other cheek, only the levers of the rack.

"We haven't the time or the money," Conrad told me as we sat in the visitation room at his prison. "Even if I win at the Supreme Court, I'll be sixty-seven at least before I get out of here and I have to build a new life."

The libel settlement was the largest in Canadian history. US$5 million for libel plus $7 million for legal costs. I found no comfort in it, viewed from the wreckage of our lives.

Like a jack-in-the-box, my husband was always springing back with some new way to defeat those arrayed against him. I lived in dread of his new schemes, which, though ingenious and business-savvy, were inevitably foiled by a new regulation invoked or, if necessary, specially created. Now he wanted to privatize what was left of the Canadian Hollinger, which still owned the *Chicago Sun-Times* and its associated small newspapers. Privatization would give us the means to fight Breeden properly and get the stock value, which was now below our ankles, moving again. I took my distance. There is only so much hope in the human soul, and mine was dry.

But it worked: after weeks and weeks of careful co-operation with staff from the Ontario Securities Commission, in November 2004 the OSC team and its compliance office approved the offer, and soon after, 85 per cent of minority shareholders approved it. (As insiders, we were excluded from voting.) As Conrad's confidence grew, I tried to steam out the wrinkles of pessimism and despair that lined my brain, but by now they were ingrained. We just kept losing. Why would privatization be any different?

"Because," said Conrad with confident determination, "this is not about us. This is on behalf of the hundreds of thousands of minority public shareholders." Funny, I thought, that's just not so. It *is* about us and only us. No one talks about the minority shareholders, no matter how often Conrad mentions them.

OSC commissioner Susan Wolburgh Jenah—her name is burned into my amygdala, not that she would know what that was—chaired the hearings on the privatization application. With unanimous staff approval, privatization ought to have whizzed through, a slam dunk, even though all sorts of convoluted legal obstacles were being dredged up by Hollinger's new brooms to try to stop it. Money greases everything—and everyone. Conrad negotiated a severance payment to the temporary directors of $600,000 each—a bargain after the $1.8 million per person they first demanded to approve privatization and wean themselves from Hollinger's generous teat. Extortion, really. Though I could see their point of view: in the real world, none of them could get mid-management jobs in a slaughterhouse.

A few days before the OSC hearings, I heard the hiss and drag of slithering creatures rising from the regulatory swamp. In quick sequence in a clearly coordinated attack they locked arms: The OSC announced that additional hearings might be held to determine whether the civil allegations of the SEC should be copycatted in Ontario. Next, an assistant U.S. attorney from Chicago rose up from his basket talking about some unidentified document he needed to keep away from the OSC hearings since there was an ongoing "criminal investigation"—a standard tainting operation to make the atmosphere around us murky. (The unidentified document, when found later, was so obscure that it was never used.) Then, in case we were getting a minute's sleep, which we weren't, in jumped the Canada Revenue Agency. They put a lien on our home in Palm Beach for about a quarter of its value, with a spokesperson helpfully telling reporters that the CRA feared they may have trouble collecting taxes. Against this backdrop Conrad's fitness to regain his company was to be judged: La trahison des bureauclercs.

This led to an absolutely anguished call from our Palm Beach house manager, dear man. He had gone to Main Street News to pick up our usual daily order of newspapers. "They told me, Lady Black," said Domenico, "that we would no longer be able to have an account there. All further purchases had to be in cash only. It was very embarrassing." Conrad had been buying his newspapers there since 1979.

The dark-hooded many-limbed creature that had taken up residence in my head began to tap its legs on my brain, tap, tap, tap.

Finally, the big showdown: Breeden himself, in person, was coming to Toronto to "talk" to the OSC. The regulators were in paradise. "I had to lecture the OSC a little," Breeden was quoted as saying. One writer said he used the word *bully.* After his visit, Jenah urged her staff to reject Conrad's offer—which they had previously approved. They refused.

Conrad and I sat by the computer in his library waiting for the OSC decision. We sat in dead silence as no word came through; we had been led to believe the announcement would be made before the opening of stock trading. I remember wanting to go to the bathroom but afraid the decision would arrive while I was away. I fidgeted. Then I went upstairs to the balcony overlooking Conrad's library so I could see him sitting at his computer. No, I thought, I'm like a vulture up here.

Just before one o'clock the decision clicked onto the screen. In what has been called by knowledgeable insiders the worst decision the OSC ever made, Jenah had defied her own staff and turned down the application. The hundreds of thousands of Canadian shareholders who had invested, some privately, some through institutions and pension plans, all these shareholders—shareholders the OSC was pledged to protect—would never see a penny. Hollinger Inc. had received $70 million from its share of the *Telegraph* sale, plus Conrad's $16 million, and not a penny of it would go to shareholders. All those millions would, courtesy of Jenah, be a slush fund for a rotating bunch of avaricious insiders who would never make an operating decision again. They could plug into Willy Wonka's money machine using Conrad's company to destroy him, and reward themselves just as they had been doing for the past twelve months. One supposes Madame Jenah was the toast of her circle. Perhaps Breeden made a charitable donation in her name.

I stood behind Conrad in front of the screen. I saw him crumple in his chair. Breeden had what he wanted. A company with loads of cash plus the *Chicago Sun-Times* and no Conrad or anyone who knew about newspapers to bother him.

During the first couple of years, I had kept waiting for a judicial Solomon in either Canada or the U.S., some blazing intellect who would see behind the smoke and mirrors and halt the rolling sludge that coated us more each day. Lying in bed at night or sitting slumped in a chair, I had a kinescope of what-to-do-next scenarios playing in my head, only to fade out, crushed by a mental heaviness like cement boots. I'd think of all my illusions about the legal system. Never mind the highbrow stuff, just the terrific films and books that seized you with tales of honest lawyers in search of truth. You know—equity and truth when mixed produces justice. It is said to exist, though it comes in very small bottles.

"The one thing that doesn't abide by majority rule is a person's conscience," says lawyer Atticus Finch in *To Kill a Mockingbird*. The judge in *Anatomy of a Murder*, based on the book by Associate Justice John D. Voelker of the Michigan Supreme Court, was played by the courageous real-life lawyer Joseph N. Welch, whose famous line "Have you no sense of decency?" is credited with finally arousing public indignation at the slanders and persecutions of Senator Joe McCarthy. That judge, both onscreen and in real life, wanted the truth.

Susan Wolburgh Jenah went to law school, and she must have had some ambitions beside swimming in the zeitgeist, but sitting up there in her raised chair at the OSC hearings judging Conrad's privatization plan, did she ever consider the hundreds of thousands of shareholders? It was all spelled out to her by her staff. But what did she know of Atticus Finch's conscience or Welch's decency? What special magic did Breeden use to befuddle her and her fellow commissioners? In my experience, you have to be reasonably clever to be evil; she was not clever. Whatever qualities she lacked made her vulnerable to manipulation by the presence of an Important American spinning his web.

Most people don't know what Conrad really went to prison for and frankly don't care. I'm warned it would bore readers to be told about it, but this is my book, and given the days and nights I spent alone, watching every bit of our life bloody well go down the drain, I think I ought to be able to at least describe how vanity and stupidity, when in the hands of a judge, can destroy a life. Besides, I suspect that I am not alone in my experience with the great legal profession in Britain, America or Canada.

Our courtroom judges were more like those in Charles Dickens's *Bleak House*: stale, unoriginal minds, yellowed and eating themselves up in a brew of precedent and deference to the crowd, held together with the glue of their vanity. I firmly believe the two Ontario Superior Court justices, Colin Campbell and James Farley, whose vainglorious actions produced the circumstances for the U.S.'s obstruction of justice charge, should themselves now be in a U.S. federal correctional institution, clothed in the dull green uniforms and lousy prison underwear, and suffering the strip searches Conrad had to undergo every visiting day.

Both judges wallowed in their own bathwater. Mr. Justice Farley appeared to believe the reviews of himself as a tough upholder of the little man against the merciless self-interests of big capitalism. This compassion expressed itself by kicking Conrad out of the office his private company owned, the pleasing old Toronto Post Office at Number 10 Toronto Street, which is a heritage building and national historic site. Conrad loved that building from the day he acquired it, thirty years earlier, even though his own office was something of a pigeonhole. Two hundred buyers now wanted the building, and it was sold for $14 million to a financial management company. Not a penny ever went to Farley's little people—the shareholders. Every dollar went to Hollinger's gravy train.

Before it was sold, the building was simply an ache in the heart. Conrad rerouted the drive to his barber so as not to pass by it. But events conspired. While we sat at home in the usual Friday gloom, waiting for Hollinger's weekend kick in the ass and the coming eviction from Toronto Street effective in three working days, the telephone rang.

"Oh, God," I moaned. "I cannot face another horror show." This was to be the worst Friday of all.

"Conrad," said Joan Maida, his assistant of eleven years, "they won't let me take your own boxes out."

Those blankety-blank bloody boxes. Most were files that had been sent to 10 Toronto Street only a few days earlier from lawyer Eddie Greenspan's office. They were the papers left over after the various SEC subpoenas, deemed irrelevant to the case, as well as copies of documents that had gone to the SEC. Some were Conrad's personal files of letters from such key people in the Hollinger story as the late Maurice Duplessis and Lyndon B. Johnson. Unfortunately, so many others had gone through those files—teams of lawyers for the special committee, Hollinger Inc. and the SEC—and many of his personal letters had been purloined, including ones from the late Canadian prime minister Louis St. Laurent and, just for the hell of it, letters of condolence on the death of Conrad's parents. Who has them framed in their recreation room? Choose your thief among the Hollinger new brooms, there were many to choose from.

The SEC had sent five subpoenas already and had received 124,000 documents. There wasn't a telephone message, a Post-it, a pack of matches or piece of wastepaper in that office that hadn't been examined at least three times by different sets of lawyers over the past twelve months. The boxes did not qualify in any way under the timeline of the completely unnecessary document retention order that a self-important Judge Campbell had put in place.

"You have to come down here, Conrad," said Joan, "if you want your personal stuff back." He went, reluctantly. Then, for just a moment, it looked like we were going to beat the Friday jinx. The acting head of Hollinger met us at the office and gave Conrad permission to remove the boxes.

Conrad, who daily lugged huge piles of books around his libraries, gave his chauffeur a hand with the boxes. More fodder for ridicule. The *New York Times*, in a sarcastic piece, congratulated him on his fitness, and other newspapers made fun of the sedentary and spoiled Conrad having to lift a box into the boot of his car, as if he had never done such a thing in his gilded life. As he went down the stairs that afternoon, Conrad pointed up at the video cameras, most of which he had installed, to indicate he was aware of them.

On seeing this video, Hollinger's lawyers scurried to court to get a contempt order against Conrad, but even Judge Campbell's hatchet grasp on the law accepted this could not be considered contempt. His disappointment was palpable. As compensation, he decided to get into showbiz. To liven things up, he held a little screening of the tape for the press. No legal reason; it was just fun.

The video was grainy and black-and-white (the one in colour was withheld). Who cared that Conrad had installed most of the cameras himself? Frames from the video looking like a bad film noir, showing Conrad holding a box, appeared on front pages all over Canada, the U.S. and the U.K., and on TV screens the world over, with the caption "Caught on Camera!"

"That won't win any prizes," a jovial Judge Campbell remarked of the video as he threw Conrad's life away. It would be good enough, though, to be the single piece of evidence that got a conviction of obstruction of justice in the U.S. The jury in Chicago would see the grainy video and, just like the newspapers, say, "Caught on camera."

There must be a legal version somewhere of Noël Coward's "Don't put your daughter on the stage, Mrs. Worthington." Please, God, no more lawyers. There are conscientious lawyers—generally protecting other lawyers from their own profession—but as both a journalist for forty years and during our terrible time, I've seen an occupation, on and off the bench, in the U.S. and Canada, that most often operates with arrogance and boundless contempt for anyone outside their legal world; they are indifferent to anything but their own success and greed.

What other profession has a 360-degree cartel: lawyers write the thousands of new regulations and laws they administer, regulate, prosecute, defend and judge, spawning a need for more and more lawyers, like an aggressively metastasizing cancer, with all the same disastrous consequences. And their damage lives on after them. Our Canadian judges, Campbell and Farley, now retired, have gone into that expanding and profitable field of "alternative dispute resolution." *Caveat emptor.*

Madame Jenah herself went from this fiasco to found a brand-new regulatory unit: the non-profit but quasi-judicial Investment Industry Regulatory Organization of Canada, with its punitive powers. With apologies to Karl Marx, "Regulators of the world, unite. You have no chains to lose." You can just put them on others. If in this Jarndyce and Jarndyce world there were any justice, Jenah, together with her mentor Richard Breeden and a lengthy list of American prosecutors, would long be disbarred.

CHAPTER TWENTY

On Being Booted

Even as Sarah Sands at *The Telegraph* was happily reassuring me "You've never been writing better," I could see distress signals. In January 2004, editor Martin Newland sent me an email beginning: "Barbara, we have a bit of a difficult situation here." Anything else would have been remarkable.

Newland's "difficult situation" was his own decision to run a very unpleasant piece by long-time *Telegraph* City editor Neil Collins, who, in the course of launching a fairly poisonous attack on Conrad, quoted my imperishable "extravagance" epithet from *Vogue* with the embellishment that my five words had started Tweedy, Browne's investigation. This was complicated by Newland's decision to run Collins's piece on the same day and same page as my weekly column.

Collins, being a "full disclosure" business writer at the time (until he wasn't and didn't disclose that he had purchased and sold shares in some of the companies he was writing about), began by stating his "apprehension" at writing on so touchy a subject as the Blacks. In my experience, journalists who want you to know of their apprehension in tackling a tricky subject are those sucking up to their bosses till their cheeks nearly implode, reiterating opinions that they already know will meet the approval of all peers including, most especially, Newland and his pro tem employer.

My deadline was in two days and I was hard at work on my column. Newland wrote that he "wanted to warn [me] as a matter of courtesy," suggesting I not write that day or that I publish another day. There it was. Or rather, there I was not. "Whatever the case," concluded Newland's email, "I hope it does not hurt our good relations."

Honestly, do people really believe they can sling such mud and you will use it for a facial? If as editor I had permitted some staff journalist to write a nasty, mendacious attack on Newland and his wife, would he have been relieved to get my assurance that, though integrity required me to publish such a piece, I was sure it would not harm our good relations?

By then, author Julia Reed, to whom I had uttered those five lethal words, had gallantly written to media outlets galore telling them the "extravagance" line was uttered in self-deprecation and was being used out of context to lampoon me. I think a couple of newspapers may actually have published an edited version of her letter, but of course that's like the apology on page twenty-nine for the year-old front-page headline.

She sent me a letter as well. "I have hated that you have been hit over the head almost daily with my piece—always with quotes taken completely out of context . . . I can only reiterate that I'm sorry the piece has come back to haunt you in such tawdry ways, you bashed time and time again with that line because of me." Julia had nothing to apologize for: the quote was accurate and she used it without malice. But it was very decent of her to write that note. The quote itself will certainly feature in any press obituary I get, no matter how short.

Earlier, Newland had told me he was resisting efforts to get rid of me. "I told them you're a good hack and a good reporter." I refrained from any high-horse comment on his description of my job—who knows, in his parlance both *hack* and *reporter* may have been synonymous with *columnist* and *feature writer*—and simply asked, "Who's them?"

The reply was vague—people in the paper. Sarah had mentioned already that Jeremy Deedes, son of Bill and now the paper's managing editor, wanted me out. Like father, like son.

"We'll carry on," Newland had said, also ever so bravely, "and if things change, I'll write to you."

When Hollinger International replied to Conrad's $400-million lawsuit by skyrocketing theirs to over a billion and tacking me on, it seemed odd that I was not a defendant at $250 million but was at $1 billion. The reason quickly became apparent. I was in Manhattan when Penny told me there was an email from Martin Newland. I telephoned him.

"I've sent you a letter," he said.

"I haven't received it yet."

"Well, as I told you in it, the situation has changed."

"Over the weekend," Newland wrote, "you were named in the revised action by Hollinger International, a development that now meant [sic] the company is employing a person whom the parent company is suing for alleged damages. I cannot allow this." *I cannot allow this??????* Was this how he spoke to his fags?

"You, Martin Newland, can't?" I asked. "I'm not on staff and this is not a criminal charge and"—I got on my legal hind legs—"this is not yet litigated." Empty air. No sound. "Martin, are you there?"

"I am."

"Are you talking about the accusations in a civil suit that I charged twenty dollars in tips to a Bergdorf's doorman and a $140 jogging suit to the company? You know that's bullshit. Who told you to do this?"

"No one. Absolutely no one. I agonized about this all day Friday."

I tried to visualize Newland's Friday, all agony as he brought out the important Saturday paper. Had I been in his awkward situation, reporting to the new brooms, I might have said, "Look, Barbara. This is rough but I must do this—it's your job or mine. That's the way the chips fall and I'm so sorry," or something rather more elegant but at least frank. He might even have said that he was never, ever comfortable with my column in the paper so long as I was the proprietor's wife and had felt that way when I was writing in the *National Post* and he was deputy editor there. Anyway, my column was kaput.

My writing then was probably better than it ever had been, for the evident reason that it was all I had. Each column and article was a work of defiance written in pints of blood. Away from the lawyers and the gobbling sound of invoices from all and sundry, I had my own world in my workroom. They can jeer and sneer, I told myself, but they can't silence my voice so long as that voice is as strong as I can make it and—unlike the notional tree in the forest with no one to hear it—a published voice.

The ending of my *Telegraph* column was like a myocardial infarction. Nothing in my life, not clothes, jewellery or love, had given me the feeling of accomplishment and a life lived the way having a column first at *Maclean's*, then at *The Times* and *Sunday Times*, and then at *The Telegraph* had. Which may show an impoverished life or really skewed values, but there it is. I couldn't ever see life without working, and although a life of regular column deadlines is one of indentured labour and slavery (metaphorically speaking, not you understand to be compared with life under Boko Haram), they are also a terrific luxury for a writer.

I left our apartment on Park Avenue, omitting to remind myself of the number of homeless people in the world (an estimated 150 million, with another 1.6 billion lacking adequate housing—I looked this up for a column), never mind those that do not live on Park Avenue, and walked in the rain to Fifth Avenue, aimless really, going nowhere, as it were. A bench on Fifth Avenue is not quite the shores of Babylon, but there I sat by the traffic and wept.

Five months later, in June, Michael Benedict, an associate editor and my copy editor for years at *Maclean's*, telephoned. "I have some sad—no, bad news. Your contract is up next month and Tony"— editor Anthony-Wilson Smith—"has decided not to renew it." He said this hurriedly, in one breath, so I knew he didn't like doing it at all. "This is not just aimed at you. He's making a lot of changes and a redesign at the magazine. You can write a last farewell column." This was the Canadian version of Martin Newland's firing, although it lacked even the cover of a lawsuit.

A deep breath followed (mine). Pause (mine). "Michael, I've lived through at least five redesigns in my twenty-eight years at *Maclean's*." He was silent. I didn't envy him the job of making the call that Tony was too squeamish to make or, more likely given his nature, felt it more insulting to me to do this way.

Now the magazine would be *judenfrei*. Not in the sense of no

Jews, because I had no idea whether there were other Jewish writers at *Maclean's*, which you probably won't believe, thinking, as so many like Deborah Orr and the *Guardian* lot do, that were I a restaurant critic, I'd give out Stars of David for good eats. What I mean is that *Maclean's* would be free of that sort of *Commentary* magazine neo-conservatism they thought I represented and which has a viewpoint so very un-Canadian. (*Commentary* was founded in 1945 by the American Jewish Committee, but separated from it in 2007, after the AJC had kipups over its drift away from soft-left politics. It is a brilliantly edited and written magazine that remains an influential cultural and political voice.)

A few days later Michael sent me an email.

> Barbara:
> You should know this: you stand out from the pack and deserve to be considered one of the top serious columnists writing today. Unlike those of too many of your colleagues, your columns are thoroughly researched. . . . No doubt the last six months or so have taken their toll, but I never had the sense that you let that impinge on your Maclean's column, never missing a deadline and continuing to produce sparkling work. Another distinction, you remain original no matter how many years have passed. I always looked forward to reading your columns because they were unpredictable. . . . Frequently you made me think of issues in a different way.

There was quite a bit more in this complimentary vein. Okay, it was probably over the top, but when you're scuttling along the bottom, over the top is really good news.

The Spectator's letter to me that same month was one perfectly clear sentence: "I am writing to advise you that following a board meeting of The Telegraph Group Limited the shareholders of The Spectator (1828) Limited resolved to remove you as a Director with effect from 19 May 2004." A *retroactive* firing. Did they hold up hands around the table or just nod heads agreeably and discuss the wine column next?

And then there was the column I lost that I didn't even have. According to *The Times*, "More humiliation for Barbara Amiel . . . a promised column in *The Spectator* has been withdrawn after alleged pressure on the editor, Boris Johnson." I hadn't been aware that such a column was being considered, so didn't miss losing it until I read I might have it.

Getting into the spirit of the times, British Airways revoked their Premier card, which, as they pointed out, "is by invitation to selected individuals." University College at the University of Toronto removed me from its UC Committee, with the assurance made on the telephone by a man I had known since university days "that this removal is coincidental to the matters you are facing outside the university."

And so it went.

The pain of losing my work was sufficiently intense that I didn't even notice the chorus of triumph in the Canadian and U.K. press noting the demise of my columns. I hadn't even brought the temple down on the Philistines, though they had cut my hair and left me shorn. Indeed, Robert Gage, my hairdresser for over ten years, fired me. When I called to make my appointment I was told by him: "It would be embarrassing for everyone to have you here." Apparently, he was doing the hair of local Hollinger people. I thought things were getting really bad when the hairdresser who had proudly hung my photo on the wall wouldn't seat me in his salon. The *Daily Mail* nicknamed a toad Amiel. London's National Portrait Gallery removed India Jane Birley's portrait of us, which, frankly, all Birley's undeniable gifts notwithstanding, I was relieved to hear.

The day I lost my column in *The Telegraph*, the *Guardian* PR department rang up to speak to me, and my assistant, Penny, asked them to put any request in an email. Said email arrived promptly from columnists Matthew Norman and Marina Hyde. "Dear Barbara: We are very sorry to hear about your little difficulties and are interested in helping alleviate them with the offer of some work. We propose a weekly column of no more than 45 words and to be featured in the

Diary, to be entitled Good Husbandry with Barbara Amiel. You will treat readers to tips about stretching one's pay packet to the end of the week, such as drawing an eyeliner down the back of one's leg to suggest the presence of stocking." And so on. In mitigation, Marina was only twenty-nine years old and had not yet become the rather witty—if incautious—lefty columnist she is now. Matthew went on to a more temperamentally suitable environment as a restaurant and wine critic. They published their offer to me in the paper, which really wasn't very nice.

Various school chums and friends were contacted for "personal anecdotes." *Vanity Fair*'s Duff McDonald did a call-around, assuring my friends that "it's fine by me if they are complimentary—I just want to be able to deliver more about C & B as people, not caricatures." I've tried that one myself and even meant it. At first I made impassioned pleas to friends like Miriam to answer such enquiries with accounts of my joy in the simple life, but soon I realized that it was hellishly unpleasant for close friends to get caught constantly in this choppy experience, and if I kept on at them they would find me more of a liability than a friend.

The same day my firing from *The Telegraph* was announced, I received a letter from John Witherow, editor of the *Sunday Times*, for whom I had been working when the price war forced me to leave for *The Telegraph*. "I was sorry to hear that your column at The Telegraph has finished. I always looked forward to reading it and the paper will not be the same without its firepower." His offer was to write a piece for the *Sunday Times* News Review on "how recent developments regarding Hollinger have affected you." As a codicil he suggested that the subject might not interest me "and you may have something entirely different to say."

The subject really did interest me, but short of writing in cuneiform, the whole notion was strewn with pitfalls, both legal and personal. But given the poisonous atmosphere, I was grateful for the note, very grateful, even though Witherow within a day cancelled the lunch we had scheduled for the following week as he was going to Scotland—or possible the Bonga oilfield in Nigeria. Whatever the reason, there seemed no absolute fatwa against me writing for the *Sunday Times*, and I did a column shortly after on the efforts to introduce sharia law into Ontario.

Not unexpectedly, I was becoming gun-shy of my profession. Murdoch's *New York Post* specialized in fantasy, making up stories about how I careened around in Manhattan cafés lecturing strangers on my importance. In the U.K. I read about how I screamed at staff, selfishly diverted Conrad's chauffeur from urgent trips for employees in order to stop and pick up my cleaning or go shopping or simply ride around being important. I knew by now that the people quoted (always anonymous), if they existed, had convinced themselves in the endless telling and retelling of these outrages that such behaviour by me really happened.

I am sure there are psychological studies to explain and prove this transmutation of wish-think to established fact, but I don't have them at hand and you wouldn't believe them anyway. But I will refer you to Willem Wagenaar's book *Identifying Ivan: A Case Study in Legal Psychology*, which assessed memory and showed how unreliable it was after one week, never mind forty years—as in the trial of accused concentration camp guard John Demjanjuk—or two or three years, as in the tales about me.

So perhaps when I said to our car driver, "Can we take another route to avoid this traffic?" while driving with a *Telegraph* employee, they remembered it as "Let's go and get my dry cleaning" while their child or mother at home writhed in desperate pain and possibly died? That version played better in the newsroom and in print. Although I must tell you that I have no recollection of any instance whatsoever driving with a *Telegraph* employee in distress. Nor could our driver when asked.

The Spectator decided time was ripe for a cover story. The cover was drawn by the intriguing artist Jonathan Wateridge, no mean talent. His art has developed considerably from this issue, which hit the newsstands in 2004, but it had all his classic elements; his website describes his technique as "elaborately crafted 'non-events', that have the trappings of a real occurrence but for the most part are entirely fabricated"—not a bad description of what was happening to us.

Wateridge's *Spectator* cover was a mix of editor Boris Johnson's enthusiasm at cashing in on us, leavened by his backstopping (not stabbing) sense that we just might not be totally over. So sufficient ambiguity needed, in case of recovery. In the design, I am wearing one of my worst mistakes, a woven leather and fringed gown from Alexander McQueen Haute Couture—my Minnehaha dress, as Conrad named it—ideal to match the wolves and reindeer at the bottom of the cover, depicting, I suppose, our Canadian connections. You can spot a corporate jet flying through clouds of black smoke over a mosque that suggests a bombing, and—if you use a magnifying glass—you can see the plane's cabin door is open and a male figure stands in it, trying to see where he is going? possibly having launched a bomb? or getting ready to jump? Some existential crisis, obviously.

The cover slash, "The Lost Tycoon," by Peter Oborne, was promisingly subtitled "A Shattering Tale of Ambition, Love and Board Room Passions." I could almost hear word for word the conversation between Boris, good friend of the Lost Tycoon in question, and writer Peter Oborne when the article was commissioned. A middle road had to be walked carefully, just in case it needed to be walked backwards— but not at the expense of leaving out the sheer joy of us as targets. Boris would adopt a Brechtian tone, I suspected—something like scene 12 of *The Life of Galileo* when the Pope instructs the Grand Inquisitor to refrain from actually using the torture tools on Galileo but delicately suggests, "At the very most he can be shown the instruments."

Oborne opened with an account of a meeting between Conrad and the private equity firm Cerebus at our apartment in New York in 2004. Conrad was on a desperate hunt to refinance Hollinger Inc. "Executives were endeavouring to bring home to Conrad Black the full horror of his personal and corporate predicament," wrote Oborne, as if only Cerebus had known of this and it wasn't keeping us awake day and night and in between, "when a sight met their eyes. His wife Barbara, clad only in a leotard and shades, had swept into the room. For a moment nobody spoke. 'Oh Conrad,' Barbara Black proclaimed: 'Let's just get out of here, they hate us.'"

God, I thought. Oborne's a genius. That is exactly how I felt. If a bubble could have been put over my head, Oborne's words would undoubtedly have been in it, together with a few profanities. Accurate though his intuition was, in fact I hadn't said a word. Because we didn't have staff in New York—one of the reasons I loved the place—Conrad had asked me to see if anyone needed refreshments. Given how I felt about gougers like Cerebus, a shaker laced with arsenic would have come in handy or a glass of blood. I was working on a column in my usual provocative writing gear of long-sleeved T-shirt and leggings, sometimes intoxicatingly varied by long-sleeved T-shirt and jeans. Having no inclination to change clothes for the task, I made one enquiry in said leggings and shirt, got one glass of something for some-one, before silently, without comment, returning to work.

I assumed Oborne had been directed by Hollinger's Paul Healy, something of a wit and now, I guessed, fabricator-in-chief with a team of scriptwriters. I suspected the many fake lines of mine were made up at the Hollinger office when they (temporarily) ran out of new legal suits to file against us. Journalists particularly glommed onto a comment I was supposed to have made on our corporate travel. "It's always best to have two planes," they claimed I'd remarked as if talking about a spare pair of pantyhose, "because however well one plans ahead one always finds one is on the wrong continent."

No question it is the sort of po-faced remark I would like to have made as a quip, but it wasn't mine, although the use of *one* as a per-sonal pronoun was very much my style. Hollinger did have two planes: an older one used almost exclusively by David Radler for his American newspapers, and the leased G4 we used. Under the circum-stances, the remark practically put me in a Leona Helmsley league.

Endless articles ridiculed our need and longing to hang out with the billionaires we weren't. I had absolutely no illusions about the monetary gulf that separated us from the society in which we moved in New York. So long as the super-rich people around us knew I recognized that gulf, I felt okay. So when the subject of the new yacht, plane, apartment, Schiele painting or Magnificent Jewel Auction came up together with the loaded enquiry "And will you be bidding, Barbara?" my response "Can't afford it" just about let me swallow the roundelay of villas and jewels.

If we're really getting into the mental slime of commentators and the press in general—and believe me, *slime* doesn't begin to cover it—my real complaint was with the way my husband was slagged off by people who had absolutely no idea at all of what made Conrad run but suddenly became nasty little experts on the topic. I don't want to sound like Hadassah Lieberman at the 2000 Democratic National Convention doing her "Let me tell you about my Joey," which admittedly made me all but throw up, though that was largely because a political convention ought not to be about wives coated in syrup telling you "about" their husbands—but this is my book and my game.

Let me tell you a thing or two about my Conrad, because it's perfectly clear the trolls at the national press in Canada and the U.S. and the U.K.—not to mention thug-in-chief Tom Bower, U.K. author of the nastiest lies between hard covers—wrote out of spite. Their work was so clearly reliant on magpie runs of newspaper clippings without any desire to know the man himself.

We can't choose our parents—yet—even if we can now choose our gender. It was not Conrad's fault that he was born to a wealthy family rather than the more useful—in public relations terms—single mum on skid row, and that he was sent to Upper Canada College, a leading boys private school, rather than a Native residential school. The wealthy do reproduce, and their offspring should be allowed to do something other than become drug addicts or work for Doctors Without Borders.

Conrad's ambition was certainly to acquire huge wealth and move in circles of the Great and Good, which in his eyes did not necessarily include Park and Fifth socialites, who were a diversion or, like Jayne Wrightsman, simply old friends. Neither were his gods hedge fund billionaires. The greasy pole of society was a distraction, but his climb was on a different part of the mountain, where great statesmen, politicians and diplomats frolicked. (To me this was about as engaging as having a libidinous orgy with the inhabitants of Madame Tussauds. Still, each to their own.) I could see a jolly good conversation with accomplished historians each topping one another—which is what they do, like any other lot, only with bigger words and more interesting anecdotes—and Conrad galloping along with them. He was always happiest when he could lasso dinner with real eggheads—Hugh Thomas, Andrew Roberts, Niall Ferguson, Alistair Horne, Martin Gilbert, Hugh Trevor-Roper, Asa Briggs, David Pryce-Jones, Sir Michael Howard, John Keegan, etc.—but that side of his life didn't offer the press any meat for ridicule.

Self-importance, of which he was always being accused—pompous and showing off—wasn't really a part of it either: his talks with important people were so enjoyable for him that it translated into an enthusiasm that could be misread—body language with his large hands moving to emphasize points and his face leaning towards his conversational partners. And *enjoyed* is the key: though France, the U.S. and the U.K. held special interest for him, there wasn't a country or system of government that didn't absorb him. (Well, perhaps not Kiribati or Papua New Guinea.) That's why I knew he'd have no problems with fellow prisoners in prison. Unlike me, he is totally without snobbery and finds absolutely everyone interesting.

Probably, yes, it was showing off to recite lists of vice-presidents or senators back a few hundred years, as Conrad was, unfortunately, wont to do. In the unlikely event any journo had bench strength in a hobby outside their backbiting little world, they might do the same: babble about the world's twenty most valuable stamps, starting with British Guiana's one-cent magenta, valued at €9 million in August 2018—which is the sum total of my knowledge on that subject—or all telephone models, from Meucci's invention up to the iPhone 10X-plus. Myself, I'm unstoppable on the subjects of large-breed dogs, monarch butterflies, classic liberalism and the death of free speech. You can see my problem—sort of an upside-down trifle pudding of a mind.

American politics was Conrad's trainspotting, the equivalent of being able to identify every Köchel of Mozart chronologically, which a particularly nasty aunt on my father's side claimed she could do whenever I spoke of a Mozart work. Conrad had this passion for American political history, British history and the great battles of history, which really don't interest me very much at all. "Talk to me about the Battle of the Somme," I would say when my sleeping tablets weren't working, and I knew that I'd be asleep in about five minutes and he would probably still be talking next morning. I tried to warn Conrad that reciting lists like all the senatorial results of the 1964 U.S. election could be seen as showing off, unless he was talking to Michael Barone, another nut on U.S. elections. But reciting political outcomes was for Conrad similar to games played together by movie aficionados—go on, name every film with Elsa Lanchester.

To be honest, I could never quite fit the Park Avenue set into his vision, with the exception of Henry Kissinger. I suppose Henry, who loved his wife very much, accepted her friends—the Group—and took part in their constant socializing for her sake. Probably Henry was of two minds about the cycle of charity dinners and high-society life, just as Conrad was, and both enjoyed aspects of it. Conrad had first met Henry in 1980, at a lunch held jointly by *The Economist* and Argus (Conrad's company) in Toronto, and it was love at first sight, for Conrad at least. Kissinger was a man he admired for his role in the world and for his prose. "His memoirs are magnificent," he would say, and he read every page, every bloody sentence. I was less sanguine. You simply can't deny Kissinger's accomplishments, and his company is terrific, but being a somewhat cynical person myself, I couldn't help questioning the durability of his friendship. "Remember his good friends the South Vietnamese," I would say, which was pretty much the fate of Conrad when Henry made a peace treaty with Richard Breeden and we were left stranded and ripe for invasion.

What Conrad never cared about was showy personal possessions—unless you count his books. I spent a small fortune (in my terms) giving him the usual expensive "things" as birthday gifts. There was a Patek Philippe and a Franck Muller watch and antique sapphire cufflinks, but he lost the watches and preferred to wear his Duplessis and FDR cufflinks or some hideous combination design of the American, British and Canadian flags. I dragged him into bespoke clothes, and although he liked them, I'd still find him wearing his baggy Canadian corduroys and broken shoes. You can't take the "use it up and make do" of his Canadian Protestant mother out of the newspaper magnate.

We absolutely had too many cars—because he kept all his late father's, mother's and brother's cars as well as an old Cadillac limousine simply because Richard Nixon had once used it—they were virtually worthless and we were forever getting him towed home when he was stranded in the most inconvenient places. The exception was London—he loved his extremely expensive Bentley with its very thin double red line on the exterior and hunting green leather seats piped with red. (Carina Frost told David, "We have to have the same.") There was also a 1950s Rolls-Royce in London about which the newspapers made quite a racket later. Conrad hadn't purchased the car; it came with the Massey Ferguson company he acquired in 1978. We rode in it once, to a party at foreign secretary Michael Heseltine's country home, and that was that. It of course disappeared into the maw of Breeden's voracious Hollinger gig.

There was nothing phony about Conrad's lifelong fascination with British politics and his desire to get into the House of Lords. As a child, he was taken from Toronto to London to see the coronation. This was not exactly a Butlin's special: he and his parents sailed first-class on the *Queen Elizabeth*, settling down for a six-week visit, with one week in Claridge's and the remainder in a house on Connaught Square rented from one of the Queen's ladies-in-waiting.

His guide in London was a British woman who must have had unfathomable patience with the truly frightful little swot of an eight-year-old who wanted to visit Apsley House ten times to soak up the historical connections with the Duke of Wellington and Napoleon. "I want to see the prime minister's house as well," said the little boy. "It's only a door and we'd have to walk up to it," replied the guide. "I don't mind. Please, can we see it?" Happenstance as they walked to the door: Prime Minister Churchill came out accompanied by General

George Marshall, an official U.S. delegate to the coronation. Conrad was in heaven. His older brother, Monty, wondered if they could go and see cricket instead.

In long nights that went to three or four in the morning, Conrad and his eccentric father talked politics, literature, ideas—and drank. His father planted seeds in him that fuelled his son's ambitions—the need to be financially successful in business and the parallel need for a full intellectual life. "No one laughs at a man with ten million," his father often told the young Conrad—not quite the usual chat between dad and son. The bond between them was deep—and permanent. Premature and ugly though George Black's death was, it seemed very right to me in the telling that it happened alone with Conrad. Sometimes, I really think George Black still hangs out in Conrad's sitting room in the house to which he brought his family in 1951. Perhaps it is true that the soul of a man who courts suicide never finds peace. If so, my own father has been remarkably quiet and never popped up to mention how good my last column was. But George Black, one feels, is always here, with us. And though I never knew him, I rather rely on his company.

CHAPTER TWENTY-ONE

The Counterfeit Bitch

Parents, good or bad, alive or dead, can be tenacious. And unexpected. There in the *Mail on Sunday* was Vera. We split the double-page spread, with Vera in a wheelchair and me in my skinny best at the 2004 Chelsea Flower Show Cartier after-party, a true size zero. Next to this vision of bone and a hank of hair was the headline "Barbara Always Wanted Only One Thing—Money," alongside a series of twenty-point captions headed by the beguiling words "Parents Reveal How Lady Black's Greed Drove Her," written by a long-time gossip columnist—last seen at the *National Enquirer*— Sharon Churcher.

Parents? I thought, having pretty much forgotten I had any. Turns out Ms. Churcher had located my mother and stepfather in Kitchener, Ontario. "Although she lived in luxury a few miles away"—seventy-five miles, actually—"she rarely visited their shabby flat," wrote Churcher melodramatically. I took umbrage with that. First of all, I had never visited their flat, never mind "rarely," and secondly, I found it unlikely that my stepfather and mother would be living in shabby circumstances. My stepfather had done very well in Canada. Wherever they lived would be a matter of choice and convenience.

Ms. Churcher spotlighted such festering problems as my childhood anger at the ending of the elocution lessons I never had. Even Vera could never have come up with that one. "Even as a girl she wanted the most expensive clothes," my mother was quoted as saying.

Mother was a clothes horse—as much as one could be in the four postwar years of clothing coupons and the poverty of her early life in Canada—and she tried very hard to implant a love of dressing in me. Incredibly, as a child, I was uncooperative. Anything but my school uniform made me uncomfortable. Going to buy my lace-up Clarks shoes in the 1940s was fun because I could stand in the fluoroscope X-ray machine and see my toes wiggling inside the shoe.

The *Mail* story was a pudding of half-truths and straightforward lies. The most painful aspect was that my "parents" believed I had been trashing them in print, blaming "their cruelty that made [me] obsessed with money" for my current problems. Whatever our past together, my mother did not deserve to be targeted like this with crocodile sympathy and phony stories of the serpent's tooth.

My sister told me that my stepfather had been diagnosed with cancer the year before and was now in perilous shape. My mother had suffered another stroke and was completely dependent on him. The two of them had sold their house and moved into a small flat they could manage in their invalided condition. I wrote to my stepfather to assure him that my current problems had absolutely nothing to do with them and to ask, if he wanted to tell me, how the interview had come about.

He sent me back a three-page handwritten letter making it very clear they were media innocents.

My stepfather gave a step-by-step account of the pathetic invasion of the lives of an infirm couple approaching their eighties: telephone calls, knocks on the door, "chatter, chatter, chatter," he wrote, as Churcher carpet-bombed their home and cell phones. An offer via a note was shoved under their apartment door after they'd declined to speak to her five separate times. Page two of his letter began "Contents of Note":

1. We want to sign a contract with you both.
2. You will have a chance to read over every word before going to print.
3. We will pay you $10,000 U.S.

I was aggrieved to see I was worth so little in the *Mail on Sunday*'s vast budget, but then Judas launched Christianity for thirty pieces of silver.

"It has been a poor year for us," wrote my stepfather. "And we are under pressure. But I do believe one has to be positive." (He was going for his latest cancer results in two weeks' time. They would not be good. I would see him twice before he died.)

"Barbara," he continued. "Your letter was a joy to receive and thank you for your kind comments to both of us, regards Vera's wheelchair and my cancer problems. . . . We know that you and your husband are going to have your hands full in the future months and we hope things work out fine for both of you. We're sorry about this but we do not see the British press and did not understand it all." I could see that mental balance and health difficulties matter very little when a true love story exists; and that it did between my mother and stepfather, who worshipped her, was beyond any doubt.

My initial impulse was to go to the U.K. Press Complaints Commission. But that could mean dragging my mother's mental condition and Leonard's cancer into the public eye. My own reputation at this point would probably only tarnish the absolute respectability of my stepfather and mother. Life had become an ocean wave that swells and picks up debris, hitting out wildly as it moves towards the shore, and you can't quite tell what it will carry or where it will break.

I've often thought that gossip-type writers like Churcher, Geoffrey Levy et al., who almost exclusively cover celebs and rich people, are the ones obsessed with money because they themselves have only ordinary amounts. The reason I had defended unpopular wealthy people in my columns before and after my marriage to Conrad, including some I didn't much like (Leona Helmsley, Michael Jackson) was not because I thought money was so terrific, but because I believed they were getting a raw deal simply because of their wealth. One of the themes of my work from decades earlier had been selective justice, and the targets of selective justice change according to the zeitgeist. (God, sorry about that word, which makes my skin crawl with its overworked pretension, but the only substitutes are "fashion of the times" or "winds of fashion," and they sound like magazine supplements.) Different groups, whether of race, gender, sexual predilection or economic position, are targets of protection or opprobrium at different times, and it had always seemed to me, post-1980s, that the group singled out—the rich and celebrated—should be given equal treatment under the law no matter how unpleasant their personalities, or deeds if they turn out to be guilty. I doubted whether Harvey Weinstein or Kevin Spacey could get fair trials; meanwhile, verdicts were rendered and their punishments in process.

Like Arya Stark in *Game of Thrones*, I was accumulating a list of people to kill that I recited intermittently while visions of machine guns and bottles of acid danced in my head. The *Mail on Sunday* was an inexhaustible source of nasties, and given that I was not exactly a household name to its readers in the way of a pop star or serial murderer, I think in giving way to their own interest in a fellow journalist they misjudged the interest of their readers—an unusual failing for the fiendishly clever editor Paul Dacre. A new theme emerged predicting I was about to leave Conrad because he had lost his influence, power and, most of all, money. "All Because the Lady Loves Money" and "Queen of Excess" got replaced by musings about where I would go for the next wealthy husband.

George Jonas, always a source of wisdom and common sense, on listening to the radio chat about my next husband, remarked that had gold-digging been my ambition, he would have to say I had been a total failure. Myself, I'd never met any of these fabled creatures, the red-nailed scheming females pursuing fat wallets irrespective of the pocket they were in. Clare Boothe Luce created a great one in her play *The Women*—Crystal Allen, played by Joan Crawford in the original film. Crystal did, like Jayne Wrightsman, meet her husband while working as a counter girl in a department store, but Jayne as a gold-digger? Doesn't compute.

Anyway, there I was, clearly giving off the smell of L'Eau de Croqueuse de Diamants. I can't really blame the commentators on this one—I'd married three extremely well-off men. In Canada, the perception was helped by my usual rotten timing when I wrote the article

"Marrying Up" just after I married David Graham, in 1984. It dismissed the notion of money as the motivation for marrying up and posited the old saw—which I think is pretty much true—about women's biological programming attracting them to the partner they figure would be the best and safest provider for family. In the U.K. my reinvention as a woman in love with money started just months after I married Conrad, courtesy of the BBC's *Start the Week*. Host Melvyn Bragg asked playwright Steven Berkoff about the surprise casting of Joan Collins in his new play, and threw the discussion open to author and journalist Edward Pearce.

> Berkoff: Well I think she [Joan Collins] is a marvellous actress,
>   totally underrated and glamorous and . . . the part itself is
>   an extraordinary, kind of exaggerated woman who is, must
>   be denied nothing and so she is like a kind of very queenly
>   arrogant society spoilt bitch . . .
> Pearce: A sort of upmarket Barbara Amiel?
> Berkoff: Well yes, maybe something like that (general murmur) you
>   could say that.

Sadly, I missed this exchange and hadn't a clue who Edward Pearce or Steven Berkoff were, but fortunately the *Evening Standard* called me in Canada (a little-known secret haunt of downmarket rich bitches) and asked me what I thought of the remarks. I was unable to get clarification on the "general murmur" referred to in the transcript, but Steven Berkoff was happy to elaborate and clarify his thoughts in print. He told the *Evening Standard* that I was the sort of person that "dives in as if she had some God-given right by virtue of education and academia to do it." That is of course a well-known shortcoming of columnists, critics and taxi drivers, and the right is either God-given or, in my case at that particular moment, Rupert Murdoch–given. I suspected Mr. Berkoff would prefer all opinionated columnists to get licences from the Socialist International before being allowed to write or, in lieu of this, be an illiterate street person whose opinions would not be tainted by the "education and academia" that he apparently feels disqualifies one from enjoying such a petit bourgeois notion as freedom of speech.

But even earlier by a couple of weeks, Stephen Glover in *The Independent* had concluded that I was "so rich" that I had turned against my profession of journalism and was "looking forward to intimate parties and grand holidays, interspersed with a little gentle charity work." Where on earth do they get this stuff? Does Stephen actually know working columnists who live like that? I mean, why on earth would I be stupid enough to keep working if my preference was to pour tea or enjoy a salon? Now that I ask that question, I wonder myself. The notion of just eating eclairs and looking after abused dogs sounds pretty good as I bash this out at 3 a.m., with my eightieth birthday coming at the end of this year. Cripes.

Glover backed up his view of me with a *Sunday Times* column I had written a week or so earlier in October 1993, quoting Emperor Franz Joseph—a man not known for his advocacy of a free press— who described journalists as *canaille*, which translates as riff-raff or grubby people. As a journalist myself, I thought he was probably right. We were all pretty much merde, and our craft was merde; we have to use every trick fair or foul to get the interview, to get the dirt, but essentially and crucially, to get the truth.

Unlike the emperor, I believed our work very necessary. "We may live in a sewer," I wrote in that 1993 column, "but our sewer has a genuinely important social function. It actually prevents an even worse sewer: that of star chambers and secret power holders in high places, whom we prevent or at least curtail from operating with impunity. The press is the bridge between the centres of power and the public." The argument was somewhat more detailed, so it went over Mr. Glover's head, and he got very cross. I believed what I wrote, but ironically the argument I used was false so far as it applied to my situation.

The "star chambers and secret power holders in high places" were objects of worship by the free press when it came to Conrad and me. The point of a principle, really, is that you also have to apply it to people you find utterly despicable. It's rather a Voltairean point of view, I suppose: "I despise what you say but will defend to the death your right to say it" isn't exactly compatible with prosecution or persecution of those making politically incorrect remarks about gender or race or whatever is the going protected subject or group.

The notion that I was a bitch was nothing new to me, and indeed most women, whether rich or poor, working or unemployed, will at one point in their lives be called "bitch" *sotto voce* or in print, just as most men will be called "bastard." I came to bitch status pure and untainted by money. Detractors had labelled me a "fascist bitch" as early as 1980, when my book *Confessions* came out, long before I had a penny. The exciting notion that I was now a rich one obviously had to do with my very recent marriage to Conrad Black. So, I used my God-given right to do a column on the matter in the *Sunday Times* and, while I was at it, lay a few more landmines for myself in case I had any limbs to spare. "One of the differences between me and my sisters in the women's movement," I wrote, "is that I do not regard my husband's money as my own. Having married very wealthy men before my current husband, I can guarantee that I parted from them leaving both their fortunes and my opinions intact."

In retrospect, it was a damn mistake being so inept about marrying and divorcing. Done right, according to the feminist creed and the bilious divorce laws they had spearheaded, and I could have helped Conrad more with legal bills. My first divorce from a rich man got me zilch, since I wanted the divorce so asked for nothing and took nothing. My second divorce got me half of my own books and all of my clothes but I left behind everything else, including two years' worth of my monthly postdated cheques to my former husband to cover half his rent. If you cause pain by leaving, was my gold-digging reasoning, then you shouldn't cause additional pain to your abandoned lower-earning spouse by forcing him to move. So pay up. My third divorce, from multi-millionaire David, netted me about $20,000 Canadian.

When I married Conrad, a marriage contract was really needed, given Canadian law. My last divorce lawyer had fired me after I returned to David Graham the remainder of the $400,000 settlement he had negotiated for me. The new ones I had to employ, in order to give my signature the validity of "independent legal advice," took one look at my age, marital history, bank account and earnings and begged me not to sign the proffered contract, pointing out that if the marriage exploded in the next few years I would be unprotected, and if I hung on till later and Conrad fell for the notional younger woman (something my lawyers seemed fixated on) the amount of protection that kicked in would certainly not look after me in my old age. My view was that in the event of Conrad hopping off with the young and beautiful Roman Catholic girlfriend of my nightmares, Conrad would help me out.

So there at the time of the Rich Bitch broadcast I was. Fifty-two years old, four marriages in—with eighteen months of marriage to Conrad—and my net worth consisted of my opinions and my ability to put them on paper, my own three-year-old Volkswagen Golf that I adored and, admittedly, the expectations that came with being Mrs. Conrad Black, a position I loved but that at the time carried no private salary, a big but not especially valuable wardrobe, no additional or joint bank account, and no Hollinger or Telegraph plc salary. I had no real estate, no stocks or bonds, no jewellery, and rather a lot of books but no first editions. I was a fiscally irresponsible, over-dressed, walking example of why it would be far more helpful to give women courses in financial planning than gender studies.

The "Yes, I'm a Bitch, but Don't Call Me Rich" column I wrote (without the divorce details) ended with a paragraph that would, like the Hydra of Greek mythology, rapidly grow more and more heads complete with poisonous blood as the years passed and our business situation deteriorated. "Ultimately, I am a North London Jew who has read a bit of history," I wrote. "This means I know this: in a century that has seen the collapse of the Austro-Hungarian, British and Soviet Empires, reversal of fortune is this rich bitch's reality. One might as well keep working and have the family's Vuitton suitcases packed." A minefield in waiting.

This notion of my bolting for a richer man hung around in the papers for about eight years, after which it died, only occasionally surfacing as a chant of "Well, she's well preserved but old and out of options, so where would she go?" Some months into the 2004 media blitz, the *Mail on Sunday* featured a monstrously large headline on a column by Suzanne Moore: "Ooh, That Lady Black Is Common as Muck." I have to say it is unsettling to see a headline like that.

Female journalists on other females: God, what a rotten lot we are. My slate is reasonably clean when it comes to mixing in negative remarks about a female subject's appearance with commentary on their ideas or policies, although I may sometimes make a reference to a general look or way of presenting themselves. The one slip that sticks in my mind came early on in my writing: I encountered a thoroughly unpleasant department store women's clothes buyer in Manhattan when researching a *Maclean's* feature article. The saleswomen loathed her. She was in a bitchy mood, they said, because her recent facelift was still hurting. At that point in my education I would not have recognized a new facelift, so I asked her and she was very upset but didn't deny it. When using her quote, I slagged her off, mentioning that she spoke "with her newly tightened face." When it came out in print, my slimy bit of journalism, absolutely irrelevant to the story, only coated me in slime.

Canadian female journalists have always had a bit of an obsession with my face and figure—were they real or artificial? They slagged me off with innuendo about my Barbarella looks or my "cosmetic" appearance. One Canadian journalist criticized this obsession—only because she felt any suggestion I was still attractive as necrophilia, given my age. Not unreasonable but poor taste, I thought. British female journalists have a different take: their obsession is with my wardrobe (extent of) or money (lack of).

Auberon Waugh made the observation that autobiographies written by men are often motivated by an obscure form of revenge and "with women, there is this tremendous desire to expose themselves." He was dead right. My looks have always been problematic to me, and not in the way all those lemon-mouth female writers and the odd creepy male journalist think. On and on about my "pneumatic" appearance, which is a nasty euphemism for having a breakfront that nature did not give me, which in fact it did, and, to quote the late writer Larry Zolf, my college "beak" that went through a "nose job."

Obviously, appearance helped me get television work and quite a lot else. All the same, the concentration on my appearance when I was bashing out political stuff for both Canadian and U.K. employers was pretty odd—and especially grotty from the glorious sisterhood who pretty much gave a pass to other attractive female writers both in Canada and those, such as the very much younger and gorgeous Canadian-born Maya Even, working in London at the same time.

I did have plastic surgery on one crucial part of me and not, I might say, for the better. I'd like to blame it on Ross McLean, the CBC producer who put me on camera and would say in studio over the speaker, "Move that light or we'll get her nose shadow." But he didn't say it in a particularly nasty way, just rather matter-of-factly. I had never liked my nose, which I felt was responsible for putting me into the tacky housedresses and slacks sections of the Eaton's catalogue during my modelling days, rather than the smart upmarket sportswear and ladies' dresses. But then again, my original nose poked up in the TV face of Yardley's Oh! de London commercial, Bulova watches and two *Toronto Life* covers, among its other nasal outings. So probably it was just plain vanity, wanting to look prettier, better or different. The Jewish boys I double-dated throughout college all seemed to go out with gorgeous models, and I ached to have their chiselled perfection. Not their ski-slope or retroussé nose, as it was called in the sixties; I just wanted the part that caused the shadow—a bulbous thickening at the end—gone. Barbra Streisand had just had her nose refined at the time—"refined" meaning it was the same but just a bit less so. I imagined getting mine fixed like that would be as easy as having a tooth extracted.

These days, when by age six little girls seem to know all about facial fillers, brow lifts, butt and breast implants and so on, it is, I grant you, difficult to believe that I had utterly no idea what I was in for, but I didn't. A baby elephant was spotted in South Africa in 2018 with no trunk, and I would have done more research on how to fix its nose than I did on my own procedure, for which I did no research at all. My nose was done in the late summer of 1968. I was twenty-seven years old. I was rather like Evelyn Waugh—Auberon's father and author of *Brideshead Revisited*, *Scoop*, etc.—who lamented in a 1947 diary entry that he was tossing back brandy, opium and cocaine to ease the excruciating pain after a completely unnecessary hemorrhoidectomy: "I took no advice," he wrote, "just went to the surgeon and ordered the operation as I would have ordered new shirts. In fact I had behaved wholly irrationally and was paying for it." Good to know really clever people muck themselves up as well.

The first thing I noticed after the surgery—and you couldn't notice much because I had these huge bandages on my nose—was that my favourite mole on my upper lip had gone. That mole had not been discussed and I was very sad. I always thought of it as a rather distinctive beauty mark, and even had it listed on my early U.K. passports and Canadian citizenship under "distinguishing features." The surgeon and I barely discussed my face because he was more interested in my film director boyfriend, who he hoped would make a documentary on his work. When the bandages came off, I realized my nose had also been removed together with the mole. I had nothing where my nose had been but a snout. "It was more difficult than I anticipated," said the doctor. "And took much longer. Don't worry. It will drop."

I don't know what your worst nightmare is, but I have actually lived through at least two of my most basic nightmares: one was being imprisoned by a totalitarian regime, which happened when I managed to get imprisoned in that communist-Mozambique political prison, and the other was this, losing my looks, possibly through a motor accident or fire—I hadn't contemplated paying to have them destroyed. Of the two, I'd have to say Mozambique was probably more dangerous, given the very real chance of my being shot, starved or dying of some ghastly tropical disease. But losing my nose was like waking up to find you now have advanced leprosy.

Weeks passed and there was no "dropping"—well, a very tiny bit, but not so that the cashier at the local convenience shop across from my apartment, where I went every other day for milk, recognized me. Men didn't whistle, cars didn't stop, delivery boys didn't try to chat me up. No one opened doors for me when I was carrying groceries. No one tried to get my telephone number or asked me out. I was just an ugly girl. There must be non-fiction books or novels written about this sort of situation, but to be twenty-seven years old and go into an elective operation as a rather attractive female and to wake up being twenty-seven years old and extremely ugly is daunting. This was my personal version of *The Fly*: a baby piglet had got into the molecular transporter with me.

I now had the sort of look that Hollywood B films imply a female gets when acid is thrown into her face, except all they show is a perfectly good-looking woman with a bandage on two square inches along the side of her face covered up by her hair—à la Marlene Dietrich in the very A-list film *Witness for the Prosecution* when she pushes back her blonde hair to reveal the shattering, barely there scar. My scar was front and centre and defining. *Vanitas vanitatum.*

My film director boyfriend was going to make a feature film, shooting largely in New York, and I decided to go with him, having got the name of a brilliant reconstructive surgeon, John Marquis Converse, in Manhattan. He had been in the U.K. during the Battle of Britain and worked on reconstructing injured faces of burned and smashed RAF pilots, as well as creating a unit for casualties in North Africa and working with the Free French in Italy. I felt my appearance would definitely qualify as a smashed face. I brought my before-and-after photos. He called in an associate. "Look at this," he said, shaking his head, and offered to come to Toronto and testify if I was suing.

"All I want," I said, "is to look as much like my before self as possible."

"We may have to take bone from your hip to do it," he said.

He made me wait another six months before the surgery, so finally it was done early in 1970. He charged me virtually nothing but hospital expenses. "I do work for rich people," he said, "and can help people like you."

My changed nose was of no interest to journalists when I returned to Canada in 1972. "You looked better before," said George Jonas, not altogether reassuringly, and when I look at the *Globe and Mail* photos before May 1968, I suppose I have to agree. The new nose was now brilliantly normal but not quite as good as the old one.

Anyway, a new set of nostrils are not prurient in the way a new set of nipples might be. In interviews and cover stories that began as soon as I got steady work at *Maclean's*, the snide remarks returned, as ever, to my bosom. The routine was always the same: first three-quarters of the chat were the usual stuff about my life, ambitions, views, and then the last question that seemed to be the entire point of the interview: "Are your breasts silicone?" (At one point I considered having my husbands sign a letter confirming the authenticity of my bosom in its prime, but that seemed a trifle over the top.)

My reply was always boringly (to subsequent interviewers) the same. "If I had them done, they'd be twice as big. I don't do things by half." I'd say that sort of reply was the arrogance of youth, but in fact it wasn't arrogance—it was a headstrong confidence in the complete unimportance of shocking people. I thought the question silly, as most questions to me were, and so I developed a habit of replying flippantly. It was fun and as natural to me as my chest. This curiosity about my bosom remained a sub-theme throughout my life, usually reappearing like some invasive weed whenever I was more in the public eye, and it peaked in absurdity with a completely fictitious anecdote one female writer in Toronto hawked around the mainstream press in 2007.

The anecdote, first printed in the *Toronto Star* and picked up elsewhere, was raving mad and stated that my bosom of thirty-five years earlier was of such mesmerizing powers that a former boyfriend sentimentally kept pads I supposedly wore underneath my bra straps to ease the discomfort of lugging such heavy mammaries around, until his subsequent wife burned them—the pads, that is. Being sixty-six years old when this fantasy hit the press, I assumed one ought to be flattered. I mean, I was all but facing varicose veins and support hose at that point. I had no idea whether the journalist in question was in therapy, but one hoped so. The state of mind that had conjured this up was truly pathological.

To complete Auberon's thesis, the trajectory of my front was delayed, which may have puzzled some. My natural bosom in university was perfectly acceptable but relatively modest: the area looked more prominent due to a slightly idiosyncratic rib cage and very small waist, which I found embarrassing since I was sure any beau unveiling me would be terribly disappointed. Or, as the Toronto specialist to whom I was referred for testing said, "You don't have emphysema, only a rib construction acting rather like a shelf, which makes your lung X-rays appear a little distorted. I don't suppose it's any handicap in your social life." And I suppose such a comment now would get him struck off the medical register.

After my unplanned pregnancy—God, it's all so long ago—I was put on the contraceptive pill, steroids and bottles of stout, I expect. A proper menstrual cycle kicked in—such a nuisance after having it only once or twice a year—and my cystic breasts and I completed our physical development. Absent the steroids, my moon face went but not my chest, again emphasized by the tapered rib cage and small waist. I believe this top-to-waist ratio thing is a family trait.

My mammary glands and I continued our merry jiggle through life unaffected by any artificial additions or subtractions throughout my twenties, thirties and forties. In my very late forties, atypical hyperplasia and an extremely benign tumour scared the bejesus out of me and made it prudent to sort things out with some surgery. I confess that I think now would be a super time to update my front, which currently resembles a pair of beanbags. But each time I think perhaps I will, I think of what fodder my dying on a plastic surgeon's table would be to the press. I've given my share to them, and that seems a sacrifice too far.

After losing my nose, I never had a totally stable confidence in my looks. It isn't quite the standard "poor me, I'm so insecure" cliché of the film star and model, but rather an ambivalence watered by some upsetting times. There may be women publicly photographed and described as "beautiful" fairly often in their lives who forget about their appearance as age eats it up—I don't know any who have reached this happy state of equilibrium, and I do know a lot of once beautiful women—but I myself find having one's appearance praised early in life becomes something of a load. Physical beauty, unlike the spiritual kind that aging glossy-mag editors wax lyrical about, is a rapidly diminishing asset that keeps tripping you up when you turn on the light and face yourself in the mirror. God.

The media nadir for me came not from beauty fascists or spiteful columnists but, as ever, with my own co-operation. A pleasant woman I rather liked who had been managing editor at the *Calgary Herald*, Joan Crockatt, wrote telling me she was in the middle of "writing a fresh and definitive book on the new power of women" together with her colleague Arlene Bynon. The very fact that this overripe topic did not send me bolting for cover indicates there was by now something very askew in me. Could I give them an interview, asked Joan?

I temporized. We met five months later, the book deadline long past. "Just an off-the-record friendly chat," said Joan, which should have flashed like laser lighting outside a Hells Angels clubhouse. "I'd like to get some advice on how to be in touch with Lady Thatcher," she continued. We met at my favourite little coffee shop, where Jonas and I often went, at the Four Seasons Hotel.

Okay, stand me up against a wall and shoot. Any idiot who sees a cassette recorder placed on the table in full view and thinks she is having an "off-the-record friendly chat" is either lying or blind. Or cognitively impaired. I'll opt for the third choice. I saw the cassette recorder being placed on the table, no attempt to deceive me, and only the visual connection reached my brain. I thought it quite unconnected with our conversation. Is there a psychiatrist in the house?

That Sunday in February 2005 must have topped an unusually slow week of news, and editors in London, New York and Toronto decided to play Joan and Arlene's coffee with me big and splashy, at least two pages and photos each, catering to their own demographics with different cutlines. Essentially they all trumpeted my "first time speaking out" about "my exclusive grief." Which was particularly sick-making. The *Toronto Star* devoted the entire front page of its Life section to an absolutely huge photo I had never seen from the Trump wedding, and a grotesquely large title of "Being

Barbara" and the caption "'I shall make something good from this awful time.'"

This person was definitely not anyone I would waste time on, I thought as I read myself. She was a delusional and pathetically banal woman, if not lunatic. (I expect to see that line lifted vertically out of context.) A few days after this demolition, which ricocheted into other newspapers, I received a message from a happy Joan Crockatt, who felt that since she hadn't heard from me I must be sharing her pleasure in the success of the article. She was serious.

The *Toronto Star* photo of us at Donald and Melania Trump's 2005 wedding in Palm Beach evoked memories of that evening. NBC's Katie Couric had been placed next to Conrad at the dinner, and on seeing her placement she recoiled, as if encountering a dish of Ebola, and walked rapidly away, demanding a new seat. A 2016 *New Yorker* piece, "Memories of Trump's Wedding," by Joseph O'Neill, recounted that slap-down, which had not gone unnoticed.

The evening ended with Conrad and me romantically doing his version of dancing, namely standing on one spot and swaying, around the swimming pool at Mar-a-Lago with the water's surface reflecting hundreds of tiny decorative lights and the air full of the scent of night-blooming flowers. Just in case the moment had any durability, Conrad whispered in my ear, "That's Richard Johnson watching us over there." "Who's he?" I asked, dreamily looking up at the stars. "You know, Page Six, Murdoch's gossip columnist."

Money was becoming obsessional with us now, mainly because we didn't have enough for American lawyers driving German cars to their smart Washington, D.C., offices. The solution was unavoidable—but which house to sell first? I opted for Palm Beach, Conrad for London. "There is no future for me in London," he had written in a nighttime note to me. "I'm done and over. . . . I'm going to take back my Canadian citizenship when Chrétien is gone," he vowed. I doubted it would be quite that simple.

We compromised by putting the Toronto house on the market, without fanfare. I knew the house was probably a tear-down for the

Chinese and Russian buyers who were the main market in Toronto in those days (and still are). Who needed rooms of double-height libraries with fireplaces mounted in original seventeenth-century Grinling Gibbons carved wood decoration? Who cared that the carved ceilings were not plaster but wood or that the bannisters had three wooden spindles per stair rather than the usual two? Or that the entire 26,000-square-foot home had a copper roof of great beauty and was nestled in a prime location of eleven acres? "This house is unique," said my husband, rising once more to cope with the latest devastating situation. "Of course it will sell at a very good price."

Only it didn't. With the public nature of our troubles, all we got were bottom-feeders. They were counting on us being desperate enough that we would accept lowball offers insufficient to even cover the mortgage we had taken out for legal bills.

Then, one day, it hit me. Conrad's face was changing. The crisis was etching itself into the colour of his skin; his eyes were swollen more often than not—from exhaustion—and they appeared almost closed. His mouth, which he had always referred to jokingly as his cartoon mouth because its default position was that of a sad clown, had become a fixed half-moon of despair. He would go to dinner with various people in Toronto, some theoretically old friends from years of cozy luncheons, some acquaintances from successful business transactions of the past, who in making the dinner engagement held out the promise of loans, or deals, or ways for him to take the initiative back. He would leave the house a little tense but keen and with an aura of invincibility.

He would pay for the dinner out of some misplaced pride, not understanding he was now a hunting trophy: people wanted their own private story of Conrad Black's latest venture and hadn't the slightest intention of helping him. He would come home at one or later, sometimes with an optimistic view of promises made during dinner. "This was a very important evening," he would say, his words slightly slurred, "and I think we have a breakthrough." He would fall asleep at his desk trying to work out figures and finances. After the first couple of these evenings, one knew any promises were empty, forgotten the next day. I watched an exhausted boxer going into the ring, only to come out even more bloodied and disfigured.

His wine consumption at these dinners increased. This was a source of friction between us, for double reasons: he lost his edge, I thought, when his mind was made rosier by alcohol, and I was always afraid, fiercely worried, he would give away too much, believe too much, hope too much and hear more than was spoken. What could I do? How do you stand by and watch someone you love open their veins for the entertainment of others? Look, I know it's a rhetorical question, but think, what the hell do you do without making the situation worse and sending his morale even further down? The only answer was no solution: I just had to keep quiet, say nothing—which, let's face it, was huge for me.

As if this weren't enough, his own sensibility was dragging him deeper and deeper into gloom, along dead-end corridors. "My arrogant and belligerent contempt for the corporate governance movement," he wrote to me in an email in May 2004,

> though it was largely justified morally (though not my conceited insouciance which I now recognize), was an enormous tactical blunder. Such an error always has consequences. The failure to separate my disdain for the corporate governance movement from the company's interest could have been invoked by the directors as grounds for my dismissal. If those who terminated me had come to the task with clean hands and were decent honest people, and not the dishonest cowardly hypocrites that they are, and cited this as the reason for terminating me as chairman, I would have voted with them (like Erich Honecker voting for his own elimination as head of the government of East Germany). I would have voted for my own removal and dismissal for cause.
>
> As a conscientious Roman Catholic, I believe that I deserve to be fired and humiliated, but not in the way and by the people that I was, and not disgraced and reviled as dishonest. I was and am quite honest and absolutely law-abiding and in fact was quite a competent chairman of the company, but I have not passed the buck and failed

to recognize my own responsibility. Of course I don't deserve
the terrible debacle that has happened, but I do deserve a serious
comeuppance, and God knows I have had it.

I'd read these various notes, emails, faxes, noting abstractly that
even in moments of extreme private distress, his recourse was to
historical analogies. He needed someone he could trust to talk to, but
there was no one. His brother had died in 2002. Cardinal Carter, the
close friend who had steered his conversion to Catholicism over seven
years, would have been a sterling source of support, but he had died
in 2003.

The only person, I thought, who will be 100 per cent discreet is
George Jonas, and he tried hard to help. They met countless times.
Jonas read everything: transcripts, Hollinger releases, the dozens of
pages Conrad wrote listing factual errors in everything Hollinger
claimed. He was the only person in Canada or America—besides
writer Mark Steyn—who had grasped the case totally. But George
was facing the continuing assault of Parkinson's, and there too I was
fairly useless.

Exercise will slow down the progress of Parkinson's, I said to
George, who recoiled at the notion of exercise, so I talked about
poster boy Michael J. Fox. We argued, I reasoned, and he quite agreed
with my points, medically speaking but not temperamentally. I bought
a treadmill for his basement, which was a bright, carpeted space.
Given the difficulty of installing cable, I mounted a DVD player. My
Hungarian manicurist, Helga, brought videos George had wanted
back from her trip to Budapest. Robert Lantos added a copy of
Szindbád, a 1971 Hungarian film George was always banging on
about. Politely, exquisitely, George thanked me. Politely, exquisitely,
he congratulated me on my choice of viewing material, which he
watched upstairs on his Apple computer. And he never stepped onto
the basement stairs, let alone the treadmill.

Back in my world, I was being "tasked." "Go to London, will
you?" said Conrad. "We've got to keep the flag flying." Christ, I muttered. I was not being asked to cross the Kalahari Desert with one

bottle of water—I was being told to fly business class to London. But with each London visit and social function, I was becoming more insubstantial. A gulf was opening up between what was happening to me and this other world. And why not? How can you expect people to be oblivious to the unending double-stroke drum roll of the media accounts of our death as respectable people?

I could tell from questions that there was a general assumption Conrad had done "something." "We all pad our expense accounts," said one of my very closest friends, in a sympathetic attempt to be understanding. I looked at her and thought there is just no point in trying to explain.

Elton John called and asked if he could take me out to dinner. We sat before dinner in the small library on the ground floor of Cottesmore Gardens. "This is for you," said Elton, presenting me with a small package. It was a quite lovely pavé diamond star and chain from the jeweller Theo Fennell. "You're the star," said Elton. We went to dinner at Bibendum, in the Michelin building, just the two of us, and my awkwardness knew no bounds, and this time it wasn't irony or self-deprecation—I was tongue-tied. That he should actually give me a present and find time to take me to dinner when my own star was descending with the rapidity of a lump of meteoroid is still a mystery. There was absolutely nothing in it for him. It remains lodged in my mind as a moment of immense kindness. A mensch.

London was full of baleful signs. The muckraker Tom Bower was now scouring sewer pipes for his book on us. It was published in 2006 and would be the foulest, bar none, of all the movies, articles and books about us. That's a distinction he would be proud of, I suppose. Conrad, who retained counsel to sue Bower, gave up listing what both British and Canadian lawyers described as "verifiable errors of fact" after 165 examples, never mind the simply vicious opinions, which any writer has the freedom to voice.

Three of Canada's top lawyers went over the book carefully and were unanimous that Conrad would win any case against Bower. "But," said Guy Pratte thoughtfully after Conrad's victory at the U.S. Supreme Court, "his book was poorly reviewed, you have recovered your reputation to a very large extent, which would mitigate damages, and in Canada successful libel suits only recoup 45 per cent of costs. This would be a very expensive case." We all assumed Bower's armour was contractual indemnity provided by Rupert Murdoch, whose HarperCollins publishing company brought out the book and whose deep pockets could easily accommodate Bower's stench.

When I returned to Toronto, the house there had assumed a permanent gloom. The country I left behind always looked better these days than the one to which I was returning. In those Toronto halls, there was a thick sort of twilight, almost a fog. We had become crepuscule creatures. The house was not going to sell, and the bills and demands were mountains of paper on Conrad's desk. I suppose it was inevitable.

"Go back to London and sell the house," said Conrad virtually as I came in the door. "My London life is over. I've become a joke. It should go fast, and you can do it quietly." The fist in my stomach clenched. The announcement was so shattering that it drove away any resentment of this new task. A mixture of unhappiness and an impotent fury at the gods for such calamities would come later. Over. It was over.

"Quietly" selling Cottesmore Gardens, I feared, was going to have some similarities to the ongoing Toronto saga. This would take time and would be utterly horrid. Furthermore, in the event of success, it would be the monster of all packing. But it had to be done. Having barely unpacked, I took out my Vuitton luggage, now supplemented by the necessities of commercial travel—lightweight expanding Tumi bags—and left.

CHAPTER TWENTY-TWO

2005: En Route to Perdition

The rats were a bit of a surprise. Real rats, not the human ones. These were large brown ones and completely insouciant, unlike me when encountering them in the basement kitchen of our London home. Most Londoners, I expect, have encountered rats, there are so many of them living beneath the city, but I had simply not anticipated that in our house, so recently gutted and rebuilt and with a kitchen of vast stainless-steel vistas, there would be rats running about.

When you are living alone in a large house, there really isn't much point in screaming or fainting or jumping up on the counters—which had one of the rodents on it anyway. I just left and went back upstairs; after all, it was just me and them and they didn't seem inclined to leave the kitchen or advance elsewhere. They had their floor and I had mine. The rats were quite large too—about nine or ten inches, not counting the long tails. Well, I thought, who knew my first rat encounter would be while living in luxury in Kensington. Mice, yes, often in the laundry baskets in Toronto—they came in from the ravine. Cockroaches in Manhattan. And now rats in London.

The house had been on the market since summer 2004 "informally," which means everyone knew but we pretended it wasn't happening. When it didn't sell—this was before the London real estate market went into orbit somewhere north of Jupiter—and the noose around our windpipe was so tight the chances of our being able to sell it rather than a receiver doing so were rapidly declining, we turned it over to one of the big London real estate firms, and a very smart foldout with pages of photos was done. The house was in tip-top condition, in very "highly desirable Kensington." Given that it had air cooling and an indoor swimming pool of a considerable size with a separate Jacuzzi, which the agents called a "plunge pool," plus an elevator, back stairs, commercial kitchen (with rats), God knows how many bedrooms, all ensuite, a drawing room that stretched across an entire floor so you could fit in your few hundred guests, and a small but quite delicious garden designed by the genius Arabella Lennox-Boyd, the place was a knockout.

In 2005, the house sold, with a presumed closing date of April 30, for £13 million. (It would cost at least double that now and quite possibly a lot more.) That meant everything had to be packed up fast. What to store in the U.K., what to send to Canada, what to sell by auction at one of the big houses and what to sell in the cheaper Lots Road odds-and-sods auctions. In the madness I made frightful errors, and an exquisite pair of eighteenth-century *fauteuils* went for £450 at Lots Road Auctions listed as reproductions—I just pray it wasn't some bloody interior decorator who got them.

The house and its contents were pretty much a Rorschach of my life with Conrad. In my bathroom I pulled out the perfectly woven small wicker basket with the perfect set of brown glass chemist's bottles, all perfectly labelled: "Eucalyptus oil for fabric shoes," "Strong ammonia solution with 1 teaspoon in steamer for velvet," "Solvent ether—lipstick stains," "Surgical spirit alcohol 80% for ball point pen" and so on. This was a gift from Judy Taubman to help my "laun-dresses" maintain my clothes. There was the big box of cosmetic samples that I never used and couldn't bring myself to throw out. Old pills of every sort of painkiller in every pocket, drawer, cupboard. The plastic bag with the brush with my hair attached from the disastrous meeting with John Malkovich finally got tossed. On the mantelpiece of Conrad's office was the painted pasteboard *manqué* of the remod-elled Cottesmore Gardens house, which he had told me to destroy. I couldn't. I left it behind for someone else to smash.

The insides of our life were being cleaned out while the staff battles went on: "What are we going to do with her special clothes rack?" "She wants it to go to Toronto." "But it won't come apart. Look at the stupid way it's made." "No, you bent it when you tried to take it apart the wrong way." "Not me. Kevin did it last time he tried to move it."

After I had given staff microwave ovens, printers, kettles, mattresses, stacks of brown envelopes and reams of A4 paper and scarves and clutch bags, I wanted to donate clothing, but the rules from various charities about cleaning and sorting and age of clothes were murderous. Valuable items went missing: a gift from Lily Safra of Napoleonic artifacts, gold objects from drawing room tabletops, among others. But it was my donkey I missed most—a canvas Victorian donkey standing about eighteen inches high. I loved that donkey. It was a toy but it was alive for me, and its gentle eyes always met mine when I opened my workroom door.

When the movers left for the day, I would sit less than romantically on the closed toilet in the bathroom off my dressing room and look out its window to the gardens and terraces of houses that backed off Eldon Road, parallel to Cottesmore Gardens. You could see tiny people pottering around in little gardens and on roof terraces, and I rather hoped I'd see a *Rear Window* murder—sans the murdered dog. Backs of houses are like the inner seams of a garment, and I suppose it reminded me of the view from my childhood bedroom in Hendon, which looked out over the apple tree to the rear windows of neighbouring Westside road. In Cottesmore Gardens I'd always had a slightly peculiar fascination with the airplanes that were routed above us going to and from Heathrow. They were too high for noise but clearly visible from the bathroom window, and if you sat there you could see that every ninety seconds all day long they'd pass over, regular as clockwork. I shall be flying in one of those, I thought, looking down on this house in which I once lived. I have a master's in masochism and self-pity.

I had never liked the house quite as much as Conrad did, only because it demanded entertaining and, of course, I thought the dining room all wrong. The rest of it I loved, in spite of those huge Napoleon chairs in the drawing room gallery. I loved the light that streamed through the six pairs of French windows across that drawing room and the four trees placed inside, one in each centre-pair of windows, leafy, fresh and, unlike some of the visitors, very much alive. I loved the alcove in my dressing room with the curtained daybed where I could lie and watch soppy films like the BBC's marvellous *Pride and Prejudice* with Colin Firth and Jennifer Ehle or *Bridget Jones's Diary* with Renée Zellweger, and eat chocolate biscuits. I watched them over and over again. I knew every word and gesture and Ehle was a great comfort during the more difficult times—so calm, so elegant in her acceptance of fictional misfortune.

So here it was, the end of Cottesmore Gardens. Now, leaving it, seeing the creature stripped of our books and decoration, naked to the bones and walls and the wooden floors, our personality had gone. We were just a lot of "stuff." There was the usual game to be played out in front of the staff. This was all temporary, I explained. We would be returning to London. They knew I was bluffing, and I knew they knew but it had to be done. God it felt horrible. My insides kept spasming, but I did my Joyce Grenfell games-mistress routine: "Come along, gels. Let's put our all into it." And they would laugh but they were thirty-five years younger. And it was a mirror of what we had been doing everywhere: retreating. Everything packed up until all I had was my bed, a kettle and some mugs. Like the game you play as a child where your bed becomes an island and you amass needed articles on it as the tide retreats, leaving you stranded.

Conrad was boomeranging around in his thoughts now about where we would "settle," which was not especially helpful at this point. His "we are finished in London" had moved to a new view: "I have concluded, as you have, that we should live in England. We must retreat gradually there via Canada. Find a flat for us in Central London," he said. "Something we could both live in as a transition place while we sort things out." Hopeless, I thought, but it had to be pursued.

The number one candidate was a flat in Ennismore Gardens that had belonged to Ava Gardner yonks ago. "It has about four bedrooms,"

I told Conrad, "a reception room and a large terrace and the garden square is very pretty. And it's a lateral conversion." There must have been a substantial kickback for any agent that got it leased because I had four separate agents call me and all of them began with the identical words: "I have the purrrfect flat for you. It's gorgeous and it belonged to Ava Gardner." The agents seemed to think that I'd faint over it being Ava Gardner's flat, and yes, I was a great admirer of her beauty, but bragging rights didn't go far when it came to uneven floors, window sashes that leaked the wind, and a bad kitchen. The flat needed at least £25,000 of work, which could double easily when you're not an experienced overseer and everyone takes you to the cleaners.

The area was very chic, but only the week before, Nicola Horlick—"Supermum," as she had been christened by the media for her joint motherhood and business successes—had been accosted at gunpoint by two men just around the corner. She was pistol-whipped against a parked car when she didn't immediately hand over her ring and watch, so I felt my security concern was not entirely irrelevant, even though the real estate agents kept looking at me incredulously and doing the raised eyebrow and "This is almost Knightsbridge." The flat was in a house whose entrance had no camera, no concierge, only a dark hall beyond the locked front door. I rang the doorbell of the ground-floor flat where I had been told a single woman lived. The once-attractive woman answered and gave me a look-over.

"I'm so sorry to bother you, but I'm looking at the flat upstairs and wondered about the security in this area and building as I'll be alone a fair bit."

She carried off that casual-cigarette-smoker thing rather well, with hand holding the lit fag limp at her side; her Fair Isle cardigan hung pleasantly over an unexpected embonpoint on a slimmish build. She listened to my apology and then my question and obviously thought she could do without a complete idiot upstairs.

"Security?" she said. "We had a burglar here recently and someone got a bit of a bashed head but that was really the fault of one of the tenants who didn't properly close the front door. Fuss over nothing."

I took it that her head had not been the one bashed. I could see from the way she told this with her eyes slightly narrowed as she watched me that she thought, Well, here's one of those pampered hysterical Americans.

Ennismore Gardens was renting for £3,500 a week and I could get a year's lease. "Do it," said Conrad, but I was concerned about that cost as well as fixing it up, which the landlord was not going to do for a year's lease. The flat vanished from my list as my budget concerns grew.

Next I found a good flat at half the price in a mansion block across from the Albert Hall that I really liked, but by the time I got around to talking terms, the money for a London flat had all but evaporated, or else Conrad had decided he couldn't ever live in London again. I don't know—it was all rather muddled.

I topped up all redundancy payouts for our staff as substantially as our cash flow allowed. But I worried. "What are your plans?" I asked my assistant, Penny.

"Could you ask around?" she said, so I started calling up friends. I really didn't have to do a selling job because all our acquaintances and friends had worked with Penny and admired her. But there were no openings. I was stretching my budget to give her an extra £10,000 on top of redundancy, which would be topped up by social insurance payments. I pretended that the year she was away after she quarrelled to the death with terminally snotty butler Kevin was non-existent, so redundancy was based on the full term from the time she started. Still, that seemed inadequate.

Gritting my teeth, I went out to dinner with the purchasers of our house, he a Spaniard in the media business and the wife a former Miss Mexico. We went to Harry's and I blanked out the many evenings I had spent there with Conrad. I tried to chat merrily, but it was slow-going. Perhaps they were simply embarrassed. "May I make one recommendation?" I offered. "Penny would be a terrific help to you. Of course she has several job offers, but she is hard to match. She knows the house, knows all the contractors and has excellent manners and contacts in London and Paris." I was not dissembling—they couldn't have done better. They listened politely but didn't seem interested.

On my last day in the house, the Portuguese girls and Penny stood at the door to shake my hand goodbye as I left, in a sort of down-market *Downton Abbey*. The two girls had been with me for nine years and Penny for eleven, so I can't have been quite as ghastly to staff as the newspaper stories said. The job market for household help as superb as Adelia and Paula was robust, and every London agency tried to poach them. Now, they were crying. The front door shut behind me. I looked at the potted trees in front of the second front door, the false door left over from the amalgamation of the two houses, a useless door we had wanted to remove but one that Miranda Guinness, Lady Iveagh, who lived across the road, had fought to retain with vicious intensity and really beastly letters to Kensington and Chelsea council about our "pretensions" in wanting to create a huge porch (a quarter the size of hers). Well, you witch, I thought, you won that round. I'm leaving and the door is staying.

"Right," said Penny once I was out—this was related to me by one of the girls later, when they insisted on coming to the hotel to help me sort out all the cartons. "Out with the old, in with the new." She had been hired by the new owners but didn't tell me.

I moved into the rather fab Berkeley hotel in Knightsbridge while loose ends were being tied up. This was a madly extravagant thing to do, but it turned out they had a broom closet with a bed. Since there was some sort of electrical breakdown at the time and both the internet and lifts were wobbly, negotiating a (relatively) cheap weekly rate was slightly easier than usual, and I didn't mind a few flights of stairs very occasionally.

My comfy stay in the Berkeley lasted several weeks while I handled all the Cottesmore arrangements. To add to the general gaiety of life, who else but David Graham decided to make a return appearance. I feared the worst. The purpose, it developed, which in typical fashion came over dessert after he had prepped me with Muscat Beaumes de Venise, was to demand that I re-sign the lawyers' confidentiality agreement he had already got me to sign twice. I had just about had it with confidentiality settlements. He began turning up intermittently in the hotel lobby with the papers either in his hand or on his mind. Once I would have done anything to run into him, I thought. His agitation increased after the journalist Peter Newman published a book that contained a hideous essay on Conrad and me.

I hadn't realized that part of Newman's essay had been excerpted by the *Daily Mail* as well as *Maclean's*, and that it included a reference to David. I sympathized—why should David become part of Peter Newman's sticky, smelly fantasy world—but what could I do? Apparently, the anecdote used took place before I married Conrad and concerned an incident in which David had broken into the small house on Ebury Mews I rented from the Colombian embassy after our divorce. The "break-in" took place one weekend afternoon on grounds that he feared I was (once again) going to try to take my life and this time, instead of encouraging it, was going to save me—or not. Or perhaps make sure I was dead—who knows, I wasn't there. Only the police, David and my broken window were in evidence on my return. How Newman found out about this is a mystery.

The letter to me from David's solicitors included an excerpt of Newman's account, and I quickly saw it was both distorted and embroidered to David's disadvantage as well as mine. Unless I re-signed the confidentiality agreement now, his lawyers warned, legal action would be taken against me. I actually laughed. Hell, what did I care. His lawyers could join the queue of people suing me. I emailed David begging him, please, to sue Newman while he was at it.

The return to Toronto was not quite the joyous job-well-done reunion I had hoped for. The London house had been sold, but thanks to a new outbreak of Canada Revenue Agency rash, we were as usual in dire straits. They had decided to take Breeden's account of our enormous incomes to heart and, hand in glove with the IRS, were playing bouncy castle on top of us. What was left from our house sale of £13 million (around $30 million Canadian at the time) was approximately $136,000—and those bloody crates to unpack whenever they arrived.

Both the Palm Beach house and our Manhattan apartment were

on the market now, as well as Toronto. Whichever sold first, said Conrad, would solve our cash problems and give us a reserve fund. The Manhattan apartment was being handled by Sotheby's International Realty, and it sold fast, for US$10 million.

"Let's go to London and Monaco for a holiday," said Conrad.

"Are you completely mad?"

"I think it's important we show that we are not defeated or down and out. And anyway, we both need a rest."

"But we *are* down and out."

"Barbara, you have got to stop this Jewish pessimism. *They* want to destroy us, and we are going to show that they have not. Besides, it would be good to—"

Oh Christ, I thought, here it comes.

"—show the flag in London."

"How can we afford it?"

"Leave that to me."

In a way he was right. For those three weeks, Conrad lived in a marvellous delusion that would sustain him for the next seven years of hell. Somewhere between my lens of despair and Conrad's blurry pink, there was a truth. We had been sent invitations galore for London's season. There were country house balls and South of France weekends. Most had to be declined, since we couldn't straddle all invitations. Naturally, we came to the visit with two separate sets of eyes and two visions: lunch at Wiltons with Serena and Jacob Rothschild delighted Conrad, while I felt how odd it was that the waiters no longer knew who Conrad was after the years of deference. I was worried that our English friends felt an obligation to do the "right" thing, which is not in itself objectionable—it is even admirable—but felt sad to me. *Souvenirs perdus.* Looking now at all the notes and invitations, I think Conrad's vision was more accurate than mine.

Gossip reporters and society photographers always hang around the front entrance to Annabel Goldsmith's summer party each year, and in past times we were usually among those photographed. The only difference now was that the journalists included those making a meal living off our hard times, like *The Mail*'s Geoffrey Levy, a really smelly gossip writer who never let facts stand in the way of a sneer. According to his account, "Return of the Pariah," we had embarrassed the hell out of everyone by being there. People had been "shocked" and we had "gone around deliberately forcing people to shake hands with us." Yep, just the sort of thing we would do, using my jiu-jitsu grip.

We went to the same parties as ever in the hills of the French Riviera and visited Elton and David at their villa high above Nice. Conrad relaxed with Elton and they talked animatedly on the terrace with the Mediterranean far below. To me it had the earmarks of a farewell tour, while to Conrad it was the resumption of a life. "You see," he said to me, "nothing has changed with our real friends. They know America is mad." Idiotically, I wanted our holiday to end so I could get back to the normal routine of calamity. Honestly, living with me cannot have been helpful, but each to their own way of survival.

Our financial situation's roller coaster continued. Millions would appear from some source—sale of private newspapers, an auction sale, some piece of real estate Conrad had—and there would be a momentary lull. Then a week later all those millions would have gone, on loan interest payments (we did not exactly get prime rate), legal retainers, the sleight of hand that a particularly avaricious Canadian lawyer, Harvey Strosberg, played in getting Conrad's $16-million loan to Hollinger turned into a "gift" to Hollinger. God, he was a shocker of a lawyer and would have to eat his words over that bit of underhand spite in Tax Court, but not until 2019, by which time he had long taken his exorbitant fees (quickly got approved, i.e. "taxed," in his hometown of Windsor) and Hollinger no longer existed to pay Conrad back. Taxes for Palm Beach were over half a million a year. Monies were flowing like the river Heraclitus stuck his foot in. "No man steps into same river twice," he quipped, wittily I suppose for an Ancient Greek, "for it's not the same river and he's not the same man." And this is not the same invoice.

All I did was nervously sign. Co-sign mortgages, co-sign loans, co-sign anything in front of me. And when the money from a deal was earmarked for me, I'd turn it over to Conrad to pay bills and fees. This was the one and only time I really played the little woman. I looked once at the paper I was co-signing: it was a loan for $32 million Canadian. What if Conrad died or became incapacitated by a stroke? What would I do to repay $32 million? I had no idea. How much had I co-signed for already? I had no idea. What was I worth? I had no idea. Who would, while balanced on such shifting tectonic plates.

The press, meanwhile, was just repeating old stuff. I think they were as bored with it as we were. A new angle was required because, after all, and rightly, you can't really make it to the gardens of evil until you've been accused of, at the very least, some sort of child abuse. Fortunately, this lack was about to be remedied by the ever-vigilant columnist Jan Wong, who decided, true to character, to be proactive. In her *Globe and Mail* column, she accused Conrad of stealing twenty dollars from a crippled Asian child. Gotcha.

Her own credentials were a touch wonky, but never mind. During China's Cultural Revolution she had enthusiastically denounced a fellow student for asking for help to leave China. The student was expelled and sent off into the maw of the Chinese gulag. Thirty years later Jan hopped over to China, found the woman who had apparently slipped her mind for a few decades and apologized. They had lunch. So that's all right, then.

Now she was on a crusade to root out mean people (exempting herself) in Canada. She bought eleven children's wallets, put a twenty-dollar bill in each, a photo of an Asian family including a boy in a wheelchair, a Happy Mother's Day note presumably written by the crippled child—in this case Ms. Wong's eleven-year-old son, who one hopes survived his own childhood brainwashing—and a note with a phone number requesting the finder to call J. Wong.

Ten of the wallets were left in public places. Only one was left at a specific house. According to Wong's article, she "tossed the last wallet over a wrought-iron gate" that belonged to the home of Conrad Black. Within hours, she claimed, almost all of the wallets were returned. But not from Conrad Black. "Perhaps Lord Black could use the money," she wrote.

Heaven knows why I was so upset about this, but Jan probably does. After all, she went into a clinical depression after being hounded for another extremely problematic piece she wrote in the *Globe and Mail* that brought on death threats (sorry, Jan, had them for years, along with dead animals being dropped off at my apartment), lost her job at the newspaper—know that one too—and so on. So perhaps she might have some empathy for piling on to me at a tough time, although I think it unlikely. Our wrought-iron gates are about six hundred feet apart and I searched high and low. If I could have interrogated the groundhogs, raccoons, squirrels, deer and skunks that frequent our gardens, I would have braved odour and spit. I did ask the contract gardeners, the electricians and the Toronto gas and hydro people when they came on return visits. Not being readers of Ms. Wong, they all thought I was slightly dotty looking for a wallet in the dense bushes bordering the property. "For heaven's sake, Barbara," said Conrad, "she probably didn't throw it here." George Jonas was elegant in his put-down of her tactics in a column he wrote about the incident: "It's easier to take the girl out of the Red Guard than to take the Red Guard out of the girl."

There was another round of packing to do in New York, and I went alone. The movers, unsurprisingly, discovered various tiny microphones on the undersides of pieces of furniture. (I always thought they'd be in light bulbs or ceiling fixtures, but that's from movies.) Earlier, Conrad had been staying alone there when I was in London. Late at night he woke up to hear the sound of a person or people in the apartment. When he went to look, his computer had been turned on and correspondence opened, as well as drawers in his desk. Conrad assumed the intruders had police credentials or bribed the concierge. What he didn't understand was why this was done at night when he was there. "The point is to intimidate you as much as anything else," he was told by the American lawyers. "They do it to show you they can do it. Happens all the time." Might have been the FBI. Might have been private investigators hired by Breeden.

The Manhattan apartment was emptied in a much shorter time than London, and staying there was impossible after the first few days, so I moved into the Plaza Athénée hotel a couple of blocks away. After a morning cup of tea, I'd cross Park Avenue to our apartment, past the doorman, tenants and my furniture as it moved out. No one's eyes met mine. When the movers left in the evening, before I went back to the hotel I'd sit in the kitchen on the short pair of steps left there with a cutting tray on my knees and eat the dinner I'd cooked, either a minute steak or spaghetti. I liked that time.

"It's a horrible task," Conrad would say sympathetically when he telephoned the hotel in the evening, "but look at it this way. The apartment money will end our problems, and when this is over and everything is made right, I'll get you another New York apartment just the size you like." He meant it too. He was always saying to me, as we lost one thing after another, or I sold something, "Anything can be replaced when this works out. I promise you." I understood why he had to say it, and I'm not sure he believed it, but it was one of those agreed-upon white lies you tell each other in this sort of time.

Conrad's new lawyer was an ace in talent—and fees. Brian Mulroney had suggested Brendan V. Sullivan of Washington's Williams and Connolly firm. Brendan had represented Lieutenant Colonel Oliver North in the Iran–Contra hearings, thus satisfying Conrad's dangerous attraction to lawyers with historical-political connections. Our disastrous civil trial in Delaware was, apart from Breeden's judge-shopping, made hopeless by our clueless legal team, chosen by my husband because the firm had once had John Foster Dulles on its roster. Of Sullivan's brilliance there was no doubt. I decided it was time I started meeting the men who had my husband's life in their hands—having missed the previous lot—and it didn't take more than five minutes to see that under his quiet, courteous manner, Sullivan had the skills of a deadly cross-examiner backed up by prodigious research into any case he undertook. With him, we stood a real chance of a scorched earth.

Naturally he charged a prodigious amount of money, as his early bills of several million dollars testified. In June, Sullivan and his associate, Greg Craig, went to see Robert Kent, who was in charge of complex fraud cases in the U.S. Attorney's Office in Chicago, and the prosecutor assigned to the Hollinger investigation, Eric Sussman, a rather ferret-like, thin and kinetic man. Kent assured Sullivan that Conrad was not a target of any grand jury. "If criminal charges are in the offing," Sullivan told us afterwards, "they are a thousand years away. And you've been sent no target letter." This was, to put it mildly, a mis-assessment, though it brought glasses of wine to our Toronto terrace at the time.

By late July, rumours of criminal charges and grand jury hearings in Chicago were increasing, to the delight of media and onlookers. On one of our last days in London, on July 21, David Radler had called Conrad to wish him a happy wedding anniversary. A week later he ominously pulled out of the joint defence agreement the Hollinger executives accused by Breeden had. Our lawyers and theirs worked together, sharing documents and tactics to fight civil or criminal litigation. We knew exactly what that withdrawal meant. "He's making a deal, a plea bargain," said Conrad. "God knows what they've got on him." They had been partners for thirty-six years and would never speak again.

That same month, our Toronto butler's friend, Rolland, was diagnosed with bone cancer. He was entering the final torture of AIDS. Conrad's son Jonathan, in his twenties, was diagnosed with stage two Hodgkin's. "We've had the plague and the locusts," I wrote to my New York lawyer, Gregory Joseph. "When do we get the frogs?" Not a long wait, it turned out.

Up leapt the imposing six-foot-three, lean Patrick J. Fitzgerald, U.S. attorney for the Northern District of Illinois, at this point a celebrity prosecutor. (Later judgments would be more nuanced, as in the *Investor's Business Daily* assessment of him as a prosecutor who "can bend the truth with the proficiency of the slickest of pols.") On August 18, the Chicago grand jury handed down a seven-count indictment for fraud that included Hollinger's U.S. counsel Mark Kipnis,

Conrad's private Toronto company Ravelston, and David Radler. Radler had pleaded guilty to one count and was a "co-operating witness." So there it was. Radler had what lawyers call his "queen for a day," when you roll over to incriminate the person the prosecutors *really* want. We had no idea what the prosecutors had on him, but my view of Radler was that he could as easily be running numbers on Chicago's Southeast Side as when he sold "original" aboriginal artifacts at Canada's Expo 67.

Conrad was not charged, but Fitzgerald held a press conference sporting two large charts, one entitled "The Scheme," which detailed extensive criminal fraud in Ravelston, at the top of which was "The Chairman." "I'm not naming him," Fitzgerald told the assembled press, "but his name is a matter of public record." Jesus. In no other country in the Western world would you be able to get away with this at the pretrial level, let alone pre-charges.

Scavengers scented blood. The press was calling Brendan Sullivan's office to get comments on when he thought Conrad would be charged. Worryingly, he was giving off an ambiguous air about his representation of Conrad. As former directors of Hollinger, we all had legal indemnity insurance that would have covered a major portion of the various civil suits and SEC costs, but naturally Hollinger was refusing to honour them. The need for immediate funds was acute. "We'll have the money from the New York apartment for Sullivan while we sort out the indemnities," said Conrad confidently. "And he'll wax the floor with the prosecution."

The closing of the New York apartment kept being delayed. "Has the money arrived?" Conrad would ask our Sotheby's agent. "There are still a few details to be ironed out," she would reply. Had the buyers changed their minds? "No, no, they love the apartment." Finally, we were told the cheque would be handed over at the closing on October 10 in the Sotheby's office. Thank God and sighs of relief. Here I come, Chanel, I thought. Just one last jacket.

The cheque was handed over—handed over and seized on the spot by two FBI men who had shown up to take the envelope. Our money grew wings and soared through the air without ever touching our hands. The FBI knowingly swore a false affidavit on camera that the apartment belonged to Hollinger, which it did not. Don't talk to me about rot at the top of the FBI and the good and hard-working men and women in the field. These "field workers" were as rotten as they come. I suppose the culture of law enforcement in America has been corrupted for so long that such "shortcuts" are taken for granted, nothing special or unusual. Now the purchasers had our apartment with the housewarming gift I had left for them, the Smythson stationery engraved with the Park Avenue address in case they wanted to use it, and my thank-you note. The U.S. government had our money and we had zilch.

I sat in my Toronto workroom in a state of shock. Two houses down. Two lots of money gone. A Greek chorus arose of our American lawyers insisting that the government overreach was so extraordinary, so "over the top," we would get the seizure of our funds reversed almost immediately. "Not a chance they can keep it given the documentation of purchase, source of funds, agreement of Hollinger and renovations of $2 million you have personally made," boomed the lawyers at Sullivan and Cromwell and Baker Botts and Williams and Connolly (just three of the top U.S. firms we were paying, and there were several others, each with their own specialty). Everyone agreed in voices vibrant with confidence.

Then, gradually, in a diminuendo I had come to recognize, over the next few days the view changed. Telephone calls gave way to distanced emails. Forceful adjectives yielded to modifying adverbs. The tide was going out, revealing a floor of mud and writhing snakes. I did a quick Google search and found over 300,000 entries on the Civil Asset Forfeiture Reform Act. We would get the money back, all right, because it was legally ours and the affidavit was demonstrably false—the documented details of our purchase had been omitted at the secret court hearing to secure the FBI's seizure. But we would not get that needed money back anytime soon—not, it turned out, until after the trial and imprisonment. This is how American justice normally works. Bankrupt the defendant before any trial and prevent the hiring of decent defence counsel. Well, it's one way to get your man.

I had booked a flight to go back to London for the High Holy Days at my synagogue there—the West London Synagogue, the oldest Reform synagogue in Britain. The seizure deep-sixed any notion of flights and hotels. I cancelled everything, including arrangements to meet desperately needed friends—Miriam Gross, Annabelle Weidenfeld, Ronnie Harwood and the Pryce-Joneses. George Jonas came by to talk. We old Jews, he said, should be together on Yom Kippur. He was having a bad day physically, pale and puffy and taking his nitroglycerine. Everything I said or did upset or irritated him. Watching him walk down the stairs and putting his hand in his pocket to hide its shaking as he tried to maintain his balance drained my insides. I myself may be dying of some awful disease now, I thought, but at least I don't have to see or know it.

"You know," said George, in one of his cheery Yom Kippur asides, "Arthur Koestler had Parkinson's and he committed suicide with brandy and sleeping pills." Then he asked me to promise that when the time came, I would help him die. I promised. I had a sinking feeling that this was not a passing thought but a grim reality to come. Thank God he is not going to ask me to die like Koestler's wife Cynthia, who committed suicide with him, I thought. I filed the request away as another depressing task for the future. "You can always get the necessary drugs," he said to me. Well, at least he didn't want a plastic bag tied over his head.

George had begun taking small drinks of Unicum, a Hungarian bitters, at his desk, and his wife, Maya, would make him a nightly Tanqueray gin martini. I suppose it eased the discomfort. He would remind me that Koestler always wrote with brandy at hand. I knew that Ayn Rand used Dexedrine, Mailer used everything under the sun including cocaine, while opium was the favourite choice of writers in the nineteenth century, from Coleridge to Elizabeth Barrett Browning. But the cold, hard truth is that the writers I most admired, from Dickens to Orwell (who had tuberculosis to justify any medical enhancement), didn't rely on drugs or alcohol to fuel their creative spirit.

And the cold, hard truth, which is scarcely news, is that I am a minor codeine addict. Not exactly a big one—after sixty-plus years

I haven't had to escalate the amounts, which are relatively small, maybe 40 mg a day, at most 52 mg and sometimes less, which is a considerably smaller dose than the daily 195 mg the rap artist 360 told of in his addiction song "I'm Sorry," but I can rarely get through a day, especially a writing day, without a couple of 10-mg tablets. My friends used to joke that when they saw the yellow tablets come out of my handbag in the evening, they'd know I was bored stiff. I've never used anything but over-the-counter codeine, so perhaps calling myself an addict is a bit thick. I'm just one of those people who slightly exceeded the package warning of "Can cause addiction. Use for three days only" by about 22,000 days.

Inevitably there was a movie being done of the lives of Conrad and Barbara, which, having lived them, would, I thought, be a hacking great bore. Conrad had already been the subject of several documentaries, and by now the marketplace had to be saturated. Can't wait to see what I look like, I thought, and then: No, I really can wait—forever. They were shooting in Toronto with Lara Flynn Boyle playing, as it turned out, a totally humourless me, who in the film never actually sits down and writes, only struts, sticks her foot in faces for her at-home pedicures, and sometimes takes time off to pluck eyebrows (I wish I had them to pluck). Ken Whyte, thank God, had replaced Anthony Wilson-Smith as editor and publisher of *Maclean's*. He rehired me and, in one of those editorial inspirations that only come into younger heads, emailed, "Barbara, it would be great if you go down to the set"—they'd requested a *Maclean's* person to come and write about the production. That was one play-act too many.

Anna Wintour phoned almost immediately. Meryl Streep would be playing her in *The Devil Wears Prada*. "You've got the A-list star," I said. "Mine's a B-list." Yes, she said, but both Meryl and herself were nine years younger than me, while Lara Flynn Boyle was thirty years younger. I didn't quite see the relevance, but I think it was complimentary. I supposed this was the new status game: Who's playing you in the biopic? Made for TV or general release?

As 2005 drew to the end with bloody Christmas around the bloody proverbial corner, the one-hundredth-anniversary party of *Maclean's* magazine loomed. Ten people were to summarize the ten decades, and I'd been given a one-page summary of the events of 1955 through '65 to read to the dinner guests. I remembered that decade well—a simpler, happier time when I was just shoplifting. Conrad was in orbit because Kim Cattrall was there, looking rather gorgeous, and for him she was still Samantha from *Sex and the City*. My little recitative began with Sputnik and the space age and ended with the murder of Martin Luther King. "His words had been heard and his dream would live on" was my dramatic closing line. Yeah, I thought. My dream is fucking over.

As I lifted my head to emphasize the thought, milking it, I could feel my borrowed emerald earrings swaying. Normally I don't borrow jewellery from a shop, but I had been with a friend, Kate Daniels, at Royal de Versailles, a high-end jewellery shop in Toronto managed by an Israeli couple, Irit and Michael Shay. Kate was selecting something for her client Kim Cattrall. She was hemming and hawing and negotiating when out of the blue I was offered the earrings. I hesitated. "They'll be wonderful on you," said Irit. "Go on, try them on." They weren't really my style, but I had to admit they looked pretty nice. "Just for the evening, you understand," I replied.

I worked violently hard at looking good that evening. The atmosphere around us was thick as mud, and I knew the guest list would include some of Toronto's business and literary establishment, although I hadn't anticipated that Eddie Greenspan would serve Peter Newman for defamation of Conrad that night—over dessert—for his nasty article. Hairdresser Dennis Campeau had swept up my hair (with the aid of a large hairpiece) and my shoulders were bared, so the dangly earrings were very visible. Which was lucky for the jeweller. Two days later, when Conrad was indicted, a colour photo of us at the event was on the front page of the *Globe and Mail*, looking like a jewellery ad, the earrings so prominent. It's an ill wind that blows no good, and Irit put them in the window, possibly with the photo—I didn't dare ask—but she called to say happily that she had sold them the same day.

I learned of the criminal charges casually, while brushing my teeth. I was watching Report on Business on the TV set I had perilously perched by the sink. Home prices in the U.S. had plunged and Google had risen 3 per cent, and the market data at the bottom of the page suddenly switched to "Conrad Black indicted on eight charges." I swallowed the toothpaste.

In the splashy press conference, prosecutors said they were going to keep the money from the New York apartment sale, seize our Palm Beach house, extradite Conrad and ask for $80 million in forfeiture money. An average Thursday haul. They were also indicting Conrad's private holding company Ravelston, which, given that it was a Canadian company and didn't operate in the U.S., could refuse to accept U.S. documents alleging it had committed a criminal act. Or perhaps the company seal would take an Air Canada flight to Chicago to respond. Just how you criminally indict a company was weird and could be easily ignored, as our lawyers told Ravelston's *in loco parentis* operators. But being that it was evil Conrad Black's company, Ontario Superior Court judge James Farley gave permission for Ravelston to accept the indictment, and a short time later the seal, a.k.a. Judge Farley, naturally pleaded guilty.

Now the question of money for American lawyers was serious. Either Conrad would get bail or he'd stay in a Chicago jail for over a year. Patrick Fitzgerald was threatening to extradite Conrad if he didn't show up right away. Given that he was no longer a Canadian citizen, we had no protection in Canada. We expected bail would be set high, although we did not anticipate the $60 million prosecutor Eric Sussman would demand. We needed Brendan Sullivan at the bail hearing, and that meant we had to put down another few million. My ring, I thought. The time has come.

I realize it sounds a trifle picayune if you actually own a twenty-seven-carat D-flawless diamond ring—you'd expect such a person to know all about these things—but how the hell do you sell it fast? Toronto pawnshops weren't up for it. The auction houses needed at least a few months. Banks were barely letting me in the door. I suppose if you're in good odour, you can call a twenty-seven-carat-class friend. All I could do was call Irit Shay.

Earlier, in a burst of goodwill—and of course for my own sake—she had told me her business partner in Royale de Versailles, billionaire Joe Burnett, a man with something of an ambiguous reputation, had said after visiting our home and talking to Conrad that my husband would soon go broke. The best thing for me to do, he advised Irit, who passed this happy bit of good wifery on to me, would be to take my jewellery and run; meanwhile, he was interested in the stone—at a price.

"I can arrange a private sale of the ring," said Irit confidently, who knew that I was not going to sell it to Joe Burnett. "You have the GIA certificate? "Yes." "It's a done deal. I'll make a few calls." Next to phrases like "showing the flag," "reaching out" and the endless variations of the transitive verb *to hope*, as in, "We really hope that this matter will end well for you," which invariably meant we don't think it will, the phrase "done deal" was one I truly loathed. Done deals are almost never done.

The routine was out of *Ocean's Eleven*. I was to meet Irit in the foyer of the Four Seasons Hotel with the ring, and a Brink's van would arrive to take it to a bonded jeweller in New York City. I sat in the foyer feeling extremely glum. The saga that followed involved the jeweller refusing to accept it on arrival in NYC without certification that it legally belonged to me, and then it got held up in the mailroom of Brink's or somewhere—I had no idea what was going on, but I was by now sufficiently paranoid that I thought the FBI or Richard Breeden himself had seized it, just like the apartment, and probably even now his wife was wearing it. I must have had a series of mini strokes over the next few days. Irit chased it down masterfully and it was retrieved unsold. Conrad and I sat in our Toronto dining room looking painfully at each other over peas and mashed potatoes—my fallback cuisine. I had to tell him of my failed attempt, having tried to keep it secret from him until completed. The telephone rang. Conrad picked it up.

The voice at the other end explained he was a purchaser of stones and lived in Geneva. He had been told of the stone by Irit Shay and was interested in purchasing it. "Dy'ave papers to prove you are the owners?" the caller asked in the guttural voice of a man who, if a voice could be stereotypical, sounded like a con man of either Israeli or East European extraction.

"We have the bill of sale from Graff jewellers," said Conrad.

"No, no. You 'ave proof that the stone is yours? The courts don't have no authority over it?"

All night long we called lawyers to see who in this moment of need would give us such an assurance. There was a great deal of throat-clearing, pauses, suggestions that this was the job of lawyer X or Y or even Z, and then long-winded accounts of how it could not be done.

"I bought this with money from my own personal bank account," said Conrad, "with monies from a transaction that has not been challenged or implicated in any of the charges." No go.

The man from Geneva called back. Although he was of course deeply concerned about getting the legal ownership confirmed, he would overlook that and buy the ring at a fire-sale price. "No," said Conrad. The trial would reveal that the ring and all the rest of my jewellery had, much to the prosecution's chagrin, been purchased with legal funds, but like all good things in this tale, that was at the end of a very long yellow-brick road.

As the press covered the charges, which would escalate at their highest point to seventeen counts, possibly more—it changed continuously—there was palpable dismay in press circles that I had not been indicted. Lengthy discussions of my culpability ensued. "They are probably trying to keep this narrowly focused," apologized one legal scholar. Not that the prosecutors and U.S. government didn't try to find something bad in my tax returns and bank accounts, but there was nothing to find apart from their possible astonishment at my imprudence when it came to Chanel jackets.

Looking back on this, I can't really understand how we managed, day after day, to tell each other it would all be all right. It was so evidently all wrong. I was going to lose Conrad. He would, I knew immediately when the charges were laid, go to prison because that's how the system worked.

So—and this is truly cringe-making—I began to listen almost every day to Andrea Bocelli singing "Time to Say Goodbye" to prepare myself for the inevitable. I was not a great fan of Signor Bocelli's voice; I think if you listen to him sing with the aged Pavarotti and Plácido Domingo in that particular iteration of the Three Tenors, you can see how very short his voice falls, but given his blindness, his achievement is stupendous. I played his "Con te partirò" in my Nissan Rogue whenever I was alone driving back to Park Lane Circle, usually after visiting George Jonas during the fifteen months before the trial. Each time, I tried to construct my feelings as if Conrad were gone—no longer seated at his desk or warm and embracing at night. I'd be crying by the time I pressed the gate opener.

In my heart, I was sure that in the end Conrad would overcome triumphantly. I had no idea how, and this was antithetical to the prison scenario, yet I held the two ideas simultaneously and each had their anthem. For the triumph—the vindication after suffering—I had a picture in my mind of a huge party we would throw at the Savoy for the friends in England who had stood by us. Boyzone would come and sing their song "No Matter What" and repeat the verse that contains "No matter how they judge us." And I wouldn't even shudder as Stephen Gately dropped the double t from the "matter" in his third chorus. Conrad and I would dance alone, with friends murmuring "Isn't it wonderful, look at them," and I'd tilt my head and look up at Conrad and he would look down suffused with love as we twirled about.

I live in technicolour Hollywood: reality skewed because Conrad can't begin to twirl, can't hear the music's beat. Mark Birley secretly arranged dancing lessons early in our marriage, which Conrad called his "husband improvement classes"—honestly, you've got to love the fella. He'd get up early, telling me it was business. But you can't teach a tone-deaf man, however keen, to hear the beat. And it never occurred to me that by the time this saga ended we would both be too old to publicly gyrate around the dance floor and that many of our supportive friends would have died. And Stephen Gately, too, would be dead.

Once the New York apartment money had been seized, Brendan Sullivan asked us to post US$15 million retainer in addition to bills to be paid along the way. This of course was really "fuck off" money. When the charges were laid, Brendan regretfully told us he could not represent us at the bail hearing in Chicago because that would oblige him professionally to represent us in all court hearings on the matter, and he was not confident we would have the money to cover a lengthy trial. Toronto criminal lawyer Eddie Greenspan saved our skin by flying down to Chicago and negotiating a pocket-money $20 million which, together with bail and bond, came to about $40 million Canadian—the highest bail recorded in the U.S. at the time, we were told. The way millions were being tossed about was completely otherworldly.

By that point, we had already paid Brendan's firm about US$8 million, which Conrad estimated worked out to be $2 million per telephone call. Brendan helpfully suggested we canvass our many rich friends, which I thought was pretty rich in itself, and have them provide the money for the trial. Brian Mulroney offered to call around to raise the money, but his initial soundings weren't promising. Not surprising. I mean, who was going to contribute to a needy felon's defence?

We were, as ever, on our own.

CHAPTER TWENTY-THREE

Down the Rabbit Hole

In December 2005, I sat in the kitchen watching my husband on television as he entered the Chicago courthouse to be indicted, then was taken away for fingerprinting and mug shots. I put the TV on mute; subtitles for the hearing impaired were just fine. Was this one of those nightmares where any minute I would walk naked up the church aisle? More and more charges were piling up from the prosecutor's office, and I think we were now up to possible sentences of ninety-five years. Conrad says it came to 105 years at one point.

One of the channels was having a little discussion about my future, which in their view appeared not only bleak but probably involved unhitching myself from Conrad. Peter Newman was being interviewed, inevitably, and cleaving to the theory that I was even now packing my suitcases for the next man. "Isn't she getting a bit past the femme fatale act?" asked the interviewer with irritating common sense. Yes, I am. The decades had long passed when undoing a blouse button would get me my way. No one on air or in print seemed worried that I might actually do the Good Wife number and deprive them of a juicy flameout. Personally, I thought Conrad looked astonishingly terrific on television in this Chicago torture, better than he had for ages now that the show was finally on the road: wild horses loaded with loot couldn't pull me away from that tall, self-possessed man on the screen walking through a crowd of shoving, shouting pygmy journalists.

"They were rather nice people," Conrad told me on the telephone from Chicago that evening, speaking about the officers who had processed him. He had not been handcuffed as he expected. "We talked about FBI directors going back to Hoover, very interesting. And the fingerprint man loves camping in Canada." I could see him; Conrad was unflappable. He would be drawing out his interlocutors even as they were rolling his fingers in ink.

Meanwhile, courtesy of CNN, I discovered that the threatened lien by Canada Revenue had been put on the Palm Beach house: $14 million, they said, but I wasn't sure whether this was in Canadian or U.S. dollars. Not that it made much difference, really. Conrad's secretary had called to say there was just over twenty-six dollars in the Palm Beach account and what were we going to do about it. And a merry Christmas to you. Really, it was all enough to get one very down. I had a decorated tree up in the drawing room, but that Christmas was one of the dreariest yet.

And then there was a pause—and the sun broke through the clouds. Cue celestial choir.

We were about to be presented with a bouquet of goodies. First flower was that rose with thorns, Vice Chancellor Leo Strine of the Delaware Court of Chancery. Delaware is a tiny state where a lot of American companies are incorporated, among them Hollinger International. Strine, in his two-day non-jury hearing, had swallowed Breeden's guff and taken away *The Telegraph* from Conrad's control, having all of a sudden become an expert in newspaper valuations. All the same, Strine, being a lawyer, had a reverence for legal indemnities, which, after all, pay legal bills. He ruled Hollinger had to honour ours, which gave us between 60 per cent and 75 per cent of legal costs—Conrad was due for a refund of millions.

And I had, after much nail-biting and excruciating hold-ups, exercised options I had on Hollinger International stock at a brief moment in time when Breeden's promises had artificially buoyed up the stock before it became as worthless as Confederate bonds: that brought me in some millions.

Then, ironically, David Radler had been ordered by Chicago

prosecutors to pay Conrad monies he owed him from a loan for their privately owned newspapers. That was some millions as well, which we had long written off. Here was a perfect example of the rottenness of the U.S. system: the prosecution was forcing Radler to pay us money from a transaction that Breeden had already derided in his report as a "sham" transaction. This was to give Sussman a reason to go frothing into court with that little stiff-legged strut that a certain kind of short person has and say Conrad was lying to the court about his net worth on financial statements.

"He wants an excuse to put me in jail until the trial," said Conrad. "It won't work."

Next, in a transaction that reminded me of the Julia Child recipe for beef bourguignon I could never quite make, I had acquired and sold off a small chain of private newspapers. God knows how I did this—well, God doesn't know, only Conrad and the legal teams: I took a cup of this, a pinch of that and the whole transaction was marinated by little covens of accountants and lawyers fussing over more papers to sign. When it was ready to come slow-baked out of the oven, the heavily legalled money from the sale minus the heavily invoiced lawyers' bills was still a great deal of money. I used it to pay off more bills and debts before putting some aside in the rainy-day account that I had renamed the rainforest account. And a bonus: the Chicago judge refused prosecutor Sussman's agitated request to have my jewellery put in the court's custody. My Eres lingerie and Chanel jackets were probably worth a fortune but unlikely to fit Sussman's wife.

Not all was rosy, of course. Eddie Greenspan had filled in for Sullivan at the bail hearing and performed very well on short notice, but we still had no lawyer for the trial proper. "You're intelligent, excellent company and I know you are totally innocent," Brendan had told Conrad, which meant something since Brendan was the only American lawyer who had seriously looked at the case. "But I simply can't tie myself up for the time this is going to take without absolute financial guarantees." The trial was set for spring 2007.

We would need at least an initial five- to ten-million retainer for any proficient American criminal lawyer who had the resources to handle a seventeen-count trial with hundreds of thousands of documents. But before absolutely giving up on raising that pretrial down payment for Brendan, we entered a period of Alice in Wonderland deals, a gauntlet of would-be white knights.

Suddenly I was dusting off my social skills and doing the amusing, entertaining-couples thing. We'd dine with very rich people Conrad had known for donkey's years. We'd talk to them with their latest girlfriend or wife as if it were simply any ordinary social occasion and not life and death for us. I sat in their gorgeous homes, all spic and span like ours was once when we could keep up the non-stop maintenance that large homes require. I'd do the mandatory tour of their often awful art collections that left me baffled at their purchases, and worked hard at art chat. I was in this new and repulsive role of fawning over drunken elderly Canadian billionaires who promised Conrad everything at dinner, would keep up the pretense for several weeks and then become unavailable.

Summer came, which is the worst season to face when you are in trouble. Just too much sunlight and happy faces. There was a new man in my life by the name of Richard Bradshaw, the brilliant conductor and head of the Canadian Opera Company. An Englishman, much admired in the world of classical music, he had worked for over a decade to get a proper opera house built for the COC, and by God he did it—unfortunately, at the cost of working himself to death. The project took every last ounce of this large and genial man, and after the Four Seasons Centre for the Performing Arts opened in 2006, he died a year later, aged sixty-three, waiting at the luggage carousel at the airport.

The loss was enormous. I loved him for his devotion to music, his huge, generous personality, his wonderful British sense of humour, his kindness and unfailing support of Conrad, and the pleasure Conrad took in his company. I often wondered as he went home, completely wrung out, if he had anything left for his family. He let me attend rehearsals of Wagner's *Ring* cycle, which was opening the new house. Nipping into Wagner's world is pretty cathartic—watching the entire rotten structure of Valhalla, home of the gods, come crashing down in flames. Then the final sublime bars of *Götterdämmerung* washed over me, signifying that the world had returned to its natural order. Curtain. Exit the theatre, and our world was not in its natural order, not one bit.

All the same, if there were not a thousand points of light, as the first President Bush once famously said, we certainly had a few gleaming stars. Early on in our trek across our very own Nefud Desert sans water bottle, the phone rang, and it was not the usual call.

"I'm calling for Murray Sinclair and myself," said Canadian investment whiz and lawyer Ned Goodman to Conrad. "We thought there might be liquidity problems and were wondering if there was anything we could do to help. Would a loan of $2 million at a very minimal interest rate help?"

"I can secure the loan," replied Conrad.

"We don't need that," said Goodman. "Just your IOU will be enough. Pay it back whenever you like."

I thought it was a mirage and the two men would disappear in days. But no. Then came a cheque of $100,000 from Conrad's friend and the architect of his Toronto library, Thierry Despont, who sent it unquestioningly one day after Conrad called at another of the many crises that hit. Conrad's long-time associate Dan Colson, wealthy but not any billionaire, was stalwart throughout, never stinting with moral support and financial aid, even though saddled with huge medical bills for his family. I suspect his wife could brain both Conrad and myself. I wouldn't blame her.

I feel I should mention these joyful moments both to keep readers from drowning in the vale of tears I'm narrating and to keep me away from not only extra codeine but prussic acid or antifreeze. Reliving this stuff is not really a tonic. Now and then, even a positive press piece about me surfaced: columnist Christie Blatchford did a wonderful rebuttal to Peter Newman's comments that should be framed. Vancouver writer Liz Nickson defended me in a column, and in the U.K., Alexandra Shulman, in a very small but welcomed anecdote in the *Evening Standard*, told of a moment I was pleasant to her. Danielle Crittenden was simply marvellous, writing a long piece in

the *National Post* titled "The Barbara Amiel I Know." Not only did
I wish I were the person she described, but her prose flowed so well.
There may well have been more supporters, but searching the press
for them was like putting your bosom into a mangle.

Each morning, Conrad would get up and work the telephones
like a boiler-room stock salesman. I wondered if any rich widows
would turn up so I could do the noble thing and let them marry him,
but I suppose that only happens in Palm Beach. What I did learn was
that all those billionaire friends who'd promised financial help
spontaneously, without our solicitation—"anything you need," they
volunteered, and I thought, God, how wonderful—never materialized when we were forced to ask. Most claimed their lawyer wouldn't
let them, but the most original explanation I heard—and probably
the only truthful one—was that if they lent a couple of million of
their three billion, the wife would never give a blow job again.

The Hollinger indemnities covered civil costs but not any criminal proceedings. Our own five or six million in cash produced a lot
of suggestions from top U.S. lawyers offering "my son-in-law who
has just started up his own practice" and that sort of thing. As events
turned out, son-in-law might have been the best bet. Time got shorter
and, out of necessity, Eddie Greenspan, who had never pleaded a case
in a U.S. court, let alone a complex criminal fraud trial, became our
lead counsel. I endorsed this enthusiastically. I had known Greenspan
for over twenty-five years and thought him a highly skilled criminal
lawyer with, importantly, a whippet-fast sense of humour and engaging personality that jurors enjoyed.

By August 2006, I had levitated into a sense of calm. "St. Monica,
patron saint of patience, is with me," I told Conrad. When I told
Jonas, he suggested it was more likely Dymphna. (For a man whose
education ended when he was about fifteen, he was exasperating in
his erudition.) I looked up St. Dymphna and thought that her spotless
chastity might be a stretch for me, but in her role as patron saint of
the mentally ill she was probably well cast. Still, whatever brought on
this beatitude, the state was extremely welcome. The helicopters that
had been noisily circling overhead with cameramen departed for

newer victims. Our lawns were so green. The smell of fresh-cut grass and the bees so plentiful that the summer quite enfolded me. "I know it's an illusion," I told Jonas, "but *et in Arcadia ego*." I'd been watching *Brideshead Revisited* and that episode title evoked buttercups and dandelions waving under a warm sun.

"Enjoy it," said Jonas. "You do know that the phrase you are quoting has a sinister connotation that most often refers to death and a paradise glimpsed to which one may not return." I did not know. I am one of those people with a smattering of knowledge that uses words and quotes recklessly and very often wrongly. I just liked the sound of the phrase and I had seen a print of Poussin's painting with that title and a bunch of nymphs dancing around with garlands. I should have seen they were dancing around a tomb.

August 25, 2006, was Conrad's sixty-second birthday. This was "a night to remember," and all I can say is that we managed, somehow, unlike the *Titanic*, not to completely sink. Never mind the thousand points of light or stars; this night was an eclipse that would last twelve years and drain our blood and money.

Unlike me, my husband enjoys having his birthday marked. "Let's have the cubs over and a few people," he said, meaning his very un-cub-like three children, Jonathan, twenty-eight, Alana, twenty-four, and James, twenty. I added four or five friends. Early in the evening, I could hear Werner, our house manager, banging around in the hall. The noise was not unusual, as he generally gave loud Teutonic commands on any provocation. I left my makeup ritual and went onto the balcony overlooking the entrance hall. The front door was being held open and I saw a van with some boxes being unloaded.

"Werner?" I called. Werner was directing the placement of the boxes while an ungainly woman with a video camera filmed the scene from outside. The camera was now swivelling to view inside our house.

"Who's that taking film of our house?"

"It's all right," said our driver, John. "Your husband OK'd it—a delivery from Eddie Greenspan's office."

"What's the delivery?" I asked Werner.

"Some boxes and a letter for Lord Black," he replied, which on the face of it—videotaping delivery people—made no sense. But not much made sense these days, so I left it.

Buying gifts for any bloke is impossible, for Conrad triply so. With the usual cop-out, I bought a pair of white gold cufflinks in the shape of attractively stylized hamzas and had them engraved with "*Veritas vincit*"—truth prevails. That bit of rot is on the memorial bust of foreign minister Jan Masaryk in Prague, where the Communist Party defenestrated him rather than let truth prevail. No room on the links for Masaryk's follow-up line: "but it's going to be quite a job." As a joke, I'd also got a watch that referenced Albert Camus's *Myth of Sisyphus*: as the hands went around, a man pushed a boulder up a cliff, only to have it fall down on the stroke of twelve so that he would have to start pushing it up the hill again. "You can smash it after you win at trial," I wrote on the card. I should have smashed myself then and there.

The catered dinner was delicious. I made one of those idiotic toasts, de rigueur at times like this: "To my wonderful husband. There may be many awful things still to go through and your strength and resilience is wondrous to behold, but this time next year we will be toasting the end of all this nightmare."

Eldest son Jonathan had brought one of his identikit very young blonde girlfriends, and I noted warily that both brothers were drinking heavily, always a danger sign. In the kitchen, Werner was doing the same with gusto. Jonathan and James started interacting in a drunken way with the chef and waitstaff.

At some point, mercifully after non-family guests had left, I heard the crash of glass in the downstairs room, which turned out to be drunken son James falling through the case of one of Conrad's prize scale ship models to the fury and condemnation of his siblings. Conrad mentioned calmly that James had just managed to do more damage to the battlecruiser HMS *Repulse* than the Japanese when they sunk it off Singapore. James became quite belligerent, and he and Werner took turns wheeling about the kitchen, Werner by now being twelve sheets to the wind. I could see the chef and waiters were finding family behaviour in the home of the indicted Lord Black rather riveting.

Werner, though, was a happy drunk. James was a belligerent one, and I tried to calm him down, to no avail. He announced he was leaving. He would not accept a lift or a taxi, and it was unclear how exactly he was going to get home. I tried to involve Conrad, but he was curiously indifferent. "Let him go," he finally said at the point where it was pretty academic, as James had gone. Jonathan was now also too drunk to drive, and so I offered to drive him and girlfriend home. As we turned out of our driveway, I noticed, just a few houses north of ours, a parked police car.

On the grass behind the police car's rear bumper I saw James sitting handcuffed, with two policemen around him. James is about six foot five and quite muscular. He has grown into a very sensitive, exceptionally intelligent man, but perhaps wasn't so when a twenty-year-old aggressive inebriate. "Let me go and get him," said Jonathan in a thick wine-and-liquor-sodden voice. "Probably not the best idea," I replied, and hopped out of the car with instructions to iden-tikit girlfriend, who seemed to be the only sane factor, to keep Jonathan in the back seat.

James, I was told, had been carousing along the middle of the road creating one hell of a noise and threatening anyone who tried to approach him. The police were gearing up to take him in. I swarmed. "Officers," I begged, "this is my stepson and he has been at our house just down the road for his father's birthday. He's been under a great deal of pressure given the circumstances of his father." I mentioned Conrad's name, which at that time was pretty much a synonym for deep stress. After some back-and-forth, the police released him to me on the promise I would take him straight home to his apartment. I drove all three in my Nissan Rogue, now brimming with manly intoxication, and returned home.

By now it was about two. Conrad was downstairs talking to Alana. He was tipsy and Alana intoxicated, and both were at that ghastly sentimental point a steady evening of imbibing brings. I came upon Werner wheeling about the kitchen in his white terry-towel bathrobe, accessorized with Birkenstocks and short white socks, talking an intriguing mixture of German and English. You can't help liking Werner, but it took some persuading to get him back to bed.

After having a bath, I went to claim my husband. "I'm having a heart-to-heart with Alana," he told me. Perhaps not the time to mention James's travails, I thought, and went upstairs, it being four thirty. I put Conrad's things in the guest room with a warm note and the little model lamb that nods its head to show him I was not angry, took two sleeping tablets and told myself this too will pass and was having children something I really missed?

I awoke to a dire note under the bedroom door from Conrad. "I am dealing with an unimaginable disaster," he said. All through that birthday dinner, where, among other things, he looked after the tremulous, shaking George Jonas and tried to keep his children from killing each other, he had known of this disaster and not burdened anyone with it. From his demeanour and welcoming smiles, his gratitude for the small gifts, it would have been impossible to tell that the sky had fallen on him just before dinner.

CHAPTER TWENTY-FOUR

Marie Antoinette Under a Mareva

Hollinger's gangs were now led by Toronto financial man and lawyer Wesley Voorheis, who came onto Hollinger's board in 2006 and was then CEO until the company went into receivership in 2007. A short stay, but from the minute he arrived he used his time to collect huge fees for himself, rifle every dollar he could from the company and initiate litigation against us. What Conrad was referring to as an "unimaginable disaster" was Voorheis's pièce de résistance.

He had devised a plan with the Chicago prosecutors to launch a lawsuit freezing all of Conrad's assets—and mine: absolutely everything from bank balances to any right we might have to sell our childhood stamp collections. This draconian action is called a Mareva injunction, and, cautioned the Supreme Court of Canada in an earlier judgment, it should not be used as "litigious blackmail," which was a gentle description of what was being levied upon us. The intent of a Mareva is to prevent a defendant from dissipating assets or getting them out of the country, and cause must be shown. The Mareva had been granted to Hollinger Inc. on the basis of a sworn affidavit by Voorheis in a secret hearing—as many actions against us were—in front of the ludicrous jurist Colin Campbell.

The affidavit was a transparently fictitious statement of imagined acts done or contemplated by us that ranged from our secret bank accounts in Gibraltar and Patagonia (if only) to the flight arrangements we were making to destinations in darkest Africa—all to evade our upright pursuers. The entire complaint was swallowed whole by Campbell—unlike his B.C. Supreme Court counterpart who, after receiving precisely the same affidavit in an attempt to get a Mareva on David Radler, dismissed it, saying she could not "extract 'facts' from opinion, 'opinion' from 'hearsay' from 'invective' and 'argument.' In fact, I would describe a large portion of that affidavit as argument dressed up as evidence."

But anything could slide past Campbell's epiglottis, which reflexively opened at nasties about us. The entire *ex parte* judgment should have been thrown out and our civil lawyers were champing at the bit: Campbell had outrageously ignored the fact that Conrad was available for the hearing and had counsel to whom the affidavit should have been presented. This was an appalling action on Campbell's part. But our lawyer, Eddie Greenspan, was frightened. He didn't want the slightest possibility of any part of Campbell's madcap reasons for judgment or Voorheis's equally mad affidavit getting into the Chicago court. So long as it remained a secret hearing, the matter was sealed. Challenging it risked the possibility, however small, of its being brought into the open. The old bugger Colin Campbell had shrugged his shoulders and held a Star Chamber.

Every penny we had was now frozen. The banks and credit card companies had already been instructed not to honour any cheques or let us make any withdrawals from any of our accounts. Our credit cards were rendered invalid. We could not sell any item or contemplate any transaction—either of us. My inclusion was based on the notion that Conrad had transferred assets, secretly and illegally, to me. The holders of our mortgages had already been notified that they could not accept any payments from us—the prosecutors' intent being that we would default on mortgages and lose any home we had left, most especially the one now over our head in Toronto. Newton Glassman, of Hollinger's interim management group appointed by Justice Campbell, had already contacted the mortgage holder, offering to buy the Toronto mortgage (thus enabling him to seize our home rather than shell out funds to actually buy it).

We were gutted. All we had was the money in our pockets, literally.

"This can't be serious," I said. I mean, what would you say if told this very minute—out of the blue, no effing warning—that you had nothing but the spare change in your handbag, presuming like me you don't carry around thousands of dollars in cash, let alone hundreds. The delivery before dinner of the boxes said to be from Greenspan was just a front to serve us with the Mareva. Just for icing, this drastic and extreme injunction had been obtained two weeks earlier but saved for serving until the evening of Conrad's birthday. One could hear the squeals of delight at that little touch.

As the full extent of our situation sunk in, I remembered the thoughts I had when going into the emergency operating room in Calgary in 1997, having been unexpectedly struck down by a cecal volvulus. The condition took about eleven hours to diagnose as I writhed in pain. The wait may have had something to do with a looming nurses' strike which our *Calgary Herald* newspaper was condemning, and the sullen reminiscences of one of the emergency room doctors, forced to take his grade twelve exams over again "all because your husband stole our Upper Canada College exam papers": *ipso facto* as his wife I must be faking or exaggerating my pains.

In a morphine haze I had been resisting surgery, demanding to speak to Conrad who was visiting the Annenbergs in Palm Springs. Having overheard the surgeon tell Conrad something to the effect that I'd be dead in twenty minutes if they didn't operate, my life did not flash before my eyes, only my Amex bill for clothing which if I survived but was incapacitated after surgery, I wouldn't be able to pay.

Now the first thing that struck my pygmy mind was that, just the day before, I had made my first ever visit to Louis Vuitton in Toronto and, after very lengthy deliberation, purchased a pair of tweed trousers and matching jacket. The saleswoman had fawned over me, and I had bought a suit that I wasn't certain I liked but that made her like me. Now I would not be able to pay the credit card bill. It had to be returned—if I hurried, I could get there at opening time.

Fortunately, the clothes section was empty of customers that early. I gave back the goods and was in tears as I did so. "I'm so sorry,"

I said to the same saleswoman, who was slightly less fawning this time round. "And if you will just keep this quiet, I will be a loyal customer in the future, but at the moment I can't legally make any purchases." Had I been of sane mind, I would simply have returned the items, which still had the price tags affixed and had been in my possession for less than forty-eight hours. I could have said something anodyne about my husband not liking them. As it was, any hint of *compos mentis* was gone, I was out to lunch. With the tears rolling down my cheeks, I was gushingly grateful when issued a full refund. I was spared being a loyal customer, however, since someone from Vuitton told the press of the incident and it appeared in the *Toronto Star*.

I can't go home now, I thought. Our house will be swarming with lawyers. I called good friend Kate Daniels, who came, no questions asked, to Bloor Street, and before hitting the espresso we went into a small shop that sold soaps and colognes from Provence. Kate wanted some perfumed paper liners for her drawers; I wanted three sachets, which were fourteen dollars each, but then I realized I couldn't buy them and made up some lame tale.

Back at the house, I went upstairs and took some codeine. I hadn't had any for about three months. Bang out of the window went that bit of abstinence. Conrad was in his library, looking like death. "This is the end," he said. "I can't fight them."

But of course this was only one of many "this is the end" moments we fought. Myself, this time around, I fought not only the Mareva; I tried to fight Conrad's lawyers—and lost. That weekend a legal war conference convened. The sworn affidavit on which the Mareva injunction was granted was so outlandish that lawyer Earl Cherniak, Q.C., a man of considerable standing in the legal community, and Peter Howard (three degrees, including law from Oxford) called upon Regional Senior Judge Warren Winkler of the Ontario Superior Court of Justice (and later chief justice of Ontario) and pointed out that Campbell should immediately recuse himself from Hollinger matters on grounds of bias.

Campbell was astonished at this—his lack of judgment and legal ability apparently equalled only by his lack of self-knowledge. Though caught with his hand in the cookie jar of legal bias, so to speak, Campbell needed to save face, and, of course, the judicial system hovered protectively around him, attempting at the same time to correct this most egregious error.

A new order was negotiated. We had a newly appointed monitor who would arbitrate Conrad's expense needs. He was allowed, naturally, money for all legal bills—lawyers always look after their own. Essentially, I was released from the whole thing but had to agree to file an affidavit every three months stating that I had not spent more than $500,000 in that quarter on any non-disposable asset (travel or charity contributions, etc.) and would not spend more than $1.5 million a year without permission. And I had to keep this agreement in total secret at pain of contempt of court. Bloody hell, I said. I refused to sign.

Signing would give credence to the notion that I was trying to hide funds. Also, I had seen how insane my life had become and I didn't see why I should be bound by this. Of course a million and a half was a huge amount, of course a normal person would not spend (let alone have) anything like that on non-disposable assets; I didn't even know how much money I had, but who knew what fees or medical expenses I might encounter in the future?

We now had no insurance, no pension, every benefit cancelled, and I was in my sixties. I had not been charged with any crime, had not committed any crime, and was damned if I was going to be ordered around by wet fish Colin Campbell and be in a position that if I needed to spend a lot on, say, an old-age home or private medical bills in the U.S.—or support a dozen endangered elephants—I would have to ask some monitor to let me. "No, I won't do it," I said.

Then it began. "Barbara, you have to do it," said Conrad. "You must do it," said the lawyers. If I didn't sign, the whole deal was off—I didn't understand why and don't to this day. I think they were all bluffing me. They were terrified that if Campbell's Mad Hatter reasons for his Mareva judgment were somehow allowed into the Chicago trial it would be "very detrimental to your husband." This seemed linked to a fear that if I didn't sign, the special committee report would surface at the trial as well, and trying to undo that damage in front of a jury would be impossible. Not knowing U.S. rules of evidence, I was in the dark. "I want to get independent advice," I said stubbornly. I still had no Canadian lawyer.

"We'll get you a lawyer of your own," they said. And I was assigned David Roebuck. "But he's on Conrad's team," I replied. "He's not independent." Slowly, carefully, they all explained once again how we couldn't bring in new counsel, time was too short and a new lawyer would gum up the works. I was jeopardizing Conrad's trial and future if I didn't sign. God, I was furious. But trapped.

We went through a farcical telephone call in which I spoke with Roebuck, who offered his ho-ho "independent" advice, which consisted, unsurprisingly, of urging me to sign. I was grateful to Cherniak and Howard for extracting me from the main body of the Mareva. But I hated it. And I hated all of them, including Conrad.

The conference call from Conrad's team of lawyers came asking for my verbal agreement. "My lips are trying to say yes," I told them, "but I am having great difficulty."

Now I was under a highly modified Mareva—but I had signed, and that gave the court jurisdiction over me in some way, I thought. Every three months I had to go to a notary and sign something called a solemn declaration and I loathed it. All that night I worried about the precariousness of my financial position. Conrad would be going to prison, I was certain. All our present goods would have to be liquidated in order to defend him. Anything could be taken from us. I needed an additional job with compensation that wouldn't fall under the timeline of any forfeiture procedure. I canvassed in my mind what I could do.

My options were limited. Apart from journalism, I had no skills. No one needs milkmaids anymore. Selling little bouquets of wild violets on street corners, not really. My age was an almost insuperable handicap. Waitress? Conrad would kill me, and I had done it before but remembered it as really exhausting work, poorly paid, and I couldn't give up the column at *Maclean's* that now paid $1,400 and for which I needed to work at least forty hours per column. Salesperson? My best bet: probably I was too old but I could try. The wages would be low, but at any high-end shop on commission I'd be a very good salesperson, always had been in the past.

The worry was eating into my bones, never mind my brain—or what few cells were left. Till now, events had rolled past me, bizarre, perverse, but outside me. Now I was officially a part of it. Under the thumb of a bloody monitor. I couldn't sleep and went into the bathroom to think. Yes, my mind was hampered by medication and worry, but I could still write. The question was, how to make more money writing, given that I already had a *Maclean's* column.

Next day, I called up editor Ken Whyte and offered to write an additional column on, broadly speaking, fashion and style, including both high-end and "popular" pricing, clothes and accessories, cosmetics, health treatments, interviews and stories, retail and whatever the hell you want. And I'd do it for half the cost of my regular column. Ken agreed. He'd been trying to get more women's stuff in the magazine. I thought it would take me less time than it did. Once you are out of the style world, you have to work hard to get back in and up on it. The new column and lifestyle features started immediately. Work didn't frighten me: I was frightened only that some new court order would freeze my bank accounts for my fantastically expensive Natura Bissé face creams.

About a month later, when I was routinely putting my expenditures into the little book I had drawn up in case The Monitor ever asked, Conrad walked into my workroom. "It's one way to stop me buying Chanel jackets," I said jokingly.

Then Conrad made a huge mistake. "Why stop," he said. "Chanel jackets are an 'asset' and can't be forbidden." God, I wish he had never said that. It was like legalizing crystal meth to a recovering addict.

As the summer turned into autumn, I decided it was time to have a chat with Greenspan. I was worried. Eddie knew nothing of American court procedure, and their trials operated on entirely different rules to the ones he was familiar with in Canada.

"I'll pay you, and well," I told him, "to go to Chicago or any U.S. federal court or legal firm and get a tutorial and hands-on practical experience of American federal trials." Unfortunately, the one thing that distinguished Eddie Greenspan from virtually every lawyer I have known was that he had absolutely no avarice. Whatever drove him, and he was certainly no charitable institution, he was never a money-grabber. He didn't answer me, just gave a Cheshire cat smile. I had to be careful; I couldn't afford to antagonize him.

About a month later I approached him again. "Look, I'll pay an American lawyer to come to Toronto and go over court procedure with you."

"It's not necessary," he said. "I have read twelve volumes of Wigmore." If Eddie said he had read them, I didn't doubt that he had, although those twelve volumes would take most people, let alone working lawyers, years to plough through. Wigmore, the greatest American jurist ever, wrote his masterpiece in 1904. His work remains the basis for all modern U.S. criminal law—but laws do evolve, and, most important, court procedures in the U.S. are drastically different from Canadian ones. To have Eddie use our case for his first time out in a U.S. trial, let alone with such a complex commercial case—not his area of expertise—was more than risky, it was madness. So I pleaded with him. I begged. Go down to Chicago and stay in a courtroom. Immerse yourself in American courtroom techniques. He was dismissive.

Jonas was worried too. Parkinson's was shutting him down. In his increasing immobility, friendships meant everything, and Greenspan's was, together with fantasy fiction writer Guy Kay's, the most important to him. Caught between his own need to preserve friendships and the need of his former wife and friend to have the best legal representation, he was stymied. He decided to say nothing for the moment. Later he would tell me that he thought Eddie was not facing up to his own health problems. He said he had watched him become slower and more lethargic physically. But he hoped. And he kept quiet with me, even while urging Eddie to take up my offer of American experience.

So there we were, stranded somewhere out in the galaxy past Jupiter and its seventy-nine moons, with no way home.

Conrad went to Eddie's office. "He doesn't understand the case at all," he told me afterwards. "The entire sequence of financial and corporate events that led up to this judicial lynching are simply out of his realm. He hasn't a clue what it's about, and as far as I can tell he's done virtually no work."

"What's his plan?" I asked.

"He kept emphasizing 'reasonable doubt.' He simply hopes to grab a corner of the case that will provide reasonable doubt. Fine for a murder case, fine in Canada, but it's not going to work with a jury in Chicago as the prosecution throws all the spaghetti at the wall with more than a dozen charges. I don't think he has a clue, either, how different an American jury is from a Canadian one."

"What did you say to him?"

"I told him this was it—the chance for him to make a great name for himself in the States. The case could be won, but it needed a lot of work."

"And . . . ?"

"He pulled a piece of paper from his pocket. He had seen that famous quote of Churchill's when he visited the War Rooms in London and wrote it down to be typed out. Churchill had said it on the day King George VI called on him to be prime minister and you remember—"

I interrupted. The early months of the Second World War were secondary to our own war. "What did the paper say?"

"Churchill had said, 'All my past life had been but a preparation for this hour and for this trial.' And I must say it impressed me that Eddie had noted it."

My stomach did a series of bellyflops of panic. Were we once more to be hoisted on the petard of Conrad's love of historical allusion?

"He's got a Chicago law firm, Edward M. Genson Associates, to be his partner—the courts require you to have an American associate. Eddie's daughter Julianna interned for Genson, who's coming to see us. And Eddie showed me his preparations: a table spread out with folders for the trial. I looked through quite a few and apart from the odd deposition there were simply newspaper cuttings, photocopies of pages from my book *A Life in Progress* and from Newman's *The Establishment Man*, and bios on various people. It depressed the hell out of me. But Eddie was very proud of all those manila folders. This is worrying."

I'd like to say there was a limit to the load of manure a human being can carry, but it seems not. Pretty much nothing was real anymore. Our lives had entered deep Tony Soprano land: Conrad's secretary had been advised that her emails were not safe. We already knew ours were compromised. The RCMP co-operate with the FBI, so our telephone lines were probably bugged, either legally or illegally. We were advised not to talk on our regular cell phones but to keep buying different ones with new numbers and no contracts or plan. I would drive to different outlets after a while, since I felt—probably foolishly—that my repeat appearances were giving me the appearance of a Russian gangster's moll.

Whenever Conrad and I talked about the case, we went into rooms with running water or places with music. We'd stand huddled in the lavatory in our own home with the taps turned full on, or, especially if the winds were high and noisy, we'd go outside with music playing from the device in my pocket. Every car or van that parked outside our house for a suspiciously long time was presumed to be monitoring us. Voorheis's Hollinger Inc.? Breeden's Hollinger International? Chicago prosecutors?

We had the house swept and our phones swept, but we didn't know the sort of people who really knew how to do this. Greenspan was no modern Perry Mason. His contact for checking out surveillance at our house came a couple of times and said, "Be careful where you speak."

Then Eddie Genson, our new co-counsel from Chicago, came to Toronto. I remember, vividly, going into our round library and seeing a man who looked quite old, though in fact he was nearly a year younger than me. He was sitting in an electric wheelchair due to the polio he had contracted as a child. He could walk with a cane but not well. I listened to the conversation between Conrad and Genson and then asked a question or two myself. And went up to the bathroom for my usual bout of feeling sick, which seems to be a motif through this book and I apologize. I must have a very sensitive stomach.

"Christ," I said to Conrad after Genson had left. "He hasn't a clue about the case." I didn't say that I also took an immediate dislike to him—mutual, I think—after two sentences, or that he had an ego the size of Mount Everest and a mind that peaked before reaching its foothills.

"It's still early," said Conrad. Which it wasn't, but there was certainly still time. "And I think he wants to learn the story." Only he didn't get it until the end of the trial, by which time his dislike of Greenspan and his breakdown in health made it far too late.

So I just kept writing whenever I could for anyone reliable that would take me, which turned out largely to be *Maclean's*. Then came one of those periodic gluts, this time over Marie Antoinette. The doomed queen has been a staple of popular culture since about 1770, when at age fifteen she married Louis-Auguste, the somewhat sexually constipated Dauphin of France. After her execution, every person who had touched her hem and survived the Revolution wrote a book of memoirs, including her chambermaid, the first, second and third undermaids, the prison warden in charge of her, the governess of her children and even her executioner. Only Mops her dog managed to stay out of print. And it wasn't as if she was the first person to wear a birdcage on top of their head.

In 2006, PBS produced a two-hour documentary on her life, then Caroline Weber's book *Queen of Fashion* appeared, as well as a kiddies' book, *Moi and Marie Antoinette*, which sadly I didn't see and I wish it could be reissued now because it would have to be called *Moi, Toi, Trans-Moi and Moi Perhaps?* etc. Topping it all was the feature film *Marie Antoinette* with Kirsten Dunst, charming and exuberant, romping around for director Sofia Coppola with the script based on Antonia Fraser's biography *Marie Antoinette: The Journey.*

"Please," said Dianne de Fenoyl, managing editor at *Maclean's*, "write about her. Ken thinks you should do a feature."

"Okay, how many words?"

"Take what you need," which is my kind of music.

This is another of those "no one will believe me" moments, but I genuinely didn't think of it as a story that would inevitably bear comparison to my own life—with me as a very déclassé version of the beheaded queen. How this escaped me given the acres of (at the time unread) references to me in that role is an effing mystery. God it was in the air so thick were the references. I think one puts up psychological walls to protect which also imprison. After my piece appeared in *Maclean's*, I got a call from Susannah Herbert, the editor of *The Telegraph*'s arts and culture magazine, *Seven*, who wanted to reprint the piece for a good fee. I didn't know Herbert very well but I was an admirer of her work at both *The Telegraph* and the *Sunday Telegraph*, and she was always straightforward. I thought my piece was pretty good and rather liked the idea of showing U.K. readers that my head was not yet in the basket.

My copy of *Seven* arrived in November, well in time for Christmas. The article had been given huge play. In fact it was the entire eleven-by-twelve-inch cover, all given over to me photoshopped in crinolines and corseted bodice with full-on white pouf hair, butterflies and feathers sprouting in blooming technicolour (and a suspicious-looking Celine-type handbag lurking at my hem just to give it the contemporary-extravagance touch), with the cover line "Marie Antoinette: C'est Moi, Barbara Amiel Writes." My head was in the basket, all right.

Inside was worse: not just another full-page colour impression of me as the queen, with a swan, overflowing jewel box and the inevitable shoe, but my picture bled over into the next page for a double-spread entitled "Marie Antoinette and Me." "She was the original conspicuous consumer, her outrageous tastes first copied, then vilified by society. She was also a generous hostess, ultimately betrayed by her flatterers. Barbara Amiel knows exactly how she must have felt."

Oh God, I thought. Exhibit 23 in the trial. I could hear it: "This, ladies and gentlemen of the jury, is what made Conrad Black steal— he had Marie Antoinette as a wife. That's what the most respectable paper in London calls her. The very paper he once owned. Marie

Antoinette was the queen who was so extravagant [this for the Chicago jurors who I suspected were unlikely to read history let alone know who the blazes Marie Antoinette was] that the French people cut off her head."

That did it. I couldn't write for U.K. newspapers when even the most trustworthy editor thought it amusing to have "C'est Moi" attributed to me. They had no notion of the workings of U.S. prosecutors. Reluctantly, I cancelled an outstanding piece commissioned by *Harper's Bazaar UK*. That left only one piece that was written but not yet published.

In December 2005 I had written a column for *Maclean's* on Israeli prime minister Ariel Sharon that began with the particularly inauspicious sentence: "Weight and waist circumference are highly overrated markers of a man's health and vigour, as the rotund 77-year-old prime minister of Israel demonstrates." That wishful insight—predicated to some extent on my own worry over Conrad's weight gain—went belly up, as less than a month later my column began: "Ariel Sharon is unlikely to ever wake up again. Miracles are not unknown in the land where the Red Sea parted but, medically speaking, no Red Sea will part for him." Sharon was in the coma that lasted uninterrupted till his death, eight years later.

When the stroke occurred, despite my banned status at the time, *The Telegraph* asked me to contribute to his obituary. That was quite an honour, and I immediately did so. I couldn't see how even the most malicious obit editor could mangle my words, and the editor who commissioned the contribution was a highly responsible man. As Sharon lay comatose, we updated my piece a few times to reflect the changing political scene in Kadima, the party he had founded. But by January 2014, when Sharon was finally released from this world—my piece, like much of my life, had gone down the rabbit hole, never to be seen again.

And I was at that point all but comatose myself.

CHAPTER TWENTY-FIVE

Bubblegum and Bulgari

The trial was set to begin March 12, 2007. Probably it was unwise and certainly clichéd to read Franz Kafka on the plane to Chicago. "Someone must have been telling lies about Joseph K., for without having done anything wrong he was arrested one fine morning."

Like Joseph K., my difficulty was that the world around us remained perfectly ordinary even as personal reality somersaulted. My prescriptions kept running out because I forgot to renew them. The squirrels quarrelled under the bird feeders. Each morning when I woke up, I checked the time on my Casio alarm clock and every damn morning my clumsiness would knock it to the floor and the AA battery would roll to invisibility under the bedside chest of drawers because I had lost the clock's plastic bit that held it in.

Inside this ordinary world was a permanent cloud. Whatever Conrad saw through his rose-coloured glasses, all I could see was the oppressive presumption of guilt. Guilt reflected back from the silence of my own sister's family on Conrad's innocence—never once the reassurance of "we all know he's innocent." Even if they didn't believe it. Guilt pronounced by the stranger accosting me in the checkout line at the Dominion grocery store like a mad scarecrow with straws exploding out of her head: "You're a thief, married to a bigger thief. You're dirt." The newspapers seemed to find it remarkable that I believed my husband innocent. I was, they said, "bewildered." And another commented sarcastically, "She's living in a make-believe world where she can't understand what happened." Anything but.

And, of course, Conrad bashed out a last magnum opus column of orotund, portentous statements: "I do not go to Chicago as an innocent to Babylon. But the [U.S.] remains the indispensable country of Western civilization of the last century, a society of laws in a largely lawless world. . . . Justice will prevail and Barbara and I will celebrate with our true friends, never more easily identified. . . . I have never been prouder of being Canadian."

No way to stop him, but complete bunk. He was no longer a Canadian in any useful way, and fellow Canadians by and large disliked him. The U.S. had already proved that its society of laws had gone to Pluto, unless you think false affidavits and secret hearings are part of this great indispensable civilization. He must need to believe this, I thought, and so I just shut up for once. When you come right down to it, his brilliance and bravery aside, he was just a man. And men are like that—tunnel vision. They bang on, and in tough times reality is an inconvenience. My own, practically feminist point of view is that's what happens when you never have to cope with childbirth, periods and all that can bedevil our reproductive system. Females deal with reality: blood and gore from age twelve or thirteen on.

That aside, I had utterly no idea how on earth I was going to handle any of this.

Just before we left Toronto for the Windy City, John Fraser, master of Massey College, held a well-meaning and freakish dinner at the college for us with the Bradshaws—Richard would be dead five months later—historian Margaret MacMillan and several other friends, one and all toasting and joking in the same room as so many times before—just as if we were about to leave town for a new job rather than Conrad's inauguration as godhead of crookedness and greed.

Once in Chicago, every hope got knocked down like skittles. Our co-counsel revealed their prejudices and priorities early on—appearance rather than substance seemed their preoccupation. A huge fuss was made by both Genson and Greenspan—the "two

Eddies"—about the need to keep Alana and me away from jury selection or from ever attending court. We were too white, too well dressed and definitely too thin. Deadly combination.

Looking back, barring us from the courtroom was the first and last tactic that both our defence lawyers agreed on. Anyway, Conrad wanted us both there and so we went. I had packed my no-name wardrobe, nameless handbags and the hell with the rest of it. We were tall and kempt. And in Alana's case, quite beautiful and young, which she played down wonderfully. As it turned out, the jury admired her dedication to her father.

The first sign that Greenspan hadn't a clue what he was doing came after Conrad signed the mandatory waiver that in the event of a conviction he could not appeal on grounds that his lawyer was not familiar with American law (never a truer word). It was a standard waiver, but for Eddie Greenspan, known for his waggish quips, it was the stuff of which stand-up comedy is made. He told the *New York Times*, "I love that I've been certified as stupid by the Illinois judge. So stupid that no matter how incompetent I might be, Conrad can't rely on it." He added that he was going to frame the waiver and hang it in his Toronto law office. He hadn't a clue that this was not a variety roast with him as the star host.

Into the courtroom came our presiding judge, Amy St. Eve. Pert, petite, even attractive; a youngish woman, wearing a black robe with a small American flag pinned almost upside down on it. "It has been brought to my attention," she said to Greenspan, "that you have reportedly made a statement to the press"—Oh God, I thought, if she starts reading all the press and Eddie goes on doing his thing, which is sucking up to every journalist in sight who wants a bon mot, we will have a bonfire in here—"that I have certified you as stupid. I do not know if you made that statement but let me assure you it is patently wrong."

Eddie's reply was jovial vaudeville. "One, if I honestly believed that's what you felt, I would not be here," he assured the judge. "Number two: I happen to have a sense of humour . . . and the writer chose to pick that out of the middle . . . I was not intending in any way to insult the court." Fine, so now we have our lawyer defending himself against the judge, relying on the old saw of being quoted out of context, and the trial hasn't begun.

"You have not insulted me," replied Judge Amy.

Eddie saw an opportunity to demonstrate his wit and establish himself in Chicago as amusing and lovable, just as in Canada. "If you want to certify me that I'm smart, I would not object." Eddie felt confident he had made his debut. I thought I saw ravens on his shoulders.

Okay, this chapter is not a primer on American criminal trials, but there were moments of low farce. Jury selection was the beginning. The large pool of juror prospects had answered a list of questions and now, after the chaff had been separated from the grain, the judge was going to interview the final candidates for us. No writer of tragicomedy could match it:

Judge Amy: "You are retired, ma'am, is that correct?"

Prospective juror: "Yes."

Judge: "You indicated that you or someone close to you had been a victim of a crime. Is that correct, ma'am?"

Prospective juror: "Well he was . . . he did the crime."

Judge: "Are you comfortable talking about that in court?"

Prospective juror: "It's okay. He's not alive anymore."

(The person was her brother who had been arrested many times.)

Judge: "Generally, what were the crimes he was arrested for?"

Prospective juror: "Beating up people."

Judge: "Beating up people?"

Prospective juror: "Uh-huh."

Judge: "Did you try to keep him in line?"

Prospective juror: "It didn't help."

Right there, then, in my view, the prospective juror came from a culture that might fairly be viewed as outside that of Conrad's. Most of the jurors had some sort of experience with the law, not surprising since this was, after all, Chicago. "I was just walking out of my house when I was shot," said one. This must be, I thought, a Monty Python skit.

Judge Amy moved on to the same prospective juror's reply that tax treatments for corporations were "wrong and unfair." The judge admonished her with one of the little homilies she was going to have to make to the entire panel repeatedly, since every one of them thought any special tax arrangements, any deviation from the standard income tax codes with which they were personally familiar, were criminal and wrong. "There are legal ways," Judge Amy said firmly, "to set up tax treatment, and I will instruct you at the end of the case on what the law is."

The juror remained impassive. She indicated she didn't like this for people with "better means, more means."

Judge: "But you do not have any problems putting aside those thoughts and just decide this based on what is in the courtroom?"

Prospective juror: No response.

Judge: "Did you understand the question?"

Prospective juror: "Yeah, I do. I still have mixed emotions about it. I don't think it's fair."

This was insufficient to disqualify her, and the judge moved on to "your answer to question 51." Fifty-one? Most of the jurors looked as if they had never read anything that long.

Judge: "You indicated in your response that you do not want to serve. And you indicated in response to the question previously, about your prior jury experience, that you did not like it. Why did you not like being a juror? Be honest. There is no right or wrong answer."

Prospective juror: "Because I didn't like sitting there all day."

Judge: "Do you think you are going to have a problem sitting here all day?"

Prospective juror: "I won't like it."

Judge: "How do you know you will not like it? I want you to be honest. Why do you think you will not like it?"

Prospective juror: "Because I have to sit there all day."

Judge: "You indicated that sometimes your concentration and attention span wander. I think everybody in the courtroom could say that."

There was nothing to be done. The respondent became a juror. And in keeping with her general attitude, she slept through the entire trial.

And so it went. In response to the question "If you heard evidence that some of the defendants in this case received tens of millions of dollars, would that fact alone cause you to believe there must have been some type of misconduct?"

Prospective juror: "Yes. You don't get money for doing nothing."

Now came the money speech. "I can tell you legally, ma'am," explained the judge, "that there's nothing wrong with the fact that people might earn a lot of money. That alone doesn't mean they've done something wrong. Do you understand that?"

Prospective juror: "Yes."

Judge: "And knowing that, can you evaluate the evidence fairly as to how they received it and make your decision based on that?"

Prospective juror: "I would try."

Judge: "Do you have any doubts about that?"

Prospective juror: "Yes."

Selected.

A mist began to form over my eyes, wafting across the courtroom and filling my nostrils with the familiar smell of class warfare and greased government ethics. Almost to a person, the jurors believed that "everyone should pay the same taxes or it's not fair." One selected juror went missing during the process. Turned out he had a rap sheet that included domestic assault, battery, theft and a number of DUI convictions. "Look in the bars," the court marshals were told. When said juror was located, the judge asked him, "Can you go from 8 a.m. to 5 p.m. without drinking?" as if an all-night bender wouldn't impair his judgment during court sessions. "Yes, I can," he replied. He was excused only because he had lied so often on his questionnaire, but his dismissal only came after a lengthy discussion about whether chucking him off would violate his civil rights.

I had some sympathy for my husband when he turned back and said to one of our team, "Is this a jury of my peers?"

The prosecutors were a team of four energetic nasties whose combined four ages added up to only slightly more than the ages of our two counsels. Their grammar may have been dodgy, their acquaintance with truth accidental, but they spoke their lies crisply, with vigour and the dramatic flourishes of younger people.

Eddie Genson, our American counsel, was well known in Chicago's criminal underworld, almost a mob lawyer, I suppose, although he himself was not one of them in any way. He was the lawyer who, in a case after ours, got singer R. Kelly off child porn charges that centred around urinating into an underage girl's mouth. Genson managed to delay his trial for six and a half years, by which point she wouldn't testify and the tape itself was deemed inadequate to determine identity and age: if you are urinating and videoing at the same time, what with liquid, only two arms and hands, and all his instructions on facial positioning, the pictures might be blurry, unfocused or possibly stained. Anyway, as a defence it worked. In this world of urinators, procurers, pimps and gangsters, Genson's defence style worked a treat: procrastinate, obfuscate, confuse the jury. Sadly, in a commercial fraud case, you need clarity and coherence.

Now, sticking to his Chicago vision of life, he felt it prudent to position himself to the jury as your ordinary bloke compared with the stuck-up nutcase from Mars he was defending. Genson was folksy, ruminating, anecdotal, a spigot of unfinished thoughts. He was the neighbour you will put your head in a pail of water to escape, the man in the seat next to you that never stops talking and drives you bonkers. And to pave the way for quotes from Conrad's rather esoteric emails came Genson's own description of Conrad Black, in his opening remarks to the jury, as "snotty, arrogant and screwy." Quite unlike Genson, who, head wobbling sideways as he spoke from his wheelchair, was all geniality and plain speak, one of them, the guy they all knew, not the egotistical Conrad Black "who thinks a lot of himself." God, I thought Alana and I were going to take poison there on the spot.

Eddie Greenspan had been a brilliant lawyer in his prime, and his prime was recent and he could have returned to it. What we didn't know was that he'd had major heart surgery in 2005, since his family had kept it virtually secret. We knew he had diabetes, although it was not clear for how long, or how severe it was, but he was on insulin, did not exercise, and was overweight and managing an illness which requires disciplined eating and carefully administered medication. Neither were medical conditions that would disqualify a man from his work, but when the needed regimes are ignored, they can be devastating.We did not anticipate the widely fluctuating moods and emotional swings. We barely recognized this man who began to nod off most afternoons in front of the jury. His head would roll forward onto his jacket, hiding the closed eyes, but there was no mistaking the gentle wave and swell of afternoon napping. A trial of several months takes a tremendous physical toll on the lawyers, which is where age and health came into play. In front of our horrified eyes, this unfamiliar Greenspan disintegrated. He had moments of brilliance, the old Eddie with the quick wit and the acid cross-examination. But then he would lapse into a strange creature, lumbering slowly and ponderously into his questioning.

He could be repetitive to the point that the jury made faces and the lawyers of our co-defendants (three other Hollinger executives were in court) were in despair. At one terrible point, when Eddie was repeating and repeating himself to the point of nonsense, one of the other defence lawyers stood up and exclaimed, "Objection! Question asked and answered." Normally an objection during a defence cross-examination would come from the prosecution—coming from your co-defendant's counsel indicates a disaster. Even more dangerously, he fought bitterly with co-counsel Eddie Genson. If we were at war with the government, our two counsels were at world war with each other. They quickly became sworn enemies, like a couple of teenagers having no-speaks days.

All I could do was occasionally run to the drugstore to get a blood sugar monitor when Eddie had left his at the hotel, or desperately hunt for orange juice, biscuits, cheese, anything when his low blood sugar made him drowsy. Heigh-ho, our lawyer was about to pass out. What he was never too tired to do was talk to the press.

All normality was buried on the very first day of the trial proper. I watched the prosecutor wheel about the courtroom making his opening statement to the jury: hard, brittle lies painted in neon colours. "You're sitting in a room with four guys who stole sixty million dollars. Bank robbers wear masks and use a gun. Burglars wear dark clothing and use a crowbar. But these four . . . dressed in ties and wore a suit." He wheeled round and pointed at Conrad. "Here's your pension funds. Here's your retirement account. Here's your mutual funds." Later, on the huge screen, just like in Campbell's courtroom, the jurors could see the black-and-white video of Conrad "caught" taking evidence. "And Conrad Black did not notice the cameras were rolling that day."

I knew we had lost. How could we not? Given the thousand and one nights of Scheherazade, the jury couldn't begin to understand what had taken place. Nor, alas, did our legal team, so they couldn't tell the jury. But the tension was over. We were smashed.

I sat, temporarily stunned, with the rows of press behind me, on task, looking for some reaction from me to give a clever bit of colour to their stories: perspiration on my upper lip, a twitch, perhaps some violent outburst. I watched my husband, his head held high. I watched the jury. My God.

Looking back, I think the best thing would have been to have arrived at the federal courthouse on Dearborn Street on day one wearing the yellow garments of the condemned, lit a match on two piles of kindling and given ourselves a good and final *auto-da-fé*. And so from that very first dreadful day in court, for the next four months, I became another person. There was nothing calculated about it. In fact, it was almost robotic and evolved unaided into a perfect routine.

We were living in a rather terrific hotel corner apartment, on the thirty-first floor, thanks to Toronto's Issy Sharp, founder of the Four Seasons hotel chain that also owned Chicago's very posh Ritz-Carlton where we stayed. Alana lived a couple of floors down in a single room. When the snows of March turned into the blazing sun of July, all those happy, chatty Chicago summer people on the streets below us, going somewhere other than the courthouse each day, were, thank God, distant faceless spots of colour.

Greenspan, on beam with appearances if nothing else, was naturally dead against us living there. "It's too luxe an address," he said, and moved himself and his team into a hotel next to Chicago's "L," the rapid transit system. That lasted for a day until his entire team threatened to leave.

Our apartment came with a kitchen and was furnished in wall-to-wall pure beige, colour-coordinated to our complexions. I devised routines for the end of the day or the evening, anything to keep me away from having to listen to Conrad talk about the day's events in court. I put up a laundry line in our bathroom and washed and ironed all my lingerie, nightgowns and T-shirts. I liked plunging my stockings and underwear into the sink filled with warm water, Tide and OxiClean, while I listened to Wagner, Chopin, Presley and Beethoven on a device or the radio I brought in. Hours scrubbing Conrad's socks and smalls—as they say in England—not because I wanted to save, although hotel laundry is hugely expensive, but because this was something I could control and see through from beginning to end.

It is possible to go slightly mad around the edges without being completely off your rocker. Retrospectively, my friendship with Ethel and Frank was marginally eccentric, but I developed a firm affection and some rapport with them. Ethel and Frank were the two people on the hotel video that played as soon as you powered the TV on; they explained what to do in case of fire. "Are those really their names?" Conrad asked when he found me watching them. "Yes," I said. "They were unhappy with their nameless status."

Or I felt they were. They were appearing in a hundred or more hotel rooms and people just switched them off even as they worked away, impish in their excessive reactions, dropping to their knees with washcloths over their faces, ever alert, peering around corners, so endearing that it seemed wrong for them to be just silent nameless actors. Whenever I came back from court, I'd say hello to them. I'd watch and rewatch Ethel and Frank during their four-minute demonstration, hoping in some curious way that they would do one thing differently, take another route out of the hotel, block the fireman's way on the back staircase—or better yet, come and sit with me. Why not enter their world? The one I was in was, frankly, loony. Ethel and Frank lived in Pleasantville and made sense.

I bought a wheeled shopping trolley to go to the supermarket that was a fifteen-minute walk from the hotel. Away from the courthouse lawyers and swarming smarmy journalists, two sides of the same counterfeit coin, I was back for just an hour or two in a world with relatively sane people shopping for detergent and tinned foods, milk and bread, fruit and OxiClean. The cashiers became my friends, just as dress vendeuses had. This, at least, was a predictable bit of life. (When this section was being initially read, a note came back suggesting I was trying to get attention for myself by claiming just to be an ordinary person happily enjoying everyday life. That's the problem with this story: events were so relentlessly mad that the only relief sounds as if it's equally mad or contrived. I simply don't know a way around this except to tell you what took place and how I coped. Christ, at that point, I'd have been thrilled to be a happy peasant hoeing her field.)

"Why on earth are you doing that?" Conrad said incredulously the day I brought home my first cart of groceries and was a little out of breath. "You should be taking a taxi or a car." He didn't see it as my link to sanity. I wished there were something I could think up for him to do. I wheeled that cart along the lake every other Friday and once or twice in the week, cold and windy in March, sweltering in July.

My alarm clock rang at 6:45 every morning and, like a wind-up doll, I plodded through the same routine of makeup, coffee and the no-name trouser suit chosen the night before to evoke no envy. If I could ever have found it, I'd have worn the $140 sweatsuit I was supposed to have charged to Hollinger.

The dread began as we circled towards the Everett McKinley Dirksen courthouse. You could see a mass of some sort on your visual horizon that quickly became a swirl of black and then focused into a swarm of reporters with cameras and the long overhead arms of microphones clad in some sort of woolly covering. They shouldered each other in search of that day's detail or quote, a look at what the sacrificial lamb chops were wearing today—and on one occasion, in their eagerness, pushed me over, accidentally, hard to the sidewalk. Shrill voices would shout questions of stunning originality: "How does it feel, Conrad, to be facing ninety years in prison?" "Barbara, where did you buy that necklace? Was it paid for by Hollinger?"

Every day as we went through security I could see those TV reporters, pressed up against the large glass walls that kept them out of the courthouse building, their faces half-hidden behind cameras, their splayed limbs jostling each other to get into position, looking like some surrealist nightmare of an anthill or insect mass. With no sun to reveal their colour under the carapace of the courthouse, they were a fresco of black figures in constant motion, ready to squirt poisonous ink if you got too close. I don't think they knew how hideous a scene they created and what it was like to walk day after day through them. And then, after a day in court, the courtroom journalists would chatter and laugh, exchange sarcastic comments about Conrad's emails and deride them as "crap," indicting both the paucity of their own vocabularies and their paucity of any knowledge of what this was all about

You remember small things. At one point, all three of Conrad's children were in the courtroom. One lunchtime, in the small room assigned to us in the corridor outside the courtroom, I said, self-mockingly, "I think tomorrow I'll just put on all the heavyweight jewellery Conrad has given me and live up to the descriptions of me. They ought to have their show." I didn't have any jewellery in Chicago, of course, but as I said it, I saw, quick as a slash of lightning between sky and ground, a look go between the children. The look said, "This is what got our father into trouble." There was no way to take my words back, and I couldn't explain that I had to make fun of what was going on in there or I'd go crazy.

Alana herself was creating quite a little storm, attending court every day but one. So simply dressed, she was a showstopper. Exquisite, twenty-four years old, five foot eleven in her bare feet, slim as a reed, with virtually no makeup and a profile like a carved Nefertiti bust. She fascinated the press because she had, quite naturally, a sort of enigmatic air about her. Smile, yes. Nod, yes. Speak—no.

"Alana Black," raved *Hello!* magazine's headline, "Defines Courthouse Chic." They labelled her "media heiress," which we all hoped she would be but at that point there wasn't much to be heir to. "The style-savvy beauty recently stole the spotlight from her media mogul father and infamously extravagant stepmother Barbara Amiel Black when photographers snapped her between the pair. Her runway good looks and trendy fringed hairstyle landed her on the front page of several newspapers." What no one, apart from Mark Steyn, realized was that she had inherited her father's brain. I tried to persuade her to go into law. Long before I grasped a point in the arguments, Alana had extrapolated and made the connections with a brilliance few are given.

In one of the lowest moments of the lottery of life, some journalists got together and made a bet on who could bed Alana. Mark Steyn was offered money if he would try. The bet was relayed to Alana.

These were not the only males eyeing her bed. Early one morning, as she lay sleeping, there was a loud knocking at the door of her hotel room. Alana ignored it. She had neglected to put on the double lock and so the room was entered anyway—by six Secret Service officers plus dog. Vice President Dick Cheney was going to be staying in the room next door. "Can I pat the dog?" said Alana, who is a fierce animal lover. Terse refusal as they turned over her mattress: "He's working."

My tripwire was the second-floor lobby of the Ritz-Carlton. Just in front of the elevators were two glass display windows, one of them always featuring a Bulgari handbag. Hard to credit, I know, that there is any brand I do not own, but I had never owned a Bulgari anything apart from two watches David Graham had given me, and this was— as I said, hard to credit—the first time I had seen their handbags. For the entire time of our hotel residency, this damn shagreen Bulgari handbag, clutch size with the distinctive worked enamel clasp, was featured behind the glass plane. That bag stared back at me. "I'm the past," it said with a sneer.

I was afraid to stand too long lest a lurking journalist spot me, but the bag always evoked suppressed memories. I couldn't just "buy" it, even having some money now. Every time I saw it, I was transported to Park and Fifth avenues. I could see my opera glasses and handkerchief being put into it after getting all dolled up for a theatre opening. This was the sharp thrust of times lost, even those not in themselves particularly entrancing. And sometimes as I gazed at the bag's simple lines, I could hear other wives or girlfriends behind me saying to the men with them, "Do you like it?" Which is femme code for "I want it."

A steady stream of friends from New York and London, with some Toronto people, visited Conrad in Chicago. Those evenings were like dancing in toffee for me but thoroughly enjoyed by Conrad. Anna Wintour and her companion, Shelby Bryan, flew down for dinner—a gesture of solidarity that was completely unexpected, although, while not downplaying her loyalty, I think somewhere there may have been a lurking, uncomfortable feeling about *Vogue* being the publisher of the sink-the-ship infamous "extravagance" remark.

Anna came to dinner straight from the airport, looking extremely beguiling, largely because she was really quite imperfect for once, thank God. That is to say, her hair had not been blown dry that very moment and was a bit messed up, with the exhaustion of a day at work and the flight showing on her face. I'd like to think she let herself go especially for me, but that would be pushing the envelope.

In the courtroom I tried to pay attention, but my psyche wouldn't survive actually listening. Going there was bad enough, like attending a nineteenth-century school with cane-wielding teachers and then recreation time with gangs of roving bullies. I don't really know how to explain the feeling as you sit, deliberately devoid of expression, watching your husband being lacerated day after day in court. It's the equivalent, I suppose, of those frightful scenes in B movies where a spouse is tied up and forced to watch their husband or wife defiled and tortured. Your being is jerked back and forth till every joint is unhinged and your mind along with them. Then watching the men and women supposed to be defending him fall by the wayside, sleep through his demolition, turns pain into rage, made all the worse by the knowledge that expressing it would damage him further.

The jury sat—with the exception of one man and two of the women—completely undisturbed by the trial. The proceedings might as well have been in Urdu. If I was in an alternate universe, they were in outer space. In the front row, the blonde hairdresser, very much the prow of the jury with her impressive prow, blew her pink bubblegum to such astonishing sizes that it was hard to concentrate on anything but the point at which it was either going to pop or retract between her rouged lips.

Every now and then, I'd hear Genson trying to explain what he didn't understand to the jury: "A bunch of lawyers went and fought each other," he said, "and a bunch of lawyers went and fought each other not to get rid of the special committee, but they fought each other in order to get him back onto his board of directors. That's what happened. . . . It indicates nothing, it indicates that a whole lot of people that were mad at each other, and it indicates a whole lot of people that believe that the other person was wrong." Not inaccurate as far as it went, but it simply didn't tell the story, or what the prosecution kept referring to as "the narrative."

The jury sat blankly as this old man wheezed on forever about this Conrad Black who "has an arrogant attitude when he writes in the middle of the night or sometimes in the afternoon or even maybe in the morning . . . He writes using large words and sentence constructions and because he's a historian he knows everything." And there below them was Conrad Black, forced to sit without a word, impassive, listening to this characterization by his own team.

Several of the jurors joined now and then in a communal big sleep. The naps of Greenspan and Genson quickly earned them the epithet of the "dream team." Greenspan was lapsing into his diabetic lethargy. Genson just to the exhaustion of age and ill health. All we had at stake was the rest of our lives.

I didn't sign up for this, I thought, but Conrad didn't either, so no point repeating so obvious a phrase. As our defence team unravelled and Greenspan became more and more reclusive, I called George Jonas and asked him to come to Chicago to see what could be done. I did so very reluctantly because his Parkinson's made travel away from home so unpleasant. He arrived promptly with Maya and her seeing-eye dog, Daisy, to stay in a suite just down the hall from us. This will do it, I thought pretty confidently.

Greenspan always worked well with Jonas, who in the past had performed something of a solicitor's role to Greenspan's barrister. I couldn't see a no-speaks situation between two such old friends. The Jonases stayed for about six weeks, and George tried very hard. But it was near hopeless. Eddie was in a state of true and complete denial. When they met, he seemed oblivious to what was happening in court. "I am to blame," Jonas kept saying to me until virtually the day he went into his death coma. "I knew before the trial Eddie wasn't up to it at that point, but I hoped."

Greenspan's friend and colleague, the distinguished Earl Cherniak, came down from Toronto and worked all weekend with Eddie to successfully bring the life back into those vital cross-examinations of the audit committee that Greenspan handled so well, like the Greenspan of yore. But the night before the time came for closing statements, the cold war between our counsel was such that Greenspan could not even get Genson to tell him what he was going to say. "I don't know yet," he told Greenspan.

By trial's end the jury so disliked Greenspan ("they absolutely *hate* him," we kept being told by the other defence counsels, who blamed us for antagonizing the jury) that Greenspan, who by now was aware of the problem, used a good part of his very short closing remarks to first stroke the jury by emphasizing their role as arbiters in the great system of justice bequeathed to the Western world, then to emphasize their role as arbiters of this man's fate, and then to apologize. "I want you to know," he said, "that if any time in this trial I have pressed a point too hard, if I have been too tough or aggressive, it is only because, I assure you, of my anxiety to make sure no stone is left unturned to show you the innocence of Conrad Black. So do not hold that against Mr. Black." His delivery was splendid, but its relevance marginal to Conrad's case. Donald Trump's border wall could have been built by the stones Greenspan and Genson left unturned. After a four-month trial, neither of our counsel had managed to give the jury a straightforward explanation of what had happened. I think basically it was because neither of them understood.

We were saved from the bulk of the charges by the counsels of our co-defendants, most prominently Ronald S. Safer. He had been chief of the Criminal Division of the U.S. Attorney's Office in Chicago and, now a defence lawyer, he was one of the three or four out of the hundreds of lawyers I met in the course of this trial who was utterly incorruptible and extremely skilled. But even he couldn't save us from the one charge that none of the other defendants faced— the merciless obstruction of justice, courtesy of Colin Campbell and aided by the press with its endless inaccurate hype of "Black Caught on Camera," as if his removal of his own belongings was being done surreptitiously.

And we hadn't a chance in hell, since neither Greenspan, whose boxes of commercial documents sent only a couple of days before Conrad's eviction made up most of the ones Conrad took from his office, nor Genson, who didn't understand what had happened in Toronto, would argue the charge. "It's the easiest one to win, Eddie," George Jonas told Greenspan. From the beginning, everyone had thought this charge would be a pushover for us. As for Don Vale, the acting head of Hollinger who had given Conrad permission to remove the boxes, he received a warm communication from the prosecution team—Eric Sussman, I believe—that if he testified at trial, he might face difficulties getting into the U.S. again. He did not appear. Probably a wise decision on his part, knowing the power and spite of U.S. prosecutors, but not a bonus for us.

George Jonas, unsuccessful in persuading Greenspan to tackle the obstruction charge either during the trial or in his closing argument, sent him a despairing note the evening before closing statements were to be made. "Eddie: do you think you could persuade Genson in the morning to recap at the end of his address . . . re obstruction, a) tell the jury Conrad was obviously looking into the camera which he knew was there and could have disabled if he wanted to, and b) defy the government to identify one commercial document in the boxes the SEC did not already have. Last kick at the cat."

The cat was already stone-dead. Genson had a breakdown in his closing and had to ask the judge to end the day early so he could recover. He came back to court next day but got utterly lost in confusion.

For me, the very worst times were not even in the courtroom, nor in the din of reporters, nor even in the ache of time rushing by taking life with it and leaving us standing on a bleak and windy corner. The worst times were our intimate moments, which had always sustained us. In bed, whatever else, we were true friends; arguments disappeared, exhaustion or sickness bound us together, we could be silent or talk, but still we always had knowledge of the other. Now I dreaded seeing the sheets and white pillows. Because there was no escape. Conrad needed to tell me how well we were doing or relive some small triumph in the courtroom, and I couldn't stand it, cursed as I was like Cassandra, snakes whispering in my ear we would lose. Resentment and anger at my husband would well up inside me and I couldn't let them emerge.

This was a loneliness of the heart and brain and being, and gradually that loneliness spilled into everything for the next eleven or twelve years. To whom could I tell the truth without betrayal? The truth, as I saw it, that we were losing everything and I must pretend we were losing nothing; that my husband had convinced himself this persecution was noble, and believed, in some crazy way, that others could see the nobility. The strain of pretending to everyone—most of all to him as he told me how respected we were, how we were winning by surviving, while I knew financial and legal disaster was a hair's breadth away. I wanted to shout at him that there was nothing noble about being innocent and ground down, we've lost, lost. That was a word that was simply not allowed.

To whom could I say these things? Burden George Jonas further? And each year, the truth would become heavier and the game played on, whether Conrad was in prison or free, till finally I too was imprisoned, exhausted and ill from the very strain of endless pretense and worry. Not until this year, 2020, would the snakes begin to stop their hissing and the constriction in my stomach and abdomen—not symbolic but real—start to relent. By then I was unsure that I could ever function in the outside world again.

The verdict was an anti-climax. The jurors took their seats, and all the ones that each day had looked over at Alana and me, sizing us up or even allowing a teeny bit of acknowledged eye contact, wouldn't look at us. I knew what that meant, and although I had known it would come, I had kept hoping, hoping. After all, the criminal conviction rate in the U.S. is 99.6 per cent, and of that, 97 per cent are plea bargains because, well, with virtually no restrictions on what the prosecution can do, what's the point of fighting?

Of the sixteen charges filed, Conrad had lost four of them. The judge read out each charge and then the verdict was given. The very first one—on the obstruction of justice—was "guilty." You don't snap. You knew this was the inevitable outcome. You look over at your husband and want to run and hug him right away as you see the signs you alone understand—the set of his eyes, the jaw. He was stone.

Conrad was acquitted of all the major charges, like racketeering and looting the company. He was acquitted of the lifestyle charges, which had been thrown as envy bait, like my birthday party and the lunatic trip to Bora Bora. Sentencing was to come.

In a way, I was almost impressed with the jury. They had seen through most of the tripe, and that was far more than I had expected. Which one, I thought, was the holdout either way? Who kept them deliberating for twelve days?

Showers of exploding fireworks and joy lit the skies. The popping of corks was thundering. "Black Guilty" on CNN, newspapers, Bloomberg, everywhere. In the courtroom a blanket of bonhomie enveloped the legal teams and hands were clasped by former rivals. Judge Amy St. Eve praised everyone—the jury, the prosecutors, the "most able and effective defence teams," while the court marshal mouthed her words which were apparently a set piece at the end of all her trials regardless of the participating lawyers' skills.

The defence counsels smiled, bounced about happily picking up their papers, and all but ours shook hands with each other and then, to my horror, shook hands with the prosecutors. Everyone was so happy. God, no more bloody 8:30 mornings at the court. The show had been a huge hit. "It's entertainment," said one of the other defence lawyers, smiling to me as I stood silent. "Well, for everyone except the accused," he added, seeing the look on my face as I had one of my now routine visions of smashing a hammer into his head.

Someone once told me that there were no nervous breakdowns in the concentration camps of World War Two. Actually, that wasn't absolutely true: there were, and there were suicides too, and the conditions in those places were a zillion times worse than this, but I understood the thrust of it. I didn't have nightmares because I was living one. Every morning in court before our trial began, I had watched the parade of the wretched. A blaze of hideous orange jumpsuits on largely black men, often handcuffed, sometimes shackled, came out of one door to meet their legal defender in front of Judge Amy. A five-minute bout of camaraderie between judge, prosecutor and defence lawyer would follow, after which prosecutor and defender would shake hands, smile, perhaps make a lunch date, and the silent orange jumpsuit who had not said a word was shuffled off through a door on the opposite side. The entire process had an eerie resemblance to the Costa-Gavras movie *The Confession*, based on Stalin's 1952 Czechoslovakian show trials. Was it now going to be like that for Conrad?

In the getaway car from the court, Conrad and I sat in silence. He was going to be taken away to some horrible cage. I couldn't think beyond that. Alana cried a bit. What Conrad was thinking, I don't know. I knew it would involve a rearrangement of his reality in order to rationalize the events into something positive.

No matter how I try, there is a part of my husband that I cannot reach. It's like diving into wet cement. Somewhere in that huge cerebral cortex there must be a vulnerable group of cells, but no one can approach. I could feel the spring inside his body tighten. I could see the narrowed eyes as he sat in concentration. I could hear words that he felt he had to say, once again, back at the hotel: "I wouldn't blame you if you left me now. I promised you happiness and this is what we have." But that was no real guide to what he was feeling. "Why don't you explode or punch the wall or scream?" I wanted to ask. There's only me here.

Twelve weeks later, after Conrad had been refused permission to return to Toronto and refused bail while we waited for his appeal to be heard, we were back in court for sentencing. He politely declined making the allocution to the judge, stating remorse for his crimes, and instead expressed his "very profound regret and deep sadness" for the shareholders and employees who had been denied the benefits of the nearly $2 billion of equity he had created and that his successors at Hollinger had squandered.

That very day, the U.S. Supreme Court had released a decision allowing judges to go below sentencing guidelines. In spite of probation officer Sheila Lally's extraordinarily positive report to the court, made after extensive investigation into the case and interviews that included ones with myself and Alana separately, Judge Amy, ever the prosecutor, declined to give Conrad a reduced sentence. He was sentenced to seventy-eight months in a federal prison.

I decided to get a dog.

CHAPTER TWENTY-SIX

No Latex

How do you solve a problem like mine? Easy. You manufacture a catastrophe to eclipse everything. Works every time.

"Get a Kuvasz," George Jonas said.

"Isn't it better to rescue a dog?"

"Yes, it's an act of human decency, of which there are very few, but you have enough to cope with. Rescue dogs go to homes where the owner can concentrate on any suffering the dog may have known. You need a dog to rescue *you*."

This was an excellent formulation, and if it had been accompanied by the suggestion to get a Labrador retriever or some such breed it would have been excellent advice. George, however, remained a Hungarian patriot, no matter how he diluted it under the great civilized umbrella of an Austro-Hungarian identity. He himself had grown up with dachshunds, a breed of uncommon intelligence and mischief, but given their size, not a threat to life and limb. "Why not a dachshund?" I asked. "You loved yours."

"You may need some protection while Conrad is away. Nothing could protect us against Joseph Stalin's communism short of a great power like America or, for the local secret police, a legion of Caucasian Ovcharkas, which in turn might kill you. After the communists took most of our apartment, small dogs were the best choice. A Kuvasz will be loyal to its death." George often tended to make decisions in light of his experience with Stalin, which I was coming to see as rather more useful than initially.

Which is how I became a Kuvasz owner.

This is a breed even most dog lovers will not know and, naturally, I went into research overdrive. The Kuvasz is a livestock guardian dog, not huge but a decent size—males weigh something over a hundred pounds—and it has an adorable, very thick, all-white wavy coat. Essentially, it is a mountain dog and its cousins are the Maremma in Italy, the Cuvac in Slovakia, the Polish Tatra and the Turkish Akbash. Absolutely none of which I knew. The Kuvasz, I read, could be stubborn, protective and not always easy to train, since mountain dogs have, as the various dog sites so euphemistically put it, "been bred for generations to think for themselves and make independent decisions." Rather like Conrad in a doggy outfit, I thought.

Through the Canadian Kennel Club, I found a breeder in Ontario who sold largely to local farms. "They are excellent for protecting your animals from fox, coyotes and wolves," said Olga Schmidt. Again, a promising recommendation, given the rabid wolves and coyotes now hovering around me. Next time someone tried to come in and pull a Mareva, my Kuvasz could take service.

I went to see Olga, who lived in a part of Ontario where all addresses began with a numbered county line off a numbered rural route to be found only with knowledge of some local landmark like "the green shed with the billboard after which you turn left." Olga's kennels full of white dogs had, I noticed, fencing about ten feet high. Olga came out, her two off-leash Kuvaszok standing quietly back at her command. "I know a lovely Kuvasz, Ara, who used to be mine, and she's pregnant," she said.

I relayed my new and important standing as a potential Kuvasz owner to George Jonas, who was very impressed. "Are you getting just one?" he asked, after telling me about the Budapest junkyard Kuvasz that near killed anyone who tried to enter the yard. George tended to exaggerate, but not entirely.

"Perhaps I should get used to one before getting two," I ventured.

Sometime in late December, I went to find Ara, now owned by a unilingual Hungarian woman. She lived in a rundown farmhouse in the middle of absolutely nowhere. In her main room, right off the front door, lay Ara, the most gentle and perfect white Kuvasz with the smiling face the breed is known for. This was no junkyard canine. After careful introduction, Ara was content to lie down and have me stroke her. There was some difficulty in communication: not between myself and Ara, who gently panted a very good English, but with Irene, who didn't. I got George on the telephone to translate.

"Her Hungarian isn't very good either," he told me. "She's almost incomprehensible in two languages. Her uncle bred championship Kuvaszok in Hungary and her father bred vizslas. Her Hungarian is atrocious. She talks dog and not much of anything else."

I had looked up Ara's pedigree and seen she was championship stock all the way. The father-to-be, I was told by Irene, was from Argentina. "He's a very good dog," said Olga, who had had a hand in selecting him. The pup would be ready to leave its mum around the end of February, and after his birth, Irene emailed photos. I stuck them up everywhere. Even then the pup tugged at you. There was a look of apprehension and wistfulness, even dejection, in every photo of him.

"I'm naming him after you," I told Jonas, and Irene began using the name. When I arrived at her farm to pick him up, there was little Jonas, an eight-week-old drift of snow-white fur. "He bite," said Irene. "I bite hard on nose. No bite you now." I was unfamiliar with this as a training method.

Jonas looked like any small white furry puppy, adorable but strangely sad, with tear stains under his eyes. Jonas would remain sad-looking his entire life. He had no siblings. This was Ara's final breeding, only the one pup, my Jonas, instead of the more usual litter of six to eleven, and Irene placed a batch of newborn vizsla pups to nurse with him. Perhaps that made him sad, I thought, being surrounded by all those reddish, smooth-skinned strangers.

———

Conrad met him in Palm Beach three days before leaving for prison and immediately named him Jonas Quadruped in order to distinguish him from his biped namesake. We carefully avoided speculation on what this eight-week-old puppy would look like when he came home in six years.

His last look at the puppy was the morning of March 3 as I took Jonas through the doors of my dressing room, which opened onto a generous plot of grass now fenced in for him. He could hear the voices of the press gathered on South Ocean Drive to bear witness to Conrad going off to be locked up, thrown in the slammer, "and while they're at it, throw his wife in," as one friendly *Maclean's* reader had written.

We had received a standard letter from the United States Marshals Service of the U.S. Department of Justice that appeared to be typed by someone who had discovered the font menu options and gone bonkers. Some instructions were heavily underlined and enlarged, like one of those anonymous letters you get from disturbed readers who print filthy words or apocalyptic predictions sideways up along the margins. Basically, it was to tell Conrad to present himself at the Federal Correctional Institution Coleman at noon on March 3.

Federal prisons are in fairly barren places located away from towns. The entrance to Florida's FCI Coleman, the largest federal prison in the U.S., was marked by a marble and stone sign and a guard box, past which was a long, straight drive to a cluster of distant buildings with not a tree or flower in sight. On the other side of the road, opposite the entrance, was the media cluster of vans with big satellite dishes on top. We drove past the women's camp to the building marked "Coleman Low."

I had to speak for Conrad who, in his politeness, waited for the guard at the desk to speak first—which he didn't. "This is my husband, Conrad Black, self-surrendering," I said. We were directed into the waiting room, a room I would come to know very well, where we sat alone for about forty-five minutes. Conrad's small crumpled brown paper bag of cash for the commissary, his eyeglasses, sleeping meds and lip salve were examined, and his medications and half-used tube of lip salve handed to me. To be honest, I can't really remember much of the whole thing. We embraced, quickly, a wordless kiss. The scent of his skin. Then he walked away behind the desk and made a left turn. He didn't look back.

Okay, I thought, let's not get soap-opera about this. He is not serving life. Except that walk to the end of the hall between guards and the matter-of-fact turn with no looking back became a video loop in my brain. I did my British-gym-mistress talk to myself. All right, gels. Backs straight. Eyes front. Let's win today.

The other side of the coin only hit me when I got home and realized that I was now alone for six years and three months—if he got the 13 per cent reduction for good behaviour. I know that Scarlett O'Hara said, "I'll think about that tomorrow," but Christ, it really zonked me between the eyes. Jonas Quadruped was waiting for me. When I went to bed, I looked down at him sleeping on the floor before I put him into his crate. He was stretched out on his side giving off that sweet perfume breath of puppy smell they have for about four months. Completely defenceless except for me.

I was gripped with a feeling unlike any I had ever had in my life and have never felt since: my whole being was in a rhapsody. I found it completely puzzling. I loved my husband, but this was a weightless warmth coursing through mind and body, a fuzzy, foreign, strange emotion that seemed to suffuse everything and cannibalize every nerve ending. I wanted only to cradle and protect this little life. Forever. So intense and unexpected a feeling, I wondered if it was what mothers felt on seeing their first baby. As I looked at Jonas, I resolved: Nothing will ever hurt you.

They don't tell you that for the first few days, a new inmate can't contact the outside world. I was afraid to approach the prison in any way, not wanting to cause repercussions for Conrad, which was my first concrete understanding of the position that would face us for the next few years. That left me to the company of Jonas Q.

He was very affectionate and he bit me. His twenty-eight little deciduous teeth were quite sharpish, baby incisors and baby canines, and not wanting to use the methods of his Hungarian owner, I did not bite him back. I was reading how-to books on dogs like mad and decided on a "firm hand and reward" method. "No," I would say very firmly as he bit me. And usually he would stop. There is a decided shortage of useful books on Kuvaszok, and I have discovered that the only ones that have any truth to them are written by Hungarians, poorly translated but very accurate.

How to Train Your Kuvasz or *Know Your Kuvasz* by American dog trainers are written by charming dog people who clearly have never dealt with anything more wilful than a terrier. Jonas was completely house-trained, 100 per cent reliable—as all my Kuvaszok have been—before ten days were up. We would walk along the boardwalk late afternoon or early morning, whenever the weather was coolest, and he would meet people and other dogs. This is called socializing your dog. Jonas was polite, curious but not unpleasantly so, and I anticipated no problems. His crate had a door that was closed at night but was in sight of my bed. After a couple of weeks he rather liked it, and during the day, when I sat reading in the bedroom, he would wander spontaneously into his crate for an afternoon sleep.

We were now progressing into the appeal to Chicago's Seventh Circuit simultaneously with the pardon application, also known as the appeal for clemency. The melodic Irish tones of former prime minister Brian Mulroney were frequently on the telephone. Brian, bless him, was determined to use his considerable influence with George Bush Sr. to obtain a pardon for Conrad from George Bush Jr.

Brian had definite views about the outline I should draft presenting Conrad's case. I was to write an explanatory letter on the injustice meted out to Conrad, a letter I was told to vary according to the recipient's knowledge of Conrad and the case. The task of recapping events in two pages of snappy and accessible prose depressed the bejesus out of me as once again I reopened the sore I was trying to heal or at least not scratch. I loathed this business of begging people to write on Conrad's behalf, asking them to help my innocent husband get a pardon from George Dubya Bush because his father was going to tell him to do so. Nor, I thought, was anyone in the Bush family

going to give a fig about us even if they were convinced of this mis-
carriage of justice.

"Brian," I would say as I typed out the thirty-second summary
of the case—this task was beginning to make lovable the many
drafts of my sentencing letter to the judge. "Brian, there is no chance
of any member of the Bush family doing anything for Conrad."

"Now, Barbara. I have a very close relationship with George
Bush Sr. and he has a great deal of influence on his son. I'll be flying
down to their vacation home and will personally give him the
petition."

I knew Brian was 100 per cent sincere and doing this out of the
pure goodness of his heart—there was no reward for him—and I
knew his relationship with the former president was extremely
close. "Brian," I would repeat patiently, "Richard Breeden was head
of the SEC when George W. Bush was about to be thrashed for what
bore an uncanny resemblance to insider trading. He got a pass from
the SEC. The Bushes are loyal to such benign corruption."

Our Chicago appeal had come and—in my view—gone. Just
before we entered the courtroom, I heard a deep sigh from Andy
Frey, our distinguished appeal lawyer, deputy solicitor general of the
U.S. for thirteen years, winner of many cases before the U.S. Supreme
Court and a man I felt completely wrong for our case. I think it was
just not the right fit temperamentally. Although I tried to persuade
my husband to change, he was adamant in his refusal.

"This is not too good," Frey said. We had been speculating on
who the appeal judge would be—you don't find out until you see the
name posted outside the courtroom—and our hopes were for Frank
Easterbrook, chief judge of the appeals court. "It's Richard Posner,"
said Frey, a little more sober than even his usual default sober. "He
can be unpredictable."

Any unpredictability ended in about thirty-one seconds, and my
bet is that Frey didn't expect to get that long. Posner, flanked by two
silent judges, was sitting at a forty-five-degree angle, his chair pushed
back to a lounging position that said very clearly, "I am bored by the

necessity of having to go through this." He was said to be the intellectual on the court, and never had an intellectual been more flamboyant in his air of superiority. Now it was my turn to sigh. I was going to have to sit through this.

Posner spent the court time in a state of constant crossness laminated to an air of being exceedingly pleased with himself. Denying our appeal was perfectly within his right and he had no need to add personal animus to it. But he made a good showing. "I want to say a few words at the beginning about obstruction of justice," Frey managed to say. "This is the weakest case I've seen in forty-five years of law practice." That was as far as he got. During Frey's allotted ten minutes for opening remarks, Posner made thirty-two interventions, twenty-four of which were outright interruptions and twenty-one of which took place less than two sentences in. After all, from Posner's point of view, it was a captive audience. When a man is in love with his own voice, justice cannot be permitted to silence it.

I knew Conrad was sitting in his cell watching the time on his commissary-purchased watch, his hopes circling. "Now we're getting to a serious court," he had said to me the night before. And I knew that when he called my cell phone as arranged at lunchtime, I was going to have to break the bad news. Which I did, unvarnished. The appeal was turned down less than three weeks later. I'm not sure this is in the book of dutiful spousal rules, but I actually read Posner's reasons for his judgment—an act of sheer masochism, but I thought I might need to know its essence for whatever the next round brought. I gave up counting major factual errors after passing twenty. Clearly, he hadn't read any of the defence briefs and relied purely upon the prosecution's.

Posner himself revelled in his self-bestowed status as an iconoclast. "I still have difficulty understanding," he told *The New Yorker* in a profile. "If someone is obviously guilty, why do you have to have all this rigmarole?" He saw Conrad as "obviously guilty" and not worthy of the rigmarole of the law. We were now dead in the waters of Coleman.

———

I dreaded prison visits. They started the day before, when I tried to sort out an outfit that would please Conrad and the Bureau of Prisons rules. Not that I *wanted* to wear latex (prohibited), sleeveless blouses (prohibited even under jackets), white T-shirts (prohibited, no idea why), sweatsuits (prohibited) or anything coloured khaki, beige, green, blue or just about any colour if the admitting guard had a bad night's sleep or was colour-blind. Orange was not a permitted colour, of course, it being the colour of the jumpsuits worn by inmates in the solitary-confinement Special Housing Unit (SHU), but orange looks utterly awful on me so that was no hardship. Unfortunately, the guards were not intimate with the spectrum differences between orange, bronze, apricot and amber. We had several animated fashion discussions at the entry screening about the difference between ecru and beige, not to mention the great "cap sleeve versus sleeveless" debates.

Anything else worn had to pass the blanket rule of being "neither provocative nor enticing." There was a bit of a double standard for the very curvaceous black women who often wore trousers and tops that might as well have been latex given how tightly they clung or how amply they were filled. Black women are more voluptuous than most whites and definitely endowed with better asses. Just how they got away with their outfits while the same guards who passed them were measuring the distance between the hem of my skirt and my sixty-six-year-old kneecaps really pissed me off. About the only attractive asset I had at that point was my shapely legs—so long as they were encased in semi-opaque stockings, not for the rules but to camouflage their not so attractive texture. Conrad said it cheered him enormously to see me dressed up in attractive clothing and he rather liked to introduce me around, so I was constantly in search of an enhancing but suitably unenticing Coleman look.

Prison mornings were a bitch. I had to get up at 3:15 to take care of the dog(s) and do my makeup and hair. Leave the house by four thirty in order to get to the Turkey Point rest area on I-95 after passing through Orlando early-morning traffic in time to change into my carefully selected prison outfit. Turkey Point had a nice clean washroom. This was last stop for the brush and hairspray deal. One comb

or hairbrush was actually on the printed "Permitted Items" list for
FCI Coleman, but in fact was not always allowed.

Prison rules for visitors were like shifting ice floes. Sometimes that
month's new prohibited colour would be posted in the waiting room
and sometimes not. Most of us kept a change of clothing in our cars.
Umbrellas, scarves and shawls were definitely not allowed, and the
walk from the waiting area to the "visitation room" (BOP phraseology)
was about a hundred yards outdoors, single file, with a BOP guard
alongside barking "Keep on the yellow line!" After a couple of Florida's
subtropical rain drenchings, I bought a see-through, Saran wrap-type
hooded rain cover-up, which the guards reluctantly permitted.

We were moved through processing in groups of about fifteen
according to time of arrival. Since visits could be interrupted at any
point by lockdowns or the sudden disappearance of all guards, thus
stranding one and all in the waiting room, door locked, glass opaque
and no information on their return, it was prudent to arrive early.
This occasionally led to fraught moments in the parking lot where
all visitors had to wait, gathered in one spot like a flock of refugees,
till the BOP deigned to open the doors. I became pretty damn good
at securing my place in line, and as a "regular" got to know other
regulars. We took care of one another's "spots."

The whole visit was a crapshoot. Visiting hours could be ended
early, interrupted, shortened arbitrarily. You could find yourself sitting forlornly in the visitation room for an hour, eyes on the inmates'
entry door which opened but never to reveal your husband. This
could be for any number of reasons but was usually because a guard
"forgot" to call him out of his cell block. Requesting a follow-up
call was inadvisable for at least forty-five minutes. You just had to
wait it out.

Caste and class sorted the visitors. There was no way I was ever
going to make it as a confidante of the tight-knit group of Afro-
American women who I really wanted to pal with. They had a
smoking-hot determination not to let the system get them down and
it was wonderful to behold. In addition, they not only sported some
of the most exotic hairstyles but also the most exuberant fingernail

decoration I had ever seen. They clearly had an in-depth knowledge of the American justice system and a deep (and justified) contempt for every part of it. I was invisible to them. They exuded sensuality, no matter what the rules were; anything they wore looked bloody enticing and provocative.

If you asked me to recall my favourite moment—it is unlikely anyone will, but this is my turn—it was when one young black woman was denied entry after flunking security because the meter that "smelt" our hands registered contact with drugs. She came back to the waiting room to pick up her car keys and addressed the room with gusto: "Them motherfuckers," she said. "I called the supervisor and got them guards to put their hands in it and they flunked too. Dirty fuckin' money or they's bringing in junk." Fighting back was exhilarating; we got so worn sitting in our rows of plastic chairs waiting to be allowed to see our men, and this woman's defiance was a hit of spirit. How the hell could any of us tell what hands had handled money or anything else we touched before us? You could wash your hands in the lavatory and get the wrong smell from the doorknob afterwards. I got searched when the meter swung for me after I bought a tin of Ice Breakers at Turkey Point and was handed a couple of dollar bills in change. But in this one area, my age and pigmentation probably played a role in letting me through after the search.

And I got taken too, I think, by an elderly white woman, probably my own age but with grey hair and a beaten look. She quickly spotted me and would reveal nothing about herself. I had to draw her out—it was really rather clever—and after about four visits she began to chat about her plight. Her husband, who I met inside, was suffering from near-psychotic depression and couldn't get any treatment in the prison. She was, she said, in treatment for a reoccurrence of cancer herself and running out of money. Gangs abounded and were constantly breaking into her place because she couldn't afford to move to anywhere that had better security. I parted with $18,000 to help and we exchanged telephone numbers.

She then disappeared, after being banned from visiting when—I was told—she tried to smuggle two Valium pills to her husband, who was further punished by being placed indefinitely in the SHU, which meant isolation and no communication. The telephone number she gave me turned out not to work. Classic grifting, I thought, but if it was, elements of her plight were very real.

In theory, the waiting room was unlocked at eight o'clock to let us in, but sometimes it wasn't. The remorseless Florida sun would come up over the tarmac, and we'd stand there and broil. We got close to rebellion the day we were made to stand in the wretched parking lot in excruciating heat for an extra fifty minutes while an outside memorial service was held for some guard who had been shot. "They should get more of the motherfuckers" was the prevailing view. In my hundred or so visits, I never heard gunshots, but Conrad said they would hear them from the maximum-security areas every couple of weeks.

Several of the male guards struck me as basically decent and fair, but I never encountered a female guard who was anything but a sulking hunk of misery to be inflicted upon any civilian in her path—and likely inmates as well. The pay is pretty atrocious, but if the compensation was the power they had over our lives and those of our men, God, how those bitches swaggered about with the ever-present handcuffs and bunch of keys always well displayed, waggling from their back and side pockets, as they snarled at us.

Leaving at the end of a visit was another fuck off. About fifteen minutes before visiting time was officially over, guards lined us up: visitors on one side of the hall and inmates facing us on the other. We couldn't talk to one another from that point, only exchange looks while we waited for a guard to come from the main building to unlock the visitation centre doors for our own exit.

As we waited, inmates exited in front of us one by one—slowly, as there was a single door for them, which only opened after the previous inmate had been strip-searched for contraband before going back to their cell block for the 4 p.m. standing head count. It was excruciating. Children wanted to go over to their dads. Mothers held them back. Sometimes I'd try to end my visit before this routine began, but if I had been denied entry for an hour or two or held up in a lockdown, you had to take as much time as you could and stay to the bitter end. No matter how many times I went through this, I'd walk back down the yellow line with the guard yelling to keep on it, facing the view of high prison walls with huge circles of razor wire topping them, and want to do myself in. Newcomers often cried.

"Mulroney is confident about the pardon," Conrad told me.

"Fine, good," I replied. "But we've only got about eighty-five days left to file an appeal to the Supreme Court if it doesn't work, so we've got to find a lawyer now."

"Andy's looking it over. He isn't optimistic about them granting a hearing."

"We've *got* to get a new appeal lawyer," I said in my irritatingly repetitious way.

Conrad was reluctant. Stuck in Coleman, he didn't want the disruption of a new lawyer. The legal indemnities covered only civil matters, like the Hollinger suits and IRS matters. Criminal costs were on us. Frey was a very good lawyer, I knew that, but I just didn't think we could win with him. I decided: Too bad what Conrad wants. He's inside and I'm out. Change lawyers.

CHAPTER TWENTY-SEVEN

For Love of a Kuvasz

Back in Palm Beach I was constructing a new half-life around a growing problem. My little puppy was growing fast, and as he grew so did his biting. It was almost always directed at me, and it was unpredictable—there was no warning snarl or bared teeth. You could just be walking and he would politely turn his head up and bite into your hand or arm, then carry on walking. I had the insane idea that the way to handle this was to show no fear, simply tell him "No!" very smartly and call out "Stop" sharply. Usually it was only one bite and then he'd lick my punctured hand and look up at me with hurt, frightened eyes, but his permanent teeth came in and they were very large indeed.

The Palm Beach vet recommended a trainer. "He needs an alpha roll to show him who's in charge," said the trainer, a tall man who also owned a large daycare centre for dogs in West Palm Beach. He would force Jonas onto his side and roll him over and command "Stay." I could see from Jonas's eyes that he hated this but was complying—for the time being. Like most people in Palm Beach, including vets, the trainer had never seen a Kuvasz, and although I kept telling him the nature of the breed, he seemed to think this was like training an unruly golden retriever.

"I'll take him into our daycare, and he can socialize more with the other dogs," said the trainer. I was in all senses that are important for a Kuvasz owner utterly stupid or I would have known that an alpha roll, or putting an unhappy, insecure Kuvasz in a daycare centre away from his owner and among strange people and dogs, was essentially pulling the pin on a hand grenade. Normally, when in difficulty, the best thing to do is call the breeder. But I had made a discovery about Jonas that rather negated that possibility.

The breeding pool of Kuvaszok was low. Most had been exterminated by the Soviets at the end of World War Two; invading soldiers coming to farms were not seen as liberators by Kuvaszok, and showing the breed's courage, selflessness and good taste, they attacked—only to be shot in return. The breed had been carefully brought back, but the use of frozen sperm was pretty common. Accidentally, Ara had been impregnated by a very much alive Kuvasz with demonstrably aggressive habits, two of whose pups had already been taken back after menacing their owners.

The breeder immediately offered to take Jonas back, "get him a home on a farm where he can work alone" and replace him with a pup free of any such problems. I worried that this was a euphemism for putting Jonas down. In my love I was rejecting the only solution that would have kept him alive. Sometimes you understand these things too late.

Since his behaviour was not improving, I paid a surprise visit to the West Palm Beach daycare centre where he was receiving his "special socializing" care. The receptionist was happy to have him brought to me. "No, I want to go inside and see him."

"You can't," she replied. "The owner is off-premises today and we aren't allowed to admit anyone without him."

"Sorry, my money, my dog." She picked up the telephone.

There he was, my Jonas, sidelined alone in a nasty concrete berth with just enough room to let him take one or two steps, while the other dogs were running around freely in the large indoor ring. He was barking, his head turning almost convulsively, distraught as he looked over the concrete wall, just low enough for him to see the other dogs. Isolated and scared. My God, I thought, he's in a canine SHU.

Once outside, his tail was a windmill of gratitude. At home he lay on the bedroom floor with his head in my lap and I wondered how I was going to handle this. He was now 130 pounds of muscle, and I was paying occasional visits to emergency rooms to get patched up and get the meds to prevent cellulitis infections, which with deep puncture wounds can be rather dangerous unless treated fast.

"Ninety per cent of the time he's a normal dog," I told the third vet—Jonas having been fired from about the same number of vets as Conrad had been expelled from schools.

"He needs quiet," out house manager Domenico said, and there was something in this. Noise clearly upset Jonas. What had I done wrong? He didn't attack strangers on the street. He didn't attack the cleaning girls in the house. He never attacked when Domenico or I were brushing him. He only attacked me, out of the blue, the person who fed and loved him, and he occasionally nipped Domenico when they were in the kitchen.

What he needed, I thought, was another Kuvasz to play with. A female who would calm him down like his mother. This time I researched more than the breed; I researched the breeders. There were a number of American Kennel Club–registered breeders of Kuvaszok. I joined the online network and the chat of owners who discussed their problems. I had taken my first baby steps into the mad, mad world of Kuvasz breeders, owners, fanciers and diehard fans of the breed. This turned out to be the perfect home for me, and I would never leave.

Two highly recommended breeders appealed to me: one was in Montana—Deborah Blank of Glacier Creek Kuvasz—but there were no pups available at that point. My other choice was Gail Dash at Casablanca Kuvasz in California. "You must get a female," they both told me when I explained the situation with Jonas. Or at least when I gave a partial explanation. I was afraid if I told them the total story they would decide I was unsuitable. Good Kuvasz breeders are very picky about pup placement.

My second Kuvasz arrived from Casablanca Kuvasz in July 2009. She was twelve weeks old, slightly more than a year younger than the now huge Jonas. I named her Maya, after George Jonas's wife.

———

On January 20, 2009, George W. Bush ended his term in office by pardoning two border patrol agents in prison for shooting a Mexican drug smuggler. "Disgraced media mogul Conrad Black's request to U.S. President George W. Bush to commute his sentence appears to have ended in failure," gloated the *Toronto Star*. Bush told reporters that he wasn't going to pardon "rich," high-profile people who had "connections" and wealthy lawyers. "That's just not right," said the son whose father's high connections and rich lawyers had helped him evade SEC investigations and possible charges.

"I'm just horribly disappointed and shocked," said Brian Mulroney when he telephoned me.

All right, another dead file. I collected all the papers still scattered around my room from the "Pardon" file and put them in the filing cabinet next to the "Appeal—Seventh Circuit" and the "Sentencing" file that contained the ghastly letter I'd had to write to Judge St. Eve, together with the dozens of letters I'd collected on Conrad's behalf for her, and I thought, Oh God, I am so weary of it all. If I must do one more summary of Conrad's case for people who aren't going to do a bloody thing for us anyway, I'm going to turn him into an axe murderer just for relief. Here we were in 2009, six years into the fight and no end in sight but slow ruination as funds wore down.

The immediate problem was to find a new lawyer to ask the Supreme Court to hear our case. Our own Toronto lawyers thought me crazy to go after this. Very easy for them, with their "Barbara, you have no basis for the Supreme Court," as they worried that I would have no bank account for their own mounting bills, but it was my husband who was in a prison, twenty-four hours a day, no way to escape the constant screaming and noise. I could hear it in the background whenever we spoke on the phone, the screaming, the banging of metal on metal, the shouts and cries. No privacy, not for a single moment. Stand up for this count. Listen to the block doors being locked. Did no one understand?

The Supreme Court only accepted—granted a writ of certiorari—a little more than a hundred cases out of the seven thousand or so applications each year, which are not great odds but blooming well worth a try. Besides, the grounds on which Conrad had been convicted were so peculiar. He had been acquitted of virtually everything that was a "crime" and found guilty on matters that were underpinned by some vague notion of "honest services," which no one could quite explain to me.

I had tried to get publicity on this and had written to the editorial page editor of the *Wall Street Journal*, whom we both knew, suggesting that Conrad's conviction on the basis of the honest services statute—about which not a single journalist wrote when covering the trial—had implications for all business disputes and threw just about any company into jeopardy. But there had been no reply. In the old days, all one had to do was pick up the phone and get straight through. The old days. Now I couldn't even get a printed regret.

Out came my reinforcement cocktail—codeine, Carnation, Ribena. I had faith in my New York lawyer, Gregory Joseph, and asked his advice. Ask one excellent lawyer like him and they tell you of another lawyer in a different field, and you call them and sound them out and try to determine if they grasp the importance or show any interest and follow up their recommendations.

Which is how I came finally to Miguel Estrada at Gibson Dunn in Washington, D.C. By the time I contacted him, we had about five weeks left to file for the upcoming court session, and Miguel didn't want the brief. "Your chances of getting certiorari are very slim," he told me, "and you have Andy Frey, who is a very good lawyer. You shouldn't even be talking to me if you haven't told him that you are looking for another lawyer." But I had no time for manners. I begged him. His initial retainer was around a million U.S.; he was going to do at least triple the work he billed by the time this odyssey was over.

His clients included huge corporations, not to mention absolutely key constitutional cases. He had a burning intensity and decency that you could feel just talking to him: later on, in 2010, that same quality compelled him to support Elena Kagan, nominated to the Supreme Court by President Barack Obama, as an "impeccably qualified nominee," even though, as he said, they came from opposite ends of the political spectrum.

After I twisted his arm he got to the point of saying, "If you have a million and a half to throw away, fine. But if that money is important to you, don't do it."

"You've got to see him," I told Conrad.

Miguel and his associate, the indefatigable David Debold, flew down to Coleman. They met in a private room set aside for inmates and their lawyers. David, it emerged, was a Democrat. "I told David," Conrad said afterwards, "that the Democratic Party was a fine institution until it walked off the dock in 1968 and never got back on. Miguel agreed." I knew this was the seal of approval. Estrada started studying and writing the brief before he received his retainer so we could make the September deadline. He was erudite, amusing and loved one-upping me on literary or philosophical matters. And, almost too good to be true, he was also a dog lover. We exchanged canine photos.

I was in love. Casablanca Kuvasz Maya was the puppy of dreams. She laughed at Jonas. When he tried to bully her, she ran over the box hedges and sat perfectly balanced on their flat leafy tops while the huge Jonas could only sit on the lawn and growl at her. She was eerily self-contained even as a three-month-old, and perfectly beautiful from the start, with the long muzzle and wonderful temperament of the legendary Ghosthill kennel dogs from which she was descended. I needed no help to train Maya—a firm hand and simple "reward and praise" system did it. She listened calmly and understood immediately—and then would decide if it was a suggestion she wished to follow.

But Jonas was still another story. I didn't mind the toilet paper unravelling through three rooms; the shoes that were chewed so much I had every pair suspended from the ceiling in a fisherman's net; my bras that walked past me in his mouth as I worked. The problem remained his aggression. He was now about 140 pounds. He could not be called a handsome Kuvasz, but he was a lost soul and while the blood gushed from my arm, I loved him.

My Palm Beach doctor was growing suspicious—but not of Jonas. Only Emergency knew about my dog bites, and I always blamed them on some unknown dog running loose. I needed a local doctor for migraine meds and sleeping pills. He gave me a medical, said my blood pressure was a little high, asked about my sleeping habits but didn't quite understand my hours, which had remained essentially my writing hours—meaning I went to bed around two or three in the morning, now complicated by the need to get up for the dogs at seven thirty. "Well, you're in pretty good health," he said, "for your schedule." Then he took my hand in his and looked at my arm.

"Is there something else you want to tell me?" he said in that calming, kind voice that essentially says, "Are you bonkers? Or on crystal meth?"

"I don't think so," I replied.

"These marks. I don't condemn you. I know what you are going through. Are you cutting yourself? I can get you help."

I was baffled. Cutting myself? What was that? He pointed to the scars on my arm, usually covered by a blouse or T-shirt. Of course, I barely noticed them.

I took the doctor to the window. Domenico was below with the two dogs. "It's the male. He's been teething on me."

And on little Maya. He had been left alone in the kitchen with her one day, and I came home to a slasher movie. The walls were covered with blood—actually dripping with it. Jonas had bitten the end of her tail, badly. She had taken it in her stead and wagged her tail all around the kitchen, hitting walls and the island, repainting them blood red.

I had heard of Patty Armfield, a dog trainer who was said to be the model for the trainer in the film *Marley and Me*. She sized up the situation right away. "First we have to get you confident controlling Jonas," she said. Off we went on walks with Jonas doing what he wanted to do, which was periodically turning to start biting his leash before working on me.

"Use your behind, Barbara," said Patty. "Use your behind to control him."

"I have none." Patty was closer to the ground than me and weighed in, I estimated, at a healthy 150-plus pounds with an admirable behind.

"Just plant your feet down and let that dog know who is in control." I had to be alpha. I knew the lingo.

Although nothing could eradicate the moments of madness in his eyes, with Patty's help I began to ease up on my worry. When I had to go up to Toronto, I went to see if her home would be suitable for Jonas and Maya. Her house was about thirty minutes' drive away, with well-fenced grounds of at least an acre. On a slightly sagging verandah I saw Patty's husband, Bill, a tall man with big, broad shoulders and brawny arms, playing a guitar; he was a country singer who went by the professional name Willie Allen. I knew there would be no concrete isolation booth here for Jonas.

When I returned to Palm Beach, Patty had a good assessment of both dogs. "Never met a dog who needs people less than Maya. She'll do fine. Jonas isn't so much aggressive as defensive. Dogs are mainly dog plus predator in their makeup, and he is way over on the predator side of the line. There's something there that you aren't going to be able to fix. That's what he is."

A dog can't tell you about its demons. So long as no one else is attacked, I thought, I'll stick by him. A fellow inmate told Conrad it would never work. He was a down-south boy and knew dogs. "Doesn't matter who the dog bites, you can sort that. But if it bites its owner, that's the end."

Every vet in Florida was telling me that Jonas had to be put down. But how can you cold-bloodedly put a dog down because he is simply being himself? There must be something to do besides shoving a needle into him and saying "so long." If he was irredeemable, the fault had to be mine. I was bleeding as much in my heart as I was in my external wounds, and I couldn't seem to help either of us.

During summer, residential Palm Beach virtually closes up. All along the ocean, the big houses put up their hurricane windows and present a spectral outlook of empty, eyeless homes. Ours was the only occupied house on the long strip. At four thirty one morning I was reading in bed when the locked doorknob on one side of the bedroom turned. I sat frozen, praying I was hallucinating. Obviously not. Jonas and

Maya, who'd been resting quietly in the dressing room just down a short hall, came flying past my bed snarling and barking and hurling themselves against the locked door. I ran to my bathroom, locked the door and called the Palm Beach police, who arrived in minutes. They could find no one. The alarm was off, but that was not too hard to explain.

Domenico had fired a couple of Haitian cleaners after they were found to be practising voodoo in the house. (I didn't mind the items hidden under beds and furniture—if it worked, I wanted to learn it myself—but he was uneasy.) There's a big trade in West Palm Beach selling alarm codes. Just two nights later, about a mile away and at approximately the same time, the man used a code to turn off the alarm and enter the bedroom of another elderly lady. Her German shepherd outside the bedroom was not enough to deter him from trying to suffocate her with pillows. Her son upstairs heard the dog's barking, and he called the police and subdued the intruder.

I owe you that, my Jonas, I thought in the difficult times ahead.

I was emailing Conrad regularly about Jonas's aggression and didn't know that Jonas was becoming a source of great interest to a couple of the guards who screened all inmates' emails and listened to my anguished telephone calls with sympathy. The photos of Jonas and Maya were up in his cell (along with a photo of the behinds of Princess Letizia of Spain and Carla Bruni as they mounted a flight of stairs).

"We are the party of life," Conrad kept emailing me. "You can't let him be put down."

The absurdity—and danger—of my position came home to me one night when Jonas took up position on my bed and wouldn't let me get in.

"Off." He bared his teeth. "Off, Jonas," I repeated, thinking, I will not do this with a treat because that would be "validating" or "encouraging" his behaviour. I moved towards the bed, assuming my "I am in charge" look, and started to pull the covers back. He lunged at me full on.

Kuvaszok are pack dogs and, normally, if one attacks an animal or human, the others pile in. Not Maya. She could see what was happening as a frenzied Jonas sunk his teeth into my hand and then mauled my arm, and she was not going to join in. She remained quietly watching, an old soul at just under six months. Jonas was still holding back from a full attack, which would have killed or at least seriously injured me, but his barking and growls were ferocious, and I was bleeding from several deep bites. His mad look had taken over. I was scared stiff.

Fortunately, part of his plan was not to abandon my bed. I managed to extract myself and retreated into my dressing room and stood on the bed there. It was midnight. I called Patty, and without hesitation she arrived with Bill. I slipped out the back way. "He's in there," I said outside the bedroom door. The minute the door was opened, he stood up snarling on my bed like a kid saying, "I'm king of the castle."

Patty and Bill took him home. "He was like a lamb," she told me the next day. "Till next morning. He got into a spot near the door and when I went to reach for his collar, he bared every one of his teeth and I knew to go no further. That dog has no bite inhibition. Bill said just turn and walk slowly away."

As for the trainer with the alpha roll, Patty told me, "That's just preparing Jonas for the moment when he's big enough to get back at you for it." Bill thought there was a chance that had Jonas been put on a ranch somewhere by himself he would have been all right, doing his job, fighting wolves, coyotes, wildcats. Just a chance. Without the decency and skill of the Armfields, I really doubt I would be alive today.

"We both thought he should be put down," Patty said later. "But you had to reach that decision. You were in such a fix, so depressed, everything you had was in that dog, and we could see how much you loved him. We just had to help you survive. And when I saw how your hand and arm had already swollen up, I could only think to lecture you about getting medical help right away."

To add to the distress, the humidity and temperature in Palm Beach were as difficult for both dogs with their thick double coats as for me with my sun-averse dermatomyositis. Jonas developed terrible skin problems, with big open sores all over his stomach and genitalia. The dermatologist gave me topical ointment for him as well as oral antibiotics. He would lie on the floor while I tried to ease his pain. Gradually he was becoming easier to handle. "You can't understand it, my baby Jonas," I would say as I saw the pleading in his dark eyes. "Florida is no place for either of us."

Though I was trying hard to make it my place. Some Palm Beach friends, like Gay Gaines, the Fanjuls and Terry Kramer, were meticulous in keeping up their invitations when in town, but I had difficulty following through on their kindness. At night I just wanted to be home with the dogs, putting them in my minivan around eleven if a breeze was blowing and walking silently along Worth Avenue and into the Everglades Club parking lot—the lot where, like blacks and Jews, dogs were not allowed during the daytime but rarely spotted at night. These were the best times, the three of us sniffing the air silently and happily, me for the smells of oleander and night-blooming jasmine, Jonas and Maya for prey or food. Then I'd pass some place or item that sparked a memory of Conrad, and his absence came crashing in on me.

Now that Conrad's application for a hearing was in the hands of the Supreme Court, there was little to do but wait and see if the case was chosen. I decided to go back to Toronto and commute to Orlando for my visits with Conrad. What I had not counted on was the way in which Werner, our Toronto houseman, had brought up my three pulik. By default, they had become his dogs. They lived together in the staff apartment attached to our house, and a deep bond had formed between them. I couldn't tell Werner he had to isolate "his" dogs, and so they barked to their hearts' content in the kitchen while Werner replied non-stop in his guttural German. The noise was like a dog percussion section. Into this I brought Jonas and Maya. It was bound to lead to trouble.

I was beginning to suffer from a cardiac arrhythmia, probably aggravated by the stimulant drugs I had bullied doctors to give me in order to keep up my energy, now hampered by lack of sleep. "Your trigeminy isn't serious," said one of them, "but your last Holter had far too many extra beats. We must keep an eye on it. Avoid too much stress."

Lord, the stuff I was taking—I still do take. I was on dexmethylphenidate for energy, as well as antidepressants. Okay, to be accurate, I was living in the Valley of the Dolls, with clonazepam to put me down at night, various drugs to fight my increasing blood pressure, Focalin to get me up in the morning and see me through the evening, along with my usual codeine and caffeine. Of course it is weakness on my part to rely on such medications, but between routine tasks, the dogs, sorting out the various legal problems that were thrown almost daily at me and, most importantly, keeping my column at *Maclean's* going, at my age I simply couldn't manage nineteen- or twenty-hour days, every day, without help.

All my doctors knew all my meds—I figured my survival depended on being above board with everyone—and all of them disapproved of what I was taking but banded together to keep me going. I rather think the occasional letter they wrote updating one another after a routine examination from each would not be flattering to me, but they were bricks.

Conrad was somehow finishing his book on the events leading up to his conviction, entitled *A Matter of Principle*. He had written most of it at home in Palm Beach between the July sentencing and his March imprisonment. I was doing some rough editing and a tiny bit of rewriting, but now that he was in prison the procedure was clumsy. My emailed suggestions and corrections were hampered by the need to use code words for names or incidents that might cause trouble with the prison authorities. Naturally I got muddled up with the bloody names Conrad had chosen as pseudonyms. He liked using important battleships or some clever assonance and rhyme. I would visit him in prison and he would tell me the new code names for people, and since I wasn't allowed to take in a pencil and paper, by the time I got back to the car I had generally forgotten at least one of them.

I felt like a proper shit when I cut my visits a little, but travelling from Toronto to Coleman was a jerk backwards every time and mentally tricky. I'd fly down the night before and stay in an Orlando hotel so I could be up early to get to the prison. Thrown back to the parking lot, facing the humiliating and deadening routines in order to see him so I could fuss with the barely working microwave ovens in the hideous visitation room—inmates weren't allowed to touch the vending machines or microwaves used to heat up the god-awful chicken wings—threw me off the other world I was trying to construct.

True, my heart actually skipped—normally, that is, not from trigeminy—each time I saw him again, but I couldn't embrace him except for a second or so and the pain of leaving him was even worse than before. "God, Conrad," I would say, and the pain would pass silently between us. The schedule caught up with me and one time I passed out cold on the plane. I've never been carried off a plane in a stretcher before, and while admittedly it's a hell of a comfy way to avoid the on-board luggage trek, I could hear the muttered indignation of passengers who had to wait for me. The medical consensus was that I had to "pace myself," but that wasn't so easy. My attempt led to the catastrophe.

Jonas was more and more on edge, alarmed by the noise of barking and the rather loud voice of Werner. He was biting me much less, but deeper because his teeth were just so damn big. I'd let him run loose in the snow on our fully fenced property as often as possible after staff had left, which he loved. He could look after himself in the dark, although getting him in could sometimes be difficult. But when my heartbeat got too irregular and I felt light-headed, I'd "pace myself" and lie down, leaving Jonas alone outdoors.

"*Aber noch*, Jonas is outside," said Werner one evening as I went to lie down when my breathing was a bit awkward. "I gave him his baked salmon dinner and then he went outside." Werner is a man of routine and any deviation upset him.

"It's all right, Werner. Let him be. He can come in later." I lay on the bed in the guest room trying to count my heartbeats, feeling weak. I could hear Werner's voice shouting into the darkness repeatedly, "Jonas, Jonas. *Kommen Sie jetzt hier.*" I wondered why he was using formal German with a dog. The refrain went on and on. I got up. It was damn cold outside and I could see very little except Werner, illuminated by the lamp over the kitchen door. He was standing at the edge of the snow-covered lawn, wearing his new coat, the big padded one I had bought him the day before. I walked out to see if I could get him to stop calling. "Werner, let him be. Go home. I can manage and Jonas is perfectly all right outside."

"He has something in his mouth. Something dead."

"All for the good. It will keep him occupied."

"Jonas! *Komm hier.*" He started walking towards Jonas.

And Jonas came. Like a bolt out of the darkness at top speed, flinging himself straight at Werner's back, knocking him down to the ground and mauling him. Werner was face down on the snow with his arms protecting his head as much as he could. Jonas was pulling him and biting. He would stop, circle and go in for another attack. I tried to pull him off and he gave me a quick bite and returned to the job at hand, 140-plus pounds of four-legged frenzy. I ran inside, called 911 and went back out with a garden spade. I knew I would have to knock the dog unconscious. Every time Jonas stopped to circle, I yelled, "Werner, crawl, crawl to the kitchen!" But Werner wasn't moving. Then suddenly, as I went in with the spade, Jonas stopped.

He had spent more than five minutes in a deranged attack and now it was over. Werner was crawling to the house and Jonas was presenting me with the frozen half of a squirrel he had dropped on the ground next to Werner. He looked up at me pleadingly.

"It's no good," I said, as much to myself as to him. "Jonas, it's over." I could barely breathe. Jonas licked my hand and went through the dog door into the kitchen. Werner was sitting bent over in a chair, his coat torn and his shirt underneath shredded. I'm not sure whether it was sixteen or eighteen bites. He was in relatively better shape than I had expected, but his back and arms were a welter of bites. Jonas put his head in Werner's lap.

The police arrived and Jonas went out to greet them at the gates. One look at him and they called animal control. I watched as Jonas, now defeated and dejected, head down, proud white furry tail hanging limp between his legs, the catch pole's cable loop pulled securely around his neck, went quietly up the ramp and through the double doors of the animal control vehicle. I knew I had to attend to Werner, but all I could think was, What will they do to my dog?

Medics were taking Werner's blood pressure and attending to his wounds. "You must tell them exactly what happened yourself, Werner," I said, "and make a formal complaint." I didn't even notice the bite I had. This poor old man was not in shock but close to it. All that saved him from a severed artery or disfigurement were his own smarts, staying face down, and that brand-new heavy coat with the theoretically indestructible material.

And now Jonas was gone and I thought my heart would break.

Next day, Saturday, I tried to find out where Jonas was. Recording machines told me I would have to wait until Monday. I knew Jonas couldn't wait two days alone and penned up. I called my vet, John Reeve-Newson. He located him and got agreement for Jonas to stay at his clinic for the mandatory ten-day period while he was monitored for rabies. I said I would bring him in.

At animal control, I signed the papers. "He's in there," said the apprehensive desk clerk. Inside, in a windowless small room, shut up in a wire locker, was a silent Jonas. There were no other animals. There was nothing but an empty bowl next to him. The only sound was the air coming through the vents.

I couldn't blame them. From their point of view, they had a wolf in custody. I took out his leash and led Jonas out. We drove to the vet's, Jonas licking my face and neck, panting, making a sound like mewing. His night had clearly been as bad as mine. Reeve-Newson had a place ready for him, the size of a large shower stall and with other animals within hearing but not irritating to him. "We can handle him," said John, and I left quickly. I didn't dare look back— like my husband, I suppose, when he went into prison.

Next, an experienced "anger management" dog trainer, who had seen Jonas before the attack, came to see if the attacks could be induced by a challenge, which would determine whether they could be controlled or whether they really were irrational. I sat in the vet's waiting room and watched Jonas being fitted with a muzzle and an electric collar. He was about to be tortured to see his response.

A muzzled Jonas paced around the waiting area while the trainer administered shocks to him at increasingly higher voltages. Zzzz, and Jonas would quiver. He would try to come over to me, but the trainer held him back. He didn't attack, though clearly the shocks were causing him pain and stress. "That's weird," said the anger management man. "But he'll attack. I can get him to." Zzzz—a stronger shock. Jonas's eyes were blinking and confused. Finally, the voltage was sufficiently high that he jumped up at the stranger that was clearly the source of this pain. "That's encouraging," said the anger management chap. "It's a rational response that we can train."

"Stop this," I said. "It's no solution."

A day or two later, John Reeve-Newson told me how calmly Jonas was behaving and how he was getting along so well with Adam, the technician who was taking him out for walks and feeding him. Adam was an excellent technician, a tall man inches over six foot, confident with dogs. Then, the telephone call. Jonas unexpectedly attacked Adam. Adam was terrorized and trapped behind a door as Jonas pounded and snarled in one of his frenzies. "I'm afraid there is something wrong with the wiring of that dog," said my vet. "You can't fix it."

There was nowhere left I could responsibly go. The Ice Man Cometh. It had to be. "Give him the best meal he has ever had. Roast chicken is his favourite, and lace it with the sedation before you put the needle in. Make him comfortable." I couldn't go down. Jonas was just over two years old. Not even a fully mature Kuvasz.

On January 29, 2010, in the middle of the afternoon, the email arrived. "Dear Mrs. Black: Jonas left us peacefully and gracefully this afternoon. He was not at all anxious or nervous. Adam held his head in his lap and he seemed at ease. Your decision, painful as it was, was a wise and responsible one. Our thoughts are with you in this difficult time. John, Adam, Eric, Tara and all the staff at The Animal Clinic."

At Coleman, one of the sympathetic guards who had followed this saga in my emails went personally to tell Conrad of Jonas's death.

My arms hadn't cradled him. Where was that care I promised you, my little one?

CHAPTER TWENTY-EIGHT

Déjà Vu Re-run

Pull yourself together, woman, I thought. Remember you are em–
powered, whatever the hell that means. I played videos of Last Night
of the Proms endlessly, along with lots of "Land of Hope and Glory."
After all, I was simply blue, having ordered the murder of my dog.

I tried an unusual approach—for me. Good things, I reminded
myself constantly, were on the horizon, and I knew there was a
chance of a breakthrough at the Supreme Court with Miguel. I tried
a shot of vodka and then one night I actually sipped a few mouthfuls
of Scotch—it had worked for Margaret Thatcher—but God almighty,
how on earth does anyone swallow such foul-tasting stuff?

After Jonas died I didn't just slow down; I turned into a weeping
willow without its graceful beauty. I was boringly awful. I cried and
cried and cried. The helpless, beseeching eyes of Jonas looking for
a way out of his fear haunted everything I did. I had failed, and in my
failure a life had been taken.

Quadruped Maya was a wreck too. On the ravine walks she
loved, she'd stop and just lie down. She was off her food and sat at
the dog door, waiting for Jonas to come in and bully her. Maya wasn't
quite Odysseus's abandoned dog, Argos, waiting years among the
dung, or Hachiko the Akita waiting nine years at the Shibuya train
station for his deceased owner, but she did a pretty good imitation.
Nothing was going to quickly eradicate the memory of the dog that
had been her alpha companion since she'd arrived.

Scientists say that wonderful stare into each other's eyes between dog and owner can be measured in increased amounts of oxytocin-mediated eye-gaze bonding in both human and canine—oxytocin being a hormone associated with trust and maternal bonding. Well, that's terrific as far as it goes, but my view is that it's a ruse to get more cheddar. At night Maya lay on the bed with me, her head on my chest and her eyes searching my face. Even her interest in cheddar, my measuring rod for all canine situations, was minimal. She turned her head away. After three months of life with a four-legged Sarah Bernhardt, I gave in.

By March we had little puppy named Arpad from Glacier Creek Kuvasz. Arpad was the Cary Grant of Kuvaszok, devilishly handsome, unruffled by the sixteen-hour flight from Helena, Montana, with a change of planes and a stopover at Salt Lake City. He came out of his travel crate at Fort Lauderdale cargo bubbling with enthusiasm.

Walking Arpad was hazardous, not because of any aggression by him, but because he was just so damned gorgeous that everywhere he went he created a small mob scene. With Maya, there too I had the feeling of being one of those terribly glamorous divas in an Erté print walking two borzois. I even started to wash my hair more often and wear cleaner jeans, tart myself up a bit, because we were a threesome now and I had to live up to them.

I had not attended a Palm Beach dinner party since I had disgraced myself by walking Jonas down the beach from our house to the ocean frontage of Terry Kramer's huge mansion. On arrival, I must have looked like a piece of flotsam drifting in from Haiti. I went up to her front door, which actually was on the side, it being so grand a house that it had sufficient property to allow a winding driveway all around, while the front was a vast stone patio area overlooking the terraced gardens. I was all excited to show her Jonas. After all, Terry had a dog. A Chihuahua or a shih tzu, something that sat on a slipper cushion, so in Palm Beach terms she was a "dog person."

"Barbara," said Terry, who had been called to the door by an agitated houseman. "You walked here all the way with *that*?" as if I had just broken every rule of locomotion and sanity. My reception was pretty courteous when you consider how we looked: Jonas, huge and menacing, coat matted with sand and seaweed, and me with dirt up to my ankles, all ready to track into Terry's triple-height lobby with its marble floors and the chandelier that came down to be cleaned by the white-gloved staff when you pressed a button. Turning up without an advance telephone call is rude, but I was thinking the way I had in an earlier life: this was just a beach walk that happened to pass a friend's house. But once you left the beach and hopped over the low wall that marked the beginning of the paving to her porte cochère, it was a Palm Beach mansion, which is a whole other world. (And if you want it, at the time Terry was asking US$135 million for it, having turned down a $95-million offer. Sadly, she died in 2018, before the house was sold.) Terry tried hard to smile but it didn't work and sort of looped her face sideways. "You must be tired," she said. "Let me get you a driver home."

The Supreme Court had agreed in May 2009 to hear Conrad's case, and that announcement opened up a Niagara Falls of speculation. Miguel invited me to Miami for a celebratory lunch with him and his wife. The word *celebratory* had dropped into a bottomless well in my vocab, and when his email containing the word came up on my screen, for a moment it looked like something in Latin. My regular driver was unavailable and so I used a driver Domenico had recommended. He was, Domenico said, highly experienced and needed the work. I could see why. He was partially blind.

"That's the exit," I said as we passed it on U.S. Route 1. "Oh dear," replied the nice blind driver, and put the car into reverse on the five-lane highway (counting exit and entry lanes at that point), which was a judgment of daring even with twenty-twenty vision. I gave Miguel a lift back to his hotel after lunch, and our Supreme Court lawyer became extremely anxious as we drove through heavy traffic on a one-way street the wrong way. "I am doing my best for you," he said, a little agitated, as if I were a mobster teaching him a lesson.

For the Supreme Court hearing, I must have chosen my low-key outfit very well because according to *The Guardian* I wasn't there. I could see Judge Amy St. Eve looking very serious, as well she might, since she was about to receive one huge rap on the knuckles. Apparently, the hearing was very good for us because all the justices, including Ruth Bader Ginsburg, whom I had not previously regarded as a riotously fun judge, were taking turns to top each other by constructing amusing anomalies in the statute that convicted Conrad. They seemed to think every one of them could easily be charged under it as it stood. "Eighty or 100 million people," guesstimated Justice Stephen Breyer. That perked me up, and I wondered if I could start civil suits against a whole slew of judges. All the same, I was suspicious of where all this was going. I'd watched lawyers exchanging jollies for too long to trust any of it.

"We have a chance," I told Conrad, not wanting to get too optimistic. The court's decisions come out in text live online as they are read, and Miguel and I tuned in from April 15 on. As it was, our decision was the very last one, on June 24. "Here it comes," I said.

"Aah," said Miguel in a rather despondent tone as the words crossed the screen. I, on the other hand, thought it looked pretty good. All counts vacated and the case remanded back to the Seventh Circuit Court of Appeals to consider the error of their ways, with a thumping denouncement of Posner by Bader Ginsburg for "judicial invention" a.k.a. making up law. The *Wall Street Journal* actually produced an editorial apologizing for not paying attention to his case and placed it at the head of the page, titling it "Conrad Black's Revenge."

"I had hoped," said Miguel, "for all counts to be overturned, and then the prosecution would have to decide whether they would retry Conrad. They would know they had very little chance of getting any conviction. Going back to Posner is not ideal." The decision meant it wasn't over, and I was going to have to face another decade (I figured) of Conrad bravely and fiercely fighting for his total innocence while I fought for my teeth and hair.

I went back to Toronto and there, one day in July, while sweating in front of my desk fan and contemplating our broken-down air conditioning, across the screen came all sorts of congratulatory emails.

The evil Judge Posner had granted bail to Conrad, terms to be set by his stooge, Judge Amy St. Eve.

An elated Conrad telephoned and asked me to arrange standby extra bail money for "tomorrow in Chicago" at a hearing to determine his release conditions. "Of course, darling," I said, when actually I felt like saying, "Shove it. I've made just about enough phone calls about money." I gave it about five minutes' thought and called Roger Hertog in New York City, an old friend of Conrad's. Off he went to Chicago—quite amazingly—where Judge Amy decided the extra bail. Conrad called me a day later to arrange a car for him. "I'll put him on standby," I said, figuring "immediate release" in Bureau of Prisons terms meant three or four days.

I was still wallowing in perspiration at my desk next day when I was informed by email that Conrad was on TV. Well, *he* wasn't, but our driver was right there, ruddy well mid-screen in his car at the Coleman entrance alongside scads of cameras and journalists. St. Eve had extended Conrad's leash to a limited area of Florida, and required him to report weekly to a bail officer, for only an extra $2 mill. There'd be no going home to Canada. I couldn't get a commercial flight that day, but through friends I found a hospital plane that wasn't being used. "It's only got one seat," said Skyservice's blessed Sid McMurray, "and it's not very comfortable, but I'll just charge you the fuel. You'll get there late but tonight."

On the plane I started having these small attacks of anxiety. For the past two and a half years all my husband had seen of me was the few hours when I dolled myself up with the deliberation of a drag queen. For seven years before that, we had barely noticed each other except in bleary despair. Now we would be in that ghastly unforgiving permanent Florida sun in July, and there I would be: The Wife. Me, after all the shrapnel.

Stupidly, I didn't think the obvious, that Conrad too would have changed: all that rotten prison food, extra weight, no exercise, no sunlight and the worry of it all. It's hard to convey how artificial prison visits are—you don't actually see one another in any normal way. He himself had gone through phases of looking absolutely ghastly, but curiously—and bloody infuriatingly—once the show got on the road with the trial, he had almost seemed to blossom. Anyway, men just have so much more self-confidence; even nude they all bounce around as if they were every one an Adonis.

It was about midnight when I finally reached Palm Beach. I walked through the house towards Conrad's library and I could see the outline of his shoulders on the terrace, backlit by the patio lights. There was my husband. Free.

We had both changed. He was rougher in manners and responses. Not bad-tempered, not changed in vocabulary patterns, but sometimes curt in his responses, withdrawn. Words were missing. No "please," no "thank you," although sometimes "thanks" was said quickly. His smile was rarer. He moved differently, without enthusiasm. His eyes were cold, on the lookout. He wanted as much silence as possible at first, especially in our house—he had lived among such bedlam and noise for the last few years in prison. "You don't know," he would say, "what it is to live in twenty-four hours of screaming and clanging, non-stop. Never any quiet." There was no ambiguity in his love and warmth. He wanted to be with me, but he wasn't quite certain at first how we had been.

In prison, his bed had been simply a metal slab with a very thin mattress over it and a pillow so flat he doubled it over. After a while he paid an inmate to sew another one inside. That explained the coded emails to send "a book" or "three books"—meaning twenty-dollar bills—to various Hispanic names and addresses all over the U.S. with thank-you cards signed by "Doris" or "Glenda" in case the mail was intercepted: inmates (illegally) earning money for their families stranded outside, by cooking, sewing or taking on some service inside. Now Conrad was home, sleeping on the thick horsehair-stuffed mattress plus separate spring, with the four heavy pillows he needed. At first he would fall into bed as if the linens and pillows were going to be taken from him. Just grab them. "Conrad, you're home, it's all right," I would say, thinking he was joking.

In fact, he was like a man back from time spent in a combat zone.

He had nightmares of prison. All that time in Coleman he had been totally cool. Never complained. Never played up to the prison authorities. And now he was out and faced with nothing but more problems of his own. And temporarily a bit of a misfit.

In prison, where everyone was so crowded, each inmate devised ways to create a tiny perimeter of their own, decorated with their fantasies. That perimeter was the lifeline to sanity—or insanity when pulled too tight. A religious cellmate of Conrad's considered the space around his Bible on the locker top—normally used to sit on—to be sacred. So you never sat down there, just stood. One fairly senior Boston Mafioso whose son had been murdered on the outside by Whitey Bulger (himself later murdered in prison) had plans for a new type of children's skipping rope. Another had plans to create a fleet of vans to compete with Brink's when he got out, and had drawn up blueprints. "What do you think of modifying the swing angle of the back doors?" he would ask Conrad.

As much as he could, Conrad had kept level. He was a celebrity when he went in, and inmates respected him for "fighting the system" and not making a plea bargain. Conrad cheerfully cleaned out the lavatory stalls and told the guards brought to view the millionaire on his knees scrubbing them that he found the work "morally uplifting." He was writing three columns a week for publication either online or in print, composed by hand in his cell and then typed into the computer when he could grab one—four computers, shared by 140 men, with a forty-minute time limit. Plus he was finishing *A Matter of Principle*— also by hand and then typed into the computer, with no Google or other bells and whistles. For those of us who take a week to do one bloody column, it was extremely annoying, and made more so because I had to congratulate him on this achievement rather than swear.

Conrad's own lifeline fantasy, though, was hard for me to swallow. "Once I'm out," he would say, "I'll make us the money back quickly. Canada is a good place to make money, and I'm still a good financier. You'll see, our life will resume. We won't have the same access as a big media owner, but we'll have a better time financially. I promised you happiness and I'm going to give you that."

He had no idea of the Hydra he would be forced to slay so many times over. I didn't dare ask him how much we owed.

Christmas 2010 had the creepy feeling of life in a space capsule. We'd been in this fight for over seven years, and time was catching up to both of us. If I was trying to stave off aging; Conrad was trying to stave off reality. We were both equally unsuccessful. Conrad insisted on putting up any Christmas cards that came. And we got quite a few, although their numbers had been diminishing year by year.

"How can people do it?" Conrad would ask with what sounded like genuine astonishment. "Do they put a line through our names on some list as if we were dead? Do they say to one another after thirty years, 'Let's not send the Blacks a card this year?'" I found the question quite interesting. I'd noticed fewer cards came from mutual Canadian friends but hadn't given that excision much thought. Now it conjured up vivid pictures of the whey-faced ones I knew with matching flat voices doing just that. Most Brits continued sending cards.

"Look," I said in my best Flo Nightingale voice, "we're together. And you can go to Midnight Mass." Which he did. But notwithstanding his Lord's happy birthday, Christmas Day turned into hell when Quadruped Maya's breathing sounded as if she had tissue paper in her lungs.

A week earlier, Joaquin Garcia, an absolutely brilliant hands-on dog person in West Palm Beach, had thought a small bulla, or blister, in the lung's edge had spontaneously punctured, but her lung hadn't collapsed so he counselled leaving it alone to see if it would heal with rest. "These things often do," he said before leaving for his holidays. But now she was in bad shape.

I quickly found a twenty-four-hour emergency veterinary hospital outside West Palm Beach. After a brief examination, I was told one lung had collapsed completely and the other was on the verge. "We have to put in a breathing tube," said the anxious vet, who looked like he might need one himself to do that. I began calling up the people in Palm Beach I felt I could rely on.

Top of the animal lovers list were Emilia Fanjul and equestrienne

Arriana Boardman. Emilia managed, God knows how on Boxing Day afternoon, to rustle up the CEO of the Animal Medical Center in New York, and through her got the names of surgeons at the Small Animal Hospital at the University of Florida in Gainesville.

By January 2 the emergency vet was splattered on the ceiling. "We took out nine litres of air, but it just fills up again. In the air tube and out," he said hysterically. "She has bilateral pneumonia and large pulmonary bullae and needs a CT scan but I can't get one for at least twenty-four hours." Maya was lying quietly with an oxygen cage around her head. She focused her eyes on me and tried to reach out but the paw fell limp.

Gary Searles, who was president of the My Chauffeur company in Palm Beach and who I'd come to know whenever he did the Coleman run with me, didn't hesitate, and off we went in the small hours on the four-and-a-half hour drive to Gainesville. "With her temperature and condition she won't live through the journey," the emergency vet had said as I signed release papers. I lay in the back of our van with two-and-half-year-old Maya, listening to her laboured breathing, occasionally looking into her patient wide-open eyes, not knowing which of us was trying to calm the other.

The Gainesville Small Animal Hospital was like a studio set for a Disney film. In its vast atrium, a large St. Bernard was being wheeled with IVs attached to his stainless steel trolley and a nurse bending over him. I half expected the nurse to be a Great Dane in uniform. Maya disappeared even before I had taken out my Amex card. "She needs a CT scan right away and breathing assistance," said someone to me as I staggered to a chair.

The team came to me after the scan. "It's bad. We think the only way to save her is surgery. But we can't say she'll survive it. And there will be a strong chance of bone cancer later in her life from opening up her sternum." I nodded catatonically. They were obviously used to owners looking like hell, tears running off the ends of their (remodelled) noses. "Operate," I said. And then I walked out to the parking lot. Maya was on a table with a saw splitting her breastbone to get at the lungs.

Maya was in surgery for over five hours. Afterwards, I asked if Maya had been co-operative. "A dream," said the surgeon's assistant. "Never gave us a moment's difficulty. Still, we're used to trouble. Last week we had a full-grown Bengal tiger under anaesthetic on the table and in the middle of surgery it gave a groan. Four assistants sprung up simultaneously flourishing hypodermics."

Selling Palm Beach was now a priority. If Conrad didn't get a full acquittal from Posner, he'd be jailed again or deported. Miraculously, out of the blue, an email arrived from a determined buyer in the U.K. We didn't actually know the buyer, but his name had terrific plonk: "Alexander Chichester," said Conrad to me.

I had known Lady Chichester, wife of the Earl of Chichester, when I was on a very junior committee of the Royal Opera House. She was a delightful woman. I immediately googled Alexander. When he didn't turn up there, I went to *Debrett's*. There didn't seem to be an extant Alexander Chichester—the last one had died in 1881—but the family was extensive.

"Barbara has some familiarity with the family," Conrad told our real estate agent. Alexander was dead keen and on the telephone to Conrad constantly. "He has a speech hesitation," he told me. "I gather from Parkinson's."

"This is marvellous," said the agent.

"But he hasn't seen the property," I said.

"He has the plans and photos," she replied.

Alexander emailed that agreed-to funds were being wired as a deposit. "The funds have certainly left my account," he wrote. "When I spoke to Geneva earlier they told me that the latest SWIFT transfer would arrive is late Friday but likely to be sooner." *Geneva* and *SWIFT* was a melodic combination, conjuring up an unsmiling Swiss typing codes to send us loads of money.

"He will be here next Monday," said our agent, her blonde bouffant stiff with lacquered excitement. On the Monday she announced, "He's checked into the Four Seasons Hotel." This was beginning to sound like a treasure hunt. He checked in, he checked out, and no one, not even the hotel staff, ever saw him. It had all the trappings of the tabloids or *Private Eye*—leaving suet pudding in my stomach.

By April 2011 we found a purchaser through top agent Lawrence Moens. And, once sold, with my usual perversity I mourned the sale. My views on Palm Beach hadn't changed, but I loved that house. The sea churning up on windy days, lawns that sloped down to the inland waterway with iguanas in a stately march along the edge, the birds coming home to the mangoes and so on. I could always do lyrical about yesterday, even when everything grated in the moment. One of my late goals in life is to reverse that syndrome, to wax poetical about the now and deride what is lost.

The new owners arrived with a tall, imperious assistant who flounced about dismissing any suggestion that they keep anything of our decor. Fair enough. One always wants to make a house one's own. I wanted to tell him, Look, it's as easy to politely dismiss another's taste as to dish it. He seemed to feel his contempt made him more credible in his employers' eyes. Domenico took a very dim view of him. "He doesn't understand the point of a silver closet," he said.

My tower workroom had a custom carpet of light blue I designed, loved and was definitely taking. The carpet had the names of all the writers I revered in what looked like dark blue ink handwriting. But there he was—Kissinger. How the hell would I eradicate his name? Bleach would ruin the wool. I could try to put a piece of furniture over it, but the placing, between Milton, Faludy and Balzac, was awkward. Then I thought, Well, I could just do a big blue blot. After all, there were fake ink blots in the design, though it would have to be a really huge blot for a nine-letter name.

We had a sad goodbye, my bedroom fabric and I: the custom French quilted silk of a delicate violet and green with a hand-embroidered eighteenth-century trellis pattern covered the walls and made up the bed hangings and the curtains, bringing the gardens into the room. The frightful flouncer didn't want it, but he wouldn't let his client give or sell it to me. I wanted to apologize to the fabric, so exquisite, so many hours in the making: "You're just going to a dust heap somewhere or a barrel of ends because the purchasers don't understand your wonder but won't allow you to continue existing with me." But there it was. You sell, you take the money and the consequences.

With Toronto out of bounds, Conrad got permission to move into a small apartment in the Mark Hotel in New York City. The hotel's website said the rooms had been "re-imagined" by Jacques Grange in 2009, but I think he forgot this particular suite. Meanwhile, I was going back to Toronto to hire a driver/security man to live in Werner's house, Werner having finally retired and resettled in Bali.

In Toronto, on the back terrace of the house, I watched the woodpeckers hard at work on the pines. Another summer—like tree trunks, we could count the rings in our lives by their misfortunes. Summer of 2003, the mysteriously futile search for refinancing of Hollinger. Summer of 2004, *The Telegraph* sold. Summer of 2005, I had packed up our house in London and said goodbye to my life there, then packed up our apartment in New York and watched the U.S. government seize the proceeds. Summer of 2006 was highlighted by the serving of the Mareva injunction. Summer of 2007 we spent in Chicago awaiting Conrad's sentencing. Summer of 2008, Judge Posner turned down our appeal of the trial verdicts. Summer of 2009, I was scrambling to find a lawyer and money for the appeal to the Supreme Court.

That's when it happened. I think it was late summer 2009, but to be honest the dates get muddled in my head and this one I have no record of for reasons that will become apparent.

The voice on the telephone was that of a very famous Canadian industrialist. I knew him, though not as well as Conrad did. "Barbara, I would like to give you five million dollars," said the man, and it wasn't a television reality show or Alexander Chichester.

"I'm sorry?"

"We could start with a million or so and see how it goes. But I want you to have it."

"A loan? I don't know when I could repay it."

"No. An outright gift. To you."

"That would be wonderful," I said rather weakly, "and would help tremendously with legal retainers, which the Mareva makes awkward."

"No, this is not for Conrad or for legal fees. This is yours. You have no company pension, no special medical insurance. What if you are ill? You are older than Conrad and who knows how his troubles will work out. But there is one condition. No one must ever know. You must not use my name, and this will be dealt with between your lawyer and mine."

So I couldn't thank him, not even when we later visited him and his family, because they were not to know. His lawyer, who had for many years managed all personal affairs for him, thoroughly disapproved of this, prevaricated and groaned, and actually I understood his reluctance. Why should the family be kept ignorant of this? I supposed they shared a view that I was a bit of a worthless snip. So the lawyer put obstacles in the way of it happening. One can't possibly complain to a man who is himself very unwell and the author of such generosity that his lawyer is being a little on the swinish side. After a year of negotiations, a million dollars arrived and was put in a trust. But about two years later, when Conrad was in an utterly desperate state, searching for liquid funds, I used it to pay some of our bills. After all, my life was tied to his, and my health would not have benefited from his having a stroke.

My benefactor is dead now and I will never be able to tell him or his family what a marvellous thing he did and how in all the years of my life it will remain the purest act of kindness and charity I have ever known. They will, I think, recognize their father in this and I hope will let me thank them without naming names.

My grim seventieth birthday had loomed while Conrad was still in Florida with me, so I'd made my exciting announcement. "We're going to Long Beach," I told him. "My birthday present to us."

"Why?" Conrad did not see the immediate charm of Long Beach, apart from its being home to the *Queen Mary*.

"Because there will be 3,233 purebred dogs there," which seemed self-explanatory to me. The American Kennel Club Eukanuba National Championships were being held there, and having looked first for a Wagner *Ring* cycle to attend and not finding one, this was the second-best thing, and a very close second. But I went alone. Promises to give me happiness did not cover the palaver of getting permission from his bail officer to travel to Long Beach, which was, after all, close to the carefree freedom of Tijuana where Conrad could discuss FDR with migrants.

The official hotel of the show was the Hyatt Regency Long Beach, right by the convention centre, and the minute I crossed the lobby— together with a giant schnauzer, two pugs and a wonderful little Chinese crested something, walking in that way show dogs do with their heads held high, their coats gleaming and their eyes sparkling with the knowledge and confidence that they are eliciting waves of admiration—I thought I had landed in the closest thing to heaven on earth. After I unpacked, I took the large elevator down twelve floors with twelve paws: an Irish wolfhound, a dachshund and, oh God they are so beautiful, in one corner shielded by its handler, a Tibetan terrier.

For once the doormen were incredibly polite to this prancing clientele, opening the door for dogs who sported far more luggage than their owners, dutifully lugging favourite bedding, throws, grooming tools and crates, rather like Britney Spears bringing her own pillows and hot rollers. Being alone is a relative thing when you are in the world of dog shows, and at the Meet the Breed booths I got down on the floor to chat with the Plott hound about the shortage of wild boars and tried to give solace to the American Staffordshire terrier over human racism with breed-specific legislation aimed at them. I would call Conrad at night and he would listen patiently to my excited canine prattle. To use the popular phrase attributed to them, I feel absolute unconditional love for all dogs, purebred or mix, and would adopt a dozen if I could.

There was a final round of appeals, a final session with the bespectacled little prick, Judge Posner. God, I thought, how he whines and gets away with doing no homework so his prejudices can't be derailed by fact. I wondered if he had been the cherished little genius of proud Jewish parents who never gave him the whacking he deserved but merely stood back in awe at his school marks. He could certainly use a good caning now. Reluctantly, he dropped two of the fraud charges but hung on to the last financial charge—relating to a $285,000 payment wired to Toronto that Chicago counsel Mark Kipnis had forgotten to get Conrad's signature on, a failing already dismissed by Judge St. Eve, who had declared it a clerical error when she'd acquitted Kipnis. Her temporary flash of common sense did not extend to Conrad. But we were toast. Posner hung on to vainglorious Colin Campbell's little flash of Hollywood North, leaving the obstruction of justice charge in place.

Over sixty inmates and correctional officers had written to Sheila Lally, the court's advisor on sentencing, citing the excellent work Conrad had done in prison as a tutor. This infuriated the prosecution, and although Eric Sussman had left the U.S. Attorney's Office several years earlier, his malformed sense of justice lived on in the remaining members of his team. Sussman himself couldn't resist showing up for the re-sentencing, lurking in the back row of the courtroom and then giving "stand-up" interviews to the press later. Now his fellow prosecutors conjured up statements from two guards— female of course—claiming Conrad did no work at all while in Coleman. Given that Sheila Lally had investigated Conrad's prison record, citing his tutoring in her justification for the recommendation of no need for more prison time, this was a broad jump even for U.S. prosecutors. Still, worth a try I suppose.

"Where are these guards?" Miguel Estrada demanded. "Where are their affidavits? We must have them in court to examine."

The spectre of perjury charges suddenly loomed over the prosecution, who hurriedly withdrew the "evidence" of the female guards and the letter now dematerialized in front of us. Judge St. Eve, naturally, saved the day by saying the women's statements would be disregarded. This was apiece with her general attitude to any prosecutorial misconduct, of which there were, to put it generously, a number of instances.

There was no way to stop Conrad now. I knew he would be stupendously good but even so there are some things in life that give you a feeling of maggots crawling under your skin. He had the right to address the court before re-sentencing. And he was stupendous—flawless and extemporaneous for about twenty minutes with not a single stutter or pause. Sheer guts and conviction and I hated it. I hated it on his behalf because it was too good for the smug press listening, mocking what they could not understand or match. I hated it because he was baring his soul, every nerve laid out in that courtroom: "I never ask for mercy," he said, and it was the Gettysburg Address of court speeches.

Once over, Judge Amy was radiant and trilling on her little perch. I thought she was going to stretch her arms and let her robed self levitate like a flying nun. She had read of Conrad's work in the prison with students and told him he had "become a better person through this experience." She herself clearly had not or she would have known that he was exactly the same decent person she sentenced to seventy-eight months in prison. She was bathing in an aura of self-congratulation at having been the instigator of this miracle of rehabilitation. I could have socked her.

The whole thing was a stitch-up now. In order to get Conrad back into prison, Judge Amy needed a certain number of points on her sentencing abacus. The crimes themselves couldn't do it so she deus ex machina added points for the "complexity of the scheme" that no longer existed. Re-sentencing for forty-two months. I fainted. Plonk. Bang onto the courtroom bench.

I hadn't realized that the forty-two months included time served; she was reducing the sentence by three years and Conrad would actually serve only seven or eight months more. Still, Conrad's old fear that Posner only gave him bail in order to enjoy sending him back to prison was realized. And we had spent over another year in semi-freedom while the appeals process wound its way along. More time slipping away in half-lives bereft of joy.

One more slimy card had to be played. The two female guards whose letter had been consigned to the dustbin now objected to Conrad's return to FCI Coleman on grounds that his presence would be a danger to them. He was re-assigned to FCI Miami, a really beastly place. The night before self-surrender we stayed at Miami's Mandarin Oriental. Right, I thought, as we awoke and stood silently together on the balcony overlooking the beaming water that surrounds the hotel, the morning sunlight bright and clear—this is where once more I do our Juliet scene, or is it the preparation for the tomb number. Christ, was this life ever going to sort out?

FCI Miami was smaller than the huge complex of Coleman and considerably more uncomfortable. In a little local show of one-upmanship, we were forced to wait outside on the doorstep after knocking for entrance. We could say nothing to one another as we waited; already the gloom of what lay ahead enveloped us both. The sun lost its gold. When, finally, the door opened, I was pushed back. "The lady, she stays out," said the guard with a definite lack of decent teatime manners.

FCI Miami was originally a medium-security prison that now housed low-security inmates, but the cells had not been changed. The steel doors were locked at 10 p.m., and overcrowding meant three people were in a cell built for two and sharing an open toilet. The horror of being locked up with the proverbial rotten-apple guard trying to get a "shot" on him—citing him for a disciplinary action that might have him thrown into solitary—was always there.

You know, I never asked myself, "What if I had not married Conrad?" But I did do another "what if?" quite a lot. What if this prosecution had not happened? Would I have continued the mindless carnival of Park Avenue? Would I ever have had the character, gumption or—God, I don't know what you call it—the common sense, perhaps, to drop the great satisfaction of achieving status in Bill Cunningham's "On the Street" and "Evening Hours" photos for the *New York Times*, in exchange for a life with real friends I had in New York City: the Podhoretzes, Neal Kozodoy or those who, like Beatrice Stern, Georgette Mosbacher and Lauren Veronis, were of society but not infected by it? Would I have stopped grinding out columns and gone back to the work I had done a dozen years before marrying Conrad—writing books? Conrad would have encouraged me.

Perhaps the gods did the right thing in throwing me off the society bus. Unfortunately, unlike Pamela Winefred Paget, I did not land

on my feet. The jolt brought with it the realization of a terrible waste
of time: for me it was just as wasteful fighting the U.S. justice system
as it was spending time celebrating birthdays on Fifth and Park
avenues together with that set's "cultural" pursuits—and my work
jammed in between. I couldn't share my husband's singular view that
his fight was "noble." *He* was noble, not the fight. But what did it
matter? We had no choice: either way, *temps perdu*. Here we were, and
there was no time left to start over again.

Weeks before our marriage, Conrad took me to a *Telegraph* summer party, 1992. (Courtesy of the author)

Just married to Conrad, outside Kensington and Chelsea Register Office, July 1992. (Barry Swaebe)

Post-wedding dinner at Annabel's, London, reading hilarious *Daily Telegraph* mock-up of wedding by Editor Max Hastings. Guests left to right: Lady (Margaret) Thatcher, Conrad, Sarah, Duchess of York, Lord (George) Weidenfeld, good friend Tessa Keswick, and former U.S. Assistant Defense Secretary Richard Perle. (Courtesy of the author)

George Weidenfeld and myself enjoying friendship post our respective marriages, mid-nineties. (Courtesy of the author)

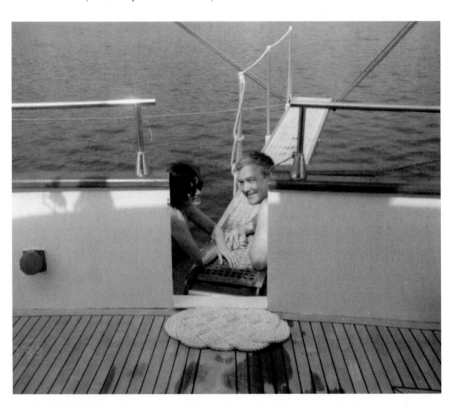

Delayed honeymoon cruising in Turkish waters, 1993. Heavenly to be alone! (Courtesy of the author)

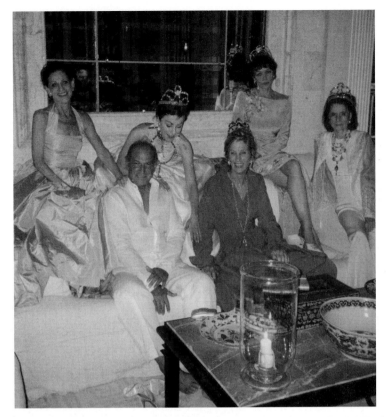

Greeting the millennium with "The Group" at the Dominican Republic home of Oscar and Annette de la Renta. Left to right Annette, Oscar, Mercedes Bass, Nancy Kissinger, me, Jayne Wrightsman. (Courtesy of the author)

With legendary Gianni Agnelli, watch on his cuff. (Courtesy of the author)

Diana Princess of Wales, with us, always discreet, witty in her observations and retorts, blessed with perfect English complexion. (Courtesy of the author)

Chivalrous former President Richard Nixon helping me out of car. I clumsily twisted my hand, smashing a new rock crystal and diamond bracelet on the ground as I not so bravely smiled and left its pieces on the road. (Peter Bregg, *Maclean's*)

Year-end Hollinger dinner, 2000, coincided with my 60th birthday. Left to right Mica Ertegun, Donald Trump (whom I had never previously met), Henry Kissinger, Tina Brown (obscured) and Charlie Rose (background). Conrad later indicted and acquitted for having the company pay one-third of the dinner's cost. (Courtesy of the author)

Classical-music-lover Oscar de la Renta, post Carnegie Hall opening at one of the last events we attended before onset of legal problems, 2003. (Courtesy of the author)

Dinner at Old Windsor home of Elton John and husband David Furnish in 2015. Elton highly intelligent, both of them loyalty and kindness personified. It mystified me why they stuck with us. (Courtesy of the author)

Editor Max Hastings and Proprietor's wife bouncing together at a *Telegraph* summer shindig. (*The Telegraph*)

OK, my worst outfit ever. Not the fault of couturier Jean Paul Gaultier, just badly worn by me, curtseying to unidentified royal at a party Dame Vivien Duffield and I threw for the Basses, Kenwood House, London, June 2000. (Courtesy of the author)

Reading the first edition of the *National Post* in the newsroom, 1998. (*National Post*)

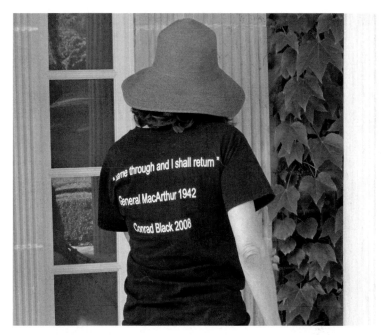

My prison-compliant T-shirt—opaque, not sleeveless, not white—made for visit to FCC Coleman on CMB's birthday, 2008, sporting one of his favorite quotes. (Courtesy of the author)

My Dick: Who is missing from this picture? but I won't be for long. Will make it all my love. your xx Conrad xx   I am, of course, a great 2012.

S.Q.Morrill 2011

Fellow inmates designed cards for Conrad to send from photos taped on his locker. This one near the end of his incarceration. (Courtesy of the author)

Literary Maya in bed with CMB, out on bail, Palm Beach 2010. (Courtesy of the author)

Dog lover Henry Kissinger in Toronto with our Kuvaszok, my gorgeous Maya and handsome Arpad, right after CMB's release, 2013. (Courtesy of the author)

CHAPTER TWENTY-NINE

Tongue-tied in High Heels

The daylight fades,
The sun is setting,
we turn to the darkness that lies within us
the hurts that never heal,
the growths of bitterness or envy that time does not dissolve,
the hatred that we can feel for others,
the dislike we can feel for ourselves. . . .
And as the gates of this world close,
open again the gates of mercy for us, and we shall enter in.
Forgive us, our Father, our King, for we have sinned.

Neilah

O ne month and one day after Conrad had planted his feet firmly
back into his hard prison shoes in Miami (soft shoe permit
denied), I planted mine into polite little low-heeled black shoes and
went off to Yom Kippur services in Toronto: twenty-four hours of
fasting, repentance and confession, during which I cheated only by
drinking a little water and one extremely teeny cup of espresso to
wash down my prescription medicines, which the rabbi had told me
were permitted. Well, permitted in a Reform temple, I suppose.

The Reform movement is the Last Chance Saloon for Jews
wanting to cling on to edges of the religious life. Unfortunately, this

necessitated listening to quite a bit about such piercingly important religious issues as aboriginal and gender rights—in the sixties it was nuclear disarmament and more recently it's welcoming Syrian refugees. Not that there is anything wrong with those issues in themselves, although I frequently saw them differently from both congregation and rabbi, but when Israel and the continuity of the Jewish people took second place to climate change at synagogue services, one suspected things were going the wrong way no matter how the rabbis managed to discern the plat du jour in the Torah's message of justice.

My mind was extremely focused that Yom Kippur of 2011, and not only because of the caffeine, dexmethylphenidate and codeine sloshed into an empty stomach, which does psych one up a bit. I needed to repent sufficiently and energetically enough to scurry inside the Gates of Mercy before they closed. Gates were very much on my mind, and if you have a musical nature like mine, which veers between passionate emotionalism and deep despair, Yom Kippur is made to measure. Gates, I kept thinking rhapsodically as the prayers to open and close them reverberated in the synagogue stuffed with Jews at the most believing moment in their year: children looking bored at their fathers' swaying rhythmically, the twenty-something daughters of the richer Jews in the front pews turning around to show off their superior seating to friends farther back, and the speakers of Hebrew letting their voices rise slightly to demonstrate they didn't need to read the prayer in English. Gates were on everyone's mind.

Mine were somewhat more specific than spiritual, specifically the opening of Conrad's prison gates at his sentence's end. Everyone was co-operating but the Canadians, and Canada was our destination. As an alien felon, Conrad would be deported by Immigration and Customs Enforcement officials the minute he stepped beyond FCI Miami's gates. But he needed proof that the country to which he was deported would take him in. Otherwise, it was off to one of ICE's notoriously dangerous prisons for alien felons, run essentially by gangs. Since home was Toronto, we had never contemplated any problems.

The U.K. was being absolutely whizzo. Consul in Orlando, Mr. Dean Churm, not only visited Conrad in prison but helped me get a brand-new U.K. passport for him. The last country I expected trouble from was Conrad's own adored Canada. But there they were, sitting tight on their Maple Leaf flag. I only wished it had a holly sprig attached to it for their behinds.

NDP members of Parliament had been asking as early as 2008 whether or not Canada would take back the felon Conrad Black on his release. Instead of quashing this right at the beginning, Stephen Harper's Conservative government decided to let it run on. I turned on the television one day in 2011 to find that the CBC's national news had taken a poll on whether Conrad should be allowed back into Canada. Apparently, the majority asked weren't keen.

"Canadians," said CBC star news anchor Peter Mansbridge quite mildly, as is his way, "don't want Conrad Black back." Once I would have been shocked or hurt, but if the years had taught me anything, it was that our lives were public property and strangers voting on what should be done with us was perfectly normal. And it was a compliment to Canada, really, that the country was so free of any real problems—say, war, poverty or violent drug cartels—that this old chestnut could occupy a nanosecond of attention.

In 2011, this growing dispute over Conrad's return to Canada was beginning to reach him and play havoc with his state of mind. They always say that "short-timers" in prison do harder time as the date of their release draws closer. In Conrad's case, with the addition of the really awful physical circumstances of his imprisonment, he was getting very depressed.

"I do not understand this, even logically," he wrote to me in an email,

> but I am subject to the fiercest attacks of demoralization I have
> had in this whole crisis except for the very worst moments, such
> as the special committee report, the OSC decision, the New York
> money seizure and the Posner performance. It makes no sense, but
> I am having the goddamnedest time getting a real sense that we are
> almost at the end, because it doesn't seem to be an end. . . . It truly
> is nerve-racking, and it just upsets me to think of you and the bears
> [the dogs] alone.

> As you know, I fight on all fronts, and I think there is no
> doubt of how much better it is going to be than it has . . . but
> the weight of the injustices and obloquy and vicious nastiness we
> have had to endure is not going to be ameliorated for a long time.

Never were truer words emailed, but I don't expect he had any idea how many years of obloquy lay ahead.

Just before Conrad returned for his last prison lap, when we didn't know he was about to be informally voted out of Canada, I'd been asked to be a presenter at Canada's prestigious Giller book prize in Toronto. A presenter delivers, live on national television, a little speech on one of the nominated books. Conrad was very keen that I take up the offer. He wanted me back in the public eye. "You'll be terrific," he said. "And it will be good for both of us."

I wasn't so sure. Since my appearance on CNN coinciding with Conrad's 2003 resignation as chairman of Hollinger International, when I had given a reasonably authentic performance as a Demented Witch, I'd only tried a couple of public performances. Both with fairly horrifying results.

The Canadian Opera Company's Richard Bradshaw had invited me on his Toronto television opera show. "You'll be wonderful," he'd said after I told him about my ghastly CNN effort. "And I'll be there if you need help. We'll just have one of our chats about *Ring* cycles you've seen." Richard asked questions and I replied. Unfortunately, my memory got stuck on one boring anecdote, which I repeated over and over again, about the smell of the audience in Bayreuth's Festspielhaus wearing their blasted 4711 eau de cologne that rose like a blanket over the boiling-hot auditorium with its closed doors and no air conditioning. This observation was a bit of minutia in those marvellous hair-raising trips to hear Wagner in the concert hall he designed. But it took over my mind. Richard tried, and sitting opposite him I could see he was trying like blazes. He coaxed, prompted, did everything but place a cue card in front of me trying to get me to budge from the subject. After the taping he showered me with praise, but we both knew.

I wondered if this was a life sentence—being an utter idiot in public speaking or on camera. Like a widow throwing herself on the suttee, I gave it one more try: the Washington-based Hudson Institute invited me to New York to give a talk, for a substantial fee. I had been led to believe I was to speak on Steven Spielberg's adaptation of George Jonas's book *Vengeance* for his 2005 film *Munich*, about the massacre of Israeli athletes at the 1972 Olympic Games. The underlying theme would have been the moral contrast between terrorism and counterterrorism. This was a topic I knew backwards, having had many discussions about it with George for his book which he dedicated to me. I had a list of points to make, plus the requisite amusing anecdotes. An excellent opportunity to kill my fears.

Unfortunately, there had been a total disconnect between the member inviting me who had suggested the topic—he was living temporarily in Budapest—and the organizers in New York who knew my work and had chosen a different topic, not specified in the letter of agreement they sent me. The large audience and I met in a smart Manhattan hotel with completely disparate expectations. About three minutes into my prepared text, as a low murmur began, I realized something had gone horribly astray, and so, to settle matters down a bit, I segued into an ad lib commentary on one of the latest horrible anti-Israel resolutions (always a reliable fallback).

My best escape route, I thought—as I determined to beat back the tempting route of dropping unconscious on the podium or talking in tongues—was to take questions. An ambassador from a Middle East country got up, perfectly politely, and asked a fairly belligerent one. I knew the answer, I knew the argument, but my mind shuffled over to an empty parking space. I stood helplessly in front of several hundred people who had paid to hear me. At the table directly to my left below the podium was author Midge Decter, sitting with her husband, *Commentary* editor Norman Podhoretz. "Come on, Barbara, you know this stuff," she said impatiently, slightly angrily, and I couldn't blame her. But I was paralyzed.

I hadn't mentioned either of these fiascos to Conrad in any detail, so he assumed when I demurred about speaking at the Giller that I was just being modest. "Test the waters," he said in an extremely welcome relief from his flag motif. "You'll see how well accepted you'll be. We'll all be back soon. It's a good beginning."

The Giller is Canada's Booker Prize, and the dinner is a gathering of the Good and Great in the country's literary world. You can imagine the atmosphere created in a room full of authors, publishers, public relations people and acolytes, all eyeing one another with the camaraderie that the prospect of a (then) $50,000 prize, and the best-selling status it bestows on the winning book, creates. The audience gave me a kind and generous reception when I stepped onto the stage to read my introduction to the nominated book, and I had none of the stop-and-start horrors of the previous occasions. But I'd forgotten the wretched amplification a microphone gives the idiosyncrasies of my voice.

Ever since CBC producer Ross McLean forced me to work with a cassette player to rid my voice of any English accent, I had realized that on tape I sounded completely different to the way I sounded in my head. Listening to the cassettes, I heard a nasal voice, with an inflection that sounded as if some words or syllables had weights attached to them and would dive off water's edge to pond's bottom throughout my sentences. I found it very affected and off-putting, which is odd because I think I have a soft, melodious voice. Perhaps many people hearing themselves on tape find their voices out of sync with their own perception. Mine only more so.

Having lived back in London for twenty years, bits of London cadence had returned, uninvited, to my speech like sequins on denim—inappropriate and worn by the tackiest of people. The result was a little sarcastic outburst in the press coverage that I was putting it on and giving everyone that night a Pygmalion to the "manor-not-born show to remember," said one newspaper account. Worse, they dug up the well-known and oft-referenced Mr. and Ms. Unnamed, who knew me and claimed to find my voice extremely artificial. My confidence pooled. Well, it pooled then. A decade later I wouldn't give a goddamn merde for how people hear me, which is the single positive outcome of slogging through waist-high crap for sixteen years. But at the time, I seemed to have become something of an ill-fitting jigsaw—you know, the puzzle where some of the pieces are a bit bent or missing and others forced to fit. This was not, I felt, a promising beginning to re-entry to Conrad's welcoming Canada.

Then, completely unexpected people helped me enormously. Arlene Perly Rae, wife of federal Liberal leader Bob Rae (formerly leader of the Ontario NDP), invited me to the PEN dinner in Ottawa as a stand-in for Conrad. Although she must have found my views on just about everything basically untenable and possibly criminal, she did her absolute best to make me feel comfortable. What a wonderful woman, I thought; she could turn me into a democratic socialist were she still of that persuasion. What was funny—not vicious but just plain funny—was that the press reflexively gave my clothes and jewellery status I no longer had. The dyed racoon and coyote scarf I wore at one function became a "must be mink scarf." I was often "loaded down with jewels" that were, in fact, either totally fake or heavy beads worth very little.

With these social swim attempts under my belt, it was something of a letdown to find that Canada might pull its welcome mat for Conrad. Earlier in 2011, *Globe and Mail* columnist Lawrence Martin pointed out that the Conservatives, who were then in power, ought to welcome Conrad back, given his role in creating their party with the help of his *National Post*. "You don't hear many prominent Conservatives defending Conrad Black today," he wrote, "but you have to wonder how much harder it would have been for their like to rise from the depths without him."

Then, on May 1, with his release four days away, Conrad wrote jubilantly to me: "It has been terribly long and difficult but all the trends are good now. Between us, I was confirmed today as the Massey lecturer for a couple of years off. The long night is ended." The Massey Lectures are a prestigious annual five-part event given by a scholar or expert on either political, cultural or business affairs, broadcast over the CBC and published by House of Anansi Press. Conrad was tailor-made to give them, and to be chosen was a real boost.

The seed for this happy news was planted back in December 2008 at a very glum time indeed, when John Fraser, then master of Massey

College, sent an email to Conrad through me. "One of your newest and greatest fans, Margaret Atwood, was harried into doing her Massey Lecture a year in advance," he wrote, "and as you know very well pulled off something of a coup . . . She and Graeme"—Gibson, her late husband—"were here at the College two nights ago for the post-mortem Massey Lecture dinner and we raised our glasses to you. And you know what? We all agreed that you would be a brilliant Massey Lecturer. . . . If you would be at all interested, I believe it could happen. We are talking 2011 or 2012 here. Anyway, something to think about."

This was followed up by a prison visit from a good friend, Scott Griffin, in his capacity as chairman of House of Anansi Press, which co-sponsors the Massey Lectures, to ask Conrad if he would do them. He gave Conrad a pep talk on the virtue of accepting the invite:

"Look," said Conrad, sitting in his prison greens, "I'm like Julia Roberts in *Pretty Woman*." I'm a sure thing."

Frankly, I couldn't believe it: too good to be true. Conrad took me to task for my "lack of faith." And he seemed to be right. In September 2010, while Conrad was still in prison, a formal invitation arrived from the CBC to deliver the Massey Lectures in 2012. The offer was balm to an exiled soul.

Still even at this late date, the turmoil was not quite over. The dogs and I were as usual sitting together eating our respective dinners in the kitchen watching the CBC news. We had weathered a number of items in the past few weeks as everyone and their auntie took polls to show that Canadians didn't want Conrad back to despoil their pine trees or something, and we had got the message. Now, on TV, we had to deal with the bearded leader of the Opposition, Thomas Mulcair, saying that this "British criminal" was getting special treatment because he was white and well connected. That takes the cake, I thought. If only I could unleash my male Kuvasz into Mulcair's office.

Irritatingly, Mulcair's anger was honest, if misdirected. "Double standard," he said, referring to the case of the black American Gary Freeman, who as a seventeen-year-old in 1969 had wounded a Chicago policeman (not necessarily a bad thing in my view, having some knowledge of Chicago's 1960s policing policies) and escaped to Canada, where he made a respectable life supporting his wife and children for nearly forty years until some bloody up-for-a-promotion Toronto cop arrested him. He languished in the luxury of the Don Jail for several years while he fought extradition, which Canadians, being U.S. lickspittles, consented to. I couldn't forgive Mulcair—two wrongs do not make a right—but Canada was now refusing to let Freeman return to his wife and children after an unblemished life in Canada, and after the U.S. all but dropped the charges.

Still, it's not exactly heartwarming to watch your husband's future being debated in Parliament unless it's for his nomination for the Nobel Prize or such. If Canada wouldn't let him in, where would we go? I had the necessary Canadian temporary resident permit, or TRP, acceptable proof for ICE, but two days before his release date we still couldn't make firm plans in case the permit was pulled for political reasons.

"Just relax," said our ever-calm immigration lawyer, Stephen Green. "I'm on top of this. It's not a government decision, it's for the Immigration people, and they have said yes. Just make no comment and tell Conrad not to." Superlative in his field though Green is, one does get a bit tense with people forever telling you to pull up a deck-chair in the minefield and relax.

Then came the unhelpful (and incorrect) contribution of immigration minister Jason Kenney, who in Conrad's defence in the House of Commons referred to Gary Freeman as a "cop killer." Put yourself in Conrad's hard prison shoes. Sitting in his cell, his head aching with worry plus the headache he got from hitting it on the steel bunk overhead because he couldn't sit up without a collision, brooding as he listened through his earbuds to tinny radio news that in the Parliament of which he was privy councillor, he was being likened to a murderer. As soon as his cell unlocked, I got an anguished call from Conrad.

I was in a mean state too. Having been told by Stephen Green that we all had to keep as mum as possible about the subject so it could just cool down, I really didn't appreciate waking up on May 2 to

Jonathan Kay's front-page story in the *National Post*, illustrated by a huge photo of Conrad and headlined "Black Cleared for Return." It began, "Two words for anyone who thinks Conrad Black shouldn't be let back into Canada: Lindsay Lohan."

Dear Jesus. First his enemies compare him with a so-called cop killer, and now his "friends" are pulling out Lindsay Lohan, the formerly alcohol- and drug-addicted actress who, Kay went on to tell us, had been caught stealing a $2,500 necklace in California, plus had multiple DUI convictions, and yet she was going to be allowed to come into Canada to film a biopic on Elizabeth Taylor. (She didn't come.) Was there no end to the helpfulness of these twerps and their insulting comparisons? Did anyone really think that the comparison with Lindsay Lohan was going to water down the toxic atmosphere in Parliament? Look, I'm a journalist, and I know when you get a good line or metaphor it's almost irresistible, and I didn't doubt Kay's good intentions but his sensibilities were in orbit.

"Can't you just tell your neo-conservative friends to shut up for two days?" I asked Conrad, which was about the last thing he needed to hear. He emailed me back:

> I love you. I telephoned you in complete innocence for reassurance. I agree that we have some pretentious little twerps who don't know anything but their intentions are good. If there is any chance of acrimony with you at this stage in my life I am not able to deal with that. I can deal with anything else.
>
> I don't have a clear picture of it from here but how could I for God's sake? I know it is agony for you too, but please try to think of my situation—after nine years to be accused of being morally indistinguishable from a murderer and to be 48 hours from the end without being sure where I am going or whether I will have a change of clothes or a cent when I get there, with you being grumpy with me at 7:10 a.m. after a sleepless night and still mired in this unspeakable place . . . I will be free as long as the arrangements with ICE hold and the Canadian government holds. But I can't be sure of either.

Suddenly the prison email was working overtime—word to Conrad of every comment on the question of his readmittance was being emailed to him via friends on his mailing list or his assistant Joan Maida. His fifth email or so of the day to me was, "Will Harper wobble?" He had just been sent an earlier remark in Parliament: Prime Minister Harper had told Mulcair, "It would be just as easy for us if Mr. Black were not allowed to come to Canada."

Naturally, I had always had visions of how it was going to end: me at the prison door in a pretty prison-banned sleeveless dress with a hemline definitely more than two inches above my knees, my hair done and a smile on my face, embracing my released husband. I live in fantasy. But even in those stark black-and-white old English movies when the ex-inmate walks out of the prison doors looking confused and lost with a bundle of belongings wrapped in paper under his arm, there is a wife or girlfriend or mother or best friend to come running up and give him a hug. That's standard release stuff.

It was not to be. But if my starring role was to be snatched from me after years of picturing it, at least it was at the expense of the press. The BOP and ICE had had enough of the media and so decided this was a good time to take the mickey out of them. Dressed in his now too-small civilian clothes, Conrad stood chatting with correctional officers just inside the prison exit. "I had a very nice talk with Mr. Kissinger," reminisced one. Another mentioned his meeting with Brian Mulroney. Then came the correctional officers' farewell. "I guess you're glad to leave and you won't be back." The standard line.

"Yes, I'm glad to leave, but it was an outrage I was ever here. The system would work better if you convicted fewer innocent people."

"It's not for us to judge. You all cross the line eventually."

"Well it is for me. I was convicted, and I didn't do anything." No yielding from Conrad. They shook hands.

Just inside the prison parking area, the BOP had a tinted-window SUV decoy with motorcycle escort complete with sirens and flashing lights. It was enough bling for a president and had everything—except Conrad. The press swarmed around the convoy as it left the prison compound for Miami. Once they were gone, Conrad was handcuffed and ushered into an inconspicuous ICE sedan. The last press person by it, a photographer, was busy packing up his tripod and didn't even notice him.

Except I wasn't there. The ruse meant I was not allowed to go to the prison. I had to stay inside the plane, on the tarmac, with instructions not to even step out on Conrad's arrival—heavens knows why not. My nose smushed against the plane's window when I saw the car drive up. The ICE agents had not put Conrad in shackles and very thoughtfully had let his hands be cuffed in front of him instead of behind as procedure dictated. "Put our names in your book," they joked, "in return for this." He did.

The handcuffs caught the sun as the two officers removed the jacket they had put over them. Had I not chartered a plane, they would have sat with him at Miami airport, taken him manacled through security and not removed the cuffs until he was on-board. I could picture the faces of the Toronto-bound passengers as Conrad came down the aisle to take his seat, with two ICE agents unlocking him so he could lock his seatbelt. Or perhaps Air Canada would have given him priority boarding along with the wheelchairs and mothers with babies strapped to them. "They were too small," Conrad said on the plane, rubbing his chafed wrists.

Canada Border Services staff were considerate and polite. Conrad had his U.K. passport, TRP, a half-used tube of lip balm, four chewed-up pens, his earplugs and the medical check-up statement that he had hypertension, anxiety, environmental problems, depressive disorder, acute upper respiratory infection and so on. What they missed was that his "acute upper respiratory infection" was early-stage idiopathic pulmonary fibrosis, an irreversible and progressive illness in which the lungs become filled with scar tissue. Normal prognosis: a lifespan of two to three years after detection.

(This happy bit of news would not come our way immediately. And thank God it didn't: that would really have been the topping on the cake. It only came later, when Conrad's constant cough caught the attention of his doctor. No one knows how you get the damn thing, but prison conditions would not have helped: the fungus in the showers, the construction dust in the AC and so on. If he had a predilection for the illness, prison would have been a great petri dish. After I had gone into something of a spiral over the news, the Toronto hospital lung clinic said there are exceptions to the disease's run and Conrad appears to be one of them; he has been virtually stable now for seven years.)

Waiting for us in Toronto was Don Reeve, looking like he had just stepped out of *The Thomas Crown Affair*—and not the overweight man who drives the getaway car. I'd hired Reeve as our driver/property manager/Mr. Fixit all in one. He was far too handsome for his job and I was deeply suspicious of him when he came to be interviewed—so very tanned, a trim build, stunning good looks, hair slicked back like Ramon Novarro. In real life he had been a police detective and then worked security for Ontario premier Mike Harris, and so was used to driving polarizing gentlemen of definite opinions. In the ghoulish sour-cream pie of petty spites and institutional oppression thrown in our faces with alarming regularity, Reeve has been the single positive ingredient—in spite of his firm disagreement with my husband on the policies and being of Donald Trump, a topic best avoided.

Don had collected us in his own 2003 grey Chrysler, and so the car got no attention from the dozens of press waiting at our gates when we drove in. The dogs came bounding out and we walked with them in Conrad's father's orchard. I'd like to say that if I could live any moment of my life over and over again it would be that moment, because for those twenty minutes it was pure unbounded joy: you know the script—the May trees in bloom, the smells of fresh-cut grass, the dogs still young and bounding happily around us, and Conrad next to me. Cue music. Cue kiss. Cue photos.

But in fact, we were both near catatonic. Conrad was substantially overweight, and his clothes didn't fit—my arm was around him to help hold up his trousers, which he couldn't do up properly. We walked to the orchard only because it had some symbolic significance to him. Frankly, we had no idea what to do next. Conrad wanted to

telephone everyone—once he figured out how to use the telephone—
to say essentially, "I'm back." I think he couldn't get over a telephone
that did not have a time limit and was free of the voice announcing
"This call is from a federal correctional facility." As for me, the first
priority was coping with the completely unforeseen situation that
Conrad had not a single pair of trousers or a jacket that would do up
on him. So, in about an hour's time, I beetled out to the big and tall
men's shop and bought him a new wardrobe.

Later, on the back terrace, I looked at him away from the press
and with none of the helicopters that had circled us when the happy
prospect of his being marched off to jail or the house being seized
loomed. It was a bit worrying. Conrad looked unwell. His pasty
complexion wasn't so much a concern because that was explicable:
FCI Miami is not Miami South Beach. During outside recreation
time, inmates weren't allowed to sit down—they had to keep walking, which was difficult with his injured knee. But while he kept
insisting he was in great shape, he coughed rather a lot.

My real worry was his state of mind. He couldn't make decisions
about small things but was full of pep about huge plans that had, once
again, the ring of prison delusions. He was going to re-enter the business world and reinstate our fortunes. He had "ideas" that he had been
working on all during his imprisonment. "You'll be astonished at how
soon we can resurrect our lives," he kept saying in one form or another.
Let it play out, I thought. Just for a while and see where it all goes.
The one good thing was that he had the Massey Lectures to look
forward to in a year or so, and that gave him a sense of self-respect.
Whatever else had happened, his intellect was still appreciated.

The fortitude of the man was nothing less than astounding. Not
simply that he had survived all the prosecution, persecution, ridicule,
caricatures and dreadful prison conditions, but that he was to all
intents undamaged. Okay, he had nightmares and was certainly pretty
violently overweight, but his morale was intact and he was raring to
start over. He was exploring the house he hadn't seen for five years,
beginning with his library.

His dressing room desk was piled high with trays of oddments, loose change from half a dozen countries, a small nodding Richard Nixon doll, loose keys, six-year-old parking numbers from valets at various Toronto restaurants, cufflinks, years-old copies of *The Spectator* and the *Catholic Herald*. The dartboard his son James had made with the faces of Breeden and other villains on it was hanging on the wall. He shuffled through some things, then sat down and just stopped.

A flash of doubt went through me. Now we had no metronome. Nothing fixed. We weren't gearing up to some court date, to a prison surrender, to a release, to a filing. We were out and on our own. I felt unmoored. For over nine years I had woken up to know that today we will fight this person, that judge. Now we had only our general circumstances: the fight to reconstruct life. Two people, one in their seventies, the other in his late sixties.

We owed $21 million, not counting the bizarre $71 million the IRS was assessing based on every last lie and exaggeration of Breeden's special committee report. "They always go for the sky" and settle somewhere below cumulus clouds, said our tax lawyer. But how on earth were we going to manage? My *Maclean's* columns and Conrad's *National Post* and *National Review* columns weren't enough to pay the hydro bill, let alone anything else. Running costs of the house were about a million a year, and freelance columnists don't live in houses in the Bridle Path unless Daddy is Ken Thomson or something. Or a pre-troubles Conrad Black.

The glow of return bathed the days in a rosier light for a little while. But not before false starts on every front. Even as the financial walls were squeezing in like some bloody Edgar Allan Poe horror story, Conrad wanted to re-establish himself socially in Toronto with "just one or two lunches or dinners and after that the invitations will be returned." I was dead against it.

"Let's show them we're back," said Conrad.

"I think they know," I replied, not completely sure who the "they" was but unequivocally sure that whoever they were, they knew.

We weren't familiar with the rising bubbles in the champagne of Toronto society even before we left for trial, being essentially London residents. Conrad's Toronto world was dated. In his ten years of absence, a new stratum had established itself. Conrad was pretty much an artifact of some historical interest to a few, but in crass terms of power and money, he was a person who could do nothing for them. Conrad had always extolled this class-free society (unlike the more hidebound European society) in which anyone could ascend to the top, and he still did. He just didn't understand the implications of his new placement in it.

A week later, Henry Kissinger flew in exclusively to see him, to "build bridges," said Conrad, which in my mind was like building a bridge over the Atlantic Ocean. Conrad of course saw him at a lunch (and later a dinner). "Small, please," I said for the lunch, "just a few male friends or writers." Historian Margaret MacMillan was in town, and Conrad had the pleasure of getting a call from Hilary Weston asking if she could come as well. Galen had accepted already, as well as Heather Reisman of the mega Indigo Books empire.

I pottered over placemats and table flowers. Why am I still doing this, I asked myself, given there was no one else to ask? Hadn't I earned my abdication from the seat left of the guest of honour through blood, tears and sweat?

"You see," Conrad said. I didn't. This was a one-off. And it was. No return invites from that. Insofar as it had given Conrad pleasure, I was grateful. Henry would come twice more.

I staggered through a mini rerun of our social lives. Frankly, it was hell. Most guests I wanted never seemed available, and speculating on why just got me nowhere. Perhaps they were in Ottawa as they regretted or Kamloops, but there were no return invites. I enjoyed the company of a number of people in Toronto and they carried on inviting us to their Christmas parties and out to dinner occasionally, but Conrad was aiming higher. I'll say this for him, he almost always accepted any social invitation and invariably enjoyed himself. I followed him for a few months, learning how to balance on high heels again, but we were adrift.

CHAPTER THIRTY

Tea, Sympathy and Strychnine

Former prime minister Margaret Thatcher died on April 8, 2013. The world isn't exactly awash with individuals whose destiny appears to be to remake it, but she was one. In my pantheon of women—next to great ballerinas, singers, queens and empresses like Catherine the Great—I list Marie Curie, Odette Hallowes, Golda Meir, Edith Wharton, Susan B. Anthony, Alice Munro, and Dian Fossey for a start. And I reserve a very special place for Maria Bochkareva, as I think Lady Thatcher would.

Feminists don't put Bochkareva on their lists but she puts them all to shame, which may be why. A peasant, born in 1889 in Russia, she suffered terrible abuse, was forced to work in a brothel, followed a husband into exile, then persuaded Minister of War Alexander Kerensky to ignore all rules and let her form the first all-female combat unit, called the Women's Battalion of Death, which fought in World War One. Harassed by male soldiers, wounded in battle, she returned to combat. She was later received by President Wilson in the U.S.A. and King George V in Britain. Determined to keep fighting for her Russia, she returned, to be executed by the Bolsheviks at age thirty. This woman did not worry about glass ceilings.

But Margaret Thatcher tops my list of greats, although in person I had little spark with her. One doesn't have to enjoy the company of someone utterly extraordinary—and I didn't.

"She deserves a state funeral," I said. The invitation came the next day. I was absolutely astonished. "They must be afraid they can't fill St. Paul's," I said in earnest.

"Are you stark raving mad?" replied Conrad. "This is a new low in your insecurity."

No one under fifty-five can remember, but this was a woman who personified True Grit. An epoch bore her name. She had physical and moral courage enough for an entire nation—actually, for the Western world at that time. Unfortunately for feminists, she wore hats and a proper little two-strand pearl necklace and had a wealthy husband. By credo, they had to disown her on some sort of *sui generis* ground that she was only herself and nothing more. Genderless. Her only fault: she had absolutely no sense of humour, which was a handicap for her speech writer Ronnie Millar, who sometimes came over to my flat to try out jokes. She couldn't deliver them—she didn't get them.

Her funeral was on a windy, wet and cold April day. My plain black felt hat—the only funeral hat I ever had, bought at a small shop in Toronto for Monty Black's funeral and subsequently described by the Canadian press in lurid and dramatic terms as if it had landed on my head from a Gainsborough painting—was pinned down but still trying to escape. The streets were lined six deep for miles. The pomp and circumstance rang out through the streets with the single bell, a dark reverberating ring, tolling as members of the armed forces carried her coffin onto a gun carriage to be wheeled to the cathedral.

They called it a ceremonial funeral, but it was hard to distinguish it from a state funeral, especially when the Queen and the Duke of Edinburgh turned up. The Queen had attended only one other prime minister's funeral—that of Winston Churchill. The Queen knew what the U.K. owed Thatcher. Every piece of music was deliriously right, as were the silent readings—T.S. Eliot's "Little Gidding" from *The Four Quartets* as we waited. I was practically back in plimsolls and monitor's badge when the first hymn was my own school hymn, number 402 from the old *English Hymnal*—"He who would valiant be." There was not a soppy sound, not a false note from beginning to end. No Earl Spencer moment, raving at his sister Princess Diana's service. This was a funeral to die for. We left to Elgar's "Nimrod" from the *Enigma Variations*—the popular piece I played constantly in my dressing room at top volume when living in London. I tried not to wallow in memory, but hell, it was like hearing the jukebox tunes you danced to as a teenager and remembering the taste of Coca-Cola.

That night, settled into Brown's Hotel, with plans next day to see girlfriends, the Mareva felt like another lifetime, or perhaps the name of a railway crossing somewhere or an Italian dessert. I giggled. A hotel suite with Conrad, no dogs to wake me, no courtroom to appear at. No effing conference calls with lawyers and accountants, no strategy meetings to combat dwellers of some dark zone.

"Alone at last." I bounced into bed hugging him with glee. I realize it's a bit late to grasp it, but you realize just like that in a hotel room what you've missed: freedom. Freedom to make your own mistakes, freedom to waste time if you want. No one in this life is ever totally "carefree," but the word has meaning. Bouncing on the bed, I suddenly knew I hadn't been carefree since the autumn of 2003. If my brain were on the outside of my head, it would show a hard, thick shell like a stale cheese blocking off every thought that could possibly interrupt my total preoccupation with "the Problem." The next day, at the Wolseley restaurant on Piccadilly, we sat in the little booth that overlooked the main floor. I was positively radiant. I had on London clothes (no jeans!). The Shawcrosses were coming to join us. My cell phone rang.

"Arpad attacked," said the staff member from Toronto, naming one of our domestic staff. So that was my holiday, all forty-eight hours of it. Back in Toronto the next day, the first thing was to settle down the remaining staff and find out what the hell had happened.

Kuvaszok are the most glorious breed I know. That intruder in Florida was not some chimera of my four-in-the-morning imagination—my dogs had saved my life. Without them, this tedious tale would long be buried with me. But they need the right environment, not simply the right owner. I had become a pretty damn good owner, but our lives had radically changed after Conrad's return. The relative peace of our home had, almost overnight, become twenty-six thousand square feet filled with strangers.

There were constantly changing domestic staff wielding brooms and vacuum cleaners, unknown persons carrying weird implements to clean the swimming pool, strange people turning up on the fiercely guarded second floor where their owners slept; unknown people to check alarm systems, maintain heat and air conditioning, clean carpets, hang curtains. Outside were a dozen gardeners wielding big rakes, leaf blowers making a god-awful racket, trucks and big electric lawn mowers going all over the place, quite a change from the calm familiar figure of Toronto's Don Reeve looking after house and garden or the becalmed lawns of Palm Beach. Add to all that innumerable delivery men—and who among us, let alone a vigilant Kuvasz, has not worried about the ominous UPS or FedEx van? Every corner of house, lawn and driveway was occupied by new people with unfamiliar smells doing unexpected tasks. They had become displaced dogs.

In a regular home, a Kuvasz could be a marvelous companion, wonderful with children, and caring therapy dogs for the sick and bedridden. On a farm they are indispensable guardians of the flocks. On Park Lane Circle, with Conrad's return the situation abruptly changed, and from the dogs' point of view, not for the better. Knowing this, I'd drawn up a protocol—pretty simple—telling each employee where they could and could not go, which rooms were off-limits when I was away. Gates were installed to section off stairs and rooms. And it worked until one employee all but dared another— who already had a fear of dogs—to burst into the room where they were sleeping, with Arpad on guard inside, lying across the door. Well, you can imagine. The details are immaterial. The damage to face and limb was material.

I had the vets come up to the house and explain to staff what had happened. "He only did his job," the vets said. "The rules are there to protect both the dog and you." I gave the remaining staff the option of staying until they got another job and then leaving with a settlement, and they all chose to stay with no settlement—except for the victim understandably, who did recover completely with time, and money.

Post-2013 Arpad meltdown, we went into the Financial Crisis phase. First, however, we had to visit the Wizard of Oz. There we would work through a series of phantasmagoric ventures that were going to make us fabulously rich, conceived by one or two delusionary inmates in prison claiming to be cousins of extremely wealthy people in Latin America. Conrad is not usually prey to this sort of madness, but prison can do odd things to your judgment.

The worst of these chimeras concerned sugar in some form or another, and I referred to it as the "sombreros scheme" since the people involved lived in Mexico primarily and latterly Brazil. "We'll make a fortune," said Conrad, explaining that this involved one of the richest industrialists in Latin America. "Why would he need you?" I asked innocently.

Whatever the answer, and I can't actually remember a credible one, conference calls took place rather often as well as intermittent calls from FCI Coleman. Just who these calls were with was difficult for me to figure out, as Conrad was, to put it mildly, elusive. Gradually they vaporized as Conrad's jubilation flattened out like a punctured tire. But for several months "the sombreros are coming" was a constant theme. They never arrived.

We needed money. Given the court constraints on the spending of funds we had and the obvious need for cash, we got legal permission to sell off assets, largely in the U.K.: antiques, paintings, furniture. This is when you find that the Oxbridge-educated art specialist with a conspicuous lack of flash and sombre demeanour denoting "I am a serious dealer" actually sold you fakes—or at least, not quite what things were said to be. There was the hidden gem: the small Van Dyck painting that when cleaned had a completely different stunning masterpiece by him underneath and fetched a handsome number of millions. But, as the situation got nastier, Conrad even began selling a little of his vast Roosevelt memorabilia. Okay, time for my ring and the large natural-pearl and diamond brooch to go. By then, there was no question as to my ownership.

"Think carefully, babe," said George Jonas when I told him. "That's your fallback, your life insurance."

Seeing off the jewellery was easier than I expected, although I had a sentimental and symbolic attachment to the ring, my sixtieth-birthday present. Before sending it off to the auction house I took it out of the bank and pranced a bit around the house. God, it was gorgeous, nearly twenty-seven carats of D-flawless shining up at me—I've never been a dedicated jewellery person, and anyway my hands were getting positively gnarled with arthritis.

When the arthritis first started I had asked New York dermatologist Pat Wexler if there was anything that could be done to tidy up my fingers so I could wear this gobsmacking stone. "You wear the ring over little net evening gloves," said Pat matter-of-factly, not understanding that by this point in life I didn't have little-net-glove evenings. "Or you can have your fingers broken and reset. Some clients do that." She sent me to a doctor down the street who I assumed was trained by one of New York's Five Families—probably the Gambino or Genovese family. Wearing splints on my typing fingers was a vanity too far.

"Is there anything that *can't* be fixed?" I asked Pat. She didn't answer, only said, "You're lucky with your earlobes. A lot of clients have to have those filled or reshaped after years of heavy earrings."

After the auction, my bank account looked rather splendid for about ten minutes. Then Conrad began to make investments. His eye settled on the *National Post*, the newspaper he had founded, which Paul Godfrey was now running as part of Postmedia. The company was in bad shape and the *National Post* itself in decline. Godfrey's only tactic was to cut costs, including ending the *Post*'s Monday edition. At Conrad's invitation, Godfrey visited our home to discuss a new plan for Postmedia.

I was dead against this. "Godfrey has an ego that makes the Empire State Building look small and is as slippery as the oiliest eel," I said helpfully.

"I think he cares about the paper," said Conrad. "But he certainly cares about what's in his best interest, and heading up a successful company instead of a stagnant and staggering one while retaining all his perks would do it."

"Yes, but his definition of 'best interest' isn't only financial," I said. "He likes the pedestal of being CEO and the publisher, and wouldn't want any improvement attributed to you."

Needless to say, Godfrey didn't want Conrad or any of Conrad's like-minded friends who also wanted to invest. He had a huge salary, perks and a golden parachute, and had got an American fund to cough up about $80 million instead, which, of course, vaporized. Godfrey then announced that Postmedia would buy Sun Media and combine the two organizations. "It's a clever idea," said Conrad. "You can merge just about every aspect except the journalists and newsprint. Costs would be dramatically cut and cash flow increased."

Out came a shiny prospectus for the merger with lots of charts and arrows upwards anticipating increased ad revenue and EBITDA. As securities law required, the prospectus began with the normal refer-ence to the danger of "forward-looking statements." Still, a prospectus is required to have some fidelity to the truth.

The terms were rather unusual. Ordinary shareholders like us had a very short time to either cough up money for new stock or see their stock extensively diluted, since Godfrey was going to issue new shares from treasury. Still, we bought in and recommended it to several friends. After all, Conrad knew the business intimately and the sav-ings were definitely there. The stock would have to go up in value.

Except it didn't. More than not go up, it had a stroke. Now there were five times as many shares outstanding, but no trading. The stock was dead in the listings. Questions on shareholder conference calls got gobbledegook answers. Godfrey temporized with solemn drivel about "accelerating revenues will come from the cornerstones of our new strategy for the years ahead." About one year later, the stock was diluted further: one share was issued for every hundred. It was a Dick Turpin deal in reverse. In the real world, the securities over-sight agency—in this case the OSC—would open up an inquiry to see if the offering document at the time of the merger contained material inaccuracies, but instead they just raised the drawbridge on the whole thing.

And Conrad paid back all the people he had encouraged to invest in it, which saw a bite of my ring proceeds. Paul Godfrey stayed on, bonuses intact, this time with another bureaucratic ploy: government money for the press. Perhaps if you have never built or created anything yourself, personal well-being is all that really counts.

"We'll sell part of the garden," said Conrad. He was referring to the two-acre lot purchased from Tom Bata some thirty years earlier adjacent to our garden. We hadn't done anything with it, although plans for a tennis court and tea house had been in the making. While we were in Chicago, somewhat preoccupied, the ravine crept up on it. Lawn became a jungle of weeds. The city flew over, noted the overgrowth and designated it as protected "ravine land." To all intents, we were expropriated. That reduced the property's value for a builder.

Nevertheless, when I'd returned to Toronto while Conrad was still in prison, I had tried to clean it up. I got shivved by the disgruntled owner of a really bad tree-maintenance company who I fired after his unethical behaviour endangered our apple trees. In revenge he ratted on us to the city bureaucrats. Up came the horrible so-called Trees and Ravine Protection people, who slapped down a stop-work order and threatened $100,000 a day in fines if I imperilled one more weed. I had to fork over about $25,000 as a deposit on weed replacement. I'd been trying to murder the buckhorn that was strangling trees as well as the dog strangling vine.

(Ironically, later on I would have been fined for *not* clearing this, when the Ontario Invasive Species Act came into effect in 2015.) These sort of "nature bureaucrats" are about as far removed from tree lovers as termites.

But they had their day and now we had their stop-work order on our property.

The lot eventually sold at a lower price, largely because of this bit of back-scratching between the tree maintenance company and the city bureaucrats. Once the lot was in the hands of a developer, the same bureaucrats seemed to give permission for seventeen trees, mostly mature Austrian pines as well as other random trees, to be hacked down at the front of the lot. Tall cranes took men up to saw off the branches one by one in a series of painful amputations. It took several days per tree, and at night the trunks stood helpless with gaping wounds and severed limbs: they had been tower blocks of protection for birds and squirrels. Arpad, Maya and I watched through the wire fence as their favourite apple tree was sawed down. I have no idea why people do not value privacy anymore and want to make sure their house has "curb appeal."

As usual, the millions from the sale was not ours. It went to pay off the blackmailers at Hollinger Inc. Lawyer Earle Cherniak wrote to me that "this is an absolute scandal and should be exposed for what it is." Instead, we had the brain-dead, moralizing OSC and so-called "business journalists" like Jackie McNish doing pastiches of clippings and press releases on our greed and missing the real story entirely. But even with tea, crumpets, and codeine, I simply can't find the energy to explain to you how it is possible, and possible it was, for a dead company to keep paying lawyers and accountants for ten years after bankruptcy for the sole purpose of enriching themselves and hounding us.

Hand in hand, the unappetizing chorus line of Justice Campbell and his Mareva ruling inspired by Wesley Voorheis, the OSC's Madame Susan Jenah, the assassin of Hollinger partnered by her pal Richard Breeden, danced around the carcass of this once-great company, indistinguishable in the consequences of their actions from the other vultures, spotted hyenas and jackals that had preyed on it. Each of them satiated, playing to their own audiences. What a banquet and bouquet of bonuses and Christmas presents for the court-appointed lawyers and auditors like Ernst & Young who billed $30 million but never discovered a thing wrong. Money for everyone except shareholders.

In 2018 we made the last payment of the $5 million negotiated to end the bloody Mareva. Our payment went in theory to Hollinger

Inc., extorted from us in exchange for winding up the lawsuits nur-
tured for ten years by the so-called "litigation committee" and its
"executives" with meaningless titles like "Restructuring Officer,"
CEO, and COO, all drawing some sort of money—whether personally or through their law firms—for attaching themselves to a dead
company operating no business. Nothing for the shareholders and
no more money from us. Every last penny sucked up and pocketed.
I made my usual whimper about paying those leeches a cent and got
back the usual ditty: "You'll win the case, but only get back 55% of
your costs, the trial will drag on for years and the Mareva will continue to tie you up."

So it was over. Not a piece of gristle left. And the whole con-
temptible matter perfectly summed up in all its greed by an eco-
nomical four word email accompanying the wind-up documents
sent out to one and all by lawyer Norm Emblem from Denton's
inaptly named Litigation and Dispute Resolution Group in Toronto:
"Twas a might run!" he chortled. You bastards all.

The triumph of destruction by lawyers, accountants and regulators was now complete. "The worst decision the OSC ever made,"
we were told time and time again by security lawyers we'd meet. No
comfort. Nor was the OSC quite finished. Conrad, bless his imperishable heart, was still alive. Just wait a little bit and they would once
more dress up in their notional robes of impartiality and make a last
attempt to grind him into the dust.

So Conrad was out of jail, finally out of the Mareva for the next
series of below-the-belt punches, this time from Canada, the country
happy to bill itself as pacesetter in the Western world for caring, compassionate policies. For years there had been talk of Conrad's Order
of Canada being rescinded—started, I think, in the *Toronto Star* in
about 2008.

"Perhaps all your friends with their Orders of Canada will get up
some sort of petition against this," I said unhopefully.

Conrad went into the ring and asked for a hearing on the matter.
No, said the advisory council who were to make a recommendation
on Conrad's fitness to keep the order to Governor General David

Johnston. No, said the Federal Court of Appeal, since, in the words of the compassionate and caring Mr. Justice John Evans, it really didn't matter whether or not Conrad got a hearing from the advisory council because ultimately the decision was in the hands of the governor general. No, said Governor General Johnston, whose official biography excels in printed cant about "caring," "learning" and "responsibility," all of which somehow deserted him when it came to Conrad Black.

"Return to sender," said the lot of them after Conrad wrote a letter to the governor general. This letter stated his case and said if this doesn't convince you, please accept this as a letter of resignation. No, came the chorus, we can't let the bastard get away with just resigning—dump him, dump him publicly without telling him first. Strap him into the ducking stool. A sharp punch in the gonads. "Liking" Conrad is not a litmus test for fairness, but treating him fairly whether you like him or not is.

Conrad woke up on a Friday morning in January of 2014 (dishonourable decisions are always made known on a Friday so the weekend press can have a good munch on them) to a press release that announced two things: his Order of Canada was removed, along with his membership in the Queen's Privy Council. A twofer. I was only surprised that the stripping didn't include a cashiering ceremony, with Conrad forced to stand in front of the massed advisory council and senior Order of Canada members while the GG ripped the decoration from his jacket.

Conrad, in my view, has always had rosy spectacles when it came to Canada. He had this stubborn belief in his country's special decency and fairness. Well, maybe. But he has a blind eye when it comes to his homeland's elites who are as intellectually lazy, morally bankrupt and cowardly as most other country's "elites" with the extra irritating addition of cloaking themselves in the so-called Canadian identity—after years of searching for it—which they tout as one of caring and fairness.

And by elites I mean the fifty to a hundred like-minded people from GG David Johnston down who ponce around heading up bureaucracy and committees in the arts, the cultural establishment, academia and our inert Canadian banks. They are separate from Canadians themselves, rich, poor, and in between, who actually work and on a one-to-one basis, not scientific, I grant you, I've never found anything but basically decent. Very occasionally you run into elites like Peter Herrndorf at the National Arts Centre, business men like Hal Jackman and Galen Weston who aren't infected by the usual hypocritical cant, but they are rare.

Astonishing to me, the gloom that descended on our house that day was about as bad as any I've seen in the years of all our fighting for survival. It had never occurred to Conrad that a man of probity, as David Johnston was reputed to be, would not only judge his case without knowledge but behave in so vindictive a manner.

"It's only a lapel pin," I said in my role as official cheerer-upper. "Don't pin this on the man in the street. Most people in this country would give you a hearing at least. Canadians really do have a sense of fairness. Just not this lot. They're too important to entertain bourgeois ideas like that."

"Barbara, you don't understand." Truth is, I didn't.

For hours he sat in absolute silence. Conrad's was a depression of the soul that comes from a disappointment in an article of faith—his Canada. God, he was so proud to be Canadian. No pretense when he was in the U.K.: Canada was his land. He believed that a country that is sufficiently sure of itself to dispense its own honours should be sovereign. He had been convicted in a foreign country on two counts that in that country were still very much a matter of contention among legal minds as high as the former attorney general of the U.S., believing the trial and convictions to be the persecution of an innocent man. Even his business enemy, Rupert Murdoch, who followed the case with particular attention, opined that the entire prosecution was a disgrace and a sham. In effect, by heaving Conrad without benefit of their own independent study and a hearing, Rideau Hall and the prime minister were announcing that America would decide who could be a member of the Order of Canada. I simply thought that the Ottawa lot led by Johnson and PM Stephen Harper were either not bright enough to understand this or were small enough to enjoy punching below the belt. Probably both.

One month after the OC betrayal, Conrad's inbox contained a short email from Chris Boyce, executive director of Radio and Audio at the CBC. "I am writing to you on behalf of the CBC, House of Anansi Press and Massey College in the University of Toronto. . . . As you know we have not corresponded about the Massey Lectures for some time. In the meantime, we have reconsidered our programming choice regarding future lectures, and we regret to inform you that we will no longer require you to deliver the Massey Lectures." That was it. No apology, no further explanation.

With that curt dismissal, sans effort to even mimic politeness, his illusions disintegrated. The friendships he believed he had, what standing he had hoped he retained, fragmented, and each piece was like shrapnel lacerating his being.

John Fraser had been a friend of Conrad's since schooldays. Scott and Krystyne Griffin had been friends of mine for nearly thirty years. None of them had the basic decency to at least warn Conrad of the CBC email sent in their name. Lack of imagination I suppose: one one-hundredth of what Conrad had endured would have killed any of them—all those books of lies and falsehoods, the films, vicious profiles, years in prison, the injustice of it all. Ah well. Each of us has our limitations, and the sort of imagination I am talking about is very rare indeed. Conrad sent off a biting note to John Fraser, who blithely replied with careless self-indulgence that he had never thought giving him the lectures was a good thing and "you may not like hearing this but at least I am being an honest friend," which was totally mendacious since he had been the very first person to raise the subject. I resisted sending him his own email.

Scott Griffin, being a man of some principle, came traipsing up to the house, but only after being told rather firmly of Conrad's unhappiness. CBC personnel had changed, he said, and new management would not broadcast the lectures or partner with Anansi if Conrad was giving them. Fair enough. It simply depends on your horizons, I suppose. I knew, without doubt, without hesitation, that Conrad would have risked sacrificing those lectures even if it meant some financial loss, had such a cowardly blow been struck against any friend of his in his name.

That pretty much had been life, day after day. A tapestry of small defeats adding up to despair. If it ended, I wondered, would that mean happiness? And would there be any time left to actually enjoy life given my increasingly palsied limbs and moth-eaten brain? It embarrasses me to quote Albert Camus, but since he and Orwell have been my literary and ethical heroes for about fifty years, I feel entitled to without sounding hideously like a swot. "One morning," Camus writes in *The Rebel*, "after many dark nights of despair, an irrepressible longing to live will announce to us the fact that all is finished and that suffering has no more meaning than happiness." I had never understood that, really, but I did now.

CHAPTER THIRTY-ONE

Loss, Love and Vera's Revenge

There has been, I'm afraid, a definite absence of humour in this book. Fortunately, mother Vera may be counted upon to provide light relief and if this, her last appearance in the book, is chronologically a little out of order, it is to relieve the gloom I feel after narrating the last chapter and before confronting grimmish matters to come.

Sometime after Conrad had exchanged his immaculate London suits for the federal government's ghastly taste in apparel, my sister called to say that our mother had died and the funeral was to be held in Kitchener, Ontario.

Mother had not played a significant part in my life, apart from her featured appearance in the *Mail on Sunday*. Indeed, not one of my three most recent husbands had ever met her. Her last appearance had been the almost phantasmagorical 1964 "presence" in the Forest Hill penthouse of the Smith family. No, I err. She did turn up, to my great surprise and pleasure, in Manhattan in 1970 or so, when I was living with my film director. We were taking her for a ride through the city to show her the sights when suddenly, apropos of nothing, she said from her back seat, "Stop the car."

"Is something wrong?" asked Film Director in a kind but worried voice.

"I'll just throw myself into a dustbin," she said. "Just find a dustbin for me, that's all I'm worth to you." She opened the car door before we had quite stopped and was gone. Film Director found it rather upsetting. When I told sister Ruth about it later, she said this was familiar. One day her eleven-year-old son had gone into the back garden where some family event was being celebrated. "Mum," he said, "there's a strange woman in the hall purporting to be our grand-mother." She had come for an unexpected visit and her departure was made in the usual manner—though this time from a standing start, not a moving one. Early one morning, before anyone was up, she packed and made her exit.

The closest Conrad came to meeting her was after one of the huge Christmas parties we used to give in our Toronto home. "Who is Vera Somes?" he asked after all the guests had left.

I had a sinking feeling. Had she been there, behind some potted palm or ship model? "My mother."

"She sent me her kind regards and I've never laid eyes on her."

"They were delivered to you by Geoffrey Somes." I had made attempts to establish some sort of relationship with my half-brothers and invited them to our Christmas party. "You are special. He brought no message for me."

When Vera died, my filial sense kicked in, even if her maternal one had sputtered a bit, and Ruth and I set off together for Kitchener, with me driving. My driving always makes my sister a little nervous, not without cause. I do drive faster than my ability, but then I like driving fast. If God had meant us to go slow he would not have made ordinary cars that can do 120 miles an hour, which is something I wish the authorities would take into consideration when setting speed limits, following the wisdom of the non-existent speed limits on much of Germany's Autobahn. And the only accident I have ever had was when I was driving at 25 mph and the uninsured, unlicensed youth in front of me did a sudden stop.

The Kitchener funeral home held about eighty unknown people in the plainest of halls that, if it had basketball hoops, would have been a gymnasium. Ruth and I did recognize our half-brothers and a single cousin from England. In the room where the coffin lay containing Vera Somes, née Isserlis Barnett, piped-in music was playing

"Ave Maria," and above the coffin, decked with white flowers, was an extremely large crucifix.

The occasion was being conducted by a pleasant man, perhaps a minister of some Christian sect—most likely the United Church but without any external trappings or signs; I find all Christian denominations fairly interchangeable in Canada. One by one, people mounted the stage quite informally to speak of Vera in terms that to Ruth and myself were perfectly unrecognizable. Who was this woman that so liked ballroom dancing, barbecues and her family?

Ruth looked unamused. "What is this?" she asked.

"This is the funeral of Vera Isserlis Somes," I said. "Our mother."

Ruth had maintained some very occasional contact with Vera when her own children were younger. "Do you think," she asked hopefully, "there could be another Vera Somes?"

To be at the funeral of your mother who has assumed an entirely unknown life is Hitchcockian in its way. She's the lady on the train who disappeared. After the last recitation of our mother's love of square dancing or flapjack making or knotting—anything seemed possible for this Vera—Ruth turned to me. "We're going up there," she said in a determined voice, inclining her head to the platform where a speaker was declaiming Vera's enjoyment of camping. This is a quality I prize in my sister. She can be extremely obstinate at the right times as well as the wrong ones. "After all," she continued, "she was our mother and she was Jewish." I have no idea why it was so bloody important to us to establish this, but without a discussion we both came to the conclusion simultaneously.

After introducing ourselves as Vera's daughters, we referred to our existence as her "English life."

"Our mother," I said after praising the early introduction to opera and classical music she gave us both, "came from a great rabbinical family whose name is on her birth certificate." I believe Mother's friends thought I was referring to a Scottish ancestry she had—the MacRabbinicals, perhaps. Ruth followed up with some detail about the ancestry and tradition of the great sixteenth-century Rabbi Isserles. The audience, apart from our one English cousin who appreciated it, seemed not to understand a word we were saying. Without any delay, a nice woman followed us and commended my mother's cooking and generosity—two features we were both unaware of.

Ruth said, "We were too subtle. We never once mentioned the word *Jewish*."

Back in my own real life post-prison, the atrocities continued with reassuring steadiness. I had not inherited Vera's paranoia; we were, quite genuinely, being persecuted. Conrad more than me, of course. Actually, I'm really lucky that way: apart from the Reform Club in London, I've never joined a club and have never thought any organization would honour me, so there was nothing to retract. My husband, on the other hand, was thrown out of the Toronto Club with a little help from his darling "Establishment" friends. Conrad belonged to many exclusive clubs in the U.S., the U.K. and Canada, several of which far exceeded the Toronto Club in prestige and history. None of them, not one, expelled him. They were, in behaviour as well as name, the clubs of gentlemen. I believe that one—the Athenaeum in London, a club for members of "distinguished eminence in science, literature or the arts," of whom fifty-two have won Nobel Prizes, considered the matter in some detail and concluded that there was absolutely no reason to withdraw Conrad's membership.

The walls of the Toronto Club are adorned with photos of distinguished guests entertained there, of which 98 per cent are with Conrad: Conrad and Ronald Reagan, Conrad with Margaret Thatcher, Richard Nixon, Brian Mulroney, Mangosuthu Buthelezi, etc., etc. The book describing its history contains those same photos—unless it has been pulped and the walls of the club stripped in a sort of Stalinist Central Committee act erasing his existence. Conrad was given membership on his twenty-first birthday—the youngest member to be so received. But it takes your friends to chuck you out.

The expulsion required a little waiting time until members on the management committee favourable to Conrad had left and a majority, including Fred Eaton, with the apparent complicity of

Anthony Fell, an early business associate of Conrad's and a man he believed to be his friend of fifty years, his brother Fraser Fell and former jeweller Irving Gerstein—the man Conrad, Galen Weston and Hal Jackman had banded together to get into the club—could make sure he would be thrown out. The ballot was secret, but the manoeuvring beforehand was not. My poor naive husband was given the opportunity to make his case to the committee and went in with his lawyer ready to answer any questions. The matter had of course already been decided.

Meanwhile, over at the witches' coven called the Ontario Securities Commission, it was all "double, double, toil and trouble" as the cauldron heated up. Back in 2004, before every financial charge against Conrad but one was thrown out (and that a $285,000 wire fraud—a non-existent crime in Canada), before the Breeden report was revealed to be a libellous tissue of lies, the SEC seized US$9 million from Conrad and announced a lifetime ban on his being a director of a public company.

Hell, Conrad said, let's fight that one in court. Whoops, said the SEC, let's not go to court. We'll give you back $6 million if you just go along with the ban on directorships of a U.S. public company. We were financially strained at the time, knew the costs of a trial, and Conrad's feelings about being on the board of a U.S. public company were that being boiled alive would be preferable. We took the $6 million. Today we could probably get that ban overturned, but that's another book and that was 2004.

Now it was 2013, and in spite of all the dropped charges and the SEC's return of the money, the OSC was still in a froth of copycat envy of the American SEC. God, can't those miserable people ever think for themselves?

The commission decided on a hearing and appointed a wool of bat and tongue of dog in the persons of OSC Commissioners Christopher Portner and Judith N. Robertson were to hold a hearing to decide whether Conrad could participate in Ontario's public companies as a director. Their "court," as criminal lawyer Steven Skurka wrote, not a hearing at all but a "meaningless pile-on."

The OSC banned Conrad from being a director of a Canadian public company on the grounds of a single U.S. conviction of a financial crime that does not exist in Canadian law and the obstruction of justice conviction based on the removal of his boxes, a charge the Canadian courts had thrown out at the time. But, the Solomonic Canadian commissioners and their staff did not want to re-litigate the case in any way. The U.S. convictions had taken place "in a fair jurisdiction," wrote Portner and Robertson. What fairy-land did they inhabit? Conrad was found guilty of something in America, *ipso facto* he was a threat to Canadian investors—at which point one expected them to get out their U.S. prayer mats.

As Judge Amy St. Eve had said, Conrad's would be a very different case if it had not been for the obstruction charge. The OSC hearing had an opportunity to actually finally set that record straight—even the obtuse Judge Campbell had ruled that the removal of the boxes was not in contempt of his court order. In their hearing room, the OSC commssioners had the people the U.S. prosecutors had prevented from testifying to the Chicago jury by threat. Portner and Robertson listened to the head of Hollinger. They listened to Joan Maida and then they put their hands over their ears and eyes. "Fair jurisdiction."

Not only did they ban Conrad permanently from being on the boards of public companies, but they included a permanent ban (probably outside their jurisdiction) on his being on the boards of private companies as well, including any he founded, which of course they would not let him found—short of an unincorporated lemonade stand. This was what they did to a seventy-two-year-old man trying to regain his footing after a transparently unfair prosecution.

But my husband was ingenious while the OSC and its commissioners were simply self-righteous and vicious. In that contest, ingenuity will win. Conrad had finally found a promising small business. It was trading insolvent, but the chief creditor had not pushed it into bankruptcy. For a million dollars U.S., I became the largest and controlling shareholder. Since Conrad couldn't travel to the U.S. to check it out, I found myself playing Rosie the Riveter, peering thoughtfully into furnaces and checking out metal presses.

Paying for it turned out to be a bit edgy, since the Mareva was still in effect, and in order to make a full investment to get control, I had to exceed my quarterly allowance and "stretch" my affidavit. I asked my lawyers, who got all antsy.

"Oh fuck them," I said, "it's 2014. The Mareva was given by order of Mad Hatter Judge Colin Campbell in 2005 on the basis of a false affidavit, and if he wants to bring me into court, we can, to use the favourite expression of the OSC, 're-litigate.' I'll write three cheques, each just under the limit. Bring it on." Everyone else was swearing false affidavits; I figured I was owed one.

It would take three years of some fairly chilling moments for Conrad to cleanse the company of all bloodsuckers, and another two years before acquisitions would put it on a path to excellent profits. At times I was suicidal, but Conrad's intuition and business skills had not deserted him. In the meantime, the need for cash reoccurred intermittently as we struggled with the remaining Hollinger serpents that bound us and whose heads would not be chopped off until 2019.

Incredibly, my husband raised a cash income of around half a million a year. This began when Moses Znaimer, a television and business entrepreneur, contracted Conrad for a series of interviews on his *Zoomer* TV show, designed for greying Canadians with all their teeth and mental acuity. Moses thought Conrad's connections might still have some validity. Judge for yourself: Conrad did live interviews with, among others, Donald Trump on Skype (before he was a candidate), heartthrob Justin Trudeau (before he was prime minister), Boris Johnson (before he was prime minister), Nigel Farage (before his Brexit victory) and mayor of Toronto Rob Ford (during his drug scandal). In addition, he got contracts as a (rather successful) financial planner with several accomplished but disorganized "venturers" and began his career as a Canadian and American political columnist and radio commentator which quickly blossomed into five columns and two regular radio shows a week.

In 1977, I'd profiled the broken-nosed, flat-faced Canadian boxer George Chuvalo in a *Maclean's* feature. Chuvalo had been trying, almost hopelessly, to make a boxing and business comeback in his forties. In a 1967 fight against the great Joe Frazier, Chuvalo stood in the ring, feet planted down, with one eye virtually knocked out of its socket and the other one a swollen-closed slit. But he kept standing, never went down—until the referee called a TKO. He did the same with Muhammad Ali, as the great champion danced around him, throwing punches all over the stolid figure of Chuvalo. "George Chuvalo Is Still On His Feet" my article was titled. The man had guts. He never gave up. He had class, I wrote. My husband reminded me of him.

George Jonas's Parkinson's was getting to the nasty stages. Crikey, I thought, where the hell is the Sugar Plum Fairy in this story? As I drove along Rosedale Valley Road to his house, my heart would sink at what lay ahead. We had to sit very near each other in order to converse. Both his vision and hearing were going, and that meant up-close observation of all his physical infirmities: his elephantine legs bandaged to cope with the lymphoedema, the severe spinal stenosis, the frozen face. I still saw the George of earlier years behind his eyes and in his ever-brilliant observations, but those words were coming from a voice that was as bandaged as his legs.

George and I had been together one way or another for fifty years. Our lives together haunted me. Little moments—thinking how sophisticated it was when he ordered a Campari and soda; lying on the floor of our first apartment together listening to the soaring duet from Boito's *Mefistofele* between *La belle Hélène* and *Faust* and wondering how anyone could possibly condemn Faust for selling his soul to forever achieve such sensual bliss.

I sat in the worn leather chair next to him and thought what my life might have been had I not left him simply for a fleeting sexual passion and the need to free myself from his physical and emotional control. What we might have written together. How deeply embedded in my limbic system he remained. "I would have killed you or you killed me," he said suddenly, as if reading my mind. "It couldn't have worked that way, babe."

Gradually, I came to realize that I might never have really known George Jonas, or not this George. The feeling grew all the time, and it was peculiar. He was a trapezoid whose surfaces couldn't be seen all at once. I had a feeling that he might not like the person I had become but couldn't risk telling me. "Babe, I love you," he would say. "Come back soon." But I wasn't sure. Back and forth I went, twice a week, almost always on Sundays, and it was between the hammer and the anvil. At home, Conrad was sitting hunched over his desk doing "figures." On Berryman Street, in the townhouse Conrad had purchased for him in earlier good times, the beached George sat looking for anything to distract him.

"You will be my literary executor," said George, "and I've given you medical power of attorney together with Maya." Maya was doing her best. They had been together for thirty years and married for twenty, but this was not easy for her, given that she was blind. She was also thirty years younger and had weathered the suicide of her brother and her own bout of breast cancer. She wanted—and deserved—a life beyond the sickbed. Her own sense of mortality after her cancer was strong.

When George asked me not to bring the dogs anymore, I knew he was approaching the finals. He was trapped in a single bed now, on a small book-lined balcony overlooking the main room downstairs. He could see the huge ficus tree in the living room and the clouds rushing by outside as life ebbed away. Taped to the wall was the "do not resuscitate" notice.

"Can I give you a Jewish burial service?" I asked.

"No. I don't deserve to die as a Jew. I converted," he said. "My grandfather refused." No use to point out, as I did ceaselessly, that his parents converted to Lutheranism in the 1930s in the shadow of anti-Semitism. How could it be a betrayal for a Hungarian Jew in Budapest to try to survive Hitler and Hungary's Arrow Cross squads? This was my first encounter with survivor's guilt, a syndrome I had never believed existed, but there it was. It had taken till this moment, the point of death, to pry loose the tortured feelings he had about his conversion.

I had promised him, when we were married, that if either of us got to the point where we were being diapered, reduced to infants again, the other would end our life. We had reached that point. At his instruction I called his doctor, who declined to be involved but offered to help me obtain the drugs I needed. The revised Ontario legislation for medically assisted death was being debated but had not been passed.

As I drove home, I brooded on the dilemma. I owed George this. I had promised for nearly fifty years to be there when the moment came. But I was afraid. George had trouble swallowing, pills might wedge in his throat, and I despaired of using a syringe. You give your dogs subcutaneous injections, I thought. Can't you get it up to simply put the syringe into his veins?

We had a doctor assigned specifically for end-of-life patients. He was a thoughtful, patient man. He explained to me that he could take George off nourishment and liquids and administer morphine for his pain, and it would take ten or so days for him to die. He would slip into a coma from which he might emerge periodically until death. But George had to request this.

As the last two months wore on, I both wanted his death and dreaded it. God, I hope others experience this ambivalence and that I was not simply a wretched monstrosity. I knew I could talk George into the words that would begin his life's end and I struggled not to do it. He had only to reply affirmatively to a couple of questions and then he could be medically starved. A hideous charade, really, but the best that could be done. George changed his mind at every moment: he would ask me to let him go, and then when the doctor came into the room, he would give equivocal answers. I realized that all those terribly serious discussions we had when young, healthy and full of life about wanting to avoid the indignity of this stage became just that finally—discussions. He was hanging on to life for dear blazes.

About three months before George's death, Anna Porter, writer and publisher, organized a new edition of his collected poems. Margaret Atwood generously wrote a rather marvellous essay as a preface. "Did you notice, babe?" George said. "She made no reference to my poetry."

"No," I told him. "She praised you as having a great deal to say in your poetry and having said it always excellently." Atwood was straightforward about her response to his work. "George was not exactly of his time," she wrote, and she knew the word to describe his perspective: not *sardonic* or *sarcastic* but *mordant*.

George's sense of peril was fast returning together with nightmares, and he could see shadows behind the doorposts. I had never really encountered death apart from in literature or abstract contemplation. Visiting dying people in hospitals is a quick drive-by. This was my first experience, and it was a slow-motion horror film. Each frame was slightly more sallow and slower than the last. Death is a pasty, pallid shade of tallow. George's eyes watched us. He still carried on conversations, but now he was on doses of morphine just to ease the pain. "Babe, a little more," he would ask.

When he dies, I knew, in spite of twenty books of prose and poetry, the notoriety of Steven Spielberg's adaptation of his book *Vengeance*, the Mystery Writers of America Edgar we had won together, all his TV Junos, the plaudits, awards and admirers—in spite of this, he will be erased in a flash. His name will be deleted from telephones, he will exist as a trace but for a short time only when someone refers to something he said or wrote or did and then it will be back to their espressos. He fought so hard to survive and then to become a literary and intellectual presence in the English-speaking world and it should have worked, and it did to a large degree, but he never achieved quite the arc he deserved.

"I want endless sleep," he would say to me. Maya felt he had come to the end. She would sit curled up on the end of his bed stroking him. But I couldn't quite let go till he gave me permission, and Maya wanted me to make the decision. The doctor needed the rules to be followed. I could tell George precisely how to answer the questions. His eyes were watching me and I didn't know whether he was testing to see if I wanted him to go.

"George, if you really want endless sleep, you can ask the doctor and he will ask two questions which you have to answer with a positive 'yes.' If you qualify your answers as you have been doing, that's fine and you should so long as this is bearable, but he cannot give you endless sleep. Do you understand?"

"Yes, babe. I understand only too well."

The table next to his bed no longer had books, only pill bottles, swabs, Vaseline, sheets of paper to record times and amounts of morphine doses. He could no longer sit, turn, read or write. No, I thought, this was not how it was meant to be when we discussed Orwell and Louis Malle. The gods gave him the hell of Hitler and then Stalin. Couldn't they at least have given him a quick death, anything but this sordid little finish with strangers tossing his stained sheets off the bed and wiping his bottom?

"I want endless sleep," George said again. He was slowly losing some cognitive ability.

The doctor came. "He has been asking for endless sleep," I said.

George was quite conscious. "Mr. Jonas," said the doctor, "do you find the pain, mental or physical, to be unbearable? Too much for you to suffer?"

I was standing just out of the doctor's vision. George looked at me. His eyes questioning. "Yes," I mouthed.

"Yes," said George.

"Do you wish me to begin medication that will give you endless sleep?" God, who came up with that phrase? George hated euphemisms and yet he was using it. I wondered if I had missed a class on dying. "Do you want that?" asked the doctor.

George looked at me. I was numb. "Yes," I mouthed. "Yes," said George, very clearly and firmly.

Then everything moved very fast. One tube went out, another went in. "About nine or ten days," said the doctor.

Conrad had offered him a place in the Black family plot. "Thank him incredibly," George said. I had permission now from him to say a Hebrew prayer over his grave at interment. "No rabbi, babe, just you."

Maya let me move into the room next to George. I put my dog pillows on the floor as a bed and regular down pillows for my head. I washed in his bathroom, mentally cataloguing the additions that marked the stages of his disease: the dozens of pill bottles with different dates, the handrail, the special shower seat, the special toilet, the bedpans. I sat next to the bed relieving the night nurse a few times. I couldn't even cry.

The urine was darkening as organs began to fail. I could hear the breathing that would slow and stop and then, after a lengthy pause, start up again. He recovered consciousness about five days in. It was night and it was only momentary. He looked at me. "I love you, babe. I hate . . ." and then he was not conscious again. "I hate?" I hate this drawn-out business, I suppose. I hate this long journey.

On about the tenth or eleventh day, I drove home to get a change of clothing and some of my meds. Before I went, I bent down to George: "I'm just leaving for a very little while," I said, kissing his forehead. "Not more than forty-five minutes. I'll be right back." I don't think he could hear a word, although I had played music to the end, on the theory that hearing is the last sense to go. When I reached home there was a phone message. George was dead.

CHAPTER THIRTY-TWO

The Pot of Gold

And then came the day. Finally. "I've held out, but we have to sell this house." Park Lane Circle, his Toronto redoubt.

A tactical retreat, Conrad had said of other decisions to sell. We'll get a home in London again, you'll see, he had said. We'll buy back the lot next door, he had said. Now the last retreat in terms of real estate. "I can't go on under this stress," he said, his body tilted backwards with exhaustion in his desk chair. "We have to get rid of the fourteen-million mortgage plus the million and a half annual running costs." I knew he was right.

"Where will we go?"

"You can choose something you like. A rental. Or we can buy." I did not ask just how we would do that.

Conrad chose an American company to auction the house and circumvent an endless procession of curious buyers sizing up how desperate we were. But at the same time, real estate broker Barry Cohen was bringing in clients in case a deal could be made before the auction. We had the worst of both worlds. I tried the "staging" thing they show you on the cable TV channels. You tidy up, bring in modern neutral furniture with perky hits of colour. Like hell. Try that in a twenty-six-thousand-square-foot home already force-fed like a prize goose with sofas, chairs and antiques from London, Palm Beach and New York.

I went room to room with the auctioneer and real estate agent breezily telling me to "get rid" of six sofas, "axe" all those books and at least three dozen occasional chairs.

"All those books?"

"Well, keep some of the leather-bound ones and put flowers in between. Or do you have nice crystal or porcelain vases? Figurines?"

Only to break over your flat little heads, I thought.

"You need better sight lines," sighed the professionals. I had three desks in my workroom for research and writing. Two had to go. Last exit to chaos.

Each week we had two or three appointments for viewing and it was diabolical. The halls and rooms to be cleared of dog beds (over two hours alone given all the heavy waterbeds and Canadian Tire carpets to prevent four legs from slipping). Kitchen mercilessly deconstructed to create blinding white surfaces and stainless steel. Our Filipino staff together with the Portuguese employees were magnificent: they worked like an elite army unit.

For what? The Chinese family that looked at the house and its double-height libraries with incomprehension? The unfamiliar people from down the road who claimed to have always had their eye on this property?

"Look," our unfamiliar neighbour would say to his unfamiliar wife as they sized up my workroom. "Her room has such a high ceiling. We should try that in your office." I would sit impassively behind my one remaining computer hoping that somehow these horrible people would self-destruct. God, how wonderful if the tops of their heads exploded and splattered pink matter over the worn silk carpeting they were complaining about where Arpad usually sat. "You can see the fabulous view from her French windows," the agent would say, leading them past me. They would turn and stare at me more than the garden.

"It's so small, this room," Conrad would hear buyers say of the bedroom in which his mother spent the last months of her life, watching leaves change colour, with Conrad and his father taking turns at her bedside. "It has an ensuite, of course," the agent would reply.

"But no separate shower," the prospective buyers would complain, "and the sink is small, with no proper vanity space. Where's the vanity?"

"She died like a prize racehorse," her nurse had told Conrad and his father. "Never a word of complaint about the pain of her liver and bone cancer." No vanity.

The auction house's Toronto rep was keen as mustard and thick as a plank. "Why don't we advertise a public viewing, an open house, with an entrance fee to go to charity?" he said, his excitement at having so original a thought in his head akin to having discovered gravity. Is such idiocy to be found on this planet? "I don't think you will get any additional buyers that way," said Conrad mildly, as if speaking to a six-year-old. This had to be far worse for Conrad, I knew. This house of memories, his father's house, which I inhabited like a hermit crab in a shell too big for it. No, losing it could be managed all right by me, but I couldn't quite see the next act.

That spring we had the auction. It was a disaster, with only one bidder, and Conrad was not going to sell for under the mortgage. "I'll manage something," he told me. "But we have to move and the problem is your dogs. A good condo is unlikely to rent to us with two dogs over a hundred pounds each."

"Maya is only ninety pounds. Arpad, admittedly, is hitting one-twenty, but he's heavily muscled. I won't leave them."

"No, no, of course not. I'd never let them go, they're part of our life. But they are complicating the situation." Conrad had located a smashing property in Uxbridge, solar-heated in some terribly modern way and surrounded by acres and acres of land. There were even outdoor caged areas for the dogs—coyotes and wolves were very much part of the scenery—which would be a real plus, but the owners wouldn't lease, only sell, and we couldn't commit to that.

A day or two after the auction, we sat immobilized by our situation. The mortgage was due. We had to keep it up or default. The American asset was there but not yet ready to pay out dividends.

Owned by anyone else, our house and land would have reached a legitimate price. There was no escaping it: quietly, curiously, we were being watched by brokers and buyers for the moment we were bankrupt and the house, put up for sale by bank or receivers, could be got on the cheap. The feeling was unpleasant.

Back in my workroom, the intercom rang. "We have a deal," said Conrad.

"With the auction bidder?"

"No, we have a sale and leaseback." Sometimes the Red Sea does part.

The apparent saviour was Harold Perry, a man who decades earlier Conrad had helped in business. A telephone call made on his behalf, a small thing, but it opened doors and Harold had gone on to make considerable wealth. He would buy the house for a sum that would pay off the mortgage, lease it to us with a buy-back possibility, and in the event of a sale to a third party above a certain figure, he and Conrad would split the profits. We would pay the running costs, taxes, utilities and upkeep of the gardens, plus an $11,000 monthly rent. It was a very generous but fair deal for Harold. He was a bit of a diamond in the rough, with an exquisitely polite and rather sensitive wife. I wanted to place a laurel wreath on his head.

All happiness is short-lived. That would be the motto on my coat of arms. The papers were drawn up for the sale when came the familiar devil waving his pitchfork. Canada Revenue had served our tax lawyer with a "jeopardy order" on all our assets, obtained, as usual, secretly in court on, as usual, an affidavit riddled with errors.

Just how many secret courts are there in Canada anyway? Hell's bells, did I know anything about jeopardy orders any more than I had known about Mareva injunctions? This was the special little frame-up of one Jon-Paul Rebellato, titled CRA Resource Officer/Complex Case Officer. Now that we had sold the house to pay off its mortgage and remaining debts, including anything that might be owed to the CRA—pending the appeal in Tax Court against their assessment—Mr. Rebellato thought it best to prevent that solution. According to his affidavit, the price the house sold for was clearly a fake figure and we had stashed some millions some-where secret and would flee Canada any moment. He knew this because the CRA's "internal appraisers" had assessed the property at a far higher figure.

Very internal, I thought. This is an electronically gated property with cameras. Unlikely this appraiser forded the creek behind our house, crawled through thick vegetation up the steep slope of the ravine wearing camouflage, jumped seven-foot fences, outran two vigilant Kuvaszok and entered the house while shedding his camo gear for repairman's overalls. Or impersonated a potential buyer—embedded in one of those Chinese families chattering away in Cantonese. Barring this triathlon of sorts, it was hard to see this appraisal as anything more than a drive-by figure.

As usual, everything came to a crashing halt. A jeopardy order was the CRA's version of a Mareva, only tighter, equally constricting both of us. The house sale couldn't go through. Neither Conrad nor I could write a cheque, as everything was frozen. We couldn't pay the mortgage—we weren't allowed to. Understandably, Harold balked at completing his deal.

I don't know what your diary looks like—dinner celebrating your new job, dental appointment or perhaps an off-the-record ren-dezvous scribbled with a false name—but I might as well take pride in the singularity of mine since there isn't much else to recommend it: Off to Federal Court to try to unhinge Mr. Rebellato from his malice or madness—or corruption. Find money for legal bills. Fight default notice just served from Hollinger Inc., who wanted posses-sion of the house immediately if we did not pay them $1.5 million based on the staged payment due to the Mareva, which was two days late. You know, just an average day.

Fortunately, when you go to court and challenge a government order, the Department of Justice takes over, and not the OSC or the CRA. The jeopardy order was removed in return for our posting a credit note of $3 million until the CRA tax claim was assessed. A rather nervous Harold gamely returned to the party.

To help meet the deadline for the needed cash deposit, ending the jeopardy order while we waited for the tax issue to be resolved, Conrad telephoned Canadian billionaire Jimmy Pattison for help. The conversation was to the point. "What do you need?" Pattison asked. "Ideally, $1.5 million for eighteen months. "Where do I send it?" replied Pattison. "I can secure the loan," assured Conrad. "That won't be necessary. A note will be fine. We've known each other for forty years and I've always found you to be a man of integrity, and am happy to be helpful now." Men like Pattison were all that prevented Conrad from having the stroke I expected to see just about every day—although anger and hatred can be a powerful prophylactic against death.

If I didn't look strained enough, I now got my first very severe attack of shingles, which was inevitable since I had, four months earlier, at the urging of Canada Health or something, taken the recommended vaccine for the prevention of shingles—especially important, the government told us, for the elderly. My arms, neck and back looked like the craters of the moon. And the nerve pain remained after the attack had passed. Rebellato's Revenge.

Our situation was rather bizarre. Conrad was becoming something of a celebrity in his field of political commentary and books. But going to the U.S. required an application that could be delayed or refused even while he was weekly on American radio and television and his presidential biographies were referred to by authors and commentators. Naturally, the CBC held its nose, just as they always had for me, but wherever Conrad went, people wanted to be photographed with him—literally everywhere: in restaurants, on the sidewalk, any sort of gathering he attended.

"Obviously," I said with mean envy one day, after he returned home to tell of another round of besieging autograph- and selfie-hunters, "you are the nearest they can get to being photoed with Robert Pickton." Fortunately, Conrad didn't know who Pickton was—a serial killer who lived outside Vancouver and fed his victims to his pigs. Everyone in Canada knew of Pickton. The comparison was both absurd and cruel, but Conrad got the gist. He was increasingly well known, but we couldn't take it to the bank.

Banks. Well, there you are. At this point, the Toronto-Dominion asked Conrad to speak at one of their big do's, the normal fee being $100,000. Well, not quite. In Conrad's case, they self-righteously explained, the cheque would have to go to a charity of his choice (and it couldn't be us, although I was sure we deserved charitable status by now) or they couldn't hire him.

My bank in the U.K. held on until about 2015, and then, together with my Visa card, declared in a letter, sadly and reluctantly—one could almost see the blots of tears—that I belonged to a class of "Politically Exposed Persons (PEPS)" because of my "position as an associate of a Member of the House of Lords" and sadly that meant they could not continue to do business with me. The wording was excruciatingly obtuse. A "Member" must mean only this one member, Lord Black of Crossharbour, because I couldn't really see a mass jilt of House of Lords spouses.

My extremely handy NEXUS/Trusted Traveler card was due for renewal. Conditional acceptance came quickly and I scheduled my interview. No trouble anticipated: after all, the original card had been granted when Conrad was in a federal prison, a fact I had carefully revealed in the initial interview. That interviewing officer seemed fine with it. She had more difficulty with my identification documents.

"Your Canadian passport says Barbara Black."

"Yes, that's me."

"Your Ontario driver's licence says Barbara Amiel."

"Yes, that's me."

"Your U.K. passport says Lady Black of Crossharbour."

"Yes, that's me."

"Your citizenship card says Barbara Joan Amiel and your birth certificate says Barbara Joan Estelle Amiel."

I was granted a NEXUS card.

The renewal interview in Toronto was going splendidly, and the large Afro-American woman was being most cordial. Idiot-child me wanted to reaffirm my honesty. "I won't be going to the U.S. quite as much," I volunteered, "since my husband's release from the federal correctional institution." Now I could see how Lot's wife looked when she became a pillar of salt. Honestly, the change in her face, speech and body language was terrifying. She disappeared for about fifteen minutes. On her return I asked if something was wrong. "You'll get your card," she said, but I knew. I was turned down.

About eight months later, I was once again given qualified approval pending my interview. The Toronto office was booked solid and directed me to make an appointment at the Niagara Falls, New York, office. I arrived spic and polished at the small office. "What's changed?" the officer barked at me. I didn't understand the question; I'd been conditionally accepted. "You were refused. What's changed?" he kept repeating as I weakly asked what he meant. His shouting deepened. "Now you think you can sneak in across the border and get your card that way." I could see the other office staff staring. I felt like a tribute in *The Hunger Games*.

"Why are you not renewing this card?" I asked plaintively. "Don't come back," he shouted as I left. I tried Freedom of Information, as the NEXUS site helpfully suggested if you are turned down, but after over three years passed in silence I realized no FOI answer was forthcoming. When I looked up my application online I could see one thing had changed: the administrators of the Trusted Traveler program seemed to be relying on Wikipedia and not the form I had filled out. I was listed as using even more names than those I had given: I was now Barbara Bloomfield, a nod to my erroneous status as George Bloomfield's wife on Wikipedia; I was also Barbara Jones, which I supposed was a misspelling somewhere of Jonas.

Predictably, into this gloom came the shining figure of David Graham making a return appearance. He was in what I believe is fashionably called a passive-aggressive phase, in which he would make apparently pleasant comments about our earlier years in order to illustrate the contrast with his current success, as in "I am sitting in what was our bedroom in Moulins des Graniers [the home in St. Tropez we bought while married], which has been renovated several times over in the past twenty-five years. I'm adding a wing you remember the house? It's looking wonderful." David wanted me to know he was watching our progress—downwards. "Dear Bab," he wrote, "I've been following the auction of your house with interest. Two real estate agents asked to show it to me. I would have been curious but would be awkward seeing it on that basis." He had tried to enlarge his already huge property on Walton Street in London by digging downwards to add a ballroom, swimming pool, wine cellar and servants' quarters. This raised a big stink, since Walton Street is both narrow and partially residential. Neighbour Edna O'Brien, who in 2009 had inscribed her new book *Byron in Love* with the accurate observation, "To David, even though he will never read this book," was by 2012 leading the opposition to the enlargement. "Monstrous and unnecessary," said neighbour the Duchess of St. Albans, and, of course, inevitably, references were made to his marriage with me and my marriage to Conrad, which evoked this sort of newspaper comment: "What is it about Commonwealth media tycoons . . . especially the Canadian variety: they seem to think their money gives them carte blanche to ride roughshod over people."

I had already been asked by David's brothers to contribute to several eightieth-birthday projects for him—there seems to be a vogue these days to ask for "comments" or "anecdotes" on the birthday boy's life, and I find the whole approach utterly reprehensible. The final effort to get me to participate in some celebration of my former husband's life came with the biography David commissioned. I reluctantly agreed but asked if the author could tell me first what sort of thing he was looking for. An attachment arrived immediately: "Prompt Questions—Memories of A Spouse." This was followed by twenty-one questions, none of which I could answer positively. "What did you do together for fun?" Suicide attempts was not a runner. "Can you remember a sad or difficult time together?" No other sort. "How will you remember David?" Unprintable, really, except I am printing this. So strange that this person who all but killed me has no concept of that.

In keeping with my ecumenical approach to former and present spouses, as our troubles began and David began to resurface, we would see him now and then for dinner. Helpfully, Conrad had known

David before I married either of them—and indeed was on David's guest list for our 1985 dinner dance in Toronto when our secret marriage was revealed.

"He was a very stylish man, quite charming, and I could see his attraction for a woman," Conrad told me later. "But having had lunch with him a few times, I knew he was basically business oriented and your interests were very much more intellectually directed. I wondered what you would actually talk about."

Conrad viewed David's occasional overture of friendship to us with mild amusement, though I was more cynical, given that David had waited until our troubles began. But hell, why not? After all, troubles or not, I still got a frisson of pleasure at showing off my happiness to David, the man who had turned me into mashed potatoes. Sometimes we would have coffee together, and if I was taking some pleasure showing off my happiness, he was keen to show off his wealth in the form of the smashing new apartment he had just bought in Toronto.

I noticed that he was aging at a faster rate than many. His pale skin was covered with a dense grid of fine lines, his complexion increasingly pallid. I put it down to his obsession with only ordering canarino—a fancy way of saying lemon and hot water; people who go bonkers on healthy living quite often look to me like the walking dead. Jim Fixx, the man who virtually invented jogging and died of a heart attack while doing it at age fifty-two, seemed to me a salutary lesson in going overboard—this of course was my own warped rationalization for the various gym memberships I took out over the years that worked out to a cost in excess of a couple of thousand dollars per lap run or swum, given the infrequency of visits. Now, as the months passed, I saw that David, this man who was so fastidious and stylish in a laidback totally heterosexual way, was no longer grooming himself properly. He was turning up for dinner looking as if he had just got out of bed, unkempt, clothes creased and sometimes even stained.

"Can we meet," he asked. "I must talk to you." He had been to the Mayo Clinic. "I have bleeding from the brain," he said. "I am cognitively handicapped. I took tests." I told him he was not cognitively handicapped—simply that the tests didn't accurately register his personality. He was renowned for his forgetfulness, his lateness, his losing of items all his life. When we were married he would go to hail a taxi to take us home after dinner and wouldn't remember I was still sitting in the restaurant until he got home and found he had no house key. "They don't have a control study of your earlier days to compare with these new tests," I said. I think I believed it. He seemed to be in complete control of his faculties, or at least as much as usual. Only his disregard for his appearance was new.

"Don't, for God's sake, travel," I counselled. "If you've got bleeding from the brain, air pressure isn't going to help you, and you need to be within minutes of a top hospital." He left that evening for London and then to his home on St. Barts.

Shortly after the revelation of his bleeding brain, the phone rang early one morning. "David," I said, "I'm just feeding the dogs. Can I call you back?"

"I'm in St. Barts and need to speak to you."

But I plumb forgot. And next day I thought it couldn't be anything serious, I'd wait till he was back. He had a stroke that very afternoon and never recovered consciousness. His family flew him comatose to Toronto, where one of his brothers was a cardiac specialist. Another brother collected messages and letters for David, which were read to him. It was unclear whether he could hear. I wrote letters to him. They were the love letters I would have written had he remained the David I first met—the dashing, heartbreaking traveller on the seas. They were letters you could only write to a dream before it became a nightmare. I asked if I could visit him.

Bedside again. I'm not sure why I went, except I couldn't bear to think of him alone. Whenever we met over the years, he appeared lonely in his great wealth, even though he had lots of courtiers who stayed at his homes: "They're hoping they will inherit," he had told me, and I said, "They've probably earned it." There had been new girlfriends since his second divorce, usually with socially bold-faced names that he was eager to share with me, but they seemed unsubstantive. Now he was in a semi-private room with a man loudly wailing in pain next to him. A description of him taped to the wall noted that

"David's interests were travel, real estate, his chocolate Labradors and blonde lady friends." God, did he never get beyond that, I thought, this man that actually talked his way into Harvard Business School because his initial application was rejected and he seated himself in the registrar's office until he got an interview and was accepted. Or that was his story, anyway. Probably absolutely true. He could talk almost anyone into anything.

The hospital room was hideously depressing, with a big tube going into his neck and IVs everywhere. To have the man I had loved so hysterically die in this horrid little setting brought out an old pain in me. Human beings—well me, anyway—are so god-awful perverse. There it was, that hideous waxen yellow creeping into his body and squeezing out the colour of life. All that money and it comes to this: I held his hand and looked at the long nails. And then, just for a moment as I sat there for my allotted hour, I glimpsed the enchantment and dazzle, the romance in him that had blown me away. Part of me had never stopped aching. I avoided his funeral.

Well, that's two husbands down, leaving one ex I barely hear about and my own living one. And my living one had been neglected.

Between trying to write these memoirs (and failing every time another bend in the road opened up), deathbed visits and the shuttered mind I had developed to the disastrous facts of our life that tumbled like falling bricks onto our existence, Conrad had been left to his own devices. I had probably spent more conscious time with George Jonas in the last two years of his life than I had with Conrad. Now Conrad was on to a new business venture in Europe and it was extremely promising. He was back in the game. Each week he looked irritatingly younger.

I had no idea how we survived the pressure of the U.S. Department of Justice's perfectly straightforward attempt to ruin and kill us, so well abetted by Canadian mimics and minions, but survive we had. For Conrad, the best revenge really was to enjoy life. For me, the only revenge would be to see our persecutors guillotined. I had worked out a thousand and one ways to see them die, beginning with injecting them with the Ebola virus and watching. Since we live in a pacific age and an age of selective justice, that's unlikely to happen.

But then, in October 2019, I finished writing this. I hadn't washed my hair for weeks and had been cutting it myself for over a year rather than waste time at salons. The only interesting thing I discovered was that I could cut my hair pretty well and that I was only about 35 per cent grey, which means I was neither wonderfully brunette nor stunningly white-haired. Then I got a vile flu and stomach problems and whined my way around the house eating jello and losing more weight.

Time to pull my act together, I thought. And revisit my husband. Let me count my blessings, I said. I do a lot of talking to myself when I'm not talking to the dogs. I thought about what I had left. Up to another twenty years, if I turned out to be as stubborn as most of the women I knew of in my family, with a good fifteen years available for active work. Yes, I could see writing into my nineties. I began mentally reeling off the names of people who had written or composed late in life: Herman Wouk, Diana Athill, Jung Jiang; Goethe finished *Faust* at eighty-one and Verdi did *Falstaff* at eighty and his *Requiem* at eighty-five. Sophocles wrote *Oedipus Rex* at ninety, in the fifth century BC, when lifespans were probably somewhat shorter than now. Although they were all of a calibre I was unlikely to reach, that was because I only knew of the distinguished ones. There could probably be a lot of middle-range writers bashing on.

Then, I still had my butterflies. The summers would come and the monarchs would arrive and my milkweed now straddled nearly an acre. I had planted wonderful nectar arrangements too—it was a five-star Lepidoptera eatery. I could peer to my heart's content under the flat furry milkweed leaves and cut some with eggs for my hatchery and watch instar to instar and become their local sanitation department, cleaning the masses of frass caterpillars excrete, hard, dark pellets along leaves and on the floor of the cages. Until the day you come downstairs and your caterpillars are climbing along the tight netting of the cage roof, looking for a place to lie straight. They are upside down like some bloody Michelangelo painting in the Sistine Chapel except they are spinning silk from their tummies to hang from.

You've done it, you pray. Got the eggs fast enough to prevent those damn tachinid flies and wasps from laying their eggs inside them.

You watch, at least I do, for hours until the few minutes of agitated twirling on the end of their silken thread comes, and they twist off their own head to complete metamorphosis into a chrysalis. It's their equivalent of writing a book in twenty-four hours and confidently throwing out the first draft. Will they make it to Mexico or be beaten down by storms or eaten by predators? Once, when I was lamenting the death of songbirds in our garden, caught by hawks circling on wind currents and then sitting on tree branches spitting out their feathers—Christ, it's a merciless sight—Peggy Atwood looked matter-of-factly at me and said, "Eagles and hawks have to eat too. It's nature, Barbara," and I knew she was right and I would be moaning away if the hawks that soar so magnificently were dying of starvation.

Count your blessings, woman, because after this nightmare you are still alive even if nothing remains the same. All that marred my pleasure in our home was that the lot we had sold next door had finally gone through a whirlwind of a build. Looking down on us like a gigantic vampire bat was this horrid monster house shoved hard up to the property line with three long floors of windows staring over our gardens, looking into the windows of my workroom. You had to feel sorry for it, really; there was no room for the house to breathe. Even ugly houses ought to have some room to flex themselves. You can imagine how it felt as day by day its structure was extended towards the very edge of its plot and the trees that might have clothed it had all been felled.

Running, almost tripping downstairs, "I'm finished writing," I tell Conrad. He smiles, but there is something in his face that tells me he has been waiting and holding off till I had finished this manuscript to tell of one more mountain.

"We're going to have to make a decision," he says. And I feel all my blessings go very still because actually I know Conrad-speak and that means a decision has been made and it may not necessarily be to my liking. The old film memory kicks in and it's *The Godfather Part III* with Al Pacino running his hand through his hair: "Just when I thought I was out, they pull me back in."

We are going to move, one last time. Leaving the house that Conrad has lived in, off and on, for sixty-seven years. But he doesn't seem too fussed. In fact, once he tells me, he looks rather happy. "No more awful memories. No more worries," he says. "This house is costing $100,000 cash a month just to run and it needs about eighty-four new window frames and sashes, a new driveway, new roof on the indoor pool, plumbing, wiring, the works. Probably several million dollars of work right away just to bring it to liveable." I think, Oh God, I cannot look for another place. There's nothing left in my toothpaste tube. The relief at finishing the book slides into the worry of the move.

"We won't sell any of your investments if we move," he says, "and you'll make a lot of money. And I've found us a new place—not easy, given your dogs. We'll camp there for a year or so while we decide where we'll live permanently."

"Who will look after the birds and milkweed?" I say stupidly. I think about my butterflies, which is about the least of it, really, except sometimes you get to a point where what's small becomes the insurmountable, while the massive task of packing up this vast house, which has the remnants of three other residences stuffed into it, seems like just another job. And I want to say, "Don't ever use the word *permanent*, because nothing is permanent when it comes to our homes."

Of course I'll manage, and I'll manage the only way I can. By the certain knowledge that although in one way life is random, you do in the nature of things become the architect of your own chaos. This was a life I designed with what bits of character I had and with what bits I lacked. Without Conrad, life would not have been any more predictable, and even though our joint chemistry created some tripwires, for me our marriage was the one right choice I made. This could, I suppose, be a mental sedative or a survival technique, but actually it's just what I learned about myself along the way. Without Conrad, by now I would long have bumped myself off or seen my happiness sucked down into the bog of self-indulgent hysteria.

I look at Conrad. He really does look like he's dropped about half a ton of worry. "This is going to be really good for us," he says, and I know that this is not false optimism put on for me but what he genuinely believes. And he may be right. Leaving behind this house, each room filled with some frightful memory of the past sixteen years, is to shuck off the last vestiges of this murderous trek.

"What about George Black?" I ask.

"Don't worry. You'll still have him. George doesn't come with the house. He comes with me."

Now that he sees I'm settled into the news, Conrad's going out to meet a couple of younger chaps who want to discuss some new venture. He's wearing one of his cream Charvet shirts—they have five hundred shades of white, I think—and he's selected one of their ties. Smart though the shirts are, he needs some new ones. He just never notices when cuffs get worn, and I have been neglecting this. Actually, he needs new everything.

And beyond the shirts and the smart Huntsman Savile Row overcoat that turns out to have a ripped lining because no one has told me and Conrad never noticed, I see the essential man. He's alive, I think, and I'm barely here. Not ill, not dead, just bloodless. All those vampires have overtaken me. Well, it's silly, of course, but what can I do? I'm not thirty or forty, nor fifty or sixty. Soon I will be eighty. One becomes a child again. His cell phone rings and he talks about things I don't understand to people I don't know. The words from Leonard Cohen's searing song in my head: "I don't know the people/In your picture frame." I don't want to leave Conrad's table.

What I wrote on that scrap of paper I put in the envelope in 1958, sick then with longing for the first love of my life in high school but knowing something basic about myself: that I would go to the end of the rainbow, and whatever was there, for me the pot of gold would always be empty. Now I understand: that's *my* failing, not the rainbow's. I know, huge insight. Anyway, enough. I have loved and lived very nicely, thank you, but I'm tired.

Conrad has turned back now after his call. He's in a smart dark blue suit and his hair has just been cut. He's that man I saw one night at George Weidenfeld's and thought, My God, I never realized how handsome Conrad is. He's happy now as well, because the business roundabout is going and he's on it. "Why aren't you coming?" he asks. "They're young and smart. It will be fun."

"I don't know. I think I need to sleep."

"You can always sleep. You mustn't brood so much," he says. "Everything is going to be all right."

I wonder. Is it safe to think forward? Is it possible to re-enter real life after all this? My health has left me unable to eat most foods for the past year; my reclusiveness has me left-footed socially. And I can only think in clichés: Tennyson's *Ulysses*, of course. Not the stuff about always roaming with a hungry heart and smiting the furrows. Not even the lines about old age. It's those killer opening lines: "It little profits that an idle king . . . Match'd with an aged wife."

Okay, aged I am, and when I was so much younger it was impossible to even contemplate love between people of our age—let alone physical love. Revolting, one thought. But here he is: my gorgeous, glorious hero and crusader. Flawed, I suppose, but not half as much as I. And for crissakes, if Ulysses can drink life to the lees, I can at least sip it, even if I'm not blonde, not as long-legged as I'd like and not forty years younger. None of this bunk about drinking life with "those that loved me, and alone."

"Just a minute," I say as he goes towards the door. "I'm coming, I'll get dressed."

He is a Ulysses of a sort. I suppose there will be jeers. It's easy enough to do. I suppose she's giving Conrad his Spartacus moment, I can hear the *Toronto Star* or *Guardian* sneer. Go ahead, sneer, but I know what punishment he has absorbed and how painful getting up has been. But he always got up. How many of you can say that, and how many could have done what he has done?

> Made weak by time and fate, but strong in will
> To strive, to seek, to find, and not to yield.

Not ever. The pot at the end of the rainbow was not empty after all.

ABSOLUTION

On Tuesday, May 15, 2019, with advice of counsel, President Donald Trump gave Conrad a full pardon. All record of charges and convictions were expunged.

Rupert Murdoch called President Trump to congratulate him and then called Conrad. Whatever use our plight had been in the business wars between the two men, Murdoch knew the charges were specious.

On June 14, Chief Justice Eugene Rossiter of the Tax Appeal Court of Canada ruled absolutely in Conrad's favour concerning the $32.3-million tax loss he was claiming, which the Canada Revenue Agency had rejected. He awarded Conrad full costs. In his judgment, he mentioned questionable aspects of the rulings of Delaware Vice Chancellor Leo Strine. The Crown, he said, should never have resisted Conrad's appeal.

On September 3, the CRA reduced their tax claim of $18 million owed by Conrad to under $500,000. *Vincit qui patitur.*

Last Words

There should be nothing more to say. Writing this book has bled the living daylights out of me. And I don't know why. Look, when you come right down to it, I was never, ever hungry or in material want; I had a roof over my head and, frankly, it was always, right up to now, including this new move, a luxurious roof far beyond the means of 99.9 per cent of North Americans—even if at times rather precarious. Conrad was in a cell—not I. I could go to Saks Fifth Avenue and did. I could go to Chanel or Hermès and did. The price tags still hang uncut from those purchases as if at any moment they will have to be returned.

And where did it go? My life, that is. I thought I would find it in these pages. Lives must be like smoke: you can't ever really get hold of them. The shape mutates in front of you and the words can't keep up. I read about a Belgian physicist who made extensive studies of the patterns soap froth makes and reduced them to a series of laws and mathematical principles. If you can do that with the froth around my sink, then capturing a life should be kid's play.

Life's gifts to me were generous and tantalizing: I had stardust, that ephemeral something that defies explanation, but not enough. Enough to get me into trouble but not into the stars. I had writing talent, but not quite the imagination to make it soar or the intellect substantial enough for the other side of the street. I had some beauty, of face and form, but I didn't know what to do with it. Wasted during the time it bloomed and then useless. I never matched the determination of the monarchs I so admire, the ones I released four months ago after raising them from egg to full-grown beauty: my miraculous September monarchs that will attempt the flight to Mexico and succeed or kill themselves trying.

Once, briefly, in 1967, when I was twenty-six years old, I decided that Israel was where I wanted to live. My determination petered out with the end of the Six-Day War. Perhaps that is the decision I most regret. I would like to have become a citizen of a country that, for all its troubles and woes, is essentially the land to which I belong. Had I been able at languages, then perhaps I could have lived and written there. Alas, given my sterling failure to grasp French after innumerable years of tutoring, the prognosis for my fluency in a Canaanite language is poor.

So many people in the world think themselves outsiders—like I do—that one wonders where the actual insiders are. Perhaps believing oneself to be an outsider, no matter how sincerely felt, is just another manifestation of vanity, of wanting to think oneself different.

I have no forgiveness in me. Though I am not a violent person, should I have the opportunity to do harm to a clutch of people named in this book, I would, just as they did to me and my husband. I'm supposed to say this is metaphorical, but it isn't. They stole my life: irreparable, unforgiveable and deserving of capital punishment. Now all that is needed—at least, I need it—are footnotes of some sort.

To those who believe that my husband's pardon was simply a "tawdry" reward for writing favourable columns about the U.S. president, they should read Conrad's book *A President Like No Other* and see that it is not a puff piece. For all those journalists who put their derision of the pardon in print, those social acquaintances and even my family, whose silence made their view clear, for the reprehensible beings at the OSC and Toronto Club who smote their goody-goody breasts and labelled the American system of justice "a fair jurisdiction," I have a few words for you.

When this began, the lead prosecutor in charge of the case was Robert W. Kent, Jr., reputed to be a man who would at least conduct the prosecution within the rules. He left the United States Attorney's Office in Chicago in September 2006 for private practice. From that point on, the lead prosecutor, Eric Sussman, working under Kent's replacement, U.S. Attorney Patrick Fitzgerald, was like a mad dog. Nothing seemed out of bounds.

Sussman gave witnesses including the directors immunity from any charges including perjury if they co-operated in the case against Conrad, and then coached them through their testimonies which were patently false and largely seen to be so by the jury. He never gave up trying to undermine Conrad's due process, a co-defendant told us after this was all over. He tried, sometimes based on an affidavit or testimony he knew to be false, to bankrupt us and deny us access to our funds at every turn, so we would be unable to pay retainers for a proper defence.

Using the same false affidavits that had been the basis of the FBI's seizure of our sale money from that apartment, he claimed again in trial that company money had "substantially" reimbursed us for any funds we contributed to our New York apartment's renovation. He stood waving some piece of paper kinetically in court to justify this, like Neville Chamberlain returning from Munich waving his "peace for our time" agreement. Our lawyer Eddie Genson came to life, standing up straight, wheelchair behind him:

"Well, Mr. Sussman," he said, "let's see that bill." Sussman remained defiantly waving the paper, ignoring the question.

"Yes," agreed Judge St. Eve, curious for once. "How much was it for?" Less than $2,500.

"That," said Genson incredulously, in a voice I wish had been available throughout the trial, "that's your reimbursement for the $2.5 million Conrad Black personally put into the apartment cost?" One one-thousandth of our contribution.

Sussman threatened a key Canadian witness with future difficulty entering the U.S., should he come to Chicago and testify for us. Co-defendants were offered deals if they would change their testimony to fit Sussman's Procrustean bed of justice and testify against Conrad. It is of credit to them that none yielded. Only David Radler, and he had been guilty of circulation manipulation with the *Chicago*

Sun-Times, perjury in a Vancouver sale of private newspapers, lying to the board of directors and God knows what else. Even so, it took at least sixteen meetings with Sussman to get the desired story and deal.

Finally, when Conrad received President Trump's pardon an unhappy Eric Sussman assumed the default position popularized by Nancy Pelosi of being "saddened" by the news—thankfully sparing us his prayers. He reminded reporters calling him that Conrad had "robbed public shareholders of millions."

In fact, the accused in the case he prosecuted were ultimately convicted of one count of wire fraud totalling $600,000, of which Conrad's share was $285,000. The basis for this single financial conviction which should have been overturned like the rest, was in the words of the delightful Torquemada Judge Posner, "a lack of documentation." That lack of documentation was described as simply a "clerical error" by Justice St. Eve in respect of a co-defendant. In any case, the transaction had been approved by the independent directors and publicly revealed twice. The shareholders were indeed robbed of the nearly two billion dollars of value Conrad had left behind, but by the usurpers who took over a profitable company and reduced it to bankruptcy after lining their own pockets.

As for the "judge" who would impartially keep justice on the rails, Judge Amy St. Eve for all her civility would not penalize the prosecution—she too had been a prosecutor and appeared to find these tactics unremarkable. I was taught as a child that the Crown and the people could never lose: if the accused was acquitted it was simply a victory for truth. The private firm that now employs Eric Sussman is doing American justice no favours.

Now, in 2020, the diseased underbelly of the American justice system is more evident every day: FBI false affidavits, DOJ-pressured plea bargains, illegal telephone intercepts, and the strategy of defendants before trial. The names of some who may possibly be indicted themselves are familiar to us. Our American lawyers had word that the Director of the FBI at the time of our prosecution, Robert Mueller, and Deputy Attorney General James Comey were taking a direct hand in our case being prosecuted by their friend, Patrick J. Fitzgerald, now Comey's defense lawyer. Conrad was not a direct American political presence, no big whale in Washington, D.C., but he was fun to bring down, a right-wing press baron with American newspapers whose point of view (especially in Chicago) was anathema.

As for Canada, I was never able to get an independent lawyer in Canada to challenge the Mareva. I sat around tables at different firms in Toronto where they either laughed at me or told me I was a bad risk for them financially. One lawyer charged me $25,000 as a retainer and all but disappeared into an Ottawa inquiry he was heading. Finally, a rather nice man in Toronto became my lawyer of record, the man who signed the Certificate of Independent Legal Advice on the dotted line and refrained from exorbitant fees but, like everyone else, was not going into a battle that required revealing that one of Toronto's top lawyers had behaved unethically in pretending to give me independent legal advice about the Mareva. They stick together, these big boys.

I do think the legal profession—and my experience of this was greatest in Canada—is a deplorable profession. If it were possible to have a society of laws without lawyers, I'd recommend disbarment for 90 per cent of them and the strangulation at birth of any infant whose parents wish the baby to go in that direction. An impossible dream.

And having got that off my genuine chest, I'm going to try to enjoy the remaining time left to me. And bugger off to the whole damn lot of you. We're still here. You lost.

Toronto, 2020

CODA

After last words, what is there to say? This.

In early March 2020, my wonderful Kuvasz Maya, at twelve years old, began to lose her appetite. A CT scan revealed a huge tumour in her spleen and smaller tumours beyond. Inoperable.

She still loved watching passersby on the street, the dogs big and small, trotting on their walks—everyone walking now because of the COVID-19 shutdown. Gradually she became lame. She couldn't manage the stairs to sleep with us, though she tried, every cell straining to propel her. Her great pleasure became sleeping outdoors all night with the cool breezes. Don Reeve and I alternated hours until sunrise so she was never alone. The coyotes and foxes couldn't kill her, but we couldn't bear the thought of her alone in any distress.

She was still alive in June. "It's a miracle," said the vet. "But of course, it is Maya."

On June 2 she demanded a walk outside the gates. By now she was severely crippled and I couldn't see how she would do it but off we went with Arpad. The day was sunny. She had to drag one hind leg and her entire back section seemed almost detached from her trunk—onlookers stopped to see this dog, in such evident difficulty with head held high, ever regal, willing herself to walk. It was magnificent. Every few minutes she had to stop and, because it was so painful to sit down, she would stand stock-still, usually in the middle of the road she had chosen to cross. The occasional car would come by and the driver would wait quietly watching the dignified elderly dog gather strength to say her goodbye to sun and earth. When we got home, she lowered herself slowly onto the driveway and smiled. She refused water, which was unusual. Later I tried to give her food and her pills, but she refused again.

That night there was a terrible storm with large hailstones and the sheet lightening that upsets her more than the accompanying thunder. We got out the van specially fitted for her with big plump cushions but she could no longer stand up. Again and again, she tried with legs that no longer worked. Her eyes looked at us desperately as frustration and pain gripped her. Don lifted Maya up and her teeth grazed him quite unintentionally, a reflex, when he accidentally pulled on the raw abrasions fresh from her attempts to stand. Settled in the van, curled up next to him, she slept solidly till morning when miraculously she limped to the front porch and up the three stairs to her mat. She devoured almost an entire bag of her hypoallergenic biscuits and drank lots of water but refused all meds. Her eyes told me. Enough.

The vet she knew and liked performed euthanasia while she remained comfortably on her favorite seat in the van. I held her head and stroked her. As ever she was perfectly calm. She didn't move when the catheter went into her back leg—she was so used to them— but when the sedative went through it, she opened her eyes wide and looked at me, one last time. Within seconds her head dropped into my hands and then came the lethal injection. The entire procedure took less than a minute. She was gone, my gorgeous Maya.

I had created a Morton's fork when I casually mentioned the scratch on Don to the vet. He had to report it to the health authorities. I could either keep Maya in quarantine for another ten days or, after euthanasia, have her head sawn off to be sent away, somewhere, to dissect her brain for rabies. Another day, let alone ten, would have been prolonged agony for her. Better mine. On June 3, her head, that beautiful head I so loved, with the dark golden-brown eyes and the smiling Kuvasz face was hacked off, to be opened up and thrown away. I gave her a private cremation, just Maya, and in return I received the ashes of my headless dog. The autopsy confirmed no rabies.

Friends & Enemies: The Lists

Compiling lists has something of a bad odour. The word at worst invokes "blacklists," whether of Hollywood or presidents. In a more frivolous sense, it has a whiff of the schoolgirl. My intent was neither, although now I think it could be seen as vulgar.

Even so, when I came to the end of writing these memoirs, I realized that there were many people who had offered help—some with outstretched hands, some more quietly, that I had either no space or no context to mention, and I wanted to thank them publicly. Then there were those who, for whatever reason, became either poisoned by events or events allowed their poison to emerge openly. I needed to list them if only to breathe properly again. A side effect of this sort of experience, if it continues for so many years, is that burying feelings all but buries you. There needs to be a release. An end.

The names cover the period during our worst troubles and not afterwards. So new friends after Conrad returned to prison aren't included. No list can be comprehensive. Some were proactive, some there if you called. Some simply sent an email or a note of support. Sadly, given the years this covers, a number are deceased.

There will be omissions and I regret most of all the friends who my compromised memory can't retrieve. As for the enemies I forget, probably that is all for the best. The mind has its own defences.

Most journalists were not friends but, though hostile, were just doing their job. Journalists singled out under "Enemies" deliberately lied or were vicious beyond the call of duty—the same criteria is applied to non-journalists.

It would take another book to list all the lawyers who went out of their way to enjoy persecuting people they knew to be innocent, either for the sheer fun of it, monetary gain or simple nastiness—and probably all three.

In general, U.K. friends were more proactively loyal and thoughtful. U.K. politicians and business people that may or may not have liked us, refrained from any easy shots. The clubs my husband belonged to didn't throw him out, the House of Lords didn't expel him. Frankly, apart from the ordinary dislike we evoked—and admittedly, there was a fair amount of that in good times as well as bad—the atmosphere in the U.K. was not as poisonous as in Canada or even the U.S. So here goes:

U.K.

Friends

Charles Moore

Dominic Lawson

Dan and Suzanne Colson

Rt. Hon. Boris Johnson

Barry Humphries and Lizzie Spender

Hon. William Shawcross and Olga Polizzi

Theo and Louise Fennell

Sir Elton John and David Furnish

Lady Owen (Miriam Gross) and Sir Geoffrey Owen

Lord and Lady Weidenfeld (George and Annabelle)

David and Clarissa Pryce-Jones

Sir Tom Stoppard

Ronald Harwood and the late Natasha Harwood

Robin Birley

Lady Annabel Goldsmith

Dame Joan Collins and Percy Gibson

Count and Countess Edmondo di Robilant (Maya Even)

Taki Theodoracopulos

Andrew Roberts and Susan Gilchrist

Manoli Olympitis

Penny Phillips

Lord and Lady Powell (Charles and Carla)

Lord Saatchi and the late, much missed Lady Saatchi (Maurice and Josephine Hart)

Rita Konig

The late Kokoly Fallah

Minette Marrin

Simon Heffer

Simon and Santa Sebag-Montefiore

Stephen and Gloria Vizinczey

The late Sir David Tang and
Lady Tang (Lucy)

Lady Cosima Somerset

His Grace the late Duke of
Malborough (Sunny)

Andrew Neil

Naim Abboud

Lord and Lady Rothschild
(Jacob and the late Serena)

The late Lord and Lady Carrington
(Peter and Iona)

Virginia Fraser

Pilar Boxford

Mark Lloyd

The late Sir David Frost

Petronella Wyatt

Wafic and Rosemary Said

Dame Janet Wolfson de Botton

Gloria, Princess Thurn and Taxis

The late Countess Maya von
Schonburg

Peter and Rosemary Buckman

The late Rosemary Millar

Rupert and Robin Hambro

Utako and Yukio Maezawa

George and Lita Livanos

Sir Ronald and Lady Cohen
(Sharon)

Steven Isserlis and the late
Pauline Mara

The late Sir Vidia and Lady Naipaul
(Nadira)

Rt. Hon. Jacob Rees-Mogg

Rt. Hon. Michael Gove

The late Lord (William) Rees-Mogg
and Lady (Gillian) Rees-Mogg

Paul and Marigold Johnson

Daniel Johnson

Lord (Norman) Tebbit

The late Rt. Hon. Margaret Thatcher

HRH Prince and Princess Michael
of Kent

His Grace, the late Duke of
Wellington (Valerian)

Sir Evelyn de Rothschild

Duncan McLaren

The late Sir Martin Gilbert

Leonie Frieda

The late Peter Stormnth Darling

The late Lord (Hugh) Thomas of
Swinnerton

Lord William and Lady Astor

Neil and Serena Balfour

Late Sir Ronald Grierson

Victoria Mather

Annunziata Asquith

The late Claus von Bulow

Nicky Haslam

Raffaella Curiel and Gigliola Curiel

Enemies

Tom Bower

Geoffrey Levy

Borderline

Max Hastings

U.S.A.

Enemies

Richard C. Breeden
(Villain-in-Chief)
Judge Richard Posner
Judge, Vice Chancellor and now
Chief Justice Leo Strine
Patrick J. Fitzgerald
Madame Judge Amy St. Eve
Eric Sussman
Jeffrey Kramer
Julie Ruder

Edward Siskel
Gordon Paris
Paul Healy
Honourable Raymond Seitz
Former Governor of Illinois James
R. Thompson Jr.
Hon. Richard Burt
Marie-Josée Kravis
Glen Horowitz

Friends

Laura Ingraham (Gold Star)
Miguel Estrada and David Debold
Caroline Gurland
Gregory Joseph
Bryan Skarlatos
Richard and Madeline Hill
Peggy Noonan
Kimberley Strassel
Ambassador Georgette Mosbacher
Lauren and John Veronis
The late Ezra and Cecile Zilkha
Beatrice Stern
Norman Podhoretz and Midge
Decter
Neil Kosovoy
Mark Steyn and Melissa Howes
Anna Wintour
Shelby Bryan
Sid Bass
Stephen and Christine Schwarzman
The late Jayne Wrightsman
Emilia and Pepe Fanjul
Dixon Boardman and Arriana
Hohenlohe Boardman
The late Norman and Sarah Murphy

The late Terry Kramer and Nick
Simunek,
Gay and Stanley Gaines
David and Danielle Frum
Ann Coulter
Rush Limbaugh
Roger and Susan Hertog
Leonard and the late Evelyn Lauder
The late William Safire
Mica Ertegun
The late Robert S. Pirie
The late Arthur M. Schlesinger Jr.
and Alexandra
The late Arnaud de Borchgrave and
Alexandra Villard de Borchgrave
Bob Tyrell
Roger Kimball
John and Melissa O'Sullivan
Rich Lowry
Seth Lipsky and Amity Shlaes
Andre F. Leon Talley
The late William F. Buckley Jr.
Julie Nixon Eisenhower
Thierry Despont
George F. Will

Oscar de la Renta

Boaz Mazur

Louise Grunwald

Alan Dershowitz

Harold Evans and Tina Brown

Jack Fowler

Marc Sole

Late Bloomers

Henry Kissinger

Rupert Murdoch

Paul Gigot

Supportive High Office Holders

President Donald J. Trump

President William J. Clinton

CANADA

Enemies

Rt. Honourable Stephen Harper

Rt. Honorable David Johnston and Stephen Wallace

Rt. Hon Beverley McLachlin

Mr. Justice Colin Campbell

Mr. Justice James Farley

Ms. Susan Wolburgh Jenah

Former OSC Commissioner Christopher Portner

Former OSC Commissioner Judith N. Robertson

David Radler

Susan Kastner

Wesley Voorheis

Newton Glassman

Gordon Walker

Fred Eaton

Maureen Sabia

Barry Avrich

The late Allan and Sondra Gotlieb

Jacquie McNish

Peter C. Newman

Dr. Bernard Gosevitz

Anthony Wilson-Smith

Rosie DiManno

Graham Savage

Stephen A. Jarislowski

Hon. Roy MacLaren

Enemy Lawyers

(A very brief sample of the worst)

Harvey Strosberg

William Brock

Robert Staley

Tony Kelly

Megan Keenberg

Friends
(Active and Or Just There)

The late Paul and Jackie Desmarais,

Kate and David Daniels

Julian and Anna Porter

Louise Lore

Veronika von Nostitz-Wallwitz

Rosemary Speirs

Brian Stewart and Tina Srebotnjak

Peter Herrndorf and Eva Czigler

Earl Cherniak

Lisa Munro

Stanley W.L. Freedman

The late Trevor Eyton

Raymond de Souza

Gabe Gonda and Victoria Webster

Hilary and Galen Weston

Lily Alexander and Dr. Waldemar
     Pruzanski

Melanie Munk

Robert Lantos

Rudyard Griffiths

Peter White

Jack Cockwell and Lynda Bronfman

Margaret Atwood and the late
     Graeme Gibson

The late Richard, Diane and
     Jenny Bradshaw

Sam Blyth

Brian and Mila Mulroney

Ben and Jessica Mulroney

Andrew Lapham and Caroline
     Mulroney

Mark and Vanessa Mulroney

The late Dr. Robert Buckman and
     Dr. Pat Shaw

David Nathanson

Dianne de Fenoyl

Ken and Tina Whyte

Sarita Dotan

Rabbi John Moscowitz

Jeanne Beker

Carol Slatt

Ivan Fecan and the late Sandra Faire

John Fraser

Heather Reisman and Gerry Schwartz

Jorge Vargas

Scott and Krystyne Griffin

Jimmy Molloy and Bernadette
     Morra

Nancy Lockhart and the late
     Murray Frum

Catherine Nugent

Tony Scherman and Margaret Priest

The late Jack Rabinovitch

Gerry Sheff and Shanitha Kachan

Helena Leung

Phay Sengthong

Don Vale

William Thorsell

Eric and Dana Margolis

The late Christie Blatchford

Joan Maida

Ira Gluskin and Maxine Granovsky

Ron and Jessie Riley

Jeremy and Jean Riley

Kurtis Rive

The late Peter Worthington and
     Yvonne

Adam Daifallah

Olga and Adrienne Stein

Ron and Steve Joyce

Joe and Kimberley
     Newport-Mimran

Jason Kenny

The late Gordon Eberts

Liona Boyd

The late Jim Coutts

Matthew Barrett

Hon. Jason Kenny and Odette Baudoin

Robert Fulford

Terence Corcoran

Ned Goodman

The late Murray M. Sinclair and A. Murray Sinclair

Amanda Lang

Hon. David and Shelley Peterson

John McDermott

Joanna MacDonald

Howard Sokolowsky and Senator Linda Frum

Peter Brown

Rod Senft

Dr. Donald Reimer

Joe Nadler

George Lengvari

Henry Fiorillo

Carlo Fidani

Lyn Westwood

Hal (H.N.R.) and Duncan Jackman

Jim Pattison

Harold Perry

Issy and Rosalie Sharp

Allan Slaight and Emanuelle Gattuso

Edward and Suzanne Rogers

June Black

Rt. Hon. John Turner and Geills Turner

Michael and Linda Radcliffe

Late Bloomers

Anthony J. Fell

My Blessed Kuvasz Support Circle

Gail Dash and Neil Berger, Casablanca Kuvasz, California
Deborah Blank, Glacier Creek Kuvasz, Colorado
Ivonne Kuvaszczyk Kuvasz Rescue, California
Dr. John Reeve-Newson and Dr. Matthew Richardson,
Toronto Animal Clinic
Dr. Doug Mason, Veterinary Emergency Hospital, Toronto
Dr. Salvatore Zeitlin, South Dixie Animal Hospital, West Palm Beach

ACKNOWLEDGEMENTS

With gratitude to my publisher Doug Pepper at Penguin Random House Canada for his inexhaustible patience and constant encouragement to "keep at it" over many lean and uncertain years. And with very special thanks to Managing Editor Kimberlee Hesas, Maryn Alberts, and the production and design team of Christie Hanson, Terra Page, and Lisa Jager. Together, they handled a seemingly endless nightmare of changes, additions, corrections, and inserts which are the bogeys of a book of this nature with an author of this nature. I cannot thank them enough for their fortitude and skill. To my agent Georgina Capel who probably has no idea how much she bolstered my confidence. To my assistant Danella Connors, who uncomplainingly organized hundreds of thousands of pages of research material. To David Debold at Gibson Dunn LLP who through both our ordeal and this book, dug up dozens of volumes of transcripts within twenty-four hours of a call. And to my stalwart computer expert, Jorge Vargas, the receiver of many desperate calls to rescue lost and abused copy over the long years of writing. All thanks and apologies to your family.

To my medical team—Dr. John Floras at Mount Sinai Hospital, Toronto; Dr. David Naimark at Sunnybrook Hospital, Toronto; Dr. Sidney Kennedy at Toronto Western Hospital; and Dr. Owen Lewis at Columbia University in Manhattan—all of whom, without violating the boundaries of good practice, supervised a medicine regime that allowed me to work the extra hours my circumstances have required. And my go-to invaluable Dr. Robert Francis, founder of Medcan and Franmed Health, who kept gluing the pieces together when I strayed into excess. I am eternally grateful to you all.

To my late husband George Jonas and my present husband Conrad Black, who together and separately caught the balance for me. You faced extraordinary difficulties in your own lives even while unselfishly giving me refuge in the blackest of times. I salute you both.

And finally, to my beloved Kuvaszok: Without you, this book could not have been written. Apart from saving my physical life in the face of danger, your company and humour during ugly times gave me the lift and hilarity I needed to carry on. If inter-species marriages— non-sexual, I hasten to add—and polygamy were legitimized, as they should be in this unfolding landscape of relationships, I would marry both of you with Conrad in a nano-sec.

INDEX

THE LOST ART OF LISTENING

The Lost Art of Listening

❖

MICHAEL P. NICHOLS

THE GUILFORD PRESS

New York   London

©1995 Michael P. Nichols
The Guilford Press
A Division of Guilford Publications, Inc.
72 Spring Street, New York, NY 10012

Printed in the United States of America

This book is printed on acid-free paper.

Last digit is print number: 9 8 7 6 5 4 3 2 1

Library of Congress Cataloging-in-Publication Data

Nichols, Michael P.
    The lost art of listening / Michael P. Nichols.
       p. cm.
    Includes bibliographical references and index.
    ISBN 0-89862-267-0
    1. Listening. 2. Interpersonal relations. 3. Interpersonal
communication. I. Title. II. Series.
BF323.L5N53 1994
153.6'8—dc20

94-38111
CIP

*To Salvador Minuchin,
a man of compassion
who isn't afraid to tell the truth*

Contents

THE LOST ART OF LISTENING

Introduction

Nothing hurts more than the sense that people close to us aren't really listening to what we have to say. We never outgrow the need to communicate what it feels like to live in our separate, private worlds of experience. That's why a sympathetic ear is such a powerful force in human relationships—and why the failure to be heard and understood is so painful.

My ideas about listening have been sharpened by twenty years of work as a psychoanalyst and family therapist. Refereeing arguments between intimate partners, coaching parents to communicate with their children, and struggling myself to sustain empathy as my patients faced their demons ultimately has led me to the conclusion that much of the conflict in our lives can be explained by one simple but unhappy fact: we don't really listen to each other.

Jumping in to say what's on our minds—before we've even acknowledged what the other person said—short-circuits the possibility of mutual understanding. Speaking without listening, hearing without understanding is like snipping an electrical cord in two, then plugging it in anyway, hoping somehow that something will light up. Most of the time, of course, we don't deliberately set out to break the connection. In fact, we're often baffled and dismayed by a feeling of being left sitting around in the dark.

Modern culture has developed conceptions of individualism that picture us as finding our own bearings within, declaring independence from the webs of interlocution that formed us, or at least neutralizing them. It is as though when we become finished persons we outgrow

our need for attention, like training wheels. All this is not to say that we can't be autonomous, in the sense of self-directing, or even original, able to think and act on our own. But we cannot leap out of the human condition and become self-sustaining, secure, and satisfied without need for conversation—conversation in a broad sense, that is some kind of interchange with others.

We think of ourselves as individuals, but we are embedded in networks of relationship that define us and sustain us. Even as the most independent adults, we have moments when we cannot clarify what we feel until we talk about it with someone who knows us, who cares about what we think, or at least is willing to listen.

Contemporary pressures have, regrettably, shrunk our attention spans and impoverished the quality of listening in our lives. We live in hurried times, when dinner is something we zap in the microwave and keeping up with the latest books and movies means reading the reviews. That's all we've got time for. Running to and from our many obligations, we close ourselves off from the world around us with headphones, exercising strict control over what we allow in.

In the limited time we still preserve for family and friends, conversation is often preempted by soothing and passive distractions. Too tired to talk and listen, we settle instead for the lulling charms of electronic devices that project pictures, make music, or bleep across display screens. Is it this way of life that's made us forget how to listen? Perhaps. But maybe the modern approach to life is the effect rather than the cause. Maybe we lead this kind of life because we're seeking some sort of solace, something to counteract the dimming of the spirit we feel when no one is listening.

How we lost the art of listening is certainly a matter for debate. What is not debatable, my experience tells me, is that the loss leaves us with an ever-widening hole in our lives. It might begin as a vague sense of discontent, sadness, or deprivation. We miss the irreplaceable sustenance of lending an attentive ear and of receiving the same in return, but we don't know what's wrong or how to fix it. Over time this lack of listening invades our most prized relationships. Within couples and families we unnecessarily hurt each other by failing to acknowledge what each other says. Whatever the arena, our hearts experience the failure to be heard as an absence of concern.

Conflict doesn't necessarily disappear when we acknowledge each other's point of view, but it's almost certain to get worse if we don't. So why don't we take time to hear each other out?

Because the simple art of listening isn't always so simple. Often it's a burden. Not, perhaps, the perfunctory attention we grant automatically as part of the give-and-take of everyday life. But the sustained attention of careful listening—that may take heroic and unselfish restraint. To listen well we must forget ourselves and submit to the other person's need for attention.

While it's true that some people are easier to listen to than others, conversations take place between two people, both of whom contribute to the outcome. Unfortunately, when we fail to get through to each other, we have a tendency to fall back on blaming. It's his fault: he's selfish or insensitive. Or it's my fault: I'm too dependent or don't express myself well.

The fact that we experience life (and its famous complications) from inside our own skin makes it hard for us to see the circular patterns of stimulus and response between us and our conversation partners. It takes reflection to step back from the frustrations of misunderstanding and recognize the extent to which we all participate in the problems that plague us. But this is the problem of living in this world with other people: we create our own relationships and must, in turn, sustain and be sustained by them.

Most failures of understanding are *not* due to self-absorption or bad faith, but to defensive reactions that crowd out understanding and concern. Each of us has characteristic ways of reacting emotionally in key relationships. We don't hear what's said because something in the speaker's message triggers hurt, anger, or fear.

Unfortunately, all the advice in the world about "active listening" can't overcome the maddening tendency to react to each other this way. To become better listeners, and use empathy to transform our relationships, we must identify and harness the emotional triggers that generate anxiety and cause misunderstanding and conflict. We *can* understand each other, once we learn to recognize our own defensive reactions and take charge of our responses.

If this seems too formidable a task, remember that most of us are more capable than we give ourselves credit for. We concentrate pretty hard at work, and most of us still enjoy hours of earnest, open conversation with a few friends. In fact, talk with friends is a model of what conversation can be: free enough to talk about what matters; sufficiently concerned (and sufficiently unthreatened) to listen, understand, and acknowledge; honest enough to tell the truth; and tactful enough to know when not to. More relationships can be like this.

In the process of writing this book, I've tried to become a better listener, in my personal as well as professional life, to listen a little harder to my wife's complaints without getting defensive and to hear my children's opinions before giving them my own. However, several times I've had painful conversations that left me bruised and feeling defeated. My wife would speak sharply to me about not helping out more around the house (or not listening to her) and I'd feel attacked; or I'd call my editor one too many times to complain about the burdens of writing and she'd make *me* feel like a burden for calling; or my friend Rich would call me the part of your anatomy you sit on for acting like I was entitled to some special consideration. Not only didn't I listen at these times—hear and acknowledge what the other person was saying, and then give my side—but I got all knotted up inside, hurt and angry, and completely unwilling to talk to that person, ever again as long as I live.

I'm sure you know how painful such encounters with misunderstanding can be. When my wife "yelled at me," my editor was "mean to me," and my friend "picked on me," I got hurt and withdrew. But what made these incidents so especially painful was that just when I thought I was learning to listen better, these setbacks set me all the way back. Instead of just thinking that things hadn't gone well and needed repair, I felt defeated and inadequate. How could I, who couldn't even get along with the people in my own life, have the temerity to write a book about listening? How could I teach anyone anything about listening if I couldn't listen to hard things without getting blown away?

I think you know how that feels. When we try to change something in our lives, whether it's our diet or work habits or listening skills, and we experience a setback, we have a tendency to feel hopeless and give up. Suddenly all the progress we thought we were making seems like an illusion. Maybe if I were reading a book about listening and experienced these setbacks, I would have given up. But, fortunately or unfortunately, I had a commitment to finish writing this book, and so after a while of brooding in hurt silence I'd go back and try to talk to the person I'd quarreled with—only this time with a firm resolve to listen to his or her side before telling mine. In the process, I learned to see how my relationships go through cycles of closeness and distance and, even more important, how I could influence those cycles by the quality of my own listening.

This book is an invitation to think about the ways we talk and listen to each other: why listening is such a powerful force in our lives; how

to listen deeply, with sustained immersion in another's experience; and how to prevent good listening from being spoiled by bad habits.

Among the secrets of successful communication we will consider are:

- The difference between real dialogue and just taking turns talking
- Setting aside your own agenda while someone else is speaking
- Hearing what people mean, not just what they say
- How to get through to someone who never seems to listen
- How to deal with people who get defensive when you try to tell them something
- How to ask for support without getting unwanted advice
- How to get an uncommunicative person to open up
- What makes some people react so violently to criticism
- How to share a difference of opinion without making the other person feel criticized
- How to make sure both sides get heard in heated discussions
- How speakers undermine their own messages
- Responding to a speaker's feelings instead of imposing your own
- Cutting down on criticism and nagging
- Establishing credibility so that people listen to you
- Understanding how the nature of a relationship affects listening
- Facing rather than avoiding conflict

The Lost Art of Listening is divided into four sections. Part I explains why listening is so important in our lives—far more important than we usually realize—and how, for many of us, it's a lack of sympathetic attention more than stress or overwork that accounts for the loss of enthusiasm and optimism in our lives. Part II explores the hidden assumptions, unconscious needs, and emotional defensiveness that are the real reasons people don't listen. We'll see what makes listeners too defensive to hear what we're saying and how people who vent emotion rather than expressing it may not get heard, even though they have something important to say.

After exploring the major roadblocks to listening, we'll examine in Part III how people can understand and control emotional reactions to become better listeners. And I'll explain how you can make yourself heard, even in the most difficult situations, by developing a sensitivity to the reactions of your listeners and by toning down your own emotionality. Finally, in Part IV, we'll see how listening breaks down in particular types of relationship, including intimate partnerships, family relationships, between friends, and at work. I'll explain how listen-

ing is complicated by the specific dynamics of each of these various relationships and how to use that knowledge to break through to each other.

Regardless of how much we take it for granted, the importance of listening cannot be overestimated. The gift of our attention and understanding makes other people feel validated and valued. Our ability to listen, and listen well, creates goodwill that comes back to us. But effective listening is also the best way to enjoy others, to learn from them, and to make them interesting to be with. I hope this book can help take us a step in the direction of showing more of the concern we feel for each other.

PART ONE

THE YEARNING
TO BE UNDERSTOOD

"Did You Hear What I Said?"

WHY LISTENING IS SO IMPORTANT

Sometimes it seems that nobody listens anymore.

"He expects me to listen to his problems, but he's never interested in mine."

"She's always complaining."

"He never talks to me. The only time I find out what's going on in his life is when I overhear him telling someone else. Why doesn't he ever tell *me* these things?"

"I can't talk to her because she's so critical."

Wives complain that their husbands take them for granted. Husbands complain that their wives nag and ramble on, taking forever to get to the point.

She feels a violation of their connection. He doesn't trust the connection.

Few motives in human experience are as powerful as the yearning to be understood. Being listened to means that we are taken seriously, that our ideas and feelings are known and, ultimately, that what we have to say matters.

The yearning to be listened to and understood is a yearning to escape our separateness and bridge the space that divides us. We reach out and try to overcome that separateness by revealing what's on our minds and in our hearts, hoping for understanding. Getting that understanding should be simple, but it isn't.

The essence of good listening is empathy, which can be achieved only by suspending our preoccupation with ourselves and entering into the experience of the other person. Part intuition and part effort, it's the stuff of human connection.

A listener's empathy—understanding what we're trying to say *and* showing it—builds a bond of understanding, linking us to someone who understands and cares and thus confirming that our feelings are recognizable and legitimate. The power of empathic listening is the power to transform relationships. When deeply felt but unexpressed feelings take shape in words that are shared and come back clarified, the result is a reassuring sense of being understood and a grateful feeling of shared humanness with the one who understands.

If listening strengthens our relationships by cementing our connection with one another, it also fortifies our sense of self. In the presence of a receptive listener, we're able to clarify what we think and discover what we feel. Thus, in giving an account of our experience to someone who listens, we are better able to listen to ourselves. Our lives are coauthored in dialogue.

IT HURTS NOT TO BE LISTENED TO

The need to be taken seriously and responded to is frustrated every day, and not just by that one special person from whom we expect so much.Parents complain that their children don't listen. Children complain that their parents are too busy arguing or lecturing to hear their side of things. Even friends, usually a reliable source of shared understanding, are often too busy to listen to one another these days. And if we sometimes feel cut off from sympathy and understanding in the private sphere, we've grown not even to expect courtesy and attention in public settings.

Our right to be heard is often violated in small ways that we don't necessarily remember, by others who don't necessarily realize. That doesn't make it hurt any less.

When I told a psychiatrist friend that I was collecting experiences on the theme "It hurts not to be listened to," he sent me this example:

"I called a friend and colleague and left a message asking if we could meet at a particular time. He didn't answer, and I felt a little anxious and confused. Should I call again to remind him? After all, I know he's busy. Should I wait another day or two and hope he'll answer? Should I not have asked him in the first place? All this leaves me uneasy."

The first thing that struck me about this example was how even a little thing like an unanswered phone message can leave someone feeling unresponded to—and troubled. Then I was really struck—like a slap in the face—by the realization that my friend was talking about *me*. Suddenly I was embarrassed, and then defensive. The reason I hadn't returned his call—doesn't matter. (We always have reasons for not responding.) What matters is how my failure to respond confused and hurt my friend and that I never had any inkling of it.

If an oversight like that can hurt, how much more painful is it when the subject is of real importance to the speaker?

---◆---

Listening is so basic that we take it for granted. Unfortunately, most of us think of ourselves as better listeners than we really are.

---◆---

When you come home from a business trip, eager to tell your partner how it went, and he listens but after a minute or two something in his eyes goes to sleep, you feel hurt, betrayed. When you call your parents to share a triumph and they don't seem really interested, you feel deflated and slightly foolish for having allowed yourself to feel excited and to hope for appreciation.

Just as it hurts not to be listened to when you're excited about something special, it's painful not to feel listened to by some*one* special, someone you expect to be especially attuned to you.

Derek's best friend in college was Roger. They were both political science majors and shared a passion for politics. Together they followed every detail of the Watergate investigation, relishing each new revelation as though they were a series of deliciously wicked Charles Addams cartoons. But much as they took cynical delight in the exposure of corruption in the Nixon White House, their friendship went well beyond politics.

Derek remembered the wonderful feeling of talking to Roger for hours, impelled by the momentum of some deep and inexplicable sym-

pathy. There was the pleasure of being able to say anything he wanted and the pleasure of hearing Roger say everything he'd always thought but never expressed. Unlike most of Derek's other friends, Roger wasn't a competitive conversationalist. He really listened.

When they went on to graduate schools in different cities, they kept up their friendship. Derek would visit Roger or Roger would visit Derek at least once a month. They'd play pool or see a movie and go out for Chinese food; and then afterward, no matter how late it got, they'd stay up talking.

Then Derek got married, and things changed. Roger didn't become distant the way some friends do after one marries, nor did Derek's wife dislike Roger. The distance that Roger felt was a small thing, but it made a big difference. "It's difficult to describe exactly, but I often end up feeling awkward and disappointed when I speak with Derek. He listens, but somehow he doesn't seem really interested anymore. He doesn't ask questions. He used to be involved rather than just accepting. It makes me sad. I still feel excited about the things going on in my life, but telling Derek just makes me feel unconnected and alone with them."

Roger's lament says something important about listening. It isn't just not being interrupted that we want. Sometimes people appear to be listening but aren't really hearing. A lot of people are good at being silent when we talk. Sometimes they betray their lack of real attention by glancing around and shifting their weight back and forth. At other times, however, listeners show no sign of inattention, but still we know they aren't really hearing what we have to say. It feels like they don't care.

Derek's passive interest was especially painful to Roger because of the closeness they'd shared. But the friends had reached an impasse; Roger couldn't open himself to his friend the way he'd done in the past, and Derek was mystified about the dynamics that were separating them.

Friendship is voluntary, and so talking about it is optional. Roger didn't want to criticize Derek or make demands. Besides, how does one friend tell another that he feels no longer cared about? And so Roger never did talk to Derek about feeling estranged. Too bad, because when a relationship goes sour, talking about it may be the only way to make things right again.

———◆———

It's especially hurtful not to be listened to in those relationships you count on for understanding.

———◆———

After a while most of us learn to do a pretty good imitation of being grownups and shrug off a lot of slights and misunderstandings. If, in the process, we become a little calloused, well maybe that's just the price we pay for living in this world. But sometimes not being responded to leaves us feeling so wounded and bitter that it can make us retreat from relationships, even for years.

When a woman discovered that her husband was having an affair, she felt as if someone had kicked her in the guts. In her shock and grief and anger, she turned to the person she was closest to—her mother-in-law. The mother-in-law tried to be understanding and supportive, but it was, after all, very difficult to listen to the bitter things her daughter-in-law was saying about her own son. Still, she tried. Apparently, however, the support she offered wasn't enough. Eventually the marital crisis passed and the couple reconciled, but the daughter-in-law, feeling that her mother-in-law hadn't been there when she needed her most, never spoke to her again.

The mother-in-law in this sad story was baffled and hurt by her daughter-in-law's stubborn silence. Other people's hurt and consequent hurtful behavior often seem unreasonable to us. What makes it reasonable to them is their feeling wounded by lack of responsiveness.

To listen is to pay attention, take an interest, care about, take to heart, validate, acknowledge, be moved . . . appreciate. Listening is in fact so central to human existence as to often escape notice; or, rather, it appears in so many guises that it is seldom grasped as the overarching need that it is. Sometimes, as Roger, the estranged daughter-in-law, and so many others have discovered, we don't realize how important being listened to is until we feel we've been cheated out of it.

Once in a while, however, we become aware of how much it means to be listened to. You can't decide whether or not to take a new job, and so you call an old friend to talk it over. She doesn't tell you what to do, but the fact that she listens, really listens, helps you see things more clearly. Another time you're just getting to know someone but you like him so much that, after a wonderful dinner in a restaurant, you take a risk and ask him over to your place for coffee. When he says, "No thanks, I've got to get up early," you feel rejected. Convinced that he doesn't really like you and not wanting to be hurt further, you start avoiding him. After a few days, however, he asks, in a very sincere way, what's wrong, and once again you take a risk and tell him that your feelings were hurt. To your great relief, instead of arguing, he listens and accepts what you have to say.

Why can't it always be that way? I speak; you listen. It's that simple. Isn't it? Unfortunately, it isn't. Talking and listening is a unique relationship in which speaker and listener are constantly switching roles, both jockeying for position, one's needs competing with the other's. If you doubt it, try telling someone about a problem you're having and see how long it takes before he interrupts to tell you about a problem of his own, to describe a similar experience of his own, or to offer advice—advice that may suit him more than it does you (and is more responsive to his own anxiety than to what you're trying to say).

A man in therapy was exploring his relationship with his loving but distant father when he suddenly remembered the happy times they'd spent together playing with his electric trains. It was a Lionel set that had been his father's and his grandfather's before him. Caught up in the memory, the man grew increasingly excited as he recalled the joy and pride and sense of belonging he had felt sharing this family tradition with his father. As the man's enthusiasm mounted, the therapist launched into a long narrative about *his* train set and how he had gotten the other kids in the neighborhood to bring over their tracks and train cars to build a huge neighborhood setup in his basement. After the therapist had gone on at some length, the patient could no longer contain his anger about being cut off. "Why are you telling me about *your* trains?!" he demanded. The therapist hesitated, then, with that level, impersonal voice we reserve for confiding something intimate, he said lamely, "I was just trying to be friendly."

The therapist had made an all-too-common mistake (actually he'd made several, but this is Be Kind to Therapists Week). He'd assumed that establishing some common ground between him and his patient was a sign of listening, that sharing his own experience was the equivalent of empathy. In fact, though, he had switched the focus to himself, making his patient feel discounted, misunderstood, unappreciated. That's what hurt.

As is the way with words that become familiar, *empathy* may not adequately convey the elusive and immensely powerful process of genuinely appreciating the inner experience of another person. Empathic listening is like the close reading of a poem; it takes in the words and gets to what's behind them. The difference is that while empathy is actively imaginative, it is fundamentally receptive rather than creative. When we attend to a work of art, our idiosyncratic response has its

own validity, but when we attend to someone who's trying to tell us something, it's accurate empathy, not creativity, that counts.

THE IMPORTANCE OF BEARING WITNESS

Listening has not one but two purposes: taking in information and bearing witness to another's expression. By momentarily stepping out of his or her own frame of reference and into ours, the person who listens well acknowledges and affirms us. That affirmation, that validation is absolutely essential for sustaining the self-affirmation known as self-respect. Without being listened to, we are shut up in the solitude of our own hearts.

A thirty-six-year-old woman was so unnerved by a "minor incident" that she wondered if she needed psychotherapy. Marnie, who was executive vice president of a public policy institute, had arranged a meeting with the lieutenant governor to present a proposal she'd developed involving the regulation of a large state industry. Of necessity she'd invited her boss to the meeting, although she would have been able to make a more effective presentation of her proposal without him. The boss, in turn, had invited the institute's chief lobbyist, who would later have to convince legislators of the need for the proposed regulation. The meeting began, as Marnie expected, with her boss rambling on in a loose philosophical discussion that circled but never quite got to the point. When he finished, he turned not to Marnie but to the lobbyist to present the proposal. Marnie was stunned. The lobbyist began to speak, and fifteen minutes later the meeting ended, without Marnie's ever having gotten to say a word—about *her* proposal.

Marnie couldn't wait to tell her husband what had happened. Unfortunately he was out of town on business and wouldn't be back for three days. She was used to her husband's business trips; what she wasn't used to was how cut off she felt. She really needed to talk to him. As the evening wore on, Marnie's disappointment grew and then changed character. Instead of simply feeling frustrated, she began to feel inadequate. Why was she so dependent on her husband? Why couldn't she handle her own emotions?

Marnie decided that her problem was insecurity. If she were more secure, she wouldn't need anyone so much. She wouldn't be so vulnerable or so easily hurt; she'd be self-sufficient.

Marnie's complaint—the unexpected urgency to be heard—and her conclusion, that if she'd developed more self-esteem growing up, she wouldn't need to depend so much on other people's responsiveness, is a common one. Needing someone to respond to us makes us feel insecure and dependent and tempts us to believe that if we were stronger we wouldn't need other people. That way they wouldn't be able to disappoint us so much.

Being listened to helps us grow up feeling secure; but, contrary to what some people would like to believe, we never become whole and complete, finished products, like a statue or a monument. On the contrary, like any living thing, human beings require nourishment not only to grow up strong but also to maintain their strength and vitality. Listening nourishes our sense of worth.

The more insecure you are, the more reassurance you need. But all of us, no matter how secure and well adjusted, need attention to sustain us. In case this isn't immediately evident, all you need to do is note how we all have our own preferred ways of announcing our news. If my wife has news, for example, she's likely to call me at work or tell me as soon as we both get home. If she has something to say, she says it. Not me. If I have good news, I hoard it, save it up to announce with a fanfare—dying to be made a fuss over.

I once worked for months trying to land a book contract. My wife knew I was working on the book, but I didn't let her know that a contract was imminent. Waiting and hoping, and trying not to let myself hope for too much, I had extravagant fantasies about getting good news—no, about sharing it. Telling my wife would be the payoff. What I absolutely didn't want to do was simply tell her; I wanted—I needed—my announcement to be a big deal. The day the contract finally arrived I was ecstatic. But the most important part was looking forward to telling my wife. So I called her at work and told her I had a surprise for her: I was taking her out for a fancy dinner. She said fine and didn't ask any questions. (She's only known me for thirty years.)

By the time I got home, my wife had changed into a silk dress and was ready to go out. She could tell I was excited, but she waited patiently to find out why. At the restaurant, I ordered a bottle of champagne, and when it came she asked, still patient, "Do you have something to tell me?" I pulled out my contract and presented it with all the savoir-faire of a ten-year-old showing off his report card. She saw at once what it was, and her face lit up with a huge beaming grin. That look—her

love and pride—was indescribably sweet. My own smile was wet with tears.

What elaborate lengths we go to for such moments! Those of us who feel the need to arrange special occasions for our announcements share a good deal with those who don't need to calculate so. The period of time during which we're waiting to tell our news is charged with anxious anticipation. We can feel the tension building. The tension has to do with an aroused impulse—to confess or confront or show off or propose—to make an impact on another person and be responded to. The excitement comes from hope for a positive response; the anxiety comes from fear of rejection or indifference.

Whom you choose to tell what says something about your relationship to yourself—and to the other people in your life. Your presentation of self involves pride and shame—and whom you choose to share them with. With whom do you feel safe to cry? To rage? To brag? To confess something truly shameful?

◆———————◆

A good listener is a witness, not a filter for your experience.

◆———————◆

As soon as you're able to say what's on your mind—and be heard and acknowledged—you are unburdened. It's like having an ache or an itch suddenly relieved. If this completion comes quickly, as it often does in day-to-day conversations, you may hardly be aware of your need for understanding. But the disappointment you feel when you're not heard and the tension you feel waiting and hoping to be heard are signs of how important being listened to is. There are times when all that can be thought must be spoken and heard, communicated and shared, when ignorance and silence are pain, and to speak is to try to alleviate that pain.

BEING HEARD MEANS BEING TAKEN SERIOUSLY

The need to be heard, which is something we ordinarily take for granted, turns out to be one of the most powerful motive forces in human nature. Being listened to is the medium through which we discover ourselves as understandable and acceptable—or not. We care about the people who listen to us. We may even love them. But, for a time at least, we use them.

When we're activated by the need for appreciation, we relate to others as *selfobjects*, psychoanalyst Heinz Kohut's telling expression for a responsive other, someone we relate to not as an independent person with his or her own agenda but as someone-there-for-us.[1]

Perhaps the idea of using listeners as selfobjects reminds you of those bores who are always talking about themselves and don't seem to care about what you have to say. When they do listen, their hearts aren't in it; they're only waiting to change the subject back to themselves, their problems, their accomplishments.

This lack of appreciation can be especially painful when it occurs between us and our parents. It's maddening when they can't seem to let us be people in our own right, individuals with legitimate ideas and aspirations. Watching our parents listening to other people right in front of us can be especially aggravating. Why don't they show *us* a little of that attention? Here's the writer Harold Brodkey in *The Runaway Soul* dramatizing this irritating experience through the conversation of a young woman and her boyfriend. The boyfriend speaks first:

"Does your dad ever listen, or does he just do monologues?"

"He just does monologues. Doesn't he let you talk?"

"Only if I insist on it. Then we do alternate monologues."

"Well, that's it, then. He talks to you more than he does to me now."

Of course the woman's father talks to her boyfriend more than he does to her. The boyfriend is a fresh audience, new blood.

The people who hurt us the most are invariably the ones with whom we think we do have a special relationship, who make us feel that our attention and understanding are particularly important to them—until we see how easily they shift their interest to someone else. Right in the middle of confiding in us, they'll catch someone else's eye and break off to talk to *that* person. We discover that what we thought was an understanding shared only with us is something they've told a dozen other people. So much for our unique qualities as confidants! What's so hurtful about these promiscuous "intimates" isn't that they use us but that they rob us of the feeling that we're important to them, that we're special.

Although none of us likes to see (especially in ourselves) the kind of blatant narcissism that disregards the feelings of others, the truth

[1]Heinz Kohut, *The Analysis of the Self* (New York: International Universities Press, 1971).

is, much of the time we're all hopelessly absorbed with ourselves. The subject of narcissism turns out to be crucial in exploring the role of listening in the psychological birth of self-esteem. I introduce it here only to note that one aspect of our need for other people is entirely selfish. Being listened to maintains our narcissistic equilibrium—or, to put it more simply, it helps us feel whole.

When Roxanne and her parents finished unloading the station wagon, she felt a sinking sensation and was conscious for the first time of all the things she didn't have. Anxiously she watched as the other students and their families trooped into the dormitory, loaded down with beautiful pillows and quilts, ten-speed bicycles, stereo sets and cartons of records and cassettes, curling irons, personal computers, tennis rackets, and lacrosse sticks. Roxanne had never even seen a lacrosse stick. By the time her parents drove off, leaving her standing in front of South Hall, her excitement about starting college had given way to dread.

She never did get over her sense of isolation that first year. Everyone else seemed to make friends so easily. Not her. She called home a lot and tried to tell her parents how awful it was. But they said things like "Don't worry, honey; everybody's a little lonesome at first," and "You should make more friends," and "Maybe you just have to study a little harder." If only it were that easy!

Reassuring someone isn't the same as listening.

By the first of December Roxanne was skipping classes, missing meals, and crying herself to sleep. When she felt she couldn't stand it anymore, she made an appointment at the student counseling center.

Roxanne was surprised when the therapist said to call her Noreen. She wasn't used to that kind of openness in adults. Noreen turned out to be the most sympathetic and caring person Roxanne had ever met. She didn't tell Roxanne what to do or analyze her feelings; she just listened. For Roxanne, it was a new experience.

With Noreen's help, Roxanne was able to get through that first year and the three years that followed. Noreen helped her discover that her feelings of insecurity stemmed from never feeling really loved by her parents. Roxanne had always thought they were pretty good parents, but she could see now that they never actually knew her very well.

Her father was always busy, and her mother never really took her seriously as a person.

Eventually Noreen convinced Roxanne that she would never be free of her anger—and vulnerability to depression—until she worked things out with her parents. When Roxanne agreed, Noreen suggested that she get in touch with me for a few family therapy sessions; both of them knew that Roxanne's parents mistrusted Noreen because they believed she'd turned their daughter against them.

Roxanne and her parents arrived separately for our first meeting, and although they were all smiles and affability, the three of them seemed as wary as cats circling a snake. I had suggested to Roxanne over the phone that we go slow in this first meeting, that she try not to unload the full weight of her anger but rather search for some common ground with her parents. But that wasn't the truth about what she was feeling, and the truth was precisely what she was after. She started in on her father. When she was little, she'd loved him, she said, but as she got older she increasingly saw him as ridiculous and irrelevant. (He worked hard, had a crew cut, voted Republican, and was a patriot. Almost nothing in his life caused him second thoughts.) After listening to his daughter's ungenerous assessment, Roxanne's father said, "So that's how you see me?" and then retreated into silence, his own brand of armor.

Then Roxanne turned to her mother. She called her "shallow," "phony," and—the cruelest thing a child can say to a mother—"interested only in yourself." Roxanne's mother tried to listen but couldn't. "That's not true!" she protested. "Why do you have to exaggerate everything?" This only infuriated Roxanne more, and the two of them lashed back and forth at each other with increasingly shrill voices.

I tried to calm them down but wasn't very successful. Roxanne was hell-bent on *communicating*—not talking, that old-fashioned process of give-and-take, but *communicating*—that fashionable development where one insistent family member imparts some critical information to the others, "confronting" them with "the truth" whether they want to hear it or not. Eventually Roxanne's mother left the session in tears.

The following week I met with Roxanne alone. She was sorry the meeting hadn't gone differently but glad to have gotten her feelings out. She thought her mother had shown herself to be the unaccepting person Roxanne knew her to be. They weren't on speaking terms, and that was just fine with her, Roxanne said.

Six months later, much to my surprise, Roxanne called to say that

she and her parents wanted to come for another meeting. This time the conversation was friendly but superficial. Roxanne complimented her mother on her shoes and asked about her younger sister. Her mother asked how Roxanne was doing. Had she gotten over all that bitterness? Roxanne, feeling once again patronized and dismissed, tried to avoid reacting but couldn't. Furiously, she accused her mother of not really being interested in how she was feeling and caring only about polite formalities. My heart sank. But this time Roxanne's mother didn't react angrily or cut her daughter off. She didn't say much, but she didn't interrupt to defend herself either. What enabled her to listen to her daughter's angry accusations this time, I don't know. But she did.

One of a mother's heaviest burdens is being the primary target of her children's primitive swings between need and rage. The rage is directed at the hand that rocks the cradle no matter how loving its care. It's part of breaking away. Roxanne's mother seemed to sense this, seemed to remember that her little girl was still a little girl in some ways.

Roxanne seemed to expect retaliation from her mother. But when it wasn't forthcoming, she calmed down considerably. She had wanted, it seemed, only to be heard.

After that, Roxanne's relationship with her family changed dramatically. Previously limited to monologues or muteness, they entered into dialogue. Roxanne phoned and wrote. She shared confidences with her mother. Not always, of course, and not always successfully, but Roxanne had become much more open to her mother as a person, rather than perceiving her simply as a mother, who was somehow supposed to make everything right. She, in turn, became less a child and more a young woman, ready for life on her own.

Roxanne's unfulfilled need to be listened to had cut her off from other people and filled her with resentment. Unburdening herself was like breaking down a wall that had for a long time kept her from feeling connected to other people her own age. That her feelings were somewhat infantile says only that they were a long time unspoken. Talking to Noreen, who didn't have a stake in defending herself, helped Roxanne find her voice.

That second meeting with Roxanne and her parents had produced one of those moments that happen once in a while in families, when someone says something and everything shifts. Only it wasn't what Roxanne said that caused the shift; she'd said it all before. It was that her mother put aside her own claims to being right and just listened.

When we learn to hear the unspoken feelings that lie beneath another's anger or impatience, we discover the power to release the bitterness that keeps people apart. With a little effort, we can learn to hear the hurt behind expressions of hostility, the resentment behind avoidance, and the vulnerability that makes people afraid to speak and afraid to truly listen. When we understand the healing power of listening, we can even begin to listen to things that make us uneasy.

Being heard means being taken seriously. It satisfies our need for self-expression and our need to feel connected to others. The receptive listener allows us to express what we think and feel. Hearing and acknowledging us helps us clarify both the thoughts and the feelings, in the process firming our sense of ourselves. By affirming that we are understandable, the listener helps confirm our common humanity. Not being listened to makes us feel ignored and unappreciated, cut off and alone. The need to be known, to have our experience understood and accepted by someone who really listens, is meat and drink to the human heart.

Without a sufficient amount of sympathetic understanding in our lives we're haunted by an amorphous unease that leaves us anxious and lonely. Such feelings are hard to tolerate, and so we seek solace in passive escapism; we snap on the TV, treat ourselves to Ben and Jerry's, or escape into popular fiction about people whose lives are exciting. There is, of course, nothing wrong with relaxing. But why do we turn on the TV even when there's nothing to watch? And why do we feel uneasy without the car radio playing, even when it's just noise?

We usually associate passive escapism with release from stress. While it's true that many of us feel stressed out at the end of the day, it may not be overwork that wears us down, but a lack of understanding in our lives. Chief among the missing elements is the attention and appreciation of responsive selfobjects, people who care and listen to us with interest.

When the quality of our relationships isn't sufficient to maintain our equilibrium and enthusiasm—or when we're not up to making them so—we seek escape from morbid self-consciousness. We seek excitement, enthusiasm, responsiveness, gratification—the same kinds of feelings that can be had from a long heart-to-heart talk with someone we care about. But without the ballast of someone to talk to, some of us will continue to drown out the silence, as though without some kind of electronic entertainment to distract us, we may hear the low rumblings of despair.

CHAPTER TWO

"Thanks for Listening"

HOW LISTENING SHAPES US
AND CONNECTS US
TO EACH OTHER

W e define and sustain ourselves in conversation with others. Recognition—being listened to—is the response from another person that makes our feelings, actions, and intentions meaningful. It allows us to realize our own agency and authorship in a tangible way. But, as we saw in Chapter 1, the expression and recognition so fundamental to our well-being is a mutual, reciprocal process. Our lives are coauthored in dialogue. So, if being recognized through listening is to define and sustain us, it must come from someone whom we in turn recognize. Striking a balance between expression (talking) and recognition (listening) is what allows us and the people we care about to interact as sovereign equals.

If your life, or even a key relationship in it, is unbalanced—if it doesn't allow you sufficient self-expression or mutual recognition—you will be the poorer for it. This chapter will show how listening is critical to the formation of a strong and healthy self *and* to the formation of strong and healthy relationships.

What makes listening such a force in shaping character is the power of words to match and share experience—or contradict and falsify it. What is understood and accepted—"Yes, isn't that wonderful!"—

23

becomes part of your social self, the self you own and share. Some of what is not appreciated—"You shouldn't be feeling that way in the first place"—becomes part of your private self, known but not shared, split off, sometimes kept secret even from yourself. Ominously, much of what fails to find acceptance becomes part of your disavowed self, what interpersonal psychiatrist Harry Stack Sullivan called the "not me."[1] Some parents may be too anxious to tolerate a child's anger; others may be too embarrassed to tolerate their children's sexual feelings. Each of us grows up with some experiences of self so poisoned with anxiety that they aren't assimilated into the rest of our personality. Listening shapes us; lack of listening twists us.

A young mother wearing denim was berating her little girl for wanting to have a Barbie doll. It was a "stupid" thing to want; the child should be "ashamed" of herself; she should "have more self-respect." It was painful to hear. The sad irony of a mother hammering away at a little girl's pride to teach her self-respect was hard to escape. Should the mother let her daughter have a Barbie, like all the other kids? That's up to her, but she should respect her daughter's right to have opinions of her own.

Gradually, with cooperation between parent and child, a self is formed, organized by language and listening, based in part on the child's natural experience, in part on the values imposed by the parents. The listened-to child grows up relatively secure and whole. The unlistened-to child lacks the understanding that firms self-acceptance and is "bent out of shape" by the wishes and anxieties of others. This is what the famous psychotherapist Carl Rogers meant when he said that the child's innate tendency toward self-actualization is subverted by the need to please.[2]

———◆———

What never gets heard affects more than a difference between the sociably shareable and the private; it drives a split between the true self and a false self.

———◆———

The seeds of listening are sown in childhood, in the quality of the relationship between parent and child. Parents who listen make their

[1]Harry Stack Sullivan, *The Interpersonal Theory of Psychiatry* (New York: Norton, 1953).

[2]Carl Rogers, *Client-Centered Therapy* (Boston: Houghton Mifflin, 1951).

children feel worthwhile and appreciated. Being listened to helps build a strong, secure self, endowing the child with sufficient self-respect to develop his or her own unique talents and ideals and to approach relationships with confidence and tolerance.

That understanding builds self-assurance is hardly news. Most of us can picture a mother with smiling eyes listening enthusiastically to a child eagerly describing some triumph or comforting a sad-faced child crying over some minor tragedy. And we all know how bad it feels to watch a father reduce a child to tears of rage and frustration for making a mistake. Of course such scenes, repeated over and over, have an impact on a child. What may not be so obvious is how early or how profoundly the quality of listening begins to shape character.

HOW LISTENING SHAPES SELF-RESPECT

To begin with, the self is not a given, like having red hair or being tall, but a perspective on awareness, and an interpersonal one at that. The self is how we personify what we are, as shaped by our experience of being responded to by others. Character is formed in relationships, and the quality of self depends on the nature of that response, the quality of listening we receive.

Among recent findings with the most profound implications for understanding the importance of listening is the work of infant researcher Daniel Stern.[3] Stern's most radical discovery is that the infant is never totally undifferentiated (symbiotic) from the mother.

Margaret Mahler's influential psychoanalytic theory of separation and individuation was based on the implicit assumption that we grow up and out of relationships, rather than becoming more active and sovereign *within* them. But once we accept the idea that infants don't begin life as part of an undifferentiated unity, the question is not only how we separate from our parents, but also how we learn to connect. The issue isn't how we become free of people, but how we actively make ourselves heard and understood in relationship to them.

This view of the self as having a fundamental need for expression and recognition emerged not only from the observation of infants but also in consulting rooms, where psychotherapists began to hear the infant cry in the adult voice. The desperate anguish of those who feel

[3]Daniel Stern, *The Interpersonal World of the Infant* (New York: Basic Books, 1985).

empty and alone, unable to connect to themselves or to others, leads to the question "What does it take to make us feel whole?" A large part of the answer is listening.

In charting the development of children, Stern identified four progressively more complex senses of self, each defining a different domain of self-experience and social relatedness. It turns out that second only to the need for food and shelter is the need for understanding. Even infants need listening to thrive. "Listening" to an infant may sound somewhat grand, but it is precisely that—the quality of parental understanding and acknowledgment—that plays such a decisive role in making us what we are.

Let's look now at the unfolding of these four senses of self to see how listening shapes character.

"Here I Am": The Sense of an Emergent Self (Birth to 2 Months)

The infant's need for listening is simple but imperative. With the sudden pressure of physical need, life goes from lovely to all wrong. Hunger breaks over the body like an angry storm. It starts slowly; the baby has a sense of something going awry. Then fussing turns to full-throated crying as the baby tries to hurl the pain sensations out and away. This crying serves as a distress signal, like a siren, to alert the parents and demand a response from them.

Being a parent at this stage is simple. As I recall, my wife and I, our empathic sensitivities honed to razor sharpness by months of sleep deprivation, were flung into action by the slightest peep. Blessed with a disposition as placid as a howler monkey, our first little darling would ever so gently summon us for her nightly lactose intolerance test. I, never the insensitive father, was usually first to respond. "Honey," I'd coo, grinding my teeth to keep them warm, "do something!" At which my mate, ever appreciative of my support, would hasten to the little one's side to administer whatever first aid was required. Ah, parenthood.

Babies are little and cute and helpless, but their smiling, gazing, fretting, and crying are commanding messages; they must be listened to. At this stage parents, thinking primarily about satisfying the baby's needs, may not recognize the extent of the social interaction involved in the process. But even before the baby achieves self-consciousness, parents invest it with their expectations and aspirations. From day one, they relate to the baby as both an actual and a potential self.

Our impulse toward understanding is irresistible. Developmental

psychologist Aidan Macfarlane's observations of new mothers talking to their infants brought to them for the first time after delivery show that the mothers attribute meaning to each sign and sound.[4] "What's that frown for? The world's a little scary, huh?" Mothers don't really believe the infant understands, but they assign meaning to what their infants are doing and respond accordingly. In time, they create little formats of interaction, jointly constructed little worlds. This is the child's first culture.

Parents immediately ascribe to their infants intentions ("Oh, you want that"), motives ("You're doing that so Mommy will hurry up and feed you"), and authorship of action ("You did that on purpose, didn't you?"). In doing this, parents are responding to and helping create an emergent self. Such motives and intentions make human behavior understandable, and parents invariably treat their infants as understandable beings—that is, as the people they are to become (just so long as they become the people their parents want them to become).

———◆———

Who we are and what we say triggers other people's response to us. That response and our connection to others remain vital to our psychological well-being.

———◆———

When babies are too young to talk, it's important for their parents to understand what they feel but cannot say. When a baby cries, the parents must figure out what's wrong. Does he want to be fed? Does she need a diaper change? Does he want to be held? (Imagine the baby's feelings. What a chasm separates her from these two giant, nervous creatures nature has assigned as her waitpersons. Would they ever catch on?) When the baby grows up and learns to talk, she becomes better at putting her needs and feelings into words. Better, but not perfect. Sometimes we all need a little help in making ourselves understood.

Infants are helplessly dependent on their parents. When the parents are absent, angry, or otherwise unresponsive, the child is alone and terrified; he feels the bottom dropping out of the whole world. This primal connection to others begins as a matter of life and death, over which we have little control when we're infants. Gradually we become aware of our own half of the equation (some people more gradually than other).

---

[4]Aiden Macfarlane, *The Psychology of Childbirth* (Cambridge, MA: Harvard University Press, 1977).

"Hey, Look At Me!":
The Sense of a Core Self (2 to 7 Months)

Between eight and twelve weeks, infants become truly gregarious. The social smile emerges; they begin to vocalize and make eye-to-eye contact. When the baby looks up and smiles and coos, or splashes in the bath, or giggles with delight, how could you *not* love her? Surely, we would like to think, all parents respond intuitively to such communications. Unfortunately, this isn't so. Some parents are so preoccupied, depressed, or otherwise distracted that they ignore their babies. And, perhaps more common, many parents respond to their babies not as little people with their own rhythms and moods but as foils for the parents' own needs.

Every infant has an optimal level of excitement. Activity beyond that level constitutes overstimulation, and the experience becomes upsetting; below that level, stimulation is, well, unstimulating, boring. Parents must learn to read their babies. By taking their children seriously as persons, responding to the children's feelings rather than imposing their own, parents convey understanding and acceptance that children take in and transform into self-respect.

The next time you see an adult interacting with a baby, notice the difference between responding in tune with the child's level of excitement and imposing the adult's emotions on the child. If you see a parent with blunted emotions ignoring a bright-eyed baby, you're witnessing the beginning of a long, sad process by which unresponsive parents wither the enthusiasm of their children like unwatered flowers.

Having quite enough unwatered flowers at the office, thank you, I wasn't about to have any around my house. I remember tiptoeing into the baby's room at eventide, right about the time she was dozing—or pretending to. What my fiendish masculine intuition told me she really wanted was not rest but to be hurled violently up to the ceiling and then come crashing toward the floor—like a skydiver without a parachute—only to be plucked from the jaws of death by Daddy. Whee!

Too choked with joy to speak, the little mite showed her pleasure by widening her eyes like saucers while her face turned a lovely shade of blue.

Excessive enthusiasm may be less depressing, but it isn't necessarily more responsive. We've all seen grown-ups at it—"baby love"—the

fulsome tone of voice, the honeyed words, the endless marveling and exclaiming. When babies are little, it's almost automatic; babies are so animated themselves that they drive up the intensity of our response. But when this adult enthusiasm regularly exceeds the baby's own, the result is a jarring discontinuity. Loving parents share the moods of their children and show it.

———◆———

It isn't exuberance or any other emotion that conveys loving appreciation; it's being noticed, understood, and taken seriously.

———◆———

The baby whose parents tickle and poke and jiggle and shake her when she's not in the mood is as alone with her real self as the baby whose parents ignore her. This imposition of the parents' agenda is, in what psychiatrist R. D. Laing so tellingly called the "politics of experience," the mystification in which the child's reality gets lost.[5] Not being understood and taken seriously as a person in your own right— even at this early age—is the root of aloneness and insecurity. In the words of psychoanalyst Ernest Wolf, "Solitude, psychological solitude, is the mother of anxiety."[6]

"Honey, I'm Cold. Don't You Want a Sweater?": The Sense of a Subjective Self (7 to 15 Months)

By about one year of age the baby realizes that he has an inner, private mental world, with intentions, desires, feelings, thoughts, and memories, which are invisible to others unless he makes an attempt to reveal them. The possibility of sharing these invisible contents of the mind is the source of the greatest human happiness and frustration.

Imagine for a moment that you're a baby who hasn't yet learned to talk, and you want a cookie. What do you do if you see the cookie but it's out of reach? Simple. You get your mother to read your mind.

Mind reading may sound extravagant, but isn't that what communication boils down to? The baby must gain Mother's attention, express what's on his mind, and do so in a way that Mother receives and

[5]R. D. Laing, *The Politics of Experience* (New York: Pantheon, 1967).
[6]Ernest Wolf, "Developmental Line of Self-Object Relations," in Arnold Goldberg, ed., *Advances in Self Psychology* (New York: International Universities Press, 1980).

understands the message. "I want a cookie" is a simple message, easily sent and easily received, even without words. When it comes to more complicated messages, babies (like you and me) have to work harder to express themselves—and hope their listeners will work hard enough to understand.

The possibility of sharing experience creates the possibility for confirmation of the self as understandable and acceptable; it also creates the possibility of intimacy, the desire to know and be known. What's at stake is nothing less than discovering what part of the private world of inner experience is shareable and what part falls outside the pale of commonly recognized and accepted human experience.

---◆---

Being listened to spells the difference between feeling accepted and feeling isolated.

---◆---

The possibility of sharing mental states between people also raises the possibility of misunderstanding. For example, babies are remarkably eager explorers. Sitting on Mommy's or Daddy's lap, a baby may probe a finger into the parent's mouth or nose or tug at a strand of hair to see if it will come loose. The parent who takes this exploration as an act of aggression may get annoyed and attribute hostility to the baby. If so, the parent may follow up this feeling with a rebuke, a slap, or some rejection of the baby, who had only been doing what comes naturally at this age.

The misunderstood baby is confused by the parent's lack of understanding, upset and frightened by the rebuke and rejection. *Maybe it was a mistake*, the baby thinks. Then if the baby repeats the exploration, to clarify the confusion or to evoke a different response this time or even to retaliate, the baby may now do so with a more energetic assertiveness. Now the parent will assume that his or her original misunderstanding was confirmed: the baby *is* being aggressive.

If this situation is repeated, the parent's false interpretation may become the infant's (and later the child's) official and accepted one: exploration is aggression, and it's bad. The baby may come to see himself as aggressive, even hostile. Someone else's reality has become his. Misunderstanding undermines not only our trust in others, but also our trust in our own perceptions.

The word for sharing experience is *intersubjectivity*. The reason for this fancy term where an ordinary word like *communication* might do

is to keep us from forgetting that understanding is a joint achievement: one person trying to express what's on his or her mind, the other trying to read it. Reading a child's mind begins with *attunement*.

Attunement, a parent's ability to share the child's affective state, is a pervasive feature of parent–child interactions with profound consequences. It's the forerunner of empathy and the essence of human understanding. Attunement begins with the intuitive parental response of sharing the baby's mood and showing it. The baby reaches out excitedly and grabs a toy. When the toy is in her grasp, she lets out an exuberant "aah!" and looks at her mother. Mother responds in kind, sharing the baby's exhilaration and showing it by smiling and nodding and saying "Yes!" The mother has understood and shared the child's mood. That's attunement.

One demonstration of the baby's need for an attuned response is the *still-face procedure.* If a mother (or father) goes still-faced—impassive and expressionless—in the middle of an interaction, the baby will become upset and withdraw. Infants after about two-and-a-half months of age react strongly to this still face. They look about. Their smiles die away and they frown. They make repeated attempts to reignite the mother by smiling and gesturing and calling her. If they don't succeed, they finally turn away, looking unhappy and confused.[7] It hurts to reach out to someone who doesn't respond.

"No, I Don't Want a Nap! I Want to Play": The Sense of a Verbal Self (15 to 18 Months)

Learning to speak creates a new type of connection between adult and child. The acquisition of language has traditionally been seen as a major step in the achievement of a separate identity apart from the parent, next only to locomotion. But the opposite is also true: the acquisition of language is a potent force for union and intimacy.

The developmental psychologists Arnold Sameroff and Robert Emde summarize an extensive literature that shows that emotional unresponsiveness produces an infant with "a restricted range of emotional expressiveness; less clear signaling; and a predominance of disengagement, distress, or avoidance in interactions. Under these conditions, clinicians may also see a 'turning off' of affective interactions and, in extreme cases, sustained sadness or depression."[8] In other words, the

[7] Daniel Stern, *Diary of a Baby* (New York: Basic Books, 1990).

[8] Arnold Sameroff and Rober Emde, eds., *Relationship Disturbances in Early Childhood* (New York: Basic Books, 1989), 47.

child whose communications aren't appreciated and responded to eventually gives up and turns inward.

———◆———

When we see sadness or depression in someone, we tend to assume that something's wrong, that something has happened. Maybe that something is that nobody's listening.

———◆———

THE LISTENED-TO CHILD IS A CONFIDENT CHILD

By the time children get to be four or five, empathy or its absence has molded their personalities in recognizable ways. The securely understood child grows up to expect others to be available and receptive. This is demonstrated by a tendency to draw effectively on preschool teachers as resources. The listened-to child who becomes ill or injured at school will confidently turn to teachers for support. In contrast, it's particularly at such times that insecure children fail to seek contact. "A boy is disappointed and folds his arms and sulks. A girl bumps her head under a table and crawls off to be by herself. A child is upset on the last day of school; she sits frozen and expressionless on a couch."[9] Such reactions are typical—and don't change much as the unlistened-to child gets older.

At the same time, preschoolers with a history of empathic listening are more engaged and more at ease with their peers. They expect interactions to be positive and thus are more eager for them. They are able to make more friends and are happier. They are also good listeners. Already by four or five, empathic failure—not abuse or cruelty, but simple, everyday lack of understanding—results in a self that is isolated and insecure, vulnerable to rejection and therefore fearful of new people and experience.

Imagine five-year-old Tammy, weaned on understanding, telling her playmate next door about a bully in kindergarten. "And then he pushed me and hogged all the crayons!"

A tiny cloud momentarily overshadowed her friend Ryan's even tinier face. Bullies were not his favorite people. But listening sympathet-

---

[9]Alan Sroufe, "Relationships, Self, and Individual Adaptation," in Arnold Sameroff and Robert Emde, eds., *Relationship Disturbances in Early Childhood* (New York: Basic Books, 1989), 88–89.

ically, he knew, was for sissies. Confident that if his own ire were sufficiently aroused, he could demolish a grape with a single blow of his
fist, Ryan counseled war. "You should put paint in his hair and spank
him with your ruler when he does that."

Here were two kindred spirits, meeting at last on a plane of perfect
understanding. "Thanks," said Tammy gratefully, "but I think I hear
my mother calling. Nice talking to you."

The need for listening is based partly on the need to sustain our
sense of significance. The listener's understanding presence serves as
a selfobject to satisfy our need for attention and appreciation. But the
idea that listening is something one person *gives* to the other is only
partly true. Another vital aspect of listening is mutuality.

LISTENING BRIDGES THE SPACE BETWEEN US

Mutuality is a sense not merely of being understood and valued but of
sharing—of being-with another person. Here it isn't just *I* but *we* that
is important. Our experience is made fuller by sharing it with another
person.

When I want to "share" a thought or feeling that means a lot to
me, what I really want is to be understood, taken seriously and appreciated. (Calling this "sharing" is an unctuous euphemism; what we really
want is to express ourselves and be heard.) It is *I* who wants to be validated. But if I see an especially funny cartoon in *The New Yorker*, I
immediately think of someone to share *it* with. (Here, "sharing" is appropriate, because the experience sought is mutual, communal.) In this
instance I don't want to be admired or valued; I just want to share the
laughter.

As psychologist Ruthellen Josselson says in *The Space Between
Us*,[10] mutuality is a powerful but neglected aspect of human experience. When we're young and alive, before life blunts our naked nerve
endings, the yearning for mutuality takes its most intense form in the
hungering for a soul mate. We find and invent that special someone
with whom we can share light moments and deep thoughts.

Mutuality is the stuff of everyday human exchange. We swap knowing comments about the president's latest gaffe, complain about the

---

[10]Ruthellen Josselson, *The Space Between Us: Exploring the Dimensions of Human Relationships* (San
Francisco: Jossey-Bass, 1992).

weather, and chat idly about the day's schedule. Nothing important is happening, just life and shared humanity. One woman said, "That's why when I'm away on business I call my husband at the end of the day—to tell him that the meeting went OK or it's raining or I forgot to pack my good shoes." This woman doesn't *need* anything; she calls just to share the everyday observations and opinions and complaints that otherwise back up and burden us in isolation.

Most theories of human relationship emphasize one or another aspect of connection, whether it's mutuality, the selfobject function, holding, attachment, or caring. All these many modes of relatedness are ways of reaching through the space that separates us. Underlying all our agendas, however, is the fact that speech is the primary mode of relating and being listened to is the primary means of being understood and appreciated. By "appreciated" I don't necessarily mean admired, but rather perceived and accepted as we feel ourselves to be. When we talk about being down in the dumps, it doesn't help to be told how wonderful we are; we want our discontent recognized. We want to be known.

As we're reminded from time to time when we're misjudged or hurt more than anyone realizes, however, no one can really see our selves. They see what they can and are willing to see, and they know what we tell them. The rest is private, mystery.

The way we become known is through empathic responsiveness, what Heinz Kohut called "mirroring."[11] The good listener (or "mirroring selfobject") appreciates us as we are, accepting the feelings and ideas that we express as they are. In the process, we feel understood, acknowledged, and accepted.

Empathy—the human echo—is the indispensable stuff of emotional well-being. What is adequately mirrored becomes, in time, part of the true and lived self. The child who is heard and appreciated has a better chance to grow up whole. The adult who is heard and appreciated is more likely to continue to feel that way.

UNSHARED THOUGHTS DIMINISH US

Some people are good at getting appreciated, but they work too hard at it. They aren't open to all of themselves, and so what gets appreciat-

---

[11]Kohut's two great (though unfortunately dense) works are: Heinz Kohut, *The Analysis of the Self* (New York: International Universities Press, 1971); and Heinz Kohut, *The Restoration of the Self* (New York: International Universities Press, 1977).

ed is only the face they show to the world. Reassurance isn't very reassuring to the person with too many secrets.

Why, then, do some people say so little about themselves?

The answer is, life teaches them to hold back. The innocent eagerness for appreciation we bring to our earliest relationships exposes us to consequences. Some people are lucky. They get the attention they need and thereafter approach life with confidence and openness. Others aren't so lucky. They don't get listened to, and as a consequence they avoid opening up. What might appear to be modesty in some such cases may have more to do with the reluctance to reexpose old wounds. Many people learn instead to channel their need for appreciation into personal ambition or doing things for other people.

------◆------

Not being listened to is hard on the heart; and so to varying degrees we cover our need for understanding with mechanisms of defense.

------◆------

Some people become experts at avoidance and cultivate the capacity to be alone. The charm of solitude, recently elaborated by British psychiatrist Anthony Storr,[12] is that it provides space for repose and reflection, time for looking within the self, time for creative endeavor. Solitude offers rest and respite from the noisy claims of everyday social living. But some of the penchant for being alone is defensive—an accommodation to being hurt by not being heard. The defenses that form the solitary person's character support a grand illusion: the illusion of self-reliance. If we could only examine the contemplation of one's own feelings that passes for introspection, we'd discover that the silence of the solitary is often filled with imagined conversations.

Unshared thoughts diminish us not only by making us less authentic and less whole, as we've discussed, but also by eating at us relentlessly. Repression is not like putting something away on the closet shelf and forgetting about it; repression takes a constant expenditure of energy that slowly wears us slowly down.

The feeling of not being understood is one of the most painful in human experience. Not being appreciated and responded to depletes

------

[12]Anthony Storr, *Solitude: A Return to the Self* (New York: The Free Press, 1988).

our vitality and makes us feel less alive. When we're with someone who doesn't listen, we shut down. When we're with someone who's interested and responsive—a good listener—we perk up and come alive. Being listened to is as vital to our enthusiasm for life as love and work. So is listening. Understanding the dynamics of listening enables us to deepen and enrich our relationships. It involves learning how to suspend our own emotional agenda and then realizing the rewards of genuine empathy. When our own listening becomes blocked by the emotions that the speaker arouses in us, we conspire to produce our own isolation. It doesn't have to be that way.

"Why Don't People Listen?"

HOW COMMUNICATION
BREAKS DOWN

Ellen was finding it more difficult than she'd imagined to stay home all day with two small children. She had planned to go back to work soon after the children were born but then decided that it was more important to be at home with them until they started school. What she missed most about not working was having people to talk with. Listening to who wanted a cookie and who had to go to the potty and what Big Bird was up to got pretty tedious by the end of the day. Greg, Ellen's husband, was surprisingly unsympathetic. He helped put the kids to bed and spent time with them on weekends, but when he came home after work he didn't even pretend to be interested in Ellen's account of her day. She was hurt, and she was angry.

"I know Greg works hard and wants to rest. But I work hard too. All I want is a few minutes of adult conversation. But if I dare to interrupt his precious six o'clock news to try to talk to him, he just gets mad. It isn't worth it, and I've had just about all I can take." Her eyes were full of tears.

"DID YOU HEAR WHAT I SAID?"

Why don't people listen? There's no shortage of easy answers to this question. Most focus on the listener. (Husbands are notoriously unsym-

pathetic listeners.) Ellen's explanation for Greg's unavailability wasn't entirely critical—"I know he needs time to unwind"—but it was, after all, focused entirely on him. His lack of listening was *his* doing.

In fact, listening (or the lack of it) is a two-person process. According to Greg, it was frustrating to talk with Ellen about the kids. "She's always complaining. She says they won't leave her alone, even when she goes to the bathroom. But she encourages it! She smothers them. She won't let them alone to play by themselves, and she refuses to take any time for herself. And the thing that really bothers me is the way she always sides with the younger one. Everything Terri does is cute; everything Charles does is wrong. If I try to say anything, even very nicely, she starts crying and says I'm always picking on her. So I've learned to keep my mouth shut."

Ellen felt neglected because Greg wouldn't talk to her, but her contribution to the problem was not being open to his point of view. The fact that Greg's position differs from hers, and may even be critical, makes it hard to hear. Unfortunately, when two people are in conflict about something important, unless each is able to at least acknowledge the other's point of view, the result is likely to be an emotional cutoff.

Greg felt discounted because Ellen complained about a problem of her own making (as he saw it) and wouldn't listen to his opinion. And yet Greg manages neither to listen nor to get his point of view across. If he could separate listening from advising, perhaps Ellen would get some sympathy for her feelings, and then he might be able to communicate his perspective more effectively. Of course it's difficult for him to set aside his own feelings long enough to listen to his wife's, especially on a subject that he feels so strongly about. But maybe that's not a good enough excuse for a husband and father's retreat.

When people don't listen to us, we can't help feeling it's their fault: they're selfish or inconsiderate. (When *we* don't listen, it's because we're bored or tired or don't like being talked down to.) The truth is, listening is a complex process. Even though failures of listening all end in the same painful experience of not being heard, there are many reasons people don't listen.

Several years ago a young couple came to me complaining of difficulties in communicating. When I asked what the problem was, the husband said, "It's my wife; she's boring." (Who says men are reticent with their feelings?) Restraining my urge to react to this nasty crack, I asked him to explain. The man was a lawyer, working as a campaign adviser

in a gubernatorial election campaign. His days were filled with strategy sessions, speechwriting conferences, meetings with the candidate, television interviews, arranging appearances across the state, defending attacks from the opposition, and planning counterattacks. When he came home at night, his head spinning from the excitement and frustration of the crusade, he mumbled a greeting to his wife and collapsed onto the couch with a drink and the newspaper.

When I asked why he wasn't more eager to talk over the events of the day, he said his wife wasn't interested. She was a graphic design artist and not at all, he contended, concerned about politics.

She protested that although she might not know a lot about politics, she *was* interested in him and what he was doing. He wasn't convinced.

I asked him to think of someone that he *knew* was interested in the campaign, someone with whom he could talk enthusiastically. Imagine, I told him, how different you are with that person. He allowed as that might be true. Then I asked him—just for an experiment—to come home for one week and pretend that his wife was that interested person, the person he found it so exciting to talk to. He agreed to try it.

The next week they returned beaming. "Guess what?" he said. "She's not boring anymore."

This young lawyer's uncommunicativeness could have been taken as just another example of men's silences. Are men emotionally illiterate? Trapped in doing—working, playing, achieving—do they have no language of feeling? Such stereotyping ignores the interactive nature of communication and the powerful role of expectations. When people don't say much, it's less likely that they have nothing on their minds than that they don't trust the other person to be interested or tolerant enough to hear it. My suggestion to this man—that he pretend his wife *was* interested—encouraged him to break his silence. But it was his approaching her with enthusiasm, taking interest in talking to her, that broke the pattern of avoidance. The truth is that we become more interesting ourselves when we assume interest on the part of our listeners.

WHY SOMEONE DOSEN'T HEAR WHAT YOU THINK YOU SAID

Sometimes people don't hear us because they've had a bad day. They may be preoccupied with the angry things someone said or with all the

extra work they have to do and thus not be able to listen to anything at all. Or they may be turned off to us by any number of things—they assume that we're talking to them only because we want something or that we're going to give them a lecture or that we don't really care about them. Listeners often don't hear because they have a preconceived notion of what we're going to say. Or they can't hear us because they can't suspend their own needs or because what we say makes them anxious. In short, although hurt feelings may tempt us to blame failures of listening on other people's recalcitrance, the reasons for not listening are many and complex.

When the communicative process breaks down, we—who are doing our best—tend to assume that the other person didn't say what he meant or didn't hear what we were saying. Usually, both parties to misunderstanding feel that way. But it may be helpful to realize that between speaker and listener are two filters to meaning.[1]

The speaker, who has an *intention* of what he or she wants to communicate, sends a *message*, and that message has an *impact* on the listener.

Good communication means having the impact you meant to have, that is *intent* equals *impact*. But every message must pass first through the filter of the speaker's clarity of expression and second through the listener's ability to hear what was said. Unfortunately, there are many times when intent doesn't equal impact and many reasons why this is the case.

Some of the reasons for misunderstanding are simple and can be improved, like learning a skill. For example, by learning to give feedback, listeners tell speakers about the impact of their messages and give them a chance to clarify their intentions. But many more reasons for misunderstanding are less straightforward and not amenable to simple formulas for improvement. Our young lawyer's assumption that his wife wasn't interested in his work is just one example of the psychological complications of listening.

Transference and Countertransference

This dynamic, the speaker's tendency to impose certain expectations on the listener, is what, in the psychoanalytic situation, is called *transference*. For simplicity's sake, the idea of transference is often reduced

[1]John Gottman, Cliff Notarius, Jonni Gonso, and Howard Markman, *A Couples Guide to Communication* (Chicago: Research Press, 1976).

to the notion that the patient assumes that the silent analyst is a carbon copy of one of his or her parents—judging her harshly just like her father did or enthralled with his accomplishments like his mother was. In fact transference refers to *all* the ways in which a person's experience of a relationship becomes organized according to the configurations of self-image and expectations of others that unconsciously structure his or her subjective universe. Transference isn't limited to the therapeutic situation—and it isn't only distortion.

Countertransference, the psychoanalytic term for the complexity introduced by the listener, refers to how the listener's subjectivity shapes his or her experience of the conversation. Like transference, countertransference isn't simply distortion, because our expectations and reactions to each other actually shape and reshape our relationships. The woman who expects men to talk only about themselves may inquire more than she discloses, thereby confirming her expectations. The man who expects to find his wife's accounts of the day uninteresting may fail to ask the kinds of questions that might make it interesting to him; as a result, he gets out of the conversation pretty much what he puts into it.

We'll explore the speaker's contributions to misunderstanding later, though as you'll discover it's never entirely possible to separate speaker and listener.

The principal forces contributing to the listener's filter are the listener's own agenda, preconceived notions and expectations, and defensive emotional reactions.

The Listener's Own Agenda

In the summer of 1992 Ariel Dorfman's play *Death and the Maiden,* starring Glenn Close, Richard Dreyfuss, and Gene Hackman, drew large audiences on Broadway. This play of ideas in the guise of a political thriller takes place in a country that might be Chile in the immediate aftermath of a corrupt dictatorship. The setting is a beach house on the night that the lawyer, Gerardo (Richard Dreyfuss), is asked to investigate certain crimes of the recent past; his wife, Paulina (Glenn Close), was one such victim. And when Roberto Miranda (Gene Hackman) gives her husband a lift after his tire blows out, she recognizes his voice as that of the doctor who raped her. Paulina gets a gun and ties the doctor to a chair. But her husband doesn't believe her. How could she recognize the man who raped and tortured her from just his voice? He can't believe that the good Samaritan who stopped to help

him on the road could actually be the evil man who did such terrible things to his wife. She assures him that there is no mistake: she could never forget that voice. Still her husband can't believe her. The play turns on the wife's desperation and the husband's incredulity. The ending is ambiguous.

I first heard about *Death and the Maiden* from a patient who took it as an allegory of a husband's failure to listen to his wife, despite the urgency of her appeal. She knew how the woman felt. I replied that as a metaphor for misunderstanding the story was one-sided, stressing as it did only the husband's failure to listen, rather than also dealing with the wife's failure to make herself understood. I wasn't familiar with the play, but I wanted my patient to quit blaming her husband for their problems and begin to see their communication as a process that took place between them. It wasn't until later that I realized that I was recreating a similar story: a woman was trying to tell a man something—in this case that the play was profoundly affecting and that it reminded her of not being listened to by her husband—and the man was not listening.

When I finally got around to reading the play, I responded the same way my patient did. It's a powerful story about a woman desperate for understanding and desperately not understood.

I didn't listen to my patient with the best of intentions. Oh, I heard what she said all right, but I was too eager to teach her a lesson about listening to really understand what she was saying—that the play was upsetting and reminded her of her own situation. My response, "Yes, but . . . ," had the effect of making her wrong and me right. Failures of listening often take that form.

To listen well, it's necessary to let go of what's on your mind long enough to hear what's on the other person's. Feigned attentiveness doesn't work.

Remember Roger, whose friend Derek grew distant from him after he got married? Roger might have been able to talk to Derek if he'd concentrated on saying how he felt, without blaming Derek or forcing him to explain himself. If you can express your feelings without trying to compel anything from the other person, you're more likely to get heard—and more likely to hear what the other person is feeling.

Preconceived Notions

By the time we emerge from adolescence most of us have become self-protective. We know where our naked nerve endings are and don't often

expose them. We open ourselves selectively and, like any creature with a soft underbelly, retreat from unfriendly encounters. Sometimes, however, it's too late to pull back inside our shells. When the pressure of upset makes us open ourselves to someone we think we can trust, failed understanding can be as bruising as a mugging.

When his son told him he was dropping out of college, Seth tried hard to be understanding. He didn't want to burden Jamie with his own expectations, and so he did his best to hide his disappointment. Still, he was deeply disappointed and needed someone to talk to. Hoping that his brother would understand how he felt, Seth gave him a call. It wasn't easy for Seth to talk about his feelings, so he started out making small talk. After a few minutes Seth warmed to the conversation and, taking a deep breath, told his brother that Jamie had dropped out of school and that he was very upset about it. There was a pause, and then his brother went on to talk about something else. Seth was stunned—not just hurt, but amazed that his brother could act so unfeelingly. With great effort, he confronted his brother, saying "Didn't you hear what I said?" His brother replied that he had never thought of Seth as someone who needed emotional support. Both brothers were on the brink of addressing the past and present they shared; if they could only open up and listen to one another, they had an opportunity to clarify and strengthen their relationship. But it didn't happen.

The expectations with which we approach each other are, as we shall see, just one of many ways we create the listening we get. Nor can the process be reduced to the behavior of the participants—the words—and therefore always be improved by "skills training" or pretending to take an interest or other calculated strategies. (Conversation can, of course, be reduced to a behavioral analysis, but only by trivializing the thoughts and feelings, yearnings and defensiveness of the people involved.) Dialogue takes place between two people with not just ears and tongues but hearts and minds—and all the famous complications therein.

———◆———

An understanding attitude doesn't presume to know a person's thoughts and feelings. Instead, it is an openness to listen and discover.

———◆———

Emotional Reactivity

As I mentioned in the Introduction, we all have certain ways of re-acting emotionally within particular relationships. The closer the re-lationship, the more vulnerable we are to hearing something said as hurtful, frightening, threatening, or infuriating even when it wasn't meant that way. Because of the dynamics of the relationship, our expectations of the other person, or what we've become accustomed to in previous relationships, we get defensive, which makes it im-possible to listen to and understand what the speaker meant to say.

A simple "Have you taken the garbage out yet?" might be taken as a rebuke by one whose parents never expected him to do anything right. His response might be an overreactive "Can't you leave me alone for one second?!"

It's not always the listener's defensiveness, of course, that gives rise to heated emotional reactions. Sometimes it's the speaker's provo-cation.

"Why do I always have to ask you three times before you do any-thing?" when it really means "Have you taken the garbage out yet?" will almost inevitably trigger a defensive reaction. For that matter, even "Haven't you taken the garbage out yet?" could provoke an emotional response. If you don't watch how you say things as well as what you say, it's easy to provoke those you love.

Then there are those touchy subjects that can almost be counted on to set off an explosion. As I explain later, in Chapters 6 and 9, topics likely to be toxic among couples are things like money, the children, and sex. To have a really fruitful discussion about any of these, where both people really listen, requires special effort. You might have to watch not only what you say and how you say it but also where, when, and why.

This is not to imply that we need to spend our lives tiptoeing around each other. What it does mean is that all of us need to step back and calm down, being aware of what sets us off and what sets off those we want to communicate with, if we are to get through to each other.

When we don't, many exchanges degenerate to such clever re-partee as "You're such a bitch!" and "Oh, grow up!" before falling apart altogether as one or both people storm out of the room.

UNDERSTANDING THE RULES OF THE LISTENING GAME: BEYOND LINEAR THINKING

We don't usually stop to examine patterns of misunderstanding in our lives because we're stuck in our own point of view. Misunderstanding hurts, and when we're hurt we tend to look outside ourselves for explanations. But the problem isn't just that when something goes wrong we look for someone to blame. The problem is linear thinking. We reduce human interactions to a matter of personalities. "He doesn't listen because he's too preoccupied with himself." "She's hard to listen to because she goes on and on about everything." Some people blame themselves ("Maybe I'm not that interesting"), but it's almost always easier to appreciate the other person's contribution.

Attributing other people's lack of understanding to character is armor for our ignorance and passivity. That some people repeat their annoying ways with most others they come in contact with doesn't prove that lack of responsiveness is fixed in character; it only proves that these individuals trigger many people to play out the reciprocal role in their dramas of two-part disharmony.

The fixed-character position assumes that it's extremely difficult for people to change. But you don't change relationships by changing other people. You change patterns of relating by changing yourself in relation to them. Personality is dynamic, not fixed. The dynamic personality position posits that it *is* possible for people to change; all we have to do is change our response to each other. We are not victims—we are participants, in a real way, and the consequences of our participation are profound.

To participate effectively, we must know something about the rules of the game.

I remember how confused I was the first time I saw a lacrosse game. From where I sat it looked as if some kids were just standing around while the rest raced up and down the field, using their sticks to pass the ball back and forth, club each other, or both. I got the gist of it—it was like soccer played by Road Warriors—but a lot of it was hard to follow. Why, for instance, did the team that lost the ball out of bounds sometimes get it back and sometimes not? And why, sometimes when one kid whacked another with his stick, did everybody cheer, while at other times the referee called a foul? The problem was, of course, that I couldn't see the whole field and didn't know the rules of the game.

The same disadvantages—not seeing the whole field and not knowing the rules of the game—keep us from understanding our successes and failures at communicating with one another.

Earlier I said that listening is a two-person process, but even that is oversimplified. Actually, even an uncomplicated communication has several components: the listener, the speaker, the message, various implicit messages, the context, and, because the process doesn't flow one-way from speaker to listener, the listener's response. Even a brief consideration of these elements in the listening process reveals more reasons for misunderstanding than simply bad faith on the part of the listener.

"What Are You Trying to Say?"

The message is the content of what a speaker says. But the message sent isn't always the one intended.

A family of four is invited to spend Sunday afternoon at the lake house of friends of the father. When the teenage daughter asks if she can bring along one of her friends, her father says, "I don't think we should bring extra guests when we're invited to dinner." The daughter looks hurt, and the man's wife says, "You're being silly; they never mind extra company." The man gets angry and withdraws, brooding over his feeling that his wife always takes the children's side and never listens to him.

The problem here is a common one: the message sent wasn't the one intended. One of the unfortunate things we learn along with being "polite" and not being "selfish" is not to say directly what we want. Instead of saying "I want . . . " we say "We should . . . " or "Do you want . . . ?" When we're taking a trip in the car and we get hungry, we say "Isn't it getting late?" (When I was growing up I learned that guests weren't supposed to put people to any trouble. If you went to someone's house and wanted a glass of water, you didn't ask; you looked thirsty. If they did offer you something, you politely declined. Only if they insisted was it OK to accept. A really good boy waited until a glass of water was offered at least twice before accepting.)

Because this convention of indirectness is so universal, it doesn't usually cause problems. If the other person in the room says "Are you cold?" you usually know he means "*I'm* cold. Can we turn up the heat?" But indirection can cause problems when stronger feelings are involved. The father in our example didn't want his daughter to bring a friend.

Perhaps his wife was right; the people who invited them wouldn't mind. But somehow *he* minded. Maybe he wanted his daughter to remain more a part of the family and less an independent person with friends of her own. Or maybe he wanted her to be part of the grown-ups' conversation, instead of off with her friend, because he found it easier to talk about the children's doings than his own. That's the trouble with indirection: there are always a lot of *maybes*.

When we're conflicted over certain of our own needs, we may infer (rightly or wrongly) that others would object even to hearing our wishes, much less acceding to them. Because indirection leads to so much misunderstanding and so many arguments that are beside the point, it does more harm than good. Two people can't have an honest disagreement about whether or not they want to move to another city as long as they engage in diversionary arguments about whether going or staying would be better for the children.[2]

One reason others argue with us in a way that seems to negate our feelings is that we blur the distinction between our feelings and the facts. Instead of saying "I don't want her to bring a friend," the father tries to cloud his motives and bolster his argument by appealing to *shoulds*. When his wife argues with what he says instead of what he means, he feels rejected. Like every listener, he measured the intentions of other speakers by what they said—or what he heard—and asked that they measure him by what he intended to say.

As speakers we want to be heard—but not merely to be heard; we want to be understood, heard for what we think we're saying, for what we know we meant. Similar impasses occur when we insist we said one thing and our listener heard another. Instead of saying "What I meant to say was . . . ," we go on insisting what we *did* say.

"Why Don't You Say What You Mean?"

Implicit messages tell us more than what's being said; they tell us how we're meant to receive what's being said. Depending on the situation, inflection, and motives of the speaker, "Let's have lunch" could mean "I'm hungry," "I'd like to see you again," or "Please leave now; I'm busy." The statements "I love you" and "I'm sorry" are of course notorious for

---

[2]There are times, however, when the most effective statement of what you want is less then completely candid. For people who have trouble saying no, rather than trying to explain why they don't want to do something, it may be easier to say "I'd love to, but I can't."

having multiple meanings. Knowing the other person makes it easier to decode implicit messages; suspecting his or her motives can make it harder.

According to Gregory Bateson, one of the founders of family therapy, all communications have two levels of meaning: *report* and *command*.[3] The report (or message) is the information conveyed by the words. The second or command level (which Bateson also called *metacommunication*) conveys information on how the report is to be taken and a statement of the nature of the relationship.

If a wife scolds her husband for running the dishwasher when it's only half full and he says OK but turns around and does exactly the same thing two days later, she may be annoyed that he doesn't listen to her. She means the message. But maybe he didn't like the metamessage. Maybe he doesn't like her telling him what to do as though she were his mother.

In attempting to define the nature of our relationships we qualify our messages by posture, facial expression, and tone of voice. For example, a rising inflection on the last two words turns "You did that on purpose" from an accusation to a question. The whole impact of a statement may change depending on which words are emphasized. Consider the difference between "Are *you* telling me it isn't true?" and "Are you telling me it *isn't* true?" Pauses, gestures, and gaze also tell us how to interpret what is being said. Although we may not need the ponderous term *metacommunication*, misunderstandings about what is implied and how messages are to be taken are major reasons for problems in listening.

One winter when I was working hard and feeling sorry for myself, I wrote to a sympathetic friend, and in the letter I said jokingly that I was running away to spend two weeks on the white beaches of a deserted Caribbean island. The only trouble was that I didn't *say* it, I *wrote* it, and she missed the irony I intended. The medium didn't carry my tone of voice or the facial expression that modified the message. Instead of getting the sympathy I was (indirectly) asking for, I got back a rather testy note to the effect that it's nice to know that some people have the time and money to indulge themselves.

We know what we mean; problems arise when we expect others

---

[3]Jurgen Ruesch and Gregory Bateson, *Communication: The Social Matrix of Psychiatry* (New York: Norton, 1951).

to. How is our communication to be taken? Is it chat? A confession? An outpouring of emotion? When our listeners fail to grasp that we're upset and need to have our feelings listened to, who's to blame?

A woman told her husband that something her boss said made her afraid that she might be in for trouble at work. The husband responded by saying no, he didn't think so; it didn't sound that way. When she replied that he didn't listen to her, both of them got upset. She was annoyed because he didn't listen to her feelings. He was hurt because he *was* listening. He had responded sincerely. He just didn't realize how upset she was.

Perhaps to some people this woman's upset would have been apparent. Maybe a friend would have realized that she needed to have her feelings acknowledged, not disagreed with. But she wasn't married to that friend. She was married to a man who didn't automatically understand how she wanted to be listened to. (Some people try to make that clear: "I'm worried about something, and I need to talk about it." "I need your advice." "I just need you to listen.")

Occasionally—but not as often as most people think—the implicit message in a communication is a request for the speaker to do something. The teenage boy who says "I'm hungry" isn't just making small talk. (A teenage boy's appetite is not an idle thing.) Usually, however, *the* most important implicit message in what people say is the feeling behind the content.

When we're little, before we learn to act grown-up by masking our feelings, our communications are full of ill-disguised emotion. You don't have to be a neurolingustics expert to figure out what children are feeling when they say "There's monsters under my bed" or "Nobody wants to play with me." The same emotions may be implicit, if less obviously implied, when an adult says "I've got that big meeting coming up tomorrow" or "I called to see if Fred and Teddy wanted to go to the movies, but they weren't home." One of the most effective ways to improve understanding is to listen for both content and implicit feelings in what people say.

Much of communication is implicit and—when people are on the same wavelength—decoded automatically. Often, however, what is implicit—what we take for granted—is not obvious to everyone. Much misunderstanding could be cleared up if we learned to do two things: appreciate the other person's perspective and, at times, clarify what usually remains implicit.

"Is This a Good Time?"

The context of communication is the setting: the time, the place, who else is present, and, because communication cannot be reduced to the obvious, people's expectations. We ordinarily accommodate our talking and listening to the context of an exchange without even thinking about it. We don't spring bad news on people the minute they walk in the door, we don't talk loudly in public, and we don't argue in front of the kids. (As you can't see by the twinkle in my eye, I'm being ironic.)

No matter how much certain people care about us, there are times when they don't have the energy and patience to listen. If a husband calls his wife at work and starts to talk at length about something that doesn't seem terribly important, she may get impatient sooner than she would if the same conversation occurred at home. By contrast, even though her husband usually retreats behind the paper at the end of the day, a wife may succeed in getting his full attention by signaling her need for it. "Honey, I need to talk to you about something important."

Unfortunately, in many relationships spouses have different preferred times to talk. He likes to talk when he comes home at the end of the day. She's busy then and prefers to talk later, when they're watching TV or getting ready for bed. Fishing for understanding at the wrong time is like trying to catch a trout in the noonday sun.

When to talk: not when your partner needs some space or time to be alone.

The idea that timing affects the listening we get may be painfully obvious; unfortunately, when needs collide, the resulting failures of understanding are obviously painful. The end of the day can be especially difficult. Partners may be frazzled and frustrated. Worn out from running around all day, trying to make other people happy, attending mind-deadening meetings, fighting traffic, or chasing after children and answering endless questions, they have little energy left over for hearing each other.

The unhappy irony is that the domestic conversation people are too tired to engage in might provide emotional refueling: talking and listening reinvigorate us. If we take listening for granted, we may assume that the people we care about will listen to us whenever we feel

like talking. But if we realize that good listening doesn't happen automatically, we'll learn to give a little more thought to finding the right time to approach people.

Setting has an obvious physical effect on listening—in terms of privacy and noise level, for example—and an equally powerful effect in terms of conditioned cues. Familiar settings, like a therapist's office or a friend's kitchen, can be reassuring places in which to open up. Other familiar settings, like your own kitchen or bedroom, can be anything but conducive to conversation. Memories of misunderstanding and distraction cling to some rooms like the smell of wet dog.

Conversation in many settings is governed by unwritten rules, some of which are obvious (to most people). At cocktail parties, for example, where conversational subgroups constantly shift in size and membership, conversations may be warm, candid, even intimate, but they are also generally brief (which may explain the warmth and candor). Anyone who tries to talk too long in a such a setting may strain a listener's sense of decorum.

Rules of decorum are based on a shared sense of what's appropriate and probably originally derive from practical considerations, like noninterference with others and respect for special places. Thus, talking loudly in a cathedral, on a train, or at the movies is frowned on.[4] Because rules of decorum are implicit and widely shared, we tend to take them for granted, not realizing that we have done so until we or someone else breaks them.

In addition to general rules of propriety, most of us have personal preferences for settings in which we're comfortable talking. Some people like to talk on the telephone, for example. (Why, I have no idea.) Some people like to talk when they go for a ride in the car; others prefer to read or look out the window. And, of course, we may be in the mood for conversation in a particular setting at one time and not another. Often the best way to get someone's attention is to invite her away from familiar surroundings—by taking a walk, say, or going out to a restaurant. Many of these preferences are sufficiently obvious that we adjust to them automatically. We know not to call certain people at home in the evening, and we learn the most promising times and places to get the listening we need. When we don't, feelings get hurt. We

---

[4]People who get annoyed at those who talk in the movies forget that the advent of videotape rentals has blurred the distinction between movie theater and living room. They also fail to consider situational priorities that might make theater conversation understandable. Yes, even people who talk to the movies deserve consideration, and so they should be shot as painlessly as possible.

blame others for not hearing us, and, alternately, we feel put upon by their lack of consideration in imposing on us at the wrong time.

Whenever conversation takes place in the presence of others, some aspects of listening are expressively accentuated while others are suppressed. If a couple goes out to dinner and the man talks about problems at work, the woman will probably listen more intently than she does at home because the setting suggests intimacy. If they bring along the children, however, she's liable to be less attentive to him and also less likely to talk about her own concerns. Sometimes that's *why* people bring the children. Togetherness is a hedge against intimacy as well as loneliness.

Most of us have had the disconcerting experience of talking to someone who seems to be interested until someone else appears. In some situations this is unavoidable. If two people are having lunch and a third person joins them, it's not reasonable to expect to continue a private conversation. But in other instances the person talking about something important might expect the listener not to accept and encourage an interruption, to say, for example, to a telephone caller, "Sorry, I can't talk now; I'm busy." Or if two people are having a confidential conversation in a public place, one might expect the other to greet a casual acquaintance who happens by, but not to break off the conversation or signal the third person that he or she is welcome to join in. Third parties are to intimate conversation what rain is to picnics.

Sometimes the effect of third parties works the other way. An adult may show more animated and sustained interest in a child's conversation when other adults are watching. Similarly a man who often interrupts his wife at home may show more respect and forbearance when they're out with another couple.

I remember once when I was being interviewed on a morning television show how the host, a dynamic and attractive woman in her early forties, was fascinated and intrigued by the book I'd written. She sat very close, kept her eyes on mine, and asked all the right questions. Here was this radiant woman, totally engrossed in what I had to say. It was very flattering. Then a commercial break came up, and the light in her face went out like the red light on the camera. I ceased to exist. After the break the interview resumed, and so did my interviewer's intense show of interest. Her pretense, in the face of a whole audience of third parties (and my susceptibility), was disconcerting, but after all, it was her job to show interest.

There's a big difference between showing interest and really taking interest.

WHY SOME PEOPLE ARE SO HARD TO LISTEN TO

Even when you play by the rules, some people are hard to listen to. In some cases that's because their accounts run on to Homeric length. They're generous with details. You ask about their vacation and they tell you about packing the car, getting lost on the way, and all the various wrong turns. They tell you about the weather and who said what and where they ate lunch and what they had for dinner, and they keep telling you until something other than tact stops them. Others may not talk at all about what they did but instead go on at great windy length about what everyone else did, all those objectionable others who are such problems in their lives.

It's also hard to listen to people who talk incessantly about their preoccupations—a mother with a difficult child who talks of little else, a careerist who wants to talk only about his work, a man with allergies who's always complaining about his sinus trouble. One person's headache can become another's if she has to hear about it all the time. It isn't just the repetition that we tire of; it's being cast in the helpless role of one who is importuned about a problem with no solution, or at least no solution the complainer wants to consider. (If the complainer doesn't expect a solution, a simple acknowledgment of his feelings—"Gee, that's too bad"—may give a satisfactory punctuation to the exchange.)

Some people who talk too much are like that with everybody, but often, whether we appreciate it or not, some of them talk at such length with us because they talk so little with anyone else. Who other than his wife does the husband with no friends talk to? Who other than the friend who seems to have her life together and talks so little about herself does the overburdened wife talk to? Some people need our attention, but if the conversation is consistently one-sided, maybe part of the reason is that we respond too passively.

Sometimes speakers are hard to listen to because they're unaware of what they've said—or of its infuriating implications. When the listener reacts to what *wasn't* said, the speaker responds with righteous indigna-

tion, wounded by the listener's "overreaction." If a mother says to her teenage daughter "Is *that* what you're wearing to school?" and the daughter bursts into tears and says "You're always criticizing me!" the mother might protest that the daughter is reacting unreasonably. "All I said was 'Is that what you're wearing to school?' How come you get so upset about a simple question?" Such questions are as simple as parents are free of judgmentalness and children are free of sensitivity to it.

My father has a way of packing what feels like a whole lot of disconfirmation into one little innocent statement that drives me crazy. If I tell him that something is so, even when it's not something particularly unusual or controversial, he'll often say "It could be." Arghh!! I think he does this because he can't tolerate overt conflict. So if somebody tells him something that he didn't know or isn't completely convinced is the case, he says "It could be." To me, this feels much worse than an argument. An argument, you can argue with. "It could be" makes you feel discounted. One consequence of these interchanges is that I become stubborn in my opinions. Having had my fill of being doubted, I can't stand not to be believed when I'm stating a fact. Like the fact that Lake Champlain is one of the five Great Lakes.

In case you think I've slid from talking about speakers to complaining about listeners, you're right. While it's possible to separate speakers and listeners conceptually, in practice they are inextricably intertwined. Listening is codetermined.

Some people are hard to listen to because they say so little, or at least little of a personal nature. If the urge to voice true feelings to sympathetic ears is such a driving desire, why are so many people numb and silent? Because life happens to them—slights, hurts, cruelty, mockery, and shame. These things are hard on the heart.

We come to relationships wounded. Longing for attention, we don't always get it. Expecting to be taken seriously, we get argued with or ignored or treated as cute but inconsequential. Needing to share our feelings, we run into disapproval or mockery. Opening up and getting no response or, worse, humiliation, is like walking into a wall in the dark. If this happens often enough, we shut down and erect our own walls.

Although a speaker's reticence may be seen as a fixed trait of personality, such traits are really nothing more than habits based on expectations formed from past relationships. People who don't talk to us are people who don't expect us to listen.

Therapists who encounter resistance to speaking freely engage in what is called *defense analysis*—pointing out to the patient *that* he is holding back, *how* he is holding back (perhaps by talking about trivia), and speculating about *what* might be on his mind and *why* he might hesitate to bring it up. Therapists have license that the average person lacks to ask such probing questions, but it's not against the law to inquire if a friend is finding it difficult to open up for some reason or to point out gently that she doesn't seem to talk much about herself. We shape our relationships by our response.

Does the person who isn't very forthcoming with you have reason to believe that you're interested in what he thinks and feels? That you'll listen without interrupting? That you can tolerate disagreement? Anger? Openness is a product of interaction.

MEN ARE FROM MARS?

As we head further into the nineties, the social construction of gender—men do this, women do that—polarizes relations between men and women as never before. As the old complementarity gives way to a new symmetry, conflict seems to be the price for equality.

Several books in recent years have gained enormous popularity by telling us that men and women communicate differently and then explaining what those differences are. Among the most popular was John Gray's *Men Are From Mars, Women Are From Venus*, in which the author argues that men need space while women crave company. If we learn to respect the inevitable differences that crop up between two people who live together by attributing such differences to gender rather than to stubbornness or ill will, maybe that's a good thing. And if we learn not to react unsympathetically to what our partners say, that's certainly a good thing. But perhaps the most important thing is not so much to learn *how* to react to these other, alien creatures, but to learn not to *overreact* and learn instead to listen. Perhaps the best response to Freud's famous question "What do women want?" might have been "Why don't you ask—and then listen?"

Once, differences between men and women were thought to be bred in the bone, and this biological determinism was used to justify all manner of inequity. After years of effort to break down these separate but unequal categories, a new wave of feminist scholars has reasserted what they once fought: gender differences. Jean Baker Miller has emphasized

responsiveness and mutuality as especially important to women in relationships,[5] and Carol Gilligan has argued that for women the qualities of care and connection are fundamental to selfhood, organizers of
identity, and moral development.[6] According to Gilligan, men build
towers and women build webs.

Thus far the greatest impact of the new work by feminist psychologists has been a reaffirmation of gender differences—but this time with
a positive construction of the psychology of women. In her 1978 book,
The Reproduction of Mothering, Nancy Chodorow pointed out that because boys and girls are parented primarily by mothers, they grow up
with different orientations to attachment and independence.[7] Boys
must separate themselves from their mothers to claim their masculinity, which is why boys of a certain age start shrinking from their mothers'
hugs and why "sissy" and "mamma's boy" are still such powerful invec-
tives. Girls, on the other hand, do not have to renounce their mothers'
caring and connection to become women; they learn to become themselves *through* connection.

In the wake of Nancy Chodorow and Carol Gilligan, the idea of
inherent gender differences has come to define the discourse on men
and women to such an extent that many writers now take for granted
that women are *fundamentally* different from men in ways that make
them better at listening. For people who accept this premise, life is simple: all the complexities of relationship can be dispensed with in favor
of one all-purpose explanation. Men do this; women do that. End of
discussion.

This new wave of sexual typecasting is reflected in the popular reception of books that reduce every nuance, every polarity of conversation
between men and women to one gender distinction: men seek power;
women seek relationship. Sadly, a lot of people now take this for granted.

Perhaps the best way to begin making a difference in the quality
of listening between men and women is to *unmake* a difference. My
point isn't that there aren't conversational differences between men and
women but that perhaps it's time to stop exaggerating, stereotyping,
and glorifying them.

Why are so many women and men so willing to assume that we're

[5]Jean Baker Miller, *Toward a New Psychology of Women* (Boston: Beacon Press, 1976).

[6]Carol Gilligan, *In a Different Voice* (Cambridge, MA: Harvard University Press, 1982).

[7]Nancy Chodorow, *The Reproduction of Mothering: Psychoanalysis and the Sociology of Gender* (Berkeley: University of California Press, 1978).

separated by a vast gender gap, that we speak different languages, and that our destinies take us in different directions? Is it really a woman's nature to be caring and seek connection? Is it really a man's nature to be independent and seek power? Or do these polarities reflect the ways our culture has—thus far—shaped the universal yearning to be appreciated?

Sometimes social and political factors provide the underlying explanation for so-called gender distinctions. Might caring, for example, which has been represented as a gender difference, be more adequately understood as a way of negotiating from a position of low power? Perhaps some women (and some men) are caring because of a need to please, which stems from a lack of a sense of personal power. Thus the same woman who appeals to the need for caring in debates with her husband may emphasize rules in arguments with her children. The same social embeddedness that promotes caring may sometimes make it difficult for women to recognize their own self-interest. Perhaps rather than our apologizing for or celebrating gender differences, it might be more useful for us to talk *with* each other, instead of about each other, and to move toward partnership, not polarization.

Perhaps if we started listening to one another we could move toward greater balance, in ourselves and our relationships. Perhaps women raised to believe that happiness is to be found in selfless service to others could learn more respect for their own strivings and capacity for independent achievement. Perhaps men who seek identity only in achievement could learn greater respect for the neglected dimensions of caring and concern. In the process of relaxing rigid definitions of what it means to be a man or a woman, perhaps fathers might learn to loosen the tight boundaries they draw around themselves and reduce the gulf across which they relate to others and guard their "masculinity." Perhaps mothers, in learning more respect for their own self-interest, would learn more respect for the boundary separating themselves and their children and allow the children greater room and freedom to become themselves.

If we can avoid thinking of gender difference as fixed and given, perhaps we might begin to entertain the possibility that boys can and should identify with their mothers' nurturance and care to become more fully realized men and better fathers. Similarly, we might begin to see that girls can identify with their fathers as well as their mothers to feel entitled to be independent persons with their own wishes. Maybe God invented the idea of two parents so that children could draw on the best of both of them.

Comforting as it may be to blame lack of understanding on other people's stubbornness or insensitivity or gender, the reasons we don't listen to each other turn out to be more complex. It isn't selfishness, but complications of character and relationship that keep us from listening and being listened to.

A fuller appreciation of the dynamics of listening makes it a little easier for us to begin hearing each other. Is it necessary to dissect every misunderstanding and analyze it according to message, subtext, context, speaker, listener, and response? Of course not. The simple, heroic act of stepping back from our own injured feelings and considering the other person's point of view is quite enough of an accomplishment.

So why are we so sensitive to misunderstanding that we have trouble seeing the other person's side of things? To answer that question and continue to move toward hearing each other, let's look more closely at the emotional factors that complicate listening.

PART TWO

THE REAL REASONS
PEOPLE DON'T LISTEN

"When Is It My Turn?"

THE HEART OF LISTENING:
THE STRUGGLE TO SUSPEND
OUR OWN NEEDS

Twenty-five years ago I took my first course in how to be a good listener. I was in graduate school, and the course was called Elementary Clinical Methods. We learned about making eye contact and asking open-ended questions and how to avoid talking about ourselves (by parrying personal questions with the therapist's famous evasion, "Why do you ask?"). We practiced on each other during role-play sessions, and I learned a lot of interesting things about my classmates. Then we went to the state hospital to practice on patients, and I learned that maybe I wasn't cut out for this work.

It was the first time I'd ever been in a mental hospital, and I was filled with fascination and horror. Maybe I expected to see an axe murderer or perhaps a scene out of *The Snake Pit*. Actually, in those days before the widespread use of tranquilizers, some of the back wards *were* like snake pits. But in the ward for new admissions, where they sent us, the patients were mostly just very unhappy people.

My first real patient was a young mother who'd become depressed after coming home from the hospital with her second baby. She looked

disheveled and lonely and empty, and I felt terribly sorry for her. I asked her why she'd come to the hospital and why she felt so hopeless and where she grew up and other things like that. She answered my questions, but the interview never really went anywhere. Every time I'd ask another question, she'd respond, but only briefly, and then wait for me to say something. Since I didn't have anything to say, it was an awkward wait.

It was my first interview, and I was sorely disappointed that it didn't go well. Eventually I learned not to ask so many questions and, if someone didn't seem to have much to say, to comment on that reticence, inviting the person to explain it rather than trying to fight it with questions. But the real problem in that first interview didn't have to do with technique. I wasn't truly interested in that woman; I was more interested in being a therapist.

This troubling experience illustrates the most vital and difficult requirement for listening. When it's genuine, listening demands taking an interest in the speaker and what he or she has to say.

Taking an interest can easily be sentimentalized by equating it with sincerity or caring. Sincerity and caring are certainly fine characteristics, but listening isn't a matter of character, nor is it something that good people do automatically. To take an interest in someone else, we must suspend the interests of the self.

---◆---

Listening is the art by which we use empathy to reach across the space between us. Passive attention doesn't work.

---◆---

Not only is listening an active process; it often takes a deliberate effort to suspend our own needs and reactions—as Roxanne's mother so bravely demonstrated by holding her own feelings in check long enough to listen to her daughter's fierce resentment. To listen well, you must hold back what you have to say and control the urge to interrupt or argue.

The act of listening requires a submersion of the self and immersion in the other. This isn't always easy. We may be interested but too concerned with controlling or instructing or reforming the other person to be truly open to his point of view. Parents have trouble hearing their children as long as they can't suspend their urgent need to set them straight. And, as I'm afraid I've demonstrated, even therapists,

presumably exemplars of understanding, are often too busy trying to change people to really listen to them. (Unfortunately, most people aren't eager to be changed by someone who doesn't take the time to understand them.) That failures of understanding occur in psychotherapy, just as everywhere else, is a fact often missed as long as therapists remain too wrapped up in their own theories and intentions to give themselves over to sustained immersion in the other person.

Although therapists may be less likely than the average person to interrupt to disagree, some are so anxious to be perceived as sympathetic that they offer sentimentality instead of compassion. "Oh yes," they say with their eyes, "*I* understand how you feel." Sympathetic or not, condescending kindness from a patronizing person isn't the same thing as listening. The superficially sensitive therapist doesn't have to listen because he already knows what he wants to say: "*Oh yes, I understand.*" Listening is a strenuous but silent activity.

Suspending the self does not of course mean *losing* the self—though that seems to be precisely what some people are afraid of. Otherwise, why do they insist on relentlessly repeating their own arguments, when a simple acknowledgment of what the other person is trying to say would be the first step toward mutual understanding? It's as though saying "I understand what you're trying to say" meant "You're right and I'm wrong." Or that to give someone who's angry at you a fair hearing and then say "I see why you're upset with me" meant "I surrender." Ironically, when the fear of never getting your turn is so strong that you don't hear the other person out, it becomes a self-fulfilling prophecy.

I'll have some practical suggestions for breaking this pattern in Chapter 7, but first it's important to understand more about the difficulty involved in the simple art of listening.

Genuine listening involves a brief suspension of self. You won't always notice this because it's reflexive and taken for granted and because in most conversations we take turns. But you might catch yourself rehearsing what you're going to say next when the other person is talking. Simply holding your tongue while the other person speaks isn't the same thing as listening. To really listen you have to suspend your own agenda, forget about what you might say next, and concentrate on being a receptive vehicle for the other person.

The listener's responsiveness is experienced subjectively by the speaker as—at least temporarily—vital to a sense of being understood, of being taken seriously. Listeners feel that pressure.

THE BURDEN OF LISTENING

Listening puts a burden on the listener. Not only do we have to suspend the needs of the self; we also feel the weight of the other person's need to be heard. Attention must be paid.

But, some people might object, isn't empathy an active expression of the self? Isn't listening something we extend to each other as a natural part of being human? Yes and no. Empathy is an active form of engagement—but it is engagement with the other. At times we're interested in and curious about what the other person is saying, and listening is effortless. But there almost inevitably comes a moment when we cease to be engrossed. We lose interest or feel the urge to interrupt. It is at this moment that listening takes self-control.

———◆———

Genuine listening means suspending memory, desire, and judgment—and, for a few moments at least, existing for the other person.

———◆———

Suppressing your own urge to talk can be harder than it sounds. After all, you have things on your mind too. To listen well, you may have to restrain yourself from disagreeing or giving advice or talking about your own experience. Temporarily, at least, listening is a one-sided relationship.

In everyday give-and-take conversations, you may not notice that burden. But you can feel the pressure to be attentive whenever another person needs to talk for more than a few moments. Even if you care about the person and are interested in what she has to say, still you're caught.

You need to be silent. You need to be selfless.

Doreen asked her father out to lunch so the two of them could have a chance to talk a little more personally than they did when her mother was around. But when they sat down at the restaurant, he started in on his usual diatribe against the bureaucracy. His bosses were "morons," and none of his co-workers cared about anything but "putting in their time until retirement."

Doreen had heard it all before a million times. She nodded and looked interested and thought about her upcoming sales conference. Once or twice she started to interrupt, but something about the way her father spoke with more feeling than usual made her heart move.

She stopped thinking about the sales conference and started listening to what he was saying. As she did, she began to hear the hurt and disappointment underneath his carping. Suddenly she was filled with intense sadness at her father's life and his isolation. The sadness had less to do with his frustrations at work than that his constant complaining about it had made other people in the family stop listening to him. Doreen's annoyance gave way to a powerful sense of sympathy and connection with her father. For the first time, she understood how lonely he felt. Later, when she said so, her father's eyes filled with tears and he thanked her for caring.

Sometimes we're so touched by what people say that listening just happens. Other times we don't realize the effort required to be a good listener because the circumstances make it seem effortless. The other person's need for our listening is obvious, and so we make ourselves available. When your child bursts into the house after school and says "Guess what happened!" you don't have work at listening.

My son was home sick yesterday, and when I called at lunchtime to ask him how he was feeling, I didn't have to make any effort to suspend my interests to tune in to his. Nor would anyone else have had to in my place. I was interested in his feelings, I intended to listen to him, and I did. We all do this dozens of times each day, at least for a few minutes.

Often, however, it's not that easy. Much of the time listening takes work.

When I came home after work, my son was lying on the couch watching MTV. Again I asked him how he was feeling, but this time it wasn't quite as easy for me to listen. As usual, he wasn't wearing a shirt or socks, and I had to suppress the urge to nag him about that. He was watching two brainless but arrogant cartoon teenagers rating videos in which everything was either "cool" or "it sucks," and I had to make an effort to ignore that. I had things on my mind that I wanted to talk about, and I wanted to go out on the back porch and read the mail before it was time for dinner. None of these considerations was terribly pressing or unusual. It took only a little effort to suppress them long enough to listen to my son for a little while. Had he needed to talk for more than a few minutes, however, I would have had to make a more active effort to suspend these other agendas—or I would not have been able to listen.

Of course suspending our needs so as to listen means more than

just allowing the other person time to talk. It doesn't mean just being willing to let a certain amount of time elapse while that person has his say, only to leap in with your own agenda when he's finished.

We're not fooled by the feigned attentiveness of the restless narcissist, who may allow us a few minutes of airtime but is waiting only to take over the stage. On the other hand, when we open up to someone we do expect to be interested and that person listens but then instead of responding changes the subject to himself, we feel betrayed. It's like a slap in the face; we feel as though he didn't hear a word we said.

David's friend Elena was telling him that she was worried about going back to school to get her master's degree after being out of school for six years. She'd been wanting to do this for a long time, and David, who had his master's degree, had encouraged her warmly. When she told him that she'd been accepted but was concerned about doing the work, David was so enthusiastic about her finally having taken the big step that he jumped in to say how great it was that she was doing this for herself and that she'd gotten into such a good program. Elena got quiet and changed the subject. David later learned that his encouragement hadn't been very encouraging. Elena was trying to tell him that she was worried, and his telling her how great it all was made her feel unresponded to. Ironically, David's expression of confidence in Elena felt like pressure, one more thing to live up to.

Like David, most people think they're better listeners than they really are. At best they allow the other person to state his case, and then they make their own private interpretation of what the other person said. At worst they're preparing their own argument while the other person is still talking.

Unfortunately, most people are more likely to react with their own interpretations of another's point of view than to listen carefully enough to make certain that they understand. David thought he was listening but wasn't able to suspend his need to have Elena not worry or for himself to be seen as supportive long enough to hear her out. A lot of us have difficulty listening when it means having to sit still and share someone's uneasiness or uncertainty. We have to say something quick to make the anxiety go away.

To listen well, we have to read the needs of the speaker and respond to the context. For example, when parents ask, "What did you do in school today?" children often answer, "Nothing." What follows is fre-

quently a battle of questions and monosyllabic answers. The parent wants to hear what happened in school but doesn't listen to what the child is saying. The child is saying something like "Nothing interesting enough for me to want to talk about right now. I just want to be left alone." A child at school is exposed and vulnerable all day. Other kids look at you and pass judgment on what you're wearing, whom you're with, what you say, how your hair is fixed, and just about anything you might do that's visible. Teachers watch to see if you did your homework and if you're paying attention and to be certain you're not making noise in the halls or generally having any fun. After being the subject of such scrutiny all day, most children want nothing more than to be left alone. Their "nothing" isn't coy or withholding; it's self-protective.

The parents' side of this conversation isn't hard to understand either. They're curious about what goes on in their children's lives. They want to know if everything is OK. They want to know if their children are doing what they should be doing. They don't want to be shut out. Besides, sometimes kids say "nothing" but really *do* have something to say. Maybe you have to show them that you're really interested to convince them to open up. Asking them about their day and really being prepared to listen shows interest. Honoring their right to respond the way they want shows respect as well as interest— interest in them and respect for their feelings. Children who sense that their parents are interested in hearing what they have to say—as opposed to anxiously interrogating or prying or living vicariously—will open up when they're ready.

If it's difficult to suspend the self with our children, imagine how much more difficult it is with another adult, whom we don't expect to have to "indulge" in any way—especially when we have our own problems.

Sometimes we fall into the habit of listening without effort because we put so much effort into other things. When we work until we're spent, we become preoccupied with our own sense of being unappreciated and careless of concern for others. It's especially hard to listen when we feel that *we* haven't gotten the attention we need. Here's an example:

A woman who's having a bad day at the office wishes she could be at home with her five-year-old. She's vexed about work and envious of her college professor husband who, because it's summer, is at home all day with the boy. When she gets home, instead of complaining about her day, she asks her husband how his day went. He complains about the burden of having to amuse a five-year-old and the difficulty of figuring

out what to do with all that unstructured time. She listens impatiently for a minute or two and then says, "Why are you complaining? You're lucky to have all this time off. Think of all the things you could do!" Her husband is hurt—first she asks him how his day went, then she criticizes him for telling her—and the woman herself is resentful. The woman in this example wasn't able to listen to her husband because she wasn't able to suspend her own feelings long enough to be receptive to his. After talking about this episode, the woman concluded that she needed to try harder to overcome or contain the stress of her work. (Perhaps it would be more reasonable for her to realize that when she comes home after a bad day she may need to talk about it before she's ready to listen.)

"But I Am Listening"

The selflessness of genuine listening is hard to sustain, and so in a number of ways we fool ourselves into thinking we're listening when in fact we aren't.

"That Reminds Me of the Time . . . " (Translation: "I can top that.")

When friends sit around having a casual conversation, they'll get on a particular subject and take turns telling their own stories. Maybe Carol will describe how her dachshund won't do his business outside in the winter because the minute he feels the icy snow on his paws he clickety-clicks over to the door and whines to be let back in. Then Murray will tell about the time his Russsian wolfhound lay at death's door for two days, until they found a small burr in his long silky fur, and when they removed it, Sasha suddenly made a miraculous recovery. Then maybe I'll tell something fascinating (to me, at least) about my cat Ralphie's latest adventure.

In this kind of friendly exchange it's OK just to take turns. The person telling a casual anecdote doesn't really need an elaborate response. However, there are times when someone has something important to say and doesn't want to hear your story until she's had a chance to tell what happened to her and how she felt—and get some acknowledgment. She needs a little time and attention. The woman who's just had her car towed away doesn't want to be interrupted to hear about the time that happened to you three years ago.

Interrupting someone to tell a similar story is a common example of how listeners don't restrain themselves. Sometimes this is annoyingly obvious, as when people call attention to themselves boorishly and blatantly by cutting in to say, "That reminds me of when. . . . " Most of us don't do that. If someone needs to talk, we listen. At times, however, the speaker's need for attention isn't obvious, and instead of devoting ourselves to receptive listening we respond from our own needs. A friend starts to tell us about an accident and, in an attempt to show empathy, we interrupt to tell her about ours—which, after all, was more upsetting to us, even though it happened six months ago.

Why do people do that? Why do we interrupt to tell our own stories? Most conversation is interactive. We're engaged, and much of what people say to us triggers something in our own experience. If I tell you something annoying that my father does, you're likely to think of something annoying that your father does. Or if I tell you about the time I fell in love for the first time, you're likely to remember your first love. But listening to people means hearing them out. Giving them sufficient time to say what's on their mind and taking sufficient interest to follow and acknowledge their experience.

"Oh, How Awful!"
(Translation: "You poor, helpless thing.
Here's another fine mess you got yourself into.")

Another example of listeners failing to restrain themselves is responding with excessive sympathy, a gift that usually means more to the giver than the receiver. Exaggerated concern may seem less selfish than turning the conversation around to yourself, but acting distressed isn't the same thing as really listening. Listening means taking in, not taking over.

Real listening requires attunement—reading and acknowledging the speaker's experience, not the kind of cranked-up sentiment that may fool small children but usually comes across to adults as patronizing and false. Expressions of concern from the person who always makes a big fuss over what you say become as meaningless as Muzak.

Once again, the problem is failing to suspend the self. Instead of holding himself back long enough to listen and to hear what you're saying, the excessive responder jumps in with an expression of sympathetic concern—as if to say, "Oh, I understand . . . (don't bother going on)."

When listening is genuine, the emphasis is on the speaker, not the listener.

When something goes wrong, Christine no longer calls her mother to get a little sympathy. She's learned that if she has the flu or one of the kids breaks a finger, not telling her mother is the only way to avoid an exaggerated show of concern. These things may not be very consequential, but she would like to share them. She doesn't, because when her mother says "Oh, that's awful" and makes too big a deal out of everything, she feels not understood, but that *her mother* is worried—as though *she's* the one with the problem.

An empathic response is restrained, largely silent; following, not leading, it encourages the speaker to go deeper into his or her experience.

Part of the problem is confusing empathy with sympathy. Sympathy is more limited and limiting; it means to feel the same as rather than to be understanding. Nor does empathy mean, as many people seem to think, worrying about, praising, cheering up, effusive gushing, consoling, or even encouraging. It means understanding.

"Well, If I Were You . . . "
(Translation: "Stop bothering me with your whining and *do* something about it.")

According to some experts, men show interest by giving advice while women show interest by sharing similar experiences.[1] Unasked-for advice is annoying. It feels like being told what to do, being told that our feelings aren't valid because we wouldn't have to have them if we'd only do what the oh-so-helpful person we're talking to suggests. (Responding with a similar story, as just discussed, can be equally unwelcome, especially if the person interrupts your story before you're finished or otherwise goes on without acknowledging what you've said.) When I'm telling someone about an experience or a problem and he or she responds with unwelcome advice, I say, "Thanks, but I don't need any advice; I just need to be listened to." (At least that's what I'd *like* to say.) Do men give more unasked-for advice than women? Maybe. Not in my experience. Perhaps in yours.

A few years ago I did something uncharacteristic for me and joined a men's group. I guess I was looking for friends. It turned out to be a

[1]Deborah Tannen, *You Just Don't Understand* (New York: William Morrow, 1990).

wonderful experience, largely because the other men in the group were all unusually thoughtful and sensitive people. One day we were talking about how we respond when a friend tells us about a problem, and I was surprised to hear most of the others say that they usually try to offer advice. I thought friends didn't do that, but just listened and tried to be understanding. I guess advice giving was trained out of me.

It's true, of course, that sometimes people *want* advice. Some individuals want advice all the time. They think that other people should have an answer for their distress and should try to alleviate it. This emotional need stirs our expectations that advice is wanted. Even if it doesn't work (or get followed), giving advice may suggest that the listener cares and takes the speaker's problems seriously.

The real issue in listening isn't whether we do or don't give advice but whether or not our response is focused on reading and responding to the other person's feelings or is simply a way of dealing with our own. Telling the person with a problem to "do something constructive" reflects a listener's inability to tolerate his or her own anxiety. So too may be pushing others to "Express your feelings" or using imperatives such as "You have to confront him about it." The difference between listening well and not is the difference between being receptive and responsive on the one hand and being reactive or introducing one's own agenda on the other. Failure to suspend the self in favor of the other reflects a lack of autonomy and a blurring of boundaries.

"Have You Heard the One About . . . ? (Translation: "Never mind what you were saying; your concerns are boring.")

Another familiar failure to restrain the self is the jokester, who's always quipping, allaying his own anxiety and calling attention to himself instead of tuning in to the speaker. There are times when your fast-quipping friend is funny and you don't mind his making a joke out of something. But there are other times when you're trying to talk and his wisecracking is annoying. What the jokester offers is the thin, unreliable rhetoric of distraction in place of authentic emotional engagement. This feeling of being distracted happens a lot when you're already having a conversation with someone and the jokester joins in. Only he doesn't join in. He doesn't tune in to you and what you're saying; he just uses something you say as a trigger to make a joke.

People who joke all the time are more or less annoying, depending

on how funny they are. We can understand their constant joking by realizing that they have a lot of nervous energy and may have learned to make jokes as a defense against boredom. But, like other failures to restrain the self, someone who always interrupts our conversation with gags can be insensitive and annoying.

"Don't Feel That Way"
(Translation: "Don't upset me with your upset.")

Do you remember the last time someone did you a really big favor and you were so grateful that you looked forward to saying thanks in a special way? Maybe you sent fresh flowers or gave the person a nice bottle of wine to show your appreciation. Or maybe you put your gratitude into words. Did the person accept your thanks or say something like "Oh, it was nothing, don't mention it?" You can understand someone's feeling embarrassed about being thanked profusely, but it leaves you feeling slightly dismissed (as if you've been told it was presumptuous for you to assume that the person would go to any real trouble for the likes of you). Wouldn't it be nice to be able to look someone in the eye and say "Thank you" and have him meet your eyes and say "You're welcome"?

You get a similar but perhaps stronger feeling of being dismissed when you tell someone about being angry or scared about something and she reassures you that there's no need to feel that way.

A lot of failed listening takes the form of telling other people not to feel the way they do. It's frustrating when people tell us we shouldn't worry or feel guilty or be so scared. The intention may be generous, but the effect is to cheat us out of having our feelings acknowledged. Most attempts to talk people out of their troubles are correctly understood as rejection—namely, "Don't upset me with your upset."

When someone is worried or upset enough to talk about it, listening to what the person's saying and acknowledging those feelings is responsive to that person. Reassuring the person that there's nothing to worry about is *not* responsive to him; it's responsive to the listener's own uneasiness.

If someone tells you that she is worried about the future, and you can control it, then by all means do so. Otherwise, hear the person out. Even if you *know* (or think you do) that things will turn out OK (in the future), saying so (predicting the future) doesn't erase the worry (in the present). Reassuring someone instead of hearing him out may ease his mind slightly, but the disconcerting effect of not being taken seriously is usually the stronger reaction. Telling someone not to worry

doesn't convince her to stop worrying; it may convince her that she shouldn't feel the way she does—or that she should give up trying to talk about her feelings to you.

The best way to keep this section simple would be to say that telling people not to feel the way they do is not listening to them and leave it at that. However, there are times when it feels OK to be reassured. You're not too happy with your new haircut, and a friend says, "No, it looks great," or you're feeling bad about not having accomplished much, and someone reminds you of all that you have accomplished and you feel better. The line between wanting to be reassured and wanting to be heard may not always be easy to discern. The more the speaker expresses self-doubt or worry or concern in a questioning or tentative way, the more likely he is to want reassurance. The stronger the feelings, the more likely he is to appreciate being heard and acknowledged. When in doubt, listen.

DO WOMEN LISTEN DIFFERENTLY FROM MEN?

My assertion that the genuine listener must suspend the self runs counter to popular linguist Deborah Tannen's idea that "Many women, when they talk among themselves in situations that are casual, friendly, and focused on rapport, use cooperative overlapping: Listeners talk along with speakers to show participation and support."[2]

Yes, there are times when mutuality and the pleasures of connection are more important than the need to be heard out by a self-reflecting other. But Tannen stereotypes the sexes by claiming that women engage in "rapport-talk," while men specialize in "report-talk." Men, according to Tannen, engage in self-display, while, "For most women, the language of conversation is primarily the language of rapport: a way of establishing connections and negotiating relationships."[3] "For most men, talk is primarily a means to preserve independence and maintain status in a hierarchical social order."[4]

Tannen gives as an example of the clashing between the sexes (which a lot of people like to think of as inevitable) a man telling a story about having to make up a shortfall in his cash register from his own pocket. The women listening to him "kept overlapping his story

[2]Tannen, 208.
[3]Tannen, 77.
[4]Tannen, 77.

with comments and expressions of sympathy, elaborating on how unfair it was. . . . "⁵ This, according to Tannen, is "rapport-talk." But the
woman (or man) who interrupts with expressions of sympathy may not
really be receptive; her frequent expressions of sympathy and elabora-
tions may be an effort to assert herself—not as a competitive self, but
as a sympathetic and appreciative person. Many "supportive" people are
like that. They don't say "Look at me, I'm terrific"; they say "Look at
me, I'm supportive."

When the people I know talk about feelings—what's really on their
minds, what they're excited about, what's troubling them—they want
to be listened to and acknowledged, not interrupted with advice or told
that someone else had a similar experience. They want listeners who
will take the time to listen and acknowledge what they're saying, not
immediately turn the focus to themselves.

The inability to set aside one's own needs for long enough to listen
is a function of personality, current state of mind, and relationship to
the speaker. Some people always turn the conversation around to themselves. Narcissism or hypochondriasis or just plain immaturity leaves
them with limited ability to consider anything but themselves. There
are certain people who rarely talk about themselves but can't listen
without imposing their own opinions on everything. These people may
not be self-centered (concerned only for themselves), but they are egocentric (stuck in their own point of view) and certainly no fun to talk to.

Being listened to through the screen of a loved one's bias or anxiety leaves us feeling isolated and lonely, as though our feelings weren't
valid, as though we didn't count. Children unlucky enough to grow up
with biased listening become alienated from their experience. Their
·view of themselves is shaped by a distorted mirror. Adults subject to
egocentric listeners who aren't open to hearing their experience from
their perspective feel shut down, angry or deflated, and alienated from
those relationships.

Those listeners who are more or less always in an unreceptive state
find themselves shut out and shunned, often with no real idea why.
They never connect because they never cross the space between themselves and others. In Chapter 7 we'll see how listeners can learn to take
in and acknowledge what people say without permeating their responses
with "me" messages.

⁵Tannen, 201.

"You Hear Only What You Want to Hear?"

HOW HIDDEN ASSUMPTIONS PREJUDICE LISTENING

Listening, as we've seen, takes effort. But sometimes that effort is prejudiced: our own internal sensitivities filter what we hear and what we say. Those sensitivities take the form of preconceived expectations and defensive emotional reactions. I'll explain how what we expect to hear filters what we do hear in this chapter and then get to emotional reactivity in the next. Understand, though, that just as it isn't always easy to separate the speaker's and listener's contributions to misunderstanding, it isn't always possible to separate expectations from emotions that interfere with listening.

HOW OUR ATTITUDE ABOUT THE SPEAKER BIASES WHAT WE HEAR

One way to learn something about the forces that influence listening is to hear the same story from two different sides.

Lucy was a special-education teacher who had a humiliating encounter with the principal of her school. When the principal wanted to find space for a new reading instructor, she sent Lucy a memo saying

that she would have to move to a small room in the basement, previously used for storage. Lucy prided herself on being flexible, but being told to move to the basement made her feel devalued and that the principal had little respect for the special needs of her children.

When Lucy called to discuss this unsatisfactory arrangement, the principal made an appointment to see her that afternoon. But when Lucy showed up at four o'clock, the principal had gone to another meeting and left a note suggesting they get together later. Ten days went by before the principal finally made time to talk to her. By that point Lucy had to make an extra effort to control her anger to make the case, as calmly as possible, that moving to the basement just wasn't acceptable. Instead of listening, the principal, who'd obviously made up her mind, got irritated and defensive. At one point, when Lucy protested that the specially equipped classroom in which the children now met had always been her room, the principal said archly, "Oh, did you bring it from home?" Lucy left the meeting in tears.

As soon as she got home, Lucy called her sister Katrine, who since their mother's recent death was the only living member of her family. But when Lucy tried to explain what had happened, Katrine kept interrupting her with questions. "What exactly did you say that made that woman so defensive? You must have said something to set her off like that." Lucy couldn't believe it. Instead of being supportive, her sister was blaming *her* for the incident. It felt like a slap in the face. "Just listen, Katrine, will you!" she pleaded. That shut Katrine up for the moment, but Lucy could tell that her sister wasn't at all sympathetic and wasn't really listening, so she said good-bye and hung up.

When Lucy told me about this incident two days later, she said that her sister just hadn't been there for her when she'd needed her most. It certainly sounded that way. But by one of those strange twists of fate that sometimes happen, I got to hear Katrine's version of the same event the following week.

According to Katrine, she's had lifelong problems talking with her sister. "Lucy has always dominated our conversations. She loves to talk about herself, but she hardly ever listens to anything I have to say. If I pause for a minute, she immediately jumps in with some comment or criticism." But the thing that bothered Katrine most was that Lucy was always complaining. "She's always telling me about hassles with somebody—other teachers, neighbors, supermarket clerks, even the nice old man in the Chinese take-out place. And it's always the other person's fault. I used to try to listen—after all, she is my sister. But as I've

gotten older, I just don't have time for her negativism." According to Katrine, Lucy was hard to listen to because she'd used up her credit.

It's common for speakers not to be heard because their credibility is low. A father's credibility, for example, may be determined by whether his wife and children think he's tuned in to what's going on in the family or too preoccupied with himself and his work to have any idea about what's happening around the house. If he's had an affair or drinks too much—even though he espouses rule-keeping to the children—they may not respect him enough to hear what he has to say. A parent's external world status also affects his or her credibility. A father who is laid off and out of work may lose credibility. This may not be because his family is judgmental, but because people who have lost self-respect in their own eyes often express themselves with a bitter or defensive edge that makes them hard to listen to. Listening is always codetermined.

The minute you pick up the phone and hear some people's voices, you're wary. They're asking you how things are going, acting interested, but you're waiting for the pitch. They call only when they want something. Even if you like them, even if you want to be friends, the one-sided nature of these relationships wears thin after a while. When you answer the phone and they say hello, they can probably hear the enthusiasm drop out of your voice. Do they have any idea why? Do you dare tell them?

Credibility is also influenced by whether you're viewed as being in an appropriate position with a particular setting. A colleague who's seen as not really caring much about what goes on at work may not be listened to even when he has something worthwhile to say. A mother who talks to her adolescent children as though they were still little kids may be experienced as out of touch and therefore incapable of having legitimate concerns and feelings.

A lot of grandparents don't get heard when they give advice about bringing up baby. Their mistake is not necessarily being pushy or intrusive but rather being out of touch with their children's anxious insecurity about being parents. The grandparents are not heard because their children perceive their advice as undermining their own shaky authority. In this case, the grandparents' mistake may be treating their children as though they were *more* grown-up, in charge and confident, than they feel.

A speaker's credibility is also affected by whether or not his or her messages are clear and pertinent. If your father-in-law muddles his mes-

sages with malapropisms and obscure metaphors, you may work at trying to understand him as part of building a relationship with your spouse's family. But if you have to work too hard at it, after a while you may give up. If your father always changes the subject to talk about himself, you will come to expect this and may get out of the habit of listening. People who abuse the privilege of listening by going on and on or by flitting from one subject to another whenever they have the floor may create the expectation that listening to them is too much work, so why bother?

When the speaker has lost credibility but the relationship has a good track record, the listener may pay attention even though he or she may not really hear. You might give the aunt who's always been nice to you the courtesy of your attention even though you don't respect her enough to really listen to what she's trying to say. But if there is relentless repetition of a message—any message—you're likely to withdraw even the courtesy of attention, replacing it with conflict or distance.

HOW OUR EXPECTATIONS MAKE US HYPERSENSITIVE: THE DISCOVERIES OF OBJECT RELATIONS THEORY

Our relationship to each other and to the world around us depends on a unique capacity to transcend immediate experience by making a reproduction of it inside the mind, where we can then manipulate the possibilities. One of the simplest examples of this is a baby learning to tolerate his mother's absence by remembering her presence and relying on her return. This mental structuralization of experience can be the source of creative alteration of circumstances or of deadening inflexibility that sets some people so at odds with the world around them.

From the start, our lives revolve around relations with others. The residue of these relationships leaves internal images of self, other, and self-in-relation-to-others. As adults we react not only to the actual other but also to an internal other. Object relations theory focuses on this internal other—the mental images we have of other people, built up from experience and expectation. (*Object relations* may seem a cold-blooded term for human intercourse, but *objects* refers to mental images of other people that are the object of our actions, not to the people themselves.)

The details of object relations theory are rich with particulars for explaining our preconceived assumptions and emotional sensitivities,

but the essence is quite simple: we relate to people in the present partly on the basis of the expectations formed by our early experience. (A
man who emerges from puppyhood with a clear picture of his father
lording it over his mother may vow always to be kind and considerate
to his own wife—at all times unstinting in his criticism and counsel.)

Contemporary relationships and earlier ones (encoded in the inner world of objects) interact in circular fashion. Life circumstances maintain internal expectations and are chosen because of them and
interpreted in light of them. The past is alive in memory—and it runs
our lives more than we know.

To understand the depth of some people's hypersensitivity to making mistakes, we might turn to Melanie Klein's notion of the *depressive
position*, namely the painful discovery that love and hurt can go
together.[1] To understand other people's rage at criticism, we might
consider Ronald Fairbairn's idea that the neurotic's ego is split into an
exciting ego (leaving him longing for total love) and a *rejecting ego* (leading him to expect rejection), so that his relationships take on an "all
good" or "all bad" quality and shift dramatically from one to the other.[2]
To explain why some people attack and others withdraw when they
get hurt, we might look to the dynamic variations in how their respective families shaped their narcissistic need for attention. Some people
get attention for being good; in their families anger and assertiveness
may be beyond the pale. For others, who get attention for achievement,
vulnerability and weakness may be intolerable.

What's common to these and other object-relations formulations
is the idea that the neurotic person encounters others not as an equal
but as a fearful child, intimidated not so much by the reality of other
people as by imagined extreme expectations. In this respect, we're all
a little neurotic.

HOW WE LEARN TO OVERREACT

Some of the expectations we bring to our conversations are built up
from the history of our relationships with those specific individuals. But
some of what we expect to hear is part of the deep structure of our per-

---

[1]Melanie Klein, "Notes on some schizoid mechanisms," *International Journal of Psycho-Analysis*,
1946, *27*, 99–110.

[2]Ronald Fairbairn, *An Object-Relations Theory of the Personality* (New York: Basic Books, 1952).

sonalities, the residue of our earliest relationships. To understand listening and the dynamics of relationship it's necessary to consider not only what goes on between people but also what goes on inside them.

More than we like to realize, we continue to live in the shadow of the families we grew up in.

The sometimes vast difference between words spoken and thoughts intended is nothing compared to the often vaster gulf between what is said and what is heard. Whenever someone, speaker or listener, seems to be responding to a private interpretation, it might be useful to ask: What *would* make that response understandable? Once you start thinking this way—namely, that people act the way they do for a reason—you'll know something about the way they were treated by their parents.

One reason we carry oversensitivities from home around with us rather than having resolved them is that most of us leave home somewhere in the transition from adolescent to mature adult responsiveness. In the busy time of our twenties, when we're making a start on love and work, we react to the expectation that we can't really talk to our parents by distancing ourselves from them. But then, often somewhere in our thirties, we decide to close the gap and rebuild our relationship with our parents, this time on a firmer, more mature footing.

People who do decide to work on their relationship with their parents often go at it with certain unfortunate expectations. They imagine themselves settling old scores and righting ancient wrongs, like avenging angels, or suddenly waking sleeping intimacy, as though family ties, cherished, strained, or severed, could be refashioned overnight. The truth is, when you go home, you're more like one of nature's humbler creatures, and you have to keep your wits about you to avoid getting stuck on the family's emotional flypaper.

Peggy and her parents agreed on many things—the value of hard work, the need to build something for the future, the importance of family. But agreement is something children and parents can always overcome, and Peggy and her parents managed to get into a shouting match on just about every visit. Most visits would start off well. Love and news would carry them through the first couple of days, but the inevitable blowup was like a ticking time bomb, set for three days and waiting to go off.

Like most people, Peggy couldn't stop wishing her parents were different. She loved them, and they loved her; she just wished they would
grow up. Her mother was loud and abrasive, always eager for company
but always complaining and never with a kind word to say about anybody. Her father was altogether a quieter soul, self-possessed, cool, some
would say aloof. He showed his love by offering advice, whether you
asked for it or not, and by repairing things around the house, whether
they needed it or not. Peggy found him impossible to talk to. When
she tried to tell him what was going on in her life, he never really
listened.

Unlike most people, who acknowledge the turmoil they feel on family visits but don't recognize their own contribution, Peggy *was* willing to look at her part in the cycles of conflict with her parents. First
she figured out what it was that her parents did that made her reactive.
Her mother assumed the right to criticize anything and anyone, but
her meanest comments were reserved for family members who did anything assertively independent. When Peggy's brother's wife decided to
start her own business, Peggy's mother wanted to know, "Who does she
think she is!" She was totally unsupportive when Peggy's cousin got a
divorce, even though it had been a disastrous marriage from the start.
And when another cousin decided to move out of her parents' house
(she wasn't getting married), Peggy's mother said, "There's only one reason
a twenty-year-old woman gets her own apartment, and *I* don't happen
to approve of that."

Next Peggy learned to see how her mother's negativism and intrusiveness triggered anxiety and rage in her. The fact that she'd learned
to expect it made her hypersensitive. The minute her mother started
in on someone, Peggy got upset, anxious and angry at the same time.
She felt she was being pressured to join her mother in anger and criticalness, and if she resisted she felt as though she herself were under
attack. She usually held her tongue, but the effort to repress protest
only put her anger under pressure, which after a while led to an erup-
tion. The longer she held back, the more her feelings of neglect and
rage would build. When she finally did blow up, her mother would get
hurt and withdraw, leaving Peggy feeling helpless and despicable at the
same time.

Peggy also began to see that although she rebelled against her
mother's criticalness, she had learned from her mother and had incorporated the habit of assuming responsibility for other people's feelings
and reactions. Whereas her mother was hostile and controlling, Peggy

was benignly controlling—worrying excessively about her own children, always doing things for other people. The expectation of merging with those you love was the same for mother and daughter—only their way of showing it was different. The "nicer" and more "helpful" Peggy was, the more she expected there to be no walls between herself and those she cared for. She felt guilty for not doing enough and repressed her anger for not getting enough. Eventually, when her children or her friends or her husband did something that made her feel shut out, she'd erupt in angry criticism, just as she'd done with her mother. These scenes never changed anything. As you've no doubt noticed, venting anger is not the same as voicing feelings in a way that makes them heard.

When she first consulted me about the relationship with her mother, Peggy said that she had tried everything. Her "everything" ran the gamut from A to C, appeasement to confrontation. The alternative, calmly stating her own point of view, never occurred to her, because by the time she finally responded to her mother's criticism she was so angry that she lost control.

The word for impetuous lack of control and unrestrained emotionalism is *childish*. The place where we learn (or don't learn) restraint is in our families. But it isn't in childhood that we overcome childishness; that isn't in the cards. As young children, we looked up to our parents. (But then we were short and looked up to everything.) Later, if they said something to incite or provoke us, we either absorbed it or cried. It was as teenagers that we began to see through our parents; we stopped putting up with the exasperating things they said and started fighting back.

Most teenagers become so hypersensitive to their parents that they flare up at the least hint of indignity, like dry grass struck by lightning. (If you have a teenager in captivity, you know what I mean.) If adolescence is a time for becoming your own person, late adolescence is a time for transforming your relationship with your parents from a childish basis to an adult one. Unfortunately, most of us leave home in the midst of that transformation. Distance and infrequent contact afford us the illusion that we're grown up, but for most of us who left home at eighteen or so, our relationships with our parents remain frozen in adolescent patterns.

Only one thing robs Superman of his mature powers: kryptonite, a piece of his home planet. A surprising number of adult men and women are similarly rendered helpless by even a brief visit with their parents.

Superman becomes mortal in contact with kryptonite; mortals become teenagers in contact with their parents. We revert to childish roles when we get anxious because we never fully learn to resist parental provocation.

Our parents may be the most important unfinished business of our lives.

OUR DIVIDED SELVES

We don't easily face our own shortcomings, and it's particularly painful to confront our inability to listen. When we do, it's natural to become critical and get discouraged: "I'm a lousy listener," "I'm selfish," "I'm too controlling." Instead of thinking of ourselves in such global, negative terms, it's possible to realize that only a particular part of ourselves is having trouble listening. Using a little imagination to personify our parts as subpersonalities (residues of early object relations) may lead us to their source.[3]

Take, for example, a husband who regularly finds himself shutting his ears when his wife tries to tell him that she needs more from him. With a little introspection, he might discover a part of himself that feels like a little boy who expects to be reprimanded by his mother. The little boy doesn't want to hear it; his mother's criticism makes him feel disapproved of and controlled; he wants to be left alone. The husband can calm down his "little boy part" by realizing—really getting it—that his wife isn't his mother. She's not trying to control him. Even if she sounds critical, what she's really trying to express is her loneliness and her need for him. It's not we who are afraid to listen; it's those

---

[3]According to Henry A. Murray, "A personality is a full congress of orators and pressure groups, of children, demagogues, Macchiavellis . . . Caesars and Christs. . . . " "What Should Psychologists Do About Psychoanalysis?" *Journal of Abnormal and Social Psychology* 35, (1940): 160–61.

Eric Berne's transactional analysis personified Freud's superego, ego, and id as parent, adult, and child. *Transactional Analysis in Psychotherapy* (New York: Grove Press, 1967).

In literature we find Pirandello's *Six Characters in Search of an Author* and Stevenson's tortured Dr. Jekyll and Mr. Hyde.

Although many people have used the metaphor of subpersonalities, I have found the "internal family systems" model of Richard Schwartz particularly useful. "Our Multiple Selves." *Family Therapy Networker* 11, (1987): 25–31; 80–83. Richard Schwartz, Know thy selves. *Family Therapy Networker* 12, (1988): 21–29.

fearful parts of us that, once triggered, reduce us to childish insecurity and the anxiety that accompanies it.

Some of our subpersonalities manifest themselves in warring inner voices that fuel those painful and tedious arguments we have with ourselves. The rival voices are normally apparent only when we're in conflict—facing a difficult decision or torn between two choices. This is when it's wise to remember that calm fosters unity; conflict sunders it. The next time you find yourself caught up in internal debate, consider the possibility that the thoughts and feelings on either side of the argument aren't just transient and situational. Maybe those competing voices have a lot to say. Maybe they've been saying similar things to you all your life, and maybe they've been fighting those same other voices that they're fighting now. We usually listen to one part, the one that represents the overdeveloped parts of our personalities. Here's an example:

Once or twice a year David Berlow takes time off from teaching at the university to spend a week by himself at a friend's house on Cape Cod. He likes to get away to spend some concentrated time writing and unwinding. But each time he goes he gets into a debate with himself about whether to spend most of his time working or relaxing. One voice says that he should really concentrate on working because that's the most important thing. The other voice counters that he's always working and that this is his only chance to really relax by himself. Each time the debate is the same, and always quite frustrating. He really wants to do both, get a lot of work done and spend a few whole days swimming and fishing. But even though the debate is always hard fought, the voice that tells him to work always wins.

The people who know us can usually predict our choices, even if we still agonize over them. In David Berlow's case, the voice that says work always wins over the one that says play. His wife could tell you that. And she's learned, after much trial and error, that the only way for her and the children to get the attention of the part of David that likes to play is to reassure the part that worries about getting enough work done. She knows, for example, that he won't be able to relax on the family vacation unless he brings along some work to do in the morning. And if she tries to get him to visit her parents for the weekend, she always helps him find a little time to get some work done. She's not just thoughtful; she's smart.

A good opportunity to learn more about the opposing voices inside you is the next time you find it necessary to ask someone's advice. The need to ask is a sign that the contending voices have nearly equal claim on your attention. But beyond the specifics of the situation, what is the nature of those voices? Does the question of whether or not to go to a meaningless staff meeting symbolize a debate between the dutiful child and the independent one? And if you ask someone's advice, aren't you aware of what he or she will say? And do you sometimes seek out the right person to give you the answer that part of you really wants to hear?

What does all this have to do with listening? Whenever someone asks your advice or shrinks from you or gets impatient with you, it's worthwhile to think about what parts of the person might be at war with each other. It may be useful to remember these conflicting voices when you're tempted to give obvious advice—telling people to stop drinking so much, start exercising more, do their homework, or quit smoking—rather than listening for what they really want from you. Can you tell these people anything they don't already know? If not, how about trying appreciate where they're at instead of pushing them to where you think they ought to go?

Giving predictable advice to adolescents—urging them to stop doing things that aren't good for them—is a classic mistake made by adults. The voice of "no" is one that teenagers are already well aware of. A more effective way to get through to them (or anyone else with self-destructive habits) is to adopt a more neutral attitude and simply ask them about the effects of whatever they're doing. Unfortunately, when this question comes from a person who is in fact anxious to make the child change, it won't be heard. Teenagers can smell control a mile away.

The compulsion to pursue self-destructive behavior can be pretty strong, not easy to countermand with platitudinous advice. Not only do smoking and drinking and overeating feel good, but they're also supported by inner voices that whisper, "Go on, you deserve it. To hell with all those killjoys." Sometimes our inner voices work as a team in a control and release cycle. The voice of guilty self-reproach heaps on the punishment that produces the control that eventually leads to another rebellious release.

Psychologists call the interface between the voice that says "do it" and the one that says "no" the *vertical split*.[4] Unlike the horizontal split

[4]Heinz Kohut, *The Analysis of the Self* (New York: International Universities Press, 1971).

(repression), the vertical split doesn't keep wishes out of consciousness, only on the back burner. In the case of a woman who spends too much money on clothes or drinks too much, the voice on the "do it" side of the vertical split is the one that usually doesn't get heard—no one says to her, "You're special; you deserve to be treated that way"—and that's why she acts out its dictates. It takes empathy to bring out and reassure the shy voice that says to her, *Go ahead, you need this; you deserve it.*

Thinking in terms of subpersonalities can be especially helpful in heated and reactive discussions. Instead of thinking of being at odds with someone, sometimes it's more useful to think of parts of one of you trying to change parts of the other. In a typical situation provoked by a teenager's coming home late, his father gets mad and demands to know what happened. His accusatory tone makes the boy feel judged and demeaned, and he counters angrily, which drives up the father's rage to the point where his wife tells him to calm down and stop shouting. This infuriates the father, and he leaves the house. If you were the father, you would probably think of the boy as disrespectful and the mother as interfering. If you were the boy, you'd view the father as controlling. Instead, think of the conflict as being waged among parts of them. A rebellious part of the boy activates a controlling part of the father, which in turn mobilizes a protective part of the mother to shield the boy from his father's temper. If you were any one of these people and you began to think this way, how difficult would it be to control your part? How might the problem be affected if each of you could stay calm and avoid letting your reactive parts take over?

Take another example. Does the question of whether or not to confront your partner with something that's bothering you represent the competing voices of a compliant child, who believes that she shouldn't complain or people will get mad at her; a hurt part; and an angry part? Of the last two, which one is more scared to speak up? Why? If you can identify those parts that have trouble speaking up, can you find any way to reassure them? Would it help to tell the person you have trouble speaking up to about the scared part of you? Would he (or she) be more understanding if you asked for his (or her) help to express this part of you?

Let's take a look at a familiar interaction between intimate partners, using the notion of subpersonalities. A woman has trouble listening to her husband because he often expresses himself with anger and intense frustration. Is this the sensitive and vulnerable man she mar-

ried that she hears, or is it an echo of mounting anxiety and danger from long ago? And who is the "she" who's doing the hearing? The part of her who's strong and cares deeply about her husband or a little girl part who trembled to hear her parents quarreling about her father's explosive temper and her mother's shame about it in front of others?

Finding the "parts" (obstacles or constraints) that get in the way of our receptivity and then releasing these constraints is a very different way of thinking from accusing ourselves of being immature or selfish or inadequate. It isn't that we're bad listeners; it's our hidden emotional agenda that crowds out understanding and concern. When we clear away automatic emotional reactions—criticism, fear, hurt—we get to compassion, curiosity, and tenderness. Instead of condemning ourselves for being "bad listeners," we can learn to identify and relax those parts of ourselves that interfere. In so doing, we release ourselves for effective listening.

CHAPTER SIX

"Why Do You Always Overreact?!"

HOW EMOTIONALITY MAKES US DEFENSIVE

O ne of the major reasons people don't listen is that they become
emotionally reactive. Something in the speaker's message triggers hurt,
anger, or fear, which activates defensiveness and blocks understanding. Emotional reactivity is like throwing a switch and having the elec-
tricity come on, only instead of music you get static. The static is anxiety.

"WHAT'S *REALLY* BOTHERING YOU?"

Perhaps the hardest messages for us to listen to without reacting emotionally are those that involve criticism. Most of us like to think that
we can accept constructive criticism, and, on the other hand, most of
us know people who can't.

Once a month the Outpatient Psychiatry staff at Briarcliff Medical
Center reviews a sample of patient charts to assess the treatment being
provided in the clinic. This may sound like a good idea, but the review
has become progressively more tedious as the need to monitor bureaucratic forms has crowded out time for considering the quality of care patients are receiving. At the last meeting the staff discovered that a few
of the charts selected for review had already been examined at the previ-

ous month's meeting. When the director mentioned this to the secretary, she said, "Then get them yourself—I can't do everything!" and stormed out of the room.

If you believed that this kind of reaction was common from this woman, you'd have no trouble recognizing her as one of those hypersensitive people who can't take criticism. If, on the other hand, you knew her to be one of the most even-tempered people around, you'd assume she was having a bad day. You'd be right. Her assistant had been out sick, and she'd had to stay three hours late the night before and come to work two hours early to get the charts ready. Of course she was on edge.

When people overreact uncharacteristically, we usually assume that something's bothering them. If our relationship with them has a history of goodwill, we give the person the benefit of the doubt and often try to find out what the real problem is. But what about those people who regularly respond inappropriately? Are they having a bad life?

Corinne was a very intelligent woman who couldn't allow herself to make mistakes. She kept up with *Forbes*, *Barrons*, and the *Wall Street Journal*, but she also watched ESPN and read *The Sporting News*. She especially loved baseball and took pleasure in writing a newsletter about her favorite team, the Atlanta Braves, and circulating it at the office. When one of the team's star pitchers injured his shoulder, Corinne wrote that this might turn out to be a blessing in disguise if it allowed a certain relief pitcher to prove that he was as good a starter as some insiders suspected. When Corinne read a draft of the piece over the phone to her cousin Drew, she said it was great, except for one thing: the pitcher was injured playing against Pittsburgh, not Philadelphia, as Corinne had written. Glad to get the facts straight, Corinne corrected her error. When the newsletter came out, a senior staff member told Corinne that he loved her article, but it was Philadelphia, not Pittsburgh, where the fateful injury took place.

Corinne was so humiliated by this minor mistake that she was thrown into a tailspin. She cried and felt like a fool and couldn't bring herself to go to work the next day.

She was a shy person who preferred to express herself in writing rather than conversation; to her, being listened to meant having what she wrote appreciated. Being wrong meant feeling the opposite of appreciated. Instead of getting angry at her cousin for giving her the wrong information, she was ashamed of herself for not getting the story straight.

Nobody likes to make mistakes, but clearly Corinne's reaction was excessive.

Another example of reacting inappropriately may be more familiar, in form if not intensity. Lenny was a devoted husband and father as well as a good provider. He worked hard and spent the rest of his time with the family. He did his share of household chores and was emotionally involved in the life of the family. His wife's one complaint was that he was too critical.

The only thing that struck me as unusual about this situation was the degree to which Sheila absorbed all of Lenny's complaints without objecting or answering with any complaints of her own. He was the lord and master, and it was her job to cater to him. When Lenny said, "You should clean all the snow off the car before you start to drive," Sheila protested feebly, "I was in a hurry to get to the cleaners." When Lenny countered, "You're always in too much of a hurry," Sheila capitulated, "I guess you're right."

Experience has taught me to listen not only to what people say but also for what they're not saying and to wonder why. I soon found out why Sheila hesitated to protest. Once she said, "Don't you think you're being a little unfair?" and Lenny flew into a rage. He started shouting at her. "You *never* listen to anything I say! You have *no* respect for me. You say you love me, but it's a *goddamned* lie!" It was awful. I don't really remember all of what he said because, frankly, I was too upset. What's more, the same thing happened every time Sheila said anything critical to Lenny. His reaction was so angry and intense that it was impossible to hear what he was feeling or to modulate what he was saying.

Having read these two accounts, you can probably guess something of what both Corinne and Lenny felt. But clearly the intensity of their reactions was inappropriate to the situation. Let me also tell you that these are two instances when it's a lot easier to read about something than to witness it firsthand. Corinne's abject remorse and Lenny's rage made listening to them almost impossible. What makes people respond so inappropriately? Long memories.

From these brief descriptions, some people might say that Corinne was insecure and oversensitive and Lenny suffered from unresolved aggression. Others might say that Corinne's turning her anger inward and Lenny's lashing out were typical of their genders. In fact these inferences are so general and judgmental as to constitute virtually meaning-

less clichés. For a more subtle appreciation of a person's overreaction we need to know its trigger.

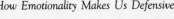

A listener's emotional reaction seems inappropriate only as long as you can't see his or her memory.

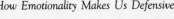

As a therapist, when I see someone responding "inappropriately," I ask myself what circumstances would make the response appropriate. (In my own relationships I just get upset like everyone else.) What circumstances would make it reasonable for a woman to feel hopelessly worthless for having made a mistake? (Hint: Most of us manage to survive childhood, but not all of us outgrow it.)

Corinne was the last in line of five children in a talented and ambitious family. She had an older sister "who was jealous and competitive" and three brothers "who never loved me." Her father was cerebral and distant; her mother was depressed, an underachiever who drank too much. Corinne was the baby, but rather than being doted on she was ignored. Early on, she decided that the only possibility of ever being loved was to be the perfect child, "docile and mediocre"—docile so as not to burden her parents, mediocre so as not to challenge her siblings. They tolerated her as long as she played the good little sister, but they couldn't acknowledge any signs of accomplishment from her. Deprived of acceptance themselves, they belittled their little sister's achievements and mocked her mistakes. They called her "lardass," "Miss Piggy," "stupid," and "retard." Even the smallest slip-up could trigger their scornful laughter. Years later Corinne was still so hypersensitive to humiliation that she sank into despair whenever she made the slightest error. The man who pointed out her mistake did not say "retard," but that's what she heard.

What made Lenny so critical of others and so unable to tolerate criticism in return? Not the kind of cruel treatment you might expect. Lenny's parents were decent and loving people. But their relative lack of involvement outside the family led them to expect a lot from each other and from their children. When they didn't get what they wanted, they criticized and complained. This alone might not have made Lenny so unable to tolerate criticism. But his parents, for all their basic goodness, never gave him the consistent empathy that would have solidified his sense of worth. Without a store of loving memories, without a sense of being taken seriously and appreciated just for himself, and

without expectations of more understanding to come, Lenny was filled with deep and ugly fears of worthlessness. Hard work and family devotion kept these repressed feelings at bay, until, that is, someone said anything remotely resembling what Lenny himself feared in his heart of hearts—that he was no good.

I once had a gray and white cat named Tina who was perfectly friendly, except that once in a while she'd lash out violently with her claws. These attacks were unexpected and unprovoked. One minute Tina would be purring to have her head stroked; the next thing you knew you'd have a bloody claw mark on the back of your hand. Eventually we took her to the vet and learned that she had a wound in her hip—possibly from a car accident when she was a kitten—so that what seemed to us like a harmless touch could actually be very painful.

Shame and insecurity are the wounds that make people react violently to criticism. Some people retreat from hurt feelings, while others attack. The most shame-sensitive individuals flare up at the slightest sign of criticism. Such people are hard to live with. But reacting to criticism with hurt and anger is something we all do. What varies is only the threshold of response.

The universal human vulnerability to criticism is related to the universal yearning for love and approval. What we really want to hear is that we're terrific (sometimes "OK" will do).

Our sensitivity to criticism varies with the situation. We're hurt most by criticism of something that feels like an important part of ourselves—our motives, for example, or the products of our creativity, or, during adolescence (and sometimes slightly beyond), our appearance. We're especially sensitive to criticism from someone whose opinion we care about. The right person saying the wrong thing can puncture the ego like a pin bursting a balloon.

What Makes Us Intolerant?

When you're trying to figure out why you or anyone else overreacts, keep in mind one of the great ironies of understanding: we're likely to be as accepting of others as we are of ourselves. That's why those lucky enough to be raised with self-respect make better listeners. Still, we needn't be stuck where we find ourselves. If we learn to respect and appreciate other people's feelings, we will learn to treat our own feelings more kindly in the process.

What we can't tolerate in others is what we can't tolerate in ourselves.

We can't listen well to other people as long as we project the mistaken idea that parts of us aren't good enough to be loved, respected, and treated fairly. A wider respect for human dignity flows from and enhances respect for ourselves. Tolerance and appreciation of our own and other people's feelings helps us hear and understand the hurt that inevitably lies behind anger and resentment. When our feelings aren't heard, our spirits are suppressed and distorted.

WHAT TURNS CONVERSATIONS INTO ARGUMENTS?

Reacting emotionally to what another person says is the number-one reason conversations turn into arguments.

If you're not sure what emotional reactivity is, take inventory of your feelings the next time you rush out of the bathroom to catch the phone on the last ring—and it turns out to be somebody selling you something. That agitation, that anxious upset that makes you want to slam down the phone, is emotional reactivity. Is it wrong or unjustified? No, of course not. But it's that feeling, in relationships that do count, that makes it hard to listen, hard to think straight, and hard to say what you want to say.

Reactivity is like a child interrupting an adult conversation—it isn't bad; it's inopportune. Our intrusive emotions may need to be hushed, but they may also need to be listened to later. Why are we reactive? What are the reactive parts of ourselves, and what are they reacting to? Disruptive feelings are messages from our inner spirit about something we need to change or pay attention to in our lives. Our reactivity can lead us to parts of ourselves that we haven't yet befriended—mute and helpless parts, frightened and lonely parts.

If Corinne were to tell a friend how stupid she felt for screwing up the newsletter, the friend might try to reassure her by telling her not to worry. After all, everyone makes mistakes, right? Yes, but when Corinne made a mistake, she could hear the savage brothers sneering at her: "Lardass! retard!" And she'd feel again what she'd been spending her whole adult life running away from: that she was ugly and stupid and helpless, and nobody loved her, and nobody would ever love her.

Lenny's always dishing out but never being able to take criticism might seem more reasonable if you realized that deep down he, too, felt worthless and inconsequential. Inside him were dark and ugly voices he anxiously shut his ears to lest he get in touch with the part of him that still felt like a little boy who was never good enough for his parents.

What turns conversations into arguments for some people (not infrequently mothers) is not so much something inside of them as the fact that they can't face, can't listen to, can't tolerate certain things in people close to them.

One of my patients doesn't want to hear what's going on in her daughter's life. It's too upsetting. The daughter was arrested for prostitution at age fifteen. Despite her mother's heroic efforts to be understanding and firm, the daughter continued to get into trouble, using drugs, hanging around with a motorcycle gang, coming home drunk night after night. Finally, when the daughter was eighteen, her parents insisted that she get her own apartment. They supported her for a while, then gradually tapered off. The daughter now works as a cocktail waitress, when she works, but her parents are reasonably sure that she's heavily involved with drugs and that she probably still prostitutes herself from time to time. They know she occasionally gets arrested for drunk and disorderly behavior, because they've had to go to the jail in the middle of the night and bail her out. Her mother still loves her of course, but finds it necessary to cushion their relationship by visiting infrequently and avoiding the details of the daughter's activities, which she finds too upsetting to listen to.

This mother's avoidance is based on a correct assessment of her own vulnerability. It isn't just worry that she's avoiding; she can't listen to her daughter's troubles without feeling the need to rescue and reform her. The temptation to tell her daughter to stop taking drugs and hanging around dangerous characters (as though these were novel ideas) interferes with listening; giving in to that temptation triggers shouting matches.

The worst thing about reactivity is that it's contagious. When anxiety jumps the gap from speaker to listener, it escalates through a series of actions and reactions, which may eventually lead to an emotional cutoff. The cutoff may be as simple—and simply frustrating—as one person walking out of the room or as sad as one person walking out of the other person's life.

The next time you have the misfortune to witness two people arguing without hearing each other, notice what each of them does to

keep the argument going. (If you're one of the parties to the argument, notice only what the other person does; the alternative is too demanding.) Notice, too, how the argument could end if either one of them would let go. In the runaway logic of reactive quarreling, both parties feel compelled to get in the last word.

The ability to listen rests on how successfully we resist the impulse to react emotionally to the position of the other. The more actions we feel compelled to take to reduce or avoid our anxiety, the less flexible we are in relationships.

Let me give you an example from the wide perspective of a public situation—before focusing on the more anxiety-arousing settings of personal exchange. The next time you attend a lecture or observe a news conference, notice the hostile questions. You'll note that many "questions" aren't really questions at all, but rhetorical attempts to prove that the speaker is wrong and the listener is right. Observe how the speaker handles these questions. Some speakers try to remain calm by finding something to agree with; others get defensive and counterattack.

A speaker is likely to get defensive if she feels that a questioner is trying to make her wrong and himself right. "Excuse me, but haven't you overlooked . . . [you dummy]?" Few such "listeners" really want answers to their questions; they just want to be right. The speaker who gets defensive and tries to counter (put down, really) the questioner often hopes to "win" the exchange by saying "No, actually . . . [I *am* right; *you're* wrong]." In rare instances a clever speaker can succeed in putting down a hostile questioner with superior intellect or knowledge of the subject. More often the questioner, who maybe wanted to make a point, feels dismissed, cheated out of the opportunity to have his voice heard.

———◆———

When neither party to an exchange is willing to break the spiral of reactivity, both of them are likely to end up feeling angry and misunderstood.

———◆———

Listening with a Clenched Mind

Listeners intent on avoiding conflict may not listen because they're too busy protecting themselves to be open to what the other is trying to say. Listeners intent on talking speakers out of unhappy feelings or independent inclinations won't hear what the speaker thinks because it

might be threatening. Even speakers who have something worthwhile to say may not get heard if they make the other person feel criticized or misunderstood; the potential listener is likely to become defensive or angry and counterattack or withdraw, making listening the last thing on his or her emotional agenda. Misunderstanding is further occluded when each one broods over the awful things the other one does and one or both of them eventually finds someone else to complain to.

Subjects Too Hot to Handle

Married couples famously have trouble talking about children, sex, and money. The immediate problem with these subjects isn't differences in points of view but the emotional reaction that the expression of those differences elicits. Even though both partners are equally reactive, they may show it in different ways. One may press for more surface calm, while the other may feel unresponded to and press for more emotional involvement. Each becomes highly attuned to slights, hurts, and criticism. Some people's radar is so good that they pick up these signals even before they're sent.

After he and Shirley have a blowup, Don becomes distant and sulky. (Sound familiar?) After a while, though, he calms down and tries to make amends. He says he's sorry for overreacting or for snapping at her for not doing something. But she never apologizes. She either just accepts Don's apology or, if she's really mad, takes it as permission to say more about how what he did upset her. Don's least favorite version of this is "You *always* do that, and I hate it!"

Finally Don told Shirley that he truly was sorry when they argued and often really could see his part in it, but it really bothered him that she never apologized. "It's like everything is my fault, like you don't have any part in our problems. It's not fair."

Shirley blew up. "What am I supposed to say, 'It's *my* fault you're so grouchy'? 'I'm sorry *you* don't like my driving'? 'I'm sorry the baby was sick'?" At this Don threw up his hands and walked out of the room.

What makes it so hard for some people to apologize? Guilty consciences. In her heart of hearts, Shirley blamed herself for everything that went wrong in her relationships. She blamed herself for Don's moods (if she was *really* a good wife, he'd be happy all the time); she blamed herself for not enjoying sex with him more (she must be inhibited); she even blamed herself when the baby got sick (if she were a better mother, nothing bad would ever happen to her child). She came from a family

that specialized in blaming. The result was extreme sensitivity to anything anyone might say that triggered her own inner self-blame. That's the nature of reactivity.

———◆———

We're most reactive to the things we secretly accuse ourselves of.

———◆———

"HOW COME YOU LISTEN TO EVERYBODY BUT ME?"

Husbands and wives often complain that their spouses never listen to what they say but come home and announce that they just heard something very interesting—and that "something" is precisely what the spouse has already told them. Recently, for example, when Marilyn told her husband that she'd decided to see a friend's chiropractor about her back, he hit the ceiling. "I've been telling you to see a chiropractor for years! Now all of a sudden when your precious friend Mary Elizabeth tells you, you listen. How come you never listen to me?"

Marilyn was so taken aback by her husband's outburst that she was unable to answer. But even if she had known what to say, her husband didn't stick around to hear it. He stormed out and slammed the door. Later, she did answer him at length, in her head, where most of us make our best comebacks.

True, he *had* told her to see a chiropractor. But she hadn't asked his advice. When she complained to him about her back, she wanted sympathy, not advice. He was always telling her what to do! Why couldn't he just listen?

When Marilyn told me about this episode, I thought her assertion that she wanted sympathy from her husband, not advice, was true as far as it went, but that it was missing something. It turned out that when her husband gave advice, it was usually in an intense, pressured way, his response to the anxiety her complaints generated in him. She usually ignored his advice, not just because she wasn't in the market for advice but because it was delivered with an emotional pressure that pushed her away.

This is typical of how messages get deflected. It isn't the content that makes people deaf; it's the emotionality behind it. A speaker's eagerness or annoyance or anxiety or tension is often felt by listeners as pressure to make them wrong or to change their way of thinking. As if it

weren't hard enough to tone down one's own emotionality, doing so is often made even more difficult by the condition of the relationship.

How Some Speakers Make Us Hard of Hearing

Even if we don't always know what to do about it, we've all had plenty of experience with listeners whose emotional reactivity makes them defensive or argumentative instead of hearing what we're trying to say. An equally important but less commonly recognized barrier to understanding is the speaker's emotionality. A speaker who expresses himself or herself in a highly emotional way makes listeners anxious and therefore hard of hearing.

———◆———

Some people have no idea how pressured and provoking their tone of voice is, but they come at you like a bad dentist.

———◆———

The hardest people to listen to are those who treat us with neglect and dictatorial disregard of our feelings. The pressured speaker may not know how he comes across, but his urgent, anxious manner of speaking, emphatic hand gestures, or conclusion of every other statement with "Right?" (apparently demanding agreement) makes us feel backed into a corner.

A Charged Atmosphere

The emotional state between speaker and listener has a lot to do with the quality of understanding that can pass between them. If the atmosphere is calm, especially if it has a history of being calm, the listener can usually hear what the speaker is trying to get across. But if there's anxiety in the air—or even just intense feeling—the listener may be too tense to take in what's said. The listener may be anxious about not wanting to be blamed, or pressured to change, or being proven wrong. Speakers who trigger such feelings, venting emotion in a way that makes listeners feel backed against the wall, may not get heard, even though they have something important to say. It's the way hard things get said that determines whether or not they get heard.

The emotional state of a relationship depends not only on the way individuals express themselves but also on the extent to which the people remain differentiated as individuals.

A differentiated individual is a mature and autonomous person who knows where his or her skin ends and other people's begin. In emotionally undifferentiated relationships anxiety becomes increasingly infectious and the partners intensely reactive to each other, especially on "hot" subjects. Among some couples money is such a charged issue that you can see the sparks begin to fly at the first mention of the word. A mother who is poorly differentiated from her small daughter may be so threatened by the familiar childish retort "I don't love you!" that she either rescinds her rules or gets into a pointless discussion that begins with "But *I* love you." A more well-differentiated parent doesn't feel so tied to and threatened by her daughter's protests. Such a parent has enough distance to realize that "I don't love you!" just means "I'm angry that you won't let me have my way." Differentiation is achieved by learning to separate what you think from what you feel—and by learning to be yourself while respecting other people's right to be themselves.

When boundaries between people are blurred and individuals become emotionally fused, almost any emotion from the speaker will make a listener reactive. As differentiation decreases, individuality is less well defined, and emotional reactivity becomes more intense. Poorly differentiated and highly reactive people may come across as emotionally demanding or avoidant.

An "independent" husband may be aware of his "dependent" wife's emotional reactivity but blind to his own. He sees her attachment because she shows it directly. When he gets mad at her for objecting to his wanting to go off by himself, he says, "You're so dependent! Why don't you develop some interests of your own and quit hanging on me?" She cries and accuses him of being selfish. As far as he's concerned, she's emotionally immature. She's so dependent that he can't even complain without her getting hysterical. What he *doesn't* see is how vulnerable and dependent *he* is on her feeling positively toward him, so much so that he's completely unable to hear her complaints as an expression of her feelings. He hears what she says only as a judgment and threat to himself and a constraint on what he wants to do. And so he goes off and broods in self-righteous hurt and anger about his wife's inability to respond to him without reacting emotionally.

Gail just had to talk to Leon about needing some help around the house. She knew it was a sore subject because they'd both grown up with the expectation that cooking and washing dishes and doing the laundry was something wives did. But, damn it, with both of them working and the kids to look after, this family couldn't afford the luxury

of a wife. For three months since starting her new job, Gail had put off asking Leon for help because she didn't want to start a fight. But she was finding it impossible to get dinner on the table before the kids started getting cranky, and so she just had to talk to him.

So that night after dinner Gail told Leon how unfair it was for her to have to do all the cooking and cleaning now that she was working. As she spoke, the anger and frustration she'd been sitting on for three months came pouring out.

Leon, who knew he wasn't doing his share, listened as Gail talked about how hurt she was that he hadn't even offered to help. But as she went on about all she had to do and how little he did, Gail started talking faster and more pressured, waving her hands about as though her words couldn't keep pace with her feelings. Leon listened with growing upset.

What started out sounding like a legitimate request turned into a tirade. Instead of listening and feeling like cooperating, he started feeling attacked and got defensive. "Why do you have to go *on and on* about everything? And why do you have to exaggerate so: You do *everything*, and I do *nothing*. Who earns the real money in this family?"

That did it. Gail burst out crying, and Leon, who couldn't take it anymore, stormed out of the room and slammed the door. Gail was left alone crying in the living room, feeling how unfair it was that Leon was too selfish to care about her.

Sometimes the speaker's emotion stirs emotions in the listener, making it particularly difficult for the listener to be the receptive vehicle that the speaker requires. When it comes to telling your side, particularly in a relationship with a history of tension, the best way to be heard is to tone down your emotionality. Even if you don't make the mistake of blaming the other person, he or she may feel attacked if you express yourself in an anxious or pressured manner. The trouble is, sometimes it's hard not to.

The reason we don't recognize the impact of our tone of voice is that we hear what we feel like, not what we sound like.

Elise gets annoyed because Jay takes the other side of almost every issue she brings up. This is a common complaint. Most subjects are complex enough to have two sides; when someone close to us points to

one side, we have a natural tendency to think of the other. The trouble is, it doesn't feel good to say the cup is half empty only to be told "No, it's half full." Jay's tendency always to take the opposite position made Elise feel not just disagreed with but also negated.

Once she commented that the neighbor's porch railing looked as if it was in bad shape and might break; someone might get hurt. Jay looked at the railing—which was in halfway good shape—and said, "I don't think so; it looks OK to me." When Elise tried to tell him what she was feeling—"I hate it when you disagree with everything I say"— Jay felt attacked and controlled. "Must I agree with everything you say?" he wanted to know. Like many reasonable married people, they discussed the issue without raising their voices or hearing each other.

Elise could understand Jay's feeling that it wasn't fair for him to have to agree with everything she said; but that wasn't what she wanted. She just wanted him to acknowledge her feelings. He heard that, sort of, but didn't know what he was supposed to do. "If you say the porch railing looks like it's going to break, and I don't think it is, how am I supposed to know that you're just expressing your feelings and that I'm only supposed to acknowledge them? How do I know what you want if you don't tell me?"

One reason Jay had trouble hearing Elise was that she often expressed herself with very strong emotion. Even clear, meaningful messages were so charged with intense feeling that Jay reacted to her anxiety rather than to her statement. Instead of getting through to him, she became something to brace against.

Elise gets excitable and raises her voice because she's been holding things in and is eager to get them out. But when she gets anxious, Jay gets tight, and he's more aware of the knot in his stomach than of what Elise is trying to tell him. When she told him how much it bothered her that he always disagreed with her, it was the upset she conveyed that made him defensive, not the message.

Even though they tried, Elise and Jay were never able to hear each other in heated discussions. Only when I interrupted and talked to them one at a time were they able to listen without a defensive response. It turned out that Elise had grown up with a father who demanded rigid adherence to his rules and had argued with and invalidated his children's every opinion. Both Jay and Elise recalled her brother and his habit of responding to even the most insignificant disagreement as though it were a declaration of war: "Either you're with me, or you're against me."

Jay and Elise aren't very different from many intimate partners who sometimes despair of ever really being heard by the other. If you want to be listened to and heard, consider how much emotionality and anxiety you have—or how much gets churned up when you speak to certain people about certain things. Listeners react to that emotion. If you can reduce your own emotional intensity, you may get heard, even when the subject is a difficult one. Remember: it isn't so much what you say as how you say it that determines whether or not you get heard. That's one reason people are often more open to what they read than to what someone says to them. (At least I hope so.)

Let's take another look at the interaction between Jay and Elise. Jay had trouble hearing his wife because she often expressed herself with anxious emotion, her sentences flapping at him like flags in a high wind. When her voice rankled and he shrank back into himself, he didn't hear the sweet, eager girl he fell in love with but an echo of harshness from long ago. The "he" who was doing the hearing wasn't the part of him who was strong and loved his wife but a little boy part, the one who could never stand to hear that harsh and powerful voice telling him that he couldn't go out to play, that he had to stay trapped in the house all afternoon, buried alive in chores.

Is it men that Medusa turns to stone, or is it the little boys inside them?

HURT FEELINGS AND BROKEN CONNECTIONS

As a family therapist, I'm often consulted about longstanding impasses in relationships. Wives complain that their husbands don't care how they feel; husbands complain that their wives nag and are more emotional than reasonable; parents complain that their children avoid them; people who feel they are treated unjustly in the family complain that they're singled out unfairly; and adult children complain that they can't get close to their parents. Many of these individuals come to therapy by themselves because the people they're concerned about refuse even to talk about the problem.

Michael's sister Susan moved to the West Coast after a bitter and acrimonious divorce. When she called from Los Angeles to talk to him, her ex-husband, who just happened to have stopped by, answered the phone. Susan was mortified, then furious. She felt betrayed and stopped

speaking to her brother. When Susan didn't return Michael's phone calls, he got so upset that he took a plane to California the next day to straighten things out. But when he got there, Susan left town for the weekend because she still wasn't ready to talk to him. Michael was livid. He could understand that she was upset, but *he* hadn't done anything wrong. And to refuse to see him after he had gone all the way to California—that he could not forgive.

The first step to healing a ruptured relationship is to understand the other person's point of view. Try to figure out what that person might be feeling and then say it in a way that invites him to elaborate. Until you acknowledge the other person's position, he's unlikely to be open to yours. He may listen, but he won't hear.

Michael tried to apologize to his sister, but his heart wasn't in it. After all, he hadn't done anything wrong. So although he was willing to say he was sorry she was upset, he just had to add that he hadn't done anything to be blamed for. Unfortunately, when someone feels wounded and aggrieved, any attempt to justify your own behavior, no matter how innocent or well meaning it was, may cancel your acknowledgment of her feelings. Michael was infuriated when his sister refused to see him, but she rightly intuited that his attempt to make up carried a lot of pressure for her to forgive him. If Susan had been less emotionally reactive or less upset, Michael's attempts to heal the breach might have worked. But when someone is really hurt and bitter, the only thing he or she wants to hear is an apology, not an apology loaded with self-justification. The greatest lesson in humility may be learning to say "I'm sorry I hurt you" without having to protest your innocence.

I saw Michael a total of three times over several months. In our first meeting I made exactly the same mistake I am here preaching against. Instead of acknowledging his hurt and anger, I advised him to reach out to his sister. Since he felt that he'd already done so and been spurned, he rejected my advice.

Our second meeting occurred five months later. He'd been getting on with his life and had calmed down about what happened between him and his sister. Time and distance had softened his anger, and he was ready for suggestions about how to patch up the break with Susan. I advised him to write her a letter acknowledging the hurt and betrayal she felt and saying that he was sorry. I cautioned him that the letter

must be absolutely devoid of two elements that would render it ineffective: any hint of self-justification, expressed or implied, and any pressure or suggestion, expressed or implied, that his sister needed to do something about his apology. It had to be an honest apology—"I'm sorry I hurt you"—nothing more and nothing less. I also warned him that his sister's first response might be an angry one—something that can be hard to take after you apologize. He understood that and said he could accept it.

Four days after Michael wrote to his sister, he received a letter from her saying how betrayed she felt when her ex-husband answered the phone at her own brother's house. How could Michael have been so insensitive? After that Susan's letter lightened. She wrote about her job in California and a new friendship and asked Michael what he was up to. They've been on good terms ever since.

"He Never Talks to Me"

How can you listen well when certain important people in your life seem to withhold themselves from you and resist all your efforts at intimacy?

People cultivate protective reticence in emotional relations because they don't want to get hurt. The introvert moves through life in a protective bubble of psychological distance not because his need for attention has ceased but because he's ceased to allow himself to feel it. Inside the prison of his defenses he preoccupies himself with other things. He keeps busy, he reads, he thinks, and he has long conversations in his head, where no one else can mess them up. Like many prisoners, he can be comfortable in his limited and protected routines, but the idea of parole into the wide world of other people and emotions terrifies him.

Although the emotional reticence of someone you care about can be powerfully frustrating, the reticent don't feel powerful. They feel vulnerable. People who withhold themselves from us are trying to insulate themselves from their own exquisite sensitivity to emotionality. It isn't all them, either. In the process of trying to get closer to someone who doesn't say much, we often set up a pursuer–distancer dynamic.

Pursuers and Distancers

One of the most easily observed conversational patterns between intimate partners is the pursuer-distancer dynamic.[1]

As you may have noticed, pursuing distancers only makes them feel
pressured and inclined to pull further away. It's a dance between one
partner who moves forward and another who moves back. The pursuer-
distancer dynamic is propelled by emotional reactivity—on the part of
both participants. The people who pull away from us aren't just "shy"
or "withholding"; they're responding to the emotionalism with which
we approach them. I can almost hear the protests: "I don't put any pressure on so-and-so; he [or she] just won't open up."

We rarely feel the emotional pressure we put on others. What we
feel is their response to it. The people who resist personal conversation
with us may indeed be more reticent than most. Still, their backing
off is not just habit but response.

Unfortunately, some of the people we find hardest to listen to are
an important part of our lives: They are our partners, our parents, our
children, our bosses, or our colleagues, and they arouse our reactivity
because our need endows them with the power to distress and please
us. When the frustrations of trying to speak and be heard, to listen and
hear get to be too much, we may be tempted to give up and pull back
into ourselves.

Facing anxious encounters tests your maturity, strengthens you if
you have the courage to stand fast and let matters unfold, or weakens
you if you fall back into reactivity and defensiveness. Making contact,
letting others be themselves while you continue to be yourself, and learning to resist automatic reactions strengthens you and transforms your
relationships. Staying open and staying calm—that's the hardest part.
You do the best you can.

If all of this seems like obvious common sense—to listen well, you
have to resist the urge to overreact—it's only obvious from an objective distance. Up close, when you're caught up in the pressure to get
the words out or the aggravation of listening to someone saying something provocative, objectivity is in short supply. Emotionality takes over.

[1]Thomas Fogarty, "The Distancer and the Pursuer," *The Family*, 7, (1979): 11-16.

GETTING THROUGH
TO EACH OTHER

"Take Your Time— I'm Listening"

HOW TO LET GO OF YOUR OWN NEEDS AND LISTEN

Effective listening requires *attention*, *appreciation*, and *affirmation*. You begin the process by tuning in to the other person, paying attention to what he has to say. Put no barriers between you. Turn off the TV, put down the newspaper, ask the kids to play in the other room, shut the door to your office. Look directly at the speaker and concentrate on what she is trying to communicate.

Practice listening whenever your partner, family member, friend, or colleague speaks to you, with the sole intention of understanding what that person is trying to express. People need to talk—and be heard—to feel understood by and connected to you.

PAYING ATTENTION

You can take the first step toward better listening by making a conscientious effort to set aside whatever is on your mind long enough to concentrate on hearing what the other person has to say.

Listening to each other never seemed to be much of a problem for Tony and Joan before the baby was born. They always had lots to talk about and, maybe more important, plenty of time to do it in. Then

the baby came along, and the pressures of parenthood seemed to squeeze the intimacy out of their relationship. They got out of the habit of going out together, and somehow neither of them seemed to have much energy for conversation in their brief and hectic evenings at home.

Tony made an effort to ask Joan about her day, but when she responded only perfunctorily, he stopped asking. Anyway, he was so tired when he came home that he didn't really mind getting off by himself with the newspaper. They weren't angry or upset with each other, but they were drifting apart.

When Tony sought my advice about the lack of intimacy in the marriage, he described his failed attempts to talk to Joan at the end of the day. I could see two mistakes he was making in trying to get Joan to open up. The first had to do with timing. Trying to have a serious conversation when he first came in the door, while Joan was cooking supper and the baby was winding down like a little clock, just didn't work. The second thing was that Joan didn't respond well to global questions like "How was your day?" Such questions may work when someone is relaxed and ready to talk, but they aren't effective when someone is wound up or distracted. Joan needed him to ask more specific questions, like "How did it go at the pediatrician's?" or "What did the baby do today?"—questions that were specific enough to trigger a response *and* show that he was aware of what was going on in her life.

I did not, however, say any of this to Tony. Instead I turned to Joan and asked if she felt lonely. She said yes. Then I asked if she felt that Tony was really interested in hearing what was going on with her. "Maybe . . . ," she said softly, "but I don't feel it."

All I said to Tony was "I guess you better try harder."

Better listening doesn't start with a set of techniques. It starts with making a sincere effort to pay attention to what's going on in your conversational partner's private world of experience.

My challenge to Tony—"I guess you better try harder"—turned out to be a one-session cure. He did try harder. It didn't occur to him to ask more specific questions; he just didn't give up so easily. Instead of offering Joan a brief moment's attention, he started showing real interest in her feelings and heartfelt concern for her well-being. In response, she began to feel once again loved and cared for—and much more like being intimate with Tony in return.

When you're trying to create a dialogue with someone who isn't revealing much of her thoughts and feelings, it may help to make

empathic guesses about what's going on inside her. Comments like "Tough day?" or "Are you worried about something?" or "Is something bothering you?" if they're on target may show enough awareness to make the other person feel that you're really interested in her. But it isn't any particular comment or any technique alone that will get someone to open up. It's taking a sincere interest in what that person has to say.

Listeners who pretend interest don't fool us for long—even though they sometimes fool themselves. The automatic smile, the hit-and-run question, the restless look in their eyes when we start to talk—all these are giveaways to the fact that they're more interested in being taken for good listeners than in really hearing what we have to say. Real listening means setting all that aside. Good listeners don't act needy. They don't charm, flatter, provoke, or interrupt. None of that *look at me, listen to me, admire me, appreciate me.* None of that. They suspend the self and listen.

APPRECIATING THE OTHER PERSON'S POINT OF VIEW

Understanding one another is a give-and-take process. The best way to get the listening you need is to make the other person feel listened to first.

————◆————

Most people won't really listen or pay attention to your point of view until they become convinced that you've heard and appreciated theirs.

————◆————

Even when you're the one initiating a discussion about something of concern to you, the best way to ensure that you'll be heard is to invite the other person to explain his viewpoint before you present yours. Suspending your agenda so as to hear the other person out enables you to understand what he thinks, helps make him feel understood, and clears the way for him to be more willing to listen to you.

Let the other person know you're interested in what he has to say by inviting him to say what's on his mind, what his opinion is, or how he feels about the issue under consideration—and then giving him your full attention.

"Can we talk about . . . ? What do you think we should do?"

"I'm not sure I really understand how you feel about. . . . What *is* your point of view?"

"I'm sorry we had this misunderstanding. I'd really like to hear what happened as far as you're concerned."

"You seem upset with me. Am I right about that?"

Elicit the other person's thoughts and feelings about the subject at hand by asking specific questions that show your grasp of what she's said and encouraging her to elaborate.

"So what you're saying is. . . . Is that right?"

"I think I understand what you're saying, but I want to be sure. Do you mean . . . ?"

"I'm not sure I really understand what you mean. You're saying . . . but I wish you'd say more about your position so I can get it straight."

"I think I understand where we disagree, but I'm not sure. Did you mean that . . . ?"

If you feel yourself getting impatient or defensive while the other person is speaking, it's important to restrain your urge to respond until you've heard her out. Just keeping your mouth shut and pretending to listen may be better than interrupting, but it isn't the same as really listening. To really listen, try hard to appreciate what the other person is feeling. Imagine how you'd feel if you were in her shoes.

Anytime you demonstrate a willingness to listen with a minimum of defensiveness, criticism, or impatience, you are giving the gift of understanding—and earning the right to have it reciprocated.

Suspending your needs long enough to hear the other person out is part of willing yourself to listen. But suspending your needs is not the same thing as becoming a nonself.

Sometimes you need to recognize that you can't suspend the self effectively until you fulfill its needs. So while it might seem selfish, in fact telling your spouse that you do want to hear about his day but you have to get your own problem off your chest first may not be. By the same token, there are times when the most considerate and honest thing you can say to someone who wants to talk when you aren't up to listen-

ing is "I really can't concentrate on what you're saying right now. Can we talk in about twenty minutes?" Trying to listen when you're really not up to it dries up your capacity to empathize.

Some listeners are so fearful of exerting their own individuality that they become nonselves, tucked into others, embedded in a safe framework of obligations and duties. These people find it easier to accommodate than to deal with conflict, threats of rejection, arguments, or signs of distress in others. Their anxious, demanding partners are frequently unaware of how much their mates accommodate to preserve harmony. They take it for granted and want more. Such compliant people may seem like good listeners, but you aren't really listening if you're nothing but a passive receptacle, a reluctant sponge.

Listening well is often silent but never passive.

Instead of listening passively, and maybe feeling a little trapped, get involved actively by asking specific questions that help the other person express his feelings or elaborate on what he's thinking.

"What does he do that bothers you the most?"

"What do you think she should do?"

"It sounds great. What was the best part?"

"What did you feel like saying to her?"

"What would you *have liked* to hear him say?"

Real listening means imagining yourself into the other's experience: concentrating, asking questions. Understanding is furthered not by knowing ("I understand") but by investigating— asking for elaboration, inquiring into the concrete particularity of the speaker's experience. The good listener is not a passive receptor but an active, open one, attuned and inquiring.

AFFIRMING YOUR UNDERSTANDING

Once in a while we all pretend we're listening when we're not. In spite of this, we're genuinely taken aback when someone accuses us of not listening when in fact we were. One reason people wonder if we're listening is that we sometimes fail to let them know that we heard them. Silence is ambiguous.

Without some sign of understanding, the speaker begins to wonder if what she's saying makes sense, if it's worth talking about. Doubts surface. *Maybe I'm boring him. Maybe I shouldn't be complaining like this.* Without some reassuring evidence of empathy, people don't trust us enough to tell us the simple truth about their feelings, much less to reveal potentially dangerous truths. Everyone is vulnerable in this sense, and everyone holds back in many ways.

Ordinarily we take turns talking. The roles of speaker and listener alternate so naturally that it may be artificial to call what one person says "the listener's response." Responding turns listeners into speakers. But listening well is a two-step process: First we take in what the speaker says, then we let him or her know it. A failed response is like an unanswered letter; you never know if you got through.

Repeating the other person's position in your own words is the best way to show that you understand. But effective listening is achieved not by summing up what the other person said as though that should be the end of it but as a means of inviting him to elaborate so that you can *really* understand.

————◆————

Effective communication isn't achieved simply by taking turns talking; it requires a concerted effort at mutual understanding.

————◆————

The best way to promote understanding is to take time to restate the other person's position in your own words, then ask her to correct or affirm your understanding of her thoughts and feelings. If you work on this process of explicit feedback and confirmation until the other person has no doubt that you grasp her position, she will feel understood—and she will then be more open to hearing from you.

"So you're saying that you don't think Kevin should join Little League because it will put a lot of unnecessary competitive pressure on him and because you'll be the one who gets stuck driving him to all the games?"

"Let me make sure I understand what you're saying. You feel that you're always the one who calls when we get together, and that makes you wonder if I really want to spend time with you. Is that right?"

"OK, I want to make sure I understand. You're saying we should hire Gloria but that we should make it very clear to her what we ex-

pect, and we should be very serious about the probationary period, and if she doesn't do the job we should let her go at the end of six months. Have I got that right?"

"So all this time you've been feeling that I'm mad at you, and that's why I've stopped being affectionate. No wonder you're upset. You must have been feeling hurt for a long time."

"You Just Don't Get It, Do You?"

When one person says, "The world is round," and the other replies, "No, it's flat," it's clear that the second person got the first person's point and disagreed. But when the subject is more personal, disagreement—without some acknowledgment of the other person's point of view—can come across as invalidating the speaker's feelings and opinions. If people spoke like self-help manuals, they might say "I see what you're saying, but I don't agree." But since most of us not only don't speak like self-help manuals but often react in heat and haste, many conversations take on the form of two-part disharmony.

------◆------

The simple failure to acknowledge what the other person says explains much of the friction in our lives.

------◆------

The more heated the exchange, the more important it is to acknowledge what the other person says. When two people are talking about something important to them, each feels an urgent need to get his or her point of view across. But without some acknowledgment, each may continue to restate his or her position, thinking *If only he [or she] would see what I'm saying, we wouldn't have to keep arguing like this.*

One Friday night, after an especially long and tedious week, Sheila said to Rob, "We never go out." Rob, feeling attacked, said, "That's not true! We went out last week." This just upset Sheila more, and she renewed her attempt to get Rob to understand what she was feeling. "You mean when we went out with Linda and John for pizza? I don't call that going out. You never want to do anything but sit around in front of that stupid TV set." Now Rob was pissed. "Listen, I work hard all week, and if I want to relax on the couch, what's so wrong with that?" By this point Sheila felt completely invalidated. "You just don't

get it, do you?" she said. Then she went upstairs to the bedroom and slammed the door.

Maybe you can identify with Sheila. Or Rob. Or both of them. The choice between going out and vegging out is one that most of us have feelings about. But what was especially unfortunate in this quarrel that left both Sheila and Rob feeling so misunderstood and unappreciated was that neither one took the time to acknowledge the other's point of view.

You don't have to be *responsible* for someone's feelings to be *aware* of them—and to acknowledge them.

When Sheila said, "We never go out," she was expressing a feeling— she's bored and a little lonely—and making a request: she wishes that she and Rob could have a little more fun, do something together, maybe be a little closer. But something about the way she said it (or he heard it) made Rob defensive. Instead of showing that he understood what she was feeling by acknowledging what she was saying, he just felt criticized. He heard her saying that he was lazy, selfish, uninvolved—just the things he worries he might be—and so he didn't listen to her feelings, much less respond calmly to her request.

Dueling Points of View

When two people keep restating their own positions without acknowledging what the other one is trying to say, the result is dueling points of view. One is tempted—especially if one is a therapist—to think of two people involved in dueling declarations as simply lacking a communicational skill, that of paraphrasing what your conversation partner says before responding. The trouble with this communication-as-skill perspective is that it leaves out conflict and anxiety, precisely the things that make understanding each other so difficult. The partners who don't acknowledge what each other says are afraid to. They're afraid that to acknowledge what the other one says means surrender—"You're right and I'm wrong." Unfortunately, as in many vicious circles, their efforts to break through to each other by restating their own positions just locks misunderstanding in place.

When the subject isn't too emotional, the result is a mildly unsatisfying sense of at least having said what you mean, even if the other

person didn't acknowledge it. But when feeling runs high, dueling declarations escalate into painful misunderstandings.

Professional advice givers often talk as though couples could get along fine if only they'd learn "to communicate"—making "I" statements and all the rest. That's nice, but it overlooks the existence of real conflict.

Although they hadn't really discussed it, Charlotte assumed that once Hugh finished his Ph.D. they would move back to the city they were from. But Hugh liked where they were living, and when he announced that he might take a teaching job at the university, Charlotte felt betrayed.

Because the question of where to live was so important to both of them, they found it difficult to talk about it without disparaging each other's point of view. When Hugh presented his arguments for staying, Charlotte would try to discredit them or say that he had a responsibility to make up to her the sacrifice she had made in leaving the city for the sake of his career. He'd respond by talking about the sacrifices he'd made for her. Later, after months of estrangement, Charlotte said that if at any point in the process Hugh had acknowledged that she had given up a lot for his schooling or had said that she would get her turn later, she could have agreed to stay. But instead of listening and acknowledging her right to feel the way she did, Hugh responded by saying that his career was more important than hers.

In another couple that faced the same issue, both wanted to move; the problem was where. Raymond was an accountant and Joyce was the dean of women at a small college. Both agreed that since he would be able to find work more easily, her search for another deanship should be given priority. Raymond, however, felt strongly about *where* he wanted to live. It wasn't so much a regional preference as wanting to live either in a big city or well out into the country—anything but suburbia, where Lawn Doctor was king. And so half the time when Joyce told him that she'd read about a job opening, he'd respond by saying "I'd never live *there.*" She'd feel defeated and angry and think he was being totally unreasonable.

Why did Hugh find it necessary to put Charlotte down by saying that his career was more important than hers? And why did Raymond have to reject so many of Joyce's possibilities so quickly? What made it so hard for these two husbands even to acknowledge what their wives were feeling?

Hugh was apparently afraid that acknowledging Charlotte's feelings would automatically lead to giving in and acting on their dictates.

Likewise, Raymond didn't seem to have the confidence that he could still say no to a potential new place after he and Joyce had visited it. Otherwise, why wouldn't he agree to at least take a look? Why weren't these two men able to listen better to their wives? Is it simply "selfishness" or "masculine insensitivity" or "immaturity" that prevents people from hearing each other? Maybe Hugh and Raymond had trouble listening to their partners because they felt anxious and insecure about their own ability to assert themselves. Maybe we—men and women—always have reasons for not listening, not understanding one another.

———◆———

Listening is hard because it involves a loss of control—and if you're afraid of what you might hear, it feels unsafe to relinquish control.

———◆———

He Says, She Says

He says, "You should have said something." She says, "You should have asked." And neither one feels heard. She talks about the things she'd like to do around the house, and he talks about being tired. He never hears what doing these things means to her, and she never hears that he wishes they could have more fun. Arguments escalate, feelings go unrecognized, and minds don't meet as long as we fail to acknowledge what the other person says before we respond with what we have to say.

———◆———

He says, she says—but neither acknowledges what the other one says.

———◆———

Behavior therapists teach married couples to paraphrase what their partners say before going on to give their side. This is a device to interrupt the cross-complaining that keeps couples in conflict from ever feeling understood, much less actually doing anything about each other's complaints. If a husband tells his wife that he wishes she would cook something different for supper, and she gets angry and complains that he's impossible to please—and he gets defensive and withdraws to brood over how unfair she is—neither one of them will feel understood. This misunderstanding—and many others like it—has less to do with being unable to resolve conflict than with being unable to tolerate it. If instead of

getting defensive and attacking, either person would simply acknowledge what the other said, it might not prove so difficult to come together.

Even when conflict is serious, we all feel better if we can at least say how we feel—what bothers us and what we wish—and have the other person say those reassuring words "I understand how you feel."

Here's an example. The vast majority of people I talk with have less than happy sex lives. Maybe mine is a biased sample, but many of the people I see who've been married for ten years or more have sex maybe once a month or every six months or even less. Even when they bring themselves to consult a therapist, few people mention this issue. Not only are they embarrassed (most people assume that most other people are successful parents and have happy sex lives), but also they've given up hope. Why talk about something so personal and painful when all their previous efforts have only made them angry and ashamed?

Once they do find the courage to talk about problems in their sexual relationship, some couples are able to make changes for the better, while others aren't. But they almost all feel better for talking about it. What makes them feel better, even if nothing changes, is being able to say how they feel about it, what they don't like, what they wish, and to admit feeling guilty and inadequate—something each partner inevitably feels and inevitably doesn't realize the other one feels.

Why do people need a therapist to have these conversations? They don't. *If* they can each say how they feel about the situation, *and* the other can *hear and acknowledge* these feelings before going on to say how he or she feels.

Most of us are reactive when it comes to sex, but some people are reactive to so many things that they fail to acknowledge what anyone else says about anything. If you complain to such people that they always argue and don't listen, they may protest that you're only asking them to agree with you. They're not aware that it takes some kind of acknowledgment of what we're saying for us to feel not agreed with but heard.

THE IMPORTANCE OF RELINQUISHING CONTROL

As I've said, I don't care to be interrupted in the middle of talking about an experience, by someone either giving advice I didn't ask for or "sharing" a similar experience. Interruption is interruption. What's missing in both cases is some kind of expression of understanding and ac-

knowledgment, something like "Gee, that's lousy." What's going on in both cases—and others—is that the listener just won't relinquish control over the exchange. Many of us are convinced that we're good listeners because we do and say all the right things. But do we? Often the speaker ends up feeling unheard, because what we're really doing is going through the motions, serving our own purposes.

"Why Don't You Just . . . ?"

A wise supervisor once told me that my treatment of a shy, overweight young man was bogged down because I was trying to change him before he felt understood and accepted by me. To me it seemed so simple: if the young man would only make a little effort to initiate conversations with people, at the same time we explored the roots of his insecurity, we could work toward change on two fronts. He, however, felt that my suggesting that he simply start doing what he found so difficult proved that I didn't understand how painfully self-conscious he was. The supervisor's technical recommendation (which had to do with transference and countertransference) was "Shut up and listen."

A Gaping Silence

If everyone followed my supervisor's advice, the world would be a better place. But if listening were only a negative accomplishment, we could concentrate (as many therapists and people playing therapist do) on restraining ourselves and not interrupting. Speakers may be gratified at being allowed to say what's on their minds but frustrated by the absence of curiosity and appreciation. This means that, taken too literally, "shut up and listen" isn't enough to convey understanding. If you're telling someone at a party about what kind of work you do and she's listening without interrupting, but her eyes are wandering around the room, you hardly feel listened to.

Whether or not someone is really listening only that person truly knows. But, on the other hand, if someone doesn't feel listened to, he doesn't feel listened to. We judge whether or not others are listening to us by the signals we see. Are they showing that they're paying attention by setting aside distractions and turning toward us?

Before they comment on what we're saying, people show interest and attention by maintaining eye contact, smiling with pleasure or frowning with concern, and making little interjections like "uh-huh" and "real-

ly?" Head nods also show attention; larger and repeated ones show agreement. You don't have to take Elementary Clinical Methods to learn these responses; they follow from taking an interest.

The Leading Question

Questions also convey interest, but sometimes the interest they convey is tangential to what we're trying to say. Sometimes the distraction is obvious. If you're trying to tell a friend about the inconsiderate things your husband did on your vacation, and she interrupts with a lot of questions about where you stayed, you certainly don't feel listened to. At other times people seem to be following but can't help trying to steer. These listeners impose their own narrative structures on our experience. Their questions assume that our stories should fit their scripts: "Problems should be denied or made to go away"; "Everyone should be together"; "Men are insensitive"; "Bullies must be confronted." By finishing our sentences, pumping us with questions, and otherwise pushing us to say what they want to hear, controlling listeners violate our right to tell our own tales.

HOW TO GET THE LISTENING YOU DESERVE

(The devil just whispered in my ear that maybe I should make that ". . . The Listening You *Want*." Maybe we already get the listening we deserve. But I'm not going to listen to that old devil.)

How to Ask for Support
without Getting Unwanted Advice

One way to get the listening you need is to tell people what you want.

"I'm upset and I need to talk to you. Just listen, OK?"

"I have a problem that I need to discuss, but I'm not ready to decide what to do, so it would be helpful if you could just listen to me."

If you don't want a reactive or intrusive response, anticipate your listener's expectations.

"I'm not asking you to agree with me, but can you understand where I'm coming from?"

"I want to tell you something and I don't want you to get mad at me. Just listen and think about what I'm saying, will you?"

"I want your opinion about something, but then I'll have to figure out what I want to do. Will you give me some advice, even if I don't end up following it?"

If someone gives advice when you just want to be listened to, by all means say so. But put the emphasis on what you want, not on how intrusive she is: "Thanks for the advice, but right now I just want to tell you what happened and have you understand how I feel" works better than "I didn't ask for advice. Just listen, will you?" or "Can't you just listen for once, without always having to tell me what to do?"

How to Handle Interruptions

If you're driving down the road and someone cuts in front of you, there's not much you can do about it. Oh, you can hit your horn and call the other person a certain member of the canine family if you wish. But you pretty much have to yield unless you want your car smashed up. The same is not true when somebody cuts in when you're talking. You can't be interrupted unless you allow it. When you're talking, you have the right of way.

If someone starts to interrupt, you can:

- Hold up your index finger.
- Say "Wait a minute, I'm not finished."
- Just keep talking: "What I was trying to say is. . . . "

If someone does cut you off:

- Instead of getting upset (or instead of *just* getting upset), practice saying, "I wasn't finished; please hear me out." Then go back to what you were saying and finish saying it.
- Comment on feeling cut off, but without lecturing or attacking:

  "I wish you'd let me finish what I was saying."

  "I'm sorry, but I can't pay attention to your story because I wasn't finished telling mine."

"I was trying to tell you something that's important to me. When you start talking about something else out of the blue, I feel like you're not interested in me or what I have to say."

"I was listening to that story on the news. I wish you'd wait a minute before breaking in."

HOW TO LISTEN TO PEOPLE WHO AREN'T EASY TO LISTEN TO

If you're unlucky enough to have someone in your life who's always talking about himself or herself, you might appreciate some advice about how to change that person. The best I can offer is the suggestion to think systemically.

People who talk too much are difficult to endure, but their need for our attention is genuine. Their neediness is a burden, but they shouldn't be made to feel ashamed of it. Shaming people for their needs makes them feel worse and intensifies the need. Even if we don't criticize someone for talking too much, our not listening to them has an isolating effect, which only increases their yearning to be heard.

When we describe someone as self-centered or say that he's always talking about himself, we are in fact describing only half of a relationship. In twenty-five years of counseling couples, I have rarely met a spouse who doesn't think he or she does an unequal share of listening in the relationship. This isn't to say that there aren't people who talk about themselves more than others, but if we turn away from the needs of those we love, we are part of the problem.

One of the secrets to dealing with the difficult people in our lives is to figure out how to play the hand we're dealt, rather than fretting and moaning about what that hand is. The reason some people in our lives remain one-dimensional is because that's as far as we go with them. Part of the reason your father-in-law always wants to talk about himself is that you rarely listen, or listen only halfheartedly. As long as he feels unlistened to himself, he's not likely to have much real interest in what anyone else has to say. If instead of stewing in the trapped anxiety of someone with nothing to do but flinch, you listen a little more to someone who talks too much, you might find the balance of the relationship shifting. Even a small shift can make a big difference.

RESISTING THE TEMPTATION TO TURN AWAY

At times when we want to control others' access to us, we may avoid looking at a person who is seeking our attention. A man watching television who doesn't wish to be interrupted may avoid looking at his wife when she tries to speak to him. Similarly, a waitress may prevent a customer from catching her eye to prevent his initiating an order or another request she's too harried to fulfill at the moment.

A paradoxical example of this responsive unavailability occurs in psychoanalysis, where the analyst sits behind the recumbent patient and out of view. The result is disconcerting. Unable to see how the therapist is responding, the patient is unsure of being understood and sympathized with. Unable to provide visible evidence of interest, the therapist may feel equally uncomfortable. Eventually, however, this constrained arrangement turns out to be liberating. The patient, who gets to trust that he won't be interrupted or prompted, learns to follow his own thoughts more fully and to express them more freely. The therapist discovers that looking off into space with no pressure to demonstrate interest enables him or her to listen more freely and to think about what's being said.

What is to be learned from the analyst being liberated to listen by not having to appear attentive? We've noted that listening well means suspending our needs, including the need to *do* something—to solve problems, to say the right thing, even to act attentive. Better to *be* attentive. Be interested. Listen hard. And overcome the need to get credit for listening.

It may not be possible in everyday life to offer that perfect and silent listening in which analytic patients are encouraged to reveal and reconstruct themselves. If people have learned not to expect careful listening from us, we may have to reassure them of our interest. But if we listen carefully, people will learn to trust us. Just listening, without interrupting or turning away, goes a long way toward establishing that trust.

"I Never Knew You Felt That Way"

EMPATHY BEGINS WITH OPENNESS

Among the unhelpful expectations we bring to listening are precon-ceived notions about *what* the speaker is going to say and *how* commu-nication should take place. Assuming you know what someone is going to say means you don't have to bother to listen.

Assumptions about how people should talk to each other aren't usual-ly conscious; they're part of the way we were brought up. Assuming that your way of communicating is the only one means you'll have trouble relating to people with different conversational styles and sensitivities. Interestingly, such assumptions come in pairs of opposites, such as: po-lite people make requests indirectly versus honest people ask directly for what they what; explanations should be short and sweet (rambling on is boring and pushy) versus explanations should be thorough and complete (make sure the other person understands exactly what you mean).

The listener who settles for confirming his expectations, like the museum-goer who looks at paintings only long enough to confirm the name of the artist, is in danger of never getting closer to another per-son's experience. There is no bridge of understanding, no touching. The listener who remains open, on the other hand, experiences from time to time surprise and delight as his assumptions topple and he discovers the speaker—child, spouse, friend—in a deeper, fuller way.

The essence of good listening is empathy, achieved by being receptive to *what* other people are trying to say and *how* they express themselves. Empathy takes an open mind to other sensibilities.

Although most people would vastly improve their listening by setting aside preconceived notions and remaining open to what the speaker is trying to say, total innocence of assumptions is neither possible nor desirable. Anticipation is useful. Anticipating how someone might react can help you express yourself more effectively; anticipating a speaker's needs and style of communicating can help you hear all levels of messages being sent. So, what am I saying? Are expectations a help or a hindrance to good listening?

Expectations hamper communication when they take the form of fixed assumptions and egocentric perspectives. Such expectations (1) are unexamined and (2) close us to other points of view. Expectations promote communication when they take the form of sensitivity to our own and other people's styles of communicating. Such sensitivities make us aware, thoughtful, and open, not biased.

CREATING A CLIMATE OF UNDERSTANDING

One of the most common expectations we bring to our conversational encounters, especially at home, is that we will be able to communicate just by doing what comes naturally. Unfortunately, the listening we do on automatic pilot is often perfunctory, precisely the kind of half-hearted or indifferent listening that makes our relationships less fulfilling than they could be, should be. If you want to make any relationship more rewarding, practice *responsive listening.*

Responsive listening means hearing the other person out, then letting him know what you understand him to be saying. If you're right, the speaker will feel a grateful sense of being understood. If you didn't quite get what he intended to say, your feedback allows him another chance to explain.

Responsive listening can be practiced like any other skill if you're willing to put in the effort. If.

Think of how many situations where familiarity, tension, or distraction, has made you get out of the habit of being attentive, considerate—concerned. The next time your partner comes home at the end of the day, or your child runs to tell you something, or someone at work wants to talk, try making an extra effort to be attentive.

Paying attention goes a long way. Your effort to listen a little longer and more carefully to others will, if you stick to it, initiate a positive spiral in all your relationships.

"I Know What You're Going to Say"

"Like hell, you do!" Have you ever felt like saying that when someone cuts you off? Unfortunately, jumping to conclusions is something we all do at times. You may not actually make the remark I've used as a head for this section, but one of the bad listening habits we all need to break is making too many assumptions about what people are going to say.

Rachel gets home at six-thirty instead of six as she'd promised and says, "I'm sorry I was late, I . . . "

"That's OK," Patrick breaks in to say, "the kids and I made spaghetti. It's all ready."

Rachel is grateful not to have to cook supper but still feels cut off. She was about to tell Patrick that she was late because her boss dumped a last-minute assignment on her, but his assumption that she was about to apologize for inconveniencing him made her feel that he didn't care. All he was interested in, it seemed to her, was his supper.

She could have told him anyway, right? Maybe. But if he's in the habit of cutting her off, she may get tired of trying to force him to listen to her.

Cutting someone off to take over conversational control can certainly be annoying, but so can jumping in before a speaker is finished with words of encouragement, agreement, or to tell a similar story.

At first Hank appreciated Sharon's habit of interjecting little expressions of support when he talked to her. Her *wows*, *gees*, and *what a shames* made him think she was tuned in to his feelings. But after a while these expressions seemed effusive and predictable. They began to make him feel that she was more interested in coming across as supportive than in really listening to him.

Being supportive means neither anticipating nor exceeding a speaker's own expression of feeling. I knew a woman who was so supportive that waves of compassion radiated from her like hot air from a clothes dryer. She may have been trying to be sensitive, but after a while I was

reminded of the Al Franken refrain: "You're good enough, you're smart enough, and doggone it, people like you!"

"Oh, I know what you mean!" Celia said. "My principal treats me the same way." Though she intends to establish empathy, Todd is annoyed. He doubts that her principal really does give her as many last-minute assignments as his boss gives him. Besides, that wasn't his point. He never got to make his point because Celia cut him off to demonstrate that she understood.

The best way to avoid cutting people off is to concentrate on what they're trying to say. Give them a chance to make their point, acknowledge it, and *then* say your piece. Don't pounce at the first pause. Let the other person finish. Inhibit the impulse to switch the focus to you and what's on your mind. Don't tell every story that crops into your head. (I wince as I write this.) Stop and consider whether your comment would contribute to the conversation or disrupt it.

If you make a habit of talking out of turn, people will consider you intrusive. If you get excited and do jump in before the other person has finished, try to catch yourself and back off politely. Say "Go ahead" or even those magic words "I'm sorry."

Even if you *do* know what somebody is going to say, he or she still needs to say it—and have you listen and then acknowledge it—before feeling understood. If conversation were an aerial dogfight, maybe it would be expedient to anticipate the other person's moves so as to shoot them down as fast as possible. But conversation needn't be like that. The person who has something to say wants to express both an idea and a feeling. Listening with an open mind gives you a chance to discover what's on her mind and gives her a chance to clarify her own thinking and feeling. The gift of your silent attention allows you to understand—and the other person to *feel* understood.

HOW TO MOVE BEYOND ASSUMPTIONS
TO OPENNESS AND EMPATHY

The psychoanalyst Wilfred Bion[1] said that to listen well we must "set aside memory, desire, and judgment." This admonition is a formula for openness, calling as it does for listeners to suspend preconceptions, as-

---

[1] Wilfred Bion, *Transformations* (New York: Jason Aronson, 1983).

sumptions, needs, and wishes. Real listening is an act of self-transcendence.

However much the people we live with, work with, or just hang around with care about being with us, they're still largely preoccupied with their own agendas: worries, problems, projects, grudges, hopes, dreams. Even (or especially) if unspoken, such personal agendas are compelling and absorbing. As long as they remain private, these preoccupations have a tendency to separate us from each other. Shared thoughts and feelings, on the other hand, are a step toward each other. Empathy is the bridge.

An empathic friend or family member inquires and acknowledges what we're thinking and feeling, and thus confirms our experience. In this way the empathic listener vitalizes us by emotional participation and reflection—feeding back to us—what we sometimes experience as inchoate.

People live in their own personal and subjective worlds. To meet, truly meet, means that they must open up this part of themselves, feel it, and share it. And it must be received. Much of the time we hide away our real feelings, sometimes even from ourselves. As a result our conversational encounters, like our relationships themselves, often consist of shadows dancing with each other.

Empathy bridges the gap between us, but it requires a real effort at openness. Too many assumptions are inimical to understanding. You can hardly listen and take in anything like the full richness of someone else's experience if you're only waiting for your turn to pounce. Empathy takes restraint; it takes work.

The empathic listener offers a bond of understanding in a deep sense. It's more than the friendly sympathy you might get from your Aunt Rose; it's a deeper resonance of understanding. Perhaps you remember a time when you were hurt or scared and a friend put a hand on your shoulder. Empathy is like that.

Empathic listening means working a little harder at understanding the other person before asking him to do the same for you. It means demonstrating your understanding with comments that draw out thoughts and feelings: "Uh-huh," "I see," "Yes." Simple empathic comments express understanding and help reach something unexpressed in the other person's experience. This helps break down the denial of feeling that keeps us apart. Denial is unnecessary with someone who cares and understands.

The empathic listener celebrates the naturalness of what is felt—

"No wonder you were mad!"—against a person's need to deny what he or she feels.

Empathy is achieved by suspending your own preoccupations and assumptions and placing yourself attentively at the service of the other person, being alert to what he's saying and to the emotional subtext. It means listening without being in a hurry to take over.

Empathy requires two kinds of activity. The first is receptivity and openness, like a moviegoer who allows himself to be absorbed in and moved by the actors and their stories. The second is an oscillation between thinking and feeling. This requires a deliberate shift from feeling *with* a speaker to thinking *about* her. What is she saying? Meaning? Feeling?

Suppose your mate comes home and says he's had a bad day and is upset. You know what that feels like. You're sympathetic. So you ask what happened. He says he's going to have to go out of town again next week. His boss wants him to represent the agency at a big meeting in Buffalo, and he's not looking forward to it.

You know how he feels. All that travel. And Buffalo of all dreary places! Maybe that's how *you'd* feel. You don't look forward to business travel because you don't like to be away from home.

Your own feelings make you sympathetic. But empathy, real empathy, requires a second step: thinking *about* the other person. How does *his* "not looking forward" feel?

Maybe he's excited about being chosen to speak for the agency. It's a chance to show the boss he can handle more responsibility. But maybe that makes him nervous. Speaking in public is a lot harder when your agenda is trying to prove yourself.

Whether or not your partner gets to talk about these issues, to discover and share *his* feelings, depends on how empathically you listen. If you want to know how someone feels, ask, and then listen.

————◆————

Do you rely on sympathy and presume you understand, or do you use empathy and work at it?

————◆————

Suspending preconceived notions and remaining open to what the other person has to say is easier in the absence of conflict. Being at odds with someone means that you have your own agenda and the pressure of the situation makes you anxious to press your point of view. But since two force fields can't occupy the same space at the same time, even if your only objective is to get your point of view across, the most

effective way to do so is to set aside your assumptions and hear the other person out first—make him feel understood and taken into account. Here are a couple of examples:

A few years ago someone who was editing a book on psychoanalytic therapy changed jobs and asked me to take over for him. I was delighted—until I saw that most of the chapters weren't very good. It was hard for me, a young and relatively unknown psychologist, to convince the authors, who were big shots, to do the necessary work. One of the authors, however, who was junior even to me, called every week, asking how the book was coming and offering to be my co-editor. Then I read his chapter. It wasn't the worst, but it was weak. Trying to be diplomatic, I returned the manuscript, praising its strong points and asking for a few minor but essential changes. Three months went by. Then I received a letter thanking me for my "suggestions" but saying that a couple of his friends had read over his chapter and agreed with him that it was perfect the way it was.

Argh! After counting to ten (about twenty times), I wrote saying that he seemed to be upset about something and I was interested in hearing about it. He called the day he received my letter and told me with a lot of feeling how hard he'd worked on his chapter and how much rewriting the previous editor had already put him through. I didn't really have to say anything. He was so appreciative of my listening to him that as soon as he finished complaining he thanked me for being understanding and said he'd be glad to make the changes I'd asked for.

Frankly I hadn't really been interested in this man's feelings, but to be able to negotiate with him—all I really wanted—I had to hear him out first, or he never would have been receptive.

With someone you do care about, empathic openness is more than a useful strategy. It's the essential means of discovering what things look like from inside that person's world.

Linda *knew* Andrew didn't want to spend time with her. He was married to his career. That's why she'd developed so many outside interests over the years. Now that the children had gone off into the wide world, Linda began to sense the marriage entering its second death. Maybe it was time to turn off the life supports. She dreamed of freedom. What had she expected when she married? Attention, shared interests, affection, conversation. What she had was what she did on her own.

And Andrew? After years of career success, he was becoming a failure at loneliness. He longed to be closer to Linda, to share something more

than domestic arrangements. He dreamed of love. Unfortunately they'd gotten out of the habit of talking. He went about his business in the armor of indifference.

When Linda came to talk to me—maybe a therapist would tell her what she wanted to hear—I tried to point out one reason she felt stuck: she wasn't open to the possibility of trying to talk to her husband, trying to rekindle some basis for staying together other than sharing children.

Linda had assumed that nothing would change and so it would be a waste of time talking to Andrew. When Linda tried to open up and talk to Andrew, she found out he had just assumed she no longer wanted to be involved with him, so he didn't say anything.

Such assumptions are protective. They keep us from getting our hopes up and our feelings hurt. But they also keep us from getting through to each other.

Most of our assumptions about why communication breaks down are about the other guy. We take our own input for granted.

After their talk Linda and Andrew did get a little closer. Not a lot, but enough to make a difference. Shared understanding was the first step.

You can get through to most people, even on difficult subjects, by first listening to their side of the issue and then, in a low-key but firm manner, insisting that they at least listen to your side of things.

Openness may be the key to listening, but not total openness, as in a blank screen. Real receptivity must be informed by sensitivity to the other person.

SENSITIVITY: EXPECTATIONS AT THEIR BEST

One of the things we learn after a while—sometimes a long while—is that different people have different emotional needs. If, for example, you need time alone when you're stressed out, it might be hard to remem-

ber that in the same circumstances the first thing your partner wants is to talk. Different people also have different ways of communicating.

To listen well, and be listened to in return, we have to develop some sensitivity to other people's conversational styles. The automatic rhythms and nuances of a person's conversational style include such things as whether descriptions are detailed or summarized, whether the pace of speaking is fast or slow, and whether who-said-what-to-whom or what-I'm-working-on-now is the preferred topic.

To Naomi, loud, overlapping talk is a sign of enthusiasm and mutual involvement. To Wardell, it's a sign of rudeness and not listening.

Hannah asks for details; Ivan feels interrogated.

Rick wants Sherry to get to the point. She feels that he isn't interested in what she had to say.

Veronica likes to talk things over at length. She complains that Chet is always leaving the room. Chet replies that Veronica says something and he responds, then when he's on the way to finish what he was about to do, she gets mad.

Listening between intimates often erodes over time because the only way they know to solve problems is to talk things out. But when different styles of communicating cause problems, talking doesn't help. Trying harder, if it means doing more of the same, only makes matters worse.

People who try to communicate indirectly feel that someone close to them should know what they like and dislike without having to say so. Direct communicators feel, "We should be able to tell each other what we want."

Being sensitive to other people's conversational ways doesn't mean you have to have them all figured out. It means you should be attentive and tolerant. If you're used to a New York City pace and you're listening to a languid southern speaker whose conversation is like an old hound dog that stops at every tree, relax. Be patient. You might even get to enjoy your differences.

Unfortunately, when conversational styles differ, misunderstandings multiply. It's difficult to straighten out such misunderstandings if each one is convinced of the rightness of his or her position and the wrongness of the other's.

Belinda and her husband were at a New Year's Eve party at his parents' house. Halfway through the evening, Belinda's mother-in-law

came over and whispered, "Loosen up, have some fun. Don't be so formal!"

Belinda was cut to the quick. She had been having fun. She'd had several enjoyable conversations with her husband's cousins and aunts and uncles. She wasn't being formal; she was being herself.

Belinda was pissed. *Who does that woman think she is? Did I say anything to her about cackling hysterically whenever anybody made the slightest joke?* In fact, Belinda found the mother-in-law's loud show of emotion and high-pitched, relentless chatter quite annoying. It wasn't her style.

Both of these people were behaving in self-evidently appropriate ways, the ways they were brought up to talk and listen.

Some people consider their restrained style of speaking to be "polite." They may find people with a more expressive style to be "crude," "loud," "coarse," "histrionic," "vulgar." More emotive speakers may think of themselves as "open and honest," "warm," "friendly," "unaffected," while they think of the more restrained speakers as "aloof," "standoffish," "unfriendly," "distant," "emotionless."

(Notice, incidentally, how Belinda and her mother-in-law each addressed their differences in character. The mother-in-law was "honest" or "rude," depending on your point of view. Belinda was "polite" or "insincere," as you see it.)

Sensitivity means being responsive to the feelings of others. It doesn't mean assuming you know what they're going to say, but rather being interested and open enough to find out. On the other hand, sensitivity does mean using your knowledge of other people to understand their perspective and respect their individuality.

Some of the ways you can show sensitivity are:

- Paying attention to what the other person is saying
- Acknowledging the other person's feelings
- Listening without giving an opinion
- Listening without offering advice
- Listening without immediately agreeing or disagreeing
- Noticing how the other person appears to be feeling—and then asking
- Asking about his or her day, both before and after
- Respecting the person's need for quiet times
- Respecting the person's need to address problems
- Listening to but not pushing too hard for feelings

Maybe you *won't* get through to the other person as long as you keep approaching him the same way you always do.

We're Most Insensitive to Those We Love

What makes someone insensitive to what others are saying? To figure out why a listener becomes reactive instead of listening, consider where the anxiety might be coming from. It's always something specific. Sometimes the anxiety comes from stress—real or imagined. People resist both actual and threatened change. We think of powerful people as dominating relationships and perhaps therefore as not willing to listen, but in fact it's often the powerless who have trouble listening. The man who feels that he can't get his point of view across about the children may resist his wife's efforts to talk about them. The woman who doesn't feel entitled to say what she wants (or doesn't want) may resist her husband's attempts to talk about sex. Most people begin to listen better once they realize what power they do have in a relationship.

On the other hand, sometimes a person who clearly seems to have power in a relationship—a parent, say, or a dominating spouse— habitually doesn't listen to the other person. When a dominant person doesn't listen it's usually because some hidden emotional agenda is at work, making him anxious.

One afternoon Tommy came home from a long day at school with so much restless energy that he decided to mow the lawn. The machine plowed into the deep grass, releasing its familiar sweet smell. But Tommy hadn't gone ten feet when the mower stalled, its blade clogged with high, wet grass. After several frustrating starts and stops, he shoved the insubordinate machine back into the garage, stomped into the house cursing and banging, went up the stairs into his room, and slammed the door.

By this time Tommy's parents were home and heard his outburst. When his father asked him what was the matter, Tommy told him about his lousy day at school, then coming home and the lawn mower not working. He was frustrated and angry.

Instead of empathizing, his father gave him a lecture. "When you have a problem, it doesn't do anybody any good to lose control and start yelling. You have to stop and be calm. Nothing gets accomplished

when you get upset." As his father went on, Tommy's head sank slowly toward his chest.

"You can't cut grass when it's a foot high and be in a hurry. You've got to go through it very, very slow. You can't bull your way through anything—including life."

Tommy tried to explain. "Yeah, but when you've had a bad day at school and you come home and everything goes wrong, your anger keeps building. You've got to let it out somehow."

"Remember what we talked about last night? About problems? What did I say?"

"You said you've got to swallow your tongue." Tommy had stopped looking for sympathy. Now he was just trying to hang on to some of his pride.

But his father wasn't finished. "I also told you that problems when they're compounded make bigger problems. But if you take that problem and break it down, and make individual problems out of it, you can usually solve them very easily. Remember we talked about that?"

Tommy finally gave up trying to explain himself, and the conversation was finished.

This is a story of a father's failure to listen. The father asks his son why he's upset and then, when the boy tries to tell him, instead of listening, gives him a speech on the futility of anger, a lecture for a course the boy didn't sign up for. Tommy attempts to explain his feelings because he's looking for understanding. Instead he becomes a captive audience forced to listen to an account of his own inadequacies.

What's so hurtful in this encounter (and others like it) isn't that the father has a different perspective from his son; it's that, because of the feelings his son's behavior arouses in him, he tries to allay his own anxieties by pushing his perspective on the boy. In this scenario, Father knows best; Tommy's perspective carries no weight at all. It's never even acknowledged. The real impact of Father's lessons for living may be that Tommy grows up to be one of those people, like his father, with didactic views on everything—and unable to listen.

But *why* was Tommy's father so unable to listen to him explain that he was upset? What was so threatening? Anger.

Anger is a huge impediment to listening. Some people, like Tommy's father, are so reactive to anger that they can't tolerate even normal, healthy amounts of this basic human emotion. Other people are just the opposite: at the slightest provocation they flare up like a lit

match. In the next chapter we'll see how to cope with anger and how to keep it from spoiling listening.

Sensitivity to Other People's Inner Voices

One of the most common consequences of failing to be sensitive to other people's motivating expectations is giving them unwanted advice. When you're tempted to give the obvious types of advice mentioned in Chapter 5, remember those conflicting inner voices. Doing so not only might stop you from wasting your breath (and credibility) but also may give you a fresh perspective on the person's motivations and how to approach him or her about a touchy issue.

What if the issue has already touched off a tirade? The ideal response to the partner who goes into a rage about something is to acknowledge what he's feeling. Something's bothering him, and he's trying to tell you that. But there are times when most of us find listening to someone who's shrieking at us almost impossible. And so the question becomes not how to defuse the blowup but how to repair it afterward. That's when thinking about the other person's rage and your reaction in terms of subpersonalities can help you gain a little empathy and insight. Thinking of your partner's tirade as a childish tantrum may help you figure out that he feels weak and helpless, not powerful. Powerful people don't scream. But if screaming scares you (welcome to the club), when you calm down, if you consider what kind of person the screaming reduced you to (a scared kid, say), that in itself will help you recover your objective adult self when it comes to addressing the incident later.

"Have You Got a Minute?"

One way to use your sensitivity to *get* better listening is by not jumping in without considering whether or not the person you want to talk to is busy or preoccupied. People signal their openness to conversation by their posture. The person who looks up expectantly when you enter the room or walks right up to you with a greeting is probably open to talking. The person with her head down, looking away when you approach, or reading, intent on the TV, or otherwise distracted may not feel like chatting. If you really want to talk to such a person, use an orienting question. "Have you got a minute?" "Can I interrupt? There's something I'd like to ask you." It's like knocking to enter.

Recently Seymour started getting home from work an hour earlier. On the first day of the new schedule he looked forward to having a

chance to talk to his sixteen-year-old son before dinner. He came in the door and called hi, but there was no answer. Too bad, Jeremy must have stayed after school. But then a few minutes later, he heard Jeremy's radio on upstairs.

Seymour climbed halfway up the stairs and called out, "Hey, Jeremy, it's me, Dad. Come on downstairs. I want to talk to you."

A few moments later Jeremy came into the living room and said, "What did I do now?"

Seymour felt bad. Is that what their relationship had come to?

No, not really. Jeremy just felt off guard and misconstrued what his father meant. So now on days when he expects to be home early or wants to spend some time with Jeremy on the weekend, Seymour says something to him in the morning. "I'll be home by around five-thirty. Maybe we can visit before supper."

――――◆――――

Expectations about how and when communication should take place work not when they're right or wrong but when they're shared.

――――◆――――

"I HEARD YOU THE FIRST TIME!"

As we've seen, some of the assumptions about different ways men and women communicate have more to do with roles they play in relation to one another than to anything intrinsic to their sexes. Still, few complaints are more common from men than that the women in their lives nag.

Whenever a woman is perceived by a man as nagging, it probably means she hasn't received a fair hearing for her concerns in a long time. When our feelings are listened to sympathetically, we experience a sense of understanding and release. But if no one listens, we feel alone with our feelings and angry and unsupported in the relationship.

"He never notices how much I do around here. I never get any help without having to beg for it."

Not being listened to makes people feel ignored, frustrated, and resentful. No wonder they come across as nagging.

"She acts like she's my mother. Doesn't she know I always get my share of the chores done?"

Lloyd *hates* Cathy's nagging.

Stop leaving the bedroom window open; don't turn the heat up any higher than sixty-eight degrees. Do this, do that. She's always bitching about something. This he says to himself, and he gets no argument.

Cathy's bothered by the fact that Lloyd never listens to her. "Why do I have to tell you the same things over and over again? Why can't you listen to a simple request?" This she has said to him—often. To her friend Samantha she complains, "I try to tell him something, and he just goes underground, with no warning—and I'm left there, all alone."

If You're Considered a Nag

In a series of conversations between the same people, each encounter bears the burdens as well as the fruits of earlier ones. Persistent criticism or constant repetition of the same request creates a negative atmosphere and eventually results in the other person tuning the nagger out. I'm reminded of the Gary Larson cartoon in which a man is explaining something to his dog and all the dog hears is "blah-blah-blah."

The nagger becomes a nuisance. But what do you do if your persistent pleas to put dirty clothes in the hamper or clean up the mess in the bathroom go unheeded?

You're caught in the role of nag if even though you know somebody isn't going to remember to do something, you keep bugging him anyway; you never ask for anything just once; you come at the other person in a critical or complaining way; you get annoyed by lots of things the other person does *and* you keep letting him know it; you appeal to what "should" be done rather than what you want; the other person flinches when you make your request. You may not think of yourself as nagging, but if that's how the other person feels, he or she isn't likely to listen.

Here are some turnoffs that turn you into a nag: trying to improve your partner's behavior; offering unasked-for advice; trying to manipulate or punish; not acknowledging what he does, only complaining about what he hasn't done; expressing upset indirectly with an accusation that the other person should know how you feel.

---◆---

Nagging is in the ear of the beholder.

---◆---

Cut down on the number of things you ask people to do and the number of times you remind them. No fair, you say? You have a right to gripe? True, but asking less results in getting more. Pick out your most important concerns, make your requests clearly and directly, and make them sound like requests.

Listening is hard because it involves a loss of control, and if you're afraid of what you might hear, it may not feel safe to listen. Among the things that someone who feels nagged (even though he didn't listen the first twelve times) doesn't want to hear are blame and requests he doesn't think are open to discussion.

In all our communications we struggle to maintain our independence, to resist being controlled by others without sacrificing our involvement or losing their love. If someone hears your requests or complaints as implying power over him, he may resist—not because he's unwilling to do what you ask but because he's unwilling to accept the metamessage (implied or inferred) that you're the boss.

To avoid sounding controlling or dogmatic, add "What do you think?" after making a request or giving an opinion. This helps keep the airways open and the dialogue going. Also, emphasize how important the request is to you and be sure to understand the other person's perspective—"What do you think?" Then make sure that an agreement is really an agreement. If you aren't willing to accept "no," you can't trust the "yes" you do get.

People other than our intimates are more likely to listen to us airing our frustrations because they know it isn't their fault. If you want to get heard around the house more, try telling your partner "I know it's not your fault" or "I'm not blaming you." Then if he (or she) does listen, let him (or her) know you appreciate being listened to. "I feel relieved that I can talk about this. Thanks for listening."

Saying "I really appreciate when you listen to my feelings; it means a lot to me" encourages other people to listen more.

Finally, if you want to get out of the role of a nag, try listening to the recalcitrant other's side of things. Maybe the teenager who never cleans her room doesn't think it's fair to have to. After all, it's her room, isn't it? The husband who persists in running the washing machine with less than a full load may feel that he has a right to do so if he wants. Perhaps the wife whose husband always has to remind her to buy beer

when she gets groceries doesn't want to bring her husband beer—either because she wishes he would drink less or because she's resentful about something else.

Even if you don't agree with someone's reasons for not complying with your requests, he or she will feel a whole lot more like compromising if you listen to and acknowledge that point of view.

If You Are Nagged

Those who feel nagged are often people who have trouble saying no. If a woman asks her husband or teenage son to take out the garbage, but it doesn't get done unless she issues several reminders, probably there was a false sense of agreement to do it in the first place. Some people should say no more often.

HOW TO GIVE CRITICISM WITHOUT STARTING A FIGHT

Directly related to nagging is criticizing. The problem is that your expectations, often quite legitimate, that things should be different may provoke an unwanted flare-up if the other person feels demeaned by what you say.

First decide if what the other person does that bothers you has a direct effect on you. Leaving dirty dishes around the house does, especially if you're the one who has to clean them up; your partner's ten extra pounds doesn't (unless you happen to own his or her body).

Consider your relationship to the person you're criticizing. It's one thing to tell your twelve-year-old that you want the lawn mowed more often than twice a month. Telling the same thing to your husband (or wife) may make him react with *Who does she think she is, my mother?*

Partners who expect to be treated like adults may not take kindly to being told how to fold the laundry, load the dishwasher, or park the car. If you want these things done differently, maybe you should do them yourself.

If you do decide you have a right to complain, consider whether or not the person is likely to change. Research has proven that, if properly motivated, people can learn to put their dishes in the sink. But few people lose weight or start exercising just because someone else thinks they should.

If you've told your son a thousand times not to leave his dirty dish-

es in the living room, maybe you should let it go. Maybe it's better to give up on some things—even if it's "not fair," "not right"—than continue to play out the role of constant critic, a voice against which the husband-in-training learns to deafen himself.

How you express criticism is also important. Alert the person that you want to talk.

"Something is bugging me, and I need to talk to you. How about tonight after work?"

"I have a problem and I need to discuss it with you. Can we go for a walk after supper?"

Advance notice allows a person to realize that something's coming and she'd better be prepared. Be sensitive to time and place. The best time to talk about difficult issues is when both of you are calm and relaxed. And alone.

That criticism is best given in private may seem obvious, but many parents continue to humiliate their children by mentioning their faults in front of their friends or siblings. Another version of the same mistake is praising a child's friends (with implied invidious comparison) in front of the child. Using personal comparisons to make criticisms ("Why can't you be more like . . . ?") makes a person feel judged, usually unfairly.

Some spouses take advantage of being out with another couple to criticize their partners. Often they make a joke out of their comments. It isn't funny.

Telling someone "I have a problem" and "I need your help," even if your problem is about something he or she is doing, is far more likely to be heard than direct criticism. Least likely to be heard is criticism framed as blame, put-downs, moralizing, or invidious comparisons.

"Why must you always . . . ?"

"You never. . . . "

"You should. . . . "

"Why can't you be more like . . . ?"

Emphasize your feelings, not the other person's shortcomings: "I feel bad that you don't get more dressed up when we go out. I feel more special when you wear your good clothes." This approach works better than, "Why do you always have to be so grungy when we go out?"

Describe how the situation is affecting you rather than being accusatory. Stick to behavior and make it clear that you're talking about
what you like and don't like, not what's right and wrong. Focus on how
the other person can help rather than on what he or she is doing wrong.

Even if you're the one with the complaint, remember to give the
other person a turn. Mention your concern, but before elaborating, ask
her how she feels about it. Don't get reactive even if the other person
gets defensive. Remember, you've just told her there's something wrong
with what she's doing.

If you ask someone to make a change, and he agrees without saying much, he's less likely to follow through than if you ask about and
acknowledge why he may not want to change or why changing might
be hard for him.

Wendy told Hank that she needed more help chauffeuring the kids
to all their activities. He agreed. But Wendy went further and said,
"I know you don't feel like it; otherwise you'd volunteer more often.
When do you feel *least* like driving?"

Hank really appreciated this consideration of his feelings. (Feeling
like it's OK to say no made it a lot easier to say yes.) He said he didn't
mind taking the kids places on weekends or early in the evening, but
he hated going out after nine on work nights. He also mentioned that
it's a lot easier for him if he knows a day in advance that he has to
drive them somewhere.

Then Wendy went one step further and asked, "Anything else?"

Hank paused. Then he said, "Yes, there is. Frankly, I think you
drive them far too many places. I don't think we should drive them
wherever and whenever they want to go."

Wendy, who hadn't know Hank felt this way, said that the next
time he disagreed he should say something. If she's willing to take them
anyway, even if he isn't, she'll do the driving. "But," she added, "maybe
you're right. Maybe I do drive them around too much."

On the way out of the movie theater, Ralph turned to Carmen and
said, "Wow, that was really a stinker, wasn't it?" He went on to describe
a basically good idea ruined by Robin Williams's overacting and the
director's sanctimonious moralizing.

Carmen didn't say anything. She'd enjoyed the movie. She loved
Robin Williams. Now Hank's running the picture down was ruining
it for her.

Since Carmen was the one who wanted to see this picture, she felt as if Hank was criticizing her taste and that while she was enjoying herself he had been having a lousy time.

In fact, Hank hadn't thought of this movie as Carmen's choice. She may have mentioned it first, but he too had wanted to see it. And he hadn't had a lousy time. Far from it. He enjoyed laughing with parts of the movie, and he enjoyed laughing at some of its excesses.

What should you say on your way out of a movie you didn't like, when you're with someone who apparently did? Nothing.

If two people both hate a movie or concert, their saying so brings them together. Shared experience, shared sensibilities. But if you enjoyed the performance, hearing someone else pick it apart spoils your fun.

Criticism of the movie or restaurant we liked feels like criticism of our taste. If you thought the food was lousy or the play was boring but sense that your companion liked it, let him savor his enjoyment. Save your criticism for later. Much later.

SELF-REFLECTIVE OBSERVATION

Tolerance and consideration of others help make you sensitive enough to be a better listener. But even more important is developing some capacity for self-reflective awareness. When you have trouble hearing someone or getting someone to hear you, step back and try to see the process of communication between the two of you as just that—a *process* of communication between the two of you. You'll need to get beyond thinking about personalities to thinking about specific behavior. And you'll need to get beyond the linearity of thinking that the other person *makes* you respond the way you do to seeing the process as circular.

Say that your teenage son never talks to you. Oh, he'll let you know when he needs new sneakers or a ride to a party, but you miss the talks you used to have when he was younger. Now he's so sullen. You can write your son's uncommunicativeness off to adolescence if you like, or you can try to think of it as part of a circular process.

To reflect on your part in the process, ask yourself what might stimulate reticence and what might reinforce it. Do you bug him about things that every teenager keeps private, like which of his friends smokes marijuana or drinks beer at parties? Do you bombard him with questions when he wants to retreat to the sanctuary of his room? And when he does

open up, do you listen respectfully to his opinions, or do you argue with everything he says?

How Well Do You Listen to Yourself?

The respect for other people's feelings that makes you listen to them can be turned around to yourself.[2] How well do you respect your own right to think and feel what you do? How well do you listen to yourself?

Kate suffered from chronic headaches but had given up going to doctors because it never did any good. None of them ever figured out what was wrong, and few of them even bothered to listen carefully to her complaints. Finally, at her sister's urging, she decided to go the headache clinic at a leading hospital in Boston.

One of the tests they did was a CAT scan of her brain. Afterward, Kate waited anxiously for the radiologist who would explain the results. When he finally arrived, it was clear that he was rushed. He introduced himself, but Kate didn't catch his name. Then he showed her the pictures from the CAT scan, and she pointed to a small white spot on the film. "That's just a normal calcification of your pineal gland," he said, "nothing to worry about."

As the doctor was preparing to leave, Kate felt unsatisfied and wished the conversation could have gone on a little longer. But she wasn't sure how to frame her questions and was embarrassed that she didn't remember the doctor's name.

Halfway out the door, the doctor turned and said, "Any other questions?"

Kate answered in a subdued voice, "No."

Kate heard the doctor's anxiousness to leave. But she was far less well tuned in to her own needs. Her fear and uncertainty, combined with the doctor's rushed manner, had created a cloud of fog surrounding her own needs.

———◆———

If you don't listen to yourself, it's unlikely that anyone else will.

———◆———

[2]And vice versa.

Listening to yourself means not only respecting your own feelings but also getting to know something about your own ways of communicating. This isn't always easy, and it isn't always pleasant.

I, for example, have learned that I have a penchant for making jokes and wisecracks in social situations. Maybe some of my jokes are funny, but they're often distracting. Joking around may be a defense against social anxiety, but it's also a convenient outlet for fast-paced, restless energy. Whatever the reasons for it, though, there are times when I have to make an effort to suppress the wise remarks that pop into my head.

You may find it easier to think of other people's conversational habits that you wish they would become aware of. But the effort to understand your own ways and habits will enable you to relate much more effectively to other people, regardless of what they do.

CHAPTER NINE

"I Can See This Is Really Upsetting You"

HOW TO DEFUSE EMOTIONAL REACTIVITY

We come now to the number-one reason people don't listen: reactive emotionalism. As we saw in Chapter 6, when someone says something that triggers emotional attack or withdrawal, understanding goes out the window. If listening without acknowledging what the other person says turns discussions into conversational Ping Pong, overreacting can turn them into the Battle of the Bulge. If the war metaphor seems melodramatic, take inventory of your emotions next time an escalating series of attacks and counterattacks leaves you feeling wounded and bleeding in a dozen places.

Some people are so provocative that it's almost impossible to listen to them without getting upset. But after a while you may begin to discover that regardless of what other people say, your real problem is how you react.

And what about those thin-skinned individuals who fly off the handle at the slightest sign of criticism? Sure, they're overreactive, but unless your relationship to them is expendable, your challenge is finding a way to get through to them.

EMPATHY TURNS DEFENSIVENESS AROUND

Defensiveness is a paradox of the human condition: our survival and security seem to depend on self-assertion and defense, but intimacy and cooperation require that we risk being vulnerable. All human communication—whether in business dealings or personal relationships—reflects this tension between self-expression (talking) and mutual recognition (listening).

Nearly everyone is insecure to some extent. Therefore, when we feel threatened, even (or especially) emotionally, we tend to react defensively rather than opening ourselves to the other person's point of view.

One reason people pay thousands of dollars to psychotherapists is simply to be listened to. (Good therapists may do more than just listen, but they certainly do no less.) When people talk to a therapist about their troubles, the therapist doesn't (usually) feel blamed and therefore doesn't get defensive. When we talk to the people we're close to about our upsets, they feel implicated. That's why the response we get is often reactive, "No! Don't feel that way." An accepting, nonreactive response feels like "Yes? Is that how you feel?" or "Tell me more" or "What's that like for you?"

Empathy and tenderness are permission giving. Receptive, nondefensive listeners allow us to get our feelings out. They welcome unpopular parts of ourselves to speak (which allows us to do the same for ourselves). They know that even on those occasions when what we're saying about them may not be true, our feelings are.

Feelings are facts to the person experiencing them.

The simple—and often enormously difficult—act of not becoming reactive has a tremendous impact on relationships. It enables difficult people to be heard—and it empowers us to remain in control of ourselves no matter what the pressure. So let's consider how to reduce reactive emotionalism, in ourselves when we're doing the listening, and in others when we're doing the talking.

HOW TO RESIST REACTING EMOTIONALLY WHEN PROVOKED

Every so often Nadine takes out her frustration in the form of an emotional outburst about Tim's many failings:

"You're selfish and inconsiderate."

"You *never* think of anyone but yourself."

"You don't care about me; all you ever want to do is fuck me!"

Tim can't stand these outbursts. *If she's so unhappy, why can't she just say so without calling me every name in the book? If she wants something from me, why doesn't she ever ask for it, instead of expecting me to read her mind?* He tries to listen to her complaints, but by the time she's through dumping on him he just wants to go away and hide.

When Gordon complains about her handling of the kids, Jane gets furious. First he leaves everything to her, then he criticizes her for doing what she thought was right. He's always right, and she's always wrong. So she let's him know just how she feels.

All four people in these two examples have a right to their feelings. The trouble is, no one is listening. To listen without flying off the handle, you must develop the ability to tolerate a certain amount of anxiety—and to resist the "fight or flight" urge.

Don't Jump to Respond—Listen Harder

The trouble with the famous advice, "Don't get defensive" is that it's a lot harder to *stop* doing something than to *start* doing something else. If you're trying to cut down on coffee, it's easier to pour yourself a cup of tea than to sit there not drinking coffee. If want to cut down on junk food, it's easier to grab a carrot than to try to avoid the urge to rip open the potato chips. If want to cut down on emotional reactivity, concentrate on listening harder.

If either or both of the examples just given sound familiar, you probably know how it feels to be berated in an angry, assaultive way or found fault with by someone who's better at criticizing than helping. But getting reactive only makes things worse. Tim thinks his problem is Nadine's breathtaking exaggerations, one-sided view of things, and emotional explosions. But a fuller description of the problem would be that when Nadine feels ignored she tries not to say anything until she can't stand it anymore and then her feelings come pouring out—*and* Tim isn't able either to pick up her signals of unhappiness before she explodes or to listen when she does blow up without getting hurt and angry and pulling away. Likewise, Jane's problem isn't just that Gordon leaves the children to her and then complains about her handling of them. Her re-

action—getting mad and counterattacking—is part of what keeps Gordon from getting more involved.

———◆———

A full description of any listening problem always includes both parties. Ultimately, what defeats us isn't the provocative speaker but our own defensive response.

———◆———

The best way to develop awareness of and control over your emotionality is by having the courage to engage emotionally intense situations and tolerating the anxiety and internal emotional reactivity associated with that engagement. Avoiding such encounters affords only an illusion of self-containment.

Ginny didn't call her mother from college after being a passenger in a car accident because she didn't want to have to deal with her mother's frantic questions and exaggerated concern. So she burdened herself with another secret and further reinforced her own inability to deal with other people's overconcern.

Learn to resist the impulse to act out your automatic and habitual response—arguing, blaming, rebelling, dominating, or accommodating to achieve peace at any price. These automatic responses are driven by anxiety and designed to mask it by avoiding issues and defying, controlling, ignoring, or appeasing others. The courage to engage people and situations you might prefer to avoid, and learning to contain your own particular reactive reflexes, leads over time to a reduction in your level of chronic anxiety.

Even if you work on lowering the level of your emotional reactivity, sometimes the burden of listening becomes difficult to bear unless you find a way to become actively involved. The ideal way to become engaged in listening is to concentrate on the task, to be attentive, curious, and concerned. I'd call this *active* listening except that shopworn expression suggests a kind of chatty show of interest, a pretense of concern, as sincere as a car salesman's smile.

———◆———

Really listening means taking interest, not showing it.

———◆———

You can go a long way toward improving your ability to listen (and be listened to in return) by simply making a concerted effort to concentrate on what the other person is trying to communicate.

In Chapter 6, I used the example of hostile questions to illustrate how emotional reactivity escalates when an exchange starts out with provocation. Something the speaker says (or maybe it's just sitting there being lectured to) makes someone in the audience restive, and he attacks the speaker in the sublimated form of a question.

"Excuse me," said the eminent French deconstructionist, Claude Nasal-Passages, who just happened to be in the audience, "but isn't everything you've just said total blather and you're full of nothing but helium?" In big words, of course.

Unfortunately, having just stood up in front of an audience for an hour or so pouring out their ideas, some speakers get a little touchy at such moments. And I've noticed (in other speakers, you understand) a certain unfortunate tendency to respond in kind.

"Well, yes, Professor Nasal-Passages, that's an intriguing point. But you're a complete ass, and so is the horse you rode in on." Big words, again.

A better way to respond to hostile questions is to apply Formula Number One for Resisting Reactivity: hear the other person out. Instead of agreeing or disagreeing, invite the questioner to say more. Hostile inquisitors aren't really asking a question but just want to say something. So let them. The same strategy works to keep reactivity from escalating in everyday conversations.

Here's how a friend of mine used this advice to reduce the antagonism that was starting to poison his second marriage.

When Rob married Carla, they got along wonderfully well except when it came to Rob's daughter, Melanie. According to Carla, Rob spoiled her, among other things lending her money and letting her have the car whenever she wanted, even though she didn't always bring it back when she said she would. But whenever Carla raised any objection, Rob felt she was attacking his child, and so instead of listening (not necessarily agreeing, just listening), he fought back. Many second marriages are broken on this very issue.

When Rob realized that the situation had reached the point of crisis, he resolved at least to listen to Carla the next time she complained about Melanie. Two days later he got his chance. Melanie promised to have the car back by eight so Carla could go shopping, but she didn't get home until nine-thirty, after the stores were closed. When Carla complained to Rob, he felt his stomach knotting and the counterarguments surging in his mind. But instead of getting defensive, he said what

he'd prepared himself to say: "Tell me more." Carla said that overindulgence wasn't doing Melanie any good. Rob, sticking to his resolve not to judge or interrupt, kept listening, and Carla went on. She talked about how hard it was feeling like an outsider in her own house. She knew that Rob and Melanie had a special relationship, and she respected that. She had no wish to play Melanie's mother or tell Rob what to do. She just wanted to be able to talk to him when she felt concerned.

Having determined not to defend himself or argue, Rob found it remarkably easy to listen—that is, after he checked the rising emotions that Carla's first few sentences triggered in him. He stopped hearing in Carla the overbearing voice of his ex-wife, who was always so critical of the children, and started hearing how left out his new wife was feeling. Moreover, because he really listened this time, he was able to hear that Carla wasn't insisting that he change anything, just asking him to listen to her point of view. After that, things changed. They didn't always agree about how to respond to Melanie, but now that Rob knew that he could listen to Carla's opinion without necessarily following it, their differences ceased to divide them.

Anticipate and Plan for Tense Encounters

The best way to defuse reactivity is to avoid becoming reactive yourself, something more easily said than done. One thing that helps is planning, as Rob was able to do once he realized how serious his breach with Carla was becoming. You can anticipate many of the conflictual conversations in your life. If you stop to think about what the boss or your teenager is likely to say that triggers your anxiety, you can plan not to flare up in defensive fight or flight. Anticipation frees you from overreacting.

One way to remain calm is by schooling yourself to ask questions instead of reacting emotionally to the usual provocations. This is a variation of the "tell me more" strategy. Another effective way to tone down emotionality is to practice responding to rhetorical questions and sarcasm literally, instead of being provoked by their inflammatory implications into a defensive retort.

"Don't you ever think about anything but sex?"
"No, it's kind of a hobby with me. Like woodworking."

"Must you pick on every little thing I say?"
"Yes, all in the service of helping you become the perfect person I know you're capable of being."

How to Understand a Speaker's Anger

When those we care about start to cry, we have an urge to comfort them so they'll stop. Somehow, we equate the crying with the pain. In fact, crying isn't pain; it's the way people express and release that pain. The same is true with expressions of anger (even if it's a little harder to keep that in mind).

I once watched a therapist interviewing a middle-aged couple five years into a second marriage. They were having a hard time deciding how to balance their obligations to ten children and twenty grandchildren and an even harder time keeping the discussion from turning into a shouting match. They were so volatile that neither one could say anything without the other one losing it. As the wife was saying her piece and starting to go on and on, rehashing the past and finding fault, her husband's foot started twitching ominously. Sitting behind the one-way mirror, I felt apprehensive and helpless. I could see an explosion building but couldn't do anything about it.

Then the therapist, bless him, did exactly what needed to be done. He acknowledged what the wife had said and then let the husband speak—being careful to direct the husband's response to himself, who could listen, not to his wife, who at that point couldn't. Even so, the husband exploded. With hot emotion he refuted what his wife said and explained the truth of things as he saw it. But as he talked—with his wife blocked from responding—he calmed down noticeably. His jaw relaxed, the tension went out of his shoulders, and his foot stopped twitching. Not having a chance to express his anger made it build. Expressing it, *even in an angry way*, released his anger.

The hard part will be teaching this couple to hear each other out without flying off the handle so that they can learn to diffuse their own anger. It's one thing to understand that expressing anger helps detoxify it; it's another thing to be on the receiving end and try to remain calm.

The wife in the couple I observed is angry because her husband doesn't understand her point of view. She thinks one of the children, who happens to be her son, needs some financial assistance. Her husband is jealous of the attention she pays this son and feels she's neglecting him. "He's twenty-three years old. He can take care of himself." But it isn't disagreeing that causes their problems; it's getting reactive and shouting at each other. If he would concentrate on understanding what she's *feeling* and not allow himself to react defensively, he'd understand that she's worried about her boy. She might or might not actually decide to give him some money; that's just an idea, a way of expressing

her concern. Her husband's not really upset about the money but about not getting as much attention as he used to. Unfortunately, instead of talking about his feelings, he blames her for them.

---◆---

When feelings of not being understood come out as anger, hearing them, not shutting your ears or fighting back, is the key to calming things down.

---◆---

To defuse angry confrontations, don't blame the other person for upsetting you. Start by trying to understand his feelings. (Save yours for the moment. Later, after the other person feels heard, express your feelings *as your feelings*, not as something the other person is doing to you.)

Feelings don't always make sense right away, and they may come out in global and critical ways at first. It's easier to hear feelings that don't come out this way, *but if they do*, remember that they are *feelings*, not scientific statements of fact. Don't yell back, call the other person names, or bring up old issues.

---◆---

Don't tell angry people to calm down. Doing so only makes them feel like you're denying their right to be upset.

---◆---

You don't have to agree to understand your angry partner's point of view. And you don't have to understand completely to be able at least to listen and try. The harder you try to listen and acknowledge what the other person is saying, the more likely you are to understand how he or she feels.

Remember: You aren't responsible for what other people feel. Even if they blame you, what they really need is to be understood.

If someone snaps at you in an angry, assaultive way, how do you get beyond listening with a clenched mind? The obvious answer is to listen through the emotional static to what the person is trying to say. But some things are bigger than they look from a distance. When the level of frustration and anger that some people live with spills out into the relationship, our natural response is to become anxious and defensive. Learning to listen to someone who comes at you in such an intense, urgent way isn't easy. One thing that may help free you from withdrawing into a defensive posture is to hear in the anxious speaker the voice of an unhappy child demanding to be heard. That, after all,

is the part of ourselves where our most urgent feelings come from. Even though the person trying to get through to you may come off sounding nasty, he or she is hurting and needs desperately to be heard.

If, instead of focusing on the speaker and how difficult he or she is, you can focus on your own efforts to listen and avoid overreacting, the anxiety in the relationship will begin to abate. Anxiety is like electrical current. It requires conduction and amplification. If you listen and endeavor to stay cool, the angry person will feel heard and begin to calm down.

In heated discussions, repeating the other person's position in your own words shows that you understand and interrupts your own defensive response. If the heat gets so intense that you start to boil over, try squeezing your thumb and index finger together, hard. This is nothing but a momentary distraction (less hazardous to your health than "biting your tongue"), but it does allow you to channel and release tension in a way you can control.

If that doesn't work, or an emotionally reactive speaker is dumping on you and it's too upsetting, you may have to protest. Doing so before you get too upset, and without attacking, keeps your anger from boiling over: "I'm sorry, but I can't listen to this right now. I'm too upset. We'll have to talk later."

How to Take Criticism without Overreacting

He says, "You're always late."
She says, "You're always rushing me."
One point for him. One point for her. Total score: zero.

Allowing the other person to spell out his or her point of view before responding with yours is especially important and especially difficult when that someone is criticizing you. If you start to get reactive, ask yourself, Does the other person have a sincere concern about this issue? If the answer is yes, keep listening.

If your spouse complains about where you park in the driveway, you might consider that he or she has a legitimate stake in the matter. If, on the other hand, he or she criticizes how you talk to your boss, you might remember that how you decide to talk to your boss is your business. Come to think of it, remembering that might make it easier to at least listen to your partner's point of view.

If someone has a criticism of you, stay with that concern; don't switch to a different criticism of your own. Avoid cross-complaining.

"Oh yeah? Well, what about you? You never take out the garbage when I ask you to."

"I don't care if you don't like what's for supper. Maybe if you cleaned up your room once in a while like I asked, I'd feel more like cooking something you like."

After you've allowed your critic to spell out his or her complaint, agree with whatever you can or at least show appreciation for his or her concern.

"Yes, I have been a little grouchy lately. I'm sorry."

"So you think I've been favoring Cindy over Joshua?"

"Yes, I did run over your prize Pomeranian in the driveway. I'll get you a new one."

OK, so I'm saying that when someone starts to criticize you, the best thing to do is to hear him out and acknowledge his point of view before defending yourself. But isn't that a little like saying that losing ten pounds is easy—all you have to do is cut out sweets? When someone starts in on you, especially someone close to you, it isn't easy to smile and nod and say, "Oh, so you think I'm a selfish and insensitive species of barnyard animal? I see. Could you say a little more about that?"

Listening to criticism is one of the hardest things any of us ever has to do. Unfortunately, erupting, although it may be understandable, only makes things worse. To prevent yourself from doing so, train yourself to listen responsively—pay attention, appreciate what the critical other is saying, and acknowledge it. This takes practice, but in time it can become a habit. The positive effort to listen helps prevent you from becoming reactive.

Focus on the issue. Try to hear in the criticism something the other person is asking you to modify rather than a rejection or condemnation of your self. One way to help you focus on the distinction between a request and an attack is to invite the other person to explain how it bothers her.

When Sid told Nancy, "I wish we didn't have to have fish every week," she started complaining about how picky he is. "You're always

complaining," she said. "For a while there you wouldn't eat meat; now that's *all* you want."

Sid was stung. He *never* complained about what Nancy cooked. He just hated the fish she served. *Didn't he have a right to say what he liked? Wasn't it better to be honest?* This kind of internal dialogue is precisely what prevents us from appreciating the other person's point of view and what fuels the likelihood of a reactive response.

If Sid could listen to Nancy for a minute, instead of to his own hurt feelings, he might realize that it's a big job figuring out what to serve for supper every night. Add in the complication of having to accommodate spouses' and children's preferences, and that those preferences change over time, and he might begin to understand what his wife was up against. If she expresses herself with "excessive" annoyance (Sid thinks: *All I said was I wish we didn't have to have fish*), that's a sign of stored-up resentment.

What if, despite all your efforts to be a good, empathic listener, the criticism comes out as a vituperative attack?

If criticism is given in a nasty or offensive way, you have a right to react to the manner in which the message was expressed. If you can't listen to someone who berates you in an assaultive way, simply state what put you off.

"I don't appreciate being called stupid" (or compared to my mother or called a bitch or a son of one).

"I'll try to listen to your suggestion if you can say it in a less nasty way."

Actually, the word *nasty* is name-calling. Better to be concrete: "I'll try to listen to your suggestion if you can say it without telling me how selfish I am"—or "if you give me some idea of what you want instead of saying what a terrible person I am."

Will such remarks calm things down and allow the two of you to understand each other? Probably not. But sometimes you have to recognize your limits and let other people know what they are too. Even if telling someone that you can't hear him when he screams at you only makes him angrier at the moment, maybe he'll think about what you said later.

"Why Does He [or She] Have
to Talk Everything to Death?"

Jackie wishes twenty-four hours would go by without Fred's complaining about how nobody appreciates him at the office. Sometimes she feels like screaming. If he wasn't so preoccupied with himself and his precious career, maybe he'd get a little more appreciation from her and the kids. She doesn't say so, of course. He'd only get mad and sulk for a couple of days. So whenever Fred starts in on topic number one, Jackie just sits there in pained silence.

Sam wishes Cheryl would stop launching into a diatribe every time she feels overwhelmed by taking care of the house and the kids. It isn't that she doesn't have a right to complain, he thinks; it's the way she goes on and on about everything. Sometimes he tries to be sympathetic, but it isn't easy. She'll say the house is a mess or the kids are a pain, and then she'll just keep talking and talking, covering every little detail without ever really getting to the point. The worst of it, as far as Sam is concerned, is that she's always complaining about the same things. " 'Suzie doesn't have any friends,' 'Suzie wasn't nice to so-and-so,' 'Suzie this,' 'Suzie that.' Why can't she leave the poor kid alone?"

The issues that come up over and over again represent people's core concerns. (*Their* core concerns, not necessarily your greatest shortcomings.) The more understood and accepted a person feels, the safer she feels to go deeper into these issues. The mechanical and repetitive feeling of some complaints stems partly from the fact that they rarely get a sympathetic hearing. Concerned and empathic listening is the greatest gift you can give to help the other person soothe her feelings. Fred's feeling that nobody appreciates his accomplishments and Cheryl's worries about the children will never be completely healed. That's why they need to talk about these issues again from time to time.

When someone close brings up a recurring issue, some people get upset and say something like "How many times do we have to go through this?" Such retorts make sense if you feel that the speaker's complaints mean that you're responsible or that it's your job to solve whatever problem the person is complaining about. But is it really your job to resolve your mother's complaints about your sister or your partner's complaints about the children? Once you understand that other people's talking about what's bothering them makes them feel better simply for

being listened to, you can relax, knowing that just listening without becoming reactive can make both of you feel better.

———◆———

Sharing problems makes people feel better. Listening is how we help them soothe themselves and how we build closer relationships.

———◆———

For those who can get beyond blaming others for "making them upset," discovering what triggers their sensitivity leads to the questions "Where does my emotional reactivity come from?" and "What can I do about it?"

GETTING TO THE ROOT OF REACTIVITY

Reactivity originates in anxiety over self-expression and the need to be understood. The more our parents listened, took us seriously, and respected our opinions and feelings, the more secure and self-possessed we became. The less they listened, the more intolerant and critical they were, the more insecure and anxious we became. The more conditioned we were to expect attack or argument, the more we learned to become defensive. What makes us defensive more than anything else are the things our parents did that made us feel criticized, argued with, or ignored.

What happens in your family when people get anxious? Do they get into shouting matches? Break off relations and avoid each other? That's your legacy.

As long as your parents are still alive, there's still time to revisit and revise your relationship with them. Making peace with your parents (and calming the part of you that still goes around ready for war) means being in emotional contact with them, being yourself, and letting them be themselves. Changing your relationship to them doesn't mean changing them; it means changing the way you react to them. Notice what they do that drives you crazy. Notice how you respond. That you can change. The more you learn to resist the urge to flare up in the face of their provocations, the more self-possessed and unflappable you'll become in all the rest of your relationships. When it comes to emotional reactivity, your parents are the final exam.

Systems are tenacious, resistant to change; or to put it in more human terms, your parents have a long history of relating to you in a cer-

tain way. If you try to change that, you will be tense and their reaction will be intense. Have a plan when you visit them. Remember that when you reenter the family's emotional force field, your ability to think about what's going on is impaired. So do your thinking beforehand. Formulate reasonable goals. When you do test a new way of behaving, start with small steps.

Remember Peggy from Chapter 5? She was the woman whose mother's negativism provoked her into shouting matches. If you recall, Peggy learned to see how her mother's negativism triggered her own rage—and how expecting it made her hypersensitive. Seeing this pattern was one thing; changing it was another.

When Peggy decided to stop trying to change her mother and learn to accept who she was, she began to realize that her mother wasn't really a mean person, just someone who prized family togetherness so much that she was threatened when people decided to go their own way. This simple shift in Peggy's view of her mother made it a lot easier for her to listen the next time she heard her mother criticizing someone in the family for doing something different. However, she also found that simply remaining silent only made her seethe. So instead of either holding her tongue or criticizing her mother (for being critical!) she started to say, as calmly as possible, that she could see how her mother saw it but that she didn't agree.

At first Peggy's effort to clarify where she stood, rather than criticize her mother, was lost on her mother. "Oh, so you think I'm all wrong, do you?"

Much to Peggy's credit, she was able to maintain a calm, nonreactive position, even if her insides were churning. She listened until her mother was through and didn't contradict her or fight back.

When Peggy finally did speak, she said, "No, Mom, you're not hearing me. I'm not saying you're all wrong. I don't think that at all. You have a right to your opinion. I'm just saying that my opinion is different, that's all."

In the ensuing months, as Peggy made an effort to continue to speak up calmly when she disagreed with her mother's violent opinions, she tried to make it clear that she was declaring her independence but not any lack of love or respect. On the contrary, as she learned to overcome her inability to tolerate her mother's criticism, the two women began to get much closer. Peggy still occasionally slipped back into blaming and distancing, but not for long, and when this happened, instead of thinking of her mother as impossible and herself as helpless, she real-

ized that she was just getting reactive again. That made it easier to control and easier to let go of.

She and her mother still argued from time to time, but now Peggy spoke up before her emotional intensity reached the boiling point. That and the fact that instead of criticizing her mother she made a point of simply clarifying where she stood made the arguments much less toxic.

After things calmed down between her and her mother, Peggy decided to work on communication with her father. Growing up, she'd thought of him as a distant and unapproachable presence, a large and benevolent shadow at the edge of the family circle. She remembered him sitting silently behind the newspaper while she and her mother fixed dinner or chatted at the breakfast table. Now she longed to be closer to him but didn't know how to go about it. How do you talk to a shadow? After she'd married and had children she made a concerted effort to get closer to him. He'd listen politely when she told him about the children's latest doings, but as soon as she said anything about her job or her friends, his eyes would drift in the direction of the television, or he'd suddenly remember something he had to do. As far as Peggy was concerned, he might as well have slapped her in the face.

What Peggy interpreted as rejection from her father was in fact anxiety about intimate conversation. Her efforts to get closer to him took the form of pursuing a distancer, a pattern she also played out with her husband.

Intimacy has levels of intensity, from simple contact, to chitchat about neutral subjects like the weather, to semipersonal topics, to personal conversations about things that are important to you, to talking about your relationship. Everyone gets anxious at some point on this scale; precisely where depends on you and whom you're with. Peggy's father just happened to be one of those people made anxious by even mildly intimate conversations with almost anyone. It wasn't that he didn't love his daughter; he just didn't know how to talk about it.

To get closer to her father, I advised Peggy to spend a little time alone with him—which meant gently pulling him out of hiding behind the television or newspaper and away from the grandchildren—and moving the conversation only very slowly from one level of intimacy to the next, stopping as soon as either one of them started to get anxious. Pushing her father past his comfort zone would only trigger his distancing reflex and leave Peggy feeling like a fisherman after the big one got away.

Peggy lowered her expectations and decided simply to spend some

time with her father, during which she would keep the conversation light. Her primary concern would be to avoid becoming anxious or making her father feel that way. She found her father remarkably receptive to this new nondemanding approach and on her next visit hoped to move the conversation to a slightly more personal level. She had complained that her father showed no interest in her life, but she now realized that she hadn't demonstrated any interest in his, either. I suggested that she try an opening that most people will respond to: "What are you working on these days?" or "What are your worries these days?"

Peggy's father welcomed his daughter's interest, and he reciprocated by showing more interest in what was going on in her world. Once or twice when she tried to talk to him about something that made him uncomfortable—like how his retirement money was holding out—he did his old disappearing act, and Peggy once again felt rejected. But now she no longer dwelled on this feeling, and it didn't last long. Her father never did become the kind of man she could really confide in, but he was after all her father, and she loved him. What's more, now that she'd come to terms with his nature, she realized how much he loved her.

The people close to you don't have any tricks up their sleeves. Their actions surprise you only because you keep looking for them to do what you wish they'd do or what you would do. They do what they do. Once you learn this, you can stop being surprised and upset. You can let them be who they are. You might as well; they will anyway.[1]

A relationship matures when you can allow the other person to be who he is. If your mother criticizes everybody *and* you can't accept this, your life may be dominated by your attempt to stop her (and everybody else, for that matter) from criticizing anything or anybody. Once you can let your mother be a person who's critical—in other words, accept that she is who she is—you don't have to fight it or organize your life around it.

———◆———

Once you accept that the people who push your buttons are who they are, you can stop trying to change them—and stop overreacting when they do *what they've always done*.

———◆———

[1] One of my patients, a 34-year-old married woman, once told me, without irony, that her father "could be a wonderful person, if only he were different."

Peggy's more relaxed approach to her parents didn't stop her mother from being critical or her father from being withdrawn, but it did make her a whole lot less reactive to them—and to the other people in her life who touched the same raw nerves.

Making peace with your parents moves you closer to them, enables you to listen without trying to change them, and helps you overcome habitual patterns of overreaction by addressing emotional reactivity at its source. You aren't going to change your family, but you can change yourself in relationship to them.

Learning to listen without overreacting is an exercise in accepting that each of us is different and separate. You can even learn to enjoy the differences. Formerly "difficult" and "disagreeable" people begin to soften perceptively as soon as you let them be who they are.

How Emotional Reactivity Increases as Relationships Evolve

In the early stages, most relationships are fairly relaxed and balanced. The two people can talk and listen without disruptive emotionality; otherwise the relationship wouldn't have gotten this far. Such circumstances, however, are time-limited. Relationships, like unstable chemical compounds, tend to deteriorate. Once they become heated with emotional reactivity, they may have to be cooled down with emotional distance—avoidance of one another or at least of potentially upsetting subjects. But if the two parties are closeted together or try to discuss emotionally charged issues, one or both of them starts spilling over with anxiety.

One person may act to preserve harmony by adapting to the other's needs and end up doing all of the listening (though not necessarily hearing). The other person is frequently unaware of the disparity. But both of them act to preserve this inequality. The mistake the placater makes is to confuse self-abnegation with self-restraint and openness to the other. The latter strategy allows both people to win; the former makes losers of them both. But as long as one person is cowed by the other's emotionality, and the second keeps trying to express himself in the same old reactive way, both of them act inadvertently to preserve the unhappy equilibrium.

The emotional climate in a relationship varies from hot to cold, turbulent to stable, and safe to unsafe to risk being vulnerable. The

presence of unresolved conflict makes for storminess. Some relationships, for example, are dominated by dissension over togetherness versus autonomy. In this case, anything that either partner says to the other that's even vaguely related to who's going to do what with whom can trigger the anxiety that surrounds this core conflict.

When someone opens up on you with a mean mouth or listens with only feigned interest, it's natural to blame it on his personality. When someone reacts with sudden, rancorous eruptions to something you say, it's impossible not to feel this emotional backlash as coming from her. But reactivity, like everything else that happens in a relationship, is interactional. The only part of the equation you can change is your part.

Try analyzing for a week the amount of your communications that are (1) critical or instructional, (2) avoidant, or (3) affectionate or laudatory. To change the climate in a relationship, just shift from (1) or (2) to (3) and see what happens.

------◆------

Trying to avoid or control people doesn't resolve reactivity.

------◆------

A listener's invisible sensitivities fester and flourish with preoccupation about giving too much and getting too little. Unfortunately, their reactivity makes other people avoid them, which increases their sense of alienation and isolation, which increases their reactivity. As emotional maturity and self-reliance decrease, people look more to one another to provide a sense of well-being. This need raises expectations, increases sensitivity, and contributes to emotional reactivity.

------◆------

To cut down on reactivity, respect your own right to be yourself and other people's right to be themselves.

------◆------

Mature and autonomous people aren't easily threatened by loss of their own emotional integrity, and so their relationships can be flexible. Periods of closeness and distance are tolerated. Each is free to be close or involved elsewhere—and to have the other person move close or pursue outside interests. Neither is particularly threatened by the other's needs and expectations. Denying one's own emotional reactions, blaming those reactions on others, and avoiding or pursuing others to reduce anxiety are emotionally governed processes that undermine flexibility in relationships. The point is not to deny one's feelings but to think about them, then choose how to react rather than responding reflexively.

Mature listeners are responsible for their own reactions. Instead of automatically thinking, "So and so is impossible," they hear what is said, feel their reactions, and then decide how to respond. "Hearing" someone who doesn't readily open up means recognizing that he doesn't want to say much. If the reticent person is someone you care about, you may feel shut out. But if you act automatically on that feeling and pressure the other person to open up, you are projecting your own anxiety and making him feel threatened.

Pressuring someone to open up isn't listening. You may sincerely want to hear what's on his mind, you may think you can help, you may believe it would be good for him and the relationship if he talked more; but pressure is pressure.

The best way to approach emotionally reticent people is to make contact without becoming intense. Your openness without pressure helps relax the assumption that it isn't safe to open up. Respecting the integrity of the emotional boundary that allows you to be yourself (someone who wants to get closer) and the other person to be herself (someone who wants to go slow) keeps anxiety from escalating and allows you to get closer without pressure or criticism.

Releasing yourself from slavish and unrewarding obligations will stem the energy drain from a few expendable relationships. But since most of our relationships are not expendable, the most important thing you can do to avoid getting caught up in emotionally reactive transactions is to stay calm and be yourself. Staying open means honoring the speaker's individuality; staying receptive means not negating your own.

The self-contained listener is not isolated or unfeeling but nonreactive.

HOW TO TONE DOWN YOUR OWN MESSAGE AND BE HEARD

We all know how frustrating it is not to be listened to. But how many of us ever stop to think that there might be something about *the way* we express ourselves that makes others deaf to our concerns?

Several years ago my friend John tried to teach me how to tune up my temperamental English motorcycle. When he arrived on the appointed day and saw how nervous I was, he said, "The first thing you have to do is calm down." Calm down? How do you calm down know-

ing you're about to take apart a three-thousand-dollar piece of machinery on which you'll later be going over a hundred miles an hour? But he was right. The way my hands were shaking I'd never have been able to shim the diphthongs with the krenging hook. So we repaired to the kitchen for a beer and cooled off. Later I had the satisfaction of knowing that it wasn't getting all wound up that made me unable to put the damn thing back together. It's just that I'm a natural born klutz.

Why is it that when it comes to relationship problems so few of us bother to follow my friend John's advice and calm down before we start?

As we've seen, one way speakers undermine their messages is to make complaints or requests with such anger and upset that the listener becomes so anxious that he doesn't clearly register—and therefore doesn't remember—the content of the speaker's message. All that gets communicated is the upset. Suppose, for example, that once every few months a wife gets so sick and tired of her husband's always leaving the bathroom a mess that she blows up at him about it. It infuriates her that he doesn't remember—even after she's told him how upset it makes her. All he remembers is getting yelled at.

It's hard to listen to complaints—or anything else—if you feel attacked. That's why sometimes even though we've been complaining about something for years, the other person never really gets it. We've told him (or her) a million times; still he (or she) doesn't understand. Anxiety is the enemy of listening.

One message sure to give your partner's hackles a workout is your pointing out some financial extravagances, of his naturally. Here's the great humorist S. J. Perelman illustrating his technique.

> Weary of pub-crawling and eager to recapture the zest of courtship, we had stayed home to leaf over our library of bills, many of them first editions. As always, it was chock-full of delicious surprises: overdrafts, modistes' and milliners' statements my cosset had concealed from me, charge accounts unpaid since the Crusades. If I felt any vexation, however, I was far too cunning to admit it. Instead, I turned my pockets inside out to feign insolvency, smote my forehead distractedly in the tradition of the Yiddish theater, and quoted terse abstracts from the bankruptcy laws. But fiendish feminine intuition was not slow to divine my true feelings. Just as I had uncovered a bill from Hattie Carnegie for a brocaded bungalow apron and was brandishing it under her nose, my wife suddenly turned pettish.
>
> "Sixteen dollars!" I was screaming. "Gold lamé you need yet! Who do you think you are, Catherine of Aragon? Why don't you rip up the foyer and pave it in malachite?" With a single dramatic gesture, I rent open my shirt. "Go ahead!" I shouted. "Milk me—drain me dry! Marshalsea prison! A pauper's grave!"

"Ease off before you perforate your ulcer," she enjoined. "You're waking the children."

"You think sixteen dollars grows on trees?" I pleaded, seeking to arouse in her some elementary sense of shame.[2]

Notice how Perelman employs his knowledge of psychology. Shaming someone is a sure way to get her attention.

Here's Perelman a little later in the same story demonstrating how to handle the delicate subject of gratuities. He and his family are moving out of their apartment, and he's faced with the challenge of appropriately expressing his gratitude for the staff's service.

Heaped by the curb were fourteen pieces of baggage exclusive of trunks; in the background, like figures in an antique frieze, stood the janitor, the handyman, and the elevator operators, their palms mutely extended. I could see that they were too choked with emotion to speak, these men who I know not at what cost to themselves had labored to withhold steam from us and jam our dumbwaiters with refuse. Finally one grizzled veteran, bolder than his fellows, stepped forward with an obsequious tug at his forelock.

"We won't forget this day, sir," the honest chap said, twisting his cap in his gnarled hands. "Will we, mates?" A low growl of assent ran round the circle. "Many's the time we've carried you through that lobby and a reek of juniper off you a man could smell five miles down wind. We've seen some strange sights in this house and we've handled some spectacular creeps; it's kind of like a microcosm like, you might say. But we want you to know that never, not even in the nitrate fields of Chile, the smelters of Nevada, or the sweatshops of the teeming East Side, has there been a man—" His voice broke off and I stopped him gently.

"Friends," I said huskily, "I'm not rich in worldly goods, but let me say this—what little I have is mine. If you ever need anything, whether jewels, money, or negotiable securities, remember these words: you're barking up the wrong tree. Geronimo."[3]

Notice that even though Perelman's message might have been a trifle unwelcome, his delivering it in a calm, reasoned tone enabled him to drive off to a chorus of ringing cheers (or so it seemed from a distance).

But seriously, what can you do if someone you try to talk to becomes reactive? Perhaps whenever you say something the least bit critical, your partner gets hurt or angry and shuts down. Try getting less invested in being heard but remain open to the relationship on the other

[2]S. J. Perelman, *The Swiss Family Perelman* (New York: Simon & Schuster, 1950), 4–5.

[3]Perelman, 16–17.

person's terms. This can be done without compromising yourself. It's the difference between giving in (living with appeasement) and temporarily setting aside your own agenda to respond to your partner's.

For example, say that whenever a wife tells her husband, even very nicely, that he shouldn't put certain dishes in the dishwasher, he gets that wounded look and withdraws into hurt silence. Normally, she's likely to become reactive in return. She's upset and feels wronged. The same thing happens when she complains about his not making the household repairs he's promised: he sulks. She feels like she's living with a big baby. But if she can calm down enough to ask herself where her criticism comes from, she might discover that it stems from unrealistic expectations.

The people we live with have assets and limitations. If we pitch our expectations at their assets instead of their limitations, we stand a better chance of being heard. Coming to terms with the real person you're relating to, rather than agonizing over the fact that he or she isn't different, will do a lot to lower your reactivity.

Learn something about what makes certain people reactive and try to defuse it with preparatory comments. For example, "I'm not saying that it's your fault, but I'm tired of seeing the kids leave their toys all over the place." Or, "I'm not sure how to say this. . . . " If you're trying to make a request, not expressing anger or disapproval, say so. But maybe you should examine your motives a little more carefully. When you say the kids shouldn't leave their toys around, do you really feel that your partner is at fault for allowing it? Is the inference he or she reacts to accurate? Even if you don't make such criticisms explicit, they often come through.

If you want someone to hear what you have to say without getting into a snit, don't forget tone and timing. Do you bring things up at the wrong time? Do you allow a judgmental tone to creep into your voice or use accusatory language?

If someone you know gets annoyed when you offer advice, inquire before doing so. "Would you like some advice, or would you rather I just listen?" If you intend to bring up an upsetting subject, give your listener some kind of warning. What makes something traumatic is being overwhelmed. If you aren't prepared, it takes less to overwhelm you. The more reactivity you anticipate, the more important it is to set the scene. A note or phone call telling the person you need to talk to him about something will help him gird himself.

Although to some people it seems artificial, putting difficult messages in notes is an effective way to short-circuit reactivity.

Ultimately, of course, it's not the other person's overreaction that is your problem but how *you* react to that. It's hard not to, but you don't have to get upset when someone else does.

One thing to remember when emotional reactivity drowns out listening is that *it's always your move.* The temptation to wait for the other person to change—or keep hammering away until he or she does—is understandable but unproductive. Sometimes it makes sense to write off unrewarding relationships that aren't central to your life. The man or woman who's so touchy that anything you say can trigger an angry response may be more trouble than he or she is worth. Unfortunately, many people are more likely to write off those relationships that *are* central to their lives—spouses, parents, colleagues—because they're the hardest to manage.

"What's Wrong with *Him?*"

The next time someone overreacts to what you're saying, ask yourself, "Where does this emotional response come from?" "What exposed nerve must I have touched on?" rather than "What's wrong with him [or her]?"

Any of the following remarks add fuel to the fire:

"You're such a big baby!"

"Someone sure got up on the wrong side of the bed today!"

"Can't you take a simple suggestion?"

"You're so immature."

"What's the matter, is it that time of the month again?"

"What's eating you? Every time I open my mouth you snap my head off."

According to Claire, her son Jeffrey was oversensitive. The least little thing she said to him could make him fly into a rage. One time she told him that his teacher probably wouldn't pick on him so much if he acted more mature in class, and he burst into tears and ran into his room. "He's always throwing tantrums," Claire said.

A child who bursts into tears and runs out of the room isn't having a temper tantrum; he feels ashamed. Kids aren't stupid. If they pitch a fit because they want to bend you to their wishes, they do it in front of you. (If you want to inactivate a temper tantrum, remove the audience; leave the room.)

The way to understand reactivity is to try to understand it, not fall back on familiar judgmental labels. Imagine a little boy storming out of the room after his mother said something apparently innocuous to him. Why would a child get so upset? Often it's because what she said made him feel ashamed of himself. When a child (or adult) feels humiliated, he becomes foot-stompingly outraged; he is I-am-wronged! Injuries to self-respect are a bruising as muggings. If you asked him what was wrong, he'd probably say, "Mommy yelled at me" or perhaps "Nothing, leave me alone!"

Few of us, children least of all, label our experience as shame. Unfortunately, parents who don't recognize a shame reaction or can't tolerate a child's upset get into a tug of war that makes things worse. They demand to know what's wrong, as if a child convulsed with emotion could say.

Give a shamed person room to hide and lick his wounds. Shame is so painful that the child momentarily loses control of his feelings. He needs time alone to regain his composure. Let him have it.

If someone becomes enraged at something you said, it might be because he feels shamed. Think about how you might have offended his dignity. Did you treat him like a baby? Imply that his opinion is wrong or doesn't count? That his feelings aren't legitimate? The way to decode an "excessive" or "inappropriate" emotional response is not to blame the other person—or yourself—but to consider what the exposed nerve might be.

SOMETIMES IT'S A MISTAKE TO TRY TO CONTROL YOUR FEELINGS

Some people are afraid to get up and say something at funerals, wedding banquets, or other emotionally charged occasions because they might start to cry—as if crying were a sign of weakness and not compassion. "But," one woman protested when I tried to tell her there's nothing wrong with crying, "if I start to cry, I won't be able to finish what I want to say."

If you start to cry and tell yourself that's awful and try to stop, you may well have trouble speaking. It's hard to concentrate on two things at once. But if your heart moves and your feelings show, what's wrong with that?

A trick some people use to help them cope with their anxiety about formal public speaking is to accept and acknowledge rather than fight their nervousness. "Good morning. My name is so-and-so, and I want you to know that I'm a little nervous about speaking in front of such a large group." Such candor makes an audience sympathetic, not judgmental. Most of us know what it feels like to be nervous about speaking in public. Even more important, though, is the effort to accept your feelings as natural instead of trying in vain to fight them. (Incidentally, thinking about communicating *to* a group of people instead of "speaking in front of them" shifts your attention and helps you calm down.)

There's an even more important way that trying to overcontrol feelings leads to more reactivity. If you let someone know how angry you are by venting your bottled-up frustration in an emotional outburst, you're likely to come across as overwhelming and attacking. If, instead of hearing your complaints, the other person responds with angry counteraccusations or just walks out, you may conclude that it's a mistake to try to talk about your feelings. This conclusion leads to a control and release cycle. You hold everything in until you explode in tears and shouting. The solution is not more control but less.

Don't wait until your frustration builds to rage before talking about it. Describe clearly the reasons you're unhappy. Discuss conflicts openly as they arise. Speaking up sooner will make it easier for you to lower your voice and to eliminate accusatory statements.

Instead of "You never do anything around here," try "I'm overloaded with housework. I need you to help me."

Don't turn the discussion into a *zero-sum game,* in which one person can win (or be right) only if the other loses (or is wrong).

There is, however, a difference between expressing what you feel and venting your emotions. Recently I got into a heated argument with a woman who was tired of her father-in-law's belittling comments and planned to tell him off. When I suggested that she tone down her emotionality before talking to him, she blew up at me. "What's wrong with emotion? What's wrong with getting angry?" Good question.

This woman *did* have something to be angry about. Her father-in-law's cutting remarks were thoughtless and disrespectful. But if she allowed her upset to overwhelm her, her complaints would not be voiced

clearly and would not be heard. Unloading her anger, rather than voicing her complaints, would allow her father-in-law not to take her seriously, to dismiss her as "oversensitive," "bitchy," or "having a bad day."

I'm not advocating emotional detachment. Anger helps preserve our integrity and self-regard, but simply venting anger doesn't usually solve the problem it signals. The distinction I'm trying to draw is not between emotion and reason but between uncontrolled reaction and deliberate action. There's nothing wrong with emotion, and there's nothing wrong with telling someone off—if that's what you want to do. It's not responding with feeling that spoils listening and makes us feel childish and inept—it's losing control.

PART FOUR

LISTENING IN CONTEXT

"We Never Seem To Talk Anymore"

LISTENING BETWEEN INTIMATE PARTNERS

It started innocently enough. She met him at an office party, and all they did was talk. But when Maureen got home and her husband asked if she had met anybody interesting, she found herself unwilling to mention Arthur, as though he were a secret wish she didn't want to lose by telling. Arthur called the next day and invited her to lunch. One lunch followed another, and then there were drinks after work. The following week they drove up to Thatcher Park and talked, as they watched the sun setting over the valley below. Nothing happened, unless you count the brief moment when Maureen's glance left Arthur's eyes and dropped to his lips and a shiver ran through her.

It was at this point that Maureen consulted me. She felt on the brink of something that could wreck her marriage. Arthur was everything her husband wasn't: successful, self-possessed, but most of all he really listened when they talked. Telling me this, Maureen was visibly nervous. Her eyes scanned mine, looking for understanding, expecting perhaps judgment, or maybe permission to do what she longed to.

When, I asked her, did the passion in her marriage die? She looked away. Then she wiped her eyes and said that Raymond, her husband, was a good man; they'd just . . . grown apart. He never talked to her anymore.

My sympathies were with this woman. Life holds few choices as consequential as the one between satisfaction and security. Still, I'd seen too many stale marriages blamed on the other partner not to wonder what Maureen's contribution was.

When I suggested she bring her husband to our second meeting, Maureen was reluctant. She wasn't asking for marital therapy, she said, and she was terrified of Raymond's finding out about Arthur. What finally overcame her hesitation was her hope that if I saw what her relationship with Raymond was like, maybe I'd understand why she would consider leaving him.

Raymond agreed to come, and Maureen told him that she was unhappy with their marriage. He seemed sympathetic, as though accustomed to obliging, but not really involved and not willing to tell his side. Only when I asked about his work did Raymond open up and become animated. We talked for a few minutes until Maureen interrupted to complain that he never talked to her about these things. Why couldn't he ever share his feelings with her? Raymond didn't have a very good answer for that. I was encouraged. Here was a concrete problem, something to work on.

If two people can't talk, I said, something's wrong. Then I turned their chairs to face each other and asked Raymond to talk to Maureen about his work in such a way as to make her understand what he was worried about. I told her to listen in such a way as to help him bring out his feelings.

Raymond talked about the anxieties of opening a new law practice in the middle of a recession. Very little work was coming in, but he was convinced that if he could hang on for another year or so, things would start to turn around. Maureen broke in to say that he was being foolish. Things would never turn around until he got rid of that idiot Roger, his partner. They argued for a minute, and then Raymond shut up.

Here was one reason this couple didn't talk. When Raymond talked about what was on his mind, Maureen argued or advised; he protested feebly, then folded his tent. Perhaps she was comfortable with conversational give-and-take and he wasn't. Maybe he couldn't listen to her opinions because he didn't believe in his own power to decide what to do, and her strong views made him feel anxious and unsupported. In any case, here clearly was something to work on.

Before I could start to help these two sort out their relationship, I knew I had to talk separately with Maureen about Arthur. I would propose a trial nonseparation, a period of not seeing Arthur and put-

ting her energy into improving the marriage, so she could find out if it could be better.

Maureen was relieved that I'd seen her and Raymond together. "Now you can see," she said, "how bad our relationship is. It's never going to change." (Maureen was a great believer in chemistry, that famous force of attraction with more power to excite than endure.) Nothing I said about postponing any decision until she'd waited a few weeks to see if we could improve the marriage made any difference. She started seeing Arthur again that same week, and when Raymond found out the following week, he was as forgiving as most husbands.

Their divorce was finalized a year and a day after the one time I saw them together, eleven months after Maureen's affair with Arthur heated up, and eight months after it was over. Maureen was left with the house, two children, mortgage payments she couldn't keep up with, and the memory of that shiver.

Maureen viewed her marriage as a predicament, an entity, something with a history, perhaps, but one that after a while takes on a life of its own. Most of us feel this way at times. But a relationship is not a thing, not a static state; it is a process of mutual influence. A relationship isn't something you have; it's something you do.

———◆———

Couples who learn to listen to each other – with understanding and tolerance – often find that they don't need to change each other.

———◆———

The impulse to change things, to make them better, is a natural and largely constructive one. But anyone who thinks of marriage as an infinitely improvable arrangement is making a mistake. The ideal of perfectibility breeds hope of overcoming differences and solving problems. Many problems can be solved, but the problem of living with another person who doesn't always see things the way you do or want what you want isn't one of them. Perhaps marriage isn't necessarily about resolving our differences but about learning to live together with them.

WHAT GOES AROUND

When I was in the third grade my teacher, Miss Halloway, used a stroboscope to show us how light affects what we see. Late one winter afternoon when the shadows were long she took out a small fan with a metal

blade and plugged it in. She turned on the switch, and the blade began to spin and then whir. Then she turned on the stroboscope. As she adjusted the rate of flash, the fan blade slowed down and then stopped. The blade looked so still and harmless! How easy it would be, I thought, to reach out and touch it.

The blade looks stationary, Miss Halloway explained, because the stroboscope illuminates only one point in the cycle. As I came to realize later, this is the same way we usually see our relationships.

The first thing to understand about listening within couples is that *complementarity* is the governing principle of connection. Behavior doesn't take place in a vacuum but in the context of relationships in which we act and react to each other. In any two-person relationship, one person's behavior is functionally related to the other's. If at times we see only one point in the cycle—a friend's failure to call, for example, or a partner's lack of interest in what we have to say—that doesn't mean that relationships don't spin around in a circle.

The greatest impediment to understanding in our intimate relationships is the hurt and longing that make us look outside ourselves for the sources of our disappointment. We can't help wishing our mates would be a little more interested in what we have to say about ourselves and a little less defensive about what we have to say about them. At about this time, the romantic vision of marriage gives way to melodrama—the story of villain and victim that many unhappily married persons tell themselves and, when things get bad enough, anyone else who will listen.

Many couples expect too much of each other and then see their difficulties as more apocalyptic than they really are. The real tragedy of this tragic view is that our ability to see where we're going is compromised. Like Maureen, we fix on the hurtful things our partner does and think of our troubles as inevitable.

When all is said and done, marriage and its famous complications can be illuminated by focusing on one thing: the basic pattern of interaction between two partners. Start with the hurtful things your partner does—the avoidance or selfishness or irritability—but then ask yourself: What is the complementary other half of this pattern?

The only thing you can change is your response to the other person, and the best way to begin is by listening.

RHYTHMS OF CHANGE IN A COMMITTED RELATIONSHIP

Although the cycle of human life may be orderly, it isn't a steady, continuous march. Periods of growth and change are followed by times of relative stability in which changes are consolidated. The good news is that life isn't one long uphill struggle; sometimes we reach plateaus and can coast. The bad news is that we can't stay forever in one place. Partnership, too, has its cycles and seasons.

Courtship—what a lovely, old-fashioned word—is a time of opening up and testing for compatibility. Enchanted by freshness and discovery, the partners are absorbed and engaged with each other. Conversation flows, and listening comes easily. They find each other so novel and delightful. So attentive, so interesting, so *interested.*

Fascination makes them overlook or forgive gaps in listening. Something puts her in mind of high school, and she asks him what it was like for him. He talks eagerly about his experience, but when he doesn't reciprocate, doesn't ask her what it was like for her, she thinks it's an oversight. She'll get her turn later.

Young and in love, we take such pleasure in each other's company that sober considerations give way to dictates of the heart. Falling in love is an act of imaginative creation. Later, our hearts may shrink, and with it our attention spans and our eagerness to listen. But that's later. Now, although we might be more compatible with partners more like ourselves, nature's urge to mix genes draws us to the otherness of the other.

————◆————

The great challenge of courtship is to be together and still be yourself.

————◆————

With love at stake, we lie a little. We tell tender lies, a few self-protecting lies, and more than a few self-deluding lies. Looking back, we may wish we'd been more honest and hadn't tried so hard to get our partners to like us.

When courting couples move in the direction of their intentions, trying to discover how far they can go together, it's usually two steps forward and one step back. A dozen or so pairs over the years have sought me out for premarital counseling. What a good idea, I used to think. Unfortunately, these encounters often turn out to be quite frustrating. The people seeking help come not because they are amazingly precautious but because they are amazingly mismatched. Despite that, most

of them have passed an emotional point of no return and intend to marry, no matter what. Among the obstacles they will overcome is their own good judgment.

———◆———

If courtship were more conscious, people would pay more attention to the quality of one another's listening.

———◆———

Among the most important things to find in a mate is someone who's fun to talk to. Making friends and being able to really talk to each other is a far more reliable guide than a person's good looks, cleverness, or that dizzy feeling that people call "falling in love." (Try telling that to someone in love.)

HE NEEDS SPACE, SHE WANTS CLOSENESS

He wants to be left alone and she wants attention. So she gives him attention and he leaves her alone.

Jack and Irene were a handsome couple, in their mid-thirties I guessed. Irene was a pretty woman, with ash-blond hair and an energetic look. The day they came to see me she was wearing a linen suit with a silk blouse. Jack, tall and slender, wore jeans. She'd dressed up; he'd dressed down. Was it just a different approach to this interview or a different approach to life?

"What brings you to therapy?" I asked, looking at both of them.

Jack answered first. "Well, I'm a little intolerant."

"What does Irene do that's hard to tolerate?"

They exchanged looks. Irene gave Jack a faint smile, and he turned back to me. "She yammers. She makes assumptions, and there's nothing I can do about it—about what she assumes—so I give up and go on about my business."

"You mean, you pull away?"

"Well . . . Yes."

He went on to describe himself as a man who isn't very emotional, married to a woman who is.

I turned to Irene. "So, Jack is learning to be more tolerant and not react to you. What would you say you're learning?"

"I'm working real hard to identify and express my feelings to him.

But he always wants an explanation of *why* I feel upset. Sometimes you don't know why; you just know that you do."

Jack's response to Irene's distress took the familiar form of an obsessional person trying to comfort an emotional one: He barraged her with questions, all based on his own approach to emotion, which was to label and compartmentalize it. (He was an electronics expert who could figure out just about any machine on earth, but with women he wished there was an instruction manual.)

Irene felt things strongly without always being able to put them into words. At these moments her husband could have comforted her by just being there, holding her perhaps, but certainly not by demanding that she stop crying and explain herself. The truth was that when Irene cried, Jack couldn't imagine it might be about anything but him, so he felt accused and guilty. His comfort took the form of asking her to reassure him. "What's the matter?" really meant "Tell me you're not mad at me."

Jack went on to talk about Irene's anger as the reason he didn't listen better. When Irene approached Jack in an excitable or nervous way, he became anxious and responded by trying to be analytic or—if that failed—by distancing himself. His distance aggravated her emotionality, which then pushed him even further away. Their failure to listen to each other wasn't caused by Irene's emotions or by Jack's anxiety; it was the combination.

Jack could see the pattern and thought Irene should break the cycle by toning down her emotional behavior. Irene thought Jack should learn to be a little more tolerant of her feelings. Even as they talked, though, they played out the familiar progression. Irene's rising pressure made Jack anxious and defensive—or, to look at the circular pattern from another angle—Jack's inability to accept what she was saying drove up her emotionality.

Finally I interrupted and told them the story of the North Wind. "One day the North Wind and the Sun were arguing about which was the most powerful force in nature. 'I can churn up the seas and drive a blizzard,' the North Wind said. 'Yes, but I can melt the snow and dry up a flood,' the Sun replied. Just then a man wearing a heavy overcoat happened by. 'I know how to settle this,' said the Sun. 'Let's see who can make that man take off his coat.' The North Wind blew hard. But the harder he blew, the more the man bundled up. Finally the Sun said, 'My turn.' The sun shone down its warmth, and the man opened his coat. The Sun shone warmer, and the man took off his coat."

Irene and Jack smiled broadly.

"Irene, sometimes you come on like the North Wind. And I don't blame you, because it's frustrating to feel shut out. And out of that frustration, you either give up or out comes the North Wind."

"You're right. I never thought of it that way."

At this point Jack, feeling relieved, opened up and started to talk about needing space. He had a lot of pressure at work, and when he came home he needed space to decompress. And Irene was afraid to give him the breathing room he needed, the freedom to read or go for a walk or spend time with his friends.

"Jack," I said, "I could tell you understood the difference between Irene being the North Wind and being the Sun. But you know, the guy wearing the coat is in the story too. It's both of them. The North Wind blows, and he bundles up, and so the North Wind blows more, and he bundles up more. He bundles up more for a lot of good reasons— he has his moods, his job is stressful, he needs his space, he likes to read . . . I respect those things. But the bundling up is part of the problem."

"I understand that," Jack said. He went on to say that he's been making an effort. After dinner, for example, he used to get up as soon as he was finished eating and go in to watch the news, while Irene cleared the table. Now he's making an effort to stay a little longer and talk with her. But, he admitted, "It's not the easiest thing for me, to be close."

By now, the atmosphere in the session had shifted. Jack and Irene had begun to see how they were locked together in a pattern in which they both pushed each other to respond in a way they didn't like.

Once Irene learns to see very clearly that coming on strong only pushes Jack away, and *he* learns that keeping his distance only makes her more anxious and persistent, they can figure out how to break their halves of the cycle. Will that magically change everything? If you kiss a frog, will he turn into a prince? Maybe not right away.

BALANCING INTIMACY AND INDEPENDENCE

In accommodating to each other, couples must negotiate the space between them as well as that separating their couplehood from the rest of the world.

When you become intimate with someone, physically and emotionally, you open up the boundary around your private self to let the other

in close. Being in love is to want no distance between you, but a wall of privacy protecting the two of you from outside intrusion. This closeness and privacy make conversation intimate, with the obvious rewards and risks.

Minimal self-reliance exists between two people when they call each other at work all the time, when neither has separate friends or independent interests, if they come to view themselves only as a pair rather than also as two individuals. Under such pressure of togetherness conversation is constrained by the threat of conflict. When two people are alone in a lifeboat, they'd better not argue.

In contrast, couples who put autonomy over connection do little together, have their own rooms, take separate vacations, have independent checking accounts, are more invested in careers or outside relationships than in each other, and don't talk much. Listening is limited because they have so many other outlets.

Most couples don't start out disengaged; the wall that grows up between them is a product of unresolved conflict. Often it's not specific transgressions so much as the not listening, the not hearing. They both feel as if the other doesn't care. That they *do* care very much but are too afraid of conflict to listen doesn't alter the feeling of being deeply unappreciated. Some people pay a lot for peace.

Typically, partners come from families with differing degrees of separateness and togetherness. Each partner tends to be more comfortable with the sort of conversational sharing he or she grew up with. Since these expectations differ, a struggle ensues over how much to talk everything over together and how much to keep to yourself. This may be the most difficult aspect of learning to listen to a new mate—developing sensitivity and tolerance to a different conversational style.

In the early stages of a couple's relationship, raging passion can mask difficulties in communicating. Sometimes both partners have broken away wrenchingly from their families, and they come together with an unchecked urgency for connection. Such fusion, such boundarylessness, the desideratum of love's young dream, is hard to sustain, especially when those in its thrall isolate themselves from family and friends. Couples who expect that all their needs for listening will be met in one all-fulfilling relationship are in for the rudest of awakenings. One reason many people get too little out of intimate relationships is that they want too much.

Tension in a couple can be resolved in one of three ways: working it out, triangulation, or distancing. When distancing between intimate

partners is unchecked by a clear boundary around their relationship, the two often drift apart.

Brendan and Gina were very much in love when they married, also very young and very much unaware of how different their backgrounds were. Hers was a large, close-knit family whose watchword was togetherness. His was a small, fragmented family in which independence and personal achievement were the highest accomplishments.

In Brendan's opinion, Gina was addicted to attachment. She always wanted to talk. Even when they were watching TV or reading, she'd interrupt every few minutes to tell him something that popped into her head. It broke his concentration and made him furious. This he tried to signal indirectly by sighing or saying "Yes?" with a weary note in his voice. But Gina didn't get the message, or did she?

Gina took closeness for granted and found Brendan's "coldness" and "detachment" selfish and punishing. Why did he have to shut her out all the time?

Brendan and Gina each had their own point of view, at best sporadically sympathetic to the other one. It's a sad and familiar story of hurt and blaming, unfortunate misunderstandings, poor choices, inability to compromise. Two young people with too great a disparity in their backgrounds and expectations to fit together easily, and too little experience to know how to work things out.

It wasn't really their differences that made the first few years together so painful; it was their inability to talk about them. Once a week or so, Gina would get fed up with Brendan's distance. At these times, Brendan was appalled by the meanness and exaggeration of the things she'd accuse him of. The worst was "You don't give a damn about anybody but yourself!" *How could she say such things?* He certainly couldn't listen. Then, feeling the frustration of not being heard, Gina would raise her voice, which only made Brendan shrink further into himself. Finally, Gina would break down in tears and sob, "Why are you so mean to me?!" Brendan only thought it, and never more than once a day.

Like a lot of ill-matched couples, Brendan and Gina gradually did learn to live with each other. After a while they had children to cushion their couplehood. Gradually they learned to accommodate to each other. Gina got used to Brendan's silences and occasional games of golf with his friends. He learned to spend more time with her and the kids. But what they never learned very well was how to talk to each other. Brendan didn't talk to Gina because he felt that she was unreasonable in

her expectations and that she didn't respect his right to his own preferences. Gina continued to express from time to time her disappointment
with Brendan's lack of involvement, but he never really did learn to
listen. He listened well enough to pacify her—"I'm sorry"; "Yes, dear"—but
not enough to understand how she felt. He wished he could change
things, he wished he could escape, and these thoughts kept him from
ever really understanding or coming to terms with the real person he
married. Like a prisoner who thinks of nothing but freedom, he never
really did adjust to the realities of his relationship.

PURSUERS AND DISTANCERS

Pursuers (like Irene) want more connection, which makes distancers
(like Jack) feel pressured and pull away. The more she pursues, the more
he distances; the more he distances, the more she pursues. It's a game
without end, though it does have interruptions.

When pursuers get fed up with being rebuffed, they withdraw in
hurt and anger. But after a while they feel a little better or start to get
lonely, and then they begin the cycle all over again.

If you're a pursuer, try backing off. Pay less attention to the other
person for a few days. This planned distance isn't the same as reactive
distance—getting fed up and giving the other person the cold shoulder. Snubbing isn't the same as ignoring someone; it's an attempt to
punish him with silence, which of course doesn't lessen your preoccupation with him. Instead of getting angry and passive-aggressive, increase your emotional investment in other things.

When you stop pursuing, notice what happens. You'll probably find
your tension rising. This is important. Consider how much of the pursuing is an attempt to cope with your own anxiety and a lack of other
avenues of satisfaction in your life.

Accept any forward movement on the part of a distancer—even
if it's angry or critical. This, too, is important. Pursuers often say they
want their partners to share feelings with them, but what they usually
mean is positive feelings. A pursuer who experiments with shifting the
pattern should try very hard to avoid getting defensive about whatever
the distancer does express. Distancers have feelings, too, but they keep
them locked away in tightly sealed compartments. If your distancer does
start expressing his or her emotions, try to listen without getting reactive.

If you're a distancer, you know that pursuers are hard to cope with.

They put you on the defensive. It's hard to stop running when you feel someone chasing you. The first thing to realize is that it isn't just him or her chasing you; it's an interlocking pattern of pursuit and withdrawal. Instead of avoiding a pursuing partner, try initiating contact—on your terms. Call the pursuer in the middle of the day, invite him or her to go for a walk. Say what's on your mind; ask what's on your partner's.

If you shift your part in the pursuer–distancer pattern for a week, you'll discover that change is a three-step process: First you change. Second, you partner responds—usually in ways that are partly rewarding and partly annoying. Third comes your response to that response—either you change back, or you persist.

If an emotional pursuer makes a deliberate effort to stop pursuing her partner, he may not immediately respond by moving toward her. The resulting distance might make her feel cheated. She might think, *See? I changed, but he didn't.* At that critical juncture—the third step in the change process—she would either revert to her old style or persist, making an effort to remain calm, develop other interests, and give her partner space to discover his need for her.

Alternatively, if an emotional distancer decides to break the cycle of pursuit and distance by moving toward his partner, she might not immediately become calm and respond the way he wants her to. She might not, for example, be receptive to his opening up about things that are bothering him. She might be critical. If her response makes him anxious and he reverts to distancing, he might conclude, "I tried, but she'll never change." But if he *does* change back, it wouldn't be because of how his partner responded; it would be because of how he responded to her response.

Another reason the pursuer–distancer dynamic isn't so easily resolved by reversing your role in it is that pursuers and distancers tend to have constitutionally different operating styles. Pursuers have a greater affinity for relationship time; distancers prefer either time alone or activity together. (That's one reason some people are emotional distancers but sexual pursuers.) Pursuers tend to express their feelings, while distancers tend to avoid them. Pursuers have relatively permeable personal boundaries, such that they relate readily to a wide number of people. Distancers are particular and let down their defenses with only a select few people.

Although each of us has a predominant operating style as either a pursuer or a distancer, the dynamics of complementarity can trigger different roles in different relationships. For example, a man may be

a distancer with his mate and a pursuer with his mother. A woman may be a pursuer with her partner but a distancer from her father and her brother.

Distancers are unsure of themselves (in the areas where they distance); they depend on privacy for protection. Pursuing only makes them feel pressured and intruded on. (If you would approach a distancer, move slowly; don't push. Knock to enter. Give him time to anticipate company.) Distancers handle threatening issues by closing them off. Anxiety about these issues may not be acknowledged, but it is always present below the surface. The tension created by such unaddressed anxiety often triggers displaced conflict in the relationship or emotional problems in one of the partners.

Emotional pursuers handle sensitive issues by talking about them over and over again in a somewhat ritualized manner. The issues never become closed off, but the emotionality surrounding them is never dealt with. For their partners, this pseudo-communication has the effect of salt poured on an open wound.

Like other familiar complementary patterns—overfunctioning/underfunctioning, strict/lenient, fast-paced/slow-paced—the pursuer–distancer dynamic isn't static. Very little about any relationship is static.

ACCOMMODATING DIFFERENCES

Intimate partnership is a process in which two individuals restructure much of their lives into a new unit: The Couple. Friends invite The Couple over for dinner, the IRS taxes The Couple, The Couple accumulates belongings. The two separate personalities don't disappear, of course, but their relationship is now a system, their fates interactive and interdependent.

The first priority of intimate partnership is mutual accommodation to manage the myriad details of everyday living. Each partner tries to organize the relationship along familiar lines and pressures the other to accommodate. They must agree on the big things, like where to live and whether and when to have children. Less obvious, but equally important, they must coordinate daily rituals, like what to watch on television, what to eat for supper, when to go to bed, and what to do there. What's at stake is the viability of the relationship and the integrity of the partners. Unfortunately, there is a thin line between accommodation and collusion. If you don't speak up and say you don't like some-

thing, if you don't say you wish things were different, you may find yourself disappearing into your partner's ways.

Lynn was just nineteen when her mother died. After the worst of the grief gave way to emptiness, she decided to get out of New York and move to Montana. When she got off the plane, she was stunned and uplifted by the intensity of the sunlight. The last of the snow was melting, and the valley blossomed. Summer came, stretched and yawned, and then it was early fall. That's when the loneliness set in, and Lynn started wondering what she was going to do with her life. Right about then she met Travis. After all the boys she'd known in New York who couldn't stop talking about themselves, Lynn took Travis's quietness for strength. She thought he was the real deal. So when he asked her to share his trailer with him, it seemed like the right thing to do.

A year later their relationship wasn't a lot better or a lot worse. Maybe a wedding would do the trick. So Lynn gave Travis an ultimatum: either they get married or she was moving out. But even walking down the aisle, she found herself thinking, "This is never going to last." Afterward she got drunk, hoping to numb this giant step into the unknown.

Lynn got pregnant on the honeymoon, and two weeks later Travis joined the Air Force. When Travis was posted to Korea, he went ahead to get settled, and Lynn moved in with his parents. It was not a happy time. And so, six weeks later, when she boarded the plane for Inchon, it was with as much relief as anxiety.

When jet lag wore off and reality settled in, Lynn found herself alone all day with the baby in a tiny apartment. She'd written Travis to buy a car with automatic transmission because she couldn't drive a stick shift; but he hadn't listened. Not being able to drive sealed her isolation. When she tried to talk to Travis about it, he said, "What's the matter with you? You'll get the hang of it. Don't be such a big baby." What could she say?

Unfortunately, Lynn neither insisted that Travis listen to how she was feeling nor asked how he was feeling. "I nagged," Lynn says. "I was angry and bitchy. Back then I wasn't very sure of what I was feeling, and so the frustration just built up and came out as attack. Instead of telling him how I was feeling, I'd say things like 'We never do anything'; 'You never take me anywhere.' He always put it back on me. 'What's the matter with you?' That was his answer to all my complaints." She didn't really remember Travis's complaints; all she remembered was that he didn't listen to hers.

Going into the marriage, Lynn had thought that if she did all the right things, Travis could become the man she wanted—loving and affectionate. She'd grown up with a self-absorbed father, and the main question for her always had been "How do I make Daddy happy?" With Travis, she'd played the good wife, hoping for a payoff of affection and attention. But there was no affection; just sex. Lynn put up with not having her needs met because she wasn't sure how to put them into words.

When her frustration turned to bitterness, Lynn's conversations with Travis took on the form of combat. Each felt trapped and misunderstood, and both of them led with their defenses. After suffering so much neglect, Lynn was seized with rage when she tried to talk about her feelings. When she opened up on him with a mean mouth, his stomach knotted and he stopped listening. Once or twice, when she cornered him, he'd answer her accusations with an outburst of his own nursed resentment. Then they'd go back to avoiding each other.

The proximity forced on them in Korea may have kept them together longer than otherwise, or it may have put too much pressure on their shaky alliance. In any case, when Travis was posted back to the States and Lynn started school again, the marriage fell apart. With school and friends of her own, Lynn felt stronger and no longer willing to put up with a relationship that gave her so little satisfaction. Ironically, as Lynn started pulling away, Travis asked her to stay and for the first time since the early days of the relationship tried to listen to her. But it was too late.

Lynn said: "He wanted someone to mother him, to cook and clean and all that. I was willing to do it, and so he was happy. But when I wanted more from him, he couldn't deal with it, and he hated me. Then my independence gave him the room he needed, and so he started liking me again. But now I knew it had been a mistake to begin with." And so they ended it.

Travis and Lynn might have had an easier time adjusting to other mates. Maybe not. Second and third marriages don't fail because people keep picking the wrong partners; they fail because it's not our differences that matter but how they're negotiated. Maybe Lynn tried to do too much compromising, in the process leaving too little room for herself. Maybe Travis did too little compromising. He was a young man caught up in confirming his masculinity rather than achieving love, and perhaps he was afraid he'd lose himself by giving in. The trouble was, neither of them dared to listen to the other's point of view.

Travis and Lynn might have found a way to talk about their differ-

ences if they'd managed to be less emotionally reactive to each other. Instead of holding her feelings in until they exploded, Lynn might have approached Travis calmly (it isn't necessary to *feel* calm to *speak* calmly), saying, perhaps, "Something's bothering me and I need to talk to you. Is this a good time?"

———————◆———————

The best way to tone down emotionality isn't to avoid talking about problems but to discuss them openly — before the upset boils over.

———————◆———————

Travis thought that if he didn't listen to Lynn's complaints, he wouldn't have to deal with them — and he could avoid the anxiety her distress made him feel. But he found out that feelings are like any other form of energy: if they don't find direct expression, they come out in other ways.

The way to reduce your own defensiveness is to stay calm and stay open. Don't interrupt, contradict, qualify, or change the subject. If you don't understand something, ask for clarification and examples. Otherwise, shut up and listen.

"Why Can't a Woman Be More Like a Man?"

When the differences that attract turn out to be hard to live with, we may be tempted to think that intimate partnership works best with a person as similar to us as possible. Actually, that's not true. With very similar partners there is the possibility for weaknesses to combine and create exaggerated, even destructive, imbalances. Two people with explosive tempers or who are financially irresponsible often form disastrous unions.

Lynn told herself she married the wrong person. Travis was strong and good-looking and smart, but he didn't know how to trust people with the truth about his feelings. A man dedicated to autonomy, married to a woman who prized togetherness. Travis, too, thought the mistake he made was choosing the wrong mate. He never suspected that the extravagant and desirable woman he fell in love with would turn out to be a dependent nag.

Your partner doesn't have the power to say what is and forever shall be or who's right and who's wrong. Even the person who puts things that way doesn't have the power to make it so; *you* give him that power if you react as though he did.

You don't have to agree to acknowledge that the other person has a point.

The simple act of omission involved in not acknowledging what the other person is saying before countering with your own point of view may be the single greatest impediment to shared understanding. If we don't know that we've been heard, we're not about to hear what the other person is saying. Instead, we turn away or raise our voices. Maybe if we scream at her, she'll hear.

Emotionally charged discussions should be kept as brief as possible. Don't unload everything. Doing so only makes the listener feel inundated, nailed to the wall, with just two choices: fight or flight.

Nowhere to turn. That's the way a lot of unhappy people feel about their relationships—trapped in the space of a relationship with another person who has some pretty strange ways. Accommodation means finding a way to fit together, but many couples mistake fitting together as an all-or-nothing proposition.

Wise couples accept their differences and accommodate. But they also realize that accommodating doesn't mean they must become two peas in a pod. Maybe she'll never be interested in politics. Maybe he'll never really get to like her parents. Rather than battle over these differences, or be untrue to themselves by giving in entirely, realistic partners avoid dwelling on certain subjects about which they cannot agree. But instead of drifting apart or insulating themselves emotionally from each other, they search for alternative avenues of connection.

Listening and adjusting to each other's realities requires a balance between tolerance and selective coming together. Mates may tire of hearing about each other's job, but they owe each other a few minutes of listening at the end of the day. (Asking questions may make familiar stories more interesting.) But couples must also search to discover which subjects are most rewarding to talk about (with each other). The same balance applies to activities other than talking.

When Dennis returned from playing golf on Sunday morning, Lorraine was still in bed, so he took off his clothes and crawled in beside her. When he kissed her awake, she gave him a dubious look. It wasn't what he'd hoped for, but over the years he'd learned the difference between a red light and a yellow one. When they were first married, Dennis expected Lorraine to be ready for sex without warning. When she tried

to slow him down and later said no, he felt rejected and avoided her altogether. Now he read her look as saying that she was happy to see him but not really in the mood to make love. They did a lot of talking with their eyes, but he made himself say, "Let's just hug a little." They did, and after a while Lorraine relaxed enough to become more affectionate. In the end they did make gentle love.

After lunch Dennis mentioned that he was going to watch football for a while. Once he'd expected to watch football all day on Sunday, and Lorraine, who came from a family that didn't follow the national obsession, would get very angry. For years they'd alternate between his watching and her fuming to his not watching and feeling resentful. This day he watched the first half while she had a long phone conversation with a friend, read the paper, and occasionally looked up when the crowd roared. At halftime she asked if he wanted to go to the movies. He did. Movies were one thing they never had to compromise about. They went to see *Batman Returns* but didn't go shopping afterward, as he knew she would have liked and she knew he would not have. After supper, they watched television for a while, until Lorraine went into the other room and read. It was a nice day.

As this example illustrates, listening in its full sense means taking each other into account. Dennis listened to Lorraine signaling her mood; later she listened to his wish to watch football, and between them they found a balance between separateness and togetherness.

In spite of the large emotions involved, marriage isn't about monumental issues; it's about little things, about everydayness, about knowing that tomorrow morning you'll wake up with a new chance to work at it, to get it a bit more wrong or right.

GETTING BEYOND BITTERNESS

Couples who survive the break-in period continue to go through cycles of closeness and distance. Some conflicts are resolved, others are avoided, and a few keep cropping up from time to time. Arguments still occur, but the nature of these heated discussions should change over time. They become less bitter and less violent. There is less blaming and a greater feeling that both of you are in the same boat. If arguments don't become less frequent, less intense, and shorter, partners would do well to see what they're doing to keep emotionality high and listening absent.

Successful couples learn that the methods most commonly used in attempting to induce unilateral change—complaining, cajoling, sweet-talking, nagging, inducing guilt, becoming angry, and using other forms of emotional manipulation—don't work very well. When empathy doesn't come easy, successful partners work at it—making themselves listen even when they would prefer to be heard. (You don't have to *feel* sympathetic to listen. Sometimes showing concern works from the outside in, the way smiling can put you in a good mood.)

Problems arise when partners keep too many secrets, say yes when they don't mean it, or don't tell the truth about their feelings because they're afraid of arguments. The broken promises that result from being afraid to say no are too great a price to pay for avoiding honest argument. Learning to say no enables you to say yes and mean it. If you're wishing that your partner would realize this, ask yourself, why would someone lie to you?

Trust allows partners to relax vigilance. Being honest is central to establishing this trust, as is being open, listening to and acknowledging the hard things your partner says. Love that grows out of and feeds into self-respect is love for ourselves as we are, not for a partial and carefully selected portion. The person who hesitates to speak wonders if it's safe to broach certain embarrassing or controversial issues. The person who never opens up to you has already decided that it isn't safe to speak.

———◆———

If we want the truth from our partners, we must make it safe for them to tell it.

———◆———

Unfortunately, even with the best of intentions, many couples reach a point where they get bogged down in bitterness and can't hear each other at all. Pursuers get sick of pursuing and distancers get tired of all the pressure, until one or both of them pulls back so far that they reach what family therapist Phil Guerin calls an "island of invulnerability."[1] Anger and animosity build to bitter resentment, and two people who once thrilled each other now give up on each other. Giving up on satisfaction in favor of security, retreating to the island of invulnerability, is cold comfort. But even loneliness sometimes feels better than constant conflict.

[1]Philip Guerin, Leo Fay, Susan Burden, and Judith Kautto, *The Evaluation and Treatment of Marital Conflict* (New York: Basic Books, 1987).

Mates bogged down in bitterness can take a step toward releasing themselves from ice castles of frozen hope by taking a hard look at those hopes. If you're willing to let go of blaming and look for a way back together, examine your expectations. Are your conflicts based on a desire for a partner who is fundamentally different from the one you married? If you're chronically irritated with your partner for being who she or he is, rather than about some particular behavior, then you are in the wrong relationship and it's never going to be very fulfilling. The only things worth fighting about are the things that can be changed.

People come to intimate partnership with an interesting and self-contradictory pair of expectations. They expect their partners both to duplicate the good aspects of their own families and to make up for the bad. To make matters worse, these expectations are often directed toward a partner's limitations rather than his or her strengths. ("I know he could be a really sociable person, if he only tried.")

Don't judge your partner by measuring him (or her) against your strengths; measure him by his strengths. Everybody wants to be appreciated for their contributions.

────◆────

No one benefits when weaknesses or shortcomings become the principal focus of attention in a relationship.

────◆────

To move away from bitterness, concentrate on your partner's strengths. See if some of the things you find objectionable are actually the downside of attributes you appreciate, that even attracted you in the first place. If your partner were different in ways that you'd like, he or she would also be different in ways you wouldn't like. Request changes of certain behavior, but don't punish your partner for what you consider misbehavior. Find your way to forgiveness and acceptance. Tenderness and appreciation will follow.

With maturity, the human quest moves from the outside in, from conquering the world and subduing others to struggling with ourselves— to be who we are and to be connected to others. Looking for love that will simultaneously recreate and undo the past, we latch on to someone and hope for the best.

New couples are ripe with possibility. Over time they become progressively structured as a system, organized by the demands of living together and perhaps raising a family. As we've seen, the process

that transforms two people into a pair is based on accommodation and boundary making.

At first the patterns of behavior a couple establishes are free to vary; later they may become entrenched. But even then, change is possible. The key is complementarity. Those who would remake their own luck must learn to see the annoying things their partners do as one part of a pattern, a pattern that connects two people together in cycles of action and reaction. Look to your part.

"Nobody Around Here Ever Listens to Me!"

HOW TO LISTEN AND BE HEARD WITHIN THE FAMILY

As we've seen, the quality of understanding between people isn't fixed in character but depends on the *process* of their interaction. The great advantage to understanding the process of relationships is flexibility. What can be seen as a pattern of mutual influence can be changed. But there's a catch. Patterns of communication in families are often resistant to change because they're embedded in powerful but unseen structures.

FAMILY STRUCTURE

Families, like other groups, have rich possibilities for relationship and satisfaction. (Don't we marry and later bring children into the world with clear and simple hopes for happiness?) Walt Whitman said, "I contain multitudes." The same could be said of family relationships, though, sadly, many soon congeal into limited and limiting molds.

———◆———

Listening is an art that requires openness to each other's uniqueness and tolerance of differences. The greatest threats to listening in the family are rigid roles, fixed expectations, and pressures to conform.

———◆———

As they are repeated, family transactions foster expectations that establish enduring patterns.[1] Once these patterns are established, family members use only a fraction of the full range of behavior available to them. The first time the baby cries or the in-laws come to visit or a child misses the school bus, it's not determined who will do what. Will the load be shared? Will there be a quarrel? Will one person get stuck with all the work? Soon patterns will be set, roles assigned, and things take on a sameness and predictability.

When a mother tells her child to put away his toys and he ignores her until his father yells at him, an interactional pattern is initiated. If it's repeated, it creates a structure in which father is the heavy and mother is the overburdened listener.

———◆———

Family members tend to have reciprocal and complementary functions; the more one parent does for the children, the less the other is likely to do.

———◆———

The Possibilities in Every Pair

The family system differentiates and carries out its functions through *subsystems*. Every individual is a subsystem, and dyads (such as husband–wife or mother–child), as well as larger groups, make up other subsystems, determined by generation, gender, common interests, and functional responsibilities.

Individuals, subsystems, and whole families are demarcated by interpersonal *boundaries*, invisible barriers that regulate the amount of contact one has with others. Boundaries protect the autonomy of the family and its subsystems. A rule forbidding phone calls at dinnertime estab-

[1]Salvador Minuchin, *Families and Family Therapy* (Cambridge, MA: Harvard University Press, 1974); Salvador Minuchin and Michael P. Nichols, *Family Healing* (New York: The Free Press, 1993).

198 ❖ LISTENING IN CONTEXT

lishes a boundary that insulates the family from outside intrusion. When small children are permitted to freely interrupt their parents' conversations, the boundary separating the parents from the children is weak.

Subsystems that aren't adequately shielded by boundaries limit the development of understanding achievable in these subgroups. If parents always step in to settle arguments between their children, the children won't learn to fight their own battles.

These days when work and school and after-school activities consume so much of our lives, most of us have less personal time and less family time. In the little time we have left over for our families, many of us are reluctant to exclude some members of the family so that others can do things together—such as a father taking a daughter to a basketball game or a mother and son taking in a movie together. This is unfortunate.

———◆———

Time alone together allows every pair in the family a chance to talk and freedom to listen.

———◆———

The most obvious example of a relationship that suffers without time alone together is the one between wife and husband.

Lewis complained that he'd lost his wife to the children. Once Iris was his wife and his friend and his lover. Deciding to have kids and the pregnancy and the birth and those first few wonderful, exhausting months of babyhood brought them closer together. Then, as Lewis saw it, Iris just kind of pulled motherhood over her head, and that was that. They were still friends, sort of, but they were more parents than anything else. They rarely listened to each other because they rarely talked. When Lewis decided to move beyond cursing his fate and casting blame, he found that the simple act of spending time alone together with Iris was the first step in revitalizing his marriage. (In the process he discovered that two people who aren't spending time together aren't just busy; they're also anxious about the quality of their listening.)

Parents also need time alone with each of their children. One of the best ways for parents to listen to their children is to arrange little outings with each one. Once a week isn't too much to aim for. Even if a child has a good relationship with a parent, conversation and intimacy are easier away from everyday distractions. The time a parent spends taking a child out to dinner or for a hike or on a bus ride into

the city may well be the best time in both of their lives. Every pair has possibilities.

Now let's look at how some familiar structural flaws create problems in listening.

When Boundaries Are Blurred

The two biggest mistakes parents make in listening to their children both involve a blurring of boundaries: failing to establish control over their children's behavior and interfering too much in their lives.

The most important thing to keep in mind when listening to children is the difference between allowing them to *express* what they want and allowing them to *do* what they want. When a young child says "I don't want to go to bed," he or she is expressing a feeling and making a request. A wise parent distinguishes between the two and acknowledges the feeling before ruling on the request.

Of course children don't want to go to bed! They might miss something. Staying awake is their way of clutching at life. Parents who blur the distinction between expression and action get into foolish debates with their children. They say "I don't care what you want, you're going to bed anyway." Or they try to convince children that they're tired, as though obeying the rules depended on agreeing with them.

Parents who confuse love with leniency often fall into a pattern of not setting and enforcing rules. Mistaking permissiveness for understanding and democracy for respect, such parents confuse their children about who is in charge and end up too anxious about controlling the children's behavior to be able to listen to their feelings and opinions. The dichotomy between strictness and understanding is a false one; actually, they go together.

The most common alternative to effective discipline is nagging. Constant bickering with children wounds their pride and does more to engender insecurity than to establish parental authority. Effective parents take firm control early in their children's lives and use it sparingly. They make clear and consistent rules *and* back them up. Children learn from consequences. Whenever possible, parents should let them learn from the natural consequences of their behavior. If the consequence of every third or fourth thing they do is that their parents nag them, children learn that their parents are nags and that they themselves are a nuisance.

The boundary that helps parents listen to their children because they know they're in charge is related to one of the crucial elements

in listening: acknowledging what the other person says before respond-ing with what you have to say.

Remember Tommy, the boy whose father lectured him on the fu-tility of anger? If only his father had first acknowledged what Tommy was feeling, the boy might have been less upset and more open to his father's message. Seeing Tommy storm upstairs and slam his door, his father might have said, "It's frustrating when that mower doesn't work, isn't it?" or "Sounds like you had a bad day."

Being a parent in charge doesn't automatically make you a good listener, but it does release you from some of the anxiety about control that gets in the way of listening.

If you listen in on conversations between parents and children, you'll often notice how little each listens to the other. The conversation sounds like two monologues, one consisting of criticism and instruction, the other of denial and pleading. Parents anxious about authority are too easily aggravated to listen to many things children have to say.

Suppose a little girl runs into the kitchen saying, "Look, I caught a caterpillar!" The mother who responds with "Go wash your dirty hands!" is obviously deflating the child's enthusiasm. Saying, "Yes that's nice, but go and wash your hands" isn't good enough either.

"Yes, but . . . " is insufficient acknowledgment. Like adults, chil-dren need to feel heard before they can be open to a new thought. If a mother were to take a minute to acknowledge her child's enthusiasm, she might say, "What a lovely caterpillar," or "Hey, wow! Good for you." The little girl, feeling heard and appreciated, might then wash her hands without needing to be told, especially if she knows that that's the rule.

Even when they make an effort to acknowledge what the other per-son is saying before replying, many people don't make *enough* of an effort.

"Yes, but . . . " is never enough. The *but* drowns out the *yes*.

Emotional Triangles

When he came downstairs, Marshall was surprised to see his teenage daughter sitting at the breakfast table sipping hot chocolate. Before he could ask why she was still home, Paula jumped up and threw her arms around his neck: "No school!" Looking out the window, Marshall saw the yard blanketed in white.

Assuming that the driving would be bad, Marshall decided to wait until after nine before going to work. By time the roads would be

clear and the worst of the traffic would be gone. While he boiled water and ground the beans for coffee, Paula built a fire in the fireplace. When the coffee was ready and the fire blazing, they sat on the couch to watch the flames and share something that had gone out of their relationship: spending time together.

Just then the front door flew open, and in walked Paula's boyfriend, Jerry. "Guess what? School's canceled!"

"Hi, Jerry," Marshall said, none too enthusiastically. Then he went upstairs to his study. He didn't exactly slam the door, but he didn't close it very gently either.

Paula and her father, who had been so close, were growing farther and farther apart in this, her last year of high school. As Marshall sat there brooding about how Paula seemed to drop everything, including her homework, when Jerry was around, he knew he was wrong. Daughters grew up and had boyfriends; a father had to accept these things. He knew he was wrong to be so irritated by Jerry, and now he had that bitterness as well to swallow.

When Paula was born, Marshall vowed never to be one of those fathers who said, "I'll play with you tomorrow." What a remarkable thing it was to be a daddy, gifted and burdened with the power to bestow moments of total delight. As Paula grew older, they still did special things together, but he noticed that her pleasure in his company was no longer entirely spontaneous; he knew that at least part of the time they spent together now was only to please him.

Two weeks later Jerry broke up with Paula. She cried but showed no sign of real grief. These things happen. Marshall couldn't help being secretly relieved and said so to his wife, Elaine.

On Monday Paula said she couldn't face going to school. Couldn't she stay home, just for one day? It seemed little enough to ask. That afternoon Elaine decided to come home early and cheer Paula up with a little shopping expedition. Finding Paula asleep in her room, still in her nightgown, was no great surprise. After all, it wasn't easy being seventeen and having your heart broken. Elaine never knew what made her go into the little bathroom, where she found the empty bottle of aspirin in the wastebasket.

Paula spent four weeks at Twin Oaks on the adolescent unit, where she learned the importance of giving voice to her feelings. When she discovered her anger, she started raging at her mother for always wanting everything to be "nice" and for thinking that going shopping could possibly be the answer to her problems. Her mother then did a surpris-

ing thing: she listened. But when Paula directed her anger at Marshall, telling him that he'd been unfair to blame her for growing up and having a boyfriend, Marshall lashed back at her. Nothing hurts like the truth.

During the last week of Paula's stay in the hospital, Jerry came to visit her, and after she was discharged they started seeing each other again. Marshall was not happy.

Aside from his earlier objections about Jerry, he didn't think it was a good idea for Paula to put herself back into a dependent and vulnerable position. His mind filled with bitter thoughts—about this callow boy who'd hurt his daughter, and might do so again, and about Paula's unforgiving anger at *him*. Well, maybe bitter thoughts were easier than wondering, achingly, how a father lets go of his daughter.

Now when Jerry came around, Marshall was barely civil. He wanted to talk to Paula about not becoming dependent, about the importance of having many friends, but he was afraid of her anger and his own. So he started complaining to Elaine.

Paula, too, started complaining to her mother. "Why is Daddy so unfair?"

Time passed, and the crisis—for that's what Marshall called it; he couldn't bring himself to say "suicide attempt"—began to seem unreal and long ago. Routine reasserted itself, and the only truly tense moments were occasions on which Paula wanted to go somewhere with Jerry, and Marshall looked grim and said nothing. If Paula pressed him, he said sarcastically, "Ask your mother." He felt angry and bereft, but increasingly less so.

Winter passed, and then it was spring. After graduation Paula broke off with Jerry, saying she wanted to have her last summer at home free to be with her friends. Men, she had learned, can be pretty jealous and possessive.

In D. H. Lawrence's *Sons and Lovers,* Paul Morel, the young artist, doesn't feel free to become his own person until his adored mother releases him from her possessive love by dying. In the last scene, when Paul's sweetheart, Miriam, asks if he is now free to marry, he says no. He's become free to go his own way.

One of the great themes of literature is the oedipal conflict—a child's passionate attachment to one parent and rivalry with the other. In real families, children fall in and out of love with each parent many times. We expect fathers to become antagonistic to their sons—and hope they will grow out of it. But when a father becomes alienated from his daugh-

ter, as Marshall did, we seek explanations in character and circumstance. Maybe Marshall was too attached to his daughter to tolerate a rival. Maybe he was too stubborn to let go. Or perhaps we can be more generous and say that it was only natural for him to worry about Paula's relationship with Jerry, considering what happened.

The trouble with these explanations is that they may account for the conflict but not why it wasn't resolved. Most family conflicts eventually get worked out—*if* the parties involved are willing to listen to each other.

When Paula felt the innocent indignation of being misunderstood by her father, it seemed only natural to turn to her mother. Likewise, when Marshall found himself troubled but uncertain about Paula's seeing Jerry again, it seemed reasonable to complain to his wife. In turning away from each other and detouring their dispute through Elaine, Paula and her father created a triangle, one of the great roadblocks to listening.

Take a minute to think about your most difficult relationship in the family. Chances are you thought of the one between you and your spouse, or maybe one of your parents, or a child, or perhaps one of your in-laws. Actually, the relationship you thought of is almost certainly between you and that person and one or more third parties.

Virtually all emotionally significant relationships between two people are shadowed by a third—a relative, a friend, even a memory.

The most notorious triangle is the extramarital affair. An affair might compensate for something missing in a marriage, but as long as one's emotional energy is invested elsewhere, there's little chance of improving the primary relationship. Similarly, if a young husband or wife remains overly attached to his or her parents and runs to them with complaints about the new spouse, the couple in formation may never work out their difficulties. Unlike infidelity and interfering in-laws, many forms of triangulation seem so innocent that we hardly notice their destructive effect. Most parents who have pretty good relationships with their children can't seem to resist complaining to them once in a while about their spouses. "Your mother's *always* late!" "Your father *never* lets anyone else drive!" These interchanges seem harmless enough. Someone who's upset about something has to talk about it, right?

When you hear a story in which one person is a victim and the other is a villain, you're being invited into a triangle.

If something's really bothering you and you're afraid to talk about it—afraid you won't be listened to—the urge to confide in someone else is overwhelming. The trouble with triangles isn't so much that complaining or seeking solace is wrong. The problem is that many triangles become chronic diversions that corrupt and undermine listening in our family relationships.

Mary Lewis was a twenty-year-old single mother who came to the clinic because she was having trouble controlling her three-year-old. After I'd listened to her unhappiness and frustration for about forty minutes, Mary confessed that she'd been hitting the baby and was afraid she might hurt her. I was alarmed but not content to think of the problem as located only in one person, so I asked Mary to bring Tamara to the next session.

Mary, who was alone and isolated, related to her little daughter like a playmate. When the baby was building a tower with blocks, Mary grabbed away some of the blocks to make her own tower, insisting that the baby "share." Later in the session, when I was trying to talk with Mary about her life as a single mom and Tamara started throwing blocks at the door, Mary yelled at her—"Quiet down, OK? I'm talking to the doctor"—but she didn't follow up. Tamara looked up and then continued throwing blocks. She seemed used to ignoring her mother.

Over the next two sessions I helped Mary understand and practice what it means to be a mother-in-charge. Parents take charge by being parental, which consists of two things: nurture and control. (The latter makes the former easier.) Mary learned not to try to control everything the baby did but that when she did need to enforce a rule to do so with a clear, direct message and then follow through with consequences. Becoming more in charge made it easer for her to be more tolerant of Tamara in play. The language of small children is a language of action; "listening" to them means letting them take the lead in play.

Mary was a receptive learner, and her relationship with Tamara improved rapidly. They started getting along better, but in the fifth session Mary reported that she was still having trouble controlling Tamara at home. It was only then that she told me that often when Tamara

was punished, she'd run down the hall to her grandmother's apartment. Instead of supporting her daughter's authority, Mrs. Lewis tried to comfort Tamara by telling her not to worry, "Grandma loves you."

Mrs. Lewis's interference with her daughter's mothering may strike you as too obviously misguided to be of much relevance to the problems of listening in your own life. But aren't we playing the same game whenever we take one person's side against another?

Most family problems are triangular. That's why working only on a twosome may have limited results. Teaching a mother better techniques for disciplining her son won't resolve the problem that she's overinvolved with the boy as a result of her husband's emotional distance from her.

Are triangles always a problem? No. Sometimes you just *have to* talk to someone else. For example, when I complain to my friends about my wife nagging me to take out the garbage, it's just because my wife doesn't understand why I don't always feel like doing it. Besides, if I tried to discuss this directly with her, we might get into tedious and unnecessary issues, like fairness and inequality and so on.

When Rigid Boundaries Keep Us Apart

Some families (or individuals or dyads) establish rigid boundaries, so restrictive that they permit little outside contact, resulting in *disengagement*. Disengaged individuals or subsystems are independent but isolated. On the positive side this fosters autonomy, growth, and mastery. If parents don't hover over their children, telling them what to do and fighting their battles, the children will be forced to develop their own resources. On the other hand, disengagement limits warmth, affection, and nurture.

Being listened to by parents who are a reliable presence in their lives is how children build confidence in their powers of communication. Parents may not always listen, but for a daycare worker in charge of eight toddlers at once it's almost impossible to listen more than very briefly.

A visit to your child's school might result in the sober realization of how little our children are listened to, might inspire you to reoccupy center stage in your children's school-dominated lives. Spending time with your children—in whatever way you can without struggling for control—helps displace peer pressure and pedagogy that pressure your

children to conform or rebel, both of which undermine their efforts to discover themselves. The best way to help children figure out who they are is to listen to them.

Disengagement is a behavioral description for lack of involvement— spending time together, sharing activities, talking. People who are disengaged aren't necessarily uncaring, even if they do seem to spend all their time pursuing their own interests. Often these people are using distance and displacement to protect their own conversational sensitivities.

Suzanne and Rick were worried about their small son's difficulty making friends. The boy's lack of friends, as it turned out, was nothing serious, little more than a ticket of admission to therapy. Actually, Suzanne was far more concerned with lack of tenderness between her and Rick. She complained of his distance and of his not thinking about her needs, but she talked in an anxious, vague way, circling her feelings, never really saying flat out what she meant.

Rick tried to listen but wasn't very good at it. Perhaps he heard and recoiled at the underlying whininess of Suzanne's complaints. Suzanne also mentioned—"by the way"—that she was seeing an individual therapist. When I asked why, she said she needed someone to understand how she felt, and she wasn't getting that from Rick. (*Oh, great,* I thought. *She's using a therapist as her confidant at the same time she's trying to create a more confiding relationship with her husband.*)

The hard core of Suzanne's and Rick's problem with intimacy wasn't that they were busy or that the wild happiness they once knew had faded or simply that they'd gotten out of the habit of being close. It was that they had trouble talking and listening to each other. Her contribution was holding back her complaints and then making them in a nebulous but blaming way. His contribution was neither listening hard enough to penetrate Suzanne's metaphors to hear her loneliness and need nor speaking up about his own complaints. He made a typical unconscious bargain: if he wasn't satisfying her complaints, he'd better not make any of his own, lest that obligate him.

After a while they did start getting through to each other. Suzanne was able to be more direct when she realized how she'd learned to be indirect to avoid her mother's stinging remarks. Rick worked harder at listening and harder at speaking up. Then Suzanne made what felt like a confession. For years she'd spent hours every day confiding in her journal. She spoke of it almost like a child's invisible friend. This, then, was Rick's rival.

Is it wrong to complain about your spouse to an individual ther-apist? Is it wrong to keep a journal? Of course not. But the more we confide our wishes and dissatisfactions to other than the people we want to get closer to, the less pressure we feel to work directly on those rela-tionships.

Disengaged relationships don't exist in a vacuum. To close the dis-tance between yourself and someone you love, keep two things in mind: You catch more flies with honey than with vinegar. And if you want to close the distance in a disengaged relationship, be prepared to hear some complaints. Disengagement isn't just distance; it's protective distance.

When Closeness Smothers Intimacy

Sometimes the boundaries separating the family or a pair within it from the rest of the world are so rigid that the relationship becomes enmeshed, offering closeness at the expense of independence and autonomy. Iso-lation from outside contact—from conversation, broadly speaking, with the rest of the world—puts too much pressure on any relationship. In-timacy grows with time together and time apart.

Enmeshed relationships can comfort like a warm blanket on a cold night or chafe like a warm blanket on a hot night. Children enmeshed with their parents become dependent. They're less comfortable by them-selves and may have trouble relating to people outside the family.

In the back of most people's minds is the unquestioned assumption that parental involvement with children is a good thing: if children are having problems, their parents must not be sufficiently involved or caring. In some cases this is true. But in other cases the problem is a parent's anxious overinvolvement, robbing children of room to be themselves—to have problems, make mistakes, and learn to chart their own course.

A clear boundary between the generations puts the parents in charge, allows them to claim their own rights and privacy, and helps them respect the children's freedom and autonomy within their own orbit.

When family therapists encounter mothers enmeshed with their children, they certainly don't want to blame mothers for this arrange-ment (as though a family's structure were the unilateral doing of one of its members). Oh, no, they wouldn't do that.

Enmeshment, unfortunately, *is* usually blamed on mothers. Who else? They're the ones smothering their children, aren't they? (Most of

us still harbor ancient grudges against the hand that rocked the cradle.) Blaming mothers for a family structure that leaves them underinvolved with their husbands and overinvolved with their children is like saying that a car without spark plugs won't go because the pistons don't fire. Infants and mothers engulfed in the blissful intimacy of new baby love need paternal involvement. They need a supporter and a confidant, not a frustrated competitor.

Children need attachment? So do their parents, not just to their children but to each other.

Some people are togetherness oriented. They value closeness and connection, but these values can sometimes actually reduce intimacy if they result in pressure to conform. To achieve genuine closeness, you must respect all family members' sovereign individual experience, their right to their own feelings and their own point of view.

Forming a United Front

To forge an alliance that works, both parents must yield some separateness to gain in belonging. *Accommodation* is the process by which people adjust their differences to come together. It is the mechanism of compromise, sometimes a deliberate matter of agreement and cooperation, sometimes the result of instinctive mutual adjustments. Unified family leadership is based on communication, compromise, and agreement between the parents and then presented to the children as one policy. Most parents discover how important it is to accommodate their differences about nurture and control to present a united front.

---◆---

When a child's misbehavior persists, you can bet that one parent isn't backing the other up.

---◆---

If you don't feel supported by your partner in parenting, if you end up doing all the driving or always have to be the one to enforce the rules, don't start blaming your partner. Maybe he or she disagrees with what you're doing. Try asking.

"I get the feeling you don't really agree with my way of handling this. Maybe you don't think I'm interested in your opinion—but I am. I'd really like to hear what you think."

Parenting is also an excellent place to observe the other face of complementarity—polarization. Instead of coming together on certain

issues, parents move further apart. If one is too strict, the other may react by becoming more lenient. The more one harps at the children, the more the other tries to compensate by being indulgent.

Polarization is like what happens if the controls on your dual-control electric blanket accidentally get switched. The first attempt by either of you to make it warmer or colder will set off a cycle of mutual maladjustments.

Small differences drive some couples to antagonistic opposites. A mother whose threshold for telling the kids to quiet down at the dinner table is only slightly higher than her husband's may never get the chance to admonish them if he always shushes them before she feels the need. Every time he reprimands the kids she'll feel that he's being too harsh. If she complains about his impatience, he'll feel betrayed and angry. The dinner table then becomes a tense battleground, where instead of sticking together, two parents become adversaries in a game where everybody loses.

Why do couples accommodate on some issues and polarize on others? Because we accommodate where we're able but polarize in response to our own inner conflicts.

The engine that drives conflicts within us to become conflicts between us is projection. This dynamic comes into play when an ambivalent inner balance between pairs of conflicting impulses (dependence–independence; emotional expression–restraint; desire–anxiety; privacy–companionship) is resolved by projecting one's own motivation onto the other person. A man (or woman) who's afraid of anger may express it through passive control that provokes his (or her) partner. When they fight, she gets angry and he gets hurt. The man who feels only hurt may be seething with rage but can remain unaware of those feelings as long as he has a collusive, obliging mate who will act out his anger for him. In the process, the partner who shows anger may be able to avoid facing inner feelings of weakness and helplessness.

Polarized mates fight in each other denied and repudiated aspects of themselves.

Projection and polarization turn couples into antagonists and prevent partners from integrating latent possibilities in the self—because these are played out by the other. The tough man may be unable to integrate his softer side to the extent that his wife acts emotional and helpless. His dependent wishes and vulnerability are repudiated because

they're seen as her domain. She then becomes a dependent and demanding wife. This is one reason men take revenge for their dependency—that bottomless need for mother-love—by bullying and criticizing their wives for openly exhibiting the needs they themselves don't dare express.

In our day, gender differences have permeated the consciousness of the middle class. No longer do we believe that men are strong and women weak. Yet what is the current vogue of celebrating women's and men's uniqueness if not stereotyping updated? It's hard for husbands and wives to work at partnership when all around they are told that women speak in a different voice and men have strange ways of communicating.

Are we once again to believe that anatomy is destiny? So many husbands and wives run out of patience with each other that they sometimes lose hope of ever reaching understanding. This haunting feeling of despair is something that comes to all of us from time to time. If it helps some people to blame failures of understanding on irreconcilable gender differences, and if doing so seems to armor some people against their own despair, fine. But if stereotyping serves to abstract members of the opposite sex, to turn them into categories, and to avoid genuine encounter, that I think is unfortunate. Exaggerating gender differences is a weapon and a shield favored by those who fail to find understanding—no, fail to *reach* understanding.

The wounded narcissism and boundless ambition of our time also militate against self-sacrifice, compromise, and partnership. In hard and troubled times like ours, loyalty, tolerance, cooperation, and complementarity—the values necessary to create and sustain family harmony—are greatly undervalued. Too often we hear what once might have been thought of as teamwork described as codependency.

We tend not to see complementarity. Instead, we see control and submission, power and weakness, villain and victim. In trying to create more flexibility for both men and women, we are in danger of forgetting that complementarity can be mutually enhancing. Individual self-actualization does not require constant self-assertion. The sturdy self can tolerate difference and thrive on it.

LISTENING TO YOUNG CHILDREN

From two to seven months "listening" to a child boils down to paying attention and responding to the baby's moods. When new parents leave

the hospital and bring home their first baby, that smiling miracle of their own creation, they wonder, *What now? How will we know what to do?* They soon find out. The baby's needs are simple, and the crying that announces them is simply overwhelming.

Once the baby is fed and changed and has had enough sleep, parents convey their responsiveness through cuddling and play. "Listening" at this early age consists primarily of reading the baby's mood—rather than imposing the parents' moods, as though the baby were an extension of themselves. Lucky babies have parents whose temperamental styles match their own. You get a sense of this fit when you ask a mother about her baby, and she beams. "He's an easy baby, so sweet and cuddly." "He's so enthusiastic, he just loves to play!" Mismatched parents complain that theirs is a difficult child—too demanding or not responsive enough.

More reliable than luck is a parent's willingness to tune in to and follow the baby's rhythm. Long before the baby can talk, his parents demonstrate the degree to which they're able to listen. Here as elsewhere, flexibility and responsiveness demonstrate willingness to tolerate the otherness of the other. Call it sensitivity.

Being listened to creates a sense of being understandable and worthwhile. Not being listened to fosters insecurity. In practice, however, not being listened to may take forms that aren't always obvious. Here are some cues that you're not listening to your young child—despite the fact that you do indeed care very much.

"Watch Out! Don't Touch That!"

Some parents who seem attentive are more concerned with the external environment than their children. They hover over their babies and make sympathetic noises, but they don't listen. They pay attention to the hard edges of a table, sharp things on the floor, cold drafts, and hot food. Because they worry a lot, we sometimes think of them as very involved with their children. But because they're preoccupied with trying to make the world safe, they remain too anxious to share the baby's experience. These hovering "child-centered" parents provide almost no experience of intersubjectivity. The impression of closeness they convey is an illusion. Hovered-over but not-listened-to children may become "dependent," in the sense of being uneasy on their own—not because they're used to intimacy but because they suffer from a pervasive sense of aloneness, an intolerable feeling from which they use superficial relationships to distract themselves.

"Quiet Down, Go Wash Your Hands, and for Goodness' Sake Don't Touch Yourself There!"

More common than this general lack of attunement is the selective attunement by which parents convey to their infants what is shareable. In this way the parents' desires, fears, prohibitions, and fantasies affect the basic wiring of the child's self-system, leaving the child with the conviction that he is or is not a self worthy of respect.

The power of parents' selective attunement determines what behavior falls inside or outside the realm of acceptability. Is it all right to bang toys hard and noisy, to get real dirty, to masturbate? It includes preferences for people: is it all right to get mad at Grandma or sometimes to prefer to play with her rather than with Mommy? And it includes the extent to which degrees or types of internal states—joy, sadness, delight—can be experienced with another person. Is the child whose parents invariably try to jolly him out of it when he's frightened likely to come to them with his fears when he's older?

It is in the breadth of attunement—from generous to cramped— that parents help determine whether their children will feel OK about themselves and whether they will have a broad or narrow range of acceptable experience.

Suppose a one-year-old listening to *Peter and the Wolf* is happy and excited. He's moved by the music and wonders if his mother feels it too. He looks up, and she smiles back at him; her eyes are bright and she's nodding. *Yes, she feels it too!* With this attunement, the child knows that he feels something that can be shared—rather than something that's somehow not supposed to be and thus should thus be kept secret. His feeling is validated; and since the feeling is part of him, he too is validated. Being moved by music becomes part of the universe he expects to share with others.

"Don't Brag, Honey. It's Not Nice."

In addition to the lessons parents teach deliberately, they shape their children's experience and behavior with negative affective responses. When a little child proudly shows off to a parent who responds with disgust or disinterest, it's a slap in the face of the child's healthy narcissism. This is shame.

What children show off for their parents' approval isn't simply who they are and what they can do; it's also their grand fantasies of who they wish they were and what they dream of doing. They're not little

and weak—oh, no, they're big and strong. If parents squelch that wonderful wish to make an impression—for whatever reason—the child may decide that he's worthless or unlovable or that he has to achieve really big things for anybody to notice him.

Before you let negative reactions slip out, think about why you're tempted to be so critical or disapproving. Is it really a prohibition your child needs, or are you more concerned about what other people might think of your child (and yourself)? Sometimes, in an attempt to instill social graces too early, we crush a child's self-respect. Again, *listen* to what your child is saying and react to that. The little girl who shouts, "I can jump higher than Robbie" isn't putting down her toddler pal but asking for your approval of her accomplishments. Why not give it to her?

Or is your instinctive admonition based on a desire to force the child to live up to your own expectations? A little girl runs to her mother and says, "Mommy, Mommy, guess what! I got an A in spelling!" "That's nice, dear," the mother responds, sounding pleased, but not very. The daughter tries again. "There's *twenty-nine* kids, and I got the second highest score." "That's good, honey." The conversation continues another couple of minutes, with the little girl proud and excited, trying to drive up her mother's enthusiasm, and the mother pleased that her daughter did well but not wanting her to get hooked on achievement (like her father is). When the little girl persists, the mother finally says, "Don't brag so much. It isn't nice."

One minute the little girl is throbbing with excitement. Getting an A was wonderful. She rushed home to tell the good news to her mother in order to complete her experience. You could say she met with misunderstanding, but it was worse. Because a child seeking an empathic response is reaching out, exposed, a failed response is like a head-on collision.

Empathic failure can come out sounding mean: "Don't be such a baby!" "Stop showing off!" But even indifference or a simple lack of enthusiasm can hurt a child who's excited and eager for attention. When our children make the mistake of daring not to be invented by us, when they reveal, perversely, minds and wills of their own, we are put to the test.

THE PARENT'S GIFT OF EMPATHY

A parent's empathy—understanding what the child is feeling, and showing it—builds a bridge of understanding, linking the child to someone

special who listens and cares, thus confirming that the child's feelings are recognizable and legitimate. The sharing of emotional experience is the most meaningful and pervasive feature of true relatedness.

How do you empathize with a child who won't stop pestering or complaining or showing off, as though he were the center of the universe and you had no concerns of your own? The solution is not to mistake sympathy for empathy. Sympathy means to feel the same as rather than to be understanding of. It's an emotion that makes parents suffer *with* unhappy children, and that feeling motivates them to talk children out of their feelings or to do *for* them rather than to empathize with them.

Foremost among the obstacles to listening are those that stem from our need to "do something" about what someone tells us: to defend ourselves, to disagree, or to solve whatever problems are being described, because hearing about them makes us anxious. Parents are particularly prone to offer advice; it comes with the job description. But if a father's first response to his son's complaining about a sunburn is that he should have used sunblock, the boy will feel blamed rather than commiserated with. Likewise, if a little girl complains that she doesn't have any friends and her mother tells her that if she were more friendly to other children they'd reciprocate, the girl might conclude that even her mother doesn't like her.

Psychologists use the term *empathic immersion* to describe the intense and focused listening that helps therapists understand their patients' experience. It is an apt and evocative metaphor, but it is of course hyperbole. Perhaps a better metaphor for empathy would be taking someone's hand.[2] Two clasped hands are still two hands—but they are also two hands touching, the warmth and pulse of one in contact with the other.

To be better listeners parents should lead less and follow more. If a child shows signs of distress, a simple statement like "You feel bad, don't you?" is more likely to make him feel understood than pressuring him to define exactly what he feels or telling him. If an exasperated child indicates that she wants to be alone, let her. She may need time to pull herself together. If someone is having a hard time putting something into words, it's often more empathic to say something like "It's hard to explain, isn't it?" than to guess what the person is trying to say.

---

[2] I am indebted to Alfie Kohn for this metaphor. Alfie Kohn, *The Brighter Side of Human Nature: Altruism and Empathy in Everyday Life* (New York: Basic Books, 1990).

A parent who finishes a child's thoughts for him is the opposite of empathic.

Listening well is more midwifery than dentistry. In the presence of an empathic parent, children are able to discover their own minds rather than having to resist or succumb to what their parents expect them to feel.

There's no way of calculating what constitutes sufficient empathy or how much misunderstanding a child can tolerate without being damaged; but, clearly, children are remarkably resilient. The empathic failure that saps self-regard isn't as often the kind of dramatic abuse that completely rejects the child as it is a silent, invidious lack of responsiveness. Empathic failure doesn't "batter," "bruise," or "injure" children; it deflates them.

Empathy is energizing. Being listened to releases us from self-concern and mobilizes us to actively engage the world around us. Children lacking empathy grow up preoccupied with themselves, as though attention were a need that, unmet, keeps growing. The unlistened-to child remains locked in silent conversation within himself, too anxious and unavailable to enter the freedom of the moment.

Parents Are Human Too

Why do parents so often fail to acknowledge what their children tell them? Question their accounts in a way that makes them feel not taken seriously? Criticize them for feeling bad? Tell them they're lazy when they find something difficult? Say they talk too much when they only want to be heard? Because children are a trial.

Parental guilt over failures of patience and empathy isn't just foolish self-reproach. Kids *do* drive us crazy, and sometimes we *are* mean to them.

One day when my son Paul was two, I was right in the middle of screaming at him, "If you don't shut up *right now,* I'll give you something to cry about!" when Bob Pierce, my first and favorite psychotherapy supervisor, walked in the front door—he from whom I'd learned about the hurt and harm parents inflict by trampling their children's feelings. It was not my finest moment. Nor as it turned out was it the last time I would get ugly with my children for having inconvenient feelings.

Every parent has felt that blind fury, and most of us have yelled at our children, screamed at them, blistered them—and seen them

stricken. When memory stabs us with our failures, we think of these outbursts of unkindness, the times when we lost our tempers and flayed them with our anger. But it isn't these sudden storms of emotion that rob children of the listening they need; rather, it is an everyday atmosphere of unresponsiveness.

Sustaining Empathy

Thinking about sad-faced children, hurting but afraid to reach out, it's hard for us not to be touched. We want to put our arms around those little kids and love them. We know how they feel. But here's where it's possible to get confused. Empathy is generous, and so it is easy to slide into thinking of it as just another way of saying loving kindness. Empathy is loving, but it doesn't mean being affectionate or supportive or helpful or a lot of other nice things. Some parents are loving but the love they express is so intense and suffocating that it smothers a child's initiative and is anything but empathic.

❖

It's easier to listen to children's wants when parents are firm with their own wills.

❖

Other parents mistake sympathy for empathy, as we've discussed, and that often goes hand in hand with confusing lenience and love. The often overindulged children of today's harried parents don't feel appreciated; they feel anxious, uncontained by parents who are themselves floundering in a social environment that doesn't support or sustain them.

Parents who allow the boundary between generations to erode become not grown-ups-in-charge but peers and playmates, without the authority to enforce boundaries or the credibility to comfort and protect. "No" is less palatable than "yes," and so it's often served up with a lot of verbal sauce, the way some people try to get kids to eat vegetables by smothering them in butter and salt (the vegetables). These parents won't magically take charge if someone teaches them to use gold stars and time-out chairs. Setting limits and enforcing rules—beginning when the children are small—follows naturally from maintaining a clear boundary between the generations. It also permits and facilitates empathy.

When children are little, the greatest impediment to empathy is a parent's not being in charge. When children get a little older, the

most difficult part of empathy is letting them be themselves. Many parents have an easier time empathizing with children when they're little. They're comfortable with closeness. But sustaining empathy means allowing children to differentiate, to have their own wishes, their own interests, their own feelings. Children aren't merely cute or needy or headstrong; they're people, and they yearn, like you and me, to be acknowledged and taken seriously. This is the hard part: loving children not only because they're ours but also because they aren't.

"You Make Me So Mad!"

It starts with the "terrible twos," that period in the career of novice parents when they first reveal their frustration and intolerance of the fact that their small fry want to become little persons in their own right. Imagine getting worked into a temper just because a tiny child is practicing autonomy! Parents who aren't constantly anxious about controlling their children listen with pride to their children's self-assertion—even if it means hearing "No!" at sonic boom levels a thousand times a day.

The understandable but misguided ambition to raise perfect children tempts parents to cross the line between the child's rights and the parents' responsibility. Mutual respect is fostered by allowing children a voice and, where possible, a choice in matters that affect them. Notice the distinction between voice and choice. Some decisions should be left to children. Other decisions that affect the child's welfare are the parents' responsibility. In such matters, children should have a voice but not a choice.

Even a two-year-old can be asked whether she wants a half a glass of juice or a whole glass. Asking very young children what they want for breakfast may be granting too much latitude, but you can show respect for their right to choose by asking them if they want their eggs boiled or poached or their cereal hot or cold.

Perhaps the most important shift a parent can make is to move from wanting their children to be successful to being pleased with them, right now, loving them, enjoying them, and accepting that they are who they are. They are separate from us; they are themselves. Parents can begin to really hear their children only when they set aside thinking of them as unfinished products, clay for the parents to mold. None of this is meant to say that we should not control and limit our children's behavior—for our own convenience as well as for their own good. But once we accept that they are who they are, for better or worse, we can

worry less about them, relax our attempts to control and reform and manipulate and improve them, and concentrate on listening to them.

LISTENING TO TEENAGERS

One reason being a parent remains an amateur sport is that as soon as you get the hang of it, your children get a little older and throw you a whole new set of problems. Successful parents learn to shift their style of parenting to accommodate to their children's development.

As children grow, parents should allow them more volitional control and show increasing respect for their ideas and opinions. "Because I said so" may be the best answer to a small child who wants to know why he has to do something, but older children deserve an explanation. This shift conveys respect for the child and helps build self-respect as well as responsibility.

Avoiding Battles for Control

There's a lot of talk these days about how children don't respect authority. They argue with their parents and speak rudely to their teachers. Who teaches children to argue? Parents who get into needless battles of control.

"You're Right."

Most people understand that adolescent rebellion is normal and that it serves a purpose, but as adults we tend to misunderstand the child's experience by seeing it primarily in relation to ourselves. We listen to ourselves but not to our children. Parents who think of their teenagers as "defiant" confuse autonomous strivings with stubbornness. Most teenagers are strong-willed, not oppositional. They struggle not to defy their parents but to gain respect and acknowledgment, and they struggle as hard as they have to. How far they carry that struggle, how extreme their behavior, is determined largely by how tenaciously parents resist recognizing their voice in an effort to retain control.

Too many parents are afraid to say "You're right." They're afraid that letting their children be right makes them wrong and afraid that letting the children win means that the parents will lose. In fact, the opposite is true.

A girl who can't win control of how to dress for school may seek to express herself by putting on dramatic makeup after she leaves the house. If she cannot win that battle, she may escalate the conflict further, deliberately coming home late or getting into shouting matches with her mother. Or she may defy her parents by smoking cigarettes or shoplifting or experimenting with drugs. Reckless experiments, chancy relationships—all for the honor of proving she has some say in her life. Wouldn't it be easier to listen to her?

"No, because. . . ."

Some parents are willing to grant freedom but cannot tolerate rudeness. Like everything else in family life, adolescent rudeness is a function of interaction.

A frequent complaint of teenagers is that their parents don't listen to them. Teenagers are exquisitely sensitive to disrespect; they demand to be treated like people with a right to their opinions. Often without realizing, parents provoke adolescents by talking to them from the same one-up position they used when the children were small. The "rude" response is a protest against what feels like a shameful put-down. Parents can avoid escalating arguments into power struggles by tolerating the children's right to *say* whatever they think, even if it means using language parents don't like.

Parents who struggle to listen to their children even when it's hard are best able to handle the inevitable battles with their teenagers. Explain the "no." "No, I won't drive you to the concert on Sunday night, because I don't want to drive that far, and I don't want you out on a school night." But don't argue. Don't debate. And don't escalate: "And if you dare to take the bus, I'll ground you for a month." Finally, and most important, don't insist on having the last word.

Recognizing the Need to Break Away

A major reason for lack of communication between teenagers and parents is the parents' failure to recognize and accept the inevitable: if their children are to grow up, they must break away from the older generation. Translation: it's a teenager's job to criticize his parents. The same children who once looked up to Mommy and Daddy as giants who can do no wrong now look down on them as impossible old fogies who can't do anything right. This disdainful attitude is a natural stage in the evo-

lution of the family system and the development of the self. It's a necessary part of pulling away and becoming your own person. When parents are threatened and fight back, they fuel an escalating series of
conflicts, which in many cases are never settled, only broken off when
the children leave home.

It may not be pleasant to hear your teenager criticizing everything
and everybody, but it's part of the process of building self-esteem. Parents who criticize their children for being critical are fighting fire with
gasoline.

The more inflexible the parents are, the more defiant teenagers will
be. Too many put-downs wear away at children's self-esteem and prompt
them to reject everything about their parents. Some people are so
ashamed of their parents that they spend their whole lives trying not
to be like them. They're so busy *not being* their parents that there's no
room left for them to be themselves.

In the process of looking for new models of how to be, teenagers
often glom onto someone outside the family—it can be almost anyone,
just as long as he or she is different—and perhaps more willing than
the parents to take the child seriously, to listen. When this happens,
their ability to hear their parents is compromised, though they may have
a fairness channel that remains open. If a parent can listen calmly and
demonstrate openness to what a teenager is trying to say, but the child
doesn't reciprocate, the parent can say, "You're not being fair to me."
The child may then listen. Teenagers respect fairness, especially if it
is reciprocal.

You might say something like "Now that I understand your point
of view, would you be willing to let me explain mine?" The point about
fairness isn't to demand tit for tat, but that really listening to someone
frees her from being preoccupied with her point of view and makes her
more willing to listen to you.

"I understand that you're upset with me. But is it fair for me to have
heard your opinion and then you not be willing to listen to mine?"

Breaking Out of Mutual Antagonism

One reason parents and teenagers have trouble listening to each other
is that each side hears the other only as objects in relation to themselves. When teenagers, who want respect and freedom, come to expect only criticism and control, they shut their ears to what their parents
are trying to say and respond reflexively with either resistance or passive compliance.

Teenagers who notice only their parents' criticism and control forget that they themselves aspire to certain grown-up achievements, such as an education and a good job. And parents who hear their children only in response to their own worries forget that *they* also value much of what their children want—self-discovery, pursuing one's own path in life. When the narrative of control and rebellion comes to dominate the relationship, these shared values are forgotten in the ensuing strife.

When oppositional perspectives take over, parents and children fail to register inputs that don't fit with the dominant theme. An angry father may not notice or acknowledge the times his son volunteers to help his parents out. The son may not appreciate or remember the times when his father has encouraged his freedom.

Breaking out of mutual antagonism is difficult but not impossible. Listen hard and acknowledge exceptions to the dominant concern—times when your youngsters act responsibly, show restraint, and listen to your point of view. Adolescents can learn to recognize and appreciate the occasions when their parents don't push or criticize.

If a parent concerned about the dangerous attraction of smoking or drinking is lucky enough to have a child who admits or even alludes to this kind of experimentation, he or she has a rare opportunity to refrain from giving the expected lecture. Candor is built on trust.

It's also important to acknowledge your teenager's right to see things differently from you—not just because that's true but also because that's imperative to having him or her listen to your point of view. To make this explicit you might say something like "I'm not saying that I'm right and you're wrong. I'm simply trying to get you to understand how strongly I feel about this and why." When you do get the privilege of attention, it's best to start by describing what you're afraid of, not why your teenager is wrong.

Striking a Balance between Autonomy and Connection

Teenagers are still children. For all their opposition to their parents and their breathless enthusiasm for the adventures of adulthood, they still need their families. Autonomy is important, but so is connection.

Adolescents need their parents to listen to their troubles, their hopes and ambitions, even some of their farfetched plans. The more tolerant parents are, the more they remain open to hearing their children, the more possible it is to preserve connection. Talking and sharing increase when divergent ideas are admitted into the family's values and habits.

In realizing that they can disagree and argue with their parents,

adolescents come to differentiate between conventional views of relationships—as nonconflicted—and a more realistic view, namely that disagreement, conflict and confrontation, and working though differences are part of a healthy, intimate relationship.

Teenage boys still expect to be supported and understood by their parents, but perhaps more than anything else they want the freedom to be independent. Teenage girls, on the other hand, often have more complex and ambivalent relationships, especially with their mothers. As a member of Carol Gilligan's study of the relational world of adolescent girls, Sharon Rich found that mothers' dependence on their daughters troubles the daughters and makes it harder for mothers to accept daughters' independence. Daughters want mothers to be there for them, but also to trust them, accept their independence, and honor their choices. Over and over, girls reported being unhappy with mothers they described as poor listeners.

"These girls depict themselves as receiving two messages when they feel their mothers are not listening: Their mothers do not care and are not 'there' for them; and their own opinions are not important."

As one girl in the study reflected: "I sort of feel that I don't want her to know too much about me. I mean not that I'm trying to keep everything a secret, but just that I want to be more myself and less her trying to mold me. And so there are lots of things I don't tell her because I just know what she would say . . . and I don't feel like hearing it."[3]

Adolescents who don't feel listened to flare up in angry resentment, and later retreat into silence and secrecy as the best way they know to protect their vulnerable, distinct voices and themselves. In attempting to protect themselves from feeling "terrible," teenagers may cut off the primary means for changing the relationship: communication.

Unheard adolescents who flee their families are seldom really free. Protective distance affords them the illusion that they are grown up, but it is only an illusion. Adolescents who find it necessary to break off relationships with their parents remain frozen in adolescent patterns, forever vulnerable to overreaction.

Not enough discipline and too much intrusiveness make parents poor listeners, and so does failing to lead full satisfying lives of their

---

[3]Sharon Rich, "Daughters' views of their relationships with their mothers." In Carol Gilligan, Nona Lyons, and Trudy Hanmer, eds., *Making Connections: The Relational Worlds of Adolescent Girls at Emma Willard School* (Cambridge, MA: Harvard University Press, 1990), 268.

own. The boundary between generations that puts parents in charge and enables them to listen is also related to what's on the other side of that boundary—the parents and their relationship with each other.

It's possible to celebrate and enjoy family life without denying the pain and boredom that families inflict on their members. But it may not be possible to resolve those vexations that creep into our lives and break our hearts without recognizing the patterns that unite us.

Most families have problems not because there's something inherently wrong with them but because they've gotten stuck. Families resist change even more than individuals do because the structure that holds them together is supported by the actions of every single family member. That's why systems are stubborn. What we mustn't forget, though, is that even though families act like systems, it is still individual persons who do the acting—and they, as you may have noticed, can sometimes be pretty courageous.

"I Knew You'd Understand"

BEING ABLE TO HEAR
FRIENDS AND COLLEAGUES

Friends make the best listeners. They may not love us quite as much as our families do, but then they don't need quite as much from us either, and that frees them to listen better. No matter how close we are to our friends, we retain a certain autonomy that enables us to listen without needing to control them or protect ourselves.

WHY FRIENDS MAKE THE BEST LISTENERS

Sandy had just come from a terrific workshop on counseling high school students when she met her friend Roberta for lunch. If she didn't trust Roberta's unselfish support so completely, Sandy might have hesitated to tell her that she was thinking about doing something that would mean an end to their lunches. The two of them had been teaching French at the same school for nine years, and now Sandy had decided to go back and get a master's in guidance counseling. It was a big decision, scary and exciting, and she needed someone sympathetic to talk to.

Roberta was startled and dismayed by Sandy's plan. Giving up tenure and going back to school seemed a rash and risky thing to do. How did Sandy know she would like counseling? Wasn't she taking an awful chance? Besides, Roberta couldn't imagine getting along at work

without Sandy. Sandy was the only sane person in the place. It would be awful if she left. But Roberta didn't say any of this. No matter how much she questioned Sandy's decision, it was Sandy's decision, and Roberta could see how excited she was by this new dream of hers. So she listened.

It took Sandy two more days to get up the nerve to mention her idea about going back to school to her husband, Gordon. "I can't believe you'd even think of doing such a thing!" was his answer. "Are you crazy? You've *got* a perfectly good job. You *love* teaching French. How are we going to pay for you to go back to school?" Sandy started to protest, but she was really too hurt to bother, and so they finished supper in silence.

Sandy's friend's ability to listen to her was the mirror opposite of her husband's inability. Roberta could listen because she wasn't threatened—or at least not *as* threatened.

Clearly Gordon had a direct stake in whether or not his wife went back to school. He had a right to his concerns and his opinion. At some point the decision may become a joint one. But his inability even to listen to Sandy's plan not only deprived her of the chance to play with it out loud but also made her *less*, not more, likely to consider his feelings in the final decision.

Whether it's money, the kids, or your mother-in-law, there are unsafe subjects in all family relationships. A woman doesn't talk to her Catholic relatives about having an abortion. The same woman may not risk telling her husband that she might be able to sleep better if they got separate beds, if she's afraid he'd be too hurt and angry even to entertain the possibility. He might not tell her about a problem he's having at work if he's afraid she'll respond with criticism or unwanted advice. He might not want to burden her with financial worries (or share the decision making). It's not necessarily a question of keeping secrets, though most family members have a few. Rather, it's simply hard to live with someone and tell that person everything. With friends, few subjects are off limits.

In conversations between friends, little misunderstandings can be passed over or allowed to be forgotten between breaks in contact. Such differences between people who live together are harder to ignore or forget.

The relationship between friends is voluntary and optional; you can leave if you want to, and therefore it's safer to be honest and take risks.

You can talk over painful and embarrassing subjects, reveal self-doubts, try out different sides of yourself, and be who you are.

People show interest, caring, and respect by the quality of their listening. Friends who listen make *us* feel interesting, and their interest inspires us to say more interesting things. Their receptivity is transformative: by listening intently to us, our friends make us feel larger, more alive. That's the glory of friendship.

A close friend is someone with whom we can talk about almost anything. With such friends we take turns as selfobjects, caring listeners willing for a time to submerge ourselves and be there without strings for the other person. Friendship grows with mutual disclosure. So do we. The compassion and empathy friends share when they listen to our triumphs and worries deepens us; their understanding and acceptance keep us from feeling alone—and help us understand and accept ourselves.

If friendship deepens us, it also broadens us. Friendships expand our definition of ourselves and awaken unrealized possibilities in us, possibilities that weren't part of the roles we were scripted to play in our families. With many friends we can express many sides of ourselves. The intimacy of friendship, the selfobject function, strengthens us. Mutuality, the sharing function, stretches us.

With friends we are easy, but, sadly, it isn't always easy to find time for friendship. When I asked people what interfered most with their talking and listening to friends, by far the most common—and wistful—response was "I'm too busy." In crowded and hurried lives, competing obligations often squeeze out anything optional, like spending time with friends. But even though many of us are terribly preoccupied these days, it's more than lack of time that undermines our friendships.

WHEN FRIENDS TAKE SIDES

After her divorce Maggie turned to her friends. They saw her through the shock of separation and the months that followed. Though she felt somewhat adrift, at least she was not alone.

Maggie's friend Liz was also divorced and disillusioned; she understood what it was to be single again, having to start all over, the indignities and misunderstandings. The two women had known each other for nine years, ever since they met at a conference for real estate brokers (ever since, in fact, they both skipped the afternoon session and ran into each other at a local art gallery).

Liz made friends easily. She had embraced Maggie with her warmth and held her with her intelligence and her keen eye for the pretentious and foolish. They both liked to cook and have friends over, but the best times were when it was just the two of them. They met often, for lunch or breakfast or for a drink after work, reveling in endless spirited conversations about work, families, friends, what they were reading, how they felt—if any subject was off limits, they hadn't come to it yet.

Maggie met Dominic three years after her divorce. As chance would have it, he lived in Liz's building, and on several occasions she actually ran into him in the elevator or downstairs lobby. She found him attractive but couldn't imagine speaking to him; he seemed so self-possessed and unapproachable. It came as a surprise, therefore, when he started talking to her one Saturday afternoon and, after no more than five minutes, asked her out. To her equal surprise, she found herself accepting.

If opposites attract, it might have been the perfect match. Maggie had the ruddy complexion and emotional reserve of her Scottish ancestors, while Dominic was Greek, with dark hair and olive skin and an openly expressive nature. She liked the way his mind worked, all intuition and confidence. What a relief after all those pale, shadow men her friends had fixed her up with!

The passion Maggie felt with Dominic stunned her. Unfortunately, as she soon found out, the price to be paid was a series of passionate quarrels. Dominic was jealous: of her time, her friends, and just about everything else. Though he himself might sometimes be busy for days, he expected her to be available whenever he wanted to see her. When she wasn't, there would be storms, scenes, and shouting matches.

When Maggie told her friends about all the trouble she was having with Dominic, they were sympathetic. Liz got angry. She considered Dominic's possessive jealousy abusive and thought Maggie was wrong to put up with it. "I'd never let a man treat *me* that way," she said. Liz too had had expectations of men and had been disappointed. Men had come to represent an absence, an absence that they could not or would not fill.

After one particularly Vesuvian outburst, Maggie decided not to see Dominic for a while. As long as they'd been going together, Liz had held back the worst of her criticism, but now that Maggie was considering ending the relationship, Liz spoke up. Maggie would be better off without him, she said. In this opinion, Liz was not alone. All of Maggie's friends felt the same way: if Dominic was causing her so much unhappiness, she should dump him.

Unfortunately, sympathy can get in the way of empathy. Unable to suspend their own emotional response, which was to rescue Maggie from the anguish she communicated to them, her friends urged her to put an end to what was making them as well as her unhappy. That's what friends often do when we complain about another person: they take our side and push us to retaliate.

It's one thing to honor a friend's right to happiness, but far more difficult to respect her right to suffer unhappiness if she decides to go to war for love.

Maggie was buoyed by the sympathy of her friends but felt pressured by their urging her to break off with Dominic. While it's comforting to have someone to share your feelings with, it's not always comforting to be told what to do about them. Dominic's rages might be reason to leave him, but she wasn't sure. It's called ambivalence.

So after a while Maggie stopped talking to her friends about Dominic. She wasn't just angry at Dominic; she also loved him. While it's OK for you to criticize your lover or spouse or family member, it's a mistake for friends to agree. Your griping expresses one side of your ambivalence—and leaves you free to do whatever you decide about the relationship. But a friend's agreeing that someone you're close to *is* a terrible person is a judgment and a rejection. It's a boundary violation.

There is certainly no formula for an empathic response, but it may help to remember that there are two sides to every dilemma. Understanding — empathy—therefore usually means acknowledging conflict. If a person hasn't acted to resolve a problem, there's probably a reason. Statements of understanding recognize this. Liz might have said something like "You sound pretty unhappy, but I guess you're not sure about what to do?" Instead she said, "Dominic's not good enough for you. If you go back to him now, you'll hate yourself for it."

There are things that have no place in friendship, and judging is one of them.

Showing empathy to friends doesn't mean just caring about them; it means listening to their point of view, whether or not you agree with it. Friendship doesn't require total acceptance or neutrality; but before they disagree or give advice, good friends listen.

Here is an example, from Paul Auster's novel *Leviathan*, of a friend struggling to be empathic. Peter's friend Sachs is telling him about the accident in which he fell off a four-story fire escape, trying to explain

that he feels responsible because he wouldn't have been out there if he hadn't been flirting with a woman.

> There were questions I wanted to ask him then, but I didn't interrupt. Sachs was having trouble getting the story out, talking in a trance of hesitations and awkward silences, and I was afraid that a sudden word from me would throw him off course. To be honest, I didn't quite understand what he was trying to say. There was no question that the fall had been a ghastly experience, but I was confused by how much effort he put into describing the small events that had preceded it. The business with Maria struck me as trivial, of no genuine importance, a trite comedy of manners not worth talking about. In Sachs's mind, however, there was a direct connection. The one thing had caused the other, which meant that he didn't see the fall as an accident or a piece of bad luck so much as some grotesque form of punishment. I wanted to tell him that he was wrong, that he was being overly hard on himself—but I didn't. I just sat there and listened to him as he went on analyzing his own behavior.[1]

It might be argued that men and women bring different expectations to friendship, that women have a basic commitment to attachment, men to independence. Thus it may be difficult for some men to listen to themes of dependence and attachment, while some women may have trouble accepting a woman friend's choice to go her own way. This may be true in general, but relationships don't exist "in general." Relationships take place between unique individuals. While those individuals may have been conditioned to have certain expectations, the fate of our relationships doesn't depend on conditioned traits of character, but on how we choose to act toward one another.

To be with other people authentically—that is, to respond to them as they are, not as we need or imagine them to be—is no easy feat. This ability depends on an awareness of ourselves as unique and autonomous individuals who relate through listening to other separate and distinct individuals.

Maggie and Liz's attachment was built on sameness and commiseration. When Maggie began to feel differently, the friendship waned. The two friends didn't know how to change or tolerate the differences that were emerging between them. Maggie felt she was betraying Liz whenever she was happy and fulfilled. Neither of them knew how to talk about the kinds of feelings they were experiencing. Liz felt abandoned by Maggie. The differences and their inability to talk about them

---

[1]Paul Auster, *Leviathan* (New York: Viking, 1992). 131.

formed a widening gulf. As in so many situations where differences between friends cannot be talked about, the friends drifted apart.

When Maggie eventually worked things out with Dominic, she
stopped seeing Liz altogether. Years later she would say to someone,
offhand, "Oh, we just lost touch."

RESOLVING CONFLICT BETWEEN FRIENDS

Why, if Maggie was able to work things out with Dominic, her demanding and critical boyfriend, wasn't she able to resolve the conflict with
Liz, her like-minded and appreciative friend? Here is the irony of listening
in friendship:

The same elective quality of relationship that enables friends to
speak freely about so many subjects makes them less likely to speak openly
about serious problems between them.

The binding and imperative nature of romantic and family ties makes
it more urgent to speak up about our unhappiness in these relationships. While friends do sometimes voice complaints to each other, they
are less likely to talk about serious negative feelings, like envy, jealousy,
and resentment. Because the boundary around friendship is less forti-
fied than that around family, there's a greater fear that friends will abandon us if we voice serious complaints to them. Sadly, when such feelings
are strong, friends often drift apart.

People who hesitate to speak when something is bothering them
often imagine that those brave souls who do simply have more confidence and self-respect. Perhaps. But most of the people I've known to
tell friends that something is bothering them were just as worried about
speaking up as those who keep silent. What enabled them to take the
risk wasn't only respect for themselves and their right to their feelings,
but also respect for the relationship—and for their friends.

The longer you avoid telling a friend that something's bothering
you—say, that you wish your friend wouldn't make a habit of bringing
along a third person when you get together—the more preoccupied you
become with your grievance. In your internal debate about whether
or not to complain, you probably imagine phrasing your complaint
in such a clear and forceful way that your friend will have to hear
you. In fact, the most effective way to address an impasse between friends
is to take into account what you imagine your friend's position to
be.

---◆---

Acknowledging your friends' position releases them from brooding about it and opens them to hearing your side.

---◆---

Let's say that you always seem to be the one to call a certain friend about getting together. You're not the sort of person to keep score, but her never inviting you to do something troubles you. It's not that you mind calling but that you're starting to wonder if she really likes you. You hesitate to say anything because she might feel attacked and get angry. What to do? Tell her all of that. Use your ability to empathize to anticipate how your friend might feel about what you have to say. "Something's been bothering me, but I've hesitated to bring it up because I didn't want you to think that I was blaming you. Actually, this probably has to do with my own insecurity. . . ."

---◆---

Sometimes an honest complaint can save a friendship.

---◆---

Chris got tired of Arlene's constant complaining—about her jerk of a boss, her numerous aches and pains, and her awesome repertory of boyfriend troubles. But Chris didn't want to say anything. She didn't want to hurt Arlene's feelings. So instead she just stopped being available when Arlene called, and the friendship withered and died.

When friends don't speak up about negative feelings, grievances can eat away at the relationship. Even if it doesn't completely resolve the conflict, hearing each other's position makes a big difference. The best place to start to address an impasse between friends is not to state your position but to consider what the other person might be feeling and try to acknowledge that in a way that invites your friend to elaborate.

Few friendships last long if all one person does is complain to the other. We all have troubles in mind, and we can all use some sympathetic attention to our complaints. But remember that listening, especially to complaints, is a burden. If you have a friend who takes advantage of your willingness to listen, without reciprocating, you can absorb this emotional burden passively until you get fed up—like collecting enough brown stamps to trade in for the right to walk out on a friendship. Or you can say something about it.

A running friend of mine used to complain about all the trouble he was having with his stepson. I'd listen sympathetically and occasion-

ally offer advice (it's OK, I have a license). But if my friend talked for more than a few minutes, he'd get self-conscious (maybe partly *because* I have a license) and apologize. When he did, I'd remind him that in our relationship complaining was a two-way street. I didn't mind hearing about his problems because I was grateful for all the time he spent listening to mine.

When two people are locked in silent grievance, the best way to break the impasse is to elicit and acknowledge the other person's feelings. This applies especially to cases of mutual misunderstanding. Don't be too quick to tell your side. In cases of major misunderstanding, concentrate first on listening to the other person. Save your feelings for later. Of course if your friend has hurt or annoyed you and doesn't know it, saying something about how you feel may be the only way to keep your resentment from poisoning the relationship.

Alice and her husband were quite independent and regularly did things like go out to dinner or to the movies separately. Alice's friend Marie, on the other hand, had a more traditional marriage and rarely felt comfortable socializing without her husband unless he was busy at work or out of town. So the two friends sometimes got together alone, but more often they did things as couples, as Marie preferred. They both understood their different situations, but each came to feel that she was doing more of the accommodating. Gradually, they saw less and less of each other.

Marie was hurt. She envied Alice her greater freedom but was disappointed that Alice wasn't more sympathetic to her feelings. The less they saw of each other, the more Marie brooded over how hurt she felt; and the more she brooded, the more she imagined confronting Alice. Could Alice's feelings conceivably mirror her own? It was a possibility she hadn't considered, but she decided to take a risk in the interest of recovering the friendship.

Marie called and said she imagined Alice must be pretty frustrated by her having trouble getting together except as couples. Alice, greatly relieved to have her own feelings acknowledged, said yes that was true, but deep down she worried that Marie didn't really like her enough to want to do things with just the two of them.

Once Marie had broken the ice by demonstrating her concern for Alice's feelings, the two friends were able to talk about their envy and resentment—feelings that often seem too ugly to talk about. The basic conflict didn't disappear—Alice still preferred to get together alone with

Marie, and Marie still had trouble going out without her husband—but it no longer festered. The two friends now understood each other. They both felt listened to, and their friendship endured.

WHEN AND HOW TO OFFER CONSTRUCTIVE CRITICISM TO A FRIEND

Real friends are honest. There are times when just listening to a friend you feel is making a mistake is less than honest. If you feel like offering criticism or advice, it's a good idea to first ask your friend if he or she wants to hear it.

"Would you like to hear a suggestion about this?"

"Are you interested in a second opinion?"

"Have you definitely decided to . . . ?"

Even well-intended criticism can backfire. You may have been trying to be honest or simply have been thoughtless; either way your criticism may make your friend feel put down or let down. If you criticize a friend for something he or she isn't interested in changing (or likely to change), your comments, however well-intentioned they may be, can leave the friend feeling emotionally deflated and resentful.

Sometimes when we give our opinion, we feel rejected if our friend doesn't follow it.

"Why did you ask my advice in the first place, if you weren't going to take it?"

Taking your advice means considering it, not necessarily following it. The best kind of feedback has no strings attached. A good listener allows friends to accept or reject suggestions without acting slighted.

See how your friend responds to your first comments before going on. Don't become so attached to convincing a friend of the rightness of your assessment—of *her* decisions—that you are insensitive to her right to decide what to do. If your friend seems defensive about your advice, pull back and let her talk.

The time to press your point of view is when you disagree with a friend's advice about what *you* should do, not the other way around.

If you're not sure how your friend feels about your advice, ask.

"What do you think?"

"Do you want me to say more about this or not?"

"Should I go on, or have you pretty much made up your mind?"

DO FRIENDS OUTGROW EACH OTHER OR JUST FORGET HOW TO LISTEN?

For all too many people the story of their friendships is a history of se-vered or eroded connections. The divorces and separations of friends may not be as wrenching as those of people who live together and share destinies, but the process is similar. We make friends in one set of circumstances—in college, say, or starting a new job or, like Maggie and Liz, as wounded veterans of divorce. Then one or both of us changes; we move on, and the points of connection are harder to sustain.

The reasons we marry at twenty aren't the same reasons we stay married at thirty or forty; but friends, who have fewer ties to bind them, are less likely to do the maintenance it takes to sustain a relationship through major life changes. A lot of that work involves respecting each other's differences and learning to listen when it doesn't come easily.

Gil and Roy were friends in high school. Both were basketball players and good students, both intensely competitive and known for their acer-bic wit, and they gravitated together naturally. It was a friendship based on shared interests and the kind of wisecracking that teenage boys use to test themselves, experimenting with insecurity. Their listening to each other, if you can call it that, took the form of taking turns show-ing off.

As they grew older, Gil found Roy's constant ribbing exasperating but often invigorating too. Others just found it annoying: Once, when they were in their thirties, they were at a basketball game and Roy had had a few beers. It was just after the great Kareem Abdul-Jabbar had changed his name from Lew Alcindor, and for some reason he became the target of Roy's abrasive humor. Every time Jabbar missed a shot, Roy would holler, "Hey *Lew*, nice shot, *Lew!*" He was really starting to bother the people around them, but Gil didn't say anything. After the game a couple of guys confronted Roy, called him an asshole, and knocked his glasses off. Later, when Gil teased him about the incident, Roy got very upset, and the two friends stopped speaking to each other.

A couple of years later Roy called Gil, and the friendship was

renewed, only now it seemed more superficial, at least to Gil. Roy still seemed so adolescent. He was always posturing, looking for an angle, a spin, a take. By this point in his life Gil expected friends to talk and listen, not to continue showing off.

Together the two friends attended their twentieth high school re-union. Gil remembered how the waves of emotion and memory washed over him but that Roy remained his old wisecracking self. Afterward the two of them went out for a drink with Gil's old girlfriend.

Janice, who was still sensationally pretty, brought out the old competitive edge between the two friends, who spent an hour in the bar tossing barbed comments back and forth. Gil didn't think Janice was very impressed by their performance, and later he felt a little embarrassed.

Much later Gil learned that Roy had taken Janice home that night and the two of them had had an affair. The way he found out was that Roy called him, all upset, to tell him that Janice had broken off with him. Gil was furious. It seemed like such a devious and hostile thing for Roy to have done—not just to score a conquest with his old girl-friend, but to keep it secret. Why, if there was nothing sneaky in what Roy had done, hadn't he said anything to Gil about it? Still, when Roy turned to Gil to nurse him through his hurt, Gil was forgiving, the way friends are.

The next time the two friends got together was when Gil invited Roy to his annual company picnic. Roy, who'd again had a few beers, started making loud jokes about private things Gil had said to him about various members of the company. Gil was acutely embarrassed and tried to shut Roy up but wasn't very successful. The following week, Gil wrote a letter to Roy saying that he didn't trust him anymore, that he didn't plan to see him again, and that he didn't want Roy to contact him.

Gil (who would later outgrow and shed his first marriage) found this act—deliberately severing a tie that had become a burden—quite liberating. It felt like a declaration of self-respect. Thinking about the end of the friendship, he remembered Woody Allen saying that the things that mean the most in this world, the things that are the most enjoyable, come naturally. You can't work at them.

That's how we sometimes feel, but that doesn't make it so. Maybe when we're kids friendship comes easily, but as we get older we may have to work at it. Working at making friends and keeping them may go against the grain, but that's true of a lot of things worth doing. Gil's friendship with Roy may have become one of those relationships that

persist out of habit even though they are fundamentally unrewarding. But many friendships, based on a more solid connection than the one between Gil and Roy, may require repair from time to time. For friendships to grow with you, you may have to put in some effort.

One important ingredient in getting the listening you deserve is cultivating relationships based on caring and mutual exchange. This means remaining open enough to form new relationships and selective enough to drop those that are basically unproductive. Deepening relationships requires a balance between self-disclosure and reciprocal listening. But then, inevitably, many of us find ourselves stuck in a variety of relationships with people who have trouble listening. Instead of remaining bitter or fatalistic, it's possible to teach them to listen—by setting an example and, if necessary, asking for reciprocation.

Having friends means making time for them. If friends come second, if you're too busy working to be with your friends, what are you working for? Keeping friends means being willing to work at the relationship. Not all the time certainly, but listening sometimes when it's hard and speaking up sometimes when it's necessary.

For friendship to flourish the relationship must be given priority. That means finding time for each other, and it means making a real effort to listen to each other. At work, however, there are more important things than relationships. Aren't there?

GETTING YOUR POINT OF VIEW ACROSS AT THE OFFICE

Bradley Duke and Bill Nowicki were thoroughly charming to Marianne when she applied for a job at the small publishing firm where they were respectively publisher and senior editor. They asked the usual questions about her training and experience but spent more time talking about the company and the books they published, telling her what a great place it was to work. Marianne needed little convincing. Any small publisher, she felt, would be a better place to work than the huge corporate firms where editors were drowning in profit and loss statements and books of substance were considered with suspicion and irony.

Marianne felt she could learn a lot from Duke and Nowicki. She knew she had the makings of a good editor, but her experience at the large firm where she'd been a valued assistant hadn't prepared her to negotiate contracts or conduct other such business matters with ease.

Marianne was thrilled when she received a letter offering her the

job a week after her interview. She'd worked a long time for this moment, and she finally had what she wanted.

Marianne was surprised at how quickly her responsibilities built up. Who would have thought that so many of the bright young authors she was attracting to the firm (and some older ones as well) would need so much hand holding?

Duke and Nowicki seemed happy to have Marianne around. But she soon discovered that they considered themselves chiefs and her an Indian. They were friendly enough, in a superficial way, but they never thought to really include her. Between meetings and appointments they would talk to each other and not to her. They'd discuss people she didn't know and exchange inside jokes. Their constant showing off, meant to entertain and impress, made her feel that all they wanted from her was an audience.

When Marianne discovered that they went out to lunch together every Wednesday without inviting her, she felt a humiliating shock of alienation. Later she learned that the firm's small board of directors had forced them to hire a woman editor and that Duke and Nowicki resented this intrusion into what they considered their fiefdom.

Another reason Marianne felt shut out was that Duke and Nowicki were such great friends. So close were they that people invariably referred to them as Duke-and-Nowicki, as though they were inseparably a pair, a single hyphenated unit. People invited Duke-and-Nowicki to parties, the booksellers asked Duke- and-Nowicki to serve on committees, and authors and agents referred to Duke-and-Nowicki as the savviest and most devoted people in the business. The fact that they were both enormously popular with authors, literary agents, and other industry people only underscored Marianne's sense of isolation.

One reason they were so well liked was that they were so accessible. They loved publishing, they loved books, and they loved the way their authors looked up to them with the total, trusting eagerness that people whose identities are invested in their writing reserve for those who appreciate their work. So Marianne was perplexed by their response when she approached them about the manuscripts she was having problems with. Duke and Nowicki made a pretense of listening, their brows furrowed in concern like state-funded bureaucrats on autopilot, but they asked no questions. When she was done they told her just to continue to do her own good work.

These encounters left Marianne not just disappointed but humiliated. But instead of getting angry, she felt ashamed of asking for help.

She didn't really need much help; what she really wanted was simply a witness to her work. More than advice, she needed collegiality, that comforting sense of shared enterprise that had sustained her through the hard years of school and publishing apprenticeship.

Shut out socially, then judged inadequate just because she'd asked for feedback, Marianne became cold and hostile. Not wanting to give her antagonists the satisfaction of exposing her real hurt and anger, she took refuge in contempt and punished them with silence.

The atmosphere in the office became so unpleasant that Marianne thought about quitting. But she was a single mother and didn't have that luxury.

It was at this point that Marianne started dating a publishing executive at another firm, a tall man with gray eyes and a large spirit. Quinn was a man of patient sweetness, but he too was divorced, and at first he and Marianne were somewhat tentative with each other. Then love took over and work became less important.

The trouble was, as Marianne now began to see, that from the beginning she'd expected a lot from Duke and Nowicki. When she'd interviewed for the job she mistook their friendliness for an offer of friendship, and when that promise wasn't fulfilled, she became hurt and bitter. Then, too, she wanted both to be appreciated as competent and given the guidance she needed as a beginner. That these motives are somewhat contradictory doesn't make them unreasonable. Marianne's bitterness was due partly to the frustration of her own inflated expectations and partly to her colleagues being too caught up in their own lives to be open to a new person.

Things changed at work when Marianne stopped worrying so much about Duke and Nowicki. Now that her personal life was full, she was less interested in their friendship or even their approval. And now that she felt better about herself, she was no longer willing to put up with blatant unfairness.

When Duke, who was filling out the annual review, rated her "mediocre," Marianne refused to sign it. "I want to talk about this," she told him evenly. When Duke said he didn't have time, she insisted. "You *have to* talk to me. Make time." He sighed theatrically but agreed.

"You *know* I deserve a good evaluation," Marianne told him when they finally met. "What's the problem?"

"I call it as I see it," Duke said, getting up to leave.

"Please sit down," Marianne said. "We have to talk about this."

And talk they did. Marianne acknowledged that she may have ex-

pected too much when she arrived, but she also pointed out that she'd been treated from the beginning like a second-class citizen and that she was tired of it. They didn't have to be friends, she said, but they did have to get along. She spoke with dignity, but also with intensity.

When Marianne finished saying what was on her mind, Duke apologized. He changed the evaluation, and after that both he and Nowicki started treating her with more respect. In return, Marianne dropped her own belligerent attitude; but she was no longer willing to put up with not being listened to.

Why were Marianne's bosses so unresponsive for so long, and why now all of a sudden did they start to listen to her? Could it really be that all she had to do was speak up?

Duke and Nowicki had allowed their resentment about being pressured to hire a woman to turn into a grudge. Unwilling to confront *their* bosses, they took out their frustration on Marianne, shutting her out and treating her as someone to be seen but not heard. What they didn't realize was that grudges have no place at the office.

------- ◆ -------

Holding on to resentment of people you have to work with punishes you as much as it does them.

------- ◆ -------

It may be a cliché, but people who work together are a team, and sometimes it's necessary to set aside or get over personal feelings that interfere with the smooth functioning of the group.

Although Marianne had tried to complain, her expectations got in the way. Like many of us, she wanted to be liked, hoped to be friends. That's fine if it happens, but Marianne had allowed her wish to have a good relationship to take priority over doing her job and insisting on being treated fairly. It's harder to confront your boss if you need him or her to like you than it is if you just want respect.

Anxious and uncertain about speaking up—lest Duke and Nowicki not like her—Marianne spoke to them in a nervous, tentative way. At the other extreme, speaking up in a shrill voice doesn't get you much respect either. No one coached Marianne on exactly what to say or how to say it, but the greater assurance she drew from her relationship with Quinn resulted in her lowering the pitch of her voice and speaking in a firm and direct way. She didn't just want to vent her feelings; she wanted things to change.

On Secretary's Day, Duke and Nowicki gave the receptionist a dozen

white carnations with a card signed from the two of them. Marianne was furious. They responded by saying that this was a social gesture and they could do what they liked. She told them that this was an office, not a social setting, and that she wouldn't be excluded like this. The next day they apologized.

Keep in mind the difference between dissent and defiance as a response to being treated unfairly. *Defiance* means attacking the other person's position and making him wrong. *Dissent* means having the courage to stand up for what you think and feel. It's the difference between saying "You're wrong" and "This is how I feel."

Defiance is reactive, a counterphobic response to the temptation to deference. A dissenting message is much easier to hear than a defiant one.

Marianne now realized that she was entitled to be listened to, and when important issues arose, she insisted on it. Knowing she could fight back effectively made her more relaxed, and so there was less often a need for it. No longer anxious for Duke and Nowicki's approval, as though she were a child and they parents, Marianne lost her dependence, her need to please: she was an independent person. The company, as usual, published some very good books that year, and an author Marianne had brought in had a great success, both critical and commercial. She and Duke and Nowicki had a wonderful celebration with him one evening, and their gratification was genuine and shared.

Marianne's unhappy experience at the office is instructive for two reasons. First, her colleagues' extreme lack of consideration illustrates one of the greatest mistakes senior people make in work settings: not listening to their subordinates. Second, the same insensitivity placed Marianne in the kind of situation that tempts us to feel and act like victims, wearing our suffering as a rebuke to the villains we hold responsible. The fact that Marianne was a woman suffering at the hands of two men also permits those who care to to see this as an example of men as tyrants and women as martyrs. Let's look at these issues one at a time.

A GOOD MANAGER IS A GOOD LISTENER

Managers are expected to lead and direct the people under them. Unfortunately, people are promoted because they were good at the jobs they were doing, not because they've proven themselves as managers.

In fact, according to the Peter Principle, people tend to advance until they reach their level of incompetence. As a result, many principals and vice presidents and supervisors pay more attention to the product than to the people producing it—to the detriment of both.

Effective managers are proactive listeners. They don't wait for members of their staffs to come to them; they make an active effort to find out what people think and feel by asking them.

The manager who meets frequently with staff members keeps informed and, even more important, communicates interest in the people themselves.

An open-door policy allows access, but it doesn't substitute for an active campaign of reaching out and listening to people. The manager who doesn't ask questions communicates that he or she doesn't care. And if he or she doesn't listen, the message is "I'm not there for you." Even if a manager decides not to follow a subordinate's suggestion or not to give that person a raise, listening with sincere interest conveys respect and makes the employee feel appreciated.

When Duke and Nowicki hired Marianne, they were impressed by her maturity. They thought of her as a self-sufficient person who would share the load. You might think that as experienced people they would have been more sensitive to a new colleague's need for support. But the truth is, they did their best work outside the office. When they sat down to court an agent or an author, they were very sensitive.

Duke and Nowicki didn't offer Marianne any supervision because *they* never got any. What didn't occur to them was that their close friendship had sustained their own needs for support when they'd first started out. The mistake they made in dealing with Marianne was thinking about her only as a worker and not as a person. Interest in peers may come easily; but even if it doesn't come naturally, senior people must take an interest in junior people. They're the ones who get the work done.

———◆———

Communicating by memo—however witty or informal— doesn't substitute for personal contact, because it closes off the chance to listen.

———◆———

Simply going through the motions of meeting with people doesn't work. The fake listener doesn't fool anyone. Poor eye contact, shuffling feet, busy hands, and meaningless replies, like "That's interesting" and "Is that right?" give them away. The insincere listener's lack of in-

terest in the conversation betrays a larger problem: lack of interest in the person with whom the listener is communicating.

Most people don't listen with the intent to understand; they listen with the intent to reply. Even at work, where performance takes priority over relationships, listening carefully to understand the other person's point of view, before you even think about replying, is the key to productive communication.

It's important to realize that failure to listen isn't necessarily a product of meanness or insensitivity. Anxiety, preoccupation, and pressure can undermine the skills of even a good listener. The point is, really, that at work, as in every other arena of life, listening is important and may require a little effort.

Effective managers develop a routine in which communication time is an integral part. They meet with their staff and ask questions. They don't react before gathering all the facts. If they don't know what their people are thinking and feeling, they ask—and they listen.

WHAT IF YOUR BOSS DOESN'T LISTEN?

If at this point we were to leave the subject of listening at the workplace, we would have fallen into the easy habit of reducing a complex subject to a simple formula: thoughtful managers listen to what their employees have to say. Where does that leave those who don't get listened to at work? Feeling sorry for themselves.

When we don't feel heard by our superiors, few of us give up right away. We write memos, we ask to meet with them, we try to communicate our needs and convey our points of view. Then we give up. Frequently we do what Marianne did: we complain to other people.

Once Marianne came to the conclusion that her senior colleagues were uninterested and unavailable, she started griping to the receptionist.

Gossip, something we all indulge in, is a form of consciousness lowering. The rules of the game are simple: players are free to run down anybody who's not in the room. (Hint: If you play this game, don't leave the room.)

Triangulation—ventilating feelings of frustration with third parties rather than addressing conflicts at their source—takes on epidemic proportions in work settings. Letting off steam by complaining to sympathetic listeners about other people is a perfectly human thing to do. The problem is that habitual complaining about superiors locks us into

passivity and helplessness and mean-spiritedness. We may have given up trying to get through to the sons of bitches, but by God we don't mind saying what we think of them—as long as they aren't within earshot.

I once worked in a clinic with six other psychotherapists, where everyone except the director went out to lunch together. Guess what the main topic of conversation was? The director and what a rigid guy he was. And guess what the group did about it? Complained regularly among themselves, as though they were a resistible force and he were an immovable object.

But, some of you might be thinking, my boss *really is* insensitive! I've *tried* to talk to him, and he just doesn't listen.

I don't doubt it. People aren't promoted because they're good listeners. They get promoted because they're good workers, or maybe good talkers. Moreover, positions of authority encourage the directive side of human nature, often at the expense of receptivity. The mistake people make in trying to get through to unreceptive superiors is the same mistake most of us make in dealing with the difficult people in our lives: We try to change them. And when that doesn't work, we give up.

You don't change relationships by trying to control other people's behavior but by changing yourself in relation to them.

Instead, start by examining your expectations. What do you want, and how are you programmed to go about getting it? Are you, as Marianne was, expecting to have your personal needs met at the office? Do you work hard and wait patiently for the boss to tell you that you're doing a great job, like a good little boy or girl? Have you learned to try to get responded to by being clever rather than competent or by being pleasing rather than productive?

No matter how fondly we may remember the Mary Tyler Moore show, the workplace is not a family. Yet many of us relate to our bosses as though we were children and they were our parents. The alternative is to think of yourselves as two self-respecting adults who happen to occupy different positions at the office. Marianne wanted Duke and Nowicki to take her seriously, but she hadn't taken herself seriously. Trying too hard to be liked by our bosses and waiting patiently for them to recognize our worth are common examples of not taking ourselves seriously.

The chairman of the department of psychiatry once complained to me that certain faculty members responded to him as though he were their father. I had to laugh. Of course they did. One of the things that comes with a position of responsibility is becoming the object of people's attitudes toward authority. (I think it's called transference.) Supervisors should remember this when they meet with their subordinates. When employees are summoned to meet with the boss, many of them expect a reprimand—why else would the boss call you in?—rather than an open forum. Supervisors must break through this anxiety by asking questions that show interest. And listening to the answers.

LISTENING WITHIN LIMITS

Leslie was sympathetic when her secretary complained about the problems she was having at home. But once Donna discovered what a willing listener Leslie was, she started taking up more and more time talking about her problems. Donna's troubles were beginning to interfere with work getting done, and Leslie was getting annoyed. She wanted to be understanding, but she didn't want to be Donna's mother. What to do?

If you have a good relationship with someone at work and that person is burdened with a personal problem, your willingness to listen helps lighten the burden. But some people are so full of their problems that they take advantage of anyone willing to listen.

When personal conversations start keeping you from your work, cut them off, firmly but gently.

"I'd like to hear more, but I have to get back to work."

"This all sounds pretty painful. I hope you have somebody to talk to about these things?"

Listening is important at work because it enables people to understand each other, get along, and get the job done. *But:* Don't get too personal. Don't let your compassion (or desire to be appreciated) allow someone to let talking about their personal problems interfere with work. This may be happening if you're the only person he talks to or if she uses your sympathy as more than an occasional excuse for taking time off or for not getting work done. A good supervisor keeps channels of (business) communication open—and keeps them focused on the task

at hand—by asking for frequent feedback about how things are going (at work).

"What do you like and dislike so far about working here?"

"Is there anything you think we should change to make things smoother?"

"How do you feel about. . . ?"

"What's your reaction to. . . ?"

Remember that it can be intimidating for subordinates to give criticism or make suggestions. If you want them to feel safe enough to open up, reassure them that you appreciate their ideas.

"I'm glad you spoke up."

"Thanks for letting me know. . . . "

"I didn't realize . . . I'm glad you told me."

Listening to the people we work with isn't the same as becoming friends with them. Many people worry that if we allow ourselves to get personal at the office, things might get sticky. But those who think that effective teamwork isn't about listening (it's about getting things done) are wrong. Without being heard we are diminished, as workers and as people.

Epilogue

The epilogue is where an author can be expected to wax philosophical. Here, for example, I might tell you that better listening not only transforms personal and professional relationships (which it does) but can also bring understanding across the gender gap, the racial divide, between rich and poor, and even among nations. All that may actually be true, but if I'm going to indulge in the unearned right to preach, maybe I should confine myself to matters closer to home. After all, I'm a psychologist, not a philosopher.

Having read this far, you've probably been reminded of some things you already knew about listening but perhaps also come to see that careful listening is even more important and difficult than most people realize. The urge to be recognized is so compelling that even when we do listen, it's usually not with the intent to understand, but to reply. And, as if that didn't make careful listening hard enough, at times of heat and conflict we must make a heroic effort to overcome, or at least restrain, the reactive emotionalism that jolts us into anxiety and out of sympathy with each other.

As I hope you'll come to see, few things can do as much to bring mutual understanding to your relationships as reflective listening—hearing and acknowledging the other person's thoughts and feelings before voicing your own. You can make reflective listening a habit, but—like developing any new habit—this takes work, takes practice.

One of my least favorite remarks comes from some people who are in therapy to improve their relationships. They've complained about their difficulties; I've listened and sympathized; then I've suggested some

things they could do to start giving and getting the understanding they say they so urgently long for. Then comes The Comment: "Why does everything have to be so artificial? Why can't we just talk to each other naturally?" I hate it when people say that! They *are* talking naturally, and it isn't working.

I get annoyed when people say that it's unnatural to hold back their reply until they've acknowledged what the other person has to say, because this protest seems so stubborn and resistant. But the thing that really annoys me about this comment is that it's based on the truth: good listening *doesn't* come naturally.

Listening is a skill, and like any skill it can be practiced and improved. But although listening can be looked at this way—as a performance—it can also be looked at another way, as a more or less natural outgrowth of an attitude, an attitude of caring and concern for other people.

Caring about someone doesn't require a great deal of deliberate thought; it's something you feel. Caring about a person almost automatically impels you to act with consideration for him or her. This consideration isn't wholly unselfish, because to care about someone means that your well-being is tied up with theirs. When a bad thing happens to someone you care deeply about, something bad happens to you as well. But *showing* that you care, suspending your own interests and making yourself available to the other person, takes some effort. It means devoting alertness to another's well-being.

Listening a little harder—extending what we do automatically, extending ourselves a little more—is one of the ways, one of the best ways, we can be good to each other. Attending a little harder to the other person—enough to discern his feelings, enough to consider her ideas and point of view—this takes a little effort.

Caring enough to listen doesn't mean going around selflessly and automatically available to everyone you encounter. Rather, it means being alert to those situations in which the person you're with needs to be listened to.

Ironically, our ability to listen is often less flexible with our inner, intimate circle. We love, but our love gets frayed. Conflict, habit, and the pressure of our own emotions makes us listen least well where listening is most needed. As we move outside the family circle to those for whom we have personal regard but less emotional intensity, we tend

to be more open, more receptive, and more flexible. It's not—as we're sometimes accused—that we "care more about our friends than we do about our family" but that these relationships are less agglutinated with conflict and resentment.

So. We don't get far with our efforts to listen better without running into the problem of our own emotionality and reactivity. Listening better requires not only a greater openness to others but also a greater reflective awareness of ourselves. Do we express ourselves in an emotionally pressured way that makes our listeners anxious and defensive? If so, what can we do about it? (If the answer is nothing, then that's the improvement we can expect in the listening we get.) Under what circumstances do we become reactive and give advice or interrupt or make jokes instead of listening?

Concern for other people is an instinctive expression of the best part of us. Unfortunately, frustrations at home and a sense of powerlessness in the wider world mean that we don't always feel or act with generosity and concern.

Everywhere around us we're encouraged to claim our victimhood and our right to bitterness. This widespread feeling of injured entitlement can be understood as a product of insufficient emotional nourishment. The people in our lives who are hungry for attention are suffered, shunned, or shamed. We let them know in some way that their great need to be heard is excessive and selfish. And where does that leave them? Hungry for attention. And so the problem of listening, like all human problems, is circular: inadequate attention and understanding make us insecure in ourselves and less open to others. The listening we don't get is the listening we don't pass on. In this sense, the blatant clamoring for attention of the narcissist is a caricature of us all—which is why these needy, demanding people make us so uncomfortable.

Their inability to get the attention they crave leaves them feeling powerless—a feeling that's reinforced by living in a world marked by economic decline, poverty, AIDS, crime, pollution, and bureaucratic ineptitude. So it's not surprising that we've lost faith in our own capacity to make a difference. Public disillusion and private disappointment deplete and discourage us. We feel put upon and let down, and so, naturally, we turn our resentment outward and our sympathy inward.

When we're feeling beleaguered and insecure, it's natural to think about looking out for number one rather than reaching out to others.

Unfortunately, preoccupation with the self is self-defeating. Trapped in excesses of self-consciousness, men and women become polarized and resentful. Sadly, anger and despair have fueled a decline in concern and a retreat to the dead end of preoccupation with the self.

We cannot simply reverse the process of misunderstanding, but we can realize that relationship problems are circular, not linear. And circular patterns can be broken—if someone is willing to make the first move.

The great reward of making that move is that listening well allows us to be open, generous, and connected, to touch others' lives and enrich them and us in the process. Effective listening—empathic listening—promotes growth in the listener, the one listened to, and the relationship between them.

That generous listening enhances our own well-being is the natural perspective of psychology, in which all human behavior is seen as motivated by the agendas of the self. But when you narrow down human relations to a collection of selves, and the self to the early conditioning of the child, what you have left is fixed characters, and you're stuck with them. The problem with such explanations is that, in explaining the status quo, they tend to undercut our autonomy and responsibility to do something about it.

It's a dogma of American life that all actions are motivated by self-interest. But this dogma is false. The tendency to view our lives on the planet from the perspective of individualism obscures the larger view that we are part of systems within systems: the family, the extended family, the community, vast networks of associations. The truth is that looking inside ourselves can show us only part of the reason for our feeling empty and unfulfilled. Viewing the self-created world of our relationships entirely from within our own egos locks us in to a very limited view of the human condition.

Should the idea of benevolent self-interest include benevolent interest in others? Yes. Benevolent self-interest does go hand in hand with interest in others. But is it only a matter of enlightened self-interest to take an interest in others?

Trade-offs have their place in the conduct of life. But it would leave too much out of the story of human affairs to give an account of relatedness to others only in terms of narcissistic utilitarianism.

Caring about other people, which takes shape in political justice, the relief of suffering, and the love of family and friends, is fundamental to our sense of who we are and what makes our lives hang

together. Pressures that block or obscure this impulse reduce, even mutilate us.

A universal respect for human dignity doesn't mean only feeling sympathy for others or doing for them. It means respecting them enough to listen to them, to hear and respect their voices—to view them as subjects, worthy of a hearing, not just objects of our needs.

Listening to others is an ethical good, part of what it means to have just and fair dealings with other people. Listening is part of our moral commitment to respecting each other.

Learning to listen better to those we're closest to is easier when we remember that we are separate selves. Openness and autonomy are correlated. If we're to have the courage to be ourselves, to stand squarely on our own two feet, then we must accept and acknowledge that other people are themselves and entitled to their own unique points of view. The idea isn't to distance ourselves from others but to let them be themselves while we continue to be ourselves.

Learning to listen involves a paradox of control: controlling yourself and letting go of control of the relationship. It's like letting the other person drive. To listen, you have to let go.

Trying harder to understand the other person's perspective takes effort, but it isn't just a skill to be studied and practiced. Hearing someone out is an expression of caring enough to listen.

One of the things I've hoped to do in this book is to help restore a sense of balance to the way we think about relationships. First because seeing our relationships as mutually defined enables us to change what we get out of them by changing what we put into them. And second because recognizing that we live in a web of relationships, which give meaning and fullness to human life, may inspire us to a little more generosity and concern for other people.

Does talk of rebalancing relationships and rediscovering concern sound a little pious? After all, you probably picked up this book to learn a little more about listening, not to read a sermon on universal benevolence. Sorry. But maybe the natural sympathy for other people that we're born with is something we have to remind ourselves to express from time to time.

We all believe in fairness and respect for the rights of others. We believe in compassion and justice and that everyone has a right to be heard. Of course these standards are regularly violated. Of course we subscribe to them better in principle than in practice. It remains that

they are valid standards. And they do from time to time galvanize us to action—as when we somehow manage to listen instead of arguing in the midst of a heated discussion or when we remember to take a little extra time to hear what's going on in someone's life.

The obligation to listen can be experienced as a burden, and we all sometimes feel it that way. But it is quite a different thing to be moved by a strong sense that the people in our lives are eminently *worth* listening to, a sense of their dignity and value. One thing we can all add a little more of is understanding—respect, compassion, and fairness, the fundamental values conveyed by listening.

As I said at the beginning of this book, the reason we care so much about being listened to is that we never outgrow our need to communicate what it feels like to live in our separate, private worlds of experience. Unfortunately, there is no parallel need to be the one who listens. Maybe that's why listening sometimes seems to be in short supply. Listening isn't a need we have; it's a gift we give.

DATE DUE			
FEB 12 1996			
SEP 0 1 1997			
DEC 0 2 1998			
NOV 1 9 2001			
DEC 3 0 2009			